NUANCES OF BLACKNESS IN THE CANADIAN ACADEMY

Teaching, Learning, and Researching While Black

Edited by Awad Ibrahim, Tamari Kitossa, Malinda S. Smith, and Handel K. Wright

The essays in *Nuances of Blackness in the Canadian Academy* make visible the submerged stories of Black life in academia. They offer fresh historical, social, and cultural insights into what it means to teach, learn, research, and work while Black.

In daring to shift from margin to centre, the book's contributors confront two overlapping themes. First, they resist a singular construction of Blackness that masks the nuances and multiplicity of what it means to be and experience the academy as Black people. Second, they challenge the stubborn durability of anti-Black tropes, the dehumanization of Blackness, persistent deficit ideologies, and the tyranny of low expectations that permeate the dominant idea of Blackness in the white colonial imagination.

Operating at the intersections of discourse and experience, contributors reflect on how Blackness shapes academic pathways, ignites complicated and often difficult conversations, and reimagines Black pasts, presents, and futures. This unique collection contributes to the articulation of more nuanced understandings of the ways in which Blackness is made, unmade, and remade in the academy and the implications for interrelated dynamics across and within post-secondary education, Black communities in Canada, and global Black diasporas.

AWAD IBRAHIM is a professor and curriculum theorist in the Faculty of Education at the University of Ottawa.

TAMARI KITOSSA is an associate professor in the Department of Sociology at Brock University.

MALINDA S. SMITH is the inaugural vice-provost of equity, diversity, and inclusion and a professor in the Department of Political Science at the University of Calgary.

HANDEL K. WRIGHT is the inaugural senior advisor to the president on anti-racism and inclusive excellence; the director of the Centre for Culture, Identity, and Education; and a professor in the Department of Educational Studies at the University of British Columbia.

Nuances of Blackness in the Canadian Academy

Teaching, Learning, and Researching While Black

EDITED BY AWAD IBRAHIM, TAMARI KITOSSA, MALINDA S. SMITH, AND HANDEL K. WRIGHT

UNIVERSITY OF TORONTO PRESS
Toronto Buffalo London

© University of Toronto Press 2022
Toronto Buffalo London
utorontopress.com

ISBN 978-1-4875-2869-0 (cloth)   ISBN 978-1-4875-2872-0 (EPUB)
ISBN 978-1-4875-2870-6 (paper)   ISBN 978-1-4875-2871-3 (PDF)

Library and Archives Canada Cataloguing in Publication

Title: Nuances of Blackness in the Canadian academy : teaching, learning,
   and researching while Black / edited by Awad Ibrahim, Tamari Kitossa,
   Malinda S. Smith, and Handel K. Wright.
Names: Ibrahim, Awad, editor. | Kitossa, Tamari, editor. | Smith, Malinda S.,
   1962–, editor. | Wright, Handel Kashope, 1959–, editor.
Description: Includes bibliographical references.
Identifiers: Canadiana (print) 2021035125X | Canadiana (ebook) 20210351284 |
   ISBN 9781487528690 (cloth) | ISBN 9781487528706 (paper) |
   ISBN 9781487528720 (EPUB) | ISBN 9781487528713 (PDF)
Subjects: LCSH: College teachers, Black – Canada. | LCSH: Blacks –
   Education (Higher) – Canada. | LCSH: Blacks – Race identity – Canada. |
   LCSH: Discrimination in higher education – Canada.
Classification: LCC LC2804 .N83 2022 | DDC 378.1/208996071 – dc23

We wish to acknowledge the land on which the University of Toronto Press operates. This
land is the traditional territory of the Wendat, the Anishnaabeg, the Haudenosaunee, the
Métis, and the Mississaugas of the Credit First Nation.

This book has been published with the help of a grant from the Federation for the
Humanities and Social Sciences, through the Awards to Scholarly Publications Program,
using funds provided by the Social Sciences and Humanities Research Council of
Canada.

University of Toronto Press acknowledges the financial support of the Government of
Canada, the Canada Council for the Arts, and the Ontario Arts Council, an agency of the
Government of Ontario, for its publishing activities.

Canada Council   Conseil des Arts
for the Arts   du Canada

ONTARIO ARTS COUNCIL
CONSEIL DES ARTS DE L'ONTARIO
an Ontario government agency
un organisme du gouvernement de l'Ontario

Funded by the   Financé par le
Government   gouvernement
of Canada   du Canada

Canadä

Contents

Figures and Tables

Figures

Tables

Preface: The Nuances of Blackness – A Genesis and Outline

All books have a genesis story. In this book, it is difficult to pinpoint an originary moment, given that the issues addressed here have always been with us. Rather, the text could be said to have evolved from an informal meeting of academics, the subsequent formation of a loose collective, and a still emergent and evolving project. We thought it prudent to give this account, to allow readers to engage with what this book is about and to provide a genealogy for future (Black) scholars who wish to understand the product of our collective intentionality and how and why we chose to include particular authors, themes, and stories.

The primary genesis of this collection of voices and perspectives began at a bar in Victoria, British Columbia, at the 2013 Congress of the Humanities and Social Sciences. Around the table were all Black men – colleagues, friends, former graduate chums, mentors, and mentees – swapping stories: professors Boulou Ebanda de B'béri, Awad Ibrahim, Tamari Kitossa, and Handel Kashope Wright, and graduate student Emmanuel Tabi. What brought us together was the shared need for commiseration and cathartic release about our lives and careers as Black academics. Something became clear as the evening progressed: whatever our different locations across Canada, stages of career, countries of origin, sexuality, ability, home disciplines, and areas of specialization, a pattern emerged. Our experiences, despite differences, had uncanny similarities. We shared stories of joy and tribulation, of our (under)representation, including the ironic absence of women at that very gathering, and of our positions as at once privileged and marginalized subjects in the academy and in society. Invoking Stuart Hall, Handel Kashope Wright called our approach to Blackness and the intended outcome of that night the "Nuances of Blackness Project." We left the bar and that lengthy conversation with a promise to keep the discussion alive and to include other voices and perspectives and to more fully articulate the nuances of being a Black academic in the Canadian academy. We affirmed the need to engage in a kind of "code switching," one in which the Black academic exercises constant and sustained reflexivity, rather than taking for granted an uncomplicated identity and position- ality in the academy.

The year 2014 proved to be a most generative one and particularly pro- ductive in shaping the work of the Nuances of Blackness Project. Dolana Mogadime, a professor in the Faculty of Education, Brock University, who was informed about the small Victoria gathering and was a member of the Equity and Diversity Issues Steering Committee of the Federation of the Humanities and Social Sciences (FHSS), which hosts congress, was excited enough about it to broach the topic at the FHSS. Under its vice-president (Equity Issues), Malinda S. Smith, then a professor of political science at the University of Alberta, the FHSS's *Ideas-Idées* blog had run a series between 2011 and 2012 on the Black experience in the Canadian academy and society, which included contributions from Carl James, Charmaine Nelson, Rinaldo Walcott, Njoki N. Wane, Zetta Elliott, Cheryl Foggo, and Adrienne Shadd, among others.

It was thought that the Nuances of Blackness Project would continue that tradition and usefully amplify that earlier work. Subsequently, with Dolana Mogadime's background work, Handel Kashope Wright and Tamari Kitossa were invited to organize an equity committee panel at the 2014 Congress of Humanities and Social Sciences at Brock University. They organized a panel titled "The Nuances of Blackness and/in the Canadian Academy," which included papers by Annette Henry (education), Afua Cooper (history), Tamari Kitossa (sociology), and Handel Kashope Wright (education). The panellists reflected on Blackness in the context of disciplinary and sociocultural diversity, as well as the theme (and even- tually the title) of the present collection (see also Mogadime, 2015). At the same congress, at which the Canadian Society for the Study of Education was held, Handel Kashope Wright and Awad Ibrahim organized a parallel symposium titled "The Nuances of Blackness and/in Education." Papers were presented by Dolana Mogadime (Brock University), Jennifer Kelly (University of Alberta), Ali A. Abdi (University of Alberta), and Awad Ibrahim (University of Ottawa). With Handel Kashope Wright as chair and discussant, the session addressed topics relevant to Blackness from within the broad field of educational studies.

The group, which by then had started to think of itself as a loose collec- tive, led by Awad Ibrahim, Tamari Kitossa, and Handel Kashope Wright, continued its engagement with Black academics at the 2015 (University of Ottawa) Congresses (including the Canadian Society for the Study of Education (CSSE) and the different SIGs (Special Interest Groups)) by organizing what they called "The Black Café." This initiative filled a void prior to the Black Canadian Studies Association being accepted formally as an association within the congress in 2018. Awad Ibrahim led the organization of the event. The Black Café went beyond the academy to undertake "town-gown" praxis. That symposium brought together the local Black community and Black academics attending the congress to explore issues facing the local community and to showcase academic, activist, and public intellectual work that included what coalesced as the Nuances of Blackness Project. Finally, when the project took on the air of viability and reality, it was clear to us (Ibrahim, Kitossa, and Wright) that the perspective and voices of Black women leadership would be vital to the project. Given her leading research on Blackness in the academy, and following discussions among ourselves and consultation with other Black academics in Canada, we extended an invitation to Malinda S. Smith (now at University of Calgary) to join the Nuances editorial team.

As the idea of the book took shape in tandem with the evolution of the Black Canadian Studies Association, we asked ourselves the central question: Who and what is missing among topics, prospective contributors, subject positions, disciplines, and perspectives? We then approached a wide range of academics across the country and at various stages in their academic career for prospective contributions. We are very pleased with the resulting representation of Black academics in the collection. However, we are mindful of, and regret, some gaps, omissions, and (self) exclusions. For example, not everyone at the original Victoria meeting was able to participate in all the work of the collective, including this book project. Also, several colleagues whom we invited were unable to submit their contribution, be it from intensive workload or because of their precarity as graduate students, sessional instructors, or non-tenured academics. Finally, despite our every effort to ensure their inclusion, the absence of Black scholars from the science, technology, engineering, and mathematics (STEM) disciplines is notable, as is the absence of Black scholars working in critical disability studies. The late and leading Black disabilities scholar Chris Bell (2006, 2012) argues that it is vital to resist the erasure of Black disabilities in disability studies (which is, in practice, white disability studies) and in Black studies (which is in essence an ableist Black studies, sans disability). This suggests the need for the inclusion of Black disability studies within both Black studies and disability studies. While Black disability as identity and as an area of studies in Canada is raised in some chapters, it is not represented as a standalone essay in the collection.

Through our rigorous editorial team review, we also had to make the difficult decision not to include some submissions. These included contributions that did not quite fit the overall theme of the book, that duplicated ground already covered in other chapters, or that were by authors who could not undertake substantive revisions in a timely manner. Finally, as is all too common with such edited volumes, there were some voluntary withdrawals owing to the lengthy publication process. Nevertheless, we believe the contributors in this volume foreground the breadth and depth of Black scholarship in the social sciences, humanities, and fine arts; disrupt unfounded myths about Blackness, Black scholars, and scholarship; and open further the possibilities for Black studies in the Canadian academy.

Outline of the Book

The Nuances of Blackness in the Canadian Academy is divided into four sections. Each section opens with a short commentary by a leading senior Black scholar – George J. Sefa Dei, Wisdom J. Tettey, Annette Henry, and Shirley-Anne Tate. Toward extending the conversation on Blackness in the Canadian academy, the four commentators offer insights and perspectives on key concepts, themes, and linkages in chapters contained in various sections of the book.

Part 1, "Blackness: What's in a Name?," opens the volume with an animating onto-epistemic question: What happens when a Black professor or student shows up? George Sefa Dei's commentary cites Du Bois and Fanon to show how the chapters in this section centre Blackness without having to appeal to whiteness, even as they are anchored in a radical politics of unity in Black difference. He suggests that for the authors in this section, "Blackness is too rich to be contained by a singular narrative and to be written about and from a single playbook, for in their diversity *description* and *normativity* are unified as a totality without the dogma of *prescription*."

In chapter 1, "The Awkward Presence of Blackness in the Canadian Academy," Handel Kashope Wright teases out the ways in which Blackness is an awkward presence in the nation and on the campuses of institutions of higher learning, the ways in which Black knowledges and ways of knowing disrupt dominant, Eurocentric ontology, epistemology, and bodies of knowledge that are taken for granted. Utilizing autobiographical vignettes, Wright illustrates and buttresses his assertion that in the language of "inclusion" and the establishment of "equity and diversity" offices and positions notwithstanding, the Black body is always already out of place, and the Black professor is the unexpected professor on the university campus.

Situated within a Black feminist experience, in chapter 2, "Exposed! The Ivory Tower's Code Noir," Delia D. Douglas is concerned with the ways in which Black women face disregard and marginalization in the academy that is not only racism – specifically not only anti-Black racism – and not only sexism, but what she identifies as "anti-Black gendered racism." Black scholars are significantly under-represented in the academy, and Black women (at 0.7 per cent) particularly so. This under-representation is not only a matter of numbers but also perversely taken up as proof of the intellectual inferiority of Blacks in general, and Black women in particular. Douglas concludes that the specific doubled form of discrimination against Black women is also integral to the bolstering of "contemporary settler-colonial enslaved interpersonal relations and intellectual hierarchies."

Located squarely within philosophy of education, chapter 3, "The Precariat African-Canadian Academic: Problematic Historical Constructions, Perpetual Struggles for Recognition," by Ali A. Abdi, is a counter-narrative to how the presence of the persona Africana is perceived in the academy. The persona Africana, Abdi argues, is theoretically globalized, then selectively localized, but again denied the expected full entry into the promised land of contemporary Western democratic cosmopolitanism.

Using the concepts of the "socius" and the "rhizome," and discussing an empirical ethnographic study, in chapter 4, "What Have Deleuze and Guattari Got to Do with Blackness?," Awad Ibrahim offers "a rhizomatic analysis of Blackness," where Blackness is seen not in a colonial one-dimensional way but as a multicultural, multi-ethnic, and multi-lingual category.

In the final chapter in part 1, chapter 5, "Dancing with the Invisibility/ Inaudibility: Nuances of Blackness in a Francophone Context," Gina Thésée argues that the concept of Blackness does not exist in French, so, in order for her to speak as a Black francophone, she must simultaneously confront the ontological, the axiological, and the praxis. She has to engage with these dimensions, Thésée concludes, through a metaphorical dance with the invisible and the inaudible.

Part 2, "Blackness and Academic Pathways," consists of Wisdom Tetty's commentary and five chapters that explore the contradictions, nuances, and paradoxes of Blackness in relation to academic pathways into and through the academy and in engagement with the Black and wider communities.

Wisdom Tetty's commentary centres on the (1) contradictions and tensions of EDI (equity, diversity, inclusion), (2) the problematic of authentic voice and burden of representation borne by Black academics, and (3) the importance of struggle to forge alliances within and outside the university. The aim is to "facilitate the transformative change needed to realize the promise of equity and inclusion within the academy."

In chapter 6, "Hidden Figures: Black Scholars in the Early Canadian Academy," Malinda S. Smith concerns herself with the silent and invisible ways in which stories are mobilized and taken up, and narrate Black lives. Working against the idea of the single story, Smith introduces "a talented dozen," Black hidden figures in Canadian higher education, including, among others, Abraham Beverly Walker (1851–1907), Robert Sutherland (1830–79), Sophia B. Jones (1857–1932), James R. Johnson (1876–1915), Ivy Lawrence Maynier (1921–99), and Violet Henry King (1929–82). Through these towering Black figures, who are hardly known or cited in Canada, Smith examines what is at stake in the strategic silences of submerged stories of Black Canadian excellence.

In chapter 7, "Committed to Employment Equity?: Impediments to Obtaining University Appointments," Carl E. James draws on available data to argue that despite universities' declared commitment to employment equity, they "have done little to increase the number of Black faculty members."

In chapter 8, "Black Gay Scholar and the Provocation of Promotion," Wesley Crichlow deploys an autobiographical analysis to show how the sheer presence of his body as an "out" Black gay man should be acknowledged to be a form of political activism, one that challenges the presumed "naturalness" of white heterosexual academic capitalism.

In chapter 9, "'Certain Uncertainty': Phenomenology of an African Canadian Professor," Tamari Kitossa argues that in predominantly white institutions, Black professors often find themselves between a rock and a hard place, navigating the often conflicting professional and ethical commitments. He exposes the limits of the instrumentalist presumption that Black academics owe a debt to Black communities, especially where Black cultural elites seek to disqualify the Blackness of Black academicians. Drawing on foundational decolonial thinkers Frantz Fanon and Kwame Nkrumah, he asserts that Black academics need to pursue relations of liberation beyond an essentialized notion of Blackness.

Speaking to the tensions between holding high administrative office and identifying with Blackness and Black communities, in chapter 10, "Socio-Cultural Obligations and the Academic Career: The Dual Expectations Facing Black Canadian Academics," Kay-Ann Williams and Gervan Fearon address the complex and competing interests where Black Canadian scholars meet the demand of the established institutional metrics while simultaneously meeting community engagement expectations.

Part 3, "Blackness: A Complicated Canadian Conversation," begins with a commentary from Annette Henry. She identifies how questions of what it means to be Black and to belong in and to Canada and the academy are not innocent conversation starters, but righteous demands calculated to affirm Black alterity and white centrality. She calls attention to deep affectivity of "blunt, curt, clipped exchanges, slips of the tongue, imposing and impolite inferences, presuppositions, and interrogations that corrode the heart and challenge the presence and integrity of the Black Canadian body and intellect in public and intellectual spaces."

The five chapters in this section explore the nuances of Blackness in complicated Canadian conversations where the politics of identity meets arts and sociality. In chapter 11, "Fitting [Out-Fitting] In," Henry Daniel – whose compendium is a constant reminder of the importance of the body and the performative, including the Black body and the performance of Blackness – offers a meditation on the intersection of the poetic and the political in his encounter as a Black academic with the dean of his faculty.

In chapter 12, "The Caged Bird Still Sings in Harmony: The Academy, Spoken Word Poetry, and the Making of Community," Emmanuel Tabi tells the story of why we need to localize our scholarship while always struggling to speak the academic language. Here, the academy, a place pre-eminently of the written word, is meeting the community of the spoken word mutually imbricating sites of challenge, resistance, and solidarity on the margins.

Juliane Okot Bitek, in chapter 13, "States of Being: The Poet & Scholar as a Black, African, & Diasporic Woman," like Daniel and Tabi, uses the performative – in her case, poetry – to situate and ground her self-understanding at the intersections of gender, Blackness, and Africa-ness in the diaspora.

Délice Mugabo asks, in chapter 14, "Intersectionality in Blackface: When Post-Racial Nationalism Meets Black Feminism," who in francophone Canada "owns" Black studies and Black feminism. Above all, who benefits from these studies being situated in academia? If Blackness does not exist in French, Quebec included, then those who introduce intersectional studies (where "intersection" is a concept that was first introduced in Black feminism) benefit the most. To be sure, surprising to many, Mugabo contends, white francophone nationalist feminism benefits the most from Black feminism and its intersectional studies.

In chapter 15, "Re-spatializing the Boundaries of Belonging: The Subversive Blackness of Muslim Women," Jan-Therese Mendes examines how Muslim women's claim to a Black selfhood makes them walk through (so to speak) an African diasporic membership in which feeling one's Africanness is employed as an affective resource to avoid an interminable placelessness.

Part 4, "Black Pasts, Black Futurity," the final section of the volume, draws on the African indigenous conceptions of time that imagine coherence and unity in the dialectic of past and future, sutured by the present as an active moment of becoming. Centred on the politics of the affective, Tate writes that the authors of the chapters communicate the intensity of what it means to *feel* the wholeness of one's Black humanity against "suffering and self-negation even whilst they speak [their] agency with and through" suffering and self-negation. She writes that transforming Black pain into a medium for liberation is made possible by thinking about the past and present as media that enable "affective attachment and the construction of communities of Black scholars, intellectuals, and activists [who] develop ways of being beyond the anger caused by, and the pain of, anti-Blackness.

Chapter 16, "(Re)situating Black Studies at York University: Unsilencing the Past, Locating the Present, Routing Futures," is written by a group of graduate students from York University who call themselves the "York Collective." Studying the past and critically examining the present, the York Collective look into the future. They describe their efforts at centring Black studies in the academy, particularly at York University, consciously in the shadow of activism by previous Black students to establish space for Black students to move freely – intellectually and physically.

Delores V. Mullings, in chapter 17, "Community Service Learning and Anti-Blackness: The Cost of Playing with Fire on the Black Female Body," takes a similar turn as the York Collective and explores how she, as a Black feminist professor, navigates anti-Black racism and sexism from groups of white students, faculty, and staff in a social work department. Mullings's chapter, like the contribution of the York Collective, provides strategies to address the struggles and contestations faced by Black scholars in the Canadian academy.

In chapter 18, "Blackness and the Limits of Institutional Good Will," OmiSoore H. Dryden utilizes document analysis and personal narrative to make the bold argument that the dominant university policies and practices on equity, diversity, and inclusion cannot disrupt anti-Black racism. Most such policies were designed without Black people in mind, she asserts, let alone with any kind of commitment to challenge white normativity by combatting racism, racial discrimination, and racial harassment.

Like Dryden, Jennifer R. Kelly, in chapter 19, "Leadership in Neoliberal Times: A Road to Nowhere," contends that despite aspiring to leadership and administration positions, Black administrators are still subjected to anti-Black racialized power as enacted through institutional whiteness. One of Kelly's central conclusions is that neoliberalism embraces racism, especially in higher education.

Chapter 20, "Vocation of the Black Scholar in the Neoliberal Academy," is by Adelle Blackett, who calls for storytelling infused with radical love, one that advocates for the forging of radical alliance between Black scholars. The result is Black academics who together desire, advocate for, and struggle to achieve a united future, with our vocation seen as a labour of love that has the potential to transform the academy.

In chapter 21, "The Changing Same: Black Lives Matter, the Work of History, and the Historians' Craft," Barrington Walker, renowned historian of the Black experience in Canada, meditates on Black Lives Matter (BLM) as a contemporary expression of the long arc of the Black radical tradition in Canada and the Americas. He draws attention not only to history, but to historians as parties to the making and remaking of how events, experiences, and reality itself is understood in asserting Black humanity. Walker offers us no near-sighted hagiography of BLM, but instead from the historians' panoramic and microscopic view of Black resistance, we are treated to an appraisal, both appreciative and critical.

The final chapter of this collection, chapter 22, by Malinda S. Smith, is far from a conclusion, with its gesture toward a new imaginary. In "Charting Black Presence and Futures in the Canadian Academy," Smith offers one of the most comprehensive surveys of Canadian higher education in order to map Black presence and absence in the academy. The chapter maps Black Canadian studies academic programs, scholarship and fellowships, student associations and faculty caucuses, as well as the data on Black faculty educational attainment and income, and the representation of Black students, faculty, and administrators in the contemporary Canadian academy. She offers a clear view of the past, the ongoing struggles to establish Black Canadian studies, and the sites of struggle for charting a future that ensures that Black academics can claim their identities as part of the struggle to resist hegemonic whiteness and the oppressive homogenizing of anti-Blackness, and create enabling spaces for Black multiplicity.

Conclusion: Within Multiplicity

In curating this text, we as editors take the multiplicity of Blackness seriously. This means being attentive to articulating, naming, theorizing, and practising Blackness as an inclusive "socius" of difference, identity, and resistance. Notably, we have considered the ethno-phaulic epithet "nigger" and its "neutral" cognate, the "N-word," which occur periodically in the essays of contributors. As curators, we have no firm agreement among ourselves nor a convincing rationale to intervene in the authorial voice, political ideology, and relationship of our contributors to a word-as-deed that continues to affect their individual experience and the collective reality of Black people.

With the final preparation of *Nuances of Blackness in the Canadian Academy* during the COVID-19 pandemic, many of the themes explored throughout this volume reverberate in the broader society. That Black and racialized people are bearing the disproportionate brunt of the pandemic reflects, as a general matter, their greater exposure to harms from structural and systemic racism that circumscribes their lives, reflected in education, employment, income, and health outcomes. As post-COVID futures are being imagined and structured, we see signs already that Black, Indigenous, and racialized students might be left behind as a result of remote learning and home schooling. These dynamics place an even greater urgency on the Canadian academia to attend to the nuances of Blackness in the academy and the broader society. Unless we struggle to avert the inequitable design of the past being projected onto the future, a future that narrows even more the current sclerotic academic opportunities, structures, pathways, and pipelines, this generation will have failed in Fanonian terms "our historic mission."

Awad Ibrahim, University of Ottawa
Tamari Kitossa, Brock University
Malinda S. Smith, University of Calgary
Handel Kashope Wright, University of British Columbia

REFERENCES

Bell, C. 2006. "Introducing White Disability Studies: A Modest Proposal." In *The Disability Studies Reader*, edited by L.J. Davis, 53–74. New York: Routledge.
Bell, C., ed. 2012. *Blackness and Disability: Critical Examinations and Cultural Interventions*. Ann Arbor: Michigan State University Press.
Mogadime, D. 2015. "The Nuances of Blackness and/in the Canadian Academy: A Tool for Engaging with Equity Pedagogy in the Graduate Classroom." Federation for the Humanities and Social Sciences. https://www.ideas-idees.ca/blog/nuances-blackness-andin-canadian-academy-tool-engaging-equity-pedagogy-graduate-classroom.

Acknowledgments

Awad Ibrahim is thankful to all the Black scholars who made it possible for us to be, to think, and to hope. Keeping their legacies alive, he would particularly like to thank the late Stuart Hall. His gratitude to Black graduate students is profound; your hope and energy push us to the edge of a better future. Finally, Baian, my beautiful spirit, this one is for you!

Tamari Kitossa is grateful for the love, support, and forbearance of his family – Katerina, Jelani, and Adisa – and thankful for Black educators from the Black Education Project, the Harriet Tubman Centre, and the current African Canadian Heritage Association, and others who continue to nurture the intellect of African Canadian youth. He is appreciative of friends and colleagues who continue to inspire and nurture his development.

Malinda S. Smith is deeply appreciative of the many Black students and established scholars who generously responded to enquiries; Janine Brodie for generously reading and providing feedback on numerous chapter drafts; the Pierre Elliot Trudeau Foundation for the 2018 Fellowship, which supported doctoral research assistants Daisy Raphael and Jeanique Tucker; and data analysis and graph design support by postdoctoral fellow Yang S. Liu.

Handel Kashope Wright is grateful to all the folks who have helped him glimpse and appreciate the richness and variety that is Blackness, especially Samuel, who is one of the Beautiful Ones, here with us at last. He would like to acknowledge the University of Johannesburg's Department of Communications Studies, where he serves as senior research fellow and which has provided support for him to undertake his contributions to this text.

The editorial team extends its hearty appreciation to Tierney Kobryn-Dietrich for collating and formatting the draft manuscript.

NUANCES OF BLACKNESS IN THE CANADIAN ACADEMY

Introduction: A Meditation on the Nuances of Blackness in the Canadian Academy

AWAD IBRAHIM, TAMARI KITOSSA, MALINDA S. SMITH, AND HANDEL KASHOPE WRIGHT

Contextualizing the Black Canadian Academic

The presence of Blackness in Canada disrupts the imaginary of the nation. Blackness haunts the nation by making visible what is made invisible, and when it comes to the academy, it takes the signifying practice of what it means to teach, learn, and research while Black into social, historical, cultural, and psychic places that are yet to be fully explored. The chapters in this volume navigate these places and explore what happens when the unexpected is a Black body that shows up in a nice place like Canada, specifically the Canadian academy, a place that wraps itself in a blanket of civility and innocence. In raising this epistemo-ontological question, we gesture toward a signifying practice that unapologetically locates Black Canada in time and place, questioning also the adequacy of Canada as a terminus-given constant flow of the African diaspora. In doing so, Black Canada is located within histories and a politics without guarantees (Hall 1992, 1996), where nuances, not unidimensionality, is the term that best describes what it means to be Black in Canada.

Making sense of these histories and multiple moments, as demonstrated in this volume, enables Black Canada to spell its own name and write itself in a place where the dominant national narratives tend to imagine it as belonging elsewhere. But the act of writing is never innocent; it brings joy as much as pain. So the *nuances of Blackness*, the conceptual frame that is guiding this volume, oscillates between the two – joy and pain – knowing fully that histories and socio-political understandings of the nuances of Blackness in Canada, as elsewhere, require considering its situatedness within a broad historical, political, and cultural dynamic, especially as these articulate themselves in social interactions.

Daring to situate Blackness in Canada confronts the converging and diverging flux of two phenomena. First, in a broad national and academic context, Blackness in Canada has come to realize and to resist the easy seduction of an essentialized *ascribed* identity constructed by whiteness. Under the white gaze, Blackness is allowed to be only one thing, a singular essentialized identity, which eschew nuances and multiplicity that "Black Canadas" insist on carving for itself. As a defence against the onslaughts of white supremacy's bewildering combinations and permutations of "bad faith," animus tinged with plastic smiles, condescension, and "know your place-ism" (to use the words of Lewis Gordon [1995]), there is a temptation to insist on an overdetermined politics of Blackness that eschews diversity and difference. This volume reveals possibilities for an ontology of Black self-identifications, Black pride, and community construction and authentic intra-racial solidarities without abandoning a Black resistance to anti-Black racism. Second, and relatedly, there is the epistemic and practical realization that there are many "bad faith" *defining tropes* about Blackness and Black people. Against the perdurability of anti-Black tropes there seems neither escape nor refutation. But rather, as noted by Baldwin (1963) and Fanon (1967), there is forbearance until the white Other learns love of self without the need to conjure a dehumanized Black Other to hate. Since that cannot wait, priority is given to Black people figuring out not only how to exist, but also how to thrive, in spite of pervasive, persistent anti-Black racism and without resort to the barren ground of essentialism. There is, accordingly, a rather lengthy list of negations against which Black people must define their/our humanity. This must be done without overdetermining those negations as the centre of their/our existence. Thus, given this book is by Black intellectuals and engaged scholars within the academy, the principal existential and ontological negation that concerns us is the presumption that by virtue of our Blackness in the white cultural imaginary we lack *intellectual competence*, that we are always already "presumed incompetent" (Niemann et al. 2020).

From thinkers of the European Enlightenment such as Thomas Carlyle, Immanuel Kant, Georg Wilhelm Hegel, David Hume, and Thomas Jefferson, among others, to their contemporary reincarnation in scholars such as Richard J. Herrnstein, Charles Murray, William Shockley, J. Philippe Rushton, James Watson, and their liberal variants, Black intellectualism, if at all possible, is believed to rise no higher than mimicry (see Lyons 1975; Eze 1997; Simon-Aaron 2008). For some, like Kant, Blackness was itself proof positive of stupidity (Eze 1995). And while today there are fewer white scholars publicly promoting myths of biological and intellectual inferiority, the chapters in this volume show that such ideas die hard, perhaps because they are burrowed too deeply into the psyche and everyday cultural and social reproduction of the normative order in the West.

Where nothing can be taken for granted unless one's subjectivity occupies the centre of hegemonic frames, the struggle inherent in contemporary definitions of Blackness cannot escape the politics of identity (Hall 1996). If identity is taken for granted, we are arguing in this volume that depending on contexts and moments of interaction this may be the result of a certainty and simplicity demanded by a communicative logic to present and "speak" in a simple, indeed simplistic, and unnuanced voice. This recalls the colonial tropes of mimicry, of Black people lacking the capacity to do more than imitate whiteness. It may also be that the code-switching that we may engage in becomes the taken-for-granted part of ourselves that the white dominant world sees, constant in its presumed singularity, is a psychological defence against ambivalence, chaos, and uncertainty. In other words, if we cannot count on others to respect the "front-stage" identities we present to the world, largely for their benefit anyway, we can at least count on the certainty of a dignified nuanced story we have of ourselves in the "back-stage." But *self*-identity is neither the product of a singular mind nor experiences removed from historical and contemporary flows of, often conflictual, human interaction. Our identities are constituted and reconstituted through social inheritance and immediate struggles that affirm *how* one is to be and to live in the world (Hall 1996; Ibrahim 2010), in contrast to the fantasies and stereotypes projected onto us by others (Achebe 1988; Baldwin 1955, 1963; Fanon 1967). Identity is always an interplay between who we take ourselves to be and what others imagine us to be.

If these arguments are true, and we undoubtedly think they are, then to articulate Blackness is to consider how we embody, are marked as, negotiate, and sometimes resist endogenous and exogenous constructions of ourselves as Black people, as Black scholars and activists, and, importantly, as Black individuals. Given that the *fact of Blackness*, as Fanon observed, is a political struggle over how meaning is experienced psycho-culturally in the contest between colonizers, oppressors, and those who embrace the urgency to craft a new humanity, Blackness is invested in a drama over how Black humanity is to be conceptualized and lived. A Black politics of identity therefore ought to mean addressing identity in all its complexity, recognizing the need for recuperative affirmations without being stuck in the mode of *only* positive representations or the single story. We want to emphasize that conceptualizing Blackness in a broad national sociocultural and academic context means resisting the narrower dictates of identity politics. The aim is to open up refreshing constructions, interpretations, and understandings of our identities toward (re)articulations of Blackness that give free play to affirmation without ascriptions imposed by anti-Blackness.

Here we draw upon Stuart Hall by recognizing that on the cultural plane there is a need for humility in the production of the Black project and subject. There is a need to avoid what Hall referred to as the misguided and dangerous attempt to produce "the new essentially good black subject" (Hall 1988, 134). The *nuances of Blackness* instead require the suppleness to produce Black subjects "without guarantees" (Hall 1996). We are also guided in this regard by Audre Lorde who asserts, "Those of us who are Black must see that the reality of our lives and our struggle does not make us immune to the errors of ignoring and misnaming difference. Within our Black communities where racism is a living reality, differences among us often seem dangerous and suspect. The need for unity is often misnamed as a need for homogeneity, and a Black [anti-ableist, queer, anti-capitalist] feminist vision mistaken for betrayals of our common interests as Black people" (1984, 119).

It is our hope that this volume contributes to conversations about how Blackness without guarantees, and with a project of unity in difference, is to be articulated.

If the presence of Blackness in Canada haunts the imaginary of the nation, as we contend, this is especially true in the Canadian academy, where Blackness creates discomfort. That is, precisely because whiteness is marked as constituting intellectual competence, the Black student's and professor's bodies are always marked *as* and *by* unexpectedness (Wright 2013). Proof of belonging, when Black on campus – whether at the lecture podium, in an undergraduate lecture or lab, in a graduate seminar, or in a leadership position – is explicitly or implicitly demanded as evidenced by the racial profiling of Shelby McPhee at the 2019 Congress of the Humanities and Social Sciences at the University of British Columbia, and the carding of Jamal Boyce and Wiliston Mason on the campus of the University of Ottawa (Larsen 2019; Fairclough 2019; Gillis et al. 2019; Gergyek 2019; Kupfer 2019). There are too-numerous examples of Black scholars presumed to be the cleaning staff, food server, technical support, or, at best, "the academic help"[1] (Smith 2018) – a fact that has no bearing on the dignity of staff who provide indispensable service work.

As the record shows, in the Canadian academy the body of the Black scholar is likely to be read as an aberration, an anomaly, a threat, or evidence of white largesse and employment measures that bypass merit (Henry 1995; James 2017). In effect, and as this volume shows, Black scholars constantly find themselves resisting an anti-Black deficit narrative. It is therefore critical to ask, What happens when Blackness shows up in the academy without apology? How is Blackness received when, by default, it is whiteness that is expected? What is the relationship between Black academics and their work on the one hand, and Black communities and the nation more generally on the other? What do Black academics tell themselves about who they are and what they do (or ought to do)? How do Black academics navigate relations and situations laden with contradictions to contribute to the production of knowledge? For those inclined toward administration, how do they find the best in themselves and others to pursue, survive, and even thrive as chairs, deans, vice-presidents, and, more rarely, as university presidents? For those scholar-activists, engaged scholars, and/or those who are inclined toward the role of the public intellectual (Said 1994; Wiseman 2013), how do they (dare to) pursue this sort of intellectual engagement, which, too often, is institutionally unacknowledged, and therefore unrewarded labour? As well, how do they sustain high levels of public scholarly engagement while also fulfilling increased expectations and intensification for service and community engagement? Indeed, this labour is often unequally performed and when conducted by Black and other racialized scholars, inequitably recognized. How do Black scholars avoid the very real possibility of burnout?

Taken together, the chapters in this volume provide the most comprehensive and deepest engagements with the lived realities of Blackness, and Black scholars and critical Black scholarship, in the Canadian academy. The chapters explore a range of responses to some perennial as well as novel questions. They are experiential, autobiographical, empirical, historical, educational, geographical, pedagogical, and philosophical, and in every case politically contextualized and socially situated. In them, contributors explore the ways in which Blackness is made, unmade, and remade in the academy and how this is relevant to the nation, the diaspora, and local and national Black communities.

The contributors to *Nuances of Blackness in the Canadian Academy* include twenty-seven early, mid-career, and senior scholars and administrators located in over two dozen disciplinary and interdisciplinary programs across the social sciences, humanities, and fine arts in fifteen universities in seven provinces. Operating at the intersection of critical discourses, *Nuances of Blackness* is an aggregation of contrapuntal and polyphonic voices that are harmonically interdependent even when discordant. These are not metaphors redolent of Negritude, however. After all, we are not contending that all Black scholars think alike, even as many in this volume riff on shared experiences. Perhaps if there is a metaphor that captures the ways in which the chapters engage each other it is that of jazz fusion. Signifying the vitality of energy manifest in life itself, there are a variety of tones, inflections, and pitches reflecting Black difference in terms of philosophical and intellectual commitments, as well as subject positions marked by race, ability, gender, language, region, sexuality, religion, and location in the academic ranks. While chapters meditate upon these identities and positionalities, attending to how they intersect over time and space, they also resist efforts to reify such categories and, in turn, resist arriving at a fixed notion of Blackness in the academy. As Amiel Joseph (2015) argues, "identity *qua* difference" too readily can become "complicit within and a product of historically perpetrated violences" (27) – in this instance, anti-Black racism and violence rooted in colonialism and slavery that continually function to circumscribe Black freedom.

Despite the multiplicity of Blacknesses in the academy, the chapters in this volume tell stories about common experiences and the many ways that Black scholars in the student body, the professoriate, and administration across education, law, the humanities, social sciences, and performing arts go about doing their work. This volume can be said to have a four-fold focus. First, each chapter provides a specific take on Canadian Blackness and the work and positioning of the Black academic. The second focus is on the complex picture painted by the points of connection and coherence, as well as divergence and productive tension, produced by scholars from different fields, and various stages and positions in the academy. Although to some degree the foci, orientation, and flow of the contributions might have a fortunate stroke of serendipity, there is also a quality of self-organized coherency to varying chapters, which led us to situate them in the thematic sections presented. As well, we invited four leading senior Black Canadian scholars to each meditate on a section of the volume and to draw on their research, experience, and insights to offer fresh commentaries. We think these subtle notes will engage readers by providing further insights into individual chapters and themes as they resonate with these senior scholars on the sections as a whole, and how they link to historical and contemporary research on the nuances of Blackness in the academy and beyond.

Such range, variety, and commitment to difference raise questions of how we, the editors, as the curators of this collection, imagine the reading audience and the interests and specializations they bring. Given the iconoclasm in nuancing Blackness in the Canadian academy, there is the risk of dilettantism and the impression that as editors we have striven for accounts that culminate in a Blackness that is all things to all people and being for none. We accept this as one possible reading. What we have aspired for, though, is not to make such a reading impossible, but to curate a body of work that is both coherent and representative of difference and offers one possible form of structure without imposing stricture. Neither we nor our contributors propose that we have the last word here. Thus, in its breadth across and within faculties and disciplines, we hope reading audiences will find themselves engaged, "seeing" their areas of interest and specialization, and also that they will accept the invitation to engage with conversations and specializations with which they may not be familiar. While the foregoing objective of this volume is to problematize the unidimensional conception and representation of Blackness, especially in the popular imagination, it is also in a related way a Black contribution to the struggle against racism in the Canadian academy (Henry et al. 2017; Eisenkraft 2010; Henry and Tator 2009).

Acknowledging the political nature of knowledge, this text has two further objectives. First it is an unabashed Black criticism of and resistance to the aesthetic, affective, and geo-spatial distancing of academia as the "ivory tower."[2] Second this text rejects the narrative of the university as a sanctuary or "safe space" of free speech and academic freedom that insulates Black scholars within from the problems of discrimination and marginalization evident in the broader society. To be sure, heterogeneous Black communities, as much as broader publics, often perceive both academia and academics, including Black academics, as out of touch with the everyday struggles of ordinary people. All too often academics speak in a highly specialized language and restrictive discourse. While such speech codes are at times necessary, given the high level of abstraction at which some scholars work, and also some specialized short-hand among a shared community of experts is unavoidable, restrictive speech codes can also reflect self-serving provincialism, which excludes the masses in order to carve a special niche reserved for knowledge workers (Gouldner 1979).[3]

In being transparent and reflexive in laying these issues bare, this volume, in part, takes up what it means to do scholarship and to be a student, an academic, and researcher while being Black. As we discuss in the preface, this book project came out of frustration at absences, elision, and lacunae about the Black presence in the academy. Being familiar with these frustrations, we, the editors, realized that this book did not exist before we initiated it, at least not in the way in which we are presenting it in this volume. In some cases, the chapters in this book are initiating a new language and in others it is refreshing a narrative and a speech act on what it means to teach, learn, and research while Black in the Canadian academy. This volume, as far as we know, is the first comprehensive compendium on the topic in Canada. To this end, the contributors grapple with the meaning and the politics of *being* Black in a learning and working environment that is vital to coming to terms with larger existential questions of national and global Black identity (Mudimbe 1988; Gilroy 1993; Siermerling 2015).

Purposefully conceived, the emphasis in this collection is on what we might call *coherent difference*, that is, the ways in which some of the identifications that cohere as Black, Black academic, and Black Canadian academic are given space in a loose identity articulation rather than being stifled by the seduction of a unitary, uniform Black identity. Reaching toward a philosophy of Blackness in Canada, a productive tension is sustained in the collection as a whole and sometimes within individual chapters. Here the distinction and relation is two-fold: On one hand it is between the politics of difference *within* Blackness and identity made *through* difference, as Stuart Hall (1996) maintains. And on the other hand, the strategic coherence of Blackness and Black identity in the Canadian context, as Foster (1997) contends. The text takes the reader along from a general (re)conceptualization of Black Canadian and Black Canadian academic identities in part 1, through intersectionality and the politics of difference of Black (academic) identities in part 2; to the work of Black academics engaged in praxis (i.e., academics involved in or exploring performative arts and engaging in difficult or contentious conversations within Blackness) in part 3; and finally in part 4, to those who audaciously move between the past and present in a radical vision of love infused within a very real and pressing struggle that opens possibilities for a better future.

Conclusion: Resiliency and Insurgency in the Face of Marginality and Precarity

Despite limited numbers relative to their doctoral attainment, Black academics and students are punching above their weight. This, however, has always been the case. By all indications, and as presented in the chapters by Carl James and Malinda S. Smith in this volume, Black Canadian professors are significantly underrepresented. To some extent, the subtle racism of micro-aggressions as well as systemic and institutional racism evident in mis/education, low expectations, push-outs, and streaming from K-12 play a significant part in reducing the absolute numbers of Black Canadian youth pursuing higher education. For those who pursue higher education, the Eurocentricity of their invariably white instructors affirms a world view consistent with tropes of Black as (B)lack, that is, shaped by deficit thinking.

Yet the agitation and insurgency of Black students and faculty members alike to demand increased representation of Black faculty, the commitment of their institutions for the formalization of Black studies, particularly Black Canadian studies led by Black professors, and demands to ensure a high level retention of students and faculty members is setting the stage for radical transformation of the Black experience in the Canadian academy. Neither Black faculty nor students appear willing to wait in queue while diversifying whiteness (i.e., white women, LGBTQ2+, and persons with disability) takes up ever more space in the academy (Smith 2018). This resistance is evident in the emergence of the Black Canadian Studies Association in 2009 formed by some fifty students, professors, and community attendees at a meeting conceived and organized by Afua Cooper in her capacity as Ruth Wynn Woodward Chair of the Gender, Sexuality, and Women's Studies at Simon Fraser University. Indeed, the growth of Black faculty caucuses, the glacially slow rise in Black administrators, the rapid expansion of Black student associations, and ongoing activism reflect efforts to hold administrations accountable for the benefits universities derive from "diversity," especially that of representations of Blackness in glossy recruitment brochures and website images. What is at stake here is not simply the "inclusion" of Blackness, as if it were a category to be contained by colonialist concepts of Black homogeneity, but instead a radical representation of Black multiplicity.

As Black Canadian academics demand chairs in Black studies, establish professional networks to share their work, conduct research together, and mentor junior scholars, we are developing into a critical mass with shared radical consciousness. As we move into second half of the United Nations Decade for People of African Descent (2015–24), Black academics are intensifying their efforts to establish benchmarks, theorize reparations, bridge the ivory tower/community divide, and identify the policy implications of their work.

In presenting the nuances of Blackness and the rich spectrum of Black identities and identifications and the wide variety of approaches, scholarly work, orientations, and experiences of Black administrators, professors, and students, this volume mirrors in significant ways the plurality of Canadian Blackness while refusing to be contained by imposed hegemonic narratives from within and without. This is not simply an effort to find a "third way" between crude materialism at one end and poststructuralism's fundamentally political apolitical endorsement of the status quo at the other. Rather, this text is an invitation to appreciate and celebrate the richness of Blackness in general, and Black academics in particular. It is also part of an ongoing struggle by Black academics and activists to challenge and resist the anti-Blackness that constrains our lives and work. Finally, it is a statement of the enabling theories, perspectives, and vocabularies that articulate our presence and support concrete actions for the assertion, sustenance, and advancement of Black people's lives. After all, be it inside or outside the academy, all Black lives matter!

NOTES

1 We are not here disparaging non-academic administrative and custodial staff
   who are Black. Instead we are observing that Blackness is as disparaged as is
   support work and that Blackness signifies disqualification from equality with
   whiteness. We also want to acknowledge that we are (re)writing this chapter
   a few days after the murder of George Floyd in Minneapolis and Breonna
   Taylor in Louisville, USA, and as COVID-19 is disproportionately affecting
   our Black communities. The murder of George Floyd and COVID-19 remind
   us of the urgency of this book and that our work is only beginning.
2 As we were finalizing responses to the three anonymous reviewers, the
   hashtag campaigns #BlackintheIvory, #BlackInTheIvoryTower, and #Black-
   OnCampus were taking off on Twitter, and many of the stories in that digital
   archive resonate with stories told in the chapters in this volume.
3 The irony is not lost on us that even in this qualification, our mode of
   "speech" is already exclusive to an audience amenable to and cognizant of
   theoretical abstraction.

REFERENCES

Achebe, C. 1988. *Hopes and Impediments: Selected Essays 1965–87.* Harmondsworth,
   UK: Heineman.
Antwi, P., and Chariandy, D., eds. 2017. "Introduction." *Transitions* 124: 31–37.
   https://doi.org/10.2979/transition.124.1.11.
Baldwin, J. 1955. *Notes of a Native Son.* Boston: Beacon Press.
Baldwin, J. 1963. *The Fire Next Time.* New York: Dial Press.
Canadian Association of University Teachers. 2018. *Underrepresented and
   Underpaid: Diversity & Equity among Canada's Post-Secondary Education Teachers.*
   https://www.caut.ca/sites/default/files/caut_equity_report_2018-04final.pdf.
Eisenkraft, H. 2010. "Racism in the Academy." University Affairs, 12 October.
   https://www.universityaffairs.ca/features/feature-article/racism-in-the-academy/.
Eze, E.C. 1995. "The Color of Reason: The Idea of 'Race' in Kant's
   Anthropology." In *Anthropology and the German Enlightenment: Perspectives
   on Humanity,* edited by Katherine Faull, 11–23. Lewisburg, KY: Bucknell
   University Press.
Eze, E.C., ed. 1997. *Race and the Enlightenment: A Reader.* New York: Wiley-Blackwell.
Fairclough, I. 2019. "Acadia Student 'Embarrassed' by Racial Profiling at B.C.
   Conference." Saltwire, 6 June. https://www.thechronicleherald.ca/news
   /local/acadia-student-embarrassed-by-racial-profiling-at-bc-conference-319573/.
Fanon, F. 1967. *Black Skin, White Masks.* New York: Grove Press.
Foster, C. 1997. *A Place Called Heaven: The Meaning of Being Black in Canada.* New
   York: Harper Collins.

Gergyek, M. 2019. "Carding of Black U of O Student Was Racial Discrimination, Investigation Finds." *Fulcrum.* https://thefulcrum.ca/news/carding-of-black -u-of-o-student-was-racial-discrimination-investigation-finds/.

Gillis, M., Crawford, B., and Laucius, C. 2019. "'Humiliating': Black uOttawa Student Handcuffed in Campus Carding Incident." *Ottawa Citizen,* 14 June. https://ottawacitizen.com/news/local-news/humiliating-black-uottawa -student-cuffed-in-campus-carding-incident.

Gilroy, P. 1993. *The Black Atlantic: Modernity and Double Consciousness.* London: Verso Books.

Gordon, L. 1995. *Bad Faith and Antiblack Racism.* New Jersey: Humanities Press.

Gouldner, A. 1979. *The Future of Intellectuals and the Rise of the New Class: A Frame of Reference, Theses, Conjectures, Arguments, and an Historical Perspective on the Role of Intellectuals and Intelligentsia in the International Class Contest of the Modern Era.* New York: Continuum.

Hall, S. 1988. "New Ethnicities." *Stuart Hall: Critical Dialogues in Cultural Studies,* edited by D. Morley and K-H. Chen, 131–150. New York: Routledge.

Hall, S. 1992. "What Is This 'Black' in Black Popular Culture?" In *Black Popular Culture,* edited by G. Dent, 21–33. Seattle: Bay Press.

Hall, S. 1996. "Introduction: Who Needs Identity?" In *Questions of Cultural Identity,* edited by S. Hall and P. du Gay, 3–17. London: SAGE Press.

Henry, F. 1995. *The Colour of Democracy: Racism in Canadian Society.* Toronto: Harcourt Brace Canada.

Henry, F., Dua, E., James, C.E., Kobayashi, A., Li, P., Ramos, H., and Smith, M.S. 2017. *The Equity Myth: Racialization and Indigeneity at Canadian Universities.* Vancouver: University of British Columbia Press.

Henry, F., and Tator, C., eds. 2009. *Racism in the Canadian University: Demanding Social Justice, Inclusion and Equity.* Toronto: University of Toronto Press.

Ibrahim, A. 2010. "The Question of the Question Is the Foreigner: The Spectre of Blackness and the Economy of Hospitality in Canada." In *Ebony Roots, Northern Soil: Perspectives on Blackness in Canada,* edited by C. Nelson, 167–186. Newcastle: Cambridge Scholars.

James, Carl E., with S. Chapman-Nyaho. 2017. "'Would Never Be Hired These Days': The Precarious Work Situation of Racialized and Indigenous Faculty Members." In *The Equity Myth: Racialization and Indigeneity at Canadian Universities,* edited by F. Henry, E. Dua, C.E. James, A. Kobayashi, P. Li, and M.S. Smith. Vancouver: University of British Columbia Press.

Joseph, A.J. 2015. "Beyond Intersectionalities of Identity or Interlocking Analysis of Difference: Confluence and the Problematic of 'Anti'-Oppression." *Intersectionalities: A Global Journal of Social Work Analyses, Research, Polity, and Practices* 4 (1): 25–39.

Kupfer, M. 2019. "U of O Student Faced Carding Confrontation Despite New Policy." *Ottawa Citizen,* 20 September.

Larsen, K. 2019. "Nova Scotia Student Says He Was Racially Profiled at UBC-Held Congress." CBC, 5 June. https://www.cbc.ca/news/canada/british-columbia/nova-scotia-student-says-he-was-racially-profiled-at-ubc-held-congress-1.4668201.

Lorde, A. 1984. *Sister Outsider: Essays and Speeches.* Trumansburg, NY: Crossing Press.

Lyons, C. 1975. *To Wash an Aethiop White: British Ideas about Black African Educability 1530–1960.* New York: Teachers College Press.

Mudimbe, V.Y. 1988. *The Invention of Africa: Gnosis, Philosophy, and the Order of Knowledge.* Indianapolis: Indiana University Press.

Niemann, Y., Gutiérrez y Muhs, G., and Gonzalez, C., eds. 2020. *Presumed Incompetent II: Race, Class, Power, and Resistance of Women in Academia.* Logan: Utah State University Press.

Said, E. 1994. *Representations of the Intellectual: The 1993 Reith Lectures.* London: Vintage.

Siermerling, W. 2015. *The Black Atlantic Reconsidered: Black Canadian Writing, Cultural History, and the Presence of the Past.* Montreal and Kingston: McGill-Queen's University Press.

Smith, M.S. 2018. "Diversity in Theory and Practice: Dividends, Downsides, and Dead-ends." In *Contemporary Inequalities and Social Justice in Canada,* edited by Janine Brodie, 43–66. Toronto: University of Toronto Press.

Simon-Aaron, C. 2008. *Atlantic Slave Trade: Empire, Enlightenment and Cult of the Unthinking Negro.* New York: Edwin Mellen Publishers.

Wiseman, N. 2013. *The Public Intellectual in Canada.* Toronto: University of Toronto Press.

Wright, H.K. 2013. "Cultural Studies as Praxis: (Making) an Autobiographical Case." *Cultural Studies* 17 (6): 805–822. https://doi.org/10.1080/0950238032000150039.

PART ONE

Blackness: What's in a Name?

Commentary on Part One: Why the Study of Blackness Is Critical at This Historical Juncture

GEORGE J. SEFA DEI (NANA ADUSEI SEFA TWENEBOAH)

What is Blackness and why is the study of Blackness so critical, particularly at this historical juncture? As a pan-ethnic and pan-national noun or racial adjective, Blackness at one level speaks of the affirmation and acknowledgment of Black and African people's lives, cultures, and histories. At this level of abstraction, Blackness speaks also of the courage to resist/combat racism for self and others, to confront fear, to name their betrayal as a betrayal of humanity, and to aspire for what ought to be. So Blackness is about the humanity of a people and peoples denied, but also about the fullness of the fully human who resists. Blackness gestures to the particular struggles of the Black and African subjects at the interface of skin, body, psyche, hegemonies, cultures, and politics. Perhaps one reason why we are hearing about Blackness today, as opposed to the more localized articulations of the 1960s Black Power in the Cold War era, is because its opposite – anti-Blackness – is global. The end of the Cold War, like the "Northern compromise" that unified white supremacy in the United States, has unified the white supremacy of the world system. This global anti-Blackness is simultaneously negative and unloving of Blackness as much as it is extractive of our minerals and labour and expropriative of our cultural contributions. Consequently, we must affirm a different Blackness in response to raging global anti-Blackness and also to dislodge the centricity of Euro-colonial and racist whiteness.

As Fanon and others have cautioned, we must not romanticize the "greatness" of an African past patterned on the equivalency of European conceptions. We can celebrate our successes and the lessons these moments offer humanity. We can also acknowledge with racial pride the creative resistance of Black and African contributions, such as that of Haiti's gift to humanity – the first and only successful slave revolution to give rise to a state. But such recounting and acknowledgment must not be directed merely at proving our humanity to the insensibly inhuman.

Europe and whiteness are not the measure of Blackness. So, in many ways, the problem of global anti-Blackness gives us a renewed opportunity for us (as Black scholars in particular) to continue to insist on defining our Blackness on our own terms. We cannot cede intellectual territory to anyone. As the adage goes, "Nothing about us without us!" Blackness should not be just a study about us; it must be a study by/with us, for us and for humanity. It is this magnificent scope offered by this whole collection, and especially this section. What the authors show is that Blackness is too rich to be contained by a singular narrative and to be written about and from a single playbook, for in their diversity *description* and *normativity* are unified as a totality without the dogma of *prescription*.

To reiterate, Blackness conjectures about history, culture, identity, and politics. Blackness is about the ontological existence of Black and African peoples. Blackness is a way of life, a philosophical, spiritual, cultural, and socio-political expression of our existence. Blackness is also a reading of the world from competing frames of reference using the Black self/subject as site of entry and location. Such constructions of Blackness are both real and metaphorical. Blackness evokes epistemic, political, and spiritual stances. In effect, Black is/can be imagined and actualized in everyday political action. As a way of doing, acting, and coming to know oneself as thinking political beings, Blackness offers us an understanding of the nuances of human life in the wider realm of multi-geo-spaces.

The collection of chapters before us presents Blackness as a frame of reference – specifically, a non-hegemonic perspective of Blackness. The fact of, and truth about, Blackness is that it is consequential, contested, and yet rewarding and affirming. Blackness must be about freedom and liberation, even in these times and moments when globalization, capitalism, and ongoing colonization make the full realization of Black freedom an impossibility. There is an urgency for an authentic liberation of Black/African scholarship in the Western academy. The key questions coursing through the contributions in this section are: What are the ends, intents, and purposes of our performances of Blackness in relation to ontologies of Blackness? What energies are liberated, and how are we liberated when we evoke language that celebrates Blackness? These questions get to the heart of Part I of this volume – "What's in a Name?" – for it is beyond letting Blackness speak. There is an African saying that "It is not what one is called that is most important but what one responds to!"

I agree with Handel Wright, who mirrors Du Bois's and Fanon's apprehension of a self that is visibly "known" and yet always a surprise to those who construct representations of Black people as part of their ego structure. As Black scholars we have all felt the "awkward presence" of our Blackness in the Western academy. We are under constant surveillance in our educational institutions. There is a false feeling of belonging, but only if we play by the rules. But we are deemed not to belong or made to feel that way when we resist and when we assert our authentic individual and racial selves. We are loathed when we mimic Eurocentric theories and sometimes throw our own communities "under the bus" in the name of science and scholarship. But when we present counter-hegemonic stances and offer oppositional discourses that affirm and localize our cultural knowledges, we are seen as anti-intellectual, violent, angry, and unfriendly. And to make matters worse, our presence in the Western academy which has done so much to harm Black people, ironically sustains our communities' ambivalence and scepticism towards academia, even as we aspire to and embody the educational attainments so highly encouraged by our communities. Of the Black intellectual in the academy – a place of purgatory – there is surely a crisis of *being*, but there are also productive ways forward (Dei 2019).

But if in an ontological sense we are to claim Blackness as a sociopolitical identity, then it is vital to acknowledge how Blackness is lodged in the differences of ethnicity, class, gender, sexuality, religion, language, and (dis)abilities. The difference in our Blackness is eloquently portrayed in Delia Douglas's chapter. In pointing to the precarity of Black female existence in academia, Douglas simultaneously is asking us to draw upon the lessons of Black female resistance in history. These are lessons of Black female and local community resistances that can are instructive for the education of our youth through the paradigm of Black difference. The struggles of Viola Desmond, Marie Joseph Angelique, the women of Africville and Hogan's Alley, as well as our maroon foremothers suggests the complex ways Blackness (through race, class, gender, politics, history, and culture) engages as we embrace the re-writing our stories and challenge the dominant, colonial, and imperial narrative of Black people as interlopers.

Ali Abdi's philosophical musing on the historical construction of the African-Canadian academic and/or Black professoriate has an important message for understanding the nuances of Blackness. In *Black Skin, White Masks* Fanon reminds us of the dynamic that there is history, the making and unfolding of events, historicity, and the politics memory and representation. Through these dynamics Abdi reminds us that Africa and its rich and varied intellectual traditions of Black radical thought should disabuse any of the notion that the "Black academic" is an oxymoron. What is required today is for us to use our scholarship to challenge "global coloniality" in the service of our diverse global Black communities. Our roles and responsibilities go beyond our academic institutions to our local communities. We can start to meet the enormous responsibilities placed on our shoulders only by resisting the colonial entrapments of academia, remembering our histories and community struggles, and resolving to build upon the rich and enduring African human condition.

But colonialism and imperialism, not least the ceaseless wandering from humanities' earliest outpouring from the Continent to populate the world, has deposited Africa's genetic tracings the world over. The past is the present, the present the future, and all are one, but like Blackness in the "socius" created by the white man, it is always constructed, reconstructed, and being constructed: "One is not born Black," Awad Ibrahim reminds us. In his account of the vibrant adaptations and adaptability of Blackness to the malformations of whiteness, what he brings us in his "rhizomatic analysis of Blackness" is that we are not simply dealing with the deposits of historic traces, things, and subjectivities. We are instead invited into a meditation on discourses, cognitive constructs, and metaphors that, through language, literally make being and relationality possible. The language of Blackness and the Blackness of language intersect, merge, flow, and oppose each other at the vital levels of being. We cannot deny local intellectual agencies in the affirmation of one's Blackness. Still, we must guard against the naturalization of Blackness. Even when we claim Blackness as a socio-political signifier, we need some analytical clarity that bears on Blackness as a signifier of difference, identity formation, and community power. The problem of a social fabrication of Blackness is when it is made an obligation of compliance such that there is an essentialized reading and homogenization of Black body performances. Clearly, Blackness is not a homogenous category and we must speak about it differently. There is the power of speaking and writing differently about and being Black without the necessity of imperious absoluteness. For what will be gained by the false security of the mass, much more will be lost in an individual's freedom and play to adapt and to be.

Gina Thésée shows us that inasmuch as vocabulary *as* language shapes the constructedness of Blackness, language as cultural dynamic shapes ontological grammars. Here contexts, history, physical and metaphysical location in time, place, and space, and politics matter equally. In writing Blackness, she reminds us that we must capture the absences, omissions, silences, and erasures in dialogue and discursive practices. Her careful portrayal of the nuances of Blackness through epistemological framings of the French language bring to bear the complexity, heterogeneity, historicity, and discursive authorizations of Blackness as racial, socio-political, and spiritual signifier. The issue here is not only of difference but, and also, of historical and spiritual consciousness. The critical question is how to develop an awareness of our Blackness when the language and conceptual tools are missing from our schooling and educational literatures. Thésée's account offers Black scholars the opportunity to reflect on ways to develop the analytical tools critical for understanding the complexity of the Black experience as a human experience. Articulating different ontologies is about decolonization. Thésée pinpoints the importance of complicating and subverting hegemonic definitions and understandings of Blackness in ways that allow us to resist how we have become "captives of the colonial experience" (Sicherman 1995, 26) and encounters and thus our mental subversion.

It has been a joy reading the papers in part 1 of this volume. The emergence of a distinctly Black philosophic tradition specific to Canadian soil is long in coming. The fact is that in Canada and elsewhere, Blackness has always showed up in unwanted spaces with deleterious consequences for Black peoples' lives and bodies (see Adjei 2013). Refreshingly, in this book Blackness shows up as a sign of intellectual power and courage. Reading the contributions in this section have persuaded me to reflect on four epistemic and theoretical concerns framed, not so much as closing thoughts but an opening for continued dialogue.

First, the place of Black cultural knowledges and the location of such onto-epistemologies of Black subjects for understanding Black life, social existence, and activism. Learning from and extending Molefi Asante's (2003) framing of Afrocentricity, there is a form of Black episteme that can be termed "Blackcentricity" (Dei, Odozor, and Vasquez 2020) that, through the variety of our histories, offers a counter-reading of Black life as an intellectual reference point to global white historicity. Our African Indigeneities inform our Blackcentricity. More importantly the insistence on our African Indigenous epistemologies and ontologies is more than an intellectual act; it is increasingly a "matter of life and death for the victims of colonial domination" as devise strategies for our survival and collective existence in a hostile, violent world (see also Black Ink 2020, 29). Second, these chapters indicate that in our constructions of Blackness we need to be careful to heed the multidimensionality of Blackness, the complexity and diversity of Black bodies, and multiplicity of possible performances. This calls for a number of things, including the recognition of the embedded gender, class, age, ethnic, sexual, (dis)abled, culture, and language differences, as well as a knowledge of the cartographies of Blackness from multiple geo-spaces. Third, it is vital to acknowledge the place of Africa and Africanness in our constructions of Black and Blackness. There are synergies, convergences, and divergences (Dei 2017). We cannot speak of Blackness absent of an understanding of Africanness and vice versa. The fact that within diasporic contexts we continually witness the re-invention of Africanness is significant in making us whole, and as a people in the sense of our connected histories, cultures, identities, and politics. Finally, the importance of anchoring the scholarship of Blackness within the rich Black intellectual traditions is beyond question. Black and African peoples have to claim our own Indigeneities as a necessary exercise in our decolonization and to subvert the thinking that colonialism is our only story or that "Europe is the advent of human history"!

Acknowledgment

Thanks to co-editor Tamari Kitossa for sharing ideas to strengthen this commentary.

REFERENCES

Adjei, P.B. 2013. "When Blackness Shows Up Uninvited: Examining the Murder of Trayvon Martin through Fanonian Racial Interpellation." In *Contemporary Issues in the Sociology of Race and Ethnicity: A Critical Reader*, edited by G.J.S. Dei and M. Lordan, 25–42. New York: Peter Lang.

Asante, M. 2003. *Afrocentricity: A Theory of Social Change.* Trenton, NJ: Africa World Press.

Black Ink. 2020. "'Solidarity Is Not a Market Exchange': An Interview with Robin D.G. Kelley," 16 January. https://black-ink.info/2020/01/16 /solidarity-is-not-a-market-exchange-an-interview-with-robin-d-g-kelley/.

Dei, G.J.S. 2017. *Reframing Blackness and Black Solidarities through Anti-Colonial and Decolonial Prisms.* New York: Springer Publishing.

Dei, G.J.S., Odozor, E., and Vasquez, A., eds. 2020. *Cartographies of Blackness and Black Indigeneities.* Gorham, ME: Myers Educational Press.

Dei, J.S.S. 2019. "An Indigenous Afrocentric Perspective on Black Leadership." In *African Canadian Leadership: Continuity, Transition and Transformation*, edited by T. Kitossa, E. Lawson, and P. Howard, 345–369. Toronto: University of Toronto Press.

Sicherman, C. 1995. "Ngugi's Colonial Education: The Subversion ... of the African *Mind.*" *African Studies Review* 38 (3): 11–41. https://doi.org/10.2307 /524791.

1 The Awkward Presence of Blackness in the Canadian Academy[1]

HANDEL KASHOPE WRIGHT

Introduction

This chapter offers pointers to ways in which Blackness is an awkward presence, including when it is an absent presence, in the Canadian context, on at least three grounds. First, Black bodies are "bodies that do not belong," in the nation[2] or on university and college campuses. Second, Black thought and ways of knowing constitute ontologies and epistemologies and a body of knowledge that disrupts traditional paradigmatic, disciplinary, and interdisciplinary discourses. Finally, and paradoxically, Blackness is an identity that is uncomfortable with itself, especially when made to face the difference within that supposedly threatens its own coherence and unity. The chapter concentrates on addressing the first two, leaving the third, which some would consider a matter for discussion within the "family of Blackness," for another time and place.

While the focus is on Blackness in the Canadian academy, this chapter reflects the fact that, on one hand, Blackness necessarily and always already overflows the boundaries of the nation state (and indeed can never be contained within that imagined community), and on the other hand it is marked by specificities that contribute to its multiplication, which in turn troubles singularity, coherence, and community, which are taken for granted. In addressing the awkwardness of Blackness in the Canadian academy I take my cue from Stuart Hall's (1992) modest autobiographical approach to addressing Blackness,[3] which involves not only incorporating the personal and experiential but also making them the starting point and touchstone of analysis, in order to avoid attempting to speak for all Blacks or to authoritatively depict the conditions of all Blacks (Black Canadian academics in particular). I have also tried to preserve and continue the orality and presentation mode of the original presentations on which this chapter is based, and, in keeping with the approach of bell hooks (especially in her early work in 1981, 1989, and 1992), of writing in an accessible style in order to reach a wide an audience. I proceed by addressing Blackness and the Black academic in three sections: the first involves the national context, the second the academy and academic activism, and the third explores "the nuances of Blackness" and my thoughts on strategies for surviving and being effective advocates for representation and equity in Canada and in the neoliberal academy.

Oh Canada: Reading Against the Grain of the Nation's Image Text

Because multiculturalism (or, in a more comprehensive sense, comparative multiculturalism and its critical alternatives, including interculturalism and cosmopolitanism) is a focus of some of my work, I have done the usual academic and intellectual work in the area (books, chapters, journal articles, and international, national, and local referred conference presentations, invited academic and public talks, interviews, etc.). However, I was struck by what I considered a high number of international invitations I received over a few years to speak on Canadian multiculturalism and related topics to non-academic audiences.[4] I mentioned this to an Irish colleague as we chatted over a pint in a Dublin pub. He chuckled and declared, "Come now, Handel, you must know how you come off. We are just beginning to come to grips with this 'diversity thing' in Ireland and everyone thinks Canada has it nailed. And you ... " (he trailed off, gesturing to me as if he need not state the obvious, but greeted by my puzzlement he stated it anyway) ... "Well you are living proof of this: the expert on Canadian multiculturalism who is a Black immigrant from Africa!"

The title of this chapter is "the awkward presence of Blackness in the Canadian academy," and it is an understatement, of course, to speak of the presence of Black people in the Canadian academy as "awkward." I've done so taking my cue from Canada's image text (that master narrative that is a combination of official narratives and folk stories), part of which strongly reads politeness and understatement. Canada's image text also reads comfortably ethno-racially diverse (indeed major cities like Vancouver, Toronto, and Montreal are not merely diverse but have become marked by what Steven Vertovec, 2007, refers to as "super-diversity"). It reads tolerant and diversity-positive, inherently multicultural (after all, we gave the world official multiculturalism), and Canada is an "unlikely utopia" (Adams 2008) in which "multiculturalism is working" (Kymlicka 2007), and indeed is well established as an inherent, inexorable, defining characteristic of the nation, "the sticky stuff of Canada," as Janice Gross Stein (2007) puts it). It reads absolutely post-racial (perhaps always already non-racial – no need to be post-racial, since we never were racial, let alone racist). And the narrative also projects Canada as champion of human rights (e.g., recently surprised but willing to stand alone internationally in defence of women's and human rights in Saudi Arabia) and ethically, ethnically, and morally superior to most countries, including and especially our neighbour to the south, the United States of America. Given this master narrative, this national image text, the Canadian university is generally expected and indeed is perceived to be the epitome of the ivory tower of innovation, diversity, inclusion, and intellectual freedom. Hence it is a fortress where academics in particular, but staff and students also, are safe from pesky social problems, including the rare incident of discrimination that might occur in "the dirty outside world" (Hall 1990).

Critical academics, including and perhaps especially critical faculty and students from racialized and minoritized groups know different. We know this image text, this "truth" about Canada is a hegemonic, perennial myth (as Michel Foucault 1981, reminds us, knowledge and power are imbricated, and truth is the acceptance of narratives of power as irrefutable, the passing of powerful subjective knowledge into what is taken for granted to be objective truth). Colleges and universities in Canada are a microcosm of Canadian society and reflect a nation that has a long history of discrimination against and marginalization of minorities (gendered, ethno-racial, sexual, etc.), including a perennial problem of racism in the Canadian university (Stewart 2009; Henry and Tator 2009). Interestingly, the history of discrimination against and marginalization of ethno-racial others is one Canada chooses too often to not remember or to not know. This peculiar not knowing – sometimes selective amnesia, sometimes refusal of uncomfortable knowledge passing off as simple ignorance (Felman 1982) – is one a principal characteristic of Canadian racism, including and especially anti-Black racism.[5] In fact ignorance and forgetting combine in a principal tactic in the overall strategy of Canadian anti-Black racism, namely erasure. Blacks in Canada are at once non-existent (the Great White North also works as a racial signifier of a predominantly white nation)[6] and hyper-visible (as problem, epitomized by supposedly outer-national cultures and problem youth) – an apparent paradox that is in fact a unitary (mis)conception, since hyper-visibility is in fact a form of invisibility. As a result, when they come to the fore, anti-Black racist incidents (indeed, most racist incidents) are marked as strange, deviant, and in need of explication as uncharacteristic, definitely and embarrassingly un-Canadian.[7]

Canada's image text is strongly promulgated within and outside the nation state and is always in play and comes to the fore or is a particularly strong element of the background and context, especially in interactive and dialogical encounters such as academics' presentations and interviews. My Irish colleague's comment on the utility of imbricating my Blackness and expertise on multiculturalism illustrates that the national image text spills over the nation's boundaries and circulates internationally and the Other as success story can be readily appropriated, including by those outside the nation, as proof of its truth. What is rendered invisible in this picture is my struggle as a Black immigrant in Canada – someone who, despite my privileged position as a tenured academic, struggles like any other immigrant to negotiate what Linda Martin Alcoff (1999) and Jenny Burman (2006) identify as dual aspects of belonging (in my case, belonging to Greater Vancouver and having Greater Vancouver belong to me, and belonging to Canada as multicultural on the one hand and diasporic on the other). As a critical Black academic in Canada I am cognizant that I work in and attempt to contribute to a public sphere permeated by Canada's image text. As an avowed anti-racist, cultural studies scholar, and critical pedagogue, I came into multiculturalism backwards when I started my career as an academic,[8] and I therefore research and teach multiculturalism principally through critique. My work in this area (e.g., Wright 1994, 2012a, 2012b, 2016) emphasizes what troubles multiculturalism. It makes for discomfort with the nation's image text. And it reveals what Himani Bannerji (2000) has referred to as "the dark side of the nation."

For example, the long-standing common sense conception of multiculturalism as a benevolent discourse and official policy aimed at the integration of immigrants involves a concerted non-acknowledgment of race and racial hierarchies in the making of the nation's "cultural" diversity discourse and policy. To take race into account and to acknowledge that multiculturalism had its origins in the 1963 Royal Commission on Bilingualism and Biculturalism is to come to terms with the policy's history as being about resolving divisions within whiteness, about bridging the two solitudes of the "founding peoples," old stock (i.e., white) English Canada and (white) Québécois de souche (with the third founding peoples – the original peoples, First Nations – conveniently forgotten). When it was first proposed, "multiculturalism within a bilingual framework" still involved the principal issue of the English versus French divide (now with emphasis on language difference), to which recognition of other white ethnic groups was added (Haque 20012). In other words, it was still about bridging whiteness. It was much later that multiculturalism developed the focus that has now passed into common sense, as a discourse and policy of welcoming and integrating immigrants (with visible minority immigrants and refugees from the Third World, including Blacks assumed, even if not stated, to be in most need of integration). As a result, the product of multiculturalism – that ideal tolerant citizen – is articulated from a paradoxical mixture of liberal democratic principles and the continuation of the discourse and practice of long-established but now seldom-mentioned colonialism and racial hierarchization. As David Austin (2010, 19) puts it, "The image of the respectable, peaceful, multiculturalism-loving Canadian citizen, descendant of the two founding nations, France and Britain, goes hand in hand with its opposites: the Indigenous 'Indian,' the Black, the immigrant newcomer and the refugee."

Also the much-vaunted cultural mosaic as national metaphor (Canada basks in its superiority to the U.S. metaphor of the melting pot) has long been critiqued, even before it was adopted as national metaphor (Porter 1965). Far from being horizontal and equality based, Canada has a vertical mosaic[9] of racial, ethnic, and cultural groups with white English and French at the top, other white ethnics below, visible minorities, including Black people, below them, and Indigenous peoples (those forgotten founding peoples) at the very bottom. To accept the false notion of a horizontal cultural mosaic therefore is to ignore the racial reality of a Canada in which "the real inequality of power [remains] hidden by the multicultural cloak" (Moodley 1983, 325). Not surprisingly, Black academics (e.g., Dei 1996, 2010; Lee 1985; Este et al. 2018) have been at the forefront of initiating and constructing Canadian anti-racism discourse and wielding it as a sharp critique of and proposed alternative to multiculturalism.

Relatedly, Blacks, including Black academics, have been very active in the perennial struggle against the erasure of Blackness, that pernicious principal strategy in Canadian anti-Black racism. These efforts include documenting official racism, from Afua Cooper's (2007) documenting "the untold story of Canadian slavery," through Wanda Robson's collaborations on documenting her sister Viola Desmond's groundbreaking civil rights activism (Robson and Caplan 2010; Reynolds and Robson 2018), to Robyn Maynard's (2017) examination of state anti-Black racism. Also important has been the documentation of Blackness and the politics of space in general (e.g., McKittrick and Woods 2007, on Black geographies) and the erasure and (wilful) forgetting of historical Black spaces, including the myth of Southern Ontario as fairy tale end of the Underground Railroad, which de B'beri, Reid-Maroney, and Wright (2014) had to retell as early Black settlement and node of dispersal of Blackness in Canada; the story of the expulsion of the Black population of Africville, and Wayde Compton (2001) and the Black Strathcona Project's documentation of the less well-known bulldozing of a mixed ethnic neighbourhood in East Vancouver that included the only substantial Black population in BC and expulsion of its population to make way for a viaduct; and Charmaine Nelson's (2018) account of the segregated burial of enslaved and free Blacks in a town in Quebec and erasure of their histories through present-day private ownership of the land and failure of authorities to create monuments and forms of memorialization.[10]

By their very existence, creative works by Canadian Blacks refuse containment as art for art's sake and instead are already political and part of the assertion of Black existence and resilience and Black resistance to anti-Black racism. From a rich and varied Black Canadian literature examples that immediately comes to mind include David Chariandy's (2018) familial novels of complex Black Canadian lives and Marlene NourbeSe Philip's (1988) overtly political Black Canadian poetry.[11] Based in British Columbia myself, I think of the collections edited by Wayde Compton (2001) and Valerie Mason-John and Kevan "Scruffmouth" Cameron (2013), both for their poetic assertion of a Black British Columbia and a Great Black North[12] respectively, and because the editors of these works are located in British Columbia, a province in which Blackness is particularly precarious, the erasure of Blackness made all too easy because the Black population is negligible. And as a Sierra Leonean descendant of formerly enslaved Africans who has lived in the United States and Canada, I cannot help but think of Lawrence Hill's (2007) *The Book of Negroes*, with its protagonist whose movements from continental Africa to the United States on to Canada then on to Sierra Leone and then to England epitomizes the impossibility of containing Blackness within the nation; the importance of Paul Gilroy's (1993, 1994) and Stuart Hall's (1996; Hall and Back 2009) argument for "routes over roots" in the (re)conceptualization of identity and the making of Black diaspora and Black transnational identity. Loosely composed of diasporic and doubly diasporic, first- and second-generation immigrant and "settler" and "indigenous" Blacks and "Black pioneers" (Kilian 2008), Canadian Blackness is paradoxically distinctly national and outernational, and collectively there is much Black academic and intellectual work that constitutes anti-racist, Black resistance, Black affirmation activist work. It is proof that, as Peggy Bristow et al. (1994) have asserted about Black women's presence in Canada, "We're rooted here and they can't pull us up."

Blackness is and has always been an awkward presence in Canada, a constant reminder of the failure of the nation state to live up to its image text, a persistent presence that confounds repression and resists erasure and thus a veritable transruption of the multicultural myth attempting to pass as reality.[13] From slavery days we have been part of a history of marginalization and discrimination that Canada would rather forget or not know, a racist history that goes against the grain of the nation's image text and continues in the form of erasure. And from slavery days to the present we have been part of the resistance to marginalization and discrimination in Canada. Black academic and intellectual work insists on asserting our presence (whether over many generations or recent immigrant arrival), work that names and resists anti-Black racism in particular and discrimination in general.

Notes from the Unexpected Professor

As a PhD student at the Ontario Institute for Studies in Education, University of Toronto, I had the opportunity to teach undergraduate courses at York University. On the first day of one of my early morning courses I found all the students hovering around the closed door of the classroom. "What's going on?" I asked. "Well the door has not been opened yet and the instructor is not here, so join the queue" a white female student quickly replied. When I was hired three years later at the University of Tennessee, temporary parking had been arranged for faculty in front of a student dormitory. As I emerged from my car on the first day of classes, a very helpful white male student shouted at me from one of the windows of the dorm, "Hey man, you can't park there, you know. It's reserved for faculty." Some ten years later I was hired at the University of British Columbia as a Canada Research Chair. As I was being shown around by a white female administrator, we encountered an older white male faculty member and she tried to introduce me: "This is Handel," she said. "He is joining us in the Faculty." "Great to meet you!" he interrupted, shaking my hand vigorously. "Welcome to UBC. Do you know yet who you will be studying with?" And just this year, some thirteen years after that encounter, I attended a talk on campus by George Elliot Clarke at UBC's Peter Wall Institute for Advanced Studies (as a member, a Peter Wall Scholar). Before the talk, as folks mingled, a young white man came up to me and introduced himself as faculty at Simon Fraser University. I told him my name only in reply, and a slightly awkward pause ensued, which he ended by asking, "And are you a doctoral student here at UBC?" with a big smile and generous emphasis on the word "doctoral."

The Canadian academy, like much of the academy worldwide, has become the neoliberal academy in a time of extended austerity. Henry Giroux (2013, 2017) is an academic and public intellectual who has addressed this matter intensively and (in Dawes 2014, 25) offers a succinct and trenchant summary: "In the United States and increasingly in Canada, many of the problems in higher education can be linked to diminished funding, the domination of universities by market mechanisms, the rise of for-profit colleges, the intrusion of the national security state, and the diminished role of faculty in governing the university, all of which both contradict the culture and democratic value of higher education and make a mockery of the very meaning and mission of the university as a democratic public sphere."

Academic work is now highly stressful and precarious, marked by work intensification and time pressures for those lucky enough to be tenured or on tenure track, compounded by increasing casualization for many well-qualified others stuck in exploitative part-time, "sessional" positions. On the one hand, much of the administrative labour of running universities as institutions has been downloaded onto faculty, while on the other university administration has become bloated, with administrators earning exorbitant salaries. Heather Menzies and Janice Newson (2007, 83) hold that "Canadian universities have been restructured and have become nodes in the wired knowledge economy," with the result that "in struggling to manage conflicting organizational and temporal priorities, academics are adopting practices to manage these conflicts which adversely affect the quality of their teaching and research," a situation that has only become exacerbated in the ensuing decade. All of this has led to, among other things, a marked rise in burnout among academics (Malesic 2016). It is hardly surprising then that there has been an increase in the numbers leaving academia, as documented and reflected in the growing literature that has been named "quit lit" (Macharia 2013; Dunn 2013; Coin 2017).[14]

A principal characteristic of critical discussions of the neoliberal university during extended austerity is that its primary subject and audience is the tenure track academic. When it does deal with diverse constituencies, it considers the place of faculty versus administrators or the fate of tenured and tenure track faculty versus non-tenure track sessionals, and only rarely does it address graduate and undergraduate students. And when it does give thought to the disciplines, the focus is on the precarious position of the humanities and to a lesser extent the social sciences. What this literature does not address is the specifics of the sociocultural identity of these constituencies, of administrators, academics, staff, and students as embodied subjects. My position is that it is crucial and urgent that we introduce identity politics and sociocultural difference into the discussion of the neoliberal university during protracted austerity and that we also introduce the neoliberal university in a time of austerity to our discussion of Black Canadian studies and the representation of Blackness in the academy. In other words, what is needed to understand the position of Blackness in the academy is a combination of critical anti-racism and/or critical race theory and the critique of neoliberalism.

The Canadian academy is a true part of the Great White North – with serious problems in recruitment, hiring, retention, and promotion of racialized faculty and staff, including Indigenous and Blacks. The university in the West, including in Canada, was originally intended for the education of white middle-class and upper-middle-class males, and these institutions of higher education continue to be distinctly white. Indeed the very fact that diversity efforts (equity administrative positions, scholarship, offices, guidelines, and policy) are now prominent and ubiquitous at institutions of higher learning in the West (Ahmed 2012), including in Canada, is proof that there is a chronic problem in diversifying (in gender, ability, and especially race) universities at all levels (from administration and leadership positions, through faculty and staff, to students). The Canadian Employment Equity Act identifies four groups for proactive hiring – women, people with disabilities, Indigenous people and visible minorities – and given that Canadian universities have been stubbornly predominantly white, one would expect that equity policies and diversity work would emphasize the racial diversification of the university. Instead diversity work in the Canadian university has resulted largely in what Malinda Smith (2018, 55) has identified as "diversifying whiteness."[15] The result for Blackness is that the Black body is still what Lewis Gordon (2012, drawing on Frantz Fanon) referred to as an illicit appearance – a body that does not belong, that makes an unexpected appearance, in this case a body out of place on campus. As I pointed out in 2003 about teaching cultural studies within a College of Education at the University of Tennessee, "As an African and even as a Black person teaching at a decidedly white institution (the University of Tennessee has failed to date to bring the percentage of Blacks at both faculty and student level to a court mandated 6%), I am the unexpected colleague and teacher ... the unexpected pedagogue teaching the unexpected discipline" (Wright 2013, 818). Similarly, the Black academic in Canada is the unexpected professor, received, not with the crude, shocked exclamation that greeted Fanon's Negro at large – "Look Mama, a Negro!" – but rather with a polite translation of that shock and discomfort into the raised eyebrow, the furtive second glance, subtle affective reactions in which institutional white privilege and anti-Black racism melt into thin air even as they permeate everywhere (Tate 2014; Gordon 1995). Misrecognizing me and other Black faculty as students (in my case repeatedly over more than twenty years since I earned my PhD and my first position as assistant professor) is one of ways in which whiteness "generously" makes sense of and comes to grips with the awkwardness of the unexpected Black presence in the unstated but presumed white institutional space that is the university campus.

Given the neoliberalization of the Canadian university and the exacerbated effects on Black and other racialized and minoritized groups (e.g., underrepresentation on tenure track faculty and especially in leadership positions, overrepresentation in precarious sessional positions), Black academics might be forgiven for eschewing institutional politics and concentrating on career advancement or indeed on mere survival within the profession. However, some of us cannot not be politically engaged, even as that means a considerable additional burden.[16] We hold a radically different view of the nature and function of the university, captured most succinctly in Stuart Hall's (1992) trenchant assertion that "the University is a critical institution or it is nothing." Given his perspective, Hall therefore advocates that critical academics go beyond academic work to undertake intellectual work and sees the two as being distinct and complexly related: "I come back to the critical distinction between intellectual work and academic work: they overlap, they abut with one another, they feed off one another; the one provides you with the means to do the other. But they are not the same thing" (286).

Despite Hall's preference for intellectual over academic work, it is important to conceptualize the academy as inherently political and hence acknowledge that there is crucial work to be done in making institutions of higher learning more diverse and equitable, in bringing together academic and intellectual work, in doing what we might call academic activism. For the critical Black academic taking on certain "service" roles constitutes political work. The following is a brief and partial outline of some of my own academic activist work and other service work beyond the academy. First there is my long-term service work on diversity, inclusion, and equity at the University of British Columbia during twelve continuous years' membership on the original President's Advisory Committee on Equity and Diversity (2006–16) on to the renamed Vice Presidential Strategic Implementation Committee for Equity and Diversity (2016–present). Second is my role since 2016 as chair of the Race & Leadership Working Group of the Vice Presidential Strategic Implementation Committee for Equity & Diversity. Third is my work on the current Inclusion & Openness Working Group of the UBC Strategic Plan. These roles have afforded me extensive knowledge of the issues faced by the university community in general and racialized faculty in particular related to representation, inclusion, and equity. As Sara Ahmed (2012, 25) observes, such "diversity work is hard because it can involve doing *within* institutions what would otherwise be done *by* them."

I also have extensive national and international leadership service experience in representation and equity work in the form of roles in prominent academic associations, including membership on the interim executive of the interdisciplinary Black Canadian Studies Association and two consecutive three-year terms representing Africa on the executive of the international Association for Cultural Studies.

My primary "discipline" is the interdisciplinary field of cultural studies. In my case I am a professor of education but also have a background in literary studies and sociology. My academic work is focused on identity and identification, representation and conceptions of ways belonging, and equity and social justice. I have worked on the articulation of African cultural studies (and its positioning in global cultural studies), cultural studies of education (and its positioning in arts and humanities dominant cultural studies discourse), Black and youth identity and identification (and their representation in the national and international community context), and the politics of difference (race, class, gender, sexuality, culture), and/in anti-oppression education. I work on and with comparative national multiculturalism(s) and alternatives of inter-culturalism, anti-racism, critical race theory, cosmopolitanism, critical pedagogy, and postcolonial and de-colonial thought. As an academic who works on Africana studies I am cognizant that at many Canadian institutions, including my own University of British Columbia, Africana studies is at best marginal, located, in Spivak's words (1993), "outside the teaching machine." But marginality is not all negative. As bell hooks (1990, 153) reminds us, the margins are not only a site of exclusion and deprivation but also "a site of resistance … a location of radical openness and possibility." So, far from being simply a victim of discrimination and in part in reaction to it, we need to acknowledge and articulate an activist Blackness in the Canadian academy, including a growing Black Canadian Studies Association, and contributions by Black scholars to discussions on historical and contemporary race and racism in Canada.

My public pedagogy also reflects these interests in identity, representation, equity, and social justice, and includes international, national, and local public lectures, media interviews (e.g., on addressing issues such as rising Islamophobia), and local collaborative community service work (e.g., as a member of the Mayor of Vancouver's Advisory on Black History Month). In sum, my public pedagogy is principally about town–gown relationships, connecting the university and the local, wider community.

The academy should not be considered as what Edward Said (1983) called the impossibility of a hermetically sealed cosmos, with Blackness operating within those tight confines. Rather, as I hope the preceding pages illustrate, Blackness in the Canadian academy ought to be conceptualized as involving an overflow from the institutional into the national and international, and flowing back from the international and national into the institutional. It often involves both academic and intellectual discourse. Indeed, it demands (though it does not always get) social justice and representation activism. It is sometimes the overt presence and politics of Blackness and at other times the covert expectation of its unnamed presence and effect.

Academics take several stances on justice and representation at their institutions, communities, and society at large. Some eschew it completely, while others tinker in academic and community activism, and yet others come close to what Gramsci (1971) identified as the organic intellectual. I hold that irrespective of whether they choose to engage or not, Black academics are always already politicized – looked upon as real or potential radicals, equity hires, niche experts, grateful conformists, etc. There is no such thing as a neutral Black academic.

The very category of "Black academic" employs an assemblage of phenotypical characteristics in a homogenized, disparate set of subjects, a strategic essentialism employed to create a united front by us and a lazy failure to entertain difference within Blackness by others (and indeed too often by us). Blackness is a primarily diasporic identity that should not be about essentialized and romanticized genealogical roots but about evolving, complex, and contradictory geographical routes – the formation from numerous identifications of semi-solid identities, strong but pliant, definite but not definitive, clearly discernible but open to change. As Stuart Hall (1999) puts it, "Instead of asking what are people's roots, we ought to think about what are their routes, the different points by which they have come to be now; they are, in a sense, the sum of those differences ... These routes hold us in place, but what they don't do is hold us in the same place ... We need to try to make sense of the connections with where we think we were then as compared to where we are now."

Some of us, especially those of us from what V.Y. Mudimbe (1988) has called an invented Africa, were not Black back there, and coming to Canada meant becoming Black. It meant being brought directly under the white gaze and being interpellated into such identities as Black, Black-Canadian, and African-Canadian and incorporated into a hegemonic, self-congratulatory, celebratory Canadian multiculturalism incapable of coping with what Steven Vertovec has identified as "superdiversity" and uninterested in true recognition and just representation. So who are African-Canadian academics? We are francophone immigrants from Africa who speak better French than the best-educated Parisians, let alone Québécois; anglophone immigrants from the Caribbean for whom, as Marlene NourbeSe Philip (1988, 56–58) declared, "English is a foreign language ... English is a foreign anguish." We are Blacks who can trace our ancestry back as far as the Underground Railroad and the Black Loyalists, and contemporary African-Americans recently hired despite all advertisements for academic positions specifying that "preference will being given to Canadian citizens and landed immigrants." We are male, female, transgendered, intersexed; we are straight, gay, and queer; we are the ironic and sometimes ambivalent beneficiaries of the one-drop rule: dark-skinned, light-skinned, creole, browning, octoroon, yalla rose, biracial, and multiracial. We are proudly Afrikan (yes, sometimes spelt with a militant *K*) and passively hyphenated African-Canadian. We are landed and rooted but never fully belonging in the academy or in Canada. All of us are asked, as Gayatri Spivak (1990, 41) puts it, to "cathect the margins" of the academy "so that others can be defined as central," situated in the nation as what Spivak (1993) has called "not-quite-not-citizens." We are those who, irrespective of how long or short our historical roots are in Canada, are asked, "Where are you from?" We are an awkward presence, the Other in position of authority and privilege, supposedly misplaced in the middle class and at the front of the class; we are Paul Gilroy's Black Atlantic come ashore on Turtle Island; we are as Gloria Ladson Billings (2000, 269) observes, "the children of fieldhands [who] have returned to do fieldwork."

If Blackness in all its diversity is an always already politicized category, it is important to choose a position, an ideological stance from which to operate. My recommendation for critical Black academics is a risky combination of the intellectual stance Stuart Hall calls "Blackness without guarantees," and what Edward Said calls "the exile who crosses borders." Hall's Gramscian notion means that we should not consider our strategies to always be right simply because of our identity and the fact our ultimate goals of equity and recognition are right. It means taking on intersectionality – acknowledging and working with and on the nuances of difference within the category of Black, even as we sometimes employ an essentialized Blackness when necessary, and it means working on alliances with progressive Others. Said's notion means activist intellectual academic Blackness reaching out reflexively beyond the struggle for justice and representation for Blackness to acknowledge that this struggle has implications for others and their struggles. Said's notion means risking extending our politics beyond the home confines of identity politics, acknowledging that Blackness does not exist in what Said would decry as a hermetically sealed cosmos and that our struggle for justice and representation should extend to other racialized and minoritized groups and studies, including Indigenous peoples and Indigeneity.

The question then is not whether but how to reach beyond Black identity politics to work with other marginalized/minoritized others. As a starting point, we should heed the radically activist and politically sensitive approach advocated by Audrey Lorde (1984), who exhorts us to "work on the edge of each other's battles."

We should choose recognition and just representation for Blacks and Black studies within and outside the academy and indeed for all, by forging alliances with and working on the edge of the battles of other progressive racialized and minoritized peoples in a Black version of working "in the spirit of conjunctural inclusiveness and solidarity" (Spivak et al. 2014). This to me is what a critical Blackness means or ought to mean in the Canadian academy at this confluence of ineffective multiculturalism, perennial racism, neoliberalism, and austerity, on the one hand, and on the other, a multiple and pliant Blackness as part of the Canadian super-diversity (Vertovec 2007), a strategically essentialized Black agency, collaborative activism. This is how we ought to position ourselves as Black academics, in spite of or indeed precisely because of our supposed awkward presence in Canada and in the Canadian academy, so that, to paraphrase Kobina Mercer (1994), "we can live."

NOTES

1 This chapter is an expansion that updates and combines two brief presentations. The first and primary source I draw upon is a paper (Wright 2014) I presented on the invited plenary panel of the Equity Committee of the Congress of the Humanities and Social Sciences conference, Brock University, St. Catharines, Ontario, in May 2014. In some ways this chapter and mention of that panel indicate a historical marker of the evolution of the project that has culminated in the present collection. The second (Wright 2016) is a paper I presented on a plenary session of the Anti-Black Racism: Community, Resistance, Criminality conference at Ryerson University, Toronto.

2 It is not within the scope of this chapter to explore – let alone come to a conclusion on – the complex issue of whether Black people should aspire to simply belong in the nation (given its capitalist, colonialist, and imperialist nature and its perennial designation of the Black body as always already not belonging). I point to belonging and not belonging in this chapter with this as an important caveat.

3 As Hall cogently puts it, "In order not to be authoritative, I've got to speak auto-biographically" (Hall 1992, 277).

4 Taking Dublin as one example, I had been invited variously to lead an "Integration and Diversity" workshop at St. Patrick's College and Blanchardstown Area Partnership in October 2007; to lead a "Design a Policy Document on Interculturalism and Anti-Racism" workshop in October 2008; to give a keynote address at the English Language Support Teachers

Association of Ireland, also in October 2008; to coordinate a five-day "Identity and Social Justice" learning lab on at the Dublin Institute of Technology in May 2010; to chair and facilitate a "Cultural Diversity and the Arts of the Forum on Migration and Communication" learning lab in June 2012; and to give a public exit interview with British feminist cultural studies scholar Mica Nava, 2015, http://learninglabeditions.org/index.php/2013 /09/08/edition-3-identity-beyond-diversity/.

5 Slavery is perhaps the longest-standing and most persistent and pernicious example of deliberate ignorance and forgetting, resulting in erasure. Most Canadians think their country excluded the institution of slavery and indeed was as a bastion of activism against slavery in the United States, providing a haven for Blacks escaping slavery. But slavery was legal in both in New France and in Lower Canada for around two hundred years.

6 The widespread understanding is that "Great White North" refers to Canada's size as the second-largest country (Great), its long winters, covered in snow (White), and its location above the United States (North).

7 So, for example, when there were incidents of blackface on campus at Canadian universities, including at McGill in 2011, the response was shock and outrage (or even more interestingly, ready forgiveness of ignorant youthful imitation an of American historical racist performance) in a supposedly post-racial Canada.

8 I borrow the notion of coming into something backwards from Stuart Hall (1992). He was surprised that many think cultural studies is unproblematically Marxist since as a New Left, cultural studies scholar he saw Marxism as a problem – as trouble rather than as a solution. Hence when he turned to and engaged with Marxism, he came into Marxism backwards, in the struggle against the worst ways in which it was being manifested. In a similar but much more limited way, as an anti-racist, cultural studies critical pedagogue who was not allowed to teach courses on anti-racism (apparently unknown, sounding too radical) when newly hired at the University of Tennessee in the mid-1990s, I turned to, engaged with, and taught critical multiculturalism, not as a solution but as a (necessary and utilitarian) problem – as useful trouble rather than a ready solution – and in that sense I came to multiculturalism backwards.

9 John Porter's critique focused on how power operates in Canada, including and especially in terms of social class and the existence of an elite that operates at the apex of Canadian society. The resulting notion of a vertical mosaic applies just as readily if not more so to an examination of how cultures and races are located in a hierarchy in the Canadian nation state.

10 Charmaine Nelson's account is about a cemetery known as "Nigger Rock" in the small town of Saint-Armand, Quebec, in which enslaved and free Blacks were buried in the eighteenth and nineteenth centuries. Beyond

being an example of early segregation of Black bodies in death in Canada, Nelson's account illustrates how erasure of Blackness works. In this case present-day private ownership and use of the piece of land (for farming) means both obfuscation of the site as burial ground and restriction of access to the site (and hence to efforts to name, mark, and treat it as burial ground). In sum it is a local erasure of both the institution of slavery and historical Black presence.

11   Marlene NourbeSe Philip's praxis involves poetry, intellectual interventions, and activism. She has paid a heavy price for her work on the representation of Blackness in general, including activism on the exclusion of Blackness in the Canadian literary scene. The following paragraph from a review of her latest work by Paul Barrett (2018) captures Philip's position(ing) in the Canadian (and international) context:

> Philip describes herself as a "disappeared" writer who has paid the price for her activism with her erasure from Canadian literature. In a recent essay published in *The Puritan*, Kate Siklosi expertly demonstrates this disappearance and the "archive of silence around Philip and her work in Canada." While many of her contemporaries have taken up comfortable positions as creative-writing instructors or editors in publishing houses, Philip has yet to find prominent footing in the larger CanLit scene. Outside the country, she has been given the Casas de las Américas prize and a Guggenheim Fellowship among other international honours, but she has never received any major national literary award at home. Her 2008 collection, *Zong!* – about the 1781 murder of Africans thrown overboard on the orders of a slave-ship captain – was mostly ignored by Canadian critics despite being praised around the world.

12   The title, *The Great Black North*, plays on the traditional designation of Canada as The Great White North and is perhaps a particularly important collection to cite from a treasure trove of Black Canadian literature, since the two editors and hence the fountainhead of this assertion of Black presence are based in British Columbia, where Blacks still constitute less than 1 per cent of the population and hence is a province where the erasure of Blacknesss is all the easier.

13   Barnor Hesse (2000) employs the term "transruption" to describe what exposes the discrepancy between the idealized multicultural state and culture (in his case, Britain) and Black lives that belie that ideal and refuse repression. As he puts it, transruption *"comprises any series of contestatory cultural and theoretical interventions which, in their impact as cultural differences, unsettle social norms and threaten to dismantle hegemonic concepts and practices"* (p. 17; italics in original).

14   Francesca Coin (2017, 705) defines "quit lit" as "a new genre of literature made of columns and opinion editorials detailing the reasons why scholars – with or without tenure – leave academia."

15 Malinda Smith (2018, 55) identifies the phenomenon of "diversifying whiteness" as pervasive across institutions in Canada such that, "despite four decades of equity policies – corporate boards, the judiciary, and the police continue to be shaped by racial and ethnic segregation, and remain overwhelmingly white and to a lesser extent male, thus maintaining the historic colour-coded ethnic pecking order even across gender and sexual difference. I have termed this social process 'diversifying whiteness.'"

In the academy this plays out in keeping whiteness as base and adding and stirring in other identity categories related to diversity – gender and sexuality in particular. The result is that universities can bask in achieving increasing diversity in hiring, retention, promotion and in leadership and management positions – more women, more LGBTQ, more persons with disabilities, but the vast majority continue to have one characteristic in common, namely being white. Thus, by diversifying whiteness institutions of higher education can claim to diversify even as they retain and even increase whiteness as core, as majority, as leadership, as form and source of knowledge, as the very identity of the institutions.

16 One personal example is a one-day symposium I organized in April 2012 titled "Black British Columbians: Race, Space and the Historical Politics of Difference at the US/Canada Border." I was actually on sabbatical that year but took on the additional burden of the project of organizing the conference in my capacity as director of the Centre for Culture, Identity and Education, in large part because I had been troubled by the lack of representation of Blackness in BC in general and at the University of British Columbia in particular, since I took up my position at UBC in 2005. As I summed it up, "I was quite disappointed, shocked even, when I got to University of British Columbia and discovered that there was no Africana studies at this institution: no undergraduate, let alone graduate program, no African studies, no Black studies; no Africana studies; no Africa and its diaspora studies, no African-Canadian studies – call it what you may, it simply did not exist at UBC" (Wright 2007, 319).

REFERENCES

Adams, M. 2008. *Unlikely Utopia: The Surprising Triumph of Canadian Multiculturalism*. Toronto: Penguin Canada.

Ahmed, S. 2012. *On Being Included: Racism and Diversity in Institutional Life*. Durham, NC: Duke University Press.

Alcoff, L.M. 1999. Latina/o Identity Politics. In *The Good Citizen*, edited by D. Batstone and E. Mendiata, 93–112. London: Routledge.

Austin, D. 2010. "Narratives of Power: Historical Mythologies in Contemporary Quebec and Canada." *Race & Class* 52 (1): 19–32. https://doi.org/10.1177/0306396810371759.

Bannerji, H. 2000. *Dark Side of the Nation: Essays on Multiculturalism, Nationalism, and Gender.* Toronto: Canadian Scholars Press.

Barrett, P. 2018, 21 September. "The Poetic Disturbances of M. NourbeSe Philip." *The Walrus.* https://thewalrus.ca/the-poetic-disturbances-of-m-nourbese-philip/.

Bristow, P., Brand, D., Carty, L., Cooper, A., Hamilton, S., & Shadd, A. 1994. *We're Rooted Here and They Can't Pull Us Up: Essays in African Canadian Women's History.* Toronto: University of Toronto Press.

Burman, J. 2006. "Absence," "Removal," and Everyday Life in the Diasporic City: Antidetention/Antideportation Activism in Montreal. *Space and Culture* 9 (3): 279–293.

Chariandy, D. 2018. *Brother.* Toronto: McClelland & Stewart.

Coin, F. 2017. On Quitting. *ephemera* 17 (3): 705–719.

Compton, W. 2001. *Bluesprint: Black British Columbian Literature and Orature.* Vancouver: Arsenal Pulp Press.

Cooper, A. 2007. *The Hanging of Angelique: The Untold Story of Canadian Slavery and the Burning of Old Montreal.* Athens: University of Georgia Press.

Dawes, S. 2014. "Interview with Henry A. Giroux: The Neoliberalisation of Higher Education." *Media Theory, History and Regulation.* https://smdawes.wordpress.com/2014/06/26/interview-with-henry-a-giroux-the-neoliberalisation-of-higher-education/.

de B'beri, B., Reid-Maroney, N., & Wright, H.K. 2014. *The Promised Land: History and Historiography of the Black Experience in Chatham-Kent's Settlements and Beyond.* Toronto: University of Toronto Press.

Dei, G.S. 1996. *Anti-Racism Education: Theory and Practice.* Halifax: Fernwood Publishing.

Dei, G.S. 2010. *Racists Beware: Uncovering Racial Politics in Contemporary Society.* Boston: Sense Publishers.

Dunn, S. 2013. "Why So Many Academics Quit and Tell?" *Chronicle Vitae.* https://chroniclevitae.com/news/216-why-so-many-academics-quit-andtell?CID=VTKT1#sthash.2IJLtEqE.dpuf.

Este, D., Lorenzetti, L., and Gato, C. 2018. *Racism and Anti-Racism in Canada.* Halifax: Fernwood Press.

Felman, S. 1982. "Psychoanalysis and Education: Teaching Terminable and Interminable." *Yale French Studies* 63: 21–44. https://doi.org/10.2307/2929829.

Foucault, M. 1981. *The History of Sexuality* (Vol. 1). Handsworth: Penguin Books.

Gilroy, P. 1993. *Small Acts: Thoughts on the Politics of Black Cultures.* London: Serpent's Tail.

Gilroy, P. 1994. *The Black Atlantic: Modernity and Double Consciousness.* London: Verso.

Giroux, H. 2013. "Public Intellectuals against the Neoliberal University." *Truthout.* https://www.truthdig.com/articles/public-intellectuals-against-the-neoliberal-university/.

Giroux, H. 2017. "Neoliberalism's War against Higher Education and the Role of Public Intellectuals." In *The Future of University Education*, edited by M. Izak, M. Kostera, and M. Zawadzki, 13–28. Champaign: Palgrave Macmillan.

Gordon, L. 1995. *Fanon and the Crisis of European Man: An Essay on Philosophy and the Human Sciences.* London: Routledge.

Gordon, L. 2012. "Of Illicit Appearance: The L.A. Riots/Rebellion as a Portent of Things to Come." *Truthout.* https://truthout.org/articles/of-illicit -appearance-the-la-riots-rebellion-as-a-portent-of-things-to-come/.

Gramsci, A. 1971. "The Intellectuals." In *Selections from the Prison Notebooks*, edited and translated by Q. Hoare and G. Nowell Smith, 131–161. London: Lawrence & Wishart.

Gross Stein, J. 2007. "Disentangling the Debate." In *Uneasy Partner: Multiculturalism and Rights in Canada*, edited by Janice Gross Stein, 137–156. Waterloo, ON: Wilfrid Laurier University Press.

Hall, S. 1990. "The Emergence of Cultural Studies and the Crisis of the Humanities." *October* 53: 11–23. https://doi.org/10.2307/778912.

Hall, S. 1992. "Cultural Studies and Its Theoretical Legacies." In *Cultural Studies*, edited by L. Grossberg, C. Nelson, and P. Triechler, 277–294. London: Routledge.

Hall, S. 1996. "Introduction: Who Needs 'Identity'?" In *Questions of Cultural Identity*, edited by S. Hall and P. du Gay, 1–25. London: Sage Publications.

Hall, S. 1999. "A Conversation with Stuart Hall." *The Journal of the International Institute* 7 (1). https://quod.lib.umich.edu/j/jii/4750978.0007.107 /–conversation-with-stuart-hall?rgn=main;view=fulltext.

Hall, S., and Back, L. 2009. "At Home and Not at Home: Stuart Hall in Conversation with Les Back." *Cultural Studies* 23 (4): 658–687. https://doi.org /10.1080/09502380902950963.

Haque, E. 2012. *Multiculturalism within a Bilingual Framework: Language and the Racial Ordering of Difference and Belonging in Canada.* Toronto: University of Toronto Press.

Henry, F., and Tator, C. 2009. *Racism in the Canadian University: Demanding Social Justice, Inclusion, and Equity.* Toronto: University of Toronto Press.

Hesse, B. 2000. "Introduction: Un/Settled Multiculturalisms." In *Un/Settled Multiculturalisms: Diasporas, Entanglements, Transruptions*, edited by B. Hesse, 1–18. London: Zed Books.

Hill, L. 2007. *The Book of Negroes.* Toronto: Harper Collins.

hooks, b. 1981. *Ain't I a Woman: Black Women and Feminism.* Boston: South End Press.

hooks, b. 1989. *Talking Back: Thinking Feminist, Thinking Black.* Boston: South End Press.

hooks, b. 1990. *Yearning: Race, Gender, and Cultural Politics.* Boston: South End Press.

hooks, b. 1992. *Black Looks: Race and Representation*. Boston: South End Press.
Howard, P. 2017. "On the Back of Blackness: Contemporary Canadian Blackface and the Consumptive Production of Post-Racialist, White Canadian Subjects." *Social Identities* 24 (1): 87–103. https://doi.org/10.1080/13504630.2017.1281113.
Kilian, C. 2008. *Go Do Some Great Thing: The Black Pioneers of British Columbia*. Madeira Park: Harbour Publishing.
Kymlicka, W. 2007, 1 December. "Well Done, Canada: Multiculturalism Is Working." *The Globe and Mail*. https://www.theglobeandmail.com/arts/well-done-canada-multiculturalism-is-working/article726485/.
Ladson-Billings, G. 2000. "Racialized Discourses and Ethnic Epistemologies." In *Handbook of Qualitative Research*, edited by N. Denzin and Y. Lincoln, 23–45. Thousand Oaks: Sage Publications.
Lee, E. 1985. *Letters to Marcia: A Reader's Guide to Anti-Racist Education*. Toronto: Cross Cultural Communications Center.
Lorde, A. 1984. *Sister Outsider: Essays and Speeches by Audrey Lorde*. Berkeley, CA: Crossing Press.
Macharia, K. 2013. "On Quitting." *The New Inquiry*. https://thenewinquiry.com/on-quitting/.
Malesic, J. 2016, 5 October. "The 40-Year-Old Burnout: Why I Gave Up Tenure for a Yet-to-Be-Determined Career." The Chronicle of Higher Education. https://www.chronicle.com/article/the-40-year-old-burnout/.
Mason-John, V., & Cameron, K.A., eds. 2013. *The Great Black North: Contemporary African Canadian Poetry*. Calgary: Frontenac House.
Maynard, R. 2017. *Policing Black Lives: State Violence in Canada from Slavery to the Present*. Halifax: Fernwood Press.
McKittrick, K., and Woods, C., eds. 2007. *Black Geographies and the Politics of Place*. Toronto: Between the Lines Press.
Menzies, H., & Newson, J. 2007. "No Time to Think: Academics' Life in the Globally Wired University." *Time & Society* 16 (1): 83–98.
Mercer, K. 1994. *Welcome to the Jungle: New Positions in Black Cultural Studies*. New York: Routledge.
Moodley, K. 1983. "Canadian Multiculturalism as Ideology." *Ethnic and Racial Studies* 6 (3): 320–331. https://doi.org/10.1080/01419870.1983.9993416.
Mudimbe, V.Y. 1988. *The Invention of Africa: Gnosis, Philosophy, and the Order of Knowledge*. Bloomington: Indiana University Press.
Nelson, C. 2018, 28 May. "Black Cemeteries Force Us to Re-examine Our History with Slavery." *Walrus*. https://thewalrus.ca/black-cemeteries-force-us-to-re-examine-our-history-with-slavery/.
NourbeSe Philip, M. 1988. *Harriet's Daughter*. Toronto: Women's Press.
Philip, N. 1988. *She Tries Her Tongue, Her Silence Softly Breaks*. Middleton: Wesleyan University Press.

Porter, J. 1965. *The Vertical Mosaic: An Analysis of Social Class and Power in Canada.* Toronto: University of Toronto Press.

Reynolds, G., and Robson, W. 2018. *Viola Desmond: Her Life and Times.* Halifax: Fernwood Press.

Robson, W., and Caplan, R. 2010. *Sister to Courage: Stories from the World of Viola Desmond.* Sydney, NS: Cape Breton Books.

Said, E. 1983. *The World, the Text and the Critic.* Cambridge, MA: Harvard University Press.

Smith, M. 2018. "Diversity in Theory and Practice: Dividends, Downsides, and Dead-ends." In *Contemporary Inequalities and Social Justice in Canada,* edited by J. Brodie, 112–134. Toronto: University of Toronto Press.

Spivak, G. 1990. *The Post-Colonial Critic: Interviews, Strategies, Dialogues.* New York: Routledge.

Spivak, G. 1993. *Outside the Teaching Machine.* New York: Routledge.

Spivak, G., Gilbert, J., and Fisher, J. 2014. "Stuart Hall: 1932–2014." *Radical Philosophy.* https://www.radicalphilosophy.com/obituary/stuart-hall-1932–2014.

Stewart, A. 2009. *You Must Be a Basketball Player: Rethinking Integration in the University.* Halifax: Fernwood Press.

Tate, A. 2014. "I Can't Quite Put My Finger on It: Racism's Touch." *Ethnicities,* 1741–2706. https://doi.org/10.1177/1468796814564626.

Vertovec, S. 2007. "Super-Diversity and Its Implications." *Ethnic and Racial Studies* 30 (6): 1024–1054. https://doi.org/10.1080/01419870701599465.

Wright, H. 1994. "Multiculturalism, Anti-Racism, and Afrocentrism: The Politics of Race in Educational Praxis." *International Journal of Comparative Race and Ethnic Studies* 1 (2): 13–31.

Wright, H. 2007. "Is This an African I See before Me?" *Diaspora, Indigenous and Minority Education* 1 (4): 313–322. https://doi.org/10.1080/15595690701564095.

Wright, H. 2012a. "Between Global Demise and National Complacent Hegemony: Canadian Multiculturalism and Multicultural Education in a Moment of Danger." In *Precarious International Multicultural Education: Hegemony, Dissent and Rising Alternatives,* edited by H. Handel, M. Singh, and R. Race, 111–131. Rotterdam: Sense Publishers.

Wright, H. 2012b. "Is This an African I See before Me? Black/African Identity and the Politics of Western, Academic Knowledge." In *The Dialectics of African Education and Western Discourses: Appropriation, Ambivalence and Alternatives,* edited by H. Wright and A. Abdi, 123–141. New York: Peter Lang Publishing.

Wright, H. 2013. "Cultural Studies as Praxis: (Making) an Autobiographical Case." *Cultural Studies* 17 (6): 805–822. https://doi.org/10.1080/0950238032000150039.

Wright, H. 2014. "The Awkward Presence of Blackness in the Neo-Liberal, 'Non-Racial' Canadian Academy." Congress Equity Issues Panel/Canadian Society for the Study of Education, Congress of the Humanities and Social Sciences, Brock University, St. Catharines.

Wright, H. 2016. "Specificity Matters: Absent Presence Means It's Hard Being Black in British Columbia." Plenary address at Anti-Black Racism Conference: Community, Resistance, Criminalization. Ryerson University, Toronto.

Wright, H. 2018. "Decolonize This! (Youth) Activism and Academia and/as the Public Sphere." Division G Vice Presidential Invited Paper. American Educational Researchers Association conference. New York.

Wright, H., Singh, M., and Race, R., eds. 2012. *Precarious International Multicultural Education: Hegemony, Dissent and Rising Alternatives.* Rotterdam: Sense Publishers.

2 Exposed! The Ivory Tower's Code Noir

DELIA D. DOUGLAS

North ... into the Blackness

Our present landscape is both haunted *and* developed by old and new hierarchies of humanness.

– Katherine McKittrick (2006)

This chapter considers the marginal status of Black women in *our* peculiar institution – Canadian universities. My allusion to the American euphemism for enslavement acknowledges Canada's particular history of racial subjugation under British and French colonial rule. In speaking of the Code Noir, I refer to the legal, ideological, and spatial discourses that established enslavement within New France. Under this system of racial-sexual-engendered codification and violence, Blacks were legally deemed subhuman, their movements regulated by their designation as chattel or immobile objects (Winks 1997). Consequently, the *badge* of Blackness prompted a socio-spatial separation and containment, revealing the interrelationships between race, racism, the social production of places and spaces, and the creation of white settler colonial nation states (Amadahy and Lawrence 2009; Peake and Ray 2001; Razack 2002). This economy of racialized socio-economic space resulted in an "economy of violence," to borrow Bibi Bakare-Yusuf's (1999, 311) phrase, which conveyed its brutality not only in the classification of the enslaved as property, but also in the forms of subjectivity and in/humanity ascribed to Blacks, which deemed them devoid of intellect and feeling (Hartman 1997; Higginbotham 1992).

Located on unceded Indigenous territories, Canadian post-secondary institutions are evidence of continuing settler colonialism. That is, universities uphold the logic and structure of settler colonial society through geographic domination, disappearing Indigenous struggles, and protecting white property rights through a coercive system of labour (Glenn 2015; Patel 2015; Razack 2002). Furthermore, Canadian universities' white colonial culture, combined with their predominantly white faculty and Eurocentric curriculum, render them key sites in and through which white racial knowledge is re-produced and disseminated (Razack 1998; Schick 2014). I link these ideas by demonstrating how legacies of anti-Black racism and the uneven and unequal geographies created by dispossession have been reconfigured in the contemporary disregard and marginalization of Black women in the *ivory* tower (and elsewhere). My concern is with how the ethos, practices, and structures associated with the Code Noir resonate in the precarious positioning of Black women's bodies, knowledge, and experience in Canadian post-secondary institutions. In this context, my use of the word "peculiar" is also meant to draw attention to the whiteness of the academy in a nation that promotes a self-image of diversity and a commitment to social justice and equality.

For example, despite thirty years of an Employment Equity policy, Canada's university faculty remains 85 per cent white; Black faculty constitute 1.6 per cent of the country's 55,880) members.[1] Moreover, Black women comprise approximately 300 of the 894 faculty who are Black (CAUT 2010; Li 2012).[2] Given the legacy of white supremacist discourses that regard Blacks as subhuman, I maintain that our absence and marginal status holds a particular cultural and political significance, as this is readily taken as evidence of our limited intellectual abilities. I argue that because the systemic anti-Black gendered racism towards Black women has become normalized; the devaluation of Black women's lives in the *ivory* tower bolsters and protects contemporary settler-colonial-enslaved interpersonal relations and intellectual hierarchies (Cacho 2012; Lomax 2015).

The Coles Notes Black Book: Scenes of Instruction

Mythologies or national stories are about a nation's origins and history. They enable citizens to think of themselves as part of a community, defining who belongs and who does not belong to the nation.

– Razack (2002, 2)

As Razack makes clear, national narratives are central to the construction of national and cultural identities. The past is created through what is remembered and forgotten; consequently, remembering and forgetting are enduring practices that are tied to power, wherein knowledge is granted authority in the construction of the past (Adichie 2009; Failler

2009; Schick 2014). Efforts to expunge, minimize, and deny the diverse history of a Black presence have been a central feature of settler colonial projects. Before considering the precarious status of Black women in the university, I briefly address ways in which a Black presence/Black Canada has been figuratively and literally repudiated and demolished in the service of settler colonialism (McKittrick 2006).

I begin with enslavement because it is an inaugural moment in the history of anti-Black racism and because it is an inaugural moment in the history of Black resistance. A story that is frequently repeated with pride among Canadians is that Upper Canada/Ontario was the final destination of the Underground Railroad; it is the place where fugitive slaves escaped servitude, thereby furthering the claim of Canada as a refuge (Cooper 2000). Few know that slavery was practised in New France and British North America for over two centuries and that the history of a Black presence is diverse and complex, extending across the country and dating back to the 1600s.

Few know that in April 1734, in New France on unceded and occupied Mohawk/Kahnawake territory, a Black enslaved woman from Portugal, Marie Joseph Angelique, was arrested and charged with burning down the home of her enslaver along with much of Old Montreal. Under torture Angelique confessed to the crime and was publicly executed, hung by the neck until dead. She was then burned, her ashes strewn to the wind (Cooper 2006). Katherine McKittrick (2006, 115) argues that Angelique's alleged "geography of arson" and the "consequential punishment/death of blackness ... signal a spatial politics" through which other Black Canadian topographies have been shaped. She rightly explains how Angelique's presence left behind spatial evidence, as her trial, conviction, and subsequent execution ensures Blackness and Black subjectivities in a (white) nation that claims to have a "blackless past" (McKittrick 2006, 119).

We therefore live in the "afterlife of slavery" (Hartman 2007, 6), dispossession, and ongoing Indigenous struggles for sovereignty. We live in a country that promotes Canada's history as one of racial harmony and benevolence through its recognition and celebration of the Underground Railroad. Moreover, the pairing of declarations of racial innocence with the violence of disavowal maintains a white national identity that grants expressions of anti-Black racism an acceptability and licence (Martinot 2010). Therefore, acknowledging enslavement as a pre-Confederation colonial institution is a significant political statement for, as Maureen Elgersman (1999, 40) explains, this recognition "forces a reconciliation of the post-emancipation history of black status in Canada as one that is anchored in and informed by the sanctioning of slavery in that country."

In addition to sanctioning enslavement, the law has played a profound role in Black life by aiding and abetting racism and racial discrimination through oversight and in directive (Thornhill 2008). For example, in November 1946, Black entrepreneur Viola Desmond was denied the privilege of purchasing a seat on the main floor of the Roseland Theatre, located on the unceded territory of the Pictou Landing First Nation.

Refusing to accept the segregated seating policy, Desmond took up a seat in the Whites Only section of the theatre. Ultimately, the police were called and Desmond was removed with a force that resulted in injuries to her hip and knee. Held in jail overnight and denied of her right and access to counsel, Desmond was taken to court the next day and charged with violating the 1915 provincial Theatres, Cinematographs and Amusements Act. While she was accused of attempting to cheat the provincial government of one cent – the difference in tax between the two seating areas – Desmond's Blackness was not mentioned during the trial. In keeping with the pattern of legally upholding racial segregation in Nova Scotia, Desmond was convicted. Her appeal was unsuccessful. In 2010, following decades of lobbying by her sister Wanda Robson, and sixty-four years after she was dragged from the theatre, the province of Nova Scotia granted Viola Desmond a (posthumous) free pardon and official apology (Murray 2011).

I refer to Marie Joseph Angelique and Viola Desmond not simply because they (along with many other Black women) are not recognized as rebellious historical subjects, but because their actions reveal Black women's legacy of resistance against geographic-racial-gender domination (Cooper 2000, 2006; McKittrick 2006). That is, both Angelique's and Joseph's geographic and embodied experiences and knowledge of enslavement and segregation signal a refusal to accept the spatial boundaries, practices, and logics that protect and maintain white settler colonial society. Their public refusal to accept their subordinate status typifies Black women's ingenuity and subjectivity. In sum, their pursuit of freedom disrupts settler colonial claims of Black inhumanity, for, as Angela Y. Davis (1971, 6) emphasizes, "a human being thoroughly dehumanized has no desire for freedom."

Collective memory has purged the perpetuation of Blacks' consignment to inferior status through the history of segregation that restricted Blacks' access to schools, housing, theatres, hotels, and employment (Backhouse 1999; Cooper 2000). In conjunction with the exclusion of Black Canadian histories, Black geographies have been hidden or expunged. The spatialization of anti-Black racism is revealed through the desecration of slave cemeteries in Ontario and Quebec, the cross burnings on the property of Black families in Nova Scotia and New

Brunswick, the torching of the Black Loyalist Society building, and the firebombing of the Black cultural centre in Nova Scotia.

Blacks have been excluded from the imagined community of the Canadian nation through the destruction of Hogan's Alley in Vancouver (Tslaywaututh and Squamish Coast Salish territory), along with the destruction of Africville (Mi'kmak territory). Regarded as the oldest Black community in Canada, Africville was demolished in the 1960s.

The politics of remembering and forgetting are further revealed in the fact that Viola Desmond, Africville, and Hogan's Alley have all been awarded commemorative stamps by Canada Post in public recognition of a history that is presumed over and done with. The structured visibility of the past is created through practices of remembrance that suggest that recognition undoes the damage of racism (Failler 2009). Rather, this form of re-membering suppresses the ongoing tension between what McKittrick (2002, 28) describes as the "erasure and existence" of a Black Canadian presence and obscures how Canada's national identity is linked to, and depends on, anti-Black racism.

I maintain there is a link between historical and contemporary racial subjugation, as Black Canadians are not seen as real members of the nation. Our presence is interpreted as an anomaly or an exception, and we are commonly regarded as being from "elsewhere," as heard in the query, "Where are you from?" Then the reply "I'm from here" is followed with a familiar rebuff: "No. I mean, where are you really from? Originally."

We are regularly assumed to be immigrants from the Caribbean, the United States, or more recently, the African continent (Cooper 2000; Pabst 2009). Furthermore, the fact that U.S. racial discourses are "privileged" as "the generalized comparison point, the yardstick of racial experience historically understood" (Goldberg 2005, 219) supports narratives of racial guiltlessness, by allowing Canadians to imagine themselves as raceless. Moreover, our closeness to the United States, in conjunction with its overwhelming symbolic and material presence, has brought great pressure to bear upon expressions and interpretations of Blackness in Canada, as Black American cultural products and producers have achieved an overarching conspicuousness and currency.

Black Women in the Ivory Tower: The Politics of Visibility and Mis/recognition

[The] victim who is able to articulate the situation of the victim has ceased to be a victim: he, or she, has become a threat.

– James Baldwin (1976, 134)

Our geographic experiences shape our ways of seeing and being, as locations/positions shape our intellectual and political practice. Thus, locations/positions involve more than geography and refer to temporality, sex, race, and sexuality. As Chandra Mohanty (1987) explains, location is not a fixed point but a "temporality of struggle" (40) that takes place "between cultures, languages, and complex configurations of meaning and power" (42). To this end, the notion of position/location precludes notions of singular points of origin and fixed or transhistorical meanings, and takes as its foundation the temporary, multiple, and contradictory aspects of narratives of identity and identification.

Correspondingly, I write words crafted in Vancouver, British Columbia, but that bear the imprint of my movements from London, England; to Bellingham, Washington; Winnipeg, Manitoba; Oxford, Ohio; Santa Cruz, California; Tobago, Republic of Trinidad and Tobago; and beyond. The matters of which I speak/write/teach are borne out of my locations and my journeying. In the valuable edited collection, *Unsettling Relations: The University as a Site of Feminist Struggles*, Linda Carty wrote a chapter titled "Black Women in Academia: A Statement from the Periphery" (1991) in which she described her experiences as one of two Black students.[3] Carty revealed how the invisibility of Black women in the white academy caused her to consider "the great gulf which exists between what [she] knew and know[s], what [she] was taught at university, what [she] actually learned and what [she was] now teaching" (13). As one of a handful of Black female teachers in the ivory tower, her presence was deemed unusual. Nearly three decades later, her words could be mine. My experiences follow the same template: throughout my undergraduate and early graduate career I was the only Black student in my classes (until I began my doctoral studies at the University of California, Santa Cruz, where I was one of two Black women and two Black men). I am Black, female, and Canadian, and since I received my PhD in sociology I have held the status of sessional faculty.

What's Going On?

Indigenous and members of racialized minority groups are the youngest and fastest-growing members of the population and they will soon comprise the racial majority in several of Canada's major cities (Statistics Canada 2007, 2008). However, while national narratives bolster harmonious multiculturalism and inclusion, as Canada's population grows more diverse, the university remains overwhelmingly white in its administration, faculty, curriculum, and culture. After several decades of an equity policy and the related discourse of diversity, little progress has been made in hiring the four equity groups – Aboriginals, racialized minorities, women, and persons with disabilities – and their invisibility and marginalization remains a dominant feature of Canadian universities (Kobayashi 2007; Smith 2007, 2010).

As Canada grows more diverse, whites' majority status reinforces the notion that those who are there secured their job through merit alone. Consequently, whites are readily understood as authorities, and they unquestionably believe themselves to be best-suited to their respective professions. In post-secondary institutions across Canada, with few exceptions, equity has meant gender equity, as the majority of women hired have been white and able bodied. Few have acknowledged these racialized and racist outcomes. white women are becoming the new gatekeepers, poised to protect and sustain institutional practices and cultural processes that reproduce and maintain white racial domination (Henry and Tator 2007; Smith 2010, 2016). White disavowal of the relevance of race is constituted by and constitutive of settler colonial discourse, in its psychology and in its practice of denial. As Audrey Kobayashi (2007, 000) summarizes, the culture of whiteness is reflected in "the overwhelming power of white academicians which keeps the status quo in place in terms of the content and the standards of the university, in terms of research, in terms of who has access to positions." In this context it is not surprising that few whites have had the courage to speak out and challenge these structured exclusions (Douglas and Halas 2013; Smith 2007).

Moreover, the dearth of Black faculty reproduces conscious and unconscious racialized beliefs of superiority for whites, who have consistently been able to gain access to the academy. Given the legacy of white supremacist discourses, which regard Black women as subhuman and therefore fundamentally inferior, our absence holds a particular cultural and political significance, as this is readily taken as evidence of our inadequate intellectual abilities. Hence we are typically not seen as knowers and authorial figures. For instance, recently recognized for her twenty years of dedication to equity and social justice issues in Canadian universities, Malinda S. Smith, a Black professor of at the University of Alberta (located on Treat Six/Métis territory) described how when she was first hired in political science she was mis/recognized as a physical education teacher on campus (as cited in Eisenkraft 2010, para. 1).[4]

Black Women Speak

Hiring: Race-ing Value, Engendering Empire

The ongoing structure of white settler colonialism is reflected in the hiring practices of one of its key institutions, the university. As a substantial employer, the university is organized according to a powerful and exploitative system of labour; Black faculty earn approximately 75 per cent of what their white colleagues receive (Li 2012). Canadian universities have responded to shrinking budgets and nearly three decades of retirements by increasingly turning to corporations for financial support and making sure they have a steady supply of contingent faculty to maintain their workforce. The corporate neoliberal university has created an economic and moral environment that is at once an economy of value and an economy of violence, since one's worth in the system is determined by one's perceived and conceived abilities, potential, and anticipated contribution to the university and to society at large (Bakare-Yusuf 1999; Cacho 2012). The fact that those who have benefitted the most from the introduction of an equity policy have been white women reveals how race, gender, and sexuality are legible measures of corporeal value. In this context, Black women are contemporaneously hailed as evidence of the absence of racism (equity works!), or of the undermining of academic integrity (equity is political correctness gone wrong).

Hiring is key to the renewal of the department and its future. Hence this pattern of hiring: the exchange of positions between white women and men is tantamount to what Malinda S. Smith (2016) describes as the "social injustice of sameness." It is precisely because these racially structured environments are not named as such that white colonial culture is expressed through the identification of some candidates as a "better fit" – code words used to maintain a racial homogeneous faculty. This semantic strategy affirms the belief that those who are there – i.e., white men and women – are the best coincides with the exclusion of marginalized (e.g., owing to disability, sexuality, and race) "others." These expressions of "privileged obliviousness," to borrow Ruth Roach Pierson's (2004, 98) phrase, reveal the difficulties of finding allies among those who have benefited from gender equity (white women), but whose racial privilege has obscured how they have come to take up the position of the dominant in relation to Black women – along with other equity seeking groups (Smith 2007, 2010).

Two examples of Black women's experiences during the hiring process demonstrate how the continuing settler colonial structure corrupts institutions and their members (Memmi 1965). For instance, during my time as a research associate an interviewee recounted overhearing a conversation in which white female members of a hiring committee acknowledged that while a Black woman was the best applicant, they were going to vote for another candidate. The actions of the white female faculty members of the hiring committee reveal their sense of (white) entitlement to inhabit the university spatially and their power to deny employment (Ahmed 2007). Additionally, the rejection of the Black female candidate confirms to students and faculty that Black women are not qualified, reflecting the broader climate of white racial domination where the disparagement of Black women remains permissible (Lomax 2015; Martinot 2010).

At a panel discussion of anti-racist equity hiring, retention, and accountability in Canadian universities, Joanne St. Lewis (2007, 21) exposed the hierarchies among the equity-seeking groups. In her words, "Colleagues, including my progressive feminist colleagues, describe me as an equity hire. Now I find that fascinating. Why? Because there had been a hire with a number of white women candidates and they could not simply say that I had outperformed those candidates and say that to their friends. It was easier for them to say we did an equity hire, and we hired a black *child*" (emphasis added).

St. Lewis's experience demonstrates how the ethos and practices of the Code Noir have been reconfigured through the perception of the conditions of her employment. The a priori distrust and accompanying devaluation of St. Lewis's ability and credentials illustrate the psychology of settler colonial domination. Her *feminist* colleagues' certainty of their talent and "fit," combined with the demeaning of St. Lewis's accomplishments and the undermining of her intellectual ability simultaneously confirm and naturalize hierarchies of race and gender. In sum, the white female academics' interpretations are formed through their presupposition of a white university (i.e., ivory tower), a place where they belong, and this Black woman does not (Ahmed 2007).

These two examples expose the ongoing conflict between what McKittrick (2002, 28) describes as the "erasure and existence" of a Black Canadian presence. An analysis of representation of racialized and Indigenous faculty in Canada showed that even though the proportion of Chinese and South Asian faculty is twice that of Black faculty, Black faculty had more grievances in terms of race and racial discrimination and cited more instances of overt racism (Henry, Choi, and Kobayashi 2012). Moreover, the notion that the implementation of equity will result in the university being full of unqualified faculty who are members of designated groups ignores the fact that, as Jensen summarizes, "the flaws of whites are more easily forgiven. White privilege has meant that scores of second-rate white professors have slid through the system because their flaws were overlooked out of solidarity based on race, as well as on gender, class and ideology" (as cited in Lewis 2003, 169).

CURRICULA: THE PRODUCTION AND DISSEMINATION OF WHITE PROPERTY

How excellent can a department/faculty/university be if its curriculum dissemi-
nates to students only a very minuscule, highly-selected, self-perpetuating, [race
and] gender-biased representation of our collective knowledge about human
beings and the world in which we live?

– Sheinin (1998, 103)

Curricula can be considered social (race/gender) texts, or forms of representation associated with the production of cultural practices and social
relations that shape students' ways of thinking and being, offering them
possibility and identity (Pinar 1993). It is instructive that in November
2015 diverse groups of Black students (along with Indigenous and racialized minorities and their allies) expressing their outrage at systemic
anti-Black racism and racialized exclusion and hostility manifest across
Canadian campuses (and beyond). In March 2016 Black students decried
the absence of Black faculty, the deliberate marginalization or the elim-
ination of programs where Black people are the subjects of study. In an
op-ed article in the *Toronto Star*, Sefanit Habtemariam and Sandy Hudson
(2016), founding members of the Black Liberation Collective-Canada, a
pan–North American movement dedicated to eliminating anti-Black racism on college and university campuses, described how the devaluation
and erasure of Black life is achieved. In their words, "At our own institution [the University of Toronto], there are no courses where you can
study black people at the graduate level. The school of Global Affairs is
completely devoid of programs and courses that focus on the continent
of Africa. This is the largest school in Canada, often touted as the best. It's
difficult to imagine such an omission with regard to, say, Europe or Asia.
Canada itself has a long and vibrant black history. Should we not be able
to study it?" In response to their activism, they and other activists were
subject to further racist attacks through online threats, harassment, and
discriminatory comments (Habtemariam and Hudson 2016).

Yvonne Brown, an educator who fought tirelessly to bring African history into the curriculum at UBC (Musqueam territory) stated, "If you teach
European history without Africa, it's a false history. If you teach the history
of the United States without African people's presence, it's false. If you teach
Caribbean history without it, it's false" (cited in Tshegay, 2016, para. 9).[5]

This omission speaks to what Nigerian author Chimimanda Ngozi
Adichie masterfully describes in her 2009 Ted Talk as "the danger of a single story." Simply put, whose views count? Power is embedded in stories
that we learn, our understanding of everyday situations and beliefs. The

marginalization and exclusion of Black women in the ivory tower denies faculty and students of the opportunity to see the world from their perspectives, and the rejection of them as educators and scholars preserves intellectual hierarchies and spatial separation. Moreover, the erasure of the continent of Africa suggests that the history of enslavement, colonialism, and empire is relevant only to people of African descent.

Furthermore, in a climate of austerity, departments/programs claim that they can barely teach their core curriculum, that they have no money to teach anything new, or they have no money to diversify their faculty, leaving the gap between the academy and the community ever wider. Furthermore, while women's studies programs (in their various incarnations) have contributed to a significant rethinking of sex-gender relations and sexuality, they have had little to say about race (Cooper 2000; Fernández Arrigoitia et al. 2015; Gutiérrez y Muhs et al. 2012; Nash 2010; Ng 1993). The same pattern holds in Physical Education/ Kinesiology faculties where courses on "race" are rarely part of the curriculum, and courses on gender rarely consider race (Douglas and Halas 2013). More often than not, race is seen as a special topic, offered intermittently, or in competition with other courses such as those that address Indigeneity. In sum, the persistent absence of race from social theory illustrates that race remains a trait of those deemed to be "raced," while whiteness remains the unmarked norm (Henry and Tator 2007; Lipsitz 1998). Given that these patterned racialized exclusions maintain structured exclusions, we must ask ourselves at what point does the absence of race in curricula become "willful ignorance and aggression" (Baker, as cited in Pinar 1993, 62?).

INTERRACIAL/INTIMATE ENCOUNTERS: VISUALIZE THIS!

The subordinate positioning of Black women in the ivory tower extends beyond these spaces of "higher education." Black (and Indigenous) women are overrepresented in Canadian prisons. While Black people make up approximately 2.5 per cent of Canada's population they represent 9 per cent of the prison population. Between 2005 and 2015 the number of federally incarcerated Black Canadians increased by 69 per cent (Sapers 2015). In addition to experiencing higher rates of unemployment than their white counterparts, between 2000 and 2005 the annual income of Blacks decreased, their annual income almost one half that of whites (Keung 2011).

The spirit of the Code Noir and its attendant cultural practices and arrangements is conveyed through the perception and treatment of Black women in everyday life. While writing this chapter I was the target of racial profiling by both police and airport security. In the middle of the day, and five blocks from home, I was stopped by two white male police officers, seeking authentication of my presence in that neighbourhood, at that time and place. One of the officers held my driver's licence up to my face and asked me to recite my name, address, and date of birth. I was asked if I had any outstanding tickets and if I had had any run-ins with the police. The officer then took my identification to the police car and returned ten minutes later, stating, "You do some interesting work." My delayed response reactivated his suspicion, prompting him to again confirm my identity by asking, "You are still teaching at UBC aren't you?" Dumbstruck, I asked him if he had "Googled" me. He laughed and told me that "everything was fine."

Weeks later, en route from Winnipeg to Toronto with a white female colleague and co-author to present our research on equity, accountability, and social justice in Canadian Faculties of Kinesiology and Physical Education to a panel at the University of Toronto (territory of the Huron-Wendat and Petun, the Seneca, and the Mississaugas of the Credit River First Nations), I was again the target of racial profiling. I was detained by airport security while my colleague proceeded without additional screening. Well versed in the process. I always make sure to remove any item that might set off an alarm. The return trip is noteworthy because we were sent to a checkpoint that was empty. I was again stopped and subjected to a full examination, while my white female colleague was deemed a "trustworthy traveller." Both times we were told that my selection was arbitrary – "it has nothing to do with *me*," – the machine "randomly" selects its objects of investigation. While I have been a target of immigration and security agents well before September 2001, the increased frequency and hostility of these encounters is expressed in an aggressive examination of my body and the probing of my hair. I suggest that the persistent scrutiny and disciplining of my Black femaleness under the guise of the settler colonial narrative of "heightened security" offers public confirmation of the white supremacist discourse that positions Black women as a threat/threatening to the sanctity of the body politic. In both instances I am exposed; the marking of my Black female presence as "out of place" reveals how racism functions through social relations and geographic domination (McKittrick 2006; Razack 2002). The settler colonial logic that tracked my movements, challenging my corporeal integrity, echoes what Tamura A. Lomax (2015, para. 25) describes as the "deepened levels of black women's systemic and simultaneous marginalization and invisibility." As she explains, the oppression of Black women is so foundational to "empire … it's interpreted as moral" (para. 6). In sum, the marginalization of Black women in the academy and the public humiliations elsewhere confirm the interrelationship between the permanence of racism and the politics of its denial (Lubiano 1992).

Black/Out: Where Have All the Black Women Gone?

Our politics initially sprang from the shared belief that Black women are inherently valuable, that our liberation is a necessity not as an adjunct to somebody else's but because of our need as human persons for autonomy.

– Combahee River Collective (1977, 11)

We are in the long crisis. The systemic oppression of Black women is centuries old, and as such it is taken for granted. Whether captives, free persons, or people who have been erased and/or displaced, through force, compulsion, or initiative, a Black female presence has influenced the Canadian landscape. Initially captive/bodies – "stolen people on stolen land" – as enduring targets of anti-Black state violence, being Black, and female on unceded and occupied territory, simultaneously raises questions of presence, collaboration, resistance, and refusal (Amadahy and Lawrence 2009, 125).

In the context of dispossession and ongoing Indigenous struggles for sovereignty, the ivory tower is a socio-spatial expression of white settler colonial structures and racial gender hierarchies. Additionally, policies such as employment equity and multiculturalism obscure how contemporary configurations of the Code Noir renders the absence of Black women in the academy "natural." George Lipsitz (1998, 183) is correct in his assertion that we are living in a "moment of danger" wherein racism "poisons everything we are and everything we hope to be." According to Lipsitz, not only does this danger rests in political manifestations of violence that occur as a result of racial oppression. There is also a danger in the "wasted talents, and corrupt interpersonal and social relations that racism causes" (183). While acknowledgment of racial inequality does not ensure the eradication of domination, it is evident that many whites are reluctant to even engage in this form of critique. Given these dynamics, who will disrupt "hegemonic ways of seeing through which [whites] make themselves dominant" (Razack 1998, 10)? To be more precise, who will acknowledge the interests and experiences of Black women?

Our critical emancipatory democratic projects require that we hear and accept our differences and not use them to compare ourselves to each other to construct hierarchy.

If we are to secure a better understanding of our interdependence and webs of connections, and the intersections of systems of domination, we must uncover, unsettle, and reconfigure burials, denials, complicities, investments, and allegiances. The relentless practice of scrutinizing and regulating the lives of Black women, and the devaluation of our abilities and contributions speak to our defiance, and ongoing efforts to secure corporeal integrity and personhood. We keep going, because as Black women our desire, "our need, as human persons for autonomy" depends on it (Combahee River Collective 1977, 11).

NOTES

1 A 2015 UK study reports that in the entire university system of 15,905 faculty, 17 of the 85 (0.53 per cent) Black faculty are female and 92.4 per cent of faculty are white (Garner, 2015). In the United States, out of 1,852,224 faculty, 70,375 instructional staff are Black women, and 58,978 of this group are contingent faculty (also see Lomax, 2015).
2 While the Canadian census is the key source for equity data on academic staff in Canadian universities, the validity of the data has been questioned because it relies upon self-reporting. However, much anecdotal evidence supports the considerably low representation of Black female faculty across the country, as well the proportion of Black female faculty relative to their Black male counterparts. Also see "The Changing Ccademy": *CAUT Education Review*, 2010, 12 (1).
3 Joanne St. Lewis (2007) echoes a similar sentiment about her experiences as a law student at UBC.
4 The irony is that in Canada the racial composition of members of Faculties of Physical Education/Kinesiology are 94 per cent white (see Douglas and Halas 2013).
5 Dr. Brown lobbied UBC to have a course titled African/Black Women in the Americas be a part of the curriculum in the Women's and Gender Studies Program (now called The Social Justice Institute). This course is an upper division elective and has long held a precarious position within the Institute, perpetually at risk of cancellation. In 2009, the year I began teaching the course (following Dr. Brown's retirement) I was told that I would have to advertise across campus, and one year I was asked if I would be willing to include men in the course materials as a way of attracting greater student interest. Initially a 400-level course, in 2010 it was reclassified to a 300-level by senior administrators, ostensibly to increase enrolment.

REFERENCES

Adichie, C.N. 2009. "The Danger of a Single Story." Ted Talk. https://www.ted.com/talks/chimamanda_adichie_the_danger_of_a_single_story?language=en.
Ahmed, S. 2007. "A Phenomenology of Whiteness." *Feminist Theory* 8 (2): 149–168. https://doi.org/10.1177/1464700107078139.

Amadahy, Z., and Lawrence, B. 2009. "Indigenous Peoples and Black People in Canada: Settlers or Allies?" In *Breaching the Colonial Contract: Anti-Colonialism in the US and Canada*, edited by A. Kempf, 105–136. New York: Springer.

Backhouse, C. 1999. *Colour Coded: A Legal History of Racism in Canada, 1900–1950.* Toronto: The Osgoode Society.

Bakare-Yusuf, B. 1999. "The Economy of Violence: Black Bodies and the Unspeakable Terror." In *Feminist Theory and the Body: A Reader*, edited by J. Price and M. Shildrick, 311–323. New York: Routledge.

Baldwin, J. 1976. *The Devil Finds Work.* New York: Dell.

Cacho, L.M. 2012. *Social Death: Racialized Rightlessness and the Criminalization of the Unprotected.* New York: New York University Press.

Carty, L. 1991. "Black Women in Academia: A Statement from the Periphery." In *Unsettling Relations: The University as a Site of Feminist Struggles*, edited by H. Bannerji, L. Carty, K. Dehli, S. Heald, and K. McKenna, 13–44. Boston: South End Press.

"The Changing Academy." 2010. *Canadian Association of University Teachers (CAUT) Education Review* 12 (1): 1–6. https://www.caut.ca/docs/education-review/the-changing-academy-a-portrait-of-canada-rsquo-s-university-teachers-%28jan-2010%29.pdf?sfvrsn=14.

Combahee River Collective. 1977. *The Combahee River Collective Statement.* New York: Kitchen Table–Women of Color Press.

Cooper, A. 2000. "Constructing Black Women's Historical Knowledge." *Atlantis* 25 (1): 39–50.

Cooper, A. 2006. *The Hanging of Angelique: The Untold Story of Canadian Slavery and the Burning of Old Montreal.* Toronto: HarperCollins.

Davis, A.Y. 1971. "Reflections on the Black Woman's Role in the Community of Slaves." *The Black Scholar* 23: 2–15. https://doi.org/10.1080/00064246.1971.11431201.

Douglas, D.D., and Halas, J.M. 2013. "The Wages of Whiteness." *Sport, Education and Society* 18 (4): 453–474. https://doi.org/10.1080/13573322.2011.602395.

Eisenkraft, H. 2010. "Racism in the Academy." *University Affairs.* http://www.universityaffairs.ca/features/feature-article/racism-in-the-academy/.

Elgersman, M.G. 1999. *Unyielding Spirits: Black Women and Slavery in Early Canada and Jamaica.* New York: Garland Publishing.

Failler, A. 2009. "Remembering the Air India Disaster: Memorial and Counter-Memorial." *Review of Education, Pedagogy, and Cultural Studies* 31 (2 & 3): 150–176. https://doi.org/10.1080/10714410902827168.

Fernández Arrigoitia, M., Beetham, G., Jones, C.E., and Nzinga-Johnson, S. 2015. "Women's Studies and Contingency: Between Exploitation and Resistance." *Feminist Formations* 27 (3): 81–113. https://doi.org/10.1353/ff.2016.0000.

Garner, R. 2015, 3 February. "UK Study Finds Just 17 Black Female Professors." *Independent.* https://www.independent.co.uk/student/news/uk-study-finds-just-17-black-female-professors-10019201.html.

Glenn, E.N. 2015. "Settler Colonialism as Structure." *Sociology of Race and Ethnicity* 1 (1): 52–72. https://doi.org/10.1177/2332649214560440.

Goldberg, D.T. 2005. "Afterwards." In *Making Race Matter: Bodies, Space and Identity*, edited by C. Alexander and C. Knowles, 218–223. New York: Palgrave Macmillan.

Gutiérrez y Muhs, G., Niemann, Y.F., González, C.G., and Harris, A.P. 2012. *Presumed Incompetent: The Intersections of Race and Class for Women in Academia*. Logan: Utah State University Press.

Habtemariam, S., and Hudson, S. 2016, 1 March. "Canadian Campuses Have a Racism Problem." *The Toronto Star*. https://www.thestar.com/opinion/commentary/2016/03/01/canadian-campuses-have-a-racism-problem.html.

Hartman, S.V. 1997. *Scenes of Subjection*. New York: Oxford University Press.

Hartman, S.V. 2007. *Lose Your Mother*. New York: Farrar, Straus and Giroux.

Henry, F., Choi, A., and Kobayashi, A. 2012. "The Representation of Racialized Faculty at Selected Canadian Universities." *Canadian Ethnic Studies* 44 (2): 1–12. https://doi.org/10.1353/ces.2012.0008.

Henry, F., and Tator, C. 2007. "The Rightness of Whiteness: Enduring Racism in the Canadian Academy." Paper presented at the biennial meeting of the Canadian Ethnic Studies Association, Winnipeg.

Higginbotham, E.B. 1992. "African-American Women's History and the Metalanguage of Race." *Signs: Journal of Women in Culture and Society* 17 (2): 251–274. https://doi.org/10.1086/494730.

Keung, N. 2011, 21 March. "Skin Colour Matters in Access to Good Jobs." *The Toronto Star*. https://www.thestar.com/news/investigations/2011/03/21/skin_colour_matters_in_access_to_good_jobs.html.

Kobayashi, A. 2007. "Making the Visible Count: Difference and Embodied Knowledge in the Academy." Paper presented at the annual Congress of the Social Sciences and Humanities, Saskatoon.

Lewis, A.E. 2003. "Some Are More Equal than Others: Lessons on Whiteness from School." In *White Out: The Continuing Significance of Racism*, edited by A. Doane and E. Bonilla-Silva, 159–172. New York: Routledge.

Li, P.S. 2012. "Differences in Employment Income of University Professors." *Canadian Ethnic Studies* 44 (2): 39–48. https://doi.org/10.1353/ces.2012.0012.

Lipsitz, G. 1998. *The Possessive Investment in Whiteness: How White People Profit from Identity Politics*. Philadelphia: Temple University Press.

Lomax, T.A. 2015. Black Women's Lives Don't Matter in Academia Either, or Why I Quit Academic Spaces That Don't Value Black Women's Life and Labor. *The Feminist Wire*. http://www.thefeministwire.com/2015/05/black-womens-lives-dont-matter-in-academia-either-or-why-i-quit-academic-spaces-that-dont-value-black-womens-life/.

Lubiano, W. 1992. "Black Ladies, Welfare Queens, and State Minstrels: Ideological War by Narrative Means." In *Race-ing Justice, En-gendering Power:*

Essays on Anita Hill, Clarence Thomas and the Construction of Social Reality, edited by T. Morrison, 323–363. New York: Pantheon Books.

Martinot, S. 2010. *The Machinery of Whiteness*. Philadelphia: Temple University Press.

McKittrick, K. 2002. "'Their Blood Is There, and They Can't Throw It Out': Honouring Black Canadian Geographies." *Topia* 7: 27–36. https://doi.org/10.3138/topia.7.27.

McKittrick, K. 2006. *Demonic Grounds: Black Women and the Cartographies of Struggle*. Minneapolis: University of Minnesota Press.

Memmi, A. 1965. *The Colonizer and the Colonized*. New York: Beacon Press.

Mohanty, C.T. 1987. "Feminist Encounters: Locating the Politics of Experience." *Copyright* 1: 30–44.

Murray, B. 2011. *Long Road to Justice: The Viola Desmond Story*. https://www.youtube.com/watch?v=yI00i9BtsQ8.

Nash, J.C. 2010. "On Difficulty: Intersectionality as Feminist Labor." *The Scholar and Feminist Online* 8 (3). http://sfonline.barnard.edu/polyphonic/nash_01.htm.

Ng, R. 1993. "'A Woman Out of Control': Deconstructing Sexism and Racism at the University." *Canadian Journal of Education* 18 (3): 189–205. https://doi.org/10.2307/1495382.

Pabst, N. 2009. "An Unexpected Blackness." *Transition* 100: 112–132. https://doi.org/10.2979/TRS.2009.-.100.112.

Patel, L. 2015. "Desiring Diversity and Backlash: White Property Rights in Higher Education." *Urban Review* 47: 657–675. https://doi.org/10.1007/s11256-015-0328-7.

Peake, L., and Ray, B. 2001. "Racializing the Canadian Landscape: Whiteness, Uneven Geographies and Social Justice." *The Canadian Geographer* 45 (1): 180–186. https://doi.org/10.1111/j.1541–0064.2001.tb01183.x.

Pierson, R.R. 2004. White Academic Women and Imperialist and Racist Knowledge Production." *Atlantis: A Women's Studies Journal* 2: 90–102.

Pinar, W.F. 1993. "Notes on Understanding Curriculum as a Racial Text." In *Race, Identity and Representation in Education*, edited by C. McCarthy and W. Crichlow, 60–70. New York: Routledge.

Razack, S.H. 1998. *Looking White People in the Eye: Gender, Race, and Culture in Courtrooms and Classrooms*. Toronto: University of Toronto Press.

Razack, S.H. 2002. "When Place Becomes Race." In *Race, Space, and the Law*, edited by S. Razack, 1–20. Toronto: Between the Lines.

Sapers, H. 2015. *Annual Report of the Office of the Correctional Investigator 2014–2015*. http://www.oci-bec.gc.ca/cnt/rpt/pdf/annrpt/annrpt20142015-eng.pdf.

Schick, C. 2014. "White Resentment in Settler Society." *Race, Ethnicity and Education* 17 (1): 88–102. https://doi.org/10.1080/13613324.2012.733688.

Sheinin, R. 1998. "The Changing Space for Women in Academe: The 'Engendering' of Knowledge." In *The Illusion of Inclusion: Women in Post-secondary*

Education, edited by J. Stalker and S. Prentice, 94–107. Halifax: Fernwood Publishing.

Smith, M.S. 2007. "Telling Tales on White Li(v)es, Diversity-Talk, and the Ivory Tower." Paper presented at the Annual Meeting of the Canadian Federation for the Humanities and Social Sciences, Saskatoon.

Smith, M.S. 2010. "Gender, Whiteness, and 'Other Others' in the Academy." In *States of Race: Critical Race Feminism for the 21st Century*, edited by S. Razack, M. Smith, and S. Thobani, 37–58. Toronto: Between the Lines.

Smith, M.S. 2016. "Intersectionality Blues: Diversity Is the New White." Paper presented at the Race Literacies: Black Canadian Speaker Series, UBC, Vancouver.

St. Lewis, J. 2007. "Getting Radical: Racism, Complacency and Self-Deception in Academic Culture." Paper presented at the Annual Meeting of the Canadian Federation for the Humanities and Social Sciences, Saskatoon.

Statistics Canada. 2007. "2006 Census: Immigration, Citizenship, Language, Mobility and Migration." https://www150.statcan.gc.ca/n1/daily-quotidien/071204/dq071204a-eng.htm.

Statistics Canada. 2008. "Aboriginal Peoples in Canada in 2006: Inuit, Métis and First Nations." https://www12.statcan.ca/english/censUS06/analysis/aboriginal/surpass.cfm.

Thornhill, E.M.A. 2008. "So Seldom for Us, So Often against Us: Blacks and Law in Canada." *Journal of Black Studies* 38 (3): 321–337. https://doi.org/10.1177/0021934707308258.

Tseghay, D. 2016. "Challenging Anti-Black Racism on Canadian Campuses." *Rank and File.* https://www.rankandfile.ca/challenging-anti-black-racism-on-canadian-campuses/.

Winks, R.W. 1997. *The Blacks in Canada: A History.* Montreal and Kingston: McGill-Queen's University Press.

3 The Precariat African-Canadian Academic: Problematic Historical Constructions, Perpetual Struggles for Recognition

ALI A. ABDI

Introduction

The location of the African-Canadian academic in the country's higher education system remains limited, under surveillance, and relatively precarious. This complicated situation is not an accidental one, it did not just come about in the past few years, it is not necessarily the outcome of one totalizing event, and there does not seem to be one identifiable professional, politico-economic, or even socio-cultural remedy for it. The overall situation is collectively damaging, but is still sustained, at least from my reading, for and by complex and interactively connecting reasons. While these reasons are not necessarily completely attached to any specific educational or professional histories, qualifications, and/or achievements or lack thereof, of the concerned academic, they are still selectively and presumptively rationalized on all or some of those. It is with this reality in mind that a combined historical and contemporary understanding of how these perceptions and reactions to the African-Canadian academic were created and maintained should be the sine qua non of figuring out and analysing the situation. Perhaps more than anything else, the continuing precariousness of the African-Canadian academic is a deliberate actualization of the cultural and epistemic falsehoods concocted against the so-called, if analytically problematic, typical persona Africana. The external constructions, more correctly the assumptions about the persona Africana in the past 500 or so years, continue to contain heavy oppressive doses that have targeted the historical, cultural, psychological, and physical, in essence, the onto-existential platforms that define and locate the African people. With this important backdrop, and in speaking about the professional space of the African-Canadian academic therefore, I refuse not to enlist, as problematic descriptors and damaging psycho-cultural blocks and for this analysis, the colonial constructions of Africa and its peoples. By extension, I attach those to the current global African diaspora context where the previous construction of the terra nullius thesis about the continent that, with its historical fixity, is still and willy-nilly conceptualizing, theorizing about, and in epistemic terms, suppressing the scholarly and other recognitive credits due to the African-Canadian academic.

It is with that historical understanding, sustained through modernity's monocentric categorizations of the world that should help us critically comprehend the historical and current constructions of Africa and the African-Canadian academic, and especially how issues that concern knowledge and related human capacities and assumptions are constructed. From there, it is important to note how these are still technically and deliberately attached to historical/current depictions of Africa, and summatively lower the value and potential of everything African. Indeed, the unidirectional constructions of historical Africa and the persistence of such fabrications were not just about the colonial conquest of Africa and were not simplistically evidenced in relation to the intellectual and related capacities of Africans, including the knowledge and character of current African-Canadian academics. These were also designed to achieve the mental colonization that was to assure the presumed epistemic inferiority of Africans and other colonized populations (Achebe 1958/2009, 2000; wa Thiong'o 2009, 2014). Indeed, the issue becomes even more interesting and more meaningful when one realizes who were the vanguard of the systematic projects of Africa's historico-cultural and epistemic colonization. I will say more about this, but suffice it to mention here that the perpetrators were among Europe's so-called illustrious thinkers, philosophers, and academics. Perhaps as much as any other group, some of the most important thought leaders from colonizing Europe became the fabricators of baseless propaganda about the capacity of Africans, which is now influencing the way African-Canadian academics are viewed, interacted with, and professionally recognized or arbitrarily mis-recognized.

African-Canadian Academics: In the Edifice of Global Cognitive Colonization

As I have written on a related topic (Abdi 2009), the subjective constructions of African Canadians, who now number about a million, is derived from the colonial schemes where the colonized were depicted as inferior people who were worthy to be colonized. Indeed, colonialism was not necessarily only a program of political domination and economic exploitation. Of course it constituted those and related activities, but it was also, especially in its initial stages, a platform of psycho-cultural and knowledge inferioritizations and superioritizations that were established to lower the value of Africans and justify their oppressions, which was to be concomitant with free access to their lands, resources, and labour. As should be expected, one does not value people highly, then decide to colonize them. The essence of the colonial project itself was justified on the presumed inferiority of those who were to be colonized, and it was on this basis that some of Europe's most admired thinkers became spokespersons for the benighted but strategically labelled *mission civilisatrice* (civilizing mission; see Said 1993). In essence, the colonial derogatory construction of Africans still retains its select applicability to contemporary continental Africans and diasporic Africans. Its continuities can be viewed through the permanency of the continuum of racism and other exclusionary schemes that affect the lives of Africans irrespective of where they currently reside. Among those well-regarded thinkers who easily but destructively jumped on the bandwagon of colonialism were such European philosophers as the German duo Immanuel Kant and G.W.H. Hegel, the Englishman Thomas Hobbes, and even the so-labelled French thinkers of liberty and freedom Jean-Marie d'Arouet (nom de plume, Voltaire) and Charles-Louis de Secondat (Baron de la Brède et de Montesquieu), generally known as Montesquieu (Abdi 2008).

Reading what these men wrote about Africa for their European societies is painful, and more than just as temporally specific exhortations, their philosophizing about the continent and its peoples continues to have enduring cognitive imprints and outcomes. These imprints still shape the way the contemporary world perceives, views, interacts with, and decides about peoples of African descent, irrespective of their locations, circumstances, and achievements. These include African-Canadian academics who are not detached from the historical and contemporary problematic constructions of the continent, especially so in the de-historicizations, de-culturalizations, de-philosophizings, and by more than conjectural extension, the de-epistemologizations of Africa and Africans. Indeed, one need not belabour the intentions of the onslaught against Africa and its peoples, especially as it was created in the colonizing European metropolis. I have extensively written about these false but still as-knowledge-constructed platforms of European thinkers and philosophers, and while I run the risk of repeating myself, I still believe it is exceedingly important for this readership to know more about this uniquely important topic. More often than is usually expected, people should rightly develop a curiosity about how Africans were historico-epistemically externally constructed. With that, one question should be, How did Europeans – and to some extent others outside Africa – presumptively "know" Africans so well?

To address some of the queries that could arise here, the task should not be too difficult to discern, as we are aided by the writings of so-called quintessential philosophers of reason and robust rational thinking. For the sake of brevity though, and with analytical fairness, I focus here more on one important European thinker whose ideas on Africans and others is worth sharing – the German philosopher Immanuel Kant. Choosing Kant for this purpose is not based on just his relevant observations on the matter but more so because he is a founding figure in the modern philosophical traditions. Kant is also a central figure in the development of new ideas and perspectives on political rights, citizenship rights, and world governance. As such, he is depicted as an original thinker on cosmopolitanism and the possibilities of extra-national citizenship where as we could read prima facie, should recognize the full value of all. In his 1795 essay "Perpetual Peace" (Zum ewigen Frieden) Kant promoted, at least in theoretical terms, a new platform for a new global order that should be safeguarded by a consortium of nations (Kant, 1795/2016). He advised the world to think about and attempt to organize their governance structures around the political and expectedly economic principles of republicanism to keep national and international peace and establish binding human rights regimes for all citizens, irrespective of where they reside or to which countries they belong. In a quasi-contradictory note that resonates with today's global citizenship debates, Kant, while advocating for a cosmopolitan life, also promoted a potential global consortium of states, in order to avoid forcing individual countries to undertake these issues, as that could violate the sovereignty of concerned nations.

Not detached from these observations and still with oxymoronic trends, Kant also spoke about how all earth should belong to all people, which should have anticipated the currently important and expansive focus on citizenship beyond one's national boundaries. This could also have possibly contributed (at least at the ideational level) to the later germination of the concept and practices of human rights platforms and regimes that again should apply to all human beings, regardless of their background and other identifiable characteristics. In reading Kant's work more closely, though, and especially the focus of his work, *Of the Different Races of Man* [Über die verschiedenen Rassen der Menschen] (1775/2015), it is clear that he was anything but someone who believed in the equality of all peoples. In his unscientific but in temporal terms, authoritative categorization of the so-called races (currently a misnomer, as we know more about the unscientific constructions of race and racism – see, inter alia, Gould 1985; Cook 2003; Sussman 2014), Kant's elevation of Europeans over all others should be instructive of his real beliefs and racist biases. For Africans especially, the situation got worse as Kant expressly associated black skin with lack of intelligence (Eze 1997). Kant's compatriot and equally celebrated philosopher, Hegel, went one step further. He didn't just disparage Africans, he actually justified the conquest of African lands and the stealing of their resources (Hegel 1965). In his words, the oppression as well as the cheating of a child-like race such as Africans was not only justified, it was the right thing to do. Such expressions of colonial temporality were used to solidify European perceptions about Africa and, by extension, the colonization of Africans.

Contrary to the shallow presentations of the civilizing mission, therefore, colonialism was predicated on the assumed inferiority of Africans, which via the endurance of concomitant and implemented mental colonizations, has assured us the current categories of human considerations. By direct extension, these also assured the misrecognitions splashed on the psychosomatics and around the professional locations of African Canadians working in the country's universities and colleges. In reality, therefore, the location of African-Canadian academics is anything but ahistorical. It is selectively historicized and epistemically concretized via the colonial depictions of Africans which in descriptively contradictory and historically connected terms, presented them as devoid of high culture – whatever that meant in that context – and aphilosophical. With this in mind and in relaying the point with existential urgency, Ivan Van Sertima (1991) likened the damage colonialism wrought on African lives (ancient and now) to the biblical Flood story. In essence, noted Van Sertima, the basic fabric of people's lives was so torn apart that our current existence is so different from that before the Holocaust, as he labels it. That tearing up of the fabric of African societies applies to all people of African descent, including those whose ancestors were captured and transported to the Americas, the Caribbean, and elsewhere. Here the cliché of the end justifying the means was so expansive and the damage done to the psyches and bodies of Africans so immense that for over half a millennium and into this hour the onto-epistemological realities of people have not yet fully recovered. Such a reality also applies to the professional platforms of African-Canadian academics who are not exempt from this, with the continuing inferioritizations of their intellect, character, and extra-self-constructed ethical qualities. It is factually with this historical background that African-Canadian academics are tentatively admitted into the country's higher education campuses. This happened more tangibly only in the past twenty years or so, even when there were many highly qualified candidates before that who were never offered such positions. More often than otherwise, the slow admission into the halls of academia seems to have started as an experiment to discover if we could perform as well as our European-Canadian or other non-European and non-African counterparts, who, in the colonial ladder of human considerations, were collectively expected to do better than Africans.

It is with such professional conditionality and still-in-vigour experimentation that continuously renders African-Canadian academics as perennial probationary figures whose employment continuum should yield some trajectories of failure in their teaching, research, or ethics. I do know what I am talking about here. Succinctly, if you continuously and via automatic brain response elicit negative reactions from those around you and are under constant surveillance without the opportunity to gain the benefit of the doubt, sooner or later your otherwise ethical dispositions and behaviour will be constructed as unethical. There will be no shortage of racist witnesses who can affirm the normative outcome of the story. The complexity of the issue here is worth explaining. While the historical, false constructions of Africans' abilities are institutionally intact and doing their intended damage, it is equally important to comprehend the second level of mental colonization. Here non-Africans of all backgrounds and from almost everywhere outside Africa and outside the African diaspora have been successfully instructed to accept everything colonialism taught them about Africans. Indeed, the potential new damage created by such mental colonization against all African Canadians is as severe as – sometimes even more severe than – that from racism and its affiliated prejudice, stereotyping, and discrimination. The reasons for this organized racism against Africans (generally called anti-Black racism in Canada) by non-European-Canadian groups, which is possibly being shared with their offspring, shouldn't be too difficult to comprehend.

Such important and needed comprehension of these different sources of racism against African Canadians should be clear to those who suffer their effects in Canadian public and private spaces. The same applies to those of us who are willing to learn from such brilliant social psychologists and decolonization creative minds as Albert Memmi (1956/1991), Frantz Fanon (1967, 1968), and Fanon's teacher, Aimé Césaire (1972). The tragic reality, though, is that others who were also colonized and have succumbed to the idea of the supremacy of the West (Sophie Bessis, 2003) have internalized a cluster of concocted truisms about Africans, even when they had no meaningful contact or any contact at all with Africans prior to Africans' Canadianization. Likely what these non-African, non-European groups are acting upon is a need to counter-weigh the "white" racism they themselves sometimes experience. That could create a primal need to seek some psycho-cultural comfort in oppressing those they perceive as inferior to them. As Albert Memmi (1956/1991) so cogently discussed, among the sorry outcomes of global colonialism is not just what it did to a specific group of people, but also the way it earned the unconditional and often enthusiastic support of the colonized to oppress one another, which some groups of former imperial subjects have fully embraced. The way Memmi and others – including the historically most exacting observers such as Fanon (1967, 1968), Césaire (1972), and Achebe (1958/1994, 2000) – understand this (and I agree) is that once a group is historico-culturally and onto-epistemologically colonized, they begin to apply a cluster of demerit points to their being, while still yearning for superiority over someone else. And since they cannot achieve superiority over the colonizer, they seek solace in placing themselves as second-, third-, or even fourth-class citizens, as long as there are others they perceive as inferior to them. It is important to discern how such untenable categorizations were brought about. These realities seem to assure us the intended marginalization of African Canadians in general and African-Canadian academics specifically. With these facts and their interpretations and practices in mind, I term the professional life of African Canadians as precariat. In the coming pages, I will say more about that.

The Precariat Situation of African-Canadian Academics

As a starting point for this section, I note that we all are outcomes of temporal and spatial intersections that label us as soon as we are born. This outcome could be aggregated through institutionalization, which borrows from the primordial platforms, thus entrenching our existentialities, on group-based stereotypes that are heaped upon entire populations. Such stereotyping can happen without recourse to the individual qualities, intentions, experiences, and efforts that one could use to advance one's life chances and achievements. These concocted perspectives are still current and are invoked to splash doubt on the intellectual capacity and the professional integrity of African-Canadian academics and their communities. Interestingly and despite their often stellar achievements, these academics are expected to express their gratitude for being saved from and overcoming their disqualifying qualities.

As I have said, this complicated situation creates multiple sources of racism for African Canadians that can limit credit for their knowledge and, by extension, their professional liquidity and recognition. It also establishes the possible cases where these academics find themselves in the socio-institutionally contradictory situation of claiming knowledge and professional expertise while Black. What is at play here is the historical bias against associating learnedness and knowing with people of African descent. Especially worth exploring are the sources of epistemic and professional demerit realities to which professional African-Canadians are subjected. African-Canadian academics are not even minimally detached from the racist scholarship of colonial apologist thinkers such as Voltaire and Hegel.

The irony of locating Africa and Africans as outside civilization and therefore in need of the civilizing mission goes against a fundamental fact. No groups or peoples could have thrived for millennia, as pre-colonial Africans did, without the cultural, educational, economic, and technological achievements that sustained them for generations. As such, the Enlightenment-centric, rationalist thinking – that those who do not exploit their physical and temporal subjectivities and their physical environments to exhaustion are backward and primitive (Huntington 1971; Rostow 1991) – is itself a savagery that subjugates people to the whims and the desires of the elite, who continue to be the beneficiaries of such projects. In the colonization of Africa, and by extension, the colonization of the professional locations of African-Canadian academics, the latter must still respond to the de-onto-epistemologicalizations of their original lands, cultures, and knowledge achievements. Despite our own historically connected and culturally relevant readings and writings on African life systems, the work of those who have been in academia for some time, like me, is still relegated to second-class scholarship by others, including those from non-European contexts. As clearly stated above, they have been brilliantly schooled by European writings and reporting on African contexts that, as Achebe (2000) and others note, have been mostly disparaging, bent on justifying organized racism and its attendant human and environmental degradations and exploitations.

Not even the greatest achievements of Africa's most celebrated writers and academics are enough to earn the knowledge and development credits that are reserved for others with lesser claims and capacities. In his characteristic bluntness, Chinua Achebe (2000), Africa's late doyen of letters, was clear that he does not come from a disfigured and tribally disorganized social context, but from coherent and politically viable life systems that have developed their own uniquely effective ways of reading the world and rendering it more viable for their aspirations and emerging socio-cultural, political, and economic needs. Otherwise, there would be no one in his Harvard audience to hear him and appreciate what he had to say. Indeed, European writing demeaned Africans and their achievements so completely that it was useful in at least one way. It awakened Achebe to how his physical and epistemological houses were under attack, and he had no choice but to see the shattered fragments of his being, and from there try to reassemble what was lost. He was largely successful.

The knowledge situations described above are not and should not be external to the epistemic and related professional locations of

African-Canadian academics. Indeed, without reconstructing what was deconstructed and deformed by the onslaught of the de-civilizing mission, epistemic and professional redemption will not be achieved and the precariousness of our professional lives will continue. The professional lives of African-Canadian academics are interwoven with continuing mis-recognitions of the continent, its peoples, and their achievements. Indeed, the precarious professional lives of African-Canadian academics are continually cemented by the dis-associative assumptions about Africa and its epistemic currency, which is extended to spaces of work where threads of achievement doubt and the continuation of the perpetual probationary status have become fait accompli, without any official institutional announcements. Returning to the example of Achebe, he was a distinguished professor at Brown University, an Ivy League school, and he had a global legacy, his works translated into many languages. Yet he was described by European and European North American commentators as perhaps the best writer out of Africa. So what else could he have done to be recognized as among the world's best writers?

Fortunately, Achebe was aware of the conditional and limited charities of recognition. He was critical of problems that should be extrapolated to those affecting the knowledge capacity and professional credibility of African-Canadian academics and all intellectuals of African descent (1989). Achebe remains my favourite anti-colonial intellectual. His groundbreaking counter-hegemonic polemic, *Things Fall Apart* (1958/2009), notified us of the existential dangers of de-historicization and de-culturation when these are applied to people's lives. Interestingly, the naturalistic Africanist philosophy of inter-human harmony known as Ubuntu actually contributed to the initial welcome of invading Europeans who, unbeknownst to Africans, had been already fed with anti-African psycho-socializations by their influential thinkers and philosophers. Ubuntu is an original humanist African philosophy that mandates that we see ourselves through the humanity of others. In speaking about how even African intellectuals of his calibre were still expected to secure the approval of Western guardians of real knowledge and literature, Achebe wrote, "Would it be invalid for a Nigerian [African] writer seeing dissatisfaction in his society to write about it? I am being told, for Christ's sake, that before I write about a problem *or for that matter, about issues of social or other interests*, I must *first* verify whether they have it too in New York, London and Paris" (96, emphasis mine).

Achebe's cogent observation is about the externality of the problematic totalization of Africa and Africans, not only during colonialism, but in these misnamed postcolonial times as well. That is, false assumptions and concoctions about the sociocultural and knowledge capacities of

Africa and Africans became established in the thinking of Europeans and increasingly about other non-African peoples across the globe. The durability of mental colonization, as has been extensively discussed by Ngugi wa Thiong'o (1986, 2009), among others, is indeed largely responsible for most of these problematic categories we see today. More than anything else, it is this reality where the extensive perception de-patterning among peoples takes place through the presumed superiority of the powerful. Again and as we saw above, the relational project of the colonizer and the colonized was not only a two-way process, but a multi-way perspective that in Fanon's steel-bending analysis (see Fanon 1967, 1968) reconstructed the being of multi actors into contexts that denied their human qualities while inversely elevating the lot of others in relation to them. In their historical and epistemic totalities, these issues apply problematic colonial or neocolonial (not postcolonial) fixities that refuse to notice even the tangible efforts, achievements, and professional dynamism of African-Canadian academics who remain precariat but resilient in their pursuit of professional excellence in the Canadian academic landscape.

African-Canadian Academics: Struggles for Success in the Face of Multiple Challenges

In *The Souls of Black Folk* (1903/1994), W.E.B. Dubois, the public intellectual and first African American to earn a doctoral degree at Harvard, critically discussed what he saw as the habitual refusal to see the full humanity of the African person, which extends into the world of African-Canadian academics. With what Cornel West (2009) termed "snobbish gentility," he was approached by those who would rather ignore him but couldn't. In such uneasy encounter Dubois (1903/1994, 1) noted,

> Between me and the other world there, there is an unasked question: unasked by some through feelings of delicacy; by others through the difficulty of framing it. All, nevertheless, flutter around it. They approach [me] in a half-hesitant sort of way, eye me curiously or compassionately, and then, instead of say directly, how does it feel to be a problem? They say, I know an excellent colored man in my town; or I fought at Mechanicsville; or do not these southern outrages make your blood boil? At these I smile, or am amused. Or reduce the boiling to a simmer, as the occasion may require. To the real question, how does it feel to be a problem? I answer seldom a word.

What Dubois is packing into this paragraph sums up announced and unannounced interpersonal and inter-group formations. These formations establish oppression and exclusion, operationalize them for the benefit of some at the expense of others, and then normalize the unequal interactions. These also systematize the situation in the sense that it is cognitively inscribed, it slowly de-patterns mental dispositions, and once discursively officialized, it perpetuates itself. If one is reminded here of post-structural and postmodernist writings, one need not experience any epistemic dissonance. But the observational block for most people could be answering this question: Whose post-structural or post-modernist writings do I have in mind? While I appreciate the ideas and knowledge-expanding contributions of those now globally associated with these works (such as Lyotard 1979; Foucault 1980; Derrida 1980; and Baudrillard 1981, among others), I actually agree with those who recognized that the pioneers of post-structuralism and postmodernism were African and African diaspora liberation intellectuals. Indeed, while the word "postmodern" was first used in a philosophical sense by Jean-François Lyotard in *The Postmodern Condition* (1979, English translation in 1984), African liberation scholars such as Achebe (1958/2009), Kane (1963/2012), wa Thiong'o (1967), Fanon (1967, 1968), Julius Nyerere (1968), and Aimé Césaire (1972) were writing about the revival of suppressed world views, languages, knowledges, and cultures much earlier.

These African liberation intellectuals were writing about and analysing the need for epistemic justice and multi-locational knowledges, and the need to re-historicize and re-philosophize (in general terms) African ideas, cultures, knowledge systems, and achievements – that is, all those important life systems and realities denied to the continent and its peoples by European colonialist thinkers, philosophers, and administrators. Indeed, the issue moved from Africans being denied their achievements to being reduced to tolerable silhouettes. That deconstruction needed the timely responses from Dubois and others who refused to de-affirm their being and capacities, just as African-Canadian academics are doing now. Yet the task for African-Canadian academics is becoming more onerous. Indeed, during the hiring processes and as they climb the professional ladder, they must continually devise new strategies for success. Counter-intuitively-normatively, the expected failure of this dark "foreigner" on presumably progressive campuses has been thus far quashed by the stellar achievements of African-Canadian academics.

Indeed, African-Canadian academics are near or at the top in relation to comparable professoriate ranks and groups, and that should have silenced the doubters. Unfortunately, the response to their achievements is not always positive. Many non-African groups develop what I term "expectation dissonance syndrome" (EDS), which is a conflictual state of relationship with the African-Canadian academic who has violated their expectation of failure. EDS seems to more severely affect the middle group (non-Africans and non-Europeans), who could be struggling to prove their own assumed superiority over Africans. This complicates the situation for African Canadian-academics, who need allies in the co-oppressed groups. Without that support on the horizon, African-Canadian academics have no other alternative than to use whatever platforms they can to survive and succeed. Engaging in such struggles requires the excavation and restoration of disparaged cultures, usurped histories, and damaged ontologies. Without that work, personal and professional respectability and recognition might not come our way in the foreseeable future. As Anthony Bogues (2003) notes, African-Canadian academics must continuously engage in subjective redemptions and robustly display great refusals to counter more damage. Doing so would enable them to continue succeeding as individuals and as a group which should facilitate their capacity to de-validate the myths fabricated about them.

Conclusion

In this chapter I have focused on the colonial and related constructions of Africans, and how these have shaped perceptions about African-Canadian academics, who are still wrongly read, misrecognized, and subjected to suspicions about their professional capacities and ethical qualities. Indeed, the almost entirely negative constructions of Africans, and by extension African-Canadian academics, should be historically and analytically attached to the works of European thinkers and philosophers who cleared the way for colonialism. Later these were spread by colonial administrators and security forces in Africa and in other colonized spaces across the globe. Such assumptions of subjective and group inferioritzation became so widespread that they are no longer limited to people of European background and infected others from places outside Africa. The issue has become a global phenomenon that fits the colonizations of minds from multiple locations that now reside in this ineptly named pluralistic Western democracy called Canada. This pattern of cognitive colonizations aligns with the social analysis of Albert Memmi (1956/1991), among others, who discussed, not only the superior-inferior mental colonization schemes that are established between the colonizer and the colonized, but also how colonized groups oppress one another for psycho-cultural status and comfort.

Those colonialist and racist constructions are applied to the professional lives of African-Canadian academics, who represent, for others, everything assumed and said about Africans, irrespective of where they reside. As such, colonial and later de-historicizations, de-culturations, and de-epistemicalizations of Africa are also applied to African-Canadian academics, even when their qualifications and achievements are equal or superior to those of others, forcing them to perpetually prove themselves, in their academic profiles and their ethical qualities. As the African-Canadian academic is perpetually scrutinized and constructed as culpable where intersubjective adverse issues arise, while all non-Africans believe anything of this genre about all African Canadians and, by extension, about African-Canadian academics, the case can be professionally destructive. To survive and succeed in such contexts, African-Canadian academics need to read their negative historical and contemporary constructions by others, perhaps adopting the pose and perspective of W.E.B. Dubois: "I answer seldom a word." But in academia, we cannot refrain from answering. As such, we are emphatically answering with our academic achievements and impeccable ethical positions. We may not be able to distil anti-African prejudices from contemporary Canadians or others from elsewhere, but by practising our humanist philosophy of Ubuntu (unconditionally seeing our humanity – in both personal and professional terms – through the humanity of others), we need not despair of their possible recovery from such baseless assumptions about us.

REFERENCES

Abdi, A.A. 2008. "Europe and African Thought Systems and Philosophies of Education: 'Re-culturing' the Trans-Temporal Discourses." *Cultural Studies* 22 (2): 309–327. https://doi.org/10.1080/09502380701789216.

Abdi, A.A. 2009. "Re-centering the Philosophical Foundations of Knowledge: The Case of Africa and the Global Role of Teachers." *Alberta Journal of Educational Research* 55 (3): 269–283.

Abdi, A.A. 2013. "Chinua Achebe (1930–2013). A Cultural and Educational Tribute." *Postcolonial Directions in Education* 2 (1): 154–159. https://www.um.edu.mt/library/oar/bitstream/123456789/19606/1/Chinua%20Achebe%20%281930-2013%29%20%20a%20cultural%20and%20educational%20tribute.pdf.

Achebe, C. 1958/2009. *Things Fall Apart.* Toronto: Anchor Press.

Achebe, C. 1989. *Morning Yet on Creation Day: Essays.* New York: Doubleday.

Achebe, C. 2000. *Home and Exile.* New York: Oxford University Press.

Baudrillard, J. 1981. *Simulacra and Simulation.* Ann Arbor: University of Michigan Press.

Bessis, S. 2003. *Western Supremacy: The Triumph of an Idea.* London: Zed Books.

Bogues, A. 2003. *Black Prophets, Black Heretics: Radical Political Intellectuals.* New York: Routledge.

Césaire, A. 1972. *Discourse on Colonialism*. Trenton: Monthly Review Press.
Cook, M. 2003. *A Brief History of the Human Race*. New York: W.W. Norton.
Derrida, J. 1980. *Writing and Difference*. Chicago: Chicago University Press.
Dubois, W.E.B. 1903/1994. *The Souls of Black Folk*. New York: Dover.
Eze, E. 1997. *Race and the Enlightenment: A Reader*. Malden: Wiley.
Fanon, F. 1967. *Black Skin, White Masks*. New York: Grove Press.
Fanon, F. 1968. *The Wretched of the Earth*. New York: Grove Press.
Foucault, M. 1980. *Power/Knowledge: Selected Interviews and Other Writings, 1972–1977*. New York: Vintage.
Gould, S. 1985. *The Mismeasure of Man*. New York: W.W. Norton.
Hegel, G.W.F. 1965. *La raison dans l'histoire*. Paris: UGE.
Huntington, S. 1971. "The Change to Change: Modernization, Development, and Politics." *Comparative Politics* 3 (3): 283–322. https://doi.org/10.2307/421470.
Kane, H. 1963/2012. *Ambiguous Adventure*. Brooklyn: Melville Books.
Kant, I. 1775/2015. *Of the Different Races of Man* [Über die verschiedenen Rassen der Menschen]. Berlin: Klassikerverlag.
Kant, I. 1795/2016. *Perpetual Peace: A Philosophical Sketch* [Zum ewigen Frieden: Ein philosophischer Entwurf]. Konigsberg: F. Nicolovius.
Lyotard, J-F. 1979. *The Postmodern Condition: A Report on Knowledge*. Minneapolis: University of Minnesota Press.
Memmi, A. 1956/1991. *The Colonizer and Colonized*. Boston: Beacon Press.
Nyerere, J. 1968. *Freedom and Socialism: A Selection from Writings and Speeches, 1965–67*. London: Oxford University Press.
Rostow, W. 1991. *Stages of Economic Growth: A Non-Communist Manifesto*. Cambridge: Cambridge University Press.
Said, E. 1993. *Culture and Imperialism*. New York: Vintage.
Sussman, R. 2014. *The Myth of Race: The Troubling Persistence of an Unscientific Idea*. Cambridge, MA: Harvard University Press.
Van Sertima, I. 1991. *Blacks in Science: Ancient and Modern*. New Brunswick: Transaction Books.
wa Thiong'o, N. 1967. *A Grain of Wheat*. London: Heinemann.
wa Thiong'o, N. 1986. *Decolonising the Mind: The Politics of Language in African Literature*. London: Heinemann.
wa Thiong'o, N. 2009. *Re-membering Africa*. Nairobi: East Africa Educational Publishers.
wa Thiong'o, N. 2014. *Globalectics: Theory and the Politics of Knowing*. New York: Columbia University Press.
West, C. 2009. *Keeping Faith: Philosophy and Race in America*. New York: Routledge.

4 What Have Deleuze and Guattari Got to Do with Blackness? A Rhizomatic Analysis of Blackness

AWAD IBRAHIM

Take 1: A Socius Analysis

Blackness, it seems, is born into a "socius." This is a monstrous machine, a metaphor of and for society where attractors and opposites can and do co-exist. Their co-existence means a permanent presence of tension, a tug of war, and ongoing struggle. There are no simple resolutions within the socius. We are forever left with the curse of improvisation and living (with)in tension. But we humans and scholars are so immersed in the socius that we forget ourselves and the very structure of the socius itself. In fact, we even forget that we live in a socius, a very sophisticated machine that is *working on us*, primarily subconsciously and through seduction, a machine that is "under way the moment the body has had enough of organs" (Deleuze and Guattari 1987, 150).

In this socius, Blackness is naturalized, so that the social fabrication is made into a biological entity par excellence. I see you Black, therefore you are Black! But one is not born Black yet, in the socius, one has to be made Black. Blackness is not a multiplicity in the socius, it is a singular that is signified not in itself but by what it is not: whiteness. It is not an identity, it is an identity claim, a political space, and a space we embody. We do not slot ourselves into it, it is a performative category, as I argued elsewhere (Ibrahim 2014), which we perform on our bodies, in our hair, in our dress, in our talk, in our walk, in our desire, and in how we feel about ourselves and others.

When it comes to Blackness, Deleuze and Guattari (1987) distinguish between two processes. The first is linked to what they call *significance*. Here whiteness, which they refer to as "white wall," equals significance equals face: white wall = significance = face. The second process is called *subjectification*. Here Blackness, which Deleuze and Guattari call "black hole," equals subjectification equals behind-the-face: Black hole = subjectification = behind-the-face. In this sense, "The face constructs the wall that the signifier needs in order to bounce off of; it constitutes the wall of the signifier, the frame or screen. The face digs the hole that subjectification needs in order to break through; it constitutes the black hole of subjectivity as consciousness or passion, the camera, the third eye" (Deleuze and Guattari 1987, 168). It is significant to note, for Deleuze and Guattari, "The face is not a universal. It is not even that of the white man; it is White Man himself, with his broad cheeks ... The face is Christ. The face is the typical European" (176).

Thus far, for the purpose of this chapter, three things have to be pointed out. First, radically stated, we need to remember that one is not born Black. That is to say, Blackness is not a category we slot ourselves into, but a social and a historical product that we take up and perform daily, in how we walk, talk, dress, etc. Second, because it is a social and a historical product that is performed every day, there is nothing fixed or inherent about Blackness; its meaning shifts and changes every day. Having said this, there is an irony in the third and final point. Because Blackness is subjectified (to use Deleuze and Guattari's term), its meaning is fixed, thanks to the mechanism of the socius. In sum, Blackness is a signifier whose meaning is *supposed to be* open, but ironically it is not. Its meaning is actually closed and mostly in the negative. As we see throughout the chapters in this volume, our collective aim is to think through how the socius closes the meaning of Blackness and to point to the absurd nature of this closure.

Take 2: The Theatre of the Absurd

Deleuze and Guattari (1987) are not thinking about these descriptors (namely, Black, white, significance, and subjectification) in absolute terms because, if they do, one can only find the theatre of the absurd. Moving "white man" into "White Man," as Deleuze and Guattari did above, is a breakthrough into this theatre – a move from the terrain of the personal to the domain of concepts and ideas. It is only here that we can understand the subjectification of Blackness. Of course, Black people do exist and they are loud about their existence. They certainly do not need Deleuze, Guattari, Lyotard, Foucault, Bourdieu, or whomever – as a number of the authors in this volume have argued – to arrogantly state whether they do exist or not. Not without some arrogance, what Deleuze and Guattari are suggesting is how Blackness has been ontologically subjectified and epistemically colonized throughout most of our modern history. This is especially true in the Western world, especially in Europe and North America. Whiteness beams (so much that it blinds itself and its otherness: Blackness), occupies, and signifies, while Blackness is blinded by the beam, occupies holes in the wall of whiteness, and is therefore signified. Ngugi wa Thiong'o (1986) has called for Blackness to own its own signification, to name itself, to dim (if not block) the beaming light that is blinding it and decolonize the episteme that is used to define it.

In Canada, the present volume is building on a larger project where Blackness is naming itself. The work by Enid Lee (1985), Lawrence Hill (1996, 2007), Rinaldo Walcott (2000), Dionne Brand (2001), Afua Cooper (2006), George Dei (2009), Carl James et al. (2010), Joseph Mensah (2010) George Elliott Clarke (2014), Awad Ibrahim (2014), Handel Kashope Wright (2012), and Boulou Ebanda de B'béri et al. (2014), to name but very few, is the foundation of this larger political, social, historical, and epistemic project. Here Blackness speaks in its own voice; its language is not without critique, but at least it is honest enough to create and assemble a cartography of and for its subjectivity, and along the way, links its word with its world (see especially Dei 2017; Dei et al., 2020). As it does so, however, there are three notions in Deleuze and Guattari's (1987) work that I think will be of direct benefit for this project: becoming-minoritarian, deterritorialization, and rhizome.

Take 3: Becoming-Minoritarian

It is important not to confuse "minoritarian," as a becoming or process, with a "minority," as an aggregate or a state … One reterritorializes, or allows oneself to be reterritorialized. Even blacks, as the Black Panthers said, must become-black. Even women must become-women. Even Jews must become-Jewish … [Here] man constitutes the majority, or rather the standard upon which the majority is based: white, male, adult, "rational," etc., in short, the average European, the subject of enunciation. (Deleuze and Guattari, 1987, 291–2)

If Blacks must become-Black and the white man is the subject of enunciation, then the first notion we are dealing with is twofold: "becoming" and "minoritarian." For Deleuze and Guattari the term "minority" is a question of number and aggregate, while "minoritarian" is altogether different. Minoritarian is a never-ending process and state of becoming and de-re-territorialization. The majority territorializes, defines, and frames, whereas minoritarian, as a process, re- and deterritorializes, reshapes, and redefines this frame. One is never a woman or Black. One is always becoming-woman or becoming-Black. Blackness in this sense is an everyday performative category that we deploy, make use of, and refer to. Hence it is in constant definition. It is not a simple category, but extremely complex and fluid "assemblage," an ensemble of conscious and subconscious, processes the result of which is a sense of self, an identity. Blackness, moreover, becomes a political category we claim and declare as our own because, as Deleuze and Guattari (1987, 292) put it, "Becoming-minoritarian is a political affair and necessitates a labor of power (*puissance*), an active micropolitics."

Moreover, if Blackness is an everyday performative category, then whiteness, as the majority, emerges as "a gigantic memory" (Deleuze and Guattari 1987, 293) that is trying to crush Blackness, hence both end up in a constant tug of war and unresolved tension. But in this war machine, Blackness becomes "a line of becoming [that] has neither beginning nor end." This is "[a] line of becoming [that] has only a middle." For Deleuze and Guattari (1987, 293), this middle "is not an average; it is fast motion, it is the absolute speed of movement." Put otherwise, "A becoming is neither one nor two, nor the relation of the two; it is the in-between, the border or line of flight or descent running perpendicular to both." Blackness, in other words, is conceived as a decentralized and distributed category, which itself is a social and historical product. It is definitely more than skin colour, hair texture, and other phenotypical characteristics.

This is why to liberate itself from the crushing of whiteness, Blackness must realize that liberation is also messy. It is not linear, nor is it a progression in which one moves from A to B to C, etc. To liberate itself, moreover, Blackness must go through what Deleuze and Guattari call "striated" process. This is a non-linear process of struggle that is without guarantees; a harsh and sometimes extremely painful psychic agony which is emotionally taxing; and an epistemic orientation that is attempting to replace hopelessness with hopefulness through hard work.

Take 4: The Deterritorialization of Blackness

> Whenever a territorial assemblage is taken up by a movement that deterritorializes it (whether under so-called natural or artificial conditions), we say that machine is released. (Deleuze and Guattari, 1987, 333)

As a result one territorializes, that is to say one impregnates the space one occupies with one's uniqueness based on gender, class, ability, sexuality, language, culture, nationality, consciousness, etc. It is therefore both absolutely necessary but absolutely absurd to talk about "Black people." They do not exist. They are made. They are made through epistemic violence, colonization, and Western arrogance, where they become its absolute Otherness: what is objectified, studied, and talked about. Blackness is not a "natural" or even a biological category, it is a social and historical product. Blackness has to be conceived as an unfinished living entity, as a rhizome that is sitting in a middle ground receiving the sun, the snow, and the rain without ever knowing how the final product of that planting will look or how green eventually it will be; as an assemblage that is in constant movement, and as a result, its edges are never fixed.

For precisely these reasons, I am introducing the notion of the rhizome, as a third idea from Deleuze and Guattari, to the analysis of Blackness. To propose a "rhizomatic analysis of Blackness" is to propose a political project that is mindful of its necessity, given the Western epistemic violence that is crushing Black people and their creativity, but simultaneously conscious of its nuances, multiplicities, and ever-changing definition. For Deleuze and Guattari (1987), a rhizome is a crabgrass-like figuration that the authors contrast to the tree-and-root system of power distribution as it functions on individuals and society at large. A rhizome is a web-like fabric that "must be produced, constructed, a map that is always detachable, connectable, reversible, modifiable, and has multiple entryways and exits and its own lines of flight" (21). Working against facile notions of "roots" and "origins," a rhizome is always in "a middle (*milieu*) from which it grows and which it overspills" (21). As such, the rhizome resists verticality and chronological "lines of flight," where its growth is contained and conceived in a linear, arborescent, and systematic line. Line of flight means a path, a line of possibilities. Used in the plural and the singular, in the end, line of flight is about pursuing and following paths where the result is either unknown (rhizome) or assumed to be known, binary and totalizing (arborescent). As such, Deleuze and Guattari (1987) argue, the rhizome is altogether different from the arborescent. It is more complex, complicated, fluid, multiple, multiplying, and forever becoming. The rhizome is a constant flow or movement of deterritorialization. It is not a point we reach, where we say once and for all, "We are finally there!" Rather, it is a way of becoming that we are forever struggling to attain. Being open to the unknown, the rhizome is an uncontainable dimension "or rather directions in motion" (21) that are forever in "between things, interbeing, intermezzo" (7). This, for me, is how the analysis of Blackness should be approached: an extremely complex political project that is attempting to de-reterritorialize and name

> Every rhizome contains lines of segmentarity according to which it is stratified, territorialized, organized, signified, attributed, etc., as well as line of deterritorialization down which it constantly flees ... These lines always tie back to one another. That is why one can never posit a dualism or a dichotomy, even in the rudimentary form of the good and the bad. (Deleuze & Guattari 1987, 9)

itself and its subjectivity, but as it does that, it needs to be conscious that its definition is never finished. Becoming-Black is an ontological as much as it is an epistemic project. Ontologically, the pain of the Middle Passage is real, racism is real, and the killing of our people by the police, especially in the United States, is real. How this pain is talked about epistemically, however, will find itself in a constant state of flow, deterritorialization, and multiplicity. There is no simple reading and definitely no simple identity in which we slot ourselves; we are forever becoming. If we reach anything, as the chapters in this volume show, we reach what I am calling a *rhizomatic analysis of Blackness*.

Take 5: There Is No Blackness without the Black Body

Thus, there is no rhizomatic analysis of Blackness without the Black body. The Black body is both real and invented semiotic space. The latter, which Deleuze and Guattari (1987) refer to as "institutional body" (158), is the idea of Blackness that was first invented by Linnaeus and fully developed by the Western episteme to enslave, colonize and subjugate so-called Black people. As such, it does not need the individual body; in fact, the individual body (the real) is subjugated to the idea. From a white Western perspective, I see your body as Black, therefore you are Black! That is to say, I will signify your individual so-called Black body according to what I already know about Blackness.

It is important to note that the knowledge and ideas that (white) people construct about Black people is not something that people simply carry in their heads; it has direct impact and repercussion and is bodily felt by the subjugated Black body/person/subject. We thus move from the semiotic body (the idea, the institutional) to the anatomical body (the individual), but this move is bi-redirectional: there is no Black body without the idea of Blackness and there is no Blackness without the Black body. Each is dependent on the other. In the West, put otherwise, racism against the Black body can flourish only within a semiotic and a semantic framework where the idea of Blackness is already signified, drawn, and assembled.

Take 6: The Story of the Assembled Body

We were a politicized grouping of student/activists, athletes, those looking for a place to hang/out, street-wise players & partiers, and people who were just dissatisfied with not seeing enough blackness in school and in the society, generally. We *werent* "Black" where we came from in the west indies, but in toronto we had to confront the fact that we were seen as "Black," and had to check/out for ourselves what this blackness was. (Joseph Clifton, cited in Prince 2000, 16–17; emphasis added)

Joseph Clifton is talking about and living the tension between the semiotic and anatomical Black body in Canada, where the Black body is assumed to belong somewhere else when the Black body has arrived in Canada as early as 1605 (Ibrahim and Abdi 2016). Over 54 per cent of Black Canadians were born in this country. Except for Japanese Canadians, who have a higher Canadian-born rate (65 per cent), more than half of Black Canadians were born in Canada, compared to 29 per cent of South Asians and 25 per cent of Chinese (Milan and Tran 2004). Furthermore, more than 10 per cent of Black Canadians are third-generation Canadians, and in certain parts of Canada where there is a longer history of Black settlement, more than 84 per cent of Blacks are at least third-generation Canadians (James et al. 2010, 35). Clearly, the Black body in Canada has a long history and ontological (i.e., physical) presence, but has very weak (if any) epistemic presence in Canadian history and in the psychic of the nation. In other words, despite its long history in Canada, it has but a tenuous presence in Canadian history books.

This genealogy, however, has to be situated within a rhizomatic analysis where Blackness in Canada is ever-multinational, multilingual, multiethnic, and multicultural. If studied or analysed otherwise, it will fall into the trap of the striated and already framed Western analysis, where Blackness becomes a phenotype and a biological category. Unfortunately, Blackness is here defined and framed, and its meaning is already determined. My book, *The Rhizome of Blackness: A Critical Ethnography of Hip-Hop Culture, Language, Identity, and the Politics of Becoming* (2014), tells the story and the odyssey of a group of continental Africans who find themselves in Canada. Some are immigrants, but primarily they are refugees. They are a group of French- and English-speaking continental African youth living in southwestern and northeastern Ontario, Canada. Based on a series of critical ethnographic research projects (1996, 2007, 2011), I journal their odyssey into the process of *becoming Black*. This process is on the one hand marked by an *identification* with and a *desire* for North American Blackness; and it is on the other as much about gender and race as it is about language, displacement, identity, and cultural performance. In the book, I delineate the desire of these youth for and identification with Blackness through language, and I show how they are learning, not the so-called standard English as a Second Language (ESL), but Black English as a Second Language or BESL, which they access in and through Black popular culture, namely hip-hop cultural identity, language practices, and ways of being.

The main contention of the book is that once in North America, continental African youth enter, so to speak, or will be subject to a *social imaginary*: an assemblage of ideas, a discursive or a symbolic space in which they are already constructed, imagined, assembled, and positioned and thus treated by the hegemonic discourses and dominant groups, respectively, as Blacks. Here I address the arborified and dominant white everyday communicative state of mind: "Oh, they all look like Blacks to me!" These youth, I contended, had no full understanding of the Black-white binaries in North America. As such, they were not Black in Africa, but they become-Black in North America.

These youth form part of the political refugee and economic immigrant continental Africans who, especially since 1990s, have been crossing the Atlantic Ocean to North America in considerable numbers (Ibrahim 2008; StatCan 2011). Once in North America, they join the African diaspora by becoming part of it. In a sense, when continental Africans "join" diasporic Africans (in North America or Europe) or when the latter "go back" to Africa (mostly, interestingly, for tourism; otherwise in search for "roots"), both are rubbing a symbolic act of defiance in the face of history of colonialism, imperialism, and the Middle Passage. But, before joining diasporic Africans, continental Africans have to confront this history – the history of the present (Foucault 1980) – where their bodies are *already assembled*: an *assemblage* that is set and in turn sets itself against a "striated" (Deleuze and Guattari 1987, 474) and "hegemonic" (Gramsci 1971) gaze, which functions as a technology of semiotic control (Foucault 1980). This gaze, as I show in the book, turns their bodies into "Black" bodies; thus making them Black. As they *become Black*, however, they have to translate, negotiate, and answer two questions: What does "being Black" really mean in North America; that is, when Blackness is spoken, either through the body or otherwise, what kind of history and social order does it invoke? And if one is becoming-Black, what does this call for, entail, and hence produce? *The Rhizome of Blackness* was an answer to these questions, among others. What I have also shown in my book is the contiguous nature of identity: the cultures, histories, and languages that the youth brought with them from Africa. Who came from ten different African countries from east to west and from north to south, was not seen in opposition to the "new" cultures and languages they were learning. African traditions and languages were performed and uttered in the same sentence, at the same time and on the same body, thus creating what I called a "rhizomatic third space." Clearly, there is no simple reading or simple process of identity formation. Blackness is complex and uniquely occupied by each of these youth.

Talking about the rhizome and the uniqueness of Blackness in the United States, Chimamanda Ngozi Adichie (2014) addressed this episodically and with a sense of humour in her novel *Americanah*. She locates her prose within the narratives of immigration and displacement and refers to "Black" immigrants as non-American Blacks: "Dear Non-American Black, when you make the choice to come to America, you become black. Stop arguing. Stop saying I'm Jamaican or I'm Ghanaian. America doesn't care. So, what if you weren't 'black' in your country? You're in America now. We all have our moments of initiation into the Society of Former Negroes. Mine was in a class in undergrad when I was asked to give the black perspective, only I have no idea what that was" (273).

Adichie's novel and my own studies are "working through" (Derrida 2000) the nuances of Blackness, the complexity within, the rhizome, the multinational, multi-ethnic, multilingual, and multicultural nature of Blackness. Therefore we have to broaden and decolonize Blackness from this striated gaze, which locks it into unidimensionality. We need a rhizomatic analysis of Blackness, where the violent Western epistemic is confronted head-on. As the late Edward Said (1994) declared, "Gone are the binary oppositions dear to the nationalist and imperialist enterprise. Instead we begin to sense that old authority cannot simply be replaced by new authority, but that new alignments made across borders, types, nations, and essences are rapidly coming into view, and it is those new alignments that now provoke and challenge the fundamentally static notion of *identity* that has been the core of cultural thought during the era of imperialism" (xxiv, original emphasis).

And since we are not fully out of this "era of imperialism" (see McLaren and Farahampour 2005), we need to challenge this static notion of Blackness. The present volume is a serious attempt to do this. Here I am hoping my introduction to the *rhizomatic analysis of Blackness* is a rupture and a radical shift from this era of colonialism and imperialism where Blackness is conceived and represented in one dimension. As I show in *The Rhizome of Blackness*, identity – Blackness in this case – is not "as transparent or unproblematic" as we previously thought, but "a "production," which is never complete, always in process, and always constituted within, not outside, representation" (Hall 1990, 222). Without naming it as such, Stuart Hall has always called for a rhizomatic analysis of Blackness, one where, in the case of African youth, *to be* is *to become*: that is, to become a rhizomatic and an ambivalent product of two, of both here *and* there, Africa *and* Canada, to become forever born in two. This complex, fluid, multidimensional, and ever-changing product is best conceived, dealt with, and analysed within a rhizomatic analysis of Blackness. Here there is a move between things and people, an establishment of the logic of

AND, a foundation that is conscious of its own limits and its own agency and capacity for change and for liberation, an epistemic framework that is attempting to crush and demolish Western one-dimensionality, and a struggle for better conditions and hopeful future that it is working to bring into existence. Only then can we hope for an ontology, an epistemology, and a pedagogy of the oppressed (Freire 1993) that will not fall into the trap of turning us into oppressors once in positions of power.

REFERENCES

Adichie, C. 2014. *Americanah*. Toronto: Vintage.
Brand, D. 2001. *A Map to the Door of No Return: Notes to Belonging*. Toronto: Random House.
Clarke, G. 2014. *Traverse*. Toronto: Exile Editions.
Cooper, A. 2006. *The Hanging of Angélique: The Untold Story of Canadian Slavery and the Burning of Old Montreal*. Toronto: HarperCollins.
de B'béri, B., Reid-Maroney, N., and Wright, H. 2014. *The Promised Land: History and Historiography of the Black Experience in Chatham-Kent Settlements and Beyond*. Toronto: University of Toronto Press.
Dei, G. 2009. *Teaching Africa: Towards a Transgressive Pedagogy*. New York: Peter Lang.
Dei, G. 2017. *Reframing Blackness and Black Solidarities through Anti-Colonial and Decolonial Prisms*. New York: Springer Publishing.
Dei, G., Odozor, E., and Vasquez, A., eds. 2020. *Cartographies of Blackness and Black Indigeneities*. Gorham: Myers Educational Press.
Deleuze, G., and Guattari, F. 1987. *Thousand Plateaus: Capitalism and Schizophrenia*. London: Continuum.
Derrida, J. 2000. *Of Hospitality*. Stanford: Stanford University Press.
Foucault, M. 1980. *Power/Knowledge: Selected Interviews and Other Writings*. New York: Pantheon.
Freire, P. 1993. *Pedagogy of the Oppressed*. New York: Continuum.
Gramsci, A. 1971. *Selections from the Prison Notes*. New York: International Publishers.
Hall, S. 1990. "Cultural Identity and Diaspora." In *Identity, Community, Culture, Difference*, edited by J. Rutherford, 222–237. London: Lawrence & Wishart.
Hill, L. 1996. *Trials and Triumphs: The Story of African-Canadians*. Toronto: Umbrella Press.
Hill, L. 2007. *The Book of Negroes*. Toronto: HarperCollins.
Ibrahim, A. 2008. "The New *Flâneur*: Subaltern Cultural Studies, African Youth in Canada, and the Semiology of In-betweenness." *Cultural Studies* 22 (2): 234–253. https://doi.org/10.1080/09502380701789141.

Ibrahim, A. 2014. *The Rhizome of Blackness: A Critical Ethnography of Hip-Hop Culture, Language, Identity, and the Politics of Becoming.* New York: Peter Lang.

Ibrahim, A., and Abdi, A. 2016. *The Education of African Canadian Children: Critical Perspectives.* Montreal and Kingston: McGill-Queen's University Press.

James, C., Este, D., Bernard, W., Benjamin, A., Lloyd, B., and Tuner, T. 2010. *Race & Well-being: The Lives, Hopes, and Activism in African Canadians.* Halifax: Fernwood.

Lee, E. 1985. *Letters to Marcia: A Teacher's Guide to Anti-Racist Education.* Toronto: CRRF.

McLaren, P., and Farahmandpur, R. 2005. *Teaching against Global Capitalism and the New Imperialism: A Critical Pedagogy.* Lanham: Rowman & Littlefield.

Mensah, J. 2010. *Black Canadians: History, Experiences, Social Conditions.* Halifax: Fernwood.

Milan, A., and Tran, K. 2004. "Blacks in Canada: A Long History." *Canadian Social Trends* 72: 2–7.

Prince, A. 2000. *Being Black.* Toronto: Insomniac Press.

Said, E. 1994. *Culture and Imperialism.* New York: Alfred A. Knopf.

StatCan. 2011. *Immigrant Languages in Canada.* http://www12.statcan.gc.ca /census-recensement/2011/as-sa/98–314-x/98–314-x2011003_2-eng.cfm.

Walcott, R. 2000. *Rude: Contemporary Black Canadian Cultural Criticism.* Toronto: Insomniac Press.

wa Thiongo, N. 1986. *Decolonising the Mind: The Politics of Language in African Literature.* Nairobi: Heinemann.

Wright, H.K. 2012. "Is This an African I See before me? Black/African Identity and the Politics of Western, Academic Knowledge." In *The Dialectics of African Education and Western Discourses: Appropriation, Ambivalence and Alternatives,* edited by H. Wright and A. Abdi, 111–130. New York: Peter Lang Publishing.

5 Dancing with the Invisibility/Inaudibility: Nuances of Blackness in a Francophone Context

GINA THÉSÉE

Comment écrire
alors que ton imaginaire s'abreuve,
du matin jusqu'aux rêves,
à des images, des pensées, des valeurs
qui ne sont pas les tiennes?
Comment écrire
quand ce que tu es végète
en dehors des élans qui déterminent ta vie?
Comment écrire dominé?

– Patrick Chamoiseau (1997)

Introduction

How can we write of the nuances of "Blackness," within the francophone context, when the French language systematically disqualifies and invalidates the very recognition of the concept of "race"? This question is inspired by Patrick Chamoiseau (1997), whose epigraph initiates the reflection in this chapter. The perniciousness of this question cannot be disentangled from the historical, social, political, cultural, and linguistic dimensions of the context that is intertwined within the construction of "Blackness," which is emblematic of wounds, tensions, and ruptures that are experienced in multiple ways. The United Nations (2013) proclaimed the period 2015–2024 as "The International Decade for People of African Descent." Thus, this book on the "nuances of Blackness" arrives at a critical moment, offering us the opportunity to de-/co-/re-construct our paradoxical, diverse, wounded, and utopian "Blackness(es)" together.

The premise here, even in the twenty-first century, is that "Blackness" is infused in the post-traumatic misery marinated in slavery and colonialism, and that people carrying "Blackness" within themselves are character-ized, as Fanon (1968) puts it, as the "wretched of the Earth." Thus, the French expedition, experience, and reign over a significant portion of the world through slavery and colonialism, specifically in Africa and the Caribbean (as well as elsewhere) forms the background of this chap-ter. However, beyond the global francophone context, my concern lies with the issues, dilemmas, and challenges of the words spoken by those carrying and transposing their "Blackness" in relation to self (identity and interiorization) and to the "Other" (alterity and exteriorization). Thus, this chapter reflects on my observation of the epistemological quasi-impossibility of writing about my "Blackness" within a context of self-erasure, and without being relegated to a redefining by the episte-mology of the "Other."

To articulate the nuances of my own "Blackness," I am obliged to un-ravel this epistemological quasi-impossibility by re-forging the words of my discomfort and wounds with Maroon travels that have shaped my "Blackness."

Nuances of Blackness through a Maroon Hermeneutics

How can I (re-)think of the nuances of "Blackness" from my own per-spective, vantage point, and experience as a Black woman, francophone, originally from Haiti and raised in Montreal, Quebec, and as a professor in a French-language university in Montreal? This requires, as Chamoiseau (1997) has suggested, undertaking an "inventory of melancholy," which involves an epistemological process that results from "Maroon thinking" emanating from a "Maroon hermeneutic." Inspired by Paul-Austin (2017), I use her concept of "Maroon hermeneutics" and define it (1) in relation to ontology, as a dual dynamic, in same time, presence, and absence of the essence of Black identity; (2) in relation to praxis, as an action of resistance and resiliency connected to the wounds, fractures, and ruptures of Black identities; (3) in relation to epistemol-ogy, as de-/co-/re-construction of knowledge(s) aimed at healing and emancipating Black identities; (4) in relation to axiology, as an ethical duty to re-appropriate the self connected to Black identities.

In the Haitian imagination, the "Maroon" is one who has broken the chains of enslavement, who has removed the "master's" scaffolding and escaped to the refuge of the mountains. Thus, "to be Maroon is to evis-cerate and remove oneself, to be invisible," and also to not be heard, to be exiled and condemned to "fleeing" the "Other." According to Paul-Austin (2017), the Maroon's identity derives from the Other (the mas-ter) as the initial and causal factor of the situation. In this sense, Maroon thinking is a posture of resistance that advances stealthily, wearing a double mask of invisibility and inaudibility. The Maroon must not be seen or heard, for fear of being once again projected into the colonial hell. The paradoxical character of socio-linguistically deconstructing my "Blackness" (Black identity/Black alterity) allows me to reclaim the Maroon thinking and hermeneutics, as if the interpretation of myself, today, requires the reappropriation of this historical and fundamental imaginary. Ultimately, it is through this oppositional self-effacement (the development of Maroon thinking) and redefining of myself through an epistemology of the "Black self" (the development of Maroon hermeneutics) that I must navigate.

Nuances of Blackness within the Conceptual Limitations and Colonial Dynamics of the French Language

In French, there appears to be a conceptual black hole that reduces to a feigned colour-blindness and deafening silence any attempt to think, to write, to voice or to act against racism, fight for emancipation, and affirmation of Blackness. There is a confiscation of the words to say it, due to the linguistic coloniality of French language, but as Ibrahim (2016, 145) asks, "At what point do we own the language we speak?" "Blackness" has no equivalent in French, in the same way that "whiteness" does not, which renders the exploration very difficult. Race is equally problematic in French and is generally rejected or attacked, as noted earlier. Thus, it is probably better to use the same English term "Blackness" in French than to literally translate it into French. However, it is important to recognize that there are powerful Afro-Caribbean francophone texts that speak to the formation of "Black identity," which meshes into "Blackness." In French, the concepts "Negritude," "Antillanité," and "Créolité" were developed out of colonial contexts. With their use of the word "Négritude," Aimé Césaire and Leopold Sedar Sengor remained solidly in the twentieth century, tethered to the independence movement in colonial Sub-Saharan Africa. In contrast, Édouard Glissant (1981) has developed the concept of "Antillanité" as a healing process required by Caribbean societies, plagued by the ills by colonialism, to re-appropriate their identities, spaces, history, language, and cultural métissage.

Raphaël Confiant's concept of "Créolité" (1989) does not include the identity wounds that Blacks around the world suffer from, and it does not deal with the matter of colour. So the French concept of "Créolité" cannot be placed alongside Blackness. One might say that before the concept of Blackness was developed, other strong figures shaped a notion of Blackness in the Francophonie. Among them, let's recall Frantz Fanon from Martinique, Cheikh Anta Diop and Cheikh Hamidou Kane from Senegal, Amadou Kourouma from Ivory Coast, Amadou Hampate Bâ from Mali, and Mongo Béti from Cameroon. Of course, Haiti is less concerned with twentieth-century political decolonization, but figures such as Anténor Firmin, Jean Price-Mars, Jacques Roumain, Jacques-Stephen Alexis, René Dépestre, Félix-Moriseau-Leroy, Frankétienne, and Laënnec Hurbon celebrated Haitian culture rooted in its African heritage. More globally, contemporary francophone writers such as Patrick Chamoiseau and Ama Mazama from Martinique, Maryse Condé from Guadeloupe, Christiane Taubira from French Guyana, Lenora Miano from Cameroon, Aminata Sow Fall and Felwine Sarr from Senegal, and many others have re-dynamized efforts to develop a conceptual, emotional, and political framework for what we could call "francophone Blackness." However, while recognizing the strength of their contributions, we can also deplore their failure to transcend national, linguistic, or religious frontiers. For example, their books are not widely translated or known outside of the Francophonie. The racial, political, and cultural hegemony is inscribed inside the English-language linguistic hegemony.

One cannot understand "Blackness" within the francophone context without considering how the tentacles of French-language colonialism shape indigenous languages, particularly Créole. The linguistic intransigence in relation to the French language is difficult to compare with other languages, and "linguistic insecurity" is significant throughout the Francophonie, including in Canada. This can lead to and underpin, the silence that resonates in discourse, writing, debates, etc. in relation to "Blackness." For example, the French spoken by Blacks is often ridiculed as *"parler petit-nègre"* (speak as a Black child). Ultimately, speaking in Créole is a social and political marker of class, power, knowledge, and education, leading to potential marginalization.

Nuances of Blackness among Anglophone and Francophone Canadian Youth

Despite everything, there is still hope. In Canada, young Afro-Canadians have taken their identities to heart and in hand. They have embraced their lives and lived experiences and are determined to face the obstacles in their personal, academic, professional, and social conditions. Young women "go natural" with their hair, challenging the beauty myth and the need to "whiten" themselves in order to be beautiful in a white-centric world (however, there is still "whitening" or "lightening" the skin, and plastic surgery to Europeanize the nose). We can also see Black affirmation of culture and the arts through hip hop, rap, and other styles and movements in music, videos, websites, and social media. Coming from diverse origins, including sub-Saharan Africa and the anglophone and francophone Caribbean, these young Black women and men express mixed Canadian citizenships in culture, language, ethnicity, ideology, and religion. Yet they are indistinguishable from other young Canadians, embracing what others are engaged with, including an obsession with technology, smartphones, social media, and protest, such as in Black Lives Matter. However, their words, expressions, postures, dynamics, and presence in the world illustrate a particular Blackness denotes concerns and issues below the surface. Why do I have the impression that the young Black women and men that I have just described, regardless of the province of origin and residence, are more likely to be in an anglophone setting rather than in a francophone one?

In the common discourse of young Black francophones, to be "Black" is not to be "Noir." When employed by francophones, "Black" refers to resistance, transcending national and linguistic barriers, against the hegemony of social representations, the erasing of historical memory, and the dynamics of discrimination. But "Noir" only partially translates those postures. Francophones use "Noir" very prudently and in a restrained way. Again, the French language, like all languages, is not innocent, devoid of meaning and context: there is an epistemological rejection, whether conscious or unconscious, that avoids engaging with intractable social situations tinged with a racial brush. In this sense, if "francophone Blackness" exists, it is immediately suspect, conceptually impoverished, and still a social taboo in Quebec. It is a bone in the throat, and it exemplifies the identity debate that has framed the consciousness of Canada since its inception, where the social, political, linguistic, cultural, and educational place of Quebec is always framed with a question mark. There is a great need for an epistemological de-/re-/co-construction.

Nuances of Blackness in the Contemporary World

Repressed Development and Mobility: Which Blackness?

Being Black in the contemporary world is no simple task. Perhaps it is easier than before, but it still carries enormous burdens. With uninhibited hate groups such as white supremacists, neo-Nazis, and *La Meute* (the wolf pack) openly marching in the streets in many European countries, in the United States, and nearby, in Quebec City, one could and should ask, What does it mean to be Black today? Do things really change for the majority of Blacks? Of course, we can see individual successes for Black athletes, artists, business people, and academics, but what about the Black masses? It is a deplorable situation for Blacks, everywhere. Living conditions are more difficult, educational outcomes are lower, socio-economic circumstances are more challenging, life expectancy is lower, infant mortality is much higher, and development levels are (much) lower, etc. In the last few years, the Mediterranean Sea has become a liquid cemetery for anonymous Black bodies, African men, women, and children risking their lives, desperately fleeing misery in their countries, seeking hope, and dreaming of entering the perceived promised land in Italy, Germany, Spain, France, Great Britain, and elsewhere in Europe. This echoes what Haitians call "wonderful realism." Five centuries earlier, the Atlantic and the Caribbean were also transformed into liquid cemeteries for anonymous Black bodies, Africans chained and shackled by their European "masters." Today, these same Europeans are asked to accept people leaving Africa, this time voluntarily. How do the colonizing countries react? With barbed wire, blockades, refugee camps, and manoeuvres aimed to corral cattle at sea. The notion of "refugees" does not seem to apply to these people burdened by history and a Black phenotype. They are considered "cheaters," "exploiters," "queue-jumpers," and "vermin" who have no right to leave misery behind. What a cruel irony!

Sub-Saharan Representations: Which Blackness?

In sub-Saharan Africa, this misery is normalized, albeit with the obligatory indignation from the "international community." Africa seems to be burdened by its natural and cultural resources, but the first burden seems to be the children, whose youthfulness should be a celebration of innocence and hope for the future. Despite notable exceptions, the twenty-first century will likely continue its march speckled with calamities, suffering, oppression, and heartache. If present trends persist, the objectives for participation of girls and women in elementary and secondary education will be met in 2121 – in another century UNESCO (2013)! These objectives include access to basic necessities and do not delve into everything that people in the "developed" countries would consider "normal." In riveting images that paper the media and museums around the world, we are provided with iconic representations of Africa that have not entirely changed today. We can still see massive poverty, famines, epidemics, genocides, mutilations, sometimes non-existent health-care systems, anaemic educational systems, armed conflicts, endless coups d'état, displaced populations, a cavalcade of violence, human rights violations, ethnic tensions, chronic social exclusion, under-development, dictatorships that masquerade as "democracies," and difficult, if not unbearable, life conditions for girls and women. These conditions, among others, are related to a status of second-class citizens: pathological female-male relations, early and forced marriages, poor access to formal education, and cultural oppression and violence, including sexual violence. Within this context, what is the signification of "Blackness" for sub-Saharan Africans and for those in the African diaspora spread around the world and broadly represented in North America?

African Diaspora Context or People of African Descent: Which Blackness?

It is worth noting that the United Nations proclaimed 2011 as the "International Year for People of African Descent" and designated the period 2015–2024 as the "International Decade for People of African Descent" (UN 2009, 2013; Thésée and Carr 2012).

> People of African descent are acknowledged in the Durban Declaration and Programme of Action as a specific victim group who continue to suffer racial discrimination as the historic legacy of the transatlantic slave trade. Even Afro-descendants who are not directly descended from slaves face the racism and racial discrimination that still persist today, generations after the slave trade ended. (UN 2009)

> Millions of human beings continue to be victims of racism, racial discrimination, xenophobia and related intolerance, including their contemporary manifestations, some of which take violent forms. (UN 2013)

What about people of African descent today throughout the world, especially in the Americas? Has the twenty-first century altered the terrain of the "independence" and decolonization movements of colonized territories that took place during the twentieth century? How is our Blackness linked to Mother Africa today, taking into account the pervasive negative representations of Africa?

Haitian Socio-Environmental Erosion: Which Blackness?

What a sad paradox: Haiti is the first Black republic in history, and by every indicator, it is also near the bottom of all countries in the world! The enslaved French colony of Saint-Domingue overthrew the French colonizers in 1804. More than two centuries later, Haiti faces complete environmental, social, political, economic, and educational erosion. What is Blackness when one is of Haitian origin? How does one embrace Blackness when one's country of origin is continually in the international media for all the wrong reasons, often pity, critic, condemnation, and incomprehension? Does such a backdrop render self-affirmation utter nonsense? What is the effect of Blackness on a descendant of the world's first Black republic, one that is so maligned, so caricaturized, so consistently left off the table of meaningful human activities?

However, in the first Black republic, like in other countries in Americas, racism takes on an insidious form of "colourism," creating a hierarchy of skin colours, leading to the same dynamics of discrimination, disqualification, marginalization, and exclusion that are well known in racialized societies. In this overt/covert racist context, how do we even start to deconstruct the embedded practice of "colourism"? From these societies, how to write about "Blackness" when the skin colour, hair texture, nose shape, body shape, etc. are described with negative words for Black phenotypes (associated with ugliness) and with positive terms for white phenotypes (associated with beauty)?

Peregrinations/Migrations of Haitians on the Roads of the Americas: Which Blackness?

In the fall of 2017, long lines of Haitian refugees, dreaming of freedom again, were walking to the border, their life's possessions and children in tow, making the journey north, many of them fleeing the "American Dream," which had become the "American nightmare," to arrive in the eldorado of peace: Canada! The doors were open, and there was a welcome, a bed, services, and a semblance of decency. Could anyone believe that some of the Haitians heading north started their long march in Chile, walking like pilgrims across the Americas? Were they refugees or were they deported? Were they illegals or asylum-seekers? This is not a question merely of semantics but one of fundamental importance. The reaction in the traditional and social media reflected the racism of Henry and Tator (2009). Racist commentary caught fire. Concurrently, many in the mainstream media and on social media categorically rejected the concept of systemic racism. Could Quebec afford to open its doors to those in need, or was it a purely economic question that obfuscated the long-term interests of citizens and newcomers alike?

No, it is not easy being Black in Quebec either. In 2017 we witnessed a terrorist attack on a mosque in Quebec City. There are frequent polemical debates or reports about Blacks. There are many examples in the popular media that can only make (Black) people cringe, including blackface to parody Blacks; missing references to Blacks whatsoever in publicity campaigns to celebrate Montreal's 375th anniversary; mockery of Obama as a potential thief on the year-end television special that is one of the most viewed shows of the year; arrest of the former secretary-general of the Francophonie, Abdou Diouf, by immigration authorities; objects thrown at P.K. Subban, arguably one of the most talented hockey players, who played in Montreal but was traded because, at least in part, "he wasn't good in the change-room" (this must be a euphemism of sorts because it does not appear to make sense at any level); casting four Black youth to carry a float surrounded by dozens of white folks singing the praises of Quebec's national day, la Saint-Jean-Baptiste; negative social representations of Montréal-Nord, a neighbourhood with a high concentration of Haitian residents; the installation of a banner at the entrance of in the Saguenay cemetery in the village of Saint-Honoré, outside of urban centres, that read "Saguenay, ville blanche" (white city); the infamous exchanges on reasonable accommodation in the Charte des valeurs québécoises (Quebec Values Charter); and a litany of racialized and racist articles and reports in the media that fly under the radar, which is why some media no longer permit comments.

Other manifestations in the media also leave room for questions, such as the common insults and negative references made about former journalist and governor-general of Canada, later head of the Francophonie, Michaëlle Jean. Or denigrating comments made about the Haitian writer Dany Laferrière, who was made a member of the Académie française when many would have preferred a more "Québécois" (translation: "white") writer be the first member of that auspicious body. These individuals, in their Blackness, have fully contributed to Quebec society and culture, so where is the problem? There are no words in French for a possible response. How can we understand the decision of the Government of Quebec, on 18 October 2017, to reverse its decision to organize a consultation on systemic racism an explosion of voices in the media denouncing the exercise itself as being racist? Within the context of Black Lives Matter, one cannot help but believe that conducting debate on race, racism, and racialization within the French-language context is so awkward and debilitating that it is highly discouraged in almost all sectors that should be involved in such matters.

Nuances of Blackness Facing the Dynamics of Democratic Racisms

Democratic Racism: Which Blackness?

In the context of Canadian society, Henry and Tator have developed the concept of "democratic racism" in relation to discourse analysis, which translates value conflicts that can trivialize racism in Canadian society: "Commitments to democratic principles such as justice, equality, and fairness conflict but coexist with attitudes and behaviours that include negative feelings about minority groups, differential treatment, and discrimination against them" (quoted by Satzewich and Liodakis 2013, 193). Democratic racism takes place through "democratic political correctness," including the following:

- The discourse of "colour blindness," which negates discussion of race in a racialized society in which racism is a lived experience for everyone.
- The discourse of "equal opportunity," which postulates that treating people equally will lead to social justice, excluding recognition of white power and privilege and institutional power.
- The discourse of "blame the victim," which suggests that racialized groups are responsible for the racism they are subjected to.
- The discourse of "multiculturalism," which hypothesizes that belief in tolerance and harmony can be achieved simply through accommodating diversity in organizations and in society in general.

Other discourses that could be considered present Canada as a non-colonizing and non-slave-holding country, or eliminate the presence of Blacks in Canada for over four hundred years, or represents Canada as a non-racist country.

These discourses are difficult to deconstruct because they express a continuous buy-in to white supremacy and whiteness (as well as neocolonial dynamics) while dissimulating behind the mask of egalitarianism, inclusion, and respect. The concept of "decolonial democratic racism" provides us with a space to complexify new forms of racism anchored in new discourses of justification. From the biological discourse (Blacks are the inferior race), to the civilizational discourse (Blacks are not civilized), the economic discourse (Blacks are predisposed for slavery), the social discourse (Blacks as second-class citizens), the cognitive discourse (Blacks have a low IQ), the aesthetic discourse (Blacks are absent from the beauty myth and canon, and the democratic discourse (Blacks play the victim and are incapable of taking advantage of equal opportunities), societies have continued to sharpen the grindstone of discourses that justify racism in subtle, sophisticated, and insidious ways.

Anti-Black Racism(s) within Democratic Racism: Which Blackness?

The first time that Paul R. Carr and I presented the concept of "anti-Black racism" – which was developed by our colleague George Sefa Dei (1996, 2006) and others before him – it was in 2005 to an international conference on interculturalism within the Francophonie (a large number of the 400 participants were French-speaking Europeans). Our objective was to discuss the implacable character of anti-Black racism(s) by examining three characteristics: systemic racism (everywhere within social spheres and systems), systematic racism (in everything, in all domains, touching all humans), and chronic racism (all of the time, without regard for time or circumstance). We were showered with attacks and intrigue: some were abrasive, others suggested that we were "epistemological warriors," others flatly contested the existence of a supposedly useless hierarchy of suffering, others questions the pertinence and scientific utility of the term "Black," and yet others felt that we underestimated the value and gravity of religious discrimination. The only positive comment associated us with Frantz Fanon. We should note that we were in post-conflict Algeria, engaging with a population that was still in shock after a decade of sustained violence by a group of radical Islamists. The almost unanimous rejection of our concept surprised us, especially since we had presented on the topic in English without such a virulent reaction. We first believed that the reaction was related only to this particular academic event. But over the next several years as we developed and intensified our research on race and racism, we started to understand the response to the concept of anti-Black racism. The reluctance to engage with race and anti-Black racism, as was borne out over the next thirteen years of presentations, articles, books, and engagement with the community, was painful, especially within the French-language context. We asked ourselves if it was worth continuing. One silver lining to the venture was that the incessant opposition came only from whites! So within democratic societies, can racism be questioned?

Whiteness gives the tone to anti-Black racism and provides the tent under which Blackness, as negative social representations of Black people by white people, can be analysed. Ironically, Blackness needs to be affirmed through whiteness and is positioned and contextualized by it. So is Blackness merely anti-whiteness? If so, then the difficult epistemological work of interpreting Blackness would appear to be useless. It would become an almost impossible task that would risk being hinged on dichotomization, polarization, generalization, and essentialization. However, it is through this theoretical and conceptual work that non-Blacks could potentially become sensitized to Blackness, raising the bar toward social transdisciplinary, transcultural, transnational, and trans-linguistic dialogue.

The Intersectionality of Anti-Black Racism and Anti-Black-Woman Sexism: Which Blackness?

Confronted by systemic, systematic, and chronic anti-Black racism and rejection of the concept and reality of it within the Francophonie, combined with the epistemological gap in the French-language literature and debates, how can we even think of Blackness? Blackness must surpass racism(s), but to do so it must pass through racism(s), by critically deconstructing, resisting, and transcending racism(s). This epistemological process seems far from being rectified. Is it necessary to consider francophone Blackness by avoiding fundamental social questions about anti-Black racism? Further, can Blackness be deconstructed without first examining the racism inherent in white power and privilege (whiteness).

Nuances of Blackness from My Personal Perspective, as a Black Woman in the Canadian Francophone Academy

Blackness cannot exist in isolation. In intersectionality with gender, age, social class, dis/ability, place, and other social factors, Blackness has such resonance that it is necessary to interrogate all of them. According to bell hooks (1990), it is impossible to understand Blackness without these identity markers. How do Black women and Black men live their Blackness? How do young Blacks evolve, mature, and age with their Blackness? How do Blacks who live with disability live their Blackness? How do LGBTQ Blacks live their Blackness? What socio-environmental impacts confront Blacks and Blackness? How are their living conditions, life expectancy, health, etc. affected by the way that Blackness is lived in society? We are aware of the risk for young Black males when interacting with the police (exemplified by "racial profiling"); we are aware of the negative representations that plague Blacks in all socio-cultural milieus; we are aware of the association between Blacks and certain types of work/employment; and we are aware of the perceived threat of the mere existence of the Black man. Each of these questions could lead to its own independent study. However, it is important to acknowledge that Blackness cannot be considered by shining a light on specific, individual circumstances that frame, elucidate, and underpin the lived experiences of Blackness. The Black identity is more than the sum of its parts.

While I have drafted this chapter I knew that it would lay wounds bare that never seem to heal. There is still much more to say, to ponder. I hope that one day a Black (female) writer will collect all these wounds into a monologue that will start the healing. Like Freire (quoted by Darder 2016, 5), "I refuse … to think that we are eternally destined to live the negation of our own selves."

Throughout these reflections, a fear and a question remain. The fear: discover even more wounds and suffering … after having open the lid of the "multiplex oppressions" (Dei, 2014, 2017): racisms, colourism, sexism, classism, linguism, nationalism, and so on. I have to confess that I did not dare to confront sexist oppression intertwined with racist oppression, and by not doing that, I did not confront the sexist Blackness of Black men or the racist whiteness of white women or the sexist and racist whiteness of white men. The combination of racism and sexism is so brutal for Black women that it requires special examination, in the light of bell hook's thought. And what to say about the social representation of the female white body at the top of the femininity scale? As a Black woman, my Blackness tries to find its way in some interstitial spaces, wherever is possible, drawing a "counter-relief" image, a mask of Black men (I am Black but not male), a mask of white women (I am a woman but not white), and a mask of white men (I am not male, I am not white).

My question has two faces: (1) Is Blackness damnation? And if so, is there salvation for it? (2) Is Blackness a celebration? And if so, when should it start (many decades after my ancestors were enslaved)? For me, this remains undecidable. Facing the mirror, looking at the "white masks" I have to wear every second of my life, I feel and I know that Fanon is right: my whole identity (body, heart, mind, and soul) has been dislocated, fragmented, confiscated, alienated, and diabolized. So what is the meaning of doing an archaeology of my Black identity and Black citizenship in Canada, from my non-human or non-person perspective? I'm afraid that this chapter has only prolonged the long voyage that I proposed to readers at the beginning. At the same time, I am fully aware that this epistemological autopsy is necessary for all of us as together we form a "community of pain" (Fanon 1968). Those who wish to go on with the mission to unravel, deconstruct, and critically engage with the black hole of Blackness may discover, far away, some light guiding to a world where Blackness can be lived as a celebration. I probably won't be there to be part of the celebration.

It is a tremendous epistemological undertake to pursue, collectively and continuously, in order to reveal the infinite the Blackness and help the healing of our wounded identities and citizenships. Can our identities and citizenships will arise one day from centuries of misery and open to the world in fierce engagement for peace, social justice, inclusion, and radical love? In that sense, I salute the courageous work of my colleagues, Afro-Canadian scholars, from the African diasporas, from coast to coast, including the editors of this book, who create the opportunities to de-/re-/co-/construct it, and by doing so, re/live our Blackness together. I also salute the courageous work of our non-Black colleagues who stand in solidarity with us.

The title of the Frantz Fanon's first book, in French *Les damnés de la terre* (1968), in English, *The Wretched of the Earth*, describes the existence of Blacks in colonial contexts. Inspired by Fanon (1968, 2008), Blackness can be understood in relation to the wounds that have been inflicted and the suffering that has been absorbed by the "wretched of the earth." In that sense, I consider my own Blackness as a complex equation involving my wounded identities and my wounded citizenships. The objectives of concepts such as "wounded identities" and "wounded citizenships" are to problematize, understand, and tackle the systemic, systematic, and chronic experiences of racisms lived by Blacks as a post-/continuous-traumatic syndrome (PTS/CTS). In this chapter, I have emphasized the wounds that have been inflicted and have been driven into the soul. Thus, I offer an equation that may seem simplistic but I believe is appropriate: Blackness = wounded identities + wounded citizenships. But there is no gap between the two: there is a spectrum between identity and alterity. The concept of "wounded identities" refers to four dimensions of identity construction: corporal (physical, body), emotional (affective, heart), intellectual (thought, spirit), and spiritual (sense, soul).

The concept of "wounded citizenship" echoes the notion of "failed citizenship" as described by Banks (2017, 367), "when individuals or groups who are born within a nation or migrate to it and live within it for an extended period of time do not internalize the values and ethos of the nation-state, feel structurally excluded within it, and have highly ambivalent feeling toward it." More specifically, "wounded citizenship" refers to the deployment of identities within the social spheres in the light of the bio-psycho-social development model of Bronfenbrenner and Morris (2006). This model includes the ego-sphere (self); the micro-sphere (family, community); the meso-sphere (education and work in professional milieus as well as in institutions such as schools, churches/places of worship, community centres, cultural and sports centres, etc.); the exo-sphere (society, laws, policies); the macro-sphere (world, values, ideologies, etc.); and the chrono-sphere (rhythms, evolutions, moments of détente and movements, etc.). Table 5.1 summarizes the conjugation of wounded identities and wounded citizenships within the expression of Blackness. Four columns list the four dimensions of wounded citizenships: corporal, emotional, intellectual, and spiritual. Six rows of the table address wounded citizenships inspired by the Bronfenbrenner's work (Bronfenbrenner and Morris 2006). Each sphere is associated with one level or more of racism (Scheurich and Young 1997).

A Tentative of Generalization of My Own Wounded Identities and Wounded Citizenships

When we encounter two perspectives – individual (wounded identities or wounded relations to self) and collective (wounded citizenships or wounded relations to Others) – we can detect two fundamental points

Table 5.1. Conjugation of Wounded Identities and Wounded Citizenships within My Own Blackness

	Corporal (phenotype)	Emotional (affective)	Intellectual (cognitive)	Spiritual (metaphysical)
Eco-sphere (self)	• Ambiguous body • Foreignness in one's own body and shame	• Ambiguous emotions • Foreignness in one's own emotions and feeling of dislocation	• Ambiguous intellect • Foreignness through education, mis-education, and alienation	• Ambiguous sense of self • Foreignness of self, loss of sense of self, and self-loathing
Micro-sphere (family, community, life conditions, conventions) **Level of open and closed interpersonal racism(s)** (relations)	• Incomprehension and questioning of negative representations of Blacks bodies • Discrimination(s) against the Black in line with colourism (privileges based on phenotypes, with whites being favoured)	• Incomprehension and questioning of emotions that are awakened • Feeling of rejection through continual preference for the Other	• Incomprehension and questioning of family and community dynamics and self-sabotage • Interiorization of colourism and forms of racism based on phenotypes	• Incomprehension about and questioning of the meaning of life • Loss of self-esteem in relations with the Other, and self-loathing
Meso-sphere (institutions, education, place of work, services, regulations) **Level of open and closed interpersonal racism(s)** (relations) **Level of institutional racism(s)** (regulations)	• Dissonance in self-rapport • Discrimination(s) against the Black body executed by institutional actors, including peers • Implicit restrictions in movements, comportment, and actions	• Dissonance in relations with the Other • Feeling of marginalization and exclusion in alignment with institutional regulations, acceptance, submission, passivity	• Dissonance in knowledge(s) and power • Interiorization of cognitive racism(s) • Learned and acquired impotence	• Dissonance in relation to the world and to life • Loss of confidence in the Other, and self-loathing • Disaffection with institutions (schools, police, etc.)

Exo-sphere (society, governance, laws, policies) **Level of societal racism(s)** (representations, knowledge, media)	• Discrimination(s) against the Black body as it is represented in the media • Social body/physical disengagement (retreat)	• Feeling of inadequacy in social frameworks (political, economic, cultural, sport-based, leisure) • Socio-emotional disengagement (avoidance)	• Interiorization of racism in relation to knowledge and epistemological racism (erased memory, suffocated discourse, passivity, learned and acquired impotence) • Socio-intellectual disengagement (evisceration)	• Loss of social organization roots • Socio-spiritual disengagement (hopelessness and self-loathing)
Macro-sphere (world, civilizations, values, principles) **Level of civilizational racism(s)** (values, beliefs)	• Demonization of the Black body (exclusion of diverse canons of beauty in the media and other social spaces) • Discrimination against the Black body in beliefs, myths, values	• Demonization of emotions of Blacks • Feeling of not-belonging	• Demonization of Black cultures • Interiorization of democratic racism (through democratic values and principles), epistemological resistance, anger	• Demonization of the sense of life presented by Blacks • Loss of sense of life, and self-loathing
Chrono-sphere (rhythms, evolutions, moments of détente, and movements)	• Continuous social anchoring of discriminations against the Black body • Discomfort with rhythm of changing body shapes	• Recurrence of emotional micro-aggressions • Surviving difficult emotional journey and feeling of non-accomplishment	• Acceleration of diverse dynamics framing negative representations of Blacks • Interiorization of disqualification of the intellectual journey	• Slowing down of life project and living • Loss of sense related to time, self-interest, self-loathing, and living

Note: Underlined text signifies fundamental points of suffering that plague Blacks daily.

of suffering (underlined in Table 5.1) that plague Blacks daily. As a first dimension of wounded identities, the body is the temple of identity and the visible phenotypical expression (corporeality). But the Black body is not a temple, because it is represented as a tool possessed by and in service of the master. It is first through the visible identity of Blacks that forms of discrimination are mobilized. More deeply, the body is the seat of "viscerality," meaning the organs (*visceres*) in which pain (discomfort, estrangement, suffocation, alienation, suspicion, anger, etc.) is felt and trapped (Darder 2009). The second dimension, the heart, is the symbolic centre of emotions and thus the recipient of social micro-aggressions that are anchored in the memory by rejection, marginalization, exclusion, and the disjointed ease with which one can feel comfortable in society. Emotions are residual effects of micro-aggressions that have been experienced during a lifetime. The third dimension, the mind, is the core of intellectual activity, which produces thought, and with it, the ability to think about and dwell on wounded identities. However, as Carter G. Woodson (1933, 2017) put it almost one century ago, mis-education leads to self-alienation and blocks progressive educational engagement and emancipation. It serves to interiorize forms of epistemological racism related to to knowledge, and to the cognitive sphere. The fourth dimension, aimed at the spiritual activity (soul) is necessary to heal the wounds. Nonetheless, this activity can be undone by an interiorization of hegemonic social and cultural dynamics (religions, languages, education, etc.) that result in a loss of sense, meaning a loss of self, self-esteem, self-confidence, feeling of being recognized, sense of belonging, sense of self-power. Each dyad is unique in the combination of points of suffering, but each presents evidence of the complexity of wounds that have been inflicted as well as the establishment of a sort of dialogue between the wounds and the wounded.

Conclusion

To weave together the nuances of Blackness in French, it is imperative to first acknowledge the invisibility and inaudibility that is intertwined with the language that frames fundamental epistemological markers, processes, and foundations (for example, knowledge, concepts, words, rules), which pave the way for how race, racialization, and racism are understood, conceptualized, and addressed. To address, frame, and engage with this problematic with the French-language academy is a daunting task. My own identities as a Black, francophone, Afro-Canadian woman of Haitian origin, who was raised in Quebec and who is a professor at a francophone university in Montreal, obliges me to reflect on, interrogate, and negotiate "Blackness" and the racial question in relation to factors that include language, gender, ethnicity, the historical and geopolitical context, and diverse academic postures. Ultimately "Blackness," like other identities, involves sensitivity to intersectionality and identity formation. Migration has affected the meaning, experience, and context of "Black bodies."

As I end this reflection here, although it will continue throughout the rest of my life, some questions remain:

• Why write about "Blackness"?
• What are the dynamics framing (collective) transformation and (individual) emancipation in relation to the de-/re-/co-construction of "Blackness"?
• How can the academy – in particular the francophone academy – become a space for critical dialogue in this area?

This book is an eloquent expression of the need to further and better unpack race, racialization, and racism. The English-language sector of the Canadian academy has already established a robust and healthy space for such ongoing reflection, as exemplified by the work of Dei, Cooper, Abdi, Wright, Wane, Walcott, and others. The contribution of the French-language sector within the Canadian academy has been more muted, contested, and constrained, although there has been some work done in this area (Labelle 2010; McAndrew et al. 2008; Bataille, McAndrew, and Potvin 1998). Interestingly, in 2006 (see Carr and Thésée 2006), I highlighted the dearth of race-related work in French in Quebec and France, especially in relation to what existed in English. I might argue that Afro-Canadian francophones in the academy, especially in Quebec, are fearful of the reactions that might erupt when de-/-re-/co-constructing the realities of racism and racialization.

Within the French-language academy, we are at an epistemological cross-roads, and much has to be de-/re-/co-constructed. Many are interested in, affected by, and concerned with this problematic, and many tentacles have branched out into socio-critical perspectives, infused in and/or infusing with anti-colonialism, indigenous knowledge and studies, feminism, environmental education, and critical pedagogy, thus presenting the parameters of a "Maroon hermeneutics." It is critical that this transcultural and transdisciplinary field engage with colleagues, partners, groups, communities, and others in a range of contexts and languages. And this is where I hope that the Afro-Canadian francophone colleagues will be involved.

REFERENCES

Banks, J. 2017. "Failed Citizenship and Transformative Civic Education." *Educational Researcher* 46 (7): 366–377. https://doi.org/10.3102/0013189X17726741.

Bataille, P., McAndrew, M., and Potvin, M. 1998. "Racisme et antiracisme au Québec: analyse et approches nouvelles. *Cahier de recherche sociologique* 31: 115–144.

Bronfenbrenner, U., and Morris, P. 2006. "The Bioecological Model of Human Development." In *Handbook of Child Psychology*, edited by W. Damon and M. Lerner, 793–828. Hoboken: Wiley.

Carr, P.R., and Thésée, G. 2006. "Race and Identity in Education in Quebec." *Directions: Research and Policy on Eliminating Racism* 3 (1): 18–23.

Chamoiseau, P. 1997. *Écrire en pays dominé*. Paris: Gallimard.

Confiant, R. 1989. *Éloge de la Créolité*. Paris: Gallimard.

Darder, A. 2009. *Decolonizing the Flesh: The Body, Pedagogy, and Inequality*. New York: Peter Lang.

Darder, A. 2016. "Freire and the Body." In *Encyclopedia of Educational Philosophy and Theory*, edited by M. Peters, 1–6. Singapore: Springer.

Dei, G.S. 1996. *Anti-Racism Education: Theory and Practice*. Halifax: Fernwood Publishing.

Dei, G.S. 2014. "A Prism of Educational Research and Policy: Anti-Racism and Multiplex Oppressions." In *Politics of Anti-Racism Education: In Search of Strategies for Transformative Learning*, edited by G. Dei and M. McDermott, 15–28. Cham: Springer.

Dei, G.S. 2017. *Reframing Blackness and Black Solidarities through Anti-Colonial and Decolonial Prisms*. Cham: Springer.

Fanon, F. 1968. *Les Damnés de la terre*. Paris: Maspero.

Fanon, F. 2008. *Black Skin, White Masks*. New York: Grove Press.

Glissant, E. 1981. *Le discours antillais*. Paris: Seuil.

Henry, F., and Tator, C. 2009. *Racism in the Canadian University: Demanding Social Justice, Inclusion, and Equity*. Toronto: University of Toronto Press.

hooks, b. 1990. *Ain't I a Woman: Black Women and Feminism*. London: Pluto Press.

Ibrahim, A. 2016. "Who Owns My Language? African Canadian Youth, Postcoloniality, and the Symbolic Violence of Language in a French-Language High School in Ontario." In *The Education of African Canadian Children: Critical Perspectives*, edited by A. Ibrahim and A. Abdi, 24–35. Montreal and Kingston: McGill-Queen's University Press.

Icart, J.-C. 1987. *Négriers d'eux-mêmes*. Montreal: Les éditions du CIDIHCA.

Labelle, M. 2010. *Racisme et antiracisme au Québec: Discours et déclinaisons*. Quebec: Presses de l'Université du Québec.

McAndrew M., Ledent, J., and Ait-Said, R. 2008. *La réussite scolaire des jeunes des communautés noires au secondaire*. Montreal: Centre de recherche interuniversitaire de Montréal sur l'immigration, l'intégration et la dynamique urbaine.

Paul-Austin, L.-C. 2017. "Le Moi et l'Autre: Une approche herméneutique Marronne." In *Pensée afro-caribéenne et (psycho)traumatismes de l'esclavage et de la colonisation*, edited by J. Blanc and S. Madhère, 24–36. Montreal: Éditions sciences et bien commun.

Satzewich, N., and Liodakis, N. 2013. *"Race" and Ethnicity in Canada: A Critical Introduction*. Toronto: Oxford University Press.

Scheurich, J., and Young, M.D. 1997. "Coloring Epistemologies: Are Our Research Epistemologies Racially Biased?" *Educational Researcher* 26 (4): 4–16. https://doi.org/10.3102/0013189X026004004.

Thésée, G., and Carr, P.R. 2012. "The 2011 International Year for People of African Descent (IYPAD): The Paradox of Colonized Invisibility within the Promise of Mainstream Visibility." *Decolonization: Indigeneity, Education & Society* 1 (1): 158–180. https://jps.library.utoronto.ca/index.php/des/article/view/18626.

UN. 2009. *Resolution 64/169. International Year for People of African Descent.*

UN. 2013. *Resolution 68/237. International Decade for People of African Descent.*

UNESCO. 2013.*Education for All 2013 Global Monitoring Report*. Paris: UNESCO.

Woodson Carter, G. 1933/1990. *The Mis-Education of the Negro*. Trenton, NJ: Africa World Press.

PART TWO

Blackness and Academic Pathways

Commentary on Part Two: Blackness in the Canadian Academy: Challenges, Contestations, and Contradictions

WISDOM J. TETTEY

Introduction

Many in the Canadian academy are committed to promoting equity, diversity, and inclusion. Notwithstanding individual and institutional efforts, however, Black students, faculty, and staff can legitimately claim that they are yet to see a fundamental shift in the structures and systems that have led to their underrepresentation in the academy. Part of the reason for this is the fact that institutional interventions aimed at addressing the inequities are not situated within a historical framework that sufficiently exposes and transforms the structural power imbalances behind them. They fail to acknowledge or address the deep and continuing complicity of existing structures and processes in sustaining those imbalances. There seems to be a lack of institutional will to push for a recalibration of relations of power and a reluctance to cede or to share privilege, thereby leading to efforts that are episodic, superficial, and fleeting. Consequently, Black colleagues who make it into spaces within the academy continue to feel marginalized as they contend with the attitudinal and structural barriers that constrain their sense of belonging and success, as well as opportunities for many in their communities to join the higher education sector. The challenges of those barriers, the contestations that they spawn, and how Black scholars negotiate their place in the academy are the focus of the five chapters in this section.

In the following commentary, I will focus on three main issues: (1) contradictions that attend the dialectical tensions between the cognate concepts of equity, diversity, and inclusion; (2) the contestations regarding authentic voice and legitimacy of representation by Black academics who occupy interstitial spaces, within their institutions or between the academy and their communities outside the sector; and (3) the importance of building alliances that would facilitate the transformative change needed to realize the promise of equity and inclusion within the academy.

The analysis is framed around three distinct but interrelated conceptions of "privilege" that are woven into the ensuing commentary. Each confers a different kind of power, control, and opportunity for a select group. In the first sense, it refers to the continuing prescriptive acceptance of enduring institutional structures and practices as applicable by default, without challenging their provenance in a hierarchical order of white colonial dominance that values and imposes certain ways of knowing and conduct, while devaluing, undermining, or rejecting others. Those in charge of the institutions are clothed with power to defend these cultures and imbued with the authority to preserve them. The second meaning pertains to the automaticity of in-built, taken-for-granted benefits that white members of the academy enjoy because of a supposedly intrinsic affinity to the institutional cultures and practices, thereby validating their experiences as "normal," reinforcing their ways of knowing as the standard, and granting their bodies pride of place in the hierarchy.

Any "aberrations" from the "norm" are not seen as attributable to an intrinsic racial deficit, but as a product of constraining externalities that can be addressed with sympathy, empathy, and support to restore homeostasis with the institutional culture. Black and other racialized and Indigenous colleagues, on the other hand, suffer from the double burden of what Smith (in this volume) calls "deficit thinking" and the absence of intrinsic affinity. This combination translates into a presumed "lack of fit," which will be too disruptive and burdensome for institutions to accommodate or to "fix." Many traditionally marginalized and under-represented colleagues are then compelled to demonstrate "fit," for purposes of admission and career progression, by denying or attenuating elements of themselves and imbibing, reflecting, and promoting the normativity of the white traditions of their institutions. Black and Indigenous scholars tend to be seen as exhibiting the least propinquity to white normativity and, hence, least likely to have any assets of intrinsic affinity to institutional cultures to fall back on for concessions or conferral of the privilege to belong.

Separate from these two types of white privilege is a third privilege that we all share as academics, even if nominally, irrespective of our location within the academy. It confers status within and outside the academy and gives us the academic freedom to contribute to knowledge, to innovate, to develop generations of learners and leaders, and to speak up for the marginalized and what is right. As will be discussed below, this privilege should come with individual commitment and the responsibility to build common purpose that routinizes equity and inclusive excellence as foundational to the success of the academic mission. For Black colleagues, the privilege comes with an amalgam of expectations from self and from within and outside the academy that imposes unique challenges.

Equity, Diversity, and Inclusion: Contentions around Cognate Concepts

The devaluation of Black difference and its equation with innate deficiency in the dominant imaginary are the spurious justifications used to explain away the underrepresentation of Blacks in the academy. The challenges that Black students, faculty, and staff face is thus blamed on them and not on the constraining environment that stymies their pipelines of access, but also their experiences of integration once they enter institutions of higher education. Many Black colleagues recount experiences where accommodations and benefits of the doubt that are granted to others are not extended to them by those who control the levers of opportunity and networks of white privilege and associated power. Consequently, there is a deficit of trust between the academy and its Black members and, by extension, with the larger Black community.

Because of "deficit thinking," many interventions to address these challenges tend to be premised on reducing those deficits (e.g., extra supports to enhance learning, to create excitement about the value of higher education) and to attract with the trappings of symbolic gestures of diversity. These approaches do not address the structural roots of problems that these interventions seek to attenuate. The equity-seeking framing of these efforts has an embedded philanthropic tenor to it, whereby the benefits of access and related rights of membership have to be sought by the marginalized, with the arbiters of power and privilege determining whether they are worthy. While coming from well-intentioned efforts to address inequities, this framing connotes responsibility of the subaltern as opposed to the obligation of the powerful and the privileged to make amends from an intrinsically human rights perspective. The "equity-seeking" orientation also comes with loaded derogatory misconceptions encapsulated in divisive and incendiary uses of terms such as "entitlement" or "identity politics." Such uses are intentionally infused with pejorative connotations to suggest that those who seek equity and inclusion are asking for what they don't deserve or want to sponge off rights and benefits to which they have not contributed. They are meant to disempower through the mobilization of derision, resentment, and resistance against racialized and other marginalized peoples, ignoring their many contributions to the citizenship rights that these interlocutors enjoy. The insidiousness of these euphemistic renditions of racism, and the irony of the critics' sense of entitlement to the preservation of the status quo for the exclusive benefit of the powerful and privileged, should be exposed. In tandem with that, the terms should be rightfully (re)appropriated to reinforce the sanctity of equal rights. If the narrative moves away from "equity-seeking" to a rights-based "equity-deserving" framework, then we can make progress based on an expectation of obligatory reckoning by the powerful and the privileged. Entitlement to equity and rights of citizenship should be embraced, not denigrated. Those who mobilize and aggregate their interest around the very markers of identity that make them targets and victims of inequity and exclusion should have no compunction demanding what they deserve as a right. As I have argued elsewhere, we have to start

> thinking of, and relating to, those who are marginalized or are constrained by existing structures and practices as "equity-deserving groups," and not "equity-seeking groups" – a concept which, while well-intentioned, perpetuates a perception of these groups as interlopers.
>
> Those on the margins of our community, who feel or are made to feel that they do not belong, deserve equity as a right. They should not be given the burden of seeking it and they should not be made to feel that they get it as a privilege from the generosity of those who have the power to give it, and hence the power to take it back. (Tettey 2019)

The process of unlearning and re-learning that would facilitate a transition from the narrative of equity-seeking to one of equity-deserving requires a change in the soft systems infrastructure of the academy. That means that curricula need to change, and the composition of decision-making structures need to become more inclusive, not just of Black bodies but of Black voices, perspectives, experiences, ways of knowing, and contributions to knowledge. Furthermore, the forms and processes of community engagement that institutions pursue with Black communities need re-examination of their undergirding values, presuppositions, and the power dynamics that inform them. Values of reciprocity and approaches that conceptualize Black communities from an asset-based, as opposed to a deficit-based, frame should inform interactions between institutions and their partners. These values and approaches allow for enrichment of experiences and knowledge broadly as the diverse perspectives, knowledges, ways of knowing, and backgrounds in the Black community enter and get embedded in knowledge production, corpora of valued knowledges, and decision-making spaces within the academy. They also confer authority to challenge the status quo and to ignite change that is more inclusive and facilitating of opportunities for all. These are the steps that will engender genuine inclusion, not the truncated version that the rhetoric of diversity promises but is unable to deliver.

A good starting point is an evidence-based approach to unearthing and addressing structural inequity and exclusion within the academy. However, many institutions lack race-based data, ostensibly because of concerns about privacy and the unwillingness of many racialized students, staff, and faculty to allow such data to be collected about them. While there may be some basis for this argument, it is disingenuous in its portrayal of the issue. Indeed, many racialized members of the academy have legitimate fears about how the data might be used to profile and/or to reinforce biases against them. They are, however, not against the collection of race-based data that would enable structural inequities, such as salary inequities or admission biases, to be ascertained and addressed while ensuring that the information is not abused in ways that unfairly target them. If institutions are genuinely concerned about addressing biases and inequities, they should engage symmetrically with Black and other racialized colleagues to find mutually acceptable ways of pursuing appropriate data collection and use that allay concerns about misappropriation and misapplication.

The availability of such data is crucial to pursuing targeted and efficacious interventions, and for holding institutions to account, particularly if those accountabilities are situated within a rights-based, equity-deserving framework. As James (this volume) points out, the use of omnibus categories like "visible minority" is a convenient way to mask the extremely peripheral location of Black colleagues relative to other marginalized groups within an aggregated set of racialized minorities. It is incomprehensible that institutions that pride themselves as citadels of evidence-based knowledge production would be reluctant or resistant to taking steps to generate specific, but prudent, decision-support data about Black students, faculty, and staff. The foot-dragging only leads to further growth in mistrust that Blacks experience in their relationship with the academy. It serves the interest of transparency and justice for institutions to partner with Black and other members of their racialized communities to find solutions with inbuilt protections against abuse.

The condescending excuse of "protecting" racialized colleagues by not generating race-based data is moribund and untenable. Gender-based data have enabled structural inequities to be exposed and corrected. There is no reason why the same cannot be done in disaggregated form, with intersecting permutations, for groups of racialized colleagues. Institutions stand to be vindicated about the fairness of the status quo if that is what the evidence shows. On the other hand, they have to assume their obligation to ensure equality and equity if the evidence bears out the view among many Black students, faculty, and staff that they are not accorded these rights.

Navigating Contestations and Conflicts in In-Between Spaces

While many will claim acceptance of the concept of intersectionality within the Black community at large, and the Black academic community specifically, we should not lose sight of the dialectical tensions that abound in relation to the markers of social identity (e.g., Canadian-born, Caribbean, African, biracial, and LGBTQ+, among others). These tensions are amply articulated in the chapters by Crichow and Kitossa. There is a tendency to privilege some social identity markers over others in an internal system of relative hierarchy where some elements are subordinated to others, subsumed, or even denigrated. The consequence is that some in the Black community are pushed to erase elements of their avowed identities, or compelled to subsume parts of their identity within particular totalizing categories, to suit prevailing dictates of power if they are to gain acceptance and credibility as deserving bona fide members.

The reality of shared experiences should, however, not be allowed to trap individual experiences within the univocal constraints of a single narrative. The single narrative creates the fallacy of a unidimensional set of experiences and imposes its own embedded structures of privilege and marginalization. It is in this vein that some Black colleagues are chosen or expected by the predominantly white institution to speak for the collective minority or to be the institution's face in interactions with external and internal Black communities. On the other hand, Black academics are subject to coercion by some compatriots in Black communities to conform to a particular version of what a Black person in the academy should be, do, or say in their individual capacity or on behalf of their communities. In effect, these expectations assume identical experiences when, in fact, those realities can be temporally and situationally different for the same or different individuals or group(s). Contestations around loyalty, authoritative voice, legitimacy of representation, purity of Blackness, and essentialization of forms and modes of expression in various settings are at the heart of Kitossa's critique, in this volume, of the relationship between Black academics and some in the larger Black community that James (2019) categorizes as "cultural curators."

It is worth noting, however, that these conflicts do not manifest themselves in neat binary forms between those in academia and the "anti-intellectual" gatekeepers outside it. In fact, contestations about those issues and the questioning of the licence to speak a non-essentialized version of the Black story are rife among Black academics as well. Here the litmus test of purity is sometimes determined by perceptions of where Black colleagues sit in relation to the institutional sites of power and/or the form of resistance or path to transformation that they take. Accusations or insinuations of being a "sell-out" do not only come from "town" but are levelled from within "gown" as well.

The contestations that come with the in-between location of Black academics have the potential to erode their credibility in the midst of contending perceptions of loyalty, or lack thereof, to the institution, to Black colleagues, and/or to the Black community. The challenge can be even more accentuated for Black academic administrators, as they face the daunting expectation to be the panacea for the change that each party desires – a very untenable situation to find themselves in, since these expectations do not always dovetail and may, in fact, be contradictory. For Black academics, the emotional labour involved in negotiating these expectations is very taxing but tends not to be recognized and valorized in relation to institutional mechanisms for career progress and reward.

To maintain their integrity and credibility in the midst of these contending expectations, it behoves those Black colleagues who have access to spaces of influence within the academy to debunk notions of the model minority, coming from the centres of power, and to eschew related trappings and accolades, which can lull them into complacency or into tempering advocacy for what is right. Comfort with the privilege of the insider can lead to uncritical association with power structures and their preferences. Rather, they should use their locations within authority structures to make the institutions more just, more equitable, and more inclusive. They should be assets for advancing the status of the marginalized while promoting the compatible collective good of inclusive excellence for the institution as a whole.

Admittedly, this is not easy to do. The foregoing is not to suggest that these individuals should shoulder full responsibility for achieving the goals of inclusive excellence, as is the case in many institutions where racialized colleagues are left to be the only ones to invest sweat equity into diversity and inclusion. But they can make a contribution by using their accomplishments and the social capital of being an insider, even if in limited respects, to constructively challenge institutions in ways that effect change. Those in charge of the institutions should recognize the value of these individuals as allies, if the former are genuinely committed to elevating their campuses as exemplars of the innate equality of all peoples and hence enablers of the substantive rights of all members of our society to work and learn in a conducive environment devoid of discrimination. The critiques may not always be pleasant, the truth is not always easy to hear, but they are necessary forebears to disruptive, yet constructive, reflective, and progressive action.

The embrace of critique and critical reflection is also applicable to Black members of the academy and their kin in the larger community, as part of their mutual responsibility and accountability to one another. Some Black colleagues have been unfairly branded as unsupportive lackeys of the institutional power structure because they have good reason not to engage in uncritical solidarity for its own sake. Not every challenging situation faced by a Black student, staff, or faculty member is attributable or reducible to racial discrimination. There are legitimate cases where institutional policies and standards are appropriately applied and the individual just happens to be Black. They are a healthy way of enhancing and supporting career growth. Such actions should not be maligned, and honest critique and feedback should not be seen as a lack of support.

Uncritical solidarity can be damaging to credibility when there are indeed legitimate performance issues that are not connected to structural systemic or procedural bias. It undermines support for valid cases of bias and retribution for perceived erosion of the privileges of whiteness, whether in intellectual thought or the movement of racialized bodies into spaces of white dominance. It is important that we do not internalize and impose a "tyranny of low expectations" (Smith, this volume) through uncritical solidarity, even as we are compelled by (under)representation of Blacks in the academy to expend emotional labour and significant sweat equity to help those who look up/to us for guidance and support (see Crichlow; Williams and Fearon, this volume). While there may be a temptation to subordinate hard truths to racial solidarity, such a tendency ultimately will be inimical. It is not helpful to individuals within the Black community whose favour we may be trying to court with lack of candour; nor is it to our collective credibility. The loss of credibility will ultimately have negative repercussions for the cause of equity, diversity, and inclusion because they can feed into the frame of "deficit thinking" that Smith addresses in this volume.

In pursuing the struggle for radical change in the academy, it would be erroneous to elevate adversarial public expressions of dissent above other forms of progressive engagement and constructive disruption of the status quo that may not have the visibility or amplitude of the former. Both approaches to change have their place and have contributed to enabling needed outcomes. To reduce the pathway to change to only one approach or to suggest, as some do, that the latter connotes complicity in, or laxity towards, Black marginalization is to diminish the contributions of many who have quietly engendered transformative change.

Partnership, Collaboration, and Alliance

Notwithstanding the asymmetries of power and opportunity that Blacks in the academy face, we must acknowledge the relative privilege of our location and embrace the responsibility that comes with it. That responsibility includes embracing our role in promoting understanding, building support, and bringing people along to the goal of equity and inclusion. In pursuing these efforts, we should avoid the temptation to be insular, recognize and welcome genuine alliance, and not succumb to a purity test that questions the commitment of our Black peers because they do not subscribe to a monolithic approach to constructively rupturing the status quo and reconstituting it within a system of values, structures, and practices that are intentionally equitable and inclusive.

In fostering common purpose towards inclusive excellence in the academy, institutions, Black and non-Black colleagues, and Black communities should learn to reconcile the seeming contradictions that come with the ambiguities of location in in-between spaces. Black colleagues need to be able to simultaneously articulate the voices that reflect their intersecting identities within the power structures of the academy and their own realities of the Black experience, writ large. Institutions should become comfortable hearing critiques from those voices and not brand them as disloyal just because they channel the concerns and experiences of Black and racialized colleagues, articulate the urgency of addressing inequities and marginalization, call for a tempering of the self-adulation that leads to complacency of "moderation in response," and push for expedited changes to the status quo. At the same time, Black peers in the academy and compatriots in the larger community should recognize that there is no single prescription for addressing the common challenge of Black marginalization, underrepresentation, and/or exclusion within the academy. We should embrace the mutually progressive efforts that may come in different forms. Successful collaboration may require that we give some latitude to non-Black colleagues who are genuine in their commitment to change and are humble enough to learn. While we should not assume responsibility for their mistakes, we should also not deflate their determination to push for change because of fear of being castigated for mistakes that could be opportunities for learning.

While alliance is important, it is crucial that allies understand that proximate appreciation of the challenges and concerns of Black colleagues is not the same as being immersed in the latter's lived experiences. There is, therefore, a need to support the cause from a position of humility and bounded alliance. While looking in from the outside may come with its own set of emotional and other tolls, it cannot be construed as the equivalent of embodied experience of the subaltern. Aggrandizing visibility by allies diminishes the contribution of those who have carried the burden of the struggle and paid the price for their courage in challenging structures and systems of marginalization and suppression. It also disempowers them as authoritative voices in their own right. Awareness of these concerns about appropriation is key to building trust with allies, particularly because of the academy's penchant for creating hierarchies of authoritative voice. That voice tends to be limited to circuits that are largely impervious to Black scholars, even with regard to their own experiences, and where intellectual valency and recognition is accorded to a coterie of scholars and academic administrators that has, at best, minimal Black representation.

The concept of "deficit thinking" requires us to be careful about how efforts at equity and inclusion are pursued within institutions, lest we end up perpetuating stereotypes and further devaluing Blacks who surmount the structural challenges of the academy to be considered worthy of admission. While equity, diversity, and inclusion policies and practices are laudable in addressing the inequities that attend the realities of marginalized peoples on many campuses, they can be self-immolating if they focus on diversity and neglect or diminish the urgency of the other aspects of the triplet. When diversity is elevated over the other two, rather than pursued as an integral co-requisite, it may only produce a feel-good catharsis of making difference visible and assuage the consciences of the dominant without generating substantive strides towards genuine equity and intentional inclusion.

To debunk the trope of the Black person embedded in the concept of "deficit thinking," equity, diversity, and inclusion initiatives should educate the academy to accept the fact that a fundamental structural wrong has been historically and consciously perpetrated to deny access to the corridors of privilege for some members of our society. Without continuing to vigorously engage with questions of wrongs that require correction, these initiatives could be seen as acts of magnanimity from the largess of a compassionate dominant class that is not obligated to own responsibility for the correction. Highlighting the structural wrongs, such as the hidden histories of Black contributions, their erasure from institutional recognition, both physically and metaphorically, and the toll of past and continuing suppression are not always a comfortable thing to do. This is because they expose the depths of inhumanity and injustice that our societies have sunk to in order to ensure the heights of privilege that continue to be available only to some. The roots of structural inequity, therefore, have to be integral to discourses and interventions that seek to correct wrongs. These should not be seen as "dredging old complaints" or "Black hypersensitivity," comments that vilify Black students, faculty, and staff for being ungrateful for the "good" being extended to them whenever they "dare" to remind all of us about the inadequacy of out-of-pace, albeit laudable, efforts to address challenges that they face.

Conclusion

The Black presence within the Canadian academy is woefully inadequate. This is an indictment that requires structural transformations to create a system where equity, diversity, and inclusion become routinized as the default mode in institutional structures and practices. In order to facilitate this outcome, there is the need to mobilize the collective will in support of a rights-based, equity-deserving ethos. The struggle to enshrine and live these fundamental values within the Canadian higher education sector should not be left to only Black or racialized colleagues. All should invest their sweat equity in this endeavour as an obligation of institutional citizenship that comes with the privileges available in the academy, albeit to different degrees for different people. As I have noted in another context,

> Genuine embrace of different experiences, backgrounds, perspectives and identities is what will sustain a vibrant intellectual community like ours, where we strive every day to inspire limitless ingenuity, address the pressing issues of our day and generate solutions that are boundless in their impact ... [I]n order to attain and sustain our goal of inclusive excellence, it is imperative that we go beyond diversity and create an environment where every potential and current member ... feels a genuine sense of belonging and is given an equitable opportunity to make their best contribution to our academic mission ... [t]hat [we] embrace and promote the enriching contributions that come from the diverse backgrounds, ways of knowing, ideas, perspectives and experiences represented in our community. (Tettey 2019)

Moreover, the intersectional realities of Black academics make it a necessity that we avoid the pitfalls of the single experience in promoting equity and inclusion. It is, nevertheless, critical that we recognize that our ability to sustain ourselves and to make an impact, within the debilitating structures of the status quo, is exponentially difficult without the solidarity that comes with shared lived experiences and the conscience of alliance. The significance of solidarity should, however, not be construed to mean blind loyalty and the obliteration of introspective critique within institutions and within the Black community itself.

REFERENCES

James, C.E. 2019. "Black Leadership and White Logic: Models of Community Engagement." In *African Canadian Leadership: Continuity, Transition and Transformation*, edited by T, Kitossa, E. Lawson, and P. Howard, 74–88. Toronto: University of Toronto Press.

Tettey, W.J. 2019, 25 February. "Inspiring Inclusive Excellence – Professor Wisdom Tettey's Installation Address." University of Toronto Scarborough. https://utsc.utoronto.ca/news-events/inspiring-inclusive-excellence -professor-wisdom-tetteys-installation-address.

6 Hidden Figures: Black Scholars in the Early Canadian Academy[1]

MALINDA S. SMITH

Storytelling Black Lives

At the heart of this meditation is a desire to change the stories we tell about Black lives, particularly the framing of these stories and the dominant deficit lens through which they are often written. I am equally concerned about the silent and invisible ways in which stories are mobilized and taken up and used to narrate Black lives. In *Birds of Heaven*, Nigerian poet and novelist Ben Okri (1995, 34) writes, "It is easy to forget how mysterious and mighty stories are. They do their work in silence, invisibly. They work with all the internal materials of the mind and self. They become part of you while changing you." Okri offers a cautionary note on why we need to be attentive to storytellers, and the ways stories circulate, consciously and unconsciously – and, importantly, what those stories do: "Beware of the stories you read or tell; subtly, at night, beneath the waters of consciousness. They are altering your world" (Okri 1995, 34). Stories can change lives or destroy lives. In *A Way of Being Free*, Okri (1997, 120) also elaborates upon the transformative power of different stories: "If we change the stories we live by," it seems, "quite possibly we change our lives."

My aim in this chapter is to tell different kinds of stories as a way of foregrounding the multiplicity of Black lives, which are not reducible to the skin that we are in, and which, on the face of it, expose the violence of stereotypes based on Blackness as a fixed and singular identity category that can be easily profiled as skin-identity (see also chapters by Handel Wright and Awad Ibrahim in this volume). "The single story," argues Nigerian feminist and novelist Chimamanda Ngozi Adichie (2009, 000), "creates stereotypes, and the problem with stereotypes is not that they are untrue, but that they are incomplete. They make one story become the only story." My approach is also informed by Jamaican novelist, essayist, and philosopher Sylvia Wynter's understanding of storytelling and the human, by our ability to narrate our social worlds and, in the process, bring such worlds into being (McKittrick 2015). In this chapter I first turn my attention, briefly, to the dominant stories we tell about what it means to be Black in Canada and in the Canadian academy, and then, inspired by Wynter's understanding of the need to imagine alternative futures, I turn to stories rooted in our own achievements indelibly shaped by efforts to uplift ourselves from slavery, colonial racism, and the persistence of structural marginality. In this narration I hope to show meaningful connections without imposing a specific order on individual stories. Instead, I am interested in showing how the rich, complicated, and often messy stories shared about the experiences of Black lives in Canada and the Canadian academy do not follow a single path or narrative and are not reducible to the skin we are in.

Storytelling is indispensable to efforts to challenge stereotypes and institutional exclusions. Storytelling does not purport to be representative of broad statistical or conceptual categories as do, for example, demographic studies or large-N survey research. Instead, storytelling can reveal the nuances and variegated biographies as well as the shared contexts, challenges, and aspirations experienced by Black scholars. Storytelling is a profoundly personal and political-ethical act. As Adiche (2009) writes, stories can dispossess, malign, and "break the dignity of a people," but they also can inspire, educate, and "repair that broken dignity." The stories we tell, including those we tell *about* and *on* each other, matter greatly "for developing a more critical consciousness about social relations in our society" (Bell 2003, 4; see also Smith 2010, 42–44). Single stories can sustain and socially reproduce the very durable structures, barriers, biases, and discriminatory practices that we seek to transform, and thus they can – and do – indelibly shape Black lives, as well as obscure avenues to alternative pathways and futures in the academy.

Stories matter. They are saturated by power relations precisely because, as Adiche writes, they have the power to restore dignity, and, as Okri writes, they can change lives. Stories matter because they are also about "the struggle over who has the authority to tell the stories that define us" (Morales 1998, 5). Excavating and mapping the nuances of Blackness in the Canadian academy is at once a moment of careful digging and of stitching together the fragments of hidden stories of brilliant Black trailblazers and, at the same time, a moment of resisting contemporary stories of Black intellectual life shaped by deficit thinking and a tyranny of low expectations that circumscribe Black futures. Dominant narratives of Blackness, and Black Canadian capabilities, educational achievement, and employment potential, are overdetermined by deficit thinking. These narratives often frame Black Canadians in terms of low educational achievement, even *under*achievement, especially in relation to other "visible" or racialized minorities in Canada. As the singular story of Black lives, these dominant narratives not only frame, but indeed *produce*, Black Canadians as a deficit and as outliers to what is normally framed as the Canadian immigrant success story. Dominant deficit narratives inform a tyranny of low expectations and are mobilized to rationalize and explain away structural marginality. Deficit stories also trade on a historical forgetfulness that has enabled the erasure of pioneering Black scholars in the academy.

Ultimately my aim is to move from margin to centre (hooks 1984) the varied stories of Black Canadian scholars who represent "hidden figures"[2] in Canadian higher education. I use hidden figures in two senses: in the first instance, I place the emphasis on figures as in numbers, in this case the numbers that highlight the multiplicity and complexity of Black lives. In the second use of hidden figures, I place emphasis on figures in the form of Black people who are hidden, especially trailblazing Black scholars whose stories are rendered invisible in dominant narratives. Their names have been forgotten, or are at best submerged, in institutional memories, school textbooks, and university curricula. My focus on historical figures counters the decline of historical thinking in some iterations of contemporary Black Canadian studies. In what follows I briefly reflect on the first instance of hidden figures, with the remainder of the chapter focusing on the second sense of hidden figures captured through the stories of trailblazing Black scholars. Both kinds of stories complicate and unsettle any notion of a singular story of Black Canada or Black scholars.

Beyond the Single Story: Black Multiplicity

A counter-narrative to dominant conceptions about what it means to be Black in the Canadian academy requires disruption and displacement of any singular notion of Blackness, and what it means to be Black now. We can tell this story about the diversity and complexity of Black Canada through conventional data. The Canadian Census population data and Statistics Canada education data tell one kind of story. But, within any census, there are all kinds of stories and interpretative debates about the meaning and signification of the data. Here I am interested in highlighting how the data render unintelligible any idea of a single story about Black lives in Canada.

A singular Blackness never existed in the Indigenous territories that predate Canada, and this historical fact remains true. A Black population has existed in the territories for centuries (Fraser 2010). Indeed, the first

Black person to set foot on the territory is believed to have been Mathieu Da Costa, a multilingual Nigerian who served as a translator for traders. Fluent in Mi'kmaq, Portuguese, French, German, and pidgin Basque, Da Costa served as a translator for Indigenous and European nations and was part of Samuel de Champlain's excursion in 1605 (Johnston 2012). The first Black person to live in New France (now Quebec) was Olivier Le Jeune, a boy who was believed to have come from either Madagascar or Guinea and who is variously characterized as a slave and a servant to Guillaume Couillard de Lespinay (Trudel 2003). The Black population has grown in waves, as slaves, freed peoples, loyalists, refugees, students-turned-permanent-residents, and, like many non-Indigenous peoples, immigrants.

Substantial increases to the Black population occurred during the nineteenth and twentieth centuries, and especially in the twentieth-first century. According to the 2016 Canadian census, Black Canadians number 1.2 million, or 3.5 per cent, of the Canadian population (Statistics Canada 2019). Of these, one in four was born in Canada, while the remainder come from over 170 different countries. They are multi-ethnic and belong to over two hundred ethnicities, including five – Edo, Ewe, Malinké, Wolof, and Djiboutian – that were reported in the 2016 census for the first time. The Black population is Canada's most multilingual, with over one hundred different languages among them. It has both a higher proportion of people speaking primarily French at home (28 per cent) than the broader population (23.3 per cent) as well as another 28 per cent speaking primarily a language other than French or English at home (Statistics Canada 2019).

The diversity and complexity of the Black community is also shaped by generations, time, and space. Overall, the Black population is primarily young and more urban (94.3 per cent) than the broader population (71.2 per cent). In Nova Scotia, for example, almost 71.8 per cent of the Black community has been in Canada for three generations or more, whereas this is the case for only 8.6 per cent of the Black population in Canada's other provinces and territories (Statistics Canada 2019). Another 35 per cent of the Black community is second generation, while the majority, 56.4 per cent, is first generation, born outside of Canada. In the period prior to 1981, over 81 per cent of Black Canadians emigrated from the Caribbean and Bermuda, particularly Jamaica, Haiti, and Trinidad and Tobago. By 1991–2000, the Black community in Canada was equally constituted by people from the Caribbean region (46.6 per cent) and the African continent (46.9 per cent). By the period 2011–16 there was a dramatic shift in the source region for Black immigration, from the Caribbean (22.3 per cent) to the African continent (65.1 per cent).

Many of the continental African newcomers emigrated from Nigeria, Ethiopia, Somalia, Cameroon, and the Democratic Republic of the Congo (Statistics Canada 2019). In 2019, the Black population was mostly young, with a median age of 29.6, compared to 40.7 for the total population. It was also predominantly urban, with 94.3 per cent living in census metropolitan areas – primarily Toronto, Montreal, Edmonton, Calgary, and Halifax – compared to 71.2 per cent of the total population. Over 50 per cent live in Ontario, followed by Quebec, Alberta, Manitoba, and Nova Scotia, and there are smaller but growing populations living in every Canadian province and territory.

This diversity and complexity of Black communities across Canada is detailed here in order to stress how the erasure of the heterogeneity of Blackness enables the reduction of Black people to skin-stereotype, a process that is foundational to racial profiling and thus is what makes carding and profiling, at their core, fundamentally anti-Black practices. Profiling requires a process of homogenization, of a singularity to Blackness that enables one kind of story, and this process is central to the social reproduction of anti-Blackness and white normativity. Disruption and displacement of the stereotypical story are necessary because the dominant narratives function to *produce* a stereotype of Blackness that plays out in everything, from racial profiling on the streets and on university and college campuses to over-punishment in schools to professional life, where Black Canadians encounter concrete ceilings and are denied opportunities in subtle and not-so-subtle ways.

Left uncontested, the single narrative brings into being, seeks to make real, an idea of Blackness that fits, or is made to fit, the stereotype rather than the historical complexity of the lived realities and struggles of educated Black Canadians. Moreover, in the broader Canadian society and the academic community, there is a fundamental misunderstanding of the diversity and complexity of what constitutes global diasporic Blackness and, certainly, how this manifests in the heterogeneity of the Black community across Canada. At the same time, the stereotype makes possible the contemporary experiences of Black children in K–12, which highlight the disproportionate experiences of over-punishment, suspension, and expulsion that make students more likely to drop out (James and Turner 2017, 10) or lead to their being disproportionately streamed into applied rather than academic fields. In other words, the stereotype seeks a self-fulfilling prophecy to bring into existence that which it imagines as (B)lack. In this way, the stereotype of Black-as-lack makes possible and indeed *produces* the very idea of Black educational underachievement and underrepresentation in the academy.

Time to Tell a Different Story: A Talented Dozen

This chapter is also an act of historical memory. It tells the stories of Black lives resolutely pursuing their higher education aspirations across time and space, from Indigenous territories to separate British colonies, to British North America and, finally, the Dominion of Canada. I share a dozen stories that highlight the diversity and nuances of Blackness and focus on three longer stories of individuals who exemplify the scholar-activist that is a hallmark of Black lives in the academy. What these remarkable individuals all have in common is their relentless pursuit of educational and professional aspirations and, simultaneously, a necessary resistance to racism, structural exclusion, and marginality. As they pursued their own dreams, they also sought to carve alternative futures for Black lives by forcing open doors to some of Canada's premier institutions of higher education. These counter-stories of racial uplift are indispensable sources of resistance to Black erasure in Canadian studies more generally. There are several reasons to focus on figures in classics and law in the social science disciplines and humanities, and in medicine in the science, technology, engineering, and mathematics (STEM) disciplines. The earliest fields of study in the British colonies included classics, theology, law, medicine, and nursing. The stories span the vastness of Canada, from New Brunswick and Nova Scotia in Atlantic Canada to Alberta and the prairies, and they show the manifold ways in which colonial institutions – created without Black people in mind – and prevailing norms function to preserve white normativity in professional life. Black people who sought entry into these academic institutions often had to depend on the prevailing white establishment's willingness to recognize their equal humanity and, in turn, their equal ability to excel in any chosen field.

It is no small irony, then, that the denial of the Black capacity for excellence in the contemporary moment often rests upon the claim that there is no Black past worthy of note. The dozen stories I share foreground Black figures who, had they lived in a world of racial equality and justice, would be household names and listed among the great Canadians. Because of their race and the impermeable colour line, their contributions have been largely hidden from history or, at best, marginalized in the stories Canadians tell about themselves. While fragments of their stories can be found in some Canadian biographies, other bits are scattered across internet sites and sometimes relegated to footnotes in published works. In the case of many trailblazing Black women, like Myrtle Blackwood Smith, the first Black woman called to the Bar in Ontario, there is no accessible biography at all. In the case of other Black women, like physician Sophia B. Jones, there is greater recognition of her academic and community contributions in the United States than in Canada.

Perhaps unsurprisingly, in the scattered stories on the internet, as elsewhere, there are significant errors, which tend to be replicated and recirculated. There are, for example, at least three men who are identified as Canada's first Black lawyer (Stokes 2015): Abraham Beverley (1851–1907) of New Brunswick, Robert Sutherland (1830–1878) of Ontario, and James R. Johnston (1876–1915) of Nova Scotia. One of the three "firsts," Walker, was born in Belleisle Creek, a descendent of early Black Loyalists in New Brunswick. Walker's story is emblematic of the thwarted ambitions of talented Black people in the Victorian era. In pursuit of his aspirations, Walker moved to the United States to study at the National University in Washington, DC. After graduation he returned to Saint John and completed a three-year legal apprenticeship with George Godfrey Gilbert, was admitted as an attorney to the Supreme Court of New Brunswick in June 1881, and was called to the Saint John Bar in June 1882. Walker established a legal practice, but, in the absence of white clientele, and with only 1.2 per cent of the city's population being Black, it was unsustainable. Like many of his contemporaries, Walker was concerned with racism and transforming the colour line in society. Despite being "the senior Negro lawyer in the British Empire" (Cahill 1994), he was often excluded from professional gatherings and recognition by his white peers. One glaring example, which garnered public controversy and commentary about societal racism at the time, was Walker not being invited to the December 1885 banquet to commemorate the centenary of the New Brunswick Bar (Cahill 1994). The cumulative experiences of racial inequality led Walker to relocate to Atlanta, Georgia, where he had heard that the "outlook … for a lawyer of my race trained in the rigid discipline of British Courts and British institutions generally is exceedingly hopeful and encouraging" (Walker, quoted in Cahill 1994). After a two-year stint in Atlanta, Walker returned to Nova Scotia and became the first student enrolled at Saint John Law School – which became the University of New Brunswick Law School – and graduated in October 1892. He was appointed the Saint John Law Society librarian in 1892 and served until 1899. Over the course of his professional life, he wrote numerous papers, founded the *Neith,* a monthly literary and public affairs magazine that operated in Saint John from February 1903 to January 1904, wrote for the *Saint John Globe,* was president of the African Civilization Movement, and was an all-round man of letters. In his little-known text *"The Negro Problem; or, the Philosophy of Race Development from a Canadian Standpoint,"* which he first delivered at the Wheat Street Baptist Church in Atlanta, Georgia, in December 1889, and was published in

1890, Walker drew a distinction between a person's status from birth and that acquired "with knowledge, with wisdom, with learning." He further argued that in the pursuit of knowledge and learning there are "no royal roads. They open their doors to all on equal terms. Within their walls the prince is no better than the peasant, nor the peasant no better than the prince" (Walker 1890, 10). The Black community petitioned the minister of justice to recognize Walker's many contributions to law and society with a "QC" (Queen's Counsel) designation; however, successive Conservative and Liberal government ministers were reluctant to brook the opposition from the white legal establishment. To honour Walker as the University of New Brunswick's Faculty of Law's first student, whom they describe as the first Canadian-born Black lawyer, the Abraham Beverley Walker Scholarship was established initially "to promote and recognize excellence and diversity in the first-year class." In 2021, the eligibility was revised and the scholarship "is awarded to a first-year law student and now will include a caveat that a Black student be given preference" (Mallees 2021).

The story of the second figure sometimes identified as Canada's first Black lawyer was unearthed by Queen's University students. Robert Sutherland was the sixtieth student to enrol at Queen's and the institution's first Black graduate. He was called to the Ontario Bar in 1855 and, after sustained advocacy by students, the university now has many honours named after him. I will elaborate upon Sutherland in one of the longer stories below.

A third figure often characterized as Canada's first Black lawyer is Delos Rogest Davis, who was born in Colchester Township in Ontario. After completing eleven years of legal studies, Davis could not find a white lawyer who would take him on as a legal apprentice. In the end, he had to appeal to the Ontario legislature under special statute to become a solicitor. According to the special statute, "In consequence of prejudices against his colour, and because of his being of African descent he had not been articled to any attorney or solicitor" (Backhouse 1999, 375; Black 2015). Davis was called to the Ontario Bar on 15 November 1885. Facing opposition from white lawyers in the Law Society of Upper Canada, Davis again had to appeal under special statute to become a barrister in 1886 (Thomas 1998; Backhouse 1999, 177). After over two decades of legal practice, in 1910 Davis was appointed a King's Counsel, which made him the first Black person in the British Empire to attain the honour (Black 2015). While some suggest this makes Davis the second Canadian Black lawyer after Sutherland, that depends on how one understands the time and space of "Canada." Sutherland was called to the Bar in what was British North America at the time, whereas Davis was called to the Bar after Confederation. At the University of Windsor he continues to be characterized as Canada's first Black lawyer and, since 1969, the Delos Rogest Davis, K.C. Memorial Award has been given to a "student who best exemplifies the ideals of Delos Rogest Davis, especially through their community involvement and contribution."

Among the "firsts" there is, too, James Robinson Johnston. Born in Halifax on 12 March 1876, he is either the second Canadian-born Black lawyer or the fourth Black lawyer (inclusive of African American) in Canada. Johnston initially attended an inner-city and racially segregated school for Black students; however, after school reform, he became the first African Nova Scotian to attend Albo Street School, which was then an all-white school. He then completed studies at the Halifax Academy before attending university. Overcoming the legally and socially imposed disadvantages of his time, Johnston became the province's first African Nova Scotian graduate of Dalhousie University, earning a Bachelor of Literature (BLitt) in 1896 (Fingard 1998). After completing his legal studies at Dalhousie in 1898, Johnston was called to the Nova Scotia Bar in July 1900 and became the first Black lawyer to practise law in Nova Scotia. A short biography of Johnston on the Dalhousie University website notes Johnston reached these "unprecedented heights" despite having to navigate and overcome racism "at almost every step: as a young boy in a segregated and underfunded Black school system; as a Dal law student, resisting thinly veiled barbs like the last line written in his class biography ("Long may he live to be the chosen pleader for his race in the police court of the city") (Dalhousie University n.d.). After he completed his legal studies and despite his prominence in the community – for example, he was the only Black member of the community invited to participate in the royal visit of the Duke and Duchess of Cornwall in 1901 – Johnston had to face Halifax's "tokenism as the occasional currency of participation" (Dalhousie University n.d.). Johnston was actively engaged in the community, the church, and the Black Freemasons' lodge. Influenced by Booker T. Washington, he advocated for an industrial school for Black children (Cahill 1992; Fingard 1998). According to Judith Fingard, Johnston's "short career represented the apogee of 19th century African Nova Scotian ambitions" (Fingard 1998). On March 3, 1915, Johnston's life came to an early and tragic end at age 38, when he was shot in his home by his brother-in-law in still-mysterious circumstances (Cahill 2012, quoted in White 2016). In his honour, Dalhousie established the James R. Johnston Chair in Black Canadian Studies,[3] and the James R. Johnston Graduate Entrance Scholarship in the Faculty of Graduate Studies.

It was sixty-eight years after the first Black man and fifty-seven years after the first white woman were called to the Bar that Black women in Canada were able to pursue similar aspirations. Black women had to overcome the intersecting obstacles of the colour bar and the glass ceiling. Ivy Lawrence Maynier (1921–99), for example, was born in Montreal to parents from Trinidad and Tobago, obtained a BA from McGill University, was president of the Women's Debating Club, and was the first woman student to win the McGill Debating Key. Maynier went on to become the first Black woman, and woman of colour, to graduate from the University of Toronto Law School, in 1945, and the first student to graduate with an honours degree in international law. Had she stayed in Ontario or returned to Quebec, she likely would have become the first Black woman to be called to the Bar in Canada. However, Maynier was called to the British Bar in 1947 and practised law in Britain and in Trinidad, later worked with the United States Information Services in Paris, and taught in Continuing Studies at the University of the West Indies in Jamaica. This global movement reinforces the view of Lennox Bernard, a resident tutor at UWI, who said Maynier "moved with ease and panache among the upper class and the intellectual elite, but she also related directly to the various dispossessed groups and communities ... She was pragmatic, innovative, people-oriented, radical at times, strong-willed and an agent of social change" (Bernard, quoted in Meyers 2004). An endowed scholarship for marginalized students is co-named after Maynier and her classmate and former fiancé, Peter Fuld, a self-described German "half-Jew" who, like Maynier, faced discrimination and marginality in the university and broader community in 1940s Ontario (1–3). A 1968 *Ebony Magazine* article about Maynier, Fuld, and the scholarship entitled it "The Legacy of a Love Affair." The two were engaged and planned to spend their lives together, but Fuld's German mother, Fran Ida Fuld, objected and reportedly threatened to kill herself if her son married a "Negro" (Sanders 1968, 94). Fuld died of cancer and in his will bequeathed 15 per cent of his estate to Maynier; although his mother challenged the will in court, Maynier eventually prevailed. Upon her death, Maynier bequeathed $600,000 to the Faculty of Law at the University of Toronto to establish the Maynier-Fuld scholarship for marginalized students.

The person who did become Canada's first Black woman lawyer, Violet King Henry (1929–82), was born in Calgary, a descendant of Black pioneers who migrated from Oklahoma to northern Alberta in the early 1900s. Henry's story is one of the three among the talented dozen that I will further elaborate upon below.

A person about whom relatively little is known is Myrtle Blackwood-Smith, who graduated with a BA from Sir George Williams University (now Concordia University) in Montreal in 1959. Blackwood-Smith became the first Black female graduate of Osgoode Law School and was called to the Ontario Bar in 1960. The fragments of Blackwood-Smith's stories need to be collected and stitched together, along with her contributions to the broader society. While little is known, it is necessary to include her name and what we know of her achievement here.

In STEM disciplines in Canada, a number of Black hidden figures are submerged in stories about universities and colleges. They need to be made visible in the Canadian higher education landscape. The invisibility of these Black pioneers reflects the structural erasure or, at best, the misremembering of Black Canadians in Canadian history. As with the lawyers, there is a question of who the "first" Black medical student and physician in Canada was – Alexander Thomas Augusta (1825–90), Anderson Ruffin Abbott (1837–1913), or Kenneth Melville (1902–75). Among these pioneers, the Rev. Dr. Frank Wright of Quebec City (1827–1908) is nowhere to be found, and he may, in fact, be the first Canadian-born Black physician.

"Almost a century before Rosa Parks defied Alabama's racial segregation laws, Trinity [College, University of Toronto] graduate Dr. Alexander Thomas Augusta refused to give up his seat in the 'whites only' section of a Washington, DC streetcar" (Taylor 2015). Known as a man of great intellect and courage, Augusta was born in Virginia in 1825 to parents who were free Blacks and lived in Maryland as a youth. Denied access to the University of Pennsylvania because he was Black, Augusta and his Native American wife Mary O. Burgoin moved to Toronto in 1850 (Fenison 2009). He was the first Black student accepted into the University of Toronto's Medical School in the 1850s, and he went on to obtain his bachelor of medicine in 1860. Upon completion, he dedicated himself to antislavery activities and to providing medical services and advancing literacy for the poor. He excelled in his professional life, including becoming head of the Toronto City Hospital (Fenison 2009). Despite these substantial contributions to medicine and to the broader community, Augusta felt called to do more – in this case, to use his medical training to support the emancipation of Black people. He wrote to President Lincoln and asked permission to serve in the "coloured regiments" that had been created in the Union Army. A storied thirteen-year career in the United States military saw Augusta become the first Black person commissioned as a medical officer and his promotion to lieutenant colonel, at that time the highest rank achieved by a Black military officer. Nonetheless, Augusta was denied entry into the American Medical Association by white peers. Undaunted, on 15 January 1870 he and other Black doctors created a more inclusive institution, the National Medical Society of the District of Columbia. Augusta returned to the academy and achieved yet another historical milestone as the first Black professor of medicine at Howard University's Medical College in Washington, DC, where he remained until 1877. Augusta died in 1890 and, even in death, broke the colour bar as the first Black military officer to be buried in Arlington National Cemetery (Fenison 2009).

Anderson Ruffin Abbott graduated from the University of Toronto one year after Alexander Thomas Augusta. By many historical accounts, this makes Abbott, who was born in Toronto in 1837, the first Canadian-born Black person to graduate from the Toronto School of Medicine. For example, an Ontario Heritage Trust plaque in his honour in Chatham reads, "He received his medical licence in 1861, becoming the first Canadian-born doctor of African descent" (Mackey 2018, 7). A 1998 book by Dalyce Newby, which is volume 22 of the Canadian medical lives series, is entitled *Anderson Ruffin Abbott: First Afro-Canadian Doctor*. As Frank Mackey writes, however, the Rev. Dr. William Wright was "the first black medical student at McGill, and 13 years ahead of Anderson Ruffin Abbott" (7; Hauch 2018). More important than who came first is the fact that these Black trailblazers are hidden, scrubbed from historical memory, even at the institutions at which they studied and worked.

Abbott was educated at the Buxton Mission School and was among the first three Black students to be admitted at the Toronto Academy of Knox College, where he excelled and was an honour student (Hauch 2018). From 1856 to 1857 he attended Oberlin College's Preparatory Department in Ohio, a co-ed liberal arts college with an abolitionist philosophy. Abbott was admitted to the Toronto School of Medicine, an affiliate of the University of Toronto, in 1857, and worked with Alexander Thomas Augusta, who was a mentor and later a good friend. At the age of twenty-three, Abbott completed his MD at the University of Toronto in 1861 and earned his medical licence from the Medical Board of Upper Canada in 1862. Following a similar path to Augusta, in 1863 Abbott joined the Union Army and went on to become a decorated soldier. Over the course of their military service the two men's paths crossed, and, indeed, both attended events at the White House hosted by President Lincoln. In April 1865 Abbott was in attendance at President Abraham Lincoln's bedside after he had been shot by John Wilkes Booth and was among the few family and friends who were with Lincoln when he died. Later, Lincoln's wife, Mary Todd Lincoln, gave Abbott a shawl that Lincoln had used on route to the inauguration on 4 March 1861. Abbott was discharged from military service in 1865 and immediately enrolled at Trinity College in Toronto. He graduated in 1867 with a bachelor of medicine and on 5 June 1869 registered with the College of Physicians and Surgeons. Abbot practised medicine in Chatham and was the first Black person to serve as coroner, a position he held from 1874 to 1881, and also served as the president of the Chatham Medical Society. It is also notable that, like many of his generation, Abbott was actively involved in promoting literacy and education in the Black community. From 1873 to 1880 he served as president of the Wilberforce Educational Institute and worked to prepare Black students for university. Abbott died on 29 December 1913 and is buried at Toronto Necropolis.

Few, if any, of the accounts of firsts ever include William Wright, who was born in Quebec City, in what was then Lower Canada, in 1827 (Stock 2018; Mackey 2018). Perhaps this is because Wright, like his father, William Wright Sr., and his siblings, is often described in the language of the time as "Creole" and "Coloured." More likely it is because of the manifold ways in which Black history is mis-remembered, if remembered at all, and how that requires a constant reassertion of belonging. By all accounts Wright was "a brilliant student, gifted both in the medical sciences and in what was called 'the classics' – the Greek and Latin languages and literatures" (Stock 2018, 22). At age fifteen he began his medical studies as a student-apprentice with Dr. James Crawford of McGill Medical School, won numerous prizes as a student, and qualified as a physician at age twenty (Stock 2018, 22). After graduation Wright travelled across Europe, visiting Paris, London, and Dublin, and completed a medical certificate at the University of Edinburgh. When he returned to Quebec in 1849 he was a licentiate of the Royal College of Edinburgh as well as an associate member of the Surgical College of Ireland (Mackey 2018, 8). Deeply committed to serving the poor, Wright was the founding secretary of and an attending physician at a Montreal dispensary. In 1850 he was appointed to the medical faculty at McGill and began a distinguished thirty-three-year teaching and clinical career, including as a demonstrator of anatomy, as a chair-holder in medical jurisprudence, a professor and chair of Materia Medica (pharmacology) from 1854 to 1883, and co-editor with Dr. Duncan McCallum of *The Medical Chronicle or Montreal Monthly Journal of Medicine & Surgery* (Stock 2018, 22; Mackey 2018, 8). Among the articles he published was an 1858 examination of the medicinal uses of marijuana (Stock 2018, 22). Despite this contribution, Kenneth J. Melville continues to be characterized in some sources, including at McGill, simply as the institution's first Black professor and first Black chair of Pharmacology, and Abbott is characterized in some McGill publications as Canada's first Black physician (Mackey 2018).

If Wright is generally invisible in Quebec and Canadian studies, this is certainly the case for physician Sophia B. Jones (1857–92), who was born in Chatham, Ontario. "Sophia Jones exemplifies the way in which women followed the opportunities of higher education opening to them in the United States, and used that education as passage through and beyond the restrictions on women's public roles in late-Victorian Canada" (Reid-Maroney 2004, 94. Because she was a woman and Black, she was denied full access to the Toronto Medical School. Determined to pursue her aspirations, Jones moved to the United States, completed an MD in 1885, and became the first Black woman to graduate from the University of Michigan's Medical School. In that year she also became the first Black professor at Spelman College in Atlanta, Georgia. In addition to starting Spelman's nursing program, Jones was the author of a number of publications, including "Fifty Years of Negro Public Health" in 1913, which appeared in "Negro Progress," a special issue of *Political and Social Sciences*. She also obtained a patent for a "barrel trunk" in 1890 (Spelman College 2016). Over the course of her career, Jones pursued opportunities across the United States, working at Wilberforce University and practising medicine across the U.S., including St. Louis, Philadelphia, and Kansas City. Too few Canadians know about Jones; in fact, in some biographical accounts she is characterized as an African American, and in other instances as a Canadian-born American physician. At the University of Michigan there is a Sophia B. Jones Lecture in Infectious Diseases, a Sophia B. Jones conference room, and the Black students' alumni society, Fitzbutler Jones Alumni Society, is named in her honour (MF 2002, 34–5).

Now, I want to pivot and elaborate more fully the stories of three Black trailblazers who navigated segregated societies and beat what seemed like insurmountable odds, to excel in the Canadian academy: Robert Sutherland (1830–78), a graduate of Queen's University, Kenneth J. Melville (1902–75), a graduate of McGill University, and Violet King Henry (1929–82), a graduate of the University of Alberta. The stories of these hidden figures reflect centuries of grit, determination, and Black excellence in the face of colonial racism. Their stories disrupt the stereotypical figure that stands in for Black scholars in Canadian universities and colleges and that functions to preserve a normative white social order.

Robert Sutherland: From Scholar to Alumnus-Philanthropist

The inscription "May his devotion to this alma mater not pass into oblivion" is written in Latin at the gravesite of Robert Sutherland, Queen's University's first Black graduate and the alumnus who saved the university from bankruptcy when he bequeathed his estate to it (Church 2009). Given the significance of Sutherland's contribution to Queen's, one might well have expected him to be given pride of place in the hallowed halls of the university. But despite the inscription and Sutherland's devotion to his alma mater, his philanthropic contributions were largely hidden for over a century. Until the inscribed tombstone was placed at his graveside by Queen's University Principal George Monro Grant in 1878,

Sutherland had been buried in an unmarked grave in Toronto's Mt. Pleasant Cemetery. The first physical recognition of Sutherland on the Queen's University campus was not until 1975, when the City of Kingston under Mayor George Speal placed a plaque in Grant Hall (Pearce 2016).

Robert Sutherland was an accomplished student, alumnus, and philanthropist. Born into slavery in colonial Jamaica, his mother was Jamaican and his father was believed to be Scottish. He was three years old when slavery was abolished in the British Empire. At the age of nineteen, and with the financial support of his father, Sutherland moved to Canada and enrolled at Queen's College (now Queen's University). He was the sixtieth student in the institution's history. A gifted and award-winning student, Sutherland excelled in classics and mathematics. "As a freshman, he won four academic awards. By the next year, his classmates awarded him a general merit award for the quality of his schoolwork. These were just a few of the many accolades Sutherland would receive" (Pearce 2016), and by gradation he had won fourteen awards and prizes. He was a valued member, as well as treasurer, of the Dialectic Society, and led the club to victory in seven of the ten debates in which they participated. When Sutherland graduated, he was one of only eleven students in his cohort. In 1852 Sutherland became the first Black, and indeed the first student of colour, graduate from the university, completing his studies with honours in classics and mathematics. Three years later, in 1855, he achieved another first when he completed his law studies through apprenticeship and examination and became the first Black lawyer in British North America (now Canada) and in the Law Society of Upper Canada.

Upon completion of his law studies at Queen's, Sutherland relocated to the city of Berlin, now Kitchener, and then to Walkerton, where he established a law practice. In Berlin, inhabited by many Black Americans who had escaped slavery, Sutherland assisted former slaves with obtaining land title. In Walkerton he was elected the town's reeve. On 2 June 1878 Sutherland contracted and eventually succumbed to pneumonia, when he was only forty-eight years old. In his will Sutherland bequeathed his entire estate of some $13,000 (equivalent to a quarter million today) to Queen's University, a place where he felt he had been treated with dignity and respect. For Sutherland, the university had been a refuge from the plantation slavery of the Caribbean, the chattel slavery throughout the southern United States, and the colonial racism of the day. He told friends that it was a space in which "he had always been treated as a gentleman." It is in the context of this experience that the alumnus became the man who "saved Queen's University" from financial ruin (Morgan 2013). The generous gift rescued the university from possible annexation by the University of Toronto. As Anthony Morgan notes, this made Sutherland Queen's first major donor. Moreover, the size of the donation was also remarkable because "research has yet to uncover an instance of any other private individual in Canada donating to an existing Canadian university an amount equivalent to the institution's operating budget" (Morgan 2013).

What accounts for almost a century of invisibility? Duncan McDowall, a Queen's university professor and author of *Testing Tradition*, an official institutional history of the university on its 175th anniversary, suggests the location of the university in a predominantly white Anglo-Saxon community made it "convenient to forget about Sutherland" (McDowall, quoted in Bayes-Fleming 2016). This draws attention to the matter of which national memories we choose to remember and, in the case of Sutherland, which ones we somehow "forget." Despite acknowledging how space and whiteness circumscribe historical memory, McDowall understates the significance of race and colonialism and their interrelated impact on memory, and on the coloniality of knowledge and power. In fact, McDowell goes on to suggest that "Sutherland just seemed to slip out of the memory of the university. There's no conscious act of suppressing his memory – he just sort of drifted out of it" (Bayes-Fleming 2016). Yet, as we know from the university's belated acknowledgment of and apology for the Queen's Senate's decision in 1919 to accept the recommendation of Medical School Dean James Connell to expel and ban Black medical students, race – specifically whiteness – mattered to the institution's ranking and prestige (Dannetta 2019). At that time, the institution made the instrumental decision to ban Black medical students, many from the Caribbean, to appease American peer institutions that maintained and enforced the colour bar. Moreover, for over several decades, university leaders consciously misled those who inquired about the rationale for, and implications of, the ban on Black students.

In Sutherland's case, formal institutional recognition came only after a small group of determined students launched a campaign to change this invisibility and to highlight the fact that without Sutherland there might not be a Queen's University as we know it today. The students faced many institutional roadblocks, including, initially, a lack of support from the university's board of trustees. In the late 1990s, student protests were held at Queen's by members of the Alma Mater Society, which also established the AMS Robert Sutherland Task Force (RSTF), led by its first Black student president, Greg Frankson. The purpose of the student mobilization and task force was to "seek a space on campus which would be appropriate to recognize the contributions of Robert Sutherland, the university's first major benefactor and first Black graduate" (Queen's

University n.d.), In 1997 the RSTK made four recommendations: first, a Robert Sutherland Award of Excellence in Debating to recognize a member of the Queen's Debating Union; second, a Robert Sutherland Prize for a graduating self-identified student of colour who had championed diversity on campus; third, the naming of a room in the John Deutsch University Centre after Sutherland; and finally, the Robert Sutherland Visiting Lecturer position to attract diverse scholars to the campus. As well, Frankson and the AMS lobbied Queen's Planning and Development to get a building named after Sutherland.

In December 2008, efforts were once again stalled when one trustee argued that the university could not honour Sutherland with a building because the previous principal, David C. Smith, had not been given such an honour. Other trustees had doubts about whether they would be able to raise the necessary funds to honour a Black alumnus by naming a building after him, and others still thought the unnamed buildings should be used for major fundraising campaigns that would then be named after a donor. In 2008 the trustees referred the issue to Queen's University Principal Tom Williams to come up with a proposal to resolve the issue and report back at the March 2009 meeting. At that time, nothing was done because they were advised that naming buildings presented major opportunities for donors and, as Frankson noted, this was said "without understanding the irony of that statement" (Pearce 2016).

It took another decade after the students' initial efforts, and 131 years after Sutherland's death, for the Queen's Board of Trustees to vote unanimously on a student motion to recognize Sutherland by naming the policy studies building Sutherland Hall (Queen's University n.d.) At the ceremony to mark the occasion, Student Rector Leora Jackson said that the naming "marks a permanent recognition of Queen's diverse roots and the multiple individuals and communities that have shaped, and that continue to shape, the university and Canada" (Queen's Encyclopedia, n.d.) Sacha Atherly, the president of the African Caribbean Student Association, noted that the honour was a fitting way to recognize Sutherland's "great successes and contributions to Queen's and Ontario. It is important to put his donation in perspective; it is the reason that any of us are able to study and work at Queen's University today" (Queen's University n.d.) There are now seven forms of recognition for Sutherland at Queen's University: the Sutherland Hall, Plaque, and Memorial Room; those arising from the student recommendations, including the Robert Sutherland Visitorship, Prize, and Award for Excellence in Debating; and, as well, Queen's University offers the Robert Sutherland Memorial Entrance Bursary, the Sutherland Fellowships, and the Robert Sutherland–Harry Jerome Entrance Award.

Kenneth J. Melville: Community-Engaged Scholar

A second hidden-figure story I want to elaborate upon is that of Kenneth J. Melville, whose biography also disrupts conceptions of a singular Black story in the Canadian academy. For the longest time Melville was believed to have been McGill University's first Black medical student. However, that honour goes to Rev. Dr. William Wright, who was born in Quebec City and is believed to have been the first Black medical doctor in British North America. Wright also served as the fifth department chair (1854–83) of pharmacology and therapeutics. Here I focus on Melville who, in addition to having been an outstanding academic in medicine, was a scholar whose academic path reflects the indispensable role played by Black academics as community-engaged scholars and in university–community engagement. Melville was born and raised in Kingston, Jamaica, which was a British colony at the time. Melville's family immigrated to Montreal in the 1920s. Despite racism and social obstacles arising from the colour bar, Melville "attained a level of success that many would have thought impossible for a Black man of his time and place" (Fine 2016a). He obtained a bachelor of science and an MDCM (Medicinæ Doctorem et Chirurgiæ Magistrum) in 1926 and a master of science in 1931. Upon the completion of his medical studies, Melville was awarded the Holmes Gold Medal as top student in his graduating class. Subsequently, he won a postdoctoral fellowship to study at the Pasteur Institute in Paris, which was known for its pathbreaking work on biology, infectious diseases, and vaccines.

In 1953 Melville blazed yet another trail at McGill University when he became the first Black person, and the first person from the Global South, to hold the position of chair of the Department of Pharmacology and Therapeutics, a position he held until 1967 (Fine 2016a). Over the course of his illustrious career, spanning five decades, Melville published over eighty peer-reviewed scientific articles on wide-ranging topics such as the physiology of stress responses and the risks of specific recreational drugs. He was an internationally renowned pharmacologist and a founding member of the International Union of Basic and Clinical Pharmacology. He was widely respected within the university and the broader community as a teacher and mentor to students from Nigeria, Jamaica, and across the Global South, as well as a leader in Montreal's growing West Indian community (Fine 2016b). Moreover, Kenneth and Gladys Melville's daughter Enid Melville (McGill BA, MDCM 1959), a psychiatrist, was also a trailblazer as one of only two women to graduate in her year. She is believed to have been the first Black woman to graduate from the undergraduate medical program at McGill University.

For much of Melville's tenure at McGill University, Montreal was characterized by normative and legislated racism. Throughout his career Melville demonstrated a deep commitment to his academic vocation, and to the advancement of human and civil rights and community empowerment. He recognized clearly that professional success did not preclude the indignities of racial profiling and discrimination. Many private businesses engaged in "colour-coded" (Backhouse 1999) commercial practices that denied equal services to Black people in restaurants, accommodation, and other services. For example, on 11 July 1936, the York Tavern, which was attached to the Montreal Forum, refused to serve Fred Christie because he was Black (J.W. Walker 1997; Adams 2012). Montreal's Black community mobilized in solidarity with Christie, and Melville chaired a fundraising committee for Christie's resulting suit against the York Tavern (*Christie v York Corporation*) (J.W. Walker 1997; B. Walker 2012; Adams 2012).

Although Christie won his case at trial and was awarded twenty-five dollars in damages (J.W. Walker 1997), he lost on appeal, where the majority held that "a merchant or trader is free to carry on his business in the manner that he conceives to be best for that business" (J.W. Walker 1997; B. Walker 2012). The case was appealed to the higher court, and on 10 May 1939, it held that private businesses could discriminate on the basis of race. Chief Justice Lyman Poore Duff, writing for the majority – there was only one dissenting justice among the five – advanced the Canadian mythology of "polite racism" (Smith 2003) when he argued that the York Tavern employee who refused to sell beer to Christie "did so quietly, politely and without causing any scene or commotion whatsoever" (Adams 2018), and that the real problem was Christie, who "persisted in demanding beer after he had been so refused and went to the length of calling the police, which was entirely unwarranted by the circumstances" (Adams 2018). The Christie case is one among many others that disrupted the myth of Canada as a race-neutral or colour-blind society (Smith 2003). The case reminds us too of a persistent reality: education and professional standing do not inoculate Black scholars against everyday racism, racial profiling, and racial discrimination in services, accommodation, and the like. This was not the only occasion during his professional career on which Melville had to take a stand against racism and the colour line in the service industry. In the late 1960s, while attending a medical congress in Atlantic City, New Jersey, Melville and seven other physicians were arrested for demanding food at a cafeteria that refused to serve him because he was Black (Fine 2016b).

Melville's contributions to the academy and to Black upliftment were significant, and even noticed across the border, where he was featured in popular African-American periodicals such as *Ebony Magazine* and *Jet Magazine* (Cobbs 1963). Indeed, in "A New Dawn in Medicine," W. Montagne Cobbs highlighted how both "Northern and Western medical schools, which had hitherto admitted only a token Negro now and then, are now making honest efforts to secure able Negro students" (166). The article also named a number of outstanding Black scholars in medicine, whom it argued neither the profession nor the various Black communities regarded "as a racial miracle." Black excellence in medicine was increasingly seen as ordinary, and they "no longer marvel when talented and well-trained Negroes move into higher reaches of professional activity" (166).

Melville retired and became a professor emeritus at McGill in 1972. In his honour, the Melville Fellowship Prize in Pharmacology was established and is awarded annually to the best poster presentations on Pharmacology Research Day. As well, the Melville Undergraduate Research Bursary in Pharmacology and Therapeutics was established with the aim of increasing "diversity in the pharmacology graduate program by offering funding for summer research experience and mentorship to an undergraduate student from an underrepresented equity group."

Violet King: From Scholar to a Life of Public Service

Violet Pauline King Henry (hereafter King) is among the many trailblazing Black women who have largely remained hidden figures in the annals of Canadian higher education in general, and Black studies and women and gender studies in particular. "People told me it wasn't a good idea for a girl to be a lawyer, particularly a colored girl – so I went ahead" (King quoted in *Winnipeg Free Press*, 5 May 1956a). This was Violet King's response to the challenge presented by the intersections of the colour line and the glass ceiling – that is, the belief that women, particularly Black women and women of colour, should not aspire to pursue professional careers in law. King pursued her dreams and, in the process, became a woman of many firsts throughout her education and professional career in Canada and, subsequently, the United States. After entering the Faculty of Arts at the University of Alberta in 1948, she completed a BA in history in 1952. It is not known how many Black students, if any, were in the Faculty of Arts, or at the university at that time.

When King entered the Faculty of Law at the University of Alberta, she was one of only three women among 142 students. Fulfilling her high school dream – a caption on a grade 12 photo of King reads, "Violet wants to be a criminal lawyer" – she was the sole woman in her 1953 graduating class when she completed her LLB. This also made King the first Black person to graduate from the University of Alberta's Faculty of Law. After articling at the law firm of Edward J. McCormick, Q.C. in Calgary, on 2 June 1954, King became the first Black person to be called to the Alberta Bar, and the first Black woman to practise law in Canada. Marking the historic moment, the 18 June 1954 headline in *The Western Farm Leader* highlighted King's feat: "First Negro Woman in Canada Called to Bar" (*Western Farm Leader* 1954). The article elaborated that King was "setting a precedent in the annals of Canadian law ... the first negro woman to practice law in the Dominion, and one of the relatively few women now practicing." As well, the article reported that, as a student, King "distinguished herself in her studies, [and] took an active part in students' affairs at the university, where she was most popular."

Yet, despite all of this, few Canadians have ever heard of Violet King. King was born in Calgary on 18 October 1929. She was the third of four children of Stella King, a seamstress, and John King, a sleeping car porter with the Canadian Pacific Railway. King's paternal grandparents were among Alberta's Black pioneers, African Americans who emigrated from Oklahoma in 1911 and established all-Black communities in Keystone (now Breton), in central Alberta, and in places like Amber Valley in northern Alberta. Her brother, Theodore "Ted" King, was an accountant and became an Alberta civil rights leader and president of the Alberta Association for the Advancement of Coloured People, which was founded to "promote goodwill and to seek equality in social and civic activities throughout Alberta" (Mohamed 2018). During Ted King's tenure as president he legally challenged both overt and, especially, more covert racial discrimination in theatres, restaurants, and accommodation.

King excelled in her studies at Calgary's Crescent High School and in grade 12 became the president of the Girls' Club. She continued this engaged leadership throughout her studies and professional life. At the University of Alberta she was vice-president of the Students' Union (SU) and served with then-SU president Peter Lougheed, who went on to become premier of Alberta (1971–85). King, along with Don Andrews, was the Alberta representative to a three-day conference of the National Federation of Canadian University Students, held at McMaster University in Hamilton (King and Andrews 1951, 1). She co-wrote a report on that experience, one that highlighted a strong commitment to internationalism: support for foreign students, sending student delegations to India, all-varsity aid for equipment to the universities of Karachi, Jamia Millia Islamia, and Delhi, and study-abroad seminars in places such as Ceylon (Sri Lanka), then Yugoslavia, Israel, and Italy because of their capacity to host such events (2).

King's extraordinary student leadership was recognized in March 1952 at Colour Night when she and three white male student peers were awarded the Executive A Gold Ring. King was commended for her many student leadership roles, including serving "three years on the Pembina House Committee, two years on the Women's Discipline Committee, two years on the Golden Key Society, two years on the SUB House Committee, [and as] the ISS delegate to the Hamilton Conference, and her class historian" (2). The three men honoured alongside King – Peter Lougheed, Garth Fryett, and Ivan L. Head – would go on to leadership roles in law, government, and the private and non-profit sectors – all three became Queen's Counsels. As well, Lougheed, as noted previously, became premier of Alberta, Fryett became a corporate lawyer, and Ivan L. Head became a foreign policy advisor to Prime Minister Pierre Elliott Trudeau, with whom he co-wrote *The Canadian Way: Shaping Canada's Foreign Policy, 1968–1984* (Head and Trudeau 1995).

Arguably, had King not been a Black woman in a society stratified by gender and race, such doors would also have been opened to her. A young feminist, King was a member of the Blue Stocking Club, which took its name from the Blue Stockings Society of eighteenth-century England. At the University of Alberta, it was a student association that provided space for young women to discuss history and how to engage in public affairs. When King served as the Student Union's vice president and the "Senior Woman" on the SUB House Committee, she also supported junior women student leaders.

Throughout her academic and professional career, King was actively involved in advancing women's rights, women in leadership, and equal pay for equal work. After King was called to the Bar, she worked two full-time jobs – one in private practice in which she represented clients on domestic violence, estate and criminal law cases (*Winnipeg Free Press* 1956a, 49), and a second job in the claims department of a Calgary insurance company. King suggested there were not many women in private practice because women lawyers had "not come into their own yet," but she added, "I don't think enough [women] have tried private practice" (49). Her advocacy anticipated intersectional feminism with attention to gender, race, class, and religious difference. King was a sought-after speaker, and stories about her regularly appeared in the "Women's World" section of prairie newspapers. King gave a speech to the Beta Sigma Phi Sorority Banquet in Calgary in 1955, where she pointed out how the intersections of race and gender required Black women and women of colour to be twice as good to secure jobs comparable to those for white women: "It is too bad that a Japanese, Chinese or coloured girl has to outshine others to secure a position." In "Lawless Woman," a January 1956 speech at the Women's University Club at the University of Lethbridge, King noted that "despite the progress which has been made towards equality for women under the law there are many instances in which women lack cooperation and protection of the law," including in cases of wealth accruing from joint contributions to family business (*Lethbridge Herald*, 17 January 1956, 11; and 13 January 1956, 14).

Two years after being called to the Alberta Bar, King decided to take up yet another challenge that had come to interest her – working on "inter-group," or cultural, relations. This led her to accept a position as assistant to the chief liaison officer for the Canadian Department of Citizenship and Immigration (*Winnipeg Free Press*, May 4, 1956b, 4). The major newspapers across western Canada, including the *Lethbridge Herald* and the *Winnipeg Free Press*, frequently ran stories on King's contributions in law and her human rights advocacy for women's rights, racial justice, and interfaith relations. Years after she was called to the Bar, newspapers continued to highlight King as a trailblazer. In 1956 an article framed King's call to the Bar as indicative of the Canadian dream: "Blazing a trail as the first woman negro lawyer in Canada has proven this country a land of opportunity to Violet King" (*Winnipeg Free Press*, 4 May 1956a). On her way to take up the post in Ottawa, King stopped in Winnipeg, where she was a guest at the Fort Garry Hotel, and attended a citizenship ceremony for 100 new Canadians and a coffee party for them hosted by the Imperial Order of Daughters of the Empire (*Winnipeg Free Press*, 5 May 1956b, 49).

King also spoke on women's rights during a seminar on citizenship at the Banff School of Fine Arts. King is quoted as saying, "I've been discriminated against not because I'm colored, but because I'm a lawyer – a field some feel a woman shouldn't be operating in." The article elaborated that King's comment about the glass ceiling in law "made a stir among male members of the seminar ... attended by 44 persons from various races, religions and ethnic groups." A human resource expert from Toronto, Vernon Trott, added that women lawyers faced "the resistance of the male in a field he has dominated for 1,000 years," and because of their beliefs that professional women would quit their careers as soon as they got married, qualified women were passed over for leadership roles in the federal civil service. At that citizenship seminar King also addressed the question of the gender wage gap, arguing that although organizations would probably reclassify positions to evade the issue of women achieving equitable wages, the "battle for equal pay for equal work represented not so much a desire for more money among women but a desire for status" (*Lethbridge Herald* 1958). King was active in Alberta women's groups that were lobbying the Alberta Social Credit government of Ernest Manning to introduce equal pay legislation similar to what had been introduced in Manitoba under the Liberal Progressive government of Douglas Lloyd Campbell.

After seven years in Ottawa, King found other doors opened for her, this time in the United States, where she blazed new leadership trails with the YWCA. In 1963 she became the first woman to hold any executive position at the YMCA when she was recruited to Newark, New Jersey, as the executive director of the YMCA Community Branch and worked with African Americans seeking employment. In New Jersey she also met her husband, Godfrey C. Henry, and they had a daughter, Jo-Anne Henry. The family moved to Chicago in 1969 for yet another opportunity for King Henry, this time serving as the YMCA's director of manpower, planning, and staff development. King was further promoted in 1976 to executive director of the YMCA's National Council, becoming the first woman to hold a national executive position with the organization. Violet King was only fifty-two years old when she died of cancer on 30 March 1982.

Over the course of her life and career, Violet King Henry received numerous awards and honours. In June 1954 she was recognized by the International Brotherhood of Sleeping Car Porters and Maids, an affiliate of the American Federation of Labour. Union President Philip Randolph travelled from New York and Vice President Bennie Smith from Detroit in order to present King with the award in Calgary. Her trailblazing leadership roles led to her induction into the YMCA Hall of Fame in 1998. She was posthumously recognized by Ryerson University at its eleventh annual Violet Desmond Awards, when the 2019 staff award was named after King, and her daughter was present to confer the award. Until 2021, there were no scholarships or other major honours in Alberta, no Black History Month postage stamps, and no Historica Canada Heritage Minute clips recognizing the significant contributions of Canada's first Black woman lawyer. In recognition of her trailblazing contributions to Alberta and Canada, in February 2021 the Government of Alberta renamed the Federal Building Plaza, which also overlooks the Alberta legislature, the Violet King Henry Plaza. As well, led by the University of Calgary's Student Union's seventy-eighth vice president academic, Semhar Abraha, the SU launched the Violet King Engaged Scholar Award in March 2021 to recognize Black, Indigenous, and People of Colour (BIPOC) students who were contributing to the betterment of the community. In October 2021, King was included among pioneering alumni on the "Wall of Firsts" at the University of Alberta Law School.

Conclusion

Stories are indispensable to the making and unmaking of Black Canadians generally, and Black scholars in the Canadian academy in particular. Stories of Black lives are woven together with diverse threads that reflect Black multiplicity. National stories also entail negotiation, implicit and explicit, of words and actions of things we choose to remember and forget. The stories of hidden figures I tell in this chapter, the two conceptions of hidden stories, and the dozen trailblazing Black scholars, make visible Black multiplicity and at the same time unsettle and displace the stories of Black-as-lack. The stories I tell remind us of the importance of storytelling to resisting the erasure and historical forgetfulness that enable stereotypes to take hold. Excavating and recovering hidden figures, making them visible, can disrupt and displace the single story that obscures trailblazing Black Canadians in higher education. As Okri (1997, 120) rightly notes, we need these different stories because they may change our lives and help us to shape more humane and just futures.

NOTES

1 Research for this chapter was supported by a 2018 Pierre Elliott Trudeau Foundation Fellowship, and the outstanding research assistance of Daisy Raphael, Jeanique Tucker, and David Semaan.
2 I borrow "hidden figures" from the book and movie about the four forgotten Black American mathematicians at NASA (Shetterly 2016).
3 The first chair was lawyer Esmeralda M. Thornhill, who was followed by social work scholar David Devine, sociology and anthropology scholar Afua Cooper, and health and gender studies scholar OmiSoore H. Dryden, who holds the chair at time of writing.

REFERENCES

Adams, E.M. 2012. "Errors of Fact and Law: Race, Space, and Hockey in Christie v. York." *University of Toronto Law Journal* 62 (4): 463–97. https://doi .org/10.3138/9781442666801-010.

Adams, E. 2018. "Fred Christie Case (Christie v York)." In *The Canadian Encyclopedia*. Last edited 6 June 2020. https://www.thecanadianencyclopedia. ca/en/article/fred-christie-case.

Adiche, C.N. 2009. "The Danger of a Single Story." Ted Global. https://www .ted.com/talks/chimamanda_adichie_the_danger_of_a_single_story.

Ahmed, S. 2012. *On Being Included: Racism and Diversity in Institutional Life.* Durham, NC: Duke University Press.

Backhouse, C. 1999. *Colour-Coded: A Legal History of Racism in Canada, 1900– 1950.* Toronto: University of Toronto Press.

Bayes-Fleming, F. 2016. "When Canada's First Black University Grad Saved Queen's." *The Charlatan*. https://charlatan.ca/2016/02/when-canadas-first-black-university-grad-saved-queens/.

Bell, L.A. 2003. "Telling Tales: What Stories Can Tell Us about Racism." *Race Ethnicity and Education* 6 (1): 3–28. https://doi.org/10.1080/1361332032000044567.

Black, N. 2015. "Delos Davis." *The Canadian Encyclopedia, Historica Canada*. https://www.thecanadianencyclopedia.ca/en/article/delos-davis.

Brown, D.R. 2009–2010. "Robert Sutherland: Celebrating the Legacy." *Queen's Law Journal* 35 (Fall): 401.

Cahill, J.B. 1992. "The 'Colored Barrister': The Short Life and Tragic Death of James Robinson Johnston, 1876–1915." *Dalhousie Law Journal* 15: 336–379. http://core.ac.uk/download/pdf/288305002.pdf.

Cahill, J.B. 1994. "Walker, Abraham Beverley." *Dictionary of Canadian Bibliography*. http://www.biographi.ca/en/bio/walker_abraham_beverley_13E.html.

Canadian Association of University Teachers. 2010. "The Changing Academy? A Portrait of Canada's University Teachers." *CAUT Education Review* 12 (1). https://www.caut.ca/docs/education-review/the-changing-academy-a-portrait-of-canada-rsquo-s-university-teachers-(jan-2010).pdf.

Canadian Association of University Teachers. 2018. *Underrepresented and Underpaid: Diversity and Equity among Canadian Postsecondary Education Teachers*. https://www.caut.ca/sites/default/files/caut_equity_report_2018-04final.pdf.

Cargle, R.E. 2018. "When Feminism Is White Supremacy in Heels." *Harper's Bazaar*. https://www.harpersbazaar.com/culture/politics/amp22717725/what-is-toxic-white-feminism/.

Carroll, A. 2016, 7 May. "Discovering Robert Sutherland." *Queen's Gazette*. https://www.queensu.ca/gazette/stories/discovering-robert-sutherland.

Carty, L. 1991. "Black Women in Academia." In *Unsettling Relations: The University as a Site of Feminist Struggles*, edited by H. Bannerji, L. Carty, K. Delhi, S. Heald, and K. McKenna, 13–44. Toronto: Women's Press.

Church, E. 2009, 19 January. "The 1st Black Graduate of Queen's Saved His Alma Mater: Will His Story Be Told?" *Globe and Mail*. https://www.theglobeandmail.com/news/national/the-1st-black-graduate-of-queens-saved-his-alma-mater-will-his-story-be-told/article20443362/.

Cobbs, W.M. 1963. "A New Dawn in Medicine: National Doctor Shortage Offers Promising Careers in Medicine to Bright Negro Youth." *Ebony Magazine* 18: 11: 166–167, 170–171.

Crenshaw, K. 1989. "Demarginalizing the Intersection of Race and Sex: A Black Feminist Critique of Antidiscrimination Doctrine, Feminist Theory and Antiracist Politics." *University of Chicago Legal Forum*. https://chicagounbound.uchicago.edu/uclf/vol1989/iss1/8.

Dalhousie University. n.d. "James Robinson Johnstone." *Dalhousie Originals.* https://
www.dal.ca/about-dal/dalhousie-originals/james-robinson-johnston.html.

Dannetta, L. 2019, 25 April. "Queen's Formally Apologizes for Black Medical
Student Ban." *The Queen's University Journal.* https://www.queensjournal.ca
/story/2019-04-25/university/queens-formally-apologizes-for-black-medical
-student-ban/.

Douglas, D. 2012. "Black/out: The White Face of Multiculturalism and
the Violence of the Canadian Imperial Academic Project." In *Presumed
Incompetent: The Intersections of Race and Class for Women in Academia,* edited
by G. Gutiérrez, Y. Muhs, C. Nieman, Z. González, and A. Harris, 50–65.
Boulder: University Press of Colorado.

Fenison, J. 2009. "Alexander T. Augusta (1825–1890)" *Black Past.* https://www
.blackpast.org/african-american-history/augusta-alexander-t-1825-1890/.

Fine, P. 2016a. "Kenneth Melville Trailblazer: A Man of Many Firsts." *Social
Accountability and Community Engagement.* https://www.mcgill.ca
/med-saceoffice/celebrating-diversity/melville-undergraduate-research
-bursary-pharmacology/kenneth-melville-trailblazer.

Fine, P. 2016b. "A Man of Many Firsts." *Health e-News.* https://publications
.mcgill.ca/medenews/2016/02/23/a-man-of-many-firsts/.

Fingard, J. 1998. "Johnston, James Robinson." In *Dictionary of Canadian
Biography,* vol. 14. University of Toronto/Université Laval. http://www
.biographi.ca/en/bio/johnston_james_robinson_14E.html.

Fingard, J. 2003. "Johnston, James Robinson." *Dictionary of Canadian Biography.*
http://www.biographi.ca/en/bio/johnston_james_robinson_14E.html.

Fleming, N.B. 2018, 25 February. "When Canada's First Black University
Graduate Saved Queen's." *The Charlatan.* https://charlatan.ca/2016/02
/when-canadas-first-black-university-grad-saved-queens/.

Fraser, F. 2010. *How the Blacks Created Canada.* Edmonton: Dragon Hill
Publishing.

The Gateway. 1952, 14 March. "Color Night Next Tuesday; Twelve to Receive
Rings: Literary and Athletic Awards to Be Presented at Banquet."

Hauch, V. 2018, 8 February. "Canada's First Canadian-Born Black Doctor Got
his MD Licence in 1861." *The Star.* https://www.thestar.com/yourtoronto
/once-upon-a-city-archives/2018/02/08/canadas-first-canadian-born-black
-doctor-got-his-md-licence-in-1861.html.

Head, I.L., and Trudeau, P.E. 1995. *The Canadian Way, 1968–1984.* Toronto:
McClelland & Stewart.

Henry, A. 2015. "'We Especially Welcome Applications from Members of
Visible Minority Groups': Reflections on Race, Gender and Life at Three
Universities." *Race, Ethnicity and Education* 18 (5): 589–610. https://doi.org
/10.1080/13613324.2015.1023787.

hooks, b. 1984. *Feminist Theory: From Margin to Center.* Boston: South End Press.

Isaac, J. 1990. "Delos Rogest Davis, K.C.: Law Society of Upper Canada." *Gazette* 24: 293–301.

James, C.E. 2011, 15 May. "Canada: Paradoxes of 'Visible Minorities' in Job Ads." *University World News*. http://www.universityworldnews.com/article.php?story=20110513185935314.

James, C., and Turner, T. 2017. *Towards Race Equity in Education: The Schooling of Black Students in the Greater Toronto Area*. https://edu.yorku.ca/files/2017/04/Towards-Race-Equity-in-Education-April-2017.pdf.

Johnston, A.J.B. 2012. "Mathieu Da Costa and Early Canada: Possibilities and Probabilities." *Parks Canada*. http://parkscanadahistory.com/publications/portroyal/dacosta-e.pdf.

Jones, S.B. 1913, 1 September. "Fifty Years of Negro Public Health in the Annals of the American Academy of Political and Social Sciences." *Annals of the American Academy of Political and Social Sciences* 49: 138–46. https://doi.org/10.1177/000271621304900116.

King, V., and Andrews, D. 1951. "U of A ISS Delegate Report on Hamilton Conference." *The Gateway* 20: 2.

Lethbridge Herald. 1956, 13 January. "Calgary Lawyer to Speak Here," 14.

Lethbridge Herald. 1956, 17 January. "Women Still Need More Legal Protection Says Lady Lawyer," 11.

Lethbridge Herald. 1958, 4 July. "Women Lawyers Resented by Men in Profession." 4: 11.

Mackey, F. 2018. "1848, 1861, 1926: Which Came First?" *Connections: Journal of the Quebec Family History Society*, July. http://quescren.concordia.ca/en/resource/2ZCTK6R4.

Malcolm, I. 1992. "Robert Sutherland: The First Black Lawyer in Canada?" *Law Society of Upper Canada Gazette* 26 (2): 183–186.

Mallees, N. 2021, 25 June. "Grave of First Canadian-Born Black Lawyer Finally Gets Headstone in Saint John." CBC News. https://www.cbc.ca/news/canada/new-brunswick/abraham-walker-headstone-1.6079117.

McDowall, D. 2016. *Testing Tradition: Queen's University* (Vol. 3), 1961–2004. Montreal and Kingston: McGill-Queen's University Press.

McKittrick, K., ed. 2015. *Sylvia Wynter: On Being Human as Praxis*. Durham, NC: Duke University Press.

Meyers, R.C. 2004. "Ivy Maynier Bursary." *Nexus* 4: 1–3.

MF. 2002. "Building the Next Generation of African American Physicians: The Fitzbutler Jones Society Re-affirms Its Commitment to Scholarship Support." *Medicine at Michigan*. http://www.medicineatmichigan.org/sites/default/files/archives/fitzjones.pdf.

Mohamed, B. 2018, 23 October. "Ted King." *The Canadian Encyclopedia*. https://www.thecanadianencyclopedia.ca/en/article/ted-king.

Morales, A.L. 1998. *Medicine Stories: History, Culture and the Politics of Integrity.* Cambridge, MA: South End Press.

Morgan, A. 2013, 3 April. "How a Black Man Saved Queen's University." *Huffington Post Canada.* https://www.huffingtonpost.ca/anthony-morgan /black-history-month-canada_b_2600011.html.

Newby, D. 1998. *Anderson Ruffin Abbott: First Afro-Canadian Doctor.* Markham, ON: Associated Medical Services and Fitzhenry & Whitside. https://web.archive .org/web/20160304192117/http://php.ams-inc.on.ca/files/a_r_abbott.pdf.

Okri, B. 1995. *Birds of Heaven.* London: Orion.

Okri, B. 1997. *A Way of Being Free.* London: Head of Zeus.

Pearce, N. 2016, 31 March. "Robert Sutherland: The First Black Grad's Long Road to Recognition." *Queen's Journal.* https://www.queensjournal.ca/story/2016-03-30 /features/robert-sutherland-the-first-black-grads-long-road-to-recognition/.

Queen's University. n.d. "Sutherland, Robert (c. 1830–1878): Queen's Alumnus, First Known University Student and Graduate of Colour in Canada, and British North America's First Known Black Lawyer." *Queen's Encyclopedia.* https://www.queensu.ca/encyclopedia/s/sutherland-robert.

Reid-Maroney, N. 2004. "African Canadian Women and the New World Diaspora (circa 1865)." *Canadian Woman Studies* 23 (2): 92–96.

Sanders, C.L. 1968. "The Legacy of a Love Affair: Will of German Millionaire Provides Millions for Children of Mixed Parentage." *Ebony* 4: 89–94.

Shetterly, M.L. 2016. *Hidden Figures: The American Dream and the Untold Story of the Black Women Mathematicians Who Helped Win the Space Race.* New York: William Morrow.

Smith, M.S. 2003. "'Race Matters' and 'Race Manners.'" In *Reinventing Canada: Politics of the 21st Century,* edited by J. Brodie and L. Trimble, 108–131. Toronto: Prentice Hall.

Smith, M.S. 2010. "Gender, Whiteness, and 'Other Others' in the Academy." In *States of Race: Critical Race Feminism for the Twentieth Century,* edited by S. Razack, M. Smith, and S. Thobani, 45–56. Toronto: Between the Lines Press.

Spelman College. 2016. *Sophia B. Jones Charts a Course of Success for African-American Doctors.* https://www.spelman.edu/about-us/news-and-events /our-stories/stories/2016/04/01/sophia-b.-jones.

Statistics Canada. 2019. *Diversity of the Black Population in Canada: An Overview.* https://www150.statcan.gc.ca/n1/pub/89-657-x/89-657-x2019002-eng.pdf.

Stock, S. 2018. "An African Inheritance: Rev. Dr. William Wright, 1827–1908." *Quebec Heritage News* 2: 21–25.

Stokes, M. 2015. "Who Was the First Black Lawyer in Canada?" *Encyclopedia: The Osgoode Society for Canadian Legal History.* https://www.osgoodesociety.ca /encyclopedia/three-first-black-lawyers-in-canada-robert-sutherland-abraham -walker-delos-davis/.

Taylor, A. 2015. "Doctor of Courage: Rejected by American Universities, Alexander Augusta Completed His Medical Degree at Trinity Medical College Then Used His Skills to Fight for Civil Rights in His Homeland." *University of Toronto Magazine*. https://magazine.utoronto.ca/campus /history/doctor-of-courage-alexander-augusta-civil-rights-hero/.

Thomas, O. 1998. "Davis, Delos Rogest." In *Dictionary of Canadian Biography*, vol. 14. University of Toronto/Université Laval. http://www.biographi.ca/en /bio/davis_delos_rogest_14E.html.

Trudel, M. 2003. "Le Jeune, Olivier." In *Dictionary of Canadian Biography*, vol. 1. University of Toronto/Université Laval. http://www.biographi.ca/en/bio /le_jeune_olivier_1E.html.

Walker, A.B. 1890. "The Negro Problem; Or, the Philosophy of Race Development from a Canadian Standpoint." A Lecture. Atlanta, GA.

Walker, B., ed. 2012. *The African Canadian Legal Odyssey: Historical Essays*. Toronto: University of Toronto Press.

Walker, J.W. 1997. *"Race," Rights and the Law in the Supreme Court of Canada*. Waterloo, ON: Wilfrid Laurier University Press.

Western Farm Leader. 1954. "First Negro Woman in Canada Called to Bar." *Western Farm Leader* 18: 11.

White, E. 2016, 22 December. "Consider the Saga of James Robinson Johnston." *The Coast*. https://www.thecoast.ca/halifax/consider-the-saga-of-james -robinson-johnston/Content?oid=5875256.

Winnipeg Free Press. 1956a. "Violet King: Colored Girl's Career in Law Leads to Ottawa." 5: 49.

Winnipeg Free Press. 1956b. "Wins Citizenship Department Post." 4: 2.

7 Committed to Employment Equity? Impediments to Obtaining University Appointments

CARL E. JAMES

Introduction

If we were to scan the academic job ads of many Canadian universities today, we would observe a version of the following statement after the job description, required qualifications, and application deadline:

> University X is strongly committed to employment equity within its community and supports diversity in its teaching, learning, and work environments. We welcome applications from all qualified candidates, including women, Indigenous people, visible minorities, persons with disabilities, and members of sexual minority groups. Members of these designated groups are encouraged to self-identify.

Some of these equity statements are brief and to the point. Others are longer and seem to be trying to convince the sceptical reader and potential applicants that the university is truly committed to equitable access and is really a "welcoming" environment (James 2011). Such attempts to "invite" and "encourage" applications from, as one statement reads "members of traditionally marginalized groups" is in keeping with the *Employment Equity Act*[1] and the Federal Contractor's Program (FCP 2020).

We might ask, Aside from the federal contractor's imperative or, more recently, threats by the then science minister, Kirsty Duncan, and heads of the Tri-Council Funding Agencies, to withdraw funds from universities that do not diversify the pool of CRCs (Hannay 2017), are Canadian universities really committed to equity and inclusivity? In terms of having a racially representative and diverse faculty (including administrators and staff) is there evidence to show that commitment? What are the chances for racialized scholars, and Black scholars in particular, getting hired and received as legitimate members of the institutions with the same rights and privileges as their white counterparts? One would expect employment equity programs to enable Black scholars to gain entry to faculty positions with the necessary structures or mechanisms in place to ensure their retention and promotion once they are hired. But is this the case in Canada?

Despite advertised or public articulation of commitment to employment equity and to having a diverse and representative workforce, many of us within universities observe disconcerting paradoxes in the stated attempts by our institutions to promote racial equity and inclusivity in their policies, programs, and practices (James 2011). In fact, in the current context of today's universities, the commitment and "welcome" articulated in employment equity statements and initiatives have done little to increase the number of Black faculty members. Because in the absence of political will, as well as changes in institutional structures, measurements, and practices (Kitossa 2016) in which race is taken to be a significant identity characteristic in universities' recruitment and retention exercises, the welcome is meaningless. In such cases, the invitation for racialized scholars to join the ranks of the professorate merely accentuates the paradoxes of the institutionalized racism that negate their presence in the academy (see Douglas 2012; Henry in his volume).

In this chapter, I discuss three concerns – the use of the "visible minority" identification, the myth of colour-blindness,[2] and the potential traps of intersectionality – that serve as impediments to the hiring and retention of Black faculty members in today's institutions. I attempt to show how current practices of grouping "visible minority" group members without disaggregating the data relating to race, sustain the myth of colour-blindness and the unjustifiable disregard for the intersectionality of identity characteristics. These practices, I argue, serve to maintain the situation in which Black scholars remain poorly represented in postsecondary institutions. But before going into this discussion, in the section that follows, I explore the how neoliberalism frames the ideas, policies, and practices within today's universities with regard to equity, diversity, and inclusivity.

Race and the Neoliberal University

Attention to race – even as a social construct – is not simply a sociological exercise to get at and/or explain issues pertaining to a population of people and racialized people in particular, but a necessary aspect of any work that aims to ensure the practice of equity, inclusivity, and social justice in society. Furthermore, any such work must address how neoliberal ideology – sustained by whiteness, colour blindness, and Canadian multiculturalism claims of cultural freedom and neutrality – conceals the insidious and inhibiting effects of structural racism. Within this context, academics who seek to engage in critical work do so, recognizing and resisting, as Clegg (2010, 21) asserts, "the stressful conditions under which they labour," but unwittingly sometimes carry out that work in the very institutions that oppress us. And insofar as the bodies of racialized scholars are inscribed with particular performative expectations and stereotypes,[3] there is an inescapable high cost of "maintaining a critical voice" (21). This high cost is, in part, sustained by the neoliberal agenda, which is affecting the work of academics, scholars, and researchers who, as Magda Lewis (2010, 2) writes, are subjected to

> the industrialization of our collective enterprise … [and] the rise of surveillance and control mechanisms such as performance audits and measures of academic production and merit, in work intensification, in the entrepreneurialization of academic work, and in academic practices that seem increasingly to close down research and scholarship aimed at critical social intervention. In AngloAmerican influenced nations, embraced by capitalist modes of production, measures of higher education performance based on research outputs, scholarship linked to research grants, and academic/corporate/industry partnerships collude with newly articulated research ethics guidelines to create frigid conditions for the investigation of these very processes of commodification. Knowledge as commodity, learning as credentialization, data as the driving force for decision making, and "excellence" measured by an explosion of audit mechanisms that require endless reporting on "productivity" disguised as standards in the name of accountability, have significantly transformed academic work over the past decade and a half from a historically creative undertaking to a largely entrepreneurial enterprise.

It is into this neoliberal university context, structured by capitalist democracy, competition, merit, individualism, personal responsibility, and risk-taking, that we, as racialized academics, are invited to enter. And while many of us do seek access to and are working in the "ivory tower," we experience self-doubt, anxiety, and stress (see Berg and Seeber 2016) that is generated as we ponder our capacity to "fit in" with the work we do (or wish to do) and meet expectations. Furthermore, the academy, as Mirowski (2013, 92) writes, is "a world where competition is the primary virtue, and solidarity a sign of weakness. Consequently, it revels in the public shaming of the failed and the hapless." Yet we enter as we must, using, as generations before us, our scholarship or writings in the language we know to articulate our ideas and have them recognized;

to make our presence known and felt; to dialogue with colleagues who otherwise would never have had opportunities for cross-racial and cross-cultural exchanges; to bring attention to the structural and institutional factors that conspire to silence us; to develop epistemologies that enable resistive agency and bring about institutional change; to expose and challenge the racist policies and practices that make it difficult to do critical intellectual work; and to open up opportunities through teaching, research, and service, for others like us to follow.

Of course, our activities, ambitions, and aspirations are rooted in our experience of navigating and negotiating the structures of racism that account for the situation in which African Canadians find ourselves. And as Magda Lewis (2005, 7), argues with reference to feminists' critique of "the corporate culture" of postsecondary institutions,

> We are able to access the workings of these larger political structures only through the [personal] stories we might tell about them. Precisely because lives are lived in the finely textured fabric of the every day, in the crevices of what happens to us in our casual encounters and conversations, it is, as Michelle Fine points out, by speaking of the "personal" that the "mystified space yawning between 'objectivity' and 'politics' is exposed as an illusion, justifying and laminating existing forms of social privilege in the name of objectivity."

Furthermore, the personal stories we tell, and the bodies from which the stories are narrated, are inextricably linked to place, space, time, and identity. So while normally place is perceived "as a passive, abstract arena in which events occur," it is "saturated with relations of domination which are relevant to the construction of identity" (Mohanram 1999, xv). And space, according to Razack (2002), not only shapes identities and difference, it also produces bodies and the ways they are viewed, read, and/or marked. Scholars indicate that space incarcerates or enables mobility of certain bodies (Cote-Meek 2014; Davis 2018; Henry 2015; Kelly 2015; Mohanram 1999; Nelson 2011; Razack 2002). In other words, marked as belonging in/to particular space or place (or environment) with knowledge, behaviours, and practices suited to that space – and depending on positionality, in terms of being a member of the dominant or subordinate group – will confine or imprison individuals to that space. For instance, if the Black body is marked as one that does not possess the abilities, skills, and aptitude for academic or intellectual work, and as such will never fit into the academy, then in such a space the person will be viewed as out of place[4] – it is a body that is imprisoned by what it lacks and will never become the norm in the academic environment.

Indeed, as Mohanram (1999, 49) proffers, "The dematerialization of the body – its unmarking – is only possible for a select group of subjects." So while the white body in an institution predicated on whiteness has "the ability to move" and to unmark itself (thus considered the norm in that space), by contrast, the Black person remains marked, for Blackness is "always static" and immobilized (M4). Hence, given the presumed fixity of Blackness, as Awad Ibrahim (in this volume) suggests, will the invitations to racialized scholars, and Black scholars in particular, to join the academy bring more of them in? This question is quite relevant, particularly when the hegemonic discourse of whiteness remains intact and its related policies and practices are never questioned or altered in order to bring about structural changes that would make these institutions "welcoming" places.

The Problem with the "Visible Minority" Identification Category

"Visible minority" is one of the four Employment Equity (EE) categories (the others are women, Aboriginal/Indigenous, people with disabilities) introduced in 1985 to define people, other than Indigenous, who are "non-Caucasian in race or non-white in colour" (Driedger and Halli 2004). This single category conceals the inter- and intra-group differences to be found among Canadians of African, Asian, and South Asian descent, among others. This shoehorning of experiences – in other words, *essentializing* of experiences – obscures the social, historical, linguistic, cultural, and other differences among the groups. In such a context, can an institution be said to have achieved "equitable representation" if it has a workforce of, say, "visible minority" members from only one or two of the fourteen groups that comprise the category? And simply matching the percentage of "visible minority" in the institution with that of the student, local, or national population, or, as the EE guidelines suggest, with that of the "available" qualified candidates within the same occupational category, is not entirely helpful. In these cases, we need to take into account how this combining of racialized peoples has become societal and institutional norms and practices that have contributed to the absence of Black academics and the "hyper-visibility" of their racialized counterparts in sciences, medicine, and engineering faculties and departments (Henry et al. 2017; Smith 2017). The use of the "visible minority" category, as a stand-in for the diverse racialized group of scholars, masks the failures, or at least the limits of these educational institutions' equity hiring initiatives for some racialized groups, while simultaneously showing success for others. Racialized group members experience different challenges and possibilities within the workplace. For instance, Picot and Hou (2011, 31) show that there are noticeable differences in the social and economic outcomes of racialized Canadians. They write that "even after controlling for education and residential location ... second-generation Blacks tend to earn less while second-generation Chinese tend to earn more than other visible minority groups." The authors suggest that economic returns for education as well as "ethnic capital" – transmitted to individuals through membership in particular ethnic groups – significantly influence outcomes for racialized members of the society. And as Block and Galabuzi (2011) found, higher unemployment and lower workforce participation and earnings are to be discovered among racialized workers compared to their non-racialized counterparts, and the gaps in these areas vary for different racialized workers. For example, compared to other racialized workers, the gap between Black and non-racialized workers tends to be greater, and more so for Black women. This speaks to the need to pay attention to variation among racialized group members if institutions are to really engage in equitable hiring, promotion, and retention.

The use of the "visible minority" category has not produced a diverse representation of racialized faculty members on today's campuses. And it has not helped, as I have written elsewhere (James 2011), that there is no data on racial identity beyond "visible minority" in which all racialized individuals (except Indigenous people) are grouped. This grouping accounts for the limitation and inadequacy of the data, hence its failure to contribute to effective evidence-based policies, programs, and practices that would address the specificity of the situation of Black scholars. Furthermore, the absence of good disaggregated data makes it difficult for institutions to assess and monitor the representation of the various "visible minority" faculty members. Surely, if institutions are to keep track of their "progress" or are to know how well their equity initiatives are working or have worked for Black scholars, then they need to look at disaggregated data. It is a paradox – indeed, contradictory – that institutions in the research business that rely on research (noting reliability, validity, and generalizability) to make their contributions to society, do not keep or examine data on race, if only for the "evidence" they are satisfying their hiring and other equity goals.

It is ironic that in a culture in which data on gender as an identity characteristic is kept and explicitly referenced and used to address the situation of women, race is not given the same identity recognition. Furthermore, Black and other racialized women ought to be disaggregated in the demographic category of women if the data is to report on the situation and representation of women. But the absence of such data poses a question: Is data are not collected and used because institutions do not want to know, keep track of, or count the racialized group members? Some institutions claim that the reason for not collecting race data (if they collect it at all) is for privacy reasons. The idea here is that the institution does not wish to "out" the one or two Black, racialized, and/or Indigenous academic/s in the faculty or department – even though the count is obvious, based crudely on the colour of the bodies within the department or institution. Indeed, confidentiality and anonymity promised in data collection are important, but so too are the policies pertaining to achieving equity, inclusivity, and representation of faculty members. It seems, therefore, that if inclusivity and equity are to be attained, institutions need to revisit and revise their policy on disclosure, particularly if representation is to go beyond increasing the number of women.

The Myth of Colour-Blindness

There is the longstanding claim by universities that it is a scholar's qualification that matters, not colour or race. This notion of colour-blindness or race neutrality belies the images, statements, and testimonies on websites and brochures, as well as the multicultural programs (e.g., Black History Month) of these institutions that seem designed to demonstrate and "celebrate" their commitment to diversity and inclusivity. And because today's student population (or financial units) of most universities – particularly in urban areas – is racially diverse, it seems logical that they would present images of these students. But interestingly, this seems not to translate into having a representative population of faculty members. Universities, in fact, tell us that the population of their local communities or the areas from which they draw their students is not what determines faculty composition, since they are national and international institutions. The implication here is that, tied as they are to the national representation of Black Canadians, these institutions will satisfy or justify themselves with less than 5 per cent Black faculty members. On the other hand, if we insist that the composition of the faculty should be aligned with the local community or its student population, then Black scholars might never show up in faculties of the institutions where there are no Black and/or other racialized students.

Presumably, the images and testimonials of racialized (including Black) people on the websites of universities are geared to the growing racialized Canadian and international student markets. As such, some might say that this makes good business sense, since institutions cannot afford to be colour-blind. So race (evidenced through skin colour) does matter, insofar as it enables institutions to make "visible" the fact that people like the students they seek to attract exist on their campuses. But seemingly, this is not the case for racialized faculty and Black faculty in particular. Why? Harvey Wingfield (2015) offers an explanation for the reluctance of U.S. universities' "to recruit and hire faculty of color":

> While students matriculate at an institution for a short period of time and then leave, the tenure system means that faculty of color may remain at a university for decades, even a lifetime. With this longer time frame, these professors develop more of a stake in the school, and may be more empowered to push the reforms many colleges resist. For universities that see no real reason to change their existing practices, traditions, and organizational cultures, bringing in a crucial mass of faculty of color is often a stated goal that never materializes.

It seems, then, that the notion of colour-blindness as conceptualized and practised by educational institutions makes a mockery of the institutions' promise of equity and inclusivity. In fact, the images, statements, and activities operate like "dark curtains"[5] through which the outside observer sees projections or images of racial diversity with representative (or reasonable) numbers of racialized people working or studying there. But in reality, the opposite is likely true. It is indeed ironic that in a society and in institutions that claim to be colour-blind, racial images are used to show diversity – a tacit admission that colour enables us to see or experience diversity. Undoubtedly, colour-blindness masks the structural, institutional, and individual racism that operate as barriers to assess inclusion and recognition of what Black scholars bring to the institutions.

Recent experimental research (Kang et al. 2016) reminds us that it makes no difference if names and all other markers of race or racial identifications (such as organizational affiliations and significant amounts of community service work – Harvey Wingfield 2015) are redacted or removed from curriculum vitae of applicants for faulty positions. In other words, "de-colouring," or as Kang and her colleagues (2016) term it, "resumé whitening," one's curriculum vitae does not work, because the premise of merit with which applicants' files are read by appointment committee members – many of whom tend to be dominant group members – remains structured by an ethic of whiteness steeped in the neoliberal paradigm of universalism, meritocracy, and individualism. Furthermore, even with names and other race or ethnic markers removed, individuals bring experiences that inform their perceptions and readings of curriculum vitae, which unwittingly operate in the assigning of identities – in terms of race, ethnicity, gender, and/or other characteristics – to applicants (Kang et al., 469).[6]

Intersectionality Is Important (but Avoid the Possible Traps)

Giving attention to intersectionality – the recognition that individuals' identities pertaining to race, gender, class, ethnicity, sexuality, disability, language, religion, and other characteristics are interrelated and are shaped by interlocking economic, political, educational, social, and cultural systems (Gillborn 2015) – is essential to any work in equity and inclusivity. Doing so allows for better understanding of how inequities are structured, created, and sustained through policies and practices that are taken as universal and normative. Intersectionality, therefore, requires that we do not treat the boxes that individuals are asked to tick (or mark) in the "employment equity" hiring or census exercises as distinct mutually exclusive identities, but as representations of our complex interrelated selves informed by the historical and contemporary contexts of our existence. So our respective "conditions of disadvantage in employment" (à la Employment Equity legislation, see Cohen 1985) cannot be merely attributed to any one identity characteristic such as gender, ethnicity, or race and related "-isms" such as sexism, racism, and classism, for these are not "autonomous sources" of oppression (King 1988). Besides, as King writes, it is "overly simplistic in assuming that the relationships among various discriminations are merely additive. These relationships [cannot be] interpreted as equivalent to the mathematical equation, racism plus sexism plus classism equals triple jeopardy," for no individual discrimination has "a single direct, and independent effect on an individual's status, wherein the relative contribution of each is readily apparent." All sources of oppression must be taken as interdependent and interactive; doing otherwise "leads to nonproductive assertions that one factor can and should supplant the other" (47).

What seems to have been missed over the years – even today – in the implementation of employment equity is attention to the intersecting and interdependent systems of identification – that is, gender along with race, class, sex and others – the consequence of which is the absence of women in some areas of the academy. In other words, while now twenty years later, employment equity has helped to bring more women into the academy, particularly in the humanities, social sciences, and education, we are yet to see similar breakthroughs in science, technology, engineering, and mathematics (STEM) (see Leggon 2010; Wulf 2016) – areas in which there is a fairly significant representation of racialized scholars except Blacks. In fact, generally speaking, Black and Indigenous scholars are inadequately represented on today's university campuses (see Henry et al. 2017). This lack of attention to intersectionality and what King (1988) refers to as the "multiple jeopardy" of racism, sexism, classism, and heterosexism accounts for the low representation of racialized women, particularly Black women, in the academy. It seems the identity of Black women's has been, as bell hooks (1981,7) writes of the American context, "socialized out of existence … We are rarely recognized as a group separate and distinct from black men, or a present part of the larger group of 'women' in this culture … When black women are talked about the focus tends to be on black men; and when women are talked about the focus tends to be on white women."[7] And as Annette Henry (2015) suggests with reference to the experiences of Black women, fear, loathing, and an expectation of maternalism also surrounds those in positions of authority.

Because identity categories are multiple and infinitely divisible, subdividing could be taken to the extreme and hence become a stalling tactic[8] that could lead to paralysis (Delgado 2011). Such practices are problematic – especially when claims of colour-blindness and post-raciality give impetus to the generalization, universalization, and ahistoricization of oppressions without regard to the specificity and the interconnection of identity categories. These categories account for the differential treatments and outcomes of members of the society. In Canada, where attention to race is considered to be contrary to its colour-blind discourse and is ascribed mainly to racialized people who, for the most part, are taken up in the aggregate as "visible minorities," the intersectional approach is of crucial importance. And while this approach fosters disaggregation, which unmasks the differential effects of racism and inequity on racialized group members, in the absence of an understanding and commitment to critical race work, individuals will likely resist or fail to disaggregate the "visible minority" category. As a consequence, there might never be a diverse representation of racialized scholars employed in the academy. Black scholars – Black women in particular – for instance, could be disadvantaged since, as hooks points out above, Black women are the only group whose identity is wrapped up with that of the men (7). In the case of Black queer scholars, the statement by a British scholar – a respondent in Bhopal's (2014) study – could be applied to our Canadian context. He said, "A Black man is threatening, but a Black queer male is even more threatening to what is considered the stereotype of what a Black male is and what he should look like" (11).

Conclusion

While job advertisements of educational institutions have asserted that racialized scholars are "welcome" to join their faculty, we are yet to see adequate representations of Black scholars at all levels of the academy. In this regard, we could look at the action of Prime Minister Justin Trudeau for a reference. Recall that in October 2015, claiming that he was opting for gender balance, Mr. Trudeau appointed a Cabinet with 50 per cent women, because, as he said then, "It's 2015." We may legitimately ask, Is this not the same as quota? Or is it seen as an acceptable goal or priority? In Canada, the idea of having representation – usually of regions – is not new, for such practice has operated in appointments to the Supreme Court of Canada, provincial and federal Cabinets, as well as boards, committees, and agencies. This practice can be interpreted as recognition that the individuals from different regions bring relevant and useful experiences and material information that are valuable to what is under consideration and the effectiveness of administration. A similar approach needs to be taken by those working in educational institutions, for colleges and universities are no less crucial to the governance and development of a democratic society.

To find out whether the welcome ads lead to the hiring, promotion, and retention of Black and other racialized faculty members, we need data. How else will we be able to go beyond the "anecdotal evidence" or the "personal stories" to advocate for needed changes in policies and practices? One wonders why institutions concerned with "research evidence" (sometimes considered "scientific" or "objective" facts) that would inform policies, practices, and decisions seem to have little to no appetite for data on race – and least of all disaggregated racialized group data. Might it be that if there is no evidence, the situation does not exist, hence there is no obligation for institutions to address the inequity? Truly, the customary reticence to talk about, take up, and acknowledge race and racism in Canadian institutions hinders real change and genuine commitment to equity and inclusivity in institutions. We know from experience that being able to reference data benefitted women (but largely white women) in the academy (Smith 2017) – not only in their representation, but also in pay equity and other factors that impede access, retention, and opportunities to fully participate at all levels of the academy.

Until we have data – essentially disaggregated racial identity data – that provides evidence of the numbers of Black scholars who manage to access universities, our numbers are unlikely to increase. But I have a concern that the racialized scholars who are fortunate enough to be employed in the academy might be those who are perceived to be ideologically or theoretically aligned with the institution. And in such contexts where colleagues are concerned with who would best "fit in," familiarity and "sameness" of racialized scholars are likely to be deciding factors.

In such cases, alternatives to present practices are unlikely to emerge. There is need to wrestle with these difficult issues if equitable hiring initiatives are to produce the desired diversity, and inclusive hiring, retention, and promotion in institutions. To the extent that the contradictions are allowed to exist and left unaddressed, Black scholars will continue to struggle to gain faculty positions in universities because of the caste-like racial system in which we are encased.

NOTES

1 The Act requires that "contractors who do business with the Government of Canada achieve and maintain a workforce that is representative of the Canadian workforce."

2 I discussed these concerns in James (2011). Many of the ideas are taken up in that posting.

3 Reporting on findings from their investigation of "black minority ethnic (BME)" in Britain's higher education institutions, Kalwant Bhopal (2014, 11) writes, "Many respondents reported a sense in which their own identity as a successful Black academic only ever emerged in a distorted fashion that was distinct from their understanding of who they were. Often the professional identity that emerged was one shaped by the particular desires and stereotypes insisted upon by white colleagues."

4 Ironically, the Black body comes into being only when it is perceived to be out of place or outside its "natural" environment or boundaries, or its function within institutions (see Mohanram 1999, xii).

5 I use this term or metaphor to refer to institutions' practice of putting racialized people or images of them upfront or on their websites for public consumption. "Dark curtain" refers to the use of Black images or Black professors, students, administrators, or staff to give the impression that they are to be found at all levels of the institution. In the same way, Asian authors use the metaphor of a "bamboo curtain" to point to the absence of Asians in these institutions.

6 It is worth noting that in Britain, the report of "The Equality Challenge Unit," as Bhopal (2014, 19) indicates in their report, suggested "that a process of anonymous shortlisting could help to address issues of inequity during the selection processes." They go on to recommend that "such robust and systematic recruitment processes can in fact help to reduce discrimination." This suggested practice is consistent with what I heard while talking with colleagues in Britain in that same year. And it is a practice that Canadians – including Canadian MP Ahmed Hussen – are advancing as a way to remove bias in hiring and to diversify workplaces.

7 Writing about the situation of Black minority ethnic female scholars in Britain, Bhopal (2014, 13) reports that those who were "understood" to be of racialized or working-class backgrounds "found their identities did not sit comfortably within the academic elites. In many respects this also appeared to contribute to the positions made available to them" – a noticeable concentration of them in most 1992 universities compared to being in older universities (Russell Group) with "expectations of self-serving, exclusionary, white middle class."

8 I refer to this situation as an "intersectionality trap" – where individuals become entangled in working through the many issues related to the multiple identities that they become trapped in, so nothing gets done.

REFERENCES

Berg, M., and Seeber, B.K. 2016. *The Slow Professor: Challenging the Culture of Speed in the Academy.* Toronto: University of Toronto Press.

Bhopal, K. 2014. *The Experience of BME Academics in Higher Education: Aspirations in the Face of Inequity.* London: Leadership Foundation for Higher Education.

Block, S., and Galabuzi, G.-E. 2011. *Canada's Colour Coded Labour Market: The Gap for Racialized Workers.* Ottawa: Canadian Centre for Policy Alternatives. https://www.policyalternatives.ca/sites/default/files/uploads/publications/National%20Office/2011/03/Colour%20Coded%20Labour%20Market.pdf.

Clegg, S. 2010. "The Possibilities of Sustaining Critical Intellectual Work under Regimes of Evidence, Audit, and Ethical Governance." *Journal of Curriculum Theorizing* 26 (3): 21–35. https://www.researchgate.net/publication/265990744_The_Possibilities_of_Sustaining_Critical_Intellectual_Work_Under_Regimes_of_Evidence_Audit_and_Ethical_Governance.

Cohen, M. 1985. "Employment Equity Is *Not* Affirmative Action." *Canadian Woman Studies/Les Cahiers de la Femme* 6 (4): 23–25.

Cote-Meek, S. 2014. *Colonized Classrooms: Racism, Trauma and Resistance in Postsecondary Education.* Halifax: Fernwood Publishing.

Davis, A. 2018. "The Black Woman Native Speaking Subject: Reflections of a Black Female Professor in Canada." *Atlantis: Critical Studies in Gender, Culture, and Social Justice* 39 (1): 70–78. https://journals.msvu.ca/index.php/atlantis/article/view/5340/pdf_57.

Delgado, R. 2011. "Rodrigo's Reconsideration: Intersectionality and the Future of Critical Race Theory." *Iowa Law Review* 96: 1247–1288. https://digitalcommons.law.seattleu.edu/cgi/viewcontent.cgi?article=1042&context=faculty.

Douglas, D. 2012. "Black/out. The White Face of Multiculturalism and the Violence of the Canadian Imperial Academic Project." In *Presumed*

Incompetent: The Intersections of Race and Class for Women in Academia, edited by G. Gutiérrez Y. Muhs, C. Nieman, Z. González, and A. Harris, 50–65. Boulder: University Press of Colorado.

Driedger, L., and Halli, S. 2004. *Race and Racism: Canada's Challenge.* Montreal and Kingston: McGill-Queen's University Press.

Federal Contractors Program. 2020. "Labour Program," Government of Canada. https://www.canada.ca/en/employment-social-development/corporate /portfolio/labour/programs/employment-equity/federal-contractors.html.

Gillborn, D. 2015. "Intersectionality, Critical Race Theory, and the Primacy of Racism: Race, Class, Gender, and Disability in Education." *Qualitative Inquiry* 2 (3): 277–287. https://doi.org/10.1177/1077800414557827.

Hannay, C. 2017, 4 May. "Ottawa to Universities: Improve Diversity or Lose Research Chair Funds." *The Globe and Mail.* https://www.theglobeandmail .com/news/politics/ottawa-to-pull-research-chair-funding-unless-diversity -issue-addressed-at-universities/article34905004/.

Harvey Wingfield, A. 2015. "The Plight of the Black Academic." *The Atlantic,* December. https://www.theatlantic.com/business/archive/2015/12 /the-plight-of-the-black-academic/420237/.

Henry, A. 2015. "'We Especially Welcome Applications from Members of Visible Minority Groups': Reflections on Race, Gender and Life at Three Universities." *Race, Ethnicity and Education* 18 (5): 589–610. https://doi.org /10.1080/13613324.2015.1023787.

Henry, F., Dua, E., James, C.E., Li, P., Ramos, H., and Smith, M.S. 2017. *The Equity Myth: Racialization and Indigeneity at Canadian Universities.* Vancouver: University of British Columbia Press.

James, C.E. 2011. "Welcoming 'Visible Minorities': Paradoxes of Equity Hiring in Canadian Universities." Federation for the Humanities and Social Sciences. http://www.ideas-idees.ca/blog/welcoming-visible-minorities -paradoxes-equity-hiring-canadian-universities.

Kang, S.K., DeCelles, K.A., Tilcsik, A. and Jun, S. 2016. "Whitened Résumés: Race and Self-Presentation in the Labor Market." *Administrative Science Quarterly* 61 (3): 469–502. https://doi.org/10.1177/0001839216639577.

Kelly, J.R. 2015. "Black Academic Leadership in Neoliberal Times: A Road to Nowhere?" Paper Presented at the Black Canadian Studies Association Conference, 22 May. Halifax, Nova Scotia.

King, D.K. 1988. "Multiple Jeopardy, Multiple Consciousness: The Context of a Black Feminists Ideology." *Signs: Journal of Woman in Culture and Society* 14 (1): 42–72. https://doi.org/10.1086/494491.

Kitossa, T. 2016. "Implicit Racism: The Need for Deep Diversity at Brock University." https://www.brockpress.com/implicit-racism-the-need -for-deep-diversity-at-brock-university/.

Leggon, C.B. 2010. "Diversifying Science and Engineering Faculties: Intersections of Race, Ethnicity, and Gender." *American Behavioral Scientist* 53 (7): 1013–1028. https://doi.org/10.1177/0002764209356236.

Lewis, M. 2005. "More Than Meets the Eye: The Underside of the Corporate Culture of Higher Education and Possibilities for a New Feminist Critique." *Journal of Curriculum Theorizing* 21 (1): 7–24.

Lewis, M. 2010. "Knowledge Commodified and the New Economies of Higher Education." *Journal of Curriculum Theorizing* 26 (3): 1–4.

Mirowski, P. 2013. *Never Let a Serious Crisis Go to Waste: How Neoliberalism Survived the Financial Meltdown.* New York: Verso.

Mohanram, R. 1999. *Black Body: Women, Colonialism and Space.* Minneapolis: University of Minnesota Press.

Nelson, C. 2011. "Toppling the 'Great White North': Tales of a Black Female Professor in the Canadian Academy." In *The Black Professoriat: Negotiating a Habitable Space in the Academy*, edited by S. Jackson and R. Johnson III, 108–134. New York: Peter Lang.

Picot, G., and Hou, F. 2011. "Seeking Success in Canada and the United States: The Determinants of Labour Market Outcomes among the Children of Immigrants." Statistics Canada, Social Analysis Division. https://www150 .statcan.gc.ca/n1/en/pub/11f0019m/11f0019m2011331-eng.pdf?st= lORFUfBU.

Razack, S. 2002. *Race, Space, and the Law: Unmapping a White Settler Society.* Toronto: Between The Lines.

Smith, M.S. 2017. "Disciplinary Silences: Race, Indigeneity, and Gender in the Social Sciences." In *The Myth: Racialization and Indigeneity at Canadian Universities*, edited by F. Henry et al., 239–262. Vancouver: University of British Columbia Press.

Wulf, W.A. 2016. "The Importance of Diversity in Engineering." *Diversity in Engineering: Managing the Workforce of the Future.* https://www.nap.edu /read/10377/chapter/4.

8 Black Gay Scholar and the Provocation of Promotion

WESLEY CRICHLOW*

Introduction

Academic institutions continue to fall short of socially transformative goals: just as Black Studies in general experiences lack of academic institutional support, so too have Black LGBTQ people felt excluded within the wider white homo-hegemony movement. There has never been a Black LGBTQ demonstration, conference, awards dinner recognition, scholarship, or institution named after one of its leaders. Black LGBTQ members are not voiceless, requiring Black heteronationalist leadership to speak for us. We are noble and courageous. I have never met any voiceless Black LGBTQ people in my community activism.

– Wesley Crichlow (2009)

We must practice revolutionary democracy in every aspect of our ... [organization's] life. Every responsible member must have the courage of his responsibilities, exacting from others a proper respect for his work and properly respecting the work of others. Hide nothing from the masses of our people. Tell no lies. Expose lies whenever they are told. Mask no difficulties, mistakes, failures. Claim no easy victories.

– Amilcar Cabral (1969)

For young Black LGBTQS+ scholars, mentors and mentoring are at a premium. Of course, mentorship from undergraduate through to the completion of PhD, sessional and contract faculty positions through to tenured track, and from associate professor through to full professor is a vital matter of concern for all Black LGBTQS+ scholars. Indeed, with so few

---

* This chapter is dedicated in loving memory to my mother, Christina, and to my niece, Justine.

Black academics and an even smaller number of Black openly LGBTQS+ professors, I especially want to provide a map of the landscape in academia that may serve as a useful guide for Black LGBTQS+ scholars and those who may be their mentors. There is considerable risk of essentializing Black LGBTQS+ mentoring, but if representation means anything, it is that where and when Black LGBTQS+ scholars possess embodied knowledge, the avenues for expanding what mentoring looks like need to be enlarged to provide more and different methods for engagement.

Thus, working from a phenomenological viewpoint of critical race storytelling, rather than a strict formal process of empirical research and citation, I detail my research, teaching, and service to the university in ways relevant to the promotion process. In particular, I reflect on the process of my recent application from associate professor to full professor as a way to narrate practical considerations for Black LGBTQS+ scholars who aspire to tenured track positions and beyond, to administration.

Since most codes and cues for surviving and thriving in academia are heel-to-toe and uttered in whispers, the arduous apprenticeship for becoming a scholar involves exceptional (open) secrecy, despite the formal presentation of collegiality, openness, and academic freedom. With so few Black LGBTQS+ scholars to mentor young Black LGBTQS+ scholars, there is a world of subtlety to academia, not least for PhDs, in knowing how to navigate postdocs, job applications, course evaluations, peer interactions, and ways to build the documentary evidence for promotion.

But inasmuch as I bring exposure to my successful attainment of full professorship, I cease to be pollyanna about it. The experience was exhausting and useful in helping me clarify what I regard as my purpose and mission in academia. To be clear, I do think that academia is among the most accommodating work and social spaces for the rights of lesbian, gay, bisexual, transgender,[1] queer, intersex,[2] and two-spirit[3] plus (LGBTQI2S+) persons in Canadian society. However, things are not perfect, particularly when one considers that courts have allowed for section 15 to be interpreted broadly, allowing not only for enumerated[4] grounds but also for analogous[5] grounds to be read in, such as personal and social characteristics other than those already listed in section 15. The Supreme Court rendered its first LGBTQI2S+ section 15 decision in *Egan v Canada*[6] in 1995, in which the courts recognized sexual orientation as an analogous[7] ground and therefore a prohibited ground of discrimination under the Charter. The establishment of sexual orientation as an analogous ground for LGBTQI2S+ protection opened the door for other human rights and Charter protections. Thus with an emphasis on marginalized sexualities, legal LGBTQI2S+ gains made in *Canada (AG) v Mossop*[8] (1993), *Vriend v Alberta*[9] (1998), and *M v H* (1999)[10] all signal victories for the federal

Civil Marriage Act,[11] legalizing same-sex marriage and serving openly in the military. These developments indicate a reduction in hostility towards LGBTQI2S+ by the courts, but not academic institutions that educated the very judges who adjudicated these cases. Clearly this makes the university academically and intellectually responsible for violence and domination against its constituents. This is most notable in LGBTQI2S+ rights, where significant Charter violations on the grounds of sexual orientation are worthy of mentioning for context of this chapter.

In the nineties I was involved with Canadian Charter of Rights legal activism in the now-defunct Foundation for Equal Families,[12] and as a board member of the 519 Church Street community centre,[13] making the argument for advancing and recognizing equality rights of the LGBTQI2S+ communities. As a member of the Foundation for Equal Families, I attended weekly Saturday morning meetings at the law offices of Eberts Symes Street Corbett & Pinto and worked alongside lawyers and other activists in supporting *M v H* and LGBTQI2S+ charter legal victories.

Good signs are appearing within the Government of Canada in advancing rights for LGBTQI2S+ that are community driven by substantive equality in the 1982 Canadian *Charter of Rights & Freedoms*.[14] The Charter equality section 15 came into effect in 1985. Since then, the courts have insisted that equality guaranteed by the Charter is more than formal equality or equality of opportunity. This is most notable in LGBTQI2S+ rights, where there are significant Charter violations on the grounds of sexual orientation, as mentioned above. They are all landmark Supreme Court cases that established that sexual orientation constitutes a prohibited basis of discrimination under section 15 of the Charter. But there is a deliberate lack of historical memory and erasure of Black gay activists from the early years of LGBTQI2S+ white activism in Canada, and by extension the Canadian academy. The Charter equality section 15 came into effect in 1985. Since then, the courts have insisted that equality guaranteed by the Charter is more than formal equality or equality of opportunity. Despite the legalizing of same-sex marriage in Canada and LGBTQS+ gains made in and victory of same-sex marriage (2005) and the right to serve openly LGBTQS+ in the military, LGBTQS+ Black and racialized academics still undergo institutional racism and homoppression in their tenure and promotion. The Wellesley Institute's definition of institutional racism assists organizations in removing barriers:

- Institutional racism is an ecological form of discrimination.
- It refers to inequitable outcomes for different racialized groups.
- There is a lack of effective action by organizations to eradicate the inequitable outcomes (McKenzie 2017).

This definition aims to move away from the paralysis caused by identifying the causes of racism. LGBTQI2S+ academics, especially those marked by disabilities and racial difference, still undergo elements of racism, and this definition can assist on action steps to address institutional racism through their tenure and promotion. While the foregoing cases are important and ground-breaking in the area of Charter activism and substantive equality, they have exposed the inadequacy of the concept of equality and the need to look at how intersectional hegemony (Crenshaw 1989) erases racial differential treatment impacts upon LGBTQS+ persons. While the white academic franchise has expanded to include upward mobility for white women and white LGBTQS+, as noted by Malinda Smith in this volume, equity for Black LGBTQS+ persons in academia, notably within tenure and promotion and higher administration, lags far behind. It has left many Black, Indigenous, and racialized LGBTQS+ scholars and activists to live in the academy without tenure, promotion administrative guarantees. We need to ask ourselves what has changed qualitatively and quantitatively for Black and racialized scholars in the academy and what the psychosocial issues are for queer bodies in the academy.

My Scholarly Interests

As noted above, my interest in Charter and judicial activist law began with Black community activism in the 1980s and the LGBTQS+ community in Toronto. In response to differential and unfair treatment against Black people, I was particularly interested in human rights, police racial carding and profiling, police shootings, discrimination in immigration and in education, disproportionate incarceration, and Black LGBTQS+ rights. As such, my research has engaged issues of human rights, law, race, and social justice. I completed my PhD at the Ontario Institute for Studies in Education of the University of Toronto (OISE-UT) primarily because of OISE'S strong interdisciplinary orientation to gender, and the sociology of law and of culture. As a student of Roger Simon, I sought to conduct research on the life and experiences of Black gay men in Toronto and Halifax. While pursuing my research projects in Black gay Caribbean diasporic culture, I continued research on Toronto's LGBTQS+ community, working with organizations organizing for LGBTQS+ equality and marriage. These interests were further prompted in the early 1990s by my project at OISE, which drew upon new developments in Black LGBTQS+ research combining praxis, critical race theory, and sociology of culture. My first published SSHRC-funded book, *Buller Men & Batty Bwoys: Hidden Men in Toronto & Halifax Black Communities* (2004), focused on interviews with Black gay men in Toronto's Caribbean diasporic community and Halifax Black community. This monograph was the first Black, scholarly, queer text to offer readers a critical insight into the complex lives of diasporic and Canadian Black gay and bisexual men. It also offered a critical analysis of racialized heterosexism within Black diasporic communities. This work was also an attempt to restore Caribbean indigenous sexual terms as a response to Western colonial politicized language of LGBTQS+ politics. This book is personal, situated in my own life, but it is also collaborative and depends on the assistance of other buller men and batty bwoys[15] living in Canada. My goal was to interrogate how these names and the associated experiences shaped the daily realities of English-speaking African-Caribbean men living in Toronto and African-Canadian men born or raised in Halifax who engaged in sexual and emotional bonding relationships and practices with other men (Crichlow 2004).

One thing that is critical to scholastic success is being able to reflect on and narrate personal academic interests. This does not mean that one's academic interests are carved in stone, never to change. As we grow through reading, conversations, and observations of key issues in the world around us, the core of our research interests takes us toward fresh, different, and deeper meanings as we gravitate toward enriching sources of inquiry. If we can continue to identify and document our growth and development, we will experience a deepening of our research competence and an enhancement of our capacity as teachers, and we will find ourselves offering service to our department, university, and/or wider community with renewed vigour.

Scrutiny of Teaching, Research, and Service

Having a stellar research, publishing, and teaching agenda, along with graduate and postdoc supervision highlighting your scholarly eminence, being familiar with your collective agreement[16] and seeking the right external reviewers are keys to attaining tenure and promotion as much as your competence in defending your work. One key thing noted by Foucault (1975/1991) is that power must be shown to academics through pervasive examination and its use as a mode of surveillance. It is little understood by undergraduate and graduate students that the lives of professors, irrespective of their greater influence and power, is characterized at a higher level of professional abstraction in being marked, graded, sorted, and sifted themselves.

For those about to undergo tenure and promotion after three years of probation, the process is nerve racking. Depending on your collective agreement, which may separate tenure from promotion, you may be granted both, or one or the other, by the majority of votes in your department, with the definite term to reapply for one or the other. Of course, being denied tenure and promotion outright is not unheard of. For those who pass this first round of hurdles after being appointed, promotion review is not as fraught as the tenure process. But despite the more relaxed attitude of your peers, the process remains debilitating and dehumanizing for Black LGBTQS+ scholars and others.

In preparing three dossiers – teaching, research, and service – you must document your publications, research projects, and teaching opinions from students in relationship to the institution at all levels. Promotion stories of Black LGBTQS+ scholars are not the same as their heterosexual colleagues', though other equity groups also experience difficulties with tenure and promotion. Because ableism, racism, heterosexism, and gender inequality are imprisoning, they also normalize self-surveillance and self-discipline. The effect is that able-bodied, heteronormative, white female and male academics' bodies and perspectives appear "normal" while keeping the rebelliousness of racialized peoples in check. To be an out Black LGBTQS+ scholar is a burdensome enactment – because one's sexual orientation is constantly up for scrutiny in all their actions by students and colleagues alike. "Difference" matters because "culture depends on giving things meaning by assigning them to different positions within a classificatory system" (Hall 1997, 236). Difference is also about constituting the "Other." "'The Other' is fundamental to the constitution of the self, to us as subjects, and to sexual identity" (237). As a Black gay scholar I employ an intersectional and critical race theory analysis in my teaching. As Foucault (1984, 84) argues, "Researchers should not be concerned with the contents, methods, or concepts of a science, but rather with the centralizing powers which are linked to the institution and functioning of an organized discourse."

My colleagues have told me prior to my promotion application that my teaching is "provocative and colourful," because my teaching employs an intersectional, queer, critical race theory analysis. Students have written that they "are not sure what I'm trying to provoke" with my teaching style. Such forms of intentional or unintentional bias can be difficult to pinpoint. However, as a Black, gay professor who teaches critical race theory and sexuality studies, I am particularly attuned to the ways such bias informs perceptions of teaching. In a similar vein, I note the Tenure and Promotion Committee's (TPC) language in the negative recommendation letter: "It was not clear to the Committee what you are trying to provoke from the students when you are engaging with them, or how you are enhancing the student experience." "Provoke" is not an appropriate synonym for teaching in any context; when used to describe a Black, gay, male professor, it is especially unfortunate and unfair. The word "provoke" is defined in the *Canadian Oxford Dictionary* as "1. Annoy, disturb, or harass ... 2. cause a person to do something by behaving in a certain esp. annoying way ... 3. cause a particular reaction in a person etc. *(her editorial provoked an angry response among readers; the goal provoked cheers from the crowd)*" (1998, 1164; italics in the original). All other variants on this verb are equally disparaging. To therefore describe my teaching with such an antagonistic term, rather than, say, "evocative," suggests a strong bias toward imagining Blackness as endangering and threatening (Fanon 1968).

My engaging students into critical thinking is not provocation. As educators, we risk difficulties associated with managing fear, resistance, and dissent in the classroom. Teaching material that may generate multiple viewpoints on current and historical social justice issues always invites healthy anger, disagreement, and frustration among students. Questions about gender, sexual orientation, criminal injustice, religious intolerance, bigotry, xenophobia, anti-Semitism, and hate are all notable for generating student discomfort and resistance, affecting student course opinions, comments, and scores.

For example, in a class on racism and the criminal justice system, how does one deal with the position held by some students that all Blacks are criminals and responsible for all moral carnage in society? When exploring Indigenous people's cultural genocide and history in Canada, students often ask, "Why do Indigenous people get so many special tax breaks on reserves"? Further, how do we respond to and manage student responses on morality and moral beliefs such as, "Employment equity is reverse discrimination and women are no longer suffering from any form of oppression and or discrimination"? And when confronting Islamophobia, "All Muslims are terrorists"? I also teach what is considered a penalized discipline and controversial subjects in which students are challenged to explore social relationships outside their comfort zones. These issues often clash with students' personal viewpoints.

Professors who are committed to creative pedagogical and non-traditional approaches are often seen as taking political risks and run the danger of being perceived as incompetent. We risk being marginalized by more traditional academics who believe in learning through lecturing and "skill and drill," "sage on the stage," rather than engaging in the interdisciplinary ethics of social justice, anti-racism, queer theory, and feminist politics via more open-ended, inquiry-oriented, student-centred approaches. The emphasis on "being" and "becoming" aware is based on trust, respect, and compassion, which compel all – teachers and learners alike – to "redefine the possible." In order to promote a more emancipatory and transformative pedagogy that invites the development of a *sociological imagination*, my course learning objectives always strive to respond to the critical faculties of all students. While Ryerson University[17] and other universities have challenged the merits and utility of student response surveys as meaningful tools for assessing pedagogy, sessional, contract, and tenured track faculty are much more vulnerable than associate professors moving toward full professorship.

Whereas student opinion surveys are given undue weight, you can balance the scale by including solicited and unsolicited letters of support in your dossier, as well as narrating how you have mentored students. Mentoring is crucial to student experience, and especially retention, so you will want to craft a narrative with supporting documentation to this effect. The invisible labour of mentoring current and former students, acting as a role model for students, doing university community outreach, offering community lectures, providing conference presentations, giving television interviews, representing the university at community events, and becoming a surrogate parent for minority students helps student retention and is good business for the university. Given what is known about UOIT's students and their university experiences according to the National Survey of Student Engagement (2014), racial minoritized students are among the most disadvantaged in the need to support their schooling through part-time and full-time employment (i.e., 46 per cent of first-year students at UOIT and 42 per cent of fourth-year students indicated that financial pressures or work obligations posed a major obstacle to their academic progress) and the lack of time to engage in student government and co-curricular activities (i.e., 52 per cent of first-year students at UOIT spend at least an hour or more per week caring for dependents living with them).[18]

Although there are no statistics on drop-out rates of racially minoritized students, we know that in 2009, 45 per cent of UOIT's graduating class self-identified as a visible minority – up from 22 per cent in 2007 (Canadian University Survey Consortium, September 2016). Given the proportion of minority students who graduated and the rates of students with pressures that limit academic engagement, it is likely that even more minority students enter UOIT but do not graduate. Therefore, it seems clear that there is a need to provide additional academic and social support for minority students.

Retention is a priority for UOIT, but there is not yet adequate identification of the students who are at risk to drop out yet who stay on as the result of the mentoring I prioritize. Faculty relating to Black, racialized, queer, and marginalized students through informal contact is critical for student retention, yet this invisible tax and work of mine is not recognized by the TPC. Teaching is more than simply classroom interaction; teaching also takes the form of mentoring and supporting students. Many students have confessed that my mentoring, teaching, and advising have assisted in their retention, completion of their degrees, and going on to grad school. As the only openly Black, gay faculty member, I often advise current and former Black, queer, and marginalized students, including every generation of Black, Indigenous, and racialized students who need extra support to navigate pre- and post-university life. Professional references, academic references, volunteer independent student supervision, telephone references for job and university applications and intervening when necessary in nuanced race-related issues that affect Black and racialized students is also invisible labour. Lack of recognition of invisible pedagogical labour in academia reinforces systemic barriers.

Full Academic Freedom

My promotion experience forced me to rethink the concept of collegiality and civility. I have come away from my experience of promotion with a simple question: how does one remain cordial, when some of colleagues camouflage long-harboured mean-spiritedness behind dehumanizing civility and painstaking scrupulousness? The university is *supposed* to be an enlightened space free of bias and prejudice, but the pursuit of this promise in my teaching and research as judged by the conduct of my peers has been hindered by structural racism, compulsory heterosexuality, heteronormativity and patriarchy.

Research scholarship on equity and diversity in higher education has documented persistent systemic barriers and implicit biases faced by members of equity-seeking groups, women, Black professors, racialized minorities, Aboriginal peoples, and persons with disabilities (Henry et al. 2017). Any attempt to place race and racism on the agenda, let alone at the centre of debate, is deeply unpopular. "In the academy, we are often told that we are being too crude and simplistic, that things are more complicated than that, that we're being essentialist and missing the real problem of social class" (Gillborn 2015, 279). The TPC evaluation reveals a need for improvement in the committee's understanding of popular culture, pedagogy and praxis, anti-racism, gender studies, masculinity studies, queer studies, and social justice, which would enhance understanding of my pedagogical approach to students. The TPC evaluation of my promotion would have been improved by a critical understanding of and ability to grapple with and overcome deeply held beliefs about race, racism, sexuality, and politics. Such critical experiences cannot be captured by standard quantitative and largely argument-oriented exams, which are more standard in the STEM and science disciplines.

Continuation

In sum, the collegial process is essential to the academy, perhaps even sacrosanct, until it runs afoul of the collective agreement. Procedural irregularities/errors indicate your colleagues' pretext to justify resistance to your candidacy and reflect their unethical haste to dispose of your candidacy for promotion. The cumulative structural barriers and biases mapped along the spectrum of my promotion application illustrate the challenges I have faced as a Black gay scholar at every point of this process. They tell a story about the obstacles to my promotion and the dynamics of subtle biases and structural barriers in my promotion application after fourteen years at UOIT. I am a Black gay scholar whose body is always racially historicized, demonized, and sexualized. The lesson my experience offers to Black LGBTQS+ professors seeking promotion to full professor is that one's file must be prepared with utmost attention to detail and for many years in preparation. In my experience, a Black LGBTQS+ professor seeking full professorship will be judged by a different standard and with an exactitude to the standards to such a degree that it is qualitatively different and therefore discriminatory. Because we are tenured, we can afford to challenge the status quo and refuse oppressive past practices that force us into cloned normativity of heterosexuality and homoppression within the academe. Our example in doing so is itself an act of mentoring and liberation.

NOTES

1 "Transgender" is an umbrella term used to describe persons who express gender nonconformity in relation to "normative" understandings of masculinity and femininity. While this term continues to be contested, I will use it here to refer specifically to transgender men and women who, either through dress, hormones, surgical technologies, or some combination of the three, live as a gender that was not assigned to them at birth.

2 "Intersex" is a term used to describe people who are not easily or neatly categorized within the binary sex system of male and female, or those who trouble this system. It is also a critical interrogation of the biomedical sciences that pathologize gender sex differences. It is worth reading Holmes's re-definition of intersex, who prefers the term "intersexuality," referring instead to a physical and/or chromosomal set of possibilities in

which features usually understood a belonging distinctly to either the male of female sex are combined into a single body (Holmes 2008, 32).

3 At the third International Gathering of American Indian and First Nations Gays and Lesbians in 1990, Myra Laramee, a Cree community member and scholar, coined the term "two-spirit." (See https://twospiritmanitoba.ca/we-belong.) Some people use it as a way to identify both their queerness and their Indigeneity (Robinson 2014, 16 May). It is a complex term that is used in many different ways and holds many different meanings for different people. However, in popular usage, the word is often simultaneously used as an umbrella term for all Indigenous people with complex genders, sexual orientations, or sexualities.

4 *Canadian Charter of Rights and Freedoms*, s 15, Part 1 of the *Constitution Act, 1982*, being Schedule B to the *Canada Act 1982* (UK), 1982, c 11. For example race, national or ethnic origin, colour, religion, sex, age, or mental or physical disability. These enumerated grounds according to the SCC are a fluid list because we do not live single identity lives. The use of the words "in particular" before this enumeration suggests that it was intended to be an open list

5 Analogous grounds are personal characteristics, similar to enumerated grounds, which are immutable, difficult to change, or changeable only at unacceptable personal cost, such as internalized homophobia and the denial of sexual expression and sexual identity.

6 *Egan v Canada*, [1995] 2 SCR 513. In 1995, the Supreme Court of Canada ruled that sexual orientation was a prohibited ground of discrimination under the Charter, even though it was not explicitly named in the Charter's equality rights clause.

7 For a more elaborate explanation, see *Corbiere v Canada (Minister of Indian and Northern Affairs).* [1999] 2 SCR 203, para 60.

8 *Canada (AG) v Mossop*, [1993] 1 SCR 554 was the first decision of the Supreme Court of Canada to consider equality rights for gays.

9 Delwin Vriend was employed as a laboratory coordinator in an Alberta college. He had received positive performance evaluations, salary increases, and promotions. He was fired when his employer found out he was gay. In *Vriend v Alberta*, [1998] 1 SCR 493, the Court held that provincial human rights legislation that left out the ground of sexual orientation violated section 15(1) (https://www.canlii.org/en/ca/scc/doc/1998/1998canlii816/1998canlii816.html).

10 In 1999, the Supreme Court of Canada upheld a decision of the Ontario Court of Appeal in recognizing the right of spousal support for same-sex couples in the case of *M v H* (1999) [1999] 2 SCR 3. The case struck down a man-woman definition of spouses in Ontario family law, paving the way for twenty years of positive changes for the LGBTQS+ communities.

11 An Act respecting certain aspects of legal capacity for marriage for civil purposes. https://laws-lois.justice.gc.ca/eng/acts/c-31.5/page-1.html.

12 The Foundation is made up of community activists and lawyers (https://
www.associations.cc/company-foundation-equal-families-in-toronto-28505).
As a young Black gay man I attended many of the early meetings to strate-
gize for *M v H*. There is a deliberate lack of historical memory and erasure
of Black gay activist from the early years of activism in Canada, by extension
the Canadian academy.

13 https://www.the519.org/. The 519 provided a space for meetings and reas-
sured safety for lesbian, gay, bisexual, transgender, and two-spirited groups
and communities in the Toronto area.

14 Part I of the *Constitution Act*, 1982, being Scheduled B to the *Canada Act*
1982, c 11.

15 In English-speaking Caribbean islands, "buller men" (i.e., "tops") and "batty
bwoys" (i.e., "bottoms") are Indigenous derogatory terms for gay men, bisexual men, and men who have sex with men (Crichlow 2004).

16 In respect to the then Ontario Tech University Collective Agreement, the
examples I provide are generalized to protect confidentiality.

17 Ryerson University v Ryerson Faculty Association, 2018.

18 UOIT is now called Ontario Tech University (OTU).

REFERENCES

Andrews v Law Society of British Columbia. 1989. 1 SCR 143.
Cabral, A. 1969. *Revolution in Guinea: Selected Texts by Amilcar Cabral.* New York:
    Monthly Review Press
Canada (AG) v Mossop. 1993. 1 SCR 554.
Canadian University Survey Consortium. 2016. https://cusc-ccreu.ca/?lang=en.
Crenshaw, K. 1989. "Demarginalizing the Intersection of Race and Sex: A Black
    Feminist Critique of Antidiscrimination Doctrine." *University of Chicago Legal
    Forum*, 1: 139–168.
Crichlow, W.E.A. 2004. *Buller Men and Batty Bwoys: Hidden Men in Toronto and
    Halifax Black Communities.* Toronto: University of Toronto Press.
Crichlow, W. 2019. "Black Consciousness and the Heteronormative Sexual
    Politics of Black Leadership in Toronto: A Commentary." In *African Canadian
    Leadership: Continuity, Transition, and Transformation*, edited by T. Kitossa, E.
    Lawson, and P. Howard, 289–310. Toronto: University of Toronto Press.
Egan v Canada. 1995. 2 SCR 513.
Fanon, F. 1968. *The Wretched of the Earth.* New York: Grove.
Foucault, M. 1984. "What Is an Author?" In *The Foucault Reader*, edited by
    P. Rabinow, 101–120. New York: Pantheon Books.

Foucault, M. 1991. *Discipline and Punish*. New York: Penguin. Original work published 1975.

Gillborn, D. 2015. "Intersectionality, Critical Race Theory, and the Primacy of Racism: Race, Class, Gender, and Disability in Education." Qualitative Inquiry 21 (3): 277–287. https://doi.org/10.1177/1077800414557827.

Hall, S., ed. 1997. *Representation: Cultural Representations and Signifying Practices*. Sage: Open University Press.

Henry, F., Dua, E., James, C.E., Li, P., Ramos, H., and Smith, M. 2017. *The Equity Myth: Racialization and Indigeneity at Canadian Universities*. Vancouver: University of British Columbia Press.

Holmes, M. (2008). *Intersex: A Perilous Difference*. Selinsgrove, PA: Susquehanna University Press.

McKenzie, K. 2017. "Rethinking the Definition of Institutional Racism." Wellesley Institute. https://www.wellesleyinstitute.com/health/rethinking-the-definition-of-institutional-racism/.

National Survey of Student Engagement (NSSE). 2014. http://nsse.indiana.edu/.

Ryerson University v Ryerson Faculty Association. 2018. CanLII 58446 (ON LA).

9 "Certain Uncertainty": Phenomenology of an African Canadian Professor[1]

TAMARI KITOSSA

Introduction

Phenomenologically, as shown by the contributions to this volume, the life-world of African Canadian professors is fraught with ambivalence, contradiction, risks, and paradox. As a group, they are a minority in the academy and within their communities. In the academy, aside from standard instructional and scholastic expectations, there is pressure to be the face of representational inclusivity and they are expected to perform a range of emotional labours (Norris 2019). In regard to their communities, they are expected to instrumentally direct their scholastic specialties and service work toward a reified Black community (see Dei 2019; Sivanandan 1977; West 1993–4). Even as I work within the frame of my reality as Black scholar, or is it a scholar who is Black, I am asking, Who and what is the Black academician? Is each of them trapped by and in Blackness? Or is Blackness an experiential and metaphoric space to theorize the human condition, liberate Black people and humanity from oppression (see Santiago-Valles 2000; Robinson 2000).

On the basis of my experience, it seems that the artificially constructed opposing tendencies between the university and the community position the Black professor between a rock, that of academia's (white) codes and modes, and a hard place, that of expectations and demands of recompense to a reified Black community. To effectively, healthily, and sanely live and make a living between, in, and within these sometimes conflicting life-worlds, Black professors must identify the relations to which they will contribute and those they will resist. To do so, the first order of business rests on the Khemetan (i.e., Egyptian) philosophy of "Know thyself," which Socrates reframed more aggressively as "The unexamined life is not worth living." The point of this chapter, then, is to promote the development of analytical capacity and to exercise critical reflexivity toward

African Canadian professors building relations of liberation within, between, and outside the academy.

There is a growing body of scholarship, op-eds, and blogs that expose and explore anti-Blackness in addition to gender and sex inequality, homophobia, and racism in academia (Nelson 2011; A. Henry 2017; F. Henry and Tator 2009; Kitossa 2016; Smith 2018; Stewart 2004). But alongside laying siege to the insulating policies and practices in the university that defend inequitable relations, it is important to share stories that centre reflexivity within the struggle to expand the domain of liberation within the university. To this end, part of my scholarship aims to add to the emergence of work the likes of Anthony Stewart (2004) and Annette Henry (2019) that offer practical considerations for African Canadian academicians at varying stages of their career.

My aim in this meditation is to critically account for my experience in the academy and my effort to navigate contexts, relationships, and situations that are imperilling, while seeking to identify persons and relationships that enable me to contribute to an organizational culture of accountability, equity, inclusivity, and transparency. But there is another struggle weighing heavily on me, besides resisting anti-Blackness in academia, and that is to identify and transcend the politics of racial debt-peonage, essentialist Black solidarity, animosity, anti-intellectualism, and instrumentalism that position Black academics as "leaders" and "servants" when not imagining them as the collective "property" of a reified "Black community." Without letting go of the centrality of Blackness, I make a case for resisting the claims of Black self-anointed gatekeepers and intellectual opinion-makers on the energy, time, and obedience of African Canadian academics. The way I've found out of the boxes and demands imposed by academia and elite guardians of conscience in the so-called Black community is to go deeper into both worlds. In doing so, my tendency is to draw on the epistemic and political philosophies of W.E.B. Du Bois, Frantz Fanon, Antonio Gramsci, Alvin Gouldner, Karl Marx, and Kwame Nkrumah as guides in the struggle for defining my existence as an academician and intellectual.

Part 1 of this chapter is a theoretical excursus on how to conceive of the Black professor. I elaborate a Fanonist and Gramscian analytic of the Black self in the white academy. I go on to argue that there is an equal need to develop an account of the African Canadian academic that resists essentialist demands and, in doing so, exposes the class and ideological conflicts between the Black intelligentsia in the academy and the (sometimes antagonistic) non-university-based Black intellectuals whom Carl James (2019) calls "cultural curators." Often the latter imagine themselves as bone fide gatekeepers and authentic interlocutors for "*the* Black community." Indeed, from a psycho-materialist vantage point, for those who generate their self-concept and a portion or all of their income from this pastoral role, it makes sense that they would erect a barrier to prevent access to "*the* Black community." And even if no material exchange is involved, the status of influencing access to "*the* Black community" amounts to a powerful controlling role tied up with symbols of esteem and reputation. But there is no single archetype of the Black intelligentsia within, between, and without the university – for the Black intelligentsia is both fractal and multidimensional, vaporizing any firm divide between the ebony ground and the ivory tower. However, analysis and reflexivity are not enough. Toward the struggle for equitable and just relations, I outline Kwame Nkrumah's (1969)[2] analytical imperatives for decolonization as a way to participate in liberation struggles within academia, between it and within African Canadian communities and the broader social order.

Parts 2 and 3 of this chapter focus on white cultural hegemony in academia and the limits to Black essentialism and instrumentalism respectively. In both instances I represent real scenarios to demonstrate my lived experience with "certain uncertainty" in the academy and African Canadian communities. I conclude with a meditation on the connections between knowledge of self, awareness of context, and the necessity to engage in the struggle to enlarge zones of liberation.

Fanon's "Certain Uncertainty" and Gramsci's Reflexivity: Toward a Philosophy of Black Professorial Ontology

As a starting point, by accepting Fanon's (1967, 85) proposition that "a given society is racist or it is not," we can accept his citing of French philosopher Karl Jaspers's contention that "comprehension in depth of a single instance will often enable us, phenomenologically, to apply this understanding in general to innumerable cases … [because] what is important in phenomenology is less the study of a large number of instances than the intuitive and deep understanding of a few individual cases" (1968, 168–9). Antonio Gramsci's (1991, 324) borrowing of the (African) Egyptian injunction "Man know thyself" asserts that we are the product of the prior relations that constitute us. In virtually every instance in this book, African Canadian scholars, in accounting for their research and their experiences in the white-dominated space of the academy, reveal further phenomenological truths that exceed purely negative accounting. Because of the specificity of each milieu within the overall hegemonic norms of whiteness, each contributor specifies from individual vantage points and perspectives, as I do here; but there is collective resonance in each testimony, irrespective of difference that is neither homogeneous nor monotonous, for each is a different perspective on a unified reality concerning the contradictions and paradoxes of what it means to be of African descent and an academician and intellectual in a social order that is both anti-Black and anti-intellectual, among other things.

I cannot speak for others, but I assert that my experiences are not exclusive to me, since nothing that is social occurs in isolation. Whether we are female, male, queer, straight, trans, light or dark-skinned, immigrant or Canadian-born, etc., we are all marked by what Du Bois called, in reference to the condemnation of Jack Johnson, this "unforgivable blackness" (1914, 181). Anticipated by Du Bois, Fanon (1977) also asserts the "fact of blackness"[3] as a white cultural psychosis that manifests in "a historico-racial schema" projected onto the world by the ontological gaze of whiteness. Locked within that gaze, the African's "body impedes the closing of the postural schema of the white man [and woman] – at the point the [African] makes [his or her] entry into the phenomenal world of the white man [and woman]" (160). A priori, marked with meaning independent of actual personality, the African-descended person is a source of neurosis, manifested in the white imaginary as a phobogenic object – a thing to be feared as much as desired, precisely because white ontology depends on it (Fanon 1977).

A regime of violence is the result, in which the African-descended person is imagined as the blameworthy cause of the effect. As I will demonstrate, this is an epistemic and symbolic violence. Because of the aggression, fantasies, fragility, and possessiveness of whiteness, I assert that African-descended professors are objects of psychic and spiritual (if not criminal) criminal violence (Christian 2017; Griffin et al. 2011; Grundy 2017; Johnson and Bryan 2017; Samuel and Wane 2005). What makes this possible?

Again I invoke Fanon, who asserts that not *aside* from the "fact of blackness" but *because* of the necessity of its alterity in the white cultural imaginary, Blackness and people of African descent embody negations that give whiteness and white people their (always) positive ontological stability. There is a context in which, given the deep denial about white racism in Canada's multicultural milieu (Stewart 2004), the body of the African Canadian professor, whether female, gender non-conforming, or male is "surrounded by a certain uncertainty" (Fanon 1977, 110–11). This means nothing is straightforward. On one hand, anti-Blackness and African peoples constitute a kind of gastronomy: the objects of a ritualized psycho-cultural consumption manifest as a cannibalizing effect that perpetuates white embodiment as an unquestioned and unproblematic cite and site of intelligibility, rationality, and reason (see Hawkesworth, 2016; Kitossa 2014). In this ontological episteme, Blackness is body and emotion, signifier of the feminine and passive, and whiteness is mind and reason, signifier of masculine and active principles. Such a deeply entrenched raciological schema finds articulation, but not origins, in the architects of the European so-called Enlightenment, including Locke, Hume, Kant, Voltaire, and even Marx and Rousseau, among many others (Ani 1994; Eze 1995; Kant 1997; Lyons 1975; Mills 2006; Simon-Aaron 2008). The entrenched perception that Blackness equates to unintelligibility articulates itself within psychic registers as "implicit bias," with effects on the experiences of African-descended academics, from undergraduates to staff and the tenured professoriate.

If my experience is anything to go by, African Canadian professors who cleave to the prerogative of intellectual autonomy and the right of academic freedom to theorize from clearly exposed values as opposed to choosing a side, run risks that are personally and professionally consequential. They must navigate anti-Blackness, nurture and mentor Black students and survive the publish-or-perish demands of the neoliberal university. And they must do so in addition to negotiating the proprietary claims on their *being*, time, and work by community pastoralists who espouse a discourse and disciplinary practice of social levelling. Relying on a false spatial geography described as "gown vs town," the "ivory tower vs the ebony street," and now the "communiversity," this politics of resentment practises bad faith in assuming that our bodies and politics do not travel with us. I suggest that this territorialization of social space negates the possibility that African Canadian academics *bring* their Black communities with them in their very personhood. To argue otherwise is to ignore the fundamental proposition that, as Robyn Maynard (2017, 11) notes, "Black lives are still imperiled and devalued by a racial calculus and a political arithmetic that were entrenched centuries ago." To argue that African-descended academicians and other elites are not also subject to anti-Blackness and endangerment in their places of work as much as in the public domain, whatever one may think of their individual politics, is a perverse alchemy of what Black existence looks like in all its diversity (Grundy 2017; Wingfield 2015; see also Benjamin 2005; Cose 1993).[4]

Within the academy and their communities, romantic ideals of tenured professors (i.e., they are a privileged lot, with a surfeit of time on their hands, since they *only* use their heads) and the mythic spatial separation of the "ivory tower" from *the* community, has three possible effects. First, it adds emotional and occupational burdens to the already heavy load on the Black tenured professoriate: the allegation of "sell-out" is always implied here. Second, it can lead to Black academicians internalizing anti-intellectualism by disparaging the merits of scholarship as a form of activism and political action (no matter how few people may read their journal articles or books); they, as a result, take on extra service work at the expense of themselves and their families. Finally, the construal of Black professors as having revoked their membership in Black communities by virtue of their professional accomplishments may give rise to three related defects: (1) the work that African Canadian professors do to resist covert and overt anti-Blackness directed at them, and Black staff and students in the academy is negated; (2) unreasonable expectations and constraints are placed upon African Canadian professors' freedom of enquiry, though I expect that this demand rarely, if ever, is applied to those in the sciences, technology, engineering, and mathematics; and (3) prospective junior Black professors may be discouraged from pursuing professoriate roles because of ideological bullying or may have their research trajectory misdirected by the instrumentalist demand that their scholarship must be "relevant" to alleviating the oppression of the Black masses.

In coming to a place of understanding and engaging with racism in the university, I have found it is vital to theorize what Fanon's "fact of blackness" (1977) means for me and other African-descended people in the intellectual culture of the Western academy. Inasmuch as it is fashionable to claim that we must get beyond the "Black and white binary paradigm," such a viewpoint is a form of anti-Blackness that negates the specific role of the aesthetic and moral anthropomorphization of the Black and white Manicheanism in Western, Levantine, and Indian subcontinental cultural complexes (Deliovsky and Kitossa 2013). Thus *because* Blackness orients alterity in the white cultural imaginary, both Blackness and African-descent people embody negations that give whiteness and "white" people their (always) positive ontological stability and presumed superior intellectual ability.

The ontology of Blackness as a "thing" to be consumed for the existential reality of whiteness paradoxically demands Black complicity: as a condition of employment and *existence*, the African-descended professor is implicitly called upon to perform the additional labour of appeasing white existential anxiety – in short, to undertake the emotional labour to make white students and sometimes peers experience the world as a safe place in the presence of a threatening Blackness (Norris 2019). Indicating just how threatening the bodies and minds of Black professors are, my well-meaning teaching assistants remind me (of the backhanded) compliment that "[white] students are intimidated by you because they think you are so smart." At other times African Canadian professors are invited to not to be "so serious" and to "smile more." Such comments indicate the line between the presumption of threat, requiring that African Canadian professors "impression manage" to make others feel comfortable, and the countenancing of Black professors as "magical negroes" is not only thin, it suggests the depth of unlearning work that is essential for non-Black people in the academy.

The point is that the corollary of producing conditions for white safety is that there is not, nor can there be, a "safe space" for Black people or Blackness. Everything about Blackness is marked and read off from the epistemic and ontological paradox of desires and endangerment that Blackness represents. But African-descended academics must bear another burden. Rooted in the European Enlightenment and "orientalist"[5] ideal of Black congenital stupidity (Simon-Aaron 2008), white peer judgments and student evaluations are mobilized as a form of violent racial literacy manifesting in marginalization and a ritualized demand for genuflection: these are yet other forms of consumption. Almost as a condition of employment, there is an implicit demand for Black emotional labour to secure, soothe, and protect white anxieties and insecurities: a fundamental reversal of racialized danger that is implicitly a condition of employment arising from white largesse. The effect of power-knowledge, in ways that Foucault did not explore from the vantage point of raciology, diffuses the power of discipline and normalizing judgment across the domain of whiteness in the academy – from student complaints and experience surveys to peer evaluations for tenure and promotion.

In the academy, then, Black academics must know their place, because such a place is imagined to exist by embodiment, performance, and force: the evidence is that African Canadian academics are held to higher and different metrics for hiring and promotion. They must tolerate being "exceptions to the rule" (i.e., the magical Negro) of Black congenital stupidity, while doing opposing things: cultivating genuine relationships with allies and mentors from among white peers and developing Teflon skin against psychic assault and career-undermining practices in order to maintain a healthy ego structure. If the African-descended academic appears paranoid, this is not a condition to be pitied: where anti-Blackness is an equal opportunity employer, "survival … depends in large measure on the development of a 'healthy' cultural paranoia … toward the motives of every white [person] and at the same time [one must] never allow this suspicion to impair [one's] grasp of reality" (Grier and Cobbs 1968, 161). But inasmuch as my experiences with racism in the academy corroborate recent research on racism (Christian 2017; Eisenkraft 2010; Fenelon 2003; Fleras 2014; Stewart 2004; F. Henry and Tator 2009), the principle of hegemony specifies that nothing in social life is absolute: there are spaces, relationships, and opportunities for cross-race resistance and solidarity that depend on elaborating alliances and solidarities with white and negatively racialized colleagues of good conscience.

On Whiteness: Certain Uncertainty and the Possibilities for Cross-Racial Solidarity

Immediately following the successful defence of my dissertation, I applied to 120 universities and colleges across Canada and the United States. Though shortlisted to 10, two job interviews at southern Ontario universities opened my eyes to the anti-Black racism I would encounter as a professor, and one institution was an amalgam of the best and worst of them. In the first interview, I was interviewed by three senior white scholars: two women and one a man. Something just did not feel right: I felt a tension between the women, who were warm and accommodating, and the man, who seemed distant and indifferent. His body language, evidence of passive aggression, bubbled over into overt aggression. In the middle of my response to a question about the distinction between social control and regulation, the white man shot to his feet, spun on his heels, and abruptly left the room – never to return. The white women apologized profusely for the conduct of their colleague and did their best to allay my misgivings. I received a call from one of the women to tell me that I was not selected for the position. I would have declined the position even if it had been offered.

The second shortlisted interview was marked by such open animosity and outright attack on my academic freedom of scholarship that I filed a complaint of human rights violation. At the Q and A with the whole department, two white men attacked me until, near the end of their harangue, another senior white male colleague suggested the conduct of his two colleagues was unbecoming. The interview was closed. One of the white men involved in the collusion to torpedo my interview was the chair of the department. He had been a model of civility and collegiality throughout the day until that critical point of the interview. Both men had done their due diligence and read my dissertation closely. They lifted quotes critical of the normalization of white supremacy in Canada, which propagates images of African Canadians as criminogenic – this to them was evidence that I was a "reverse racist." I defended my assertion that anti-Blackness and anti-Black racism are pervasive and deeply embedded in the cultural fabric of Canada. However, I was not prepared for the other white male professor, who broke into tears, to disclose that when he was a fourteen-year-old growing up in Texas, his genitals were fondled in a public washroom by an African American man. The air was sucked out of the room: my Blackness triggered his alleged memory of childhood molestation. Despite this bizarre experience, I was offered the position. Having had a concurrent offer from another university, I knew I would never subject myself to the psychological unease of working at a place where I would not be awarded tenure or I would be made to suffer for it as my reward. Nevertheless, I met with the dean to negotiate salary and perquisites. I described the unethical conduct of the faculty members to the dean, and he hired an independent lawyer to conduct an investigation. Fearing this would be a toxic workplace, I declined the offer at that institution; an assessment vindicated by the lawyer's report concerning my complaint.

But getting my foot in the door was a disciplining experience in the tyranny of whiteness. For example, early in my career, just when publishing is vital to tenure and promotion, I had an article accepted for publication in a "reputable" journal but subsequently received a communication of summary rejection. Tenure and promotion was also a time of terror, a moment for those who clearly opposed my appointment to exact revenge; more than this cannot be said. I began to learn that academia is a dangerous and hostile place and that white people with power can be terrifying. I have come to understand only recently that, without critical consciousness, strong administrators, and relations of liberation marked by colleagues' commitment to meaningful solidarity, there is little to restrain the savagery of those who would use processes and procedures (unethically) to undermine social justice. First, however, I had to learn that even after being appointed to a department that was welcoming at one level, other layers of nuance concealed the savagery of white noblesse oblige and recognition that my Blackness was to some extent an adornment. Care, however, must be taken when walking the thin line between cynicism and realistic appraisal of Black phenomenology where one's ontology is defined by "certain uncertainty."

Being "appointed" is a quaint and fatuous term of academia intended to distance the "life of the mind" from the dullness of plebian existence. Behind the urbane impressions of academia and before the drudgery of cranking out publications to satisfy the prerogatives of annual reporting, there is the ugly world of compromises, conflicts, disputes, negotiations, and general wrangling when ideological lines become more sharply defined around hiring and promotion. Since appointment decisions are supposed to be *in camera*, no party outside of the deliberations can really know what went on behind closed doors. What I wanted to know was not privileged. What I wanted to know was not who voted for me and why, but what considerations went into my being considered the right candidate – at least in the eyes of the majority. So in a private moment some years on, I asked this question of a senior colleague in the department. The answer was simple elegance: "We made a determination not to reproduce ourselves." Until that point, only two other persons "of colour" had been hired in the department, one of whom was a tenured track hire. What alarmed me was the undercurrent of my colleague's candid response. I feared that, just as white people could easily decide to hire me, they could, if enough consented, undo me. It turns out my hiring was an admixture of fit, competency, and a genuine desire for racial diversity. But just as there was no consideration of the toll upon me of being hired, in part, to fulfil the criterion of representation, fundamental questions of covert and overt anti-Black racism in the department and across the university were also beyond consideration.

For example when in 2014 there was yet another blackface incident on campus, I gave a lecture to my third-year class on the ways that neoliberalism's presumptive logic of social progress, defined by merit and individual responsibility, enables white people to be unaccountable beneficiaries of unearned privileges. Many white students felt aggrieved by the lecture. They were so angered that an alarmed student took seriously their threats to kill me. The most animated of them were four white female students. They plotted to trail me after class to identify my car and either cut my brake cables or put sugar in my gas tank.

I found this out only at the end of the semester. At the time of the incident a white male student took seriously the students' conviction to kill me and came to alert me to this fact. Before he could give me details and the names of students, I cut him off, saying that I could not listen to news of students' negative comments about me or my lectures during the semester. Even against his protest, I reasoned that I could not afford for the knowledge of racism to bias me against students and told him I needed to wait till the end of the semester. Thus at the end of the semester, when I did sit down with the student to hear what his classmates had been saying, I was stricken. How or why I came to believe it I do not know, but until that moment I had thought that anti-Black racism was a condition of my employment. I wrote about that experience in a general commentary about the racist culture at Brock University (2016). To my relief, a number of colleagues, staff, and students across the campus emailed me or spoke to me to express their outrage and solidarity – none included administrators.

In spite of clear evidence of solidarity, which is evidence of liberated relations to be discussed below, I had come to accept that the burden of racism was mine alone to bear, except for commiseration with friends who endured similar indignities. After all, as a way to get through the tyranny of white racism each semester I told myself that such violence was a condition of employment. But it was only within the past few years that I came to understand the wreckage of my mind and body is caused in part by my own complicity with white supremacy,

the indifference of administrators, and my own department's ignorance about the reality of anti-Black racism that comes with "diversity."
It was not until after my discussion with this student that I realized
that for a long time I had been losing my grip on reality, impairing
my health, and damaging relationships with my family and friends, because at the close of each semester I became paralyzed with fatigue
for about a week. Since a cathartic reflection on "certain uncertainty"
shortly after my discussion with the concerned student in 2014, I no
longer have mental and physical destructuration at the end of each
semester, because I realized that while the violence of white racism is
all around me, building relations of liberation is the surest method to
refuse a burden that is not mine to carry.

The Black Scholar and Nuancing the African Canadian Community

As for the phenomenology of the African Canadian professor, is a critique of anti-Blackness and racism all that there is for the African
Canadian professor? What of the anti-intellectualism and instrumentalist coercion that emanates from some academics of African descent and
some members of the Black cultural intelligentsia who imagine themselves "authentic" interlocutors of the Black masses? In dramatizing the
"certain uncertainty" of my experience in the academy as an African
Canadian professor, I want to address myself to the unspeakable that
further complicates and confounds what it means to be a professor of
African descent. Here I am referring to (1) animosity, disparagement,
and professional jealousy among some African Canadian academicians, and (2) the ambivalence, anti-intellectualism, and resentment of
a reified "Black community" directed toward Black academics who are
deemed to be uselessly "taking up space" in and retreating to their "cave
of solitude" in the "ivory tower," as one Black "cultural curator" accused
me. In effect by virtue of their social location, African Canadian academicians in education, the humanities, social studies, and social work are
often disparaged by self-anointed Black "organic intellectuals" within the
academy and "cultural curators" who present themselves as representatives of reified Black communities.

Queer African Canadian scholars alert us to the limits of the familial
and unitary narrative of Blackness; they expose African Canadian communities as paradoxical: sites of belonging and home but also of exclusion, marginalization, and oppression (Crichlow 2004, 2019). Through
their activism and activist-scholarship they compel us to think in more
complicated ways about how heteronormativity and rejection expose
African Canadian queer and transgender people to risks that undermine

their quality of life. "Community" and "family" are, therefore, contingent ontological sites of imagining that are challenged, recast, and reconstituted, compelling us in turn to resist hegemonic narratives and practices that exclude. In much the same way, in my capacity as an academic, I have come to experience "community" as at times exploitative, oppressive, and threatening. I suggest that if we are to explicate anti-Blackness and anti-Blackness as fundamental to our experiences in the university, we need to also think in more complicated ways about how we are positioned *in* African Canadian communities *as* academicians. There is a powerful tendency by some "cultural curators" inside and outside academia to try to display their qualifications as community gatekeepers who articulate a sharp, morally determined spatial geography between those whose incomes and attainments mark them as "bourgeois" (read white conforming) and those "organically" connected to *the* Black community.

Following a path well worn by E. Franklin Frazier (1962), Harold Cruse (1967), and many others in the United States, Black academicians are perceived to suffer from the twin crises of deformed identity and racial irresponsibility. That is to say, they do not know who they are, in part because they are too self-interested and suffer from the Stockholm Syndrome, which makes them toadies to the "white man" and his institutions. In strictly instrumental fashion, the demand is that *they*[6] serve the "Black community" to which they are expected by providence to provide leadership. The paradox is obvious. Caught between a rock and a hard place, African Canadian academics are assailed for their distance from their Black communities, both intellectual and social, at the same time they are disparaged for their "talented tenth"[7] elitism. Notably in the United States, there are efforts to resolve the intrinsic contradiction between the push force of (tenured) African American academicians as upwardly mobile petite bourgeoisie and the pull force of racial affinity.

In different contexts, degrees, and tone this self-reflexive engagement seeking to resolve the contradiction has been undertaken by scholars such as Houston Baker Jr. (2008) and Eddie Glaude Jr. (2014) in the United States. And, though less categorical and condemnatory of other ways of being a Black academic, by George Dei (2019) in Canada. I agree with these scholars that it is a right to advocate and undertake a scholar-activist role for and within Black communities. I am especially sympathetic to the frontal criticism of the ways that inclusion and upward mobility blunt the Black professoriate's capacity and willingness to challenge white supremacy and the racial state. But my agreement and sympathy end very quickly, for without major qualifications the danger of this perspective is its implicit elitism and authoritarianism. Pushed to its ultimate logic, it suggests that Black academics who do not measure up to an absolutist performance criterion of what it means to be a Black scholar in strict racial affinity have abdicated their civic, moral, and racial responsibilities to Black people.

As with Chinweizu (1975), Davis (2016), Fanon (1977), Sivanandan (1977), Rodney (1969), and other theorists in the pantheon of the Black radical tradition (Robinson 2000), my position is that Blackness is a site from which to articulate the struggle against the tyrannies of capitalist exploitation – an exploitation whose face could just as easily have been Black and not white, if historical conditions favoured it. That Martin Luther King Jr. and Malcolm X are so often invoked to assail, in a totalizing way, Black academics who are non-instrumental or who are bogged down by the intensive demands of the neoliberal university, ignores the fact that both leaders came, just at the point of their assassinations or possibly because of it, to take up a radical humanism from which Black life served as actual and metaphorical evidence of the challenge to raise the human condition. Supported by my commitment to what Alvin Gouldner (1979) calls a culture of critical discourse (CCD) and my ongoing elaboration of the position that racial affinity is not in and of itself the basis for a Black radical humanist politics, I came face-to-face with intellectual instrumentalism and the authoritarianism of "cultural curators."

Here is an example. One night in February 2014 I received a call at my home from my dean requesting a meeting to discuss the claims of injury and demands for recompense by a Black church group in St. Catharines. At issue was the fact that I reviewed the draft and supported the online publication of an article by a Fulbright MA researcher, who happens to be Black, specializing in the Underground Railroad. She described visiting the church and finding it closed. In surveying the historic site and taking pictures of the bust of Harriet Tubman, she found the bust smeared with faeces. Church officials took exception to the article, which expressed horror that Tubman's bust was vandalized. The church clerk wrote an eight-page rebuke of the student to the director of the Fulbright Scholarship Board, demanding that her funding be revoked and that she be recalled to the United States.

Holding fast to the defining characteristic of the post-Renaissance intelligentsia – a "culture of critical discourse" (Gouldner 1979, 28) – I wrote a letter in defence of the student to the director of Fulbright Canada and copied all persons and offices in the letter. I asserted that the student's right of academic freedom is in the public interest and ought not be conditional upon the pleasure of any one audience. That drew the ire of the church clerk, who wrote a four-page letter to the dean of the Faculty of Social Sciences demanding that I be fired for "conflict of interest" and that I submit a letter of apology to the church for my "error." For good measure, copies of the clerk's letter were sent to eleven officials and offices in Canada and the United States, including the Black Congressional Caucus. While the letter verged on libel and the complaint was found vexatious, it stood little chance of depriving me of employment. The calculus was simply to be an irritant, interfere with my career, and assert the authority wielded by proprietary non-academic intellectuals. It also revealed a point that I think many do not want to address in African Canadian communities – that some "cultural curators" have an aggrandizing proprietary and totalitarian disposition – neither of which is helpful or useful. But instrumentalism and anti-intellectualism combine to generate an unhealthy disrespect and ignorance about the historically specific development, special skills, and claims of professional competence of academics. In defending the Fulbright graduate scholar I was fundamentally punished for defending the knowledge community over the ignorance and punitiveness of a proprietary "cultural curator." Despite professional jealousies and ideological conflicts among African Canadian academics, they are members of a community defined by CCD. Gouldner (1979, 28) defines CCD as

> an historically evolved set of rules, a grammar of discourse, which (1) is concerned to justify its assertions, but (2) whose mode of justification does not proceed by invoking authorities, and (3) prefers to elicit the voluntary consent of those addressed solely on the basis of arguments adduced. CCD is centered on a specific speech act: Justification. It is a culture of discourse in which there is nothing that speakers will on principle permanently refuse to discuss or make problematic; indeed, they are even willing to talk about the value of talk itself and its possible inferiority to silence or to practice. This grammar is the deep structure of the common ideology shared by the New Class. The shared ideology of the intellectuals and intelligentsia is thus an ideology about discourse.

There are many problems with this definition. First, to demonstrate competence and purchase consent, CCD is a restricted community of intellectual practitioners whose authority and right to speak are seen to rely on invoking the authority of sanctified members (i.e., Angela Davis, Du Bois, Durkheim, Fanon, Foucault, Marx and Engles, Weber, etc.). Second, the "deep structure of grammar" affirms the concreteness of ideas in social life – so it is not all about talk after all, since thinking is its own form of doing that informs rational action. And finally, if intellectuals are a class, with academics being a specialized subset, they are really a dependent or subset of historically active and conscious classes in pursuit of their interests. "Organic intellectuals," then, are not self-authorized, nor have they, as is sometimes wrongly thought, chosen to side with the inchoate downtrodden. They are instead the product of and sustained by those classes who subsidize them to give expression to the ideals and values of the classes they represent (see Conforth 1977; Karabel 1976). Clearly, Black people, existing as a class and ideologically stratified race in the context of White domination, do not exist as a unified conscience collective with its own organic intellectuals as such. Be that as it may, the point to be taken is that freedom of speech and freedom of enquiry, even speech against open speech and enquiry, is the only thing that is sacred among academicians, specifically, and intellectuals, generally. This fact not only goes against Black intellectual instrumentalism, it resists the authoritarianism of Black cultural curators.

But on the other side of the ledger, we need not stretch sympathy for the devil too far in taking a nuanced position on the contradictory and paradoxical social location of Black academics. As noted by Cornel West (1993–4, 60–1), there are many in Black communities with a healthy and justifiable "distrust and suspicion … [of] the usual arrogant and haughty disposition of intellectuals toward ordinary folk, but, more importantly, from the widespread refusal of black intellectuals to remain, in some visible way, organically linked with African American cultural life." West appears sympathetic to the view that Black academics are, as a rule, "haughty," which may or may not be true. This is, however, so idiosyncratic a phenomenon that I wonder about its "falsifiability." It may come as a surprise that few Black academics were as haughty and moralizing as the much-beloved and life-long Prussophile (Barkin 2005) W.E.B. Du Bois, at least in the early stages of his career. If, as West claims, African American academics are, outside the church context, not organic intellectuals produced by the hegemonic Black community and cannot "gain the respect and support from the black community – especially the black middle class," then "haughtiness" might well be a reaction formation rather than the natural temperament of a constituency that exists largely in isolation from the social currents of which they are a part.

Rightly or wrongly, West (1993–4) is sensitive to the reasons why the African American masses might distrust African American academicians: (1) marital exogamy, (2) preoccupation with the cultural and intellectual products of white America, and (3) the self-hating flight from Blackness. While one may find as much opposing evidence in the individual circumstances used to support these claims, what is a more certain justification for communal disparagement of African American academicians is that, unlike radical activists/organizers/mobilizers and cultural artists, they are presumed to have limited immediate influence over institutions of state and cultural practices of white supremacy. In short, their utility to affect the immediacy of Black life pales in comparison to Black leaders who might direct spontaneous outrage and directly negotiate with white power elites. The problem with this viewpoint, West (1993–4, 61) notes, is that it calls attention to the masses' own capitulation to the acquisitive ethos of capitalism in which "the life of the mind is viewed as neither possessing intrinsic virtues nor harboring emancipatory possibilities [in favour of] solely short-term political gain and social status." What is more, he asserts, African American academicians themselves – mirroring tendencies within the broader African American community that reflect the capitalistic norms of U.S. culture – have a similar short-term view of the life of the mind, too often regarding academia as a means of upward mobility.

Whereas the conditions, context, and politics of Black intellectual life in the United States cannot be easily mapped onto the experiences of African Canadian academics and their communities, my experiences infer there are enough parallels that must be considered. To my knowledge, we have no studies on African Canadian academics that would cast doubt on West's contention that in the United States both Black academics and the hegemonic Black community are in a bind about anti-intellectualism and levelling as common denominators. Apart from opening public conversation about the life-world of the African Canadian professoriate, it is vital to develop relationships with "cultural curators" who may be counted as allies in resisting a politics of resentment that expresses itself as a facile dichotomy between coercive obligation and intellectual freedom. Here, in addition to my deployment of Nkrumah mentioned above, I subscribe to William Grier and Price Cobbs's (1968) articulation of the condition and role of the Black academic. First, they note that high-level accomplishment is no barrier to the blows of anti-Black racism experienced by their working-class and lumpen fictive kin: "Black intellectuals are a disenchanted lot. They have overcome incredible odds and have performed the impossible. They have had to cling to their own view of themselves amid violent contrary winds, holding fast only to ties that feel familiar and right, however strange those ties may seem to others" (142).

Second, functionally agreeing with the Marxist-Gramscian contention that academics must play a restrained role in social movements for justice, subordinating themselves to the masses to whose side they defect to facilitate the development of philosophical clarity, Grier and Cobbs combine the recognition that the white world has declared genocidal war on African peoples. It is in this context that the specialized role of the Black academics as knowledge workers is evident:

> The black intellectual must accept his [sic] exclusion from this battle. If he [sic] is called by his brothers [sic], he will leap to their aid. If they fail to call, he will continue to pursue his version of truth. He cannot force himself on them. He must be primarily devoted to truth. If the white man challenges him, the black scholar must demolish him with truth. His sword

is his science, and only when he has finally fashioned a formidable weapon can it be put to use for his people and only when he limits his thrust to his special view of the world. (Grier and Cobbs 1968, 152)

To be sure, this is but one view on the unsettled question of the role of the Black academic in particular, and academics more generally (Said 1996). To my mind, this is not an issue that can be adjudicated with absolutes, since as much as anti-Blackness establishes the general outlines of an imagined Black community, which is experienced as real in all its diversity, so too is there space to recognize there are diverse ways of being Black and an academic.

Therefore inasmuch as some Black academics in education, law, the humanities, social studies, and social work are free to direct their intellectual energies to the Black community in general and various Black communities in particular, to make this a command impoverishes the development of academics who may contribute to other ways of analysing, interpreting, and thinking about the human experience. I advocate for another type of scholasticism that walks the line between opposing ideas: the myth of the "value-free" and "free-floating intellectual" and the partisanship of "choosing a side." I am in agreement with Gouldner (1968) and Cornforth (1977) that academics in the social disciplines do not have the luxury of the precise and specifying disciplinary parameters of the natural sciences, bourgeois and state support for radical critiques of ruling relations, or the privilege of choosing sides when they themselves are as much the objects of ideology as anyone else. Their task is instead to clarify the values and principles to which they are committed and to justify them according to logically consistent criteria. Academicians must "know [themselves]" to "be on guard against [their] own hypocrisy and [their] need to be loved" by those who exercise hegemony over aesthetics, culture, materialism, and metaphysics (Gouldner 1968, 113) and to be fearless in the face of opposition. Whereas scientists, Black or otherwise, are caught in a moral rather than ideological bind because capital and the state direct and reward their labour (Cornforth 1977; Mumford 1970), critical and reflexive scholars of the humanities and social disciplines confront a milieu antithetical to their very existence.

From "Zones" to "Relations"

To the extent that the production of ideas reflects the practical realities of conflicts over authority and power in shaping the human experience, academia is a battle ground. With this observation as a "first principle," the task of writing this chapter led me to think that Nkrumah's (1969) strategic understanding of revolutionary warfare has application to the academic setting. Whereas Nkrumah theorized a blueprint of colonial resistance from the reality of the promise that armed confrontation had for a revolutionary overthrow of imperialism in Africa, he focused on the specificity of a material "topography" and relational "balance of forces." I suggest these metaphors must be substituted to adapt to a different context, even if the analogy is not watertight. The Western academy is patterned on the medievalism of the cloister and feudalism (one has only to contemplate the meaning of maces and ermine-collared robes at graduation to see this inheritance). Also the contemporary university is vital for the reproduction of social order and the undertaking of corporate and state-sponsored research and development that sustain capitalism and state apparatuses of symbolic and actual violence. We cannot escape the fact that many Canadian universities are colonial in curriculum as well as being sited on unceded Indigenous Canadian territories, as noted by George Dei (2016). The tenured and the tenure track professor and the ensemble of relations that constitute the university must be liberated from sustaining a socially repressive and ecologically insane social order. Thus, rather than, as specified by Nkrumah, military *zones* in the context of counter-colonial struggles for independence that are *liberated, under enemy control,* or *contested,* I suggest a discursive transformation and displacement in favour of *relationships* that are liberated, contested, and enemy. Since there are no such things as institutions and organizations in any concrete sense, only relationships bound by authority and power, knowledge of self and Other ought to lead to clarity and guide the search for those who shares one's values, regardless of the issue. Where individuals are not clear about their values or what those values might be, the struggle of politics is one of persuasion. Thus relationships in "contested zones" is where the struggle over meaning and, hence, action, can tip toward liberatory or oppressive relations. Within the academy or in Black communities, I have found that identifying individuals and groups who are committed, or at least open, to resistance and struggle helps to build a critical mass that bends toward the arc of justice, while expanding zones of liberated relations.

NOTES

1 I wish to express my appreciation to Anita Jack-Davies, Carl James, Delores Mullings, and Awad Ibrahim for commentary on various iterations of this chapter. Errors and omissions are mine.

2   I am grateful to Zizwe Poe for bringing this book to my attention and for engaging me in discussion about how to apply Nkrumah's ideas to the university.

3   "The Fact of Blackness" is the title of chapter five in C.L. Markmann's 1977 translation of *Black Skin, White Masks*; it is appears as "The Lived Experience of the Black Man" in the 2008 translation by R. Philcox (Fanon 2008).

4   I can think here of Henry Louis Gates arrested at his home for "breaking and entering," and Professor Ersula Ore of Arizona State University slammed to the ground for jaywalking.

5   In the strict sense, in colonial discourse and practice, the African is precluded in the genesis of the concept of orientalism by the likes of Kant, Hegel, and others as having made no culture save that brought by enslaving Arabs and Europeans. I have argued that Edward Said (1979) reified African erasure by taking no notice of this exclusion (Deliovsky and Kitossa 2013).

6   It is almost without question that the *they* in question are Black academics in education, social work, the humanities, and the social disciplines, rather than those in medicine, technology, and the sciences. The exclusion of Black scholars in technical areas from instrumentalist criticism has to do with a number of factors not limited to (1) their limited number in these areas, (2) the practical remoteness of their specializations from general apprehension and democratic control, (3) genuflection at their valorization and esteem, given their function in the context of their utility to capital, the state, and the wealthy, and (4) temporal and historical fear of their racial and socially destructive powers (see Hennessy 1992). It typically escapes attention that the doyens of Black intellectual thought were trained in these disciplines: Fanon in medicine, Chinweizu in physics, and Chaikh Anta-Diop also in physics.

7   In the early stage of his career, Du Bois asserted that an elite and talented tenth of Black men and women are essential to saving Black people. In the early 1950s as he began a move that would flower into a full-fledged Marxist position, he would substantially qualify this thesis (see Rabaka 2003).

REFERENCES

Ani, M. 1994. *Yurugu: An African Centered Critique of European Cultural Thought and Behavior.* Trenton, NJ: African World Press.

Baker, H.A., Jr. 2008. *Betrayal: How Black Intellectuals Have Abandoned the Ideals of the Civil Rights Era.* New York: Columbia University Press.

Barkin, K. 2005. "W.E.B. Du Bois' Love Affair with Imperial Germany." *German Studies Review* 28 (2): 285–302. http://www.jstor.org/stable/30038150.

Benjamin, L. 2005. *The Black Elite: Still Facing the Color Line in the Twenty-First Century.* New York: Rowman & Littlefield.

Chinweizu, I. 1975. *The West and the Rest of Us: White Predators, Black Slavers, and the African Elite*. New York: Random House.

Christian, M. 2017. "From Liverpool to New York City: Behind the Veil of a Black British Male Scholar inside Higher Education." *Race Ethnicity and Education* 20 (3): 414–428. https://doi.org/10.1080/13613324.2016.1260230.

Cornforth, M. 1977. *The Theory of Knowledge*. New York: International Publishers.

Cose, E. 1993. *The Rage of a Privileged Class: Why Are Middle-Class Blacks Angry? Why Should America Care?* New York: HarperCollins.

Crichlow, W. 2004. *Buller Men and Batty Bwoys: Hidden Men in Toronto and Halifax Black Communities*. Toronto: University of Toronto Press.

Crichlow, W. 2019. "Black Consciousness and the Sexual Politics of Black Leadership in Toronto: A Commentary." In *African Canadian Leadership: Continuity, Transition and Transformation*, edited by T. Kitossa, E. Lawson, and P. Howard, 103–119. Toronto: University of Toronto Press.

Cruse, H. 1967. *The Crisis of the Negro Intellectual*. New York: Morrow.

Davis, A.Y. 2016. *Freedom Is a Constant Struggle: Ferguson, Palestine, and the Foundations of a Movement*. Chicago: Haymarket Books.

Dei, G.S.J. 2016. "Decolonizing the University: The Challenges and Possibilities of Inclusive Education." *Socialist Studies/Études socialistes* 11 (1): 23–61. https://doi.org/10.18740/S4WW31.

Dei, G.J.S. 2019. "An Indigenous Africentric and Pan-African Perspective on Black Leadership." In *African Canadian Leadership: Continuity, Transition and Transformation*, edited by T. Kitossa, E. Lawson, and P. Howard, 345–369. Toronto: University of Toronto Press.

Deliovsky, K., and Kitossa, T. 2013. "Beyond Black and White: When Going beyond May Take Us out of Bounds." *Journal of Black Studies* 44 (2): 158–181. https://doi.org/10.1177/0021934712471533.

Du Bois, W.E.B. 1914. "The Prize Fighter." *The Crisis* 8 (4): 181. https://library.brown.edu/pdfs/1302701412421878.pdf.

Eisenkraft, H. 2010. "Racism in the Academy." *University Affairs*. https://www.universityaffairs.ca/features/feature-article/racism-in-the-academy/.

Eze, E.C. 1995. "The Color of Reason: The Idea of 'Race' in Kant's Anthropology." In *Anthropology and the German Enlightenment: Perspectives on Humanity*, edited by K. Faull, 200–241. Lewisburg, PA: Bucknell University Press.

Fanon, F. 1967. *Toward the African Revolution*. New York: Grove Press.

Fanon, F. 1977. *Black Skin, White Masks*, translated by Charles Lam Markman. New York: Grove Press.

Fanon, F. 2003. *Toward the African Revolution*, translated by Richard Philcox. New York: Grove Press.

Fanon, F. 2008. *Black Skin, White Masks*, translated by Richard Philcox. New York: Grove Press.

Fenelon, J. 2003. "Race, Research, and Tenure: Institutional Credibility and the Incorporation of African, Latino, and American Indian Faculty." *Journal of Black Studies* 34 (1): 87–100. https://doi.org/10.1177/0021934703253661.

Fleras, A. 2014. *Racisms in a Multicultural Canada: Paradox, Politics, and Resistance.* Waterloo, ON: Wilfrid Laurier University Press.

Frazier, E.F. 1962. "The Failure of the Negro Intellectual." http://www.autodidactproject.org/other/frazier_failure.html.

Glaude, E.S., Jr. 2014, 23 June. "Black Intellectuals Have Sold Their Souls." *New York Times.* http://www.nytimes.com/roomfordebate/2013/02/04/do-black-intellectuals-need-to-talk-about-race/black-intellectuals-have-sold-their-souls.

Gouldner, A. 1968. "The Sociologist as Partisan: Sociology and the Welfare State." *The American Sociologist* 3 (2): 103–116. https://www.jstor.org/stable/27701326.

Gouldner, A. 1979. *The Future of Intellectuals and the Rise of the New Class: A Frame of Reference, Theses, Conjectures, Arguments, and an Historical Perspective on the Role of Intellectuals and Intelligentsia in the International Class Contest of the Modern Era.* New York: Continuum Publishing.

Gramsci, A. 1991. *Selections from the Prison Notebooks of Antonio Gramsci.* New York: International.

Grier, W.H., and Cobbs, P.M. 1968. *Black Rage.* New York: Basic Books.

Griffin, K.A., Pifer, M.J., Humphrey, J.R., and Hazelwood, A.M. 2011. "(Re)Defining Departure: Exploring Black Professors' Experiences with and Responses to Racism and Racial Climate." *American Journal of Education* 117: 495–526. https://doi.org/10.1086/660756.

Grundy, S. 2017. "A History of White Violence Tells Us Attacks on Black Academics Are Not Ending (I Know Because It Happened to Me)." *Ethnic and Racial Studies* 40 (11): 1864–1871. https://doi.org/10.1080/01419870.2017.1334933.

Hawkesworth, M. 2016. *Embodied Power: Demystifying Disembodied Politics.* New York: Routledge.

Hennessy, A. 1992. "The Demise of the Intellectual." In *Intellectuals in the Twentieth-Century Caribbean.* Vol. 1: *Spectre of the New Class: The Commonwealth Caribbean,* edited by Hennessy, 191–200. Hong Kong: MacMillan Education.

Henry, A. 2017. "Dear White People, Wake Up: Canada Is Racist." *The Conversation.* https://theconversation.com/dear-white-people-wake-up-canada-is-racist-83124.

Henry, A. 2019. "Standing Firm on Uneven Ground: A Letter to Black Women on Academic Leadership." In *African Canadian Leadership: Continuity, Transition, and Transformation,* edited by T. Kitossa, E. Lawson, and P. Howard, 170–189. Toronto: University of Toronto Press.

Henry, F., and Tator, C. 2009. *Racism in the Canadian University: Demanding Social Justice, Equity and Inclusion.* Toronto: University of Toronto Press.

Institute of Criminology and Criminal Justice, Carleton University. 2021. "ICCJ Statement: Actions to Address Issues Related to Settler Colonialism, White Supremacy, and Systemic Racism." https://carleton.ca/criminology /wp-content/uploads/ICCJ-Statement_-Addressing-Systemic-Racism.pdf.

James, C.E. 2012. "Strategies of Engagement: How Racialized Faculty Negotiate the University System." *Canadian Ethnic Studies* 44 (2): 133–152. https://doi .org/10.1353/ces.2012.0007.

James, C.E. 2019. "Black Leadership and White Logic: Models of Community Engagement." In *African Canadian Leadership: Continuity, Transition and Transformation*, edited by T. Kitossa, E. Lawson, and P. Howard, 74–88. Toronto: University of Toronto Press.

Johnson, J., and Bryan, N. 2017. "Using Our Voices, Losing Our Bodies: Michael Brown, Trayvon Martin, and the Spirit Murders of Black Male Professors in the Academy." *Race Ethnicity and Education* 20 (2): 163–177. https://doi.org/10.1080/13613324.2016.1248831.

Kant, I. 1997. "This Fellow Was Quite Black ... A Clear Proof That What He Said Was Stupid." In *Race and the Enlightenment: A Reader*, edited by E. Eze, 38–48. Malden: Blackwell.

Karabel, J. 1976. "Revolutionary Contradictions: Antonio Gramsci and the Problem of Intellectuals." *Politics & Society* 6: 123–172. https://doi.org /10.1177/003232927600600201.

Kitossa, T. 2014. "Authoritarian Criminology and the Racial Profiling Debate in Canada: Scientism as Epistemic Violence." *African Journal of Criminology and Justice Studies* 8 (S1): 63–88.

Kitossa, T. 2016, March. "Implicit Racism: The Need for Deep Diversity at Brock University." *Brock Press*. http://brockpress.com/2016/03/implicit -racism-the-need-for-deep-diversity-at-brock-university/.

Lyons, C. 1975. *To Wash an Aethiop White: British Ideas about Black African Educability 1530–1960*. New York: Teachers College Press.

Maynard, R. 2017. *Policing Black Lives: State Violence in Canada from Slavery to the Present*. Halifax: Fernwood Publishing.

Mills, C.W. 2006. "Modernity, Persons, and Subpersons." In *Race and the Foundations of Knowledge: Cultural Amnesia in the Academy*, edited by J. Young and J. Braziel, 211–251. Urbana: University of Illinois Press.

Mumford, L. 1970. *Pentagon of Power: The Myth of the Machine*. Vol. 2. London: Harvest/HBJ.

Nelson, C. 2011. "Toppling the 'Great White North': Tales of a Black Female Professor in Canadian Academia." In *The Black Professorate: Negotiating a Habitable Space*, edited by S. Jackson and R. Johnson III, 103–113. New York: Peter Lang.

Nkrumah, K. 1969. *Handbook of Revolutionary Warfare: A Guide to the Armed Phase of the African Revolution*. New York: International.

Norris, A. 2019. "Discussing Contemporary Racial Justice in Academic Spaces: Minimizing Epistemic Exploitation While Neutralizing White Fragility." In *The Palgrave Handbook of Ethnicity*, edited by S. Ratuva, 81–94. Singapore: Palgrave Macmillan.

Rabaka, R. 2003. "W.E B. Du Bois's Evolving Africana Philosophy of Education." *Journal of Black Studies* 33 (4): 399–449. https://doi.org/10.1177 /0021934702250021.

Robinson, C. 2000. *Black Marxism: The Making of a Black Radical Tradition.* Chapel Hill: University of North Carolina Press.

Rodney, W. 1969. *The Groundings with My Brothers.* London: Bogle-L'Ouverture Publications.

Said, E. 1979. *Orientalism.* New York: Vintage Books.

Said, E. 1996. *Representation of Intellectuals.* New York: Vintage.

Samuel, E., and Wane, J. 2005. "'Unsettling Relations': Racism and Sexism Experienced by Faculty of Color in a Predominantly White Canadian University." *The Journal of Negro Education* 74 (1): 76–87. https://www.jstor .org/stable/40027232.

Santiago-Valles, W.F. 2000. "The Caribbean Intellectual Tradition That Produced James and Rodney." *Race & Class* 42 (2): 47–66.

Simon-Aaron, C. 2008. *The Atlantic Slave Trade: Empire, Enlightenment, and the Cult of the Unthinking Negro.* Lewiston, NY: Edwin Mellen.

Sivanandan, A. 1977. "The Liberation of the Black Intellectual." *Race Class* 18: 329–343. https://doi.org/10.1177/030639687701800401.

Smith, M. 2018. "Equity at Canadian Universities: National, Disaggregated and Intersectional Data." Academic Women's Association University of Alberta. https://uofaawa.wordpress.com/2018/06/22/equity-at-canadian-universities -national-disaggregated-and-intersectional-data/.

Stewart, A. 2004. "Penn and Teller: Self, Racial Devaluation and the Canadian Academy." In *Racism Eh?: A Critical Inter-disciplinary Anthology of Race and Racism in Canada*, edited by C. Nelson, and C. Nelson, 33–40. Toronto: Captus.

West, C. 1993–4. "The Dilemma of the Black Intellectual." *The Journal of Blacks in Higher Education* 2: 59–67. https://doi.org/10.2307/2962571.

Wingfield, A.H. 2015. "The Plight of the Black Academic." *The Atlantic.* https:// www.theatlantic.com/business/archive/2015/12/the-plight-of-the-black -academic/420237/.

10 Socio-Cultural Obligations and the Academic Career: The Dual Expectations Facing Black Canadian Academics

KAY-ANN WILLIAMS AND GERVAN FEARON

Introduction

This chapter is motivated by the complex nature of navigating the dual expectations associated with an academic career and community bonds. It is informative to note that statistics show there has been almost a doubling in the number of faculty in universities between 1981 and 2006 (Desjardin 2012). In contrast, census data (2016) indicate that racialized scholars represent 21 per cent of the university professoriate and, of these, Black scholars represented only 2 per cent – a figure that has not changed significantly from the 2006 census (CAUT 2018, 2, 6). Furthermore, the 2019 Universities Canada report on equity, diversity, and inclusion shows that undergraduate and graduate Black students each represent approximately 6 per cent of overall enrolment, and Black senior university leaders were at 0.8 per cent, despite 3 per cent of the Black population possessing doctorate degrees (Universities Canada 2019).

Universities and colleges place tremendous emphasis on the recruitment and retention of students through to the completion of their academic programs. Students value the opportunity to engage in discussions and gain exposure to a diversity of opinions and knowledge generated by the range of cultures and experiences of faculty and their peers. The institution also benefits from research and scholarly activities undertaken by a diverse team. Universities and colleges therefore have developed institutional principles, policies, and initiatives to foster diversity within the post-secondary education system.

Williams (1992) suggests an individual's identity is not defined solely by one's own choices but also by the social construct and categorization framework established by society and its institutions. For instance, Black faculty members are often expected to utilize their community experience and cultural competencies to advance the university's social inclusion mission, as opposed to focusing exclusively on their academic discipline. Communities may also expect Black academics to serve as a liaison between community organizations and general societal institutions to translate and interpret socio-cultural and governance contexts when there is insufficient bridging social capital between the two parties. A community's close bonds with their members simultaneously provide social capital (resiliency and capacity) to succeed in one's profession. Conversely, this expectation may compete for time and efforts needed for successful integration into the new institution and profession (Cheong et al. 2007). The Black academic must therefore navigate dual community and academic institutional expectations.

This chapter examines the complexities that Black Canadian scholars manoeuvre to achieve the established institutional metrics while meeting community expectations and the institution's social mission. The chapter is organized as follows: First, the human capital factors contributing to success within the academic profession is examined. Second, the literature on "frayed career" frames a way in which career paths and employment experiences may shape the challenges and opportunities experienced by Black community members in the academy. Third, "bridging" and "bonding" social capital concepts inform how social capital may interact with human capital and positionality to support or detract from individuals' professional success. Fourth, we explore how the institutional contract between Black academics and academic institutions as well as the social contract between Black academics and community institutions may support or detract from the individual's professional success and intergenerational knowledge transfer. Finally, the implications of the study and conclusions are presented.

This chapter uses theoretical concepts to advance an understanding of factors influencing Black academics' professional success. Additionally, the two authors' lived experiences illustrate the intertwining of commitment to community and profession, and the linkage between theory and practice.

Dr. Williams completed her undergraduate studies in Jamaica, completed her master's degree (MSc) in Sweden, worked at senior levels within the Jamaican public service and the private sector, and completed her PhD at Queen's University in Ontario in 2014. Like many recent graduates,[1] years after completing her PhD she had continued to teach on a part-time/partial load contractual basis at several educational institutions. These contractual positions assisted her in gaining teaching experience, but they rarely afforded the time to publish or access and/or utilize research networks to facilitate a full-time or tenure track position. Concurrently, members of the community look towards her for inspiration and advice in advancing their own educational and career goals. As Spafford et al. (2006) explain, being a role model for members of a society may happen even to those who are searching for mentors themselves. For Dr. Williams, her support came through a wide network that included her PhD supervisor, faculty, friends, and members of her ethnic community who were directly familiar with and had knowledge of social norms and institutions. These social networks support crucial coping and resiliency skills needed for successful careers and social connectedness. Dr. Williams currently holds a full-time faculty position.

Dr. Gervan Fearon, with a young family, completed his PhD in economics at Western University in Ontario. He had established his goal to complete his PhD during his MSc studies at the University of Guelph, where he had exposure to outstanding professors and a supportive supervisor, including several Black Canadian academics (e.g., Professors Carlton Gilles, Richard Phidd, and Clarence Munford). These tenured professors took time to interact with students from the community and motivate a generation of academics. Additionally, the West Indian Student Association was a hotbed of keen, academically oriented students aiming to make a contribution to their profession, community, and society. After two years at Western, Dr. Fearon completed his PhD comprehensive and field examinations, returning to work with the Government of Ontario. To maintain connection with the academic community, Fearon, similar to Dr. Williams, taught part-time. Dr. Fearon left his job with the government to finish his PhD thesis and to pursue an uncertain academic career.

Without the support of family and the Government of Ontario, it would not have been possible for Dr. Fearon to realize his dreams of attaining a PhD. He was then able to get a tenure track position at York University, earn tenure, serve as a visiting scholar at the University of Washington, as an associate dean at York University, and more than ten years after his first part-time/session teaching assignment at Ryerson, become the dean of the G. Raymond Chang School of Continuing Education. Dr. Fearon went on to become the provost and vice-president (academic) and then the president and vice-chancellor at Brandon University in Manitoba. In so doing, Dr. Fearon became the first Black president of a Canadian university. He then served as the president and vice-chancellor of Brock University and is currently the president of George Brown College.

Part-time teaching is a reality facing many individuals hoping to secure tenure track positions within the academic profession. Furthermore, and despite the costs to their own professional success, Black Canadian academics are often expected to support and supplement the social and institutional capital needed by the community for the betterment of its members.[2] As with Dr. Williams, members of the community also looked to Dr. Fearon to assume leadership within the community. Dr. Fearon served as the vice-president and president of Tropicana Community Services, which is a large Black Canadian and Caribbean community social services organization in the Toronto area serving about 25,000 individuals annually in thirty-five languages. In this context, this chapter also represents a mechanism for sharing social capital and supporting community development as part of the implicit social contract the authors' both accept as their own obligations and responsibilities to the community and their expressions of gratitude to those who assisted them in their own journeys and successes.

Academic Professional Success and Human Capital

Academic professional success is defined by the individual and institutional expectations that may relate to the attainment of a wide range of academic positions, such as a laboratory instructor, lecturer, assistant professor, associate professor, full professor, research chair, department chair, associate dean, dean, associate or assistant vice-president, vice-president, and, finally, president of a college, polytechnic, or university. Each of these and other positions provides value to the institution's mission through effective teaching and learning; research, scholarly and creative activities; and service. Correspondingly, an individual may fully attain career and life goals in a given position. In this sense, success is a subjective benchmark.

Daniel Munro (2015) using the National Household Survey 2011 data, notes that 39.4 per cent of PhD graduates in Ontario are employed in post-secondary education, with only 18.6 per cent of PhD holders becoming full-time university professors; 6.1 per cent are employed as part-time faculty, 7.4 per cent are research or teaching assistants, 2.9 per cent are college or polytechnic faculty, and 4.4 per cent are postdoctoral scholars. The other 60 per cent of PhD graduates are employed outside the academy.

Career success can be defined by multiple factors. It can be viewed as the utilization of one's skills, knowledge, and values (e.g., human capital) to deliver benefit to an organization, community, and society; to be appropriately compensated for the value delivered in supporting the organization (community and society) attaining its mission and mandate; and to support and inspire one's family and the next generation through one's endeavours. Indeed, the authors of this chapter have worked in jobs ranging from factories to farms, restaurants to moving companies, private to public sector. For professional success within academic institutions, there is little written to support Black Canadian academics facing dual community and institutional expectations.

Academic professional success based on the achievement of measurable outcome informs hiring, promotion, and compensation and is directly related to the human capital (competency) of the individual, which is often purported to be independent of the career path or community social context or capital. The Nobel Prize–winning economist Sir Arthur Lewis was one of the first researchers to articulate the principles of human capital in detail (Lewis 1955). Human capital was defined by three components: skill, knowledge, and values. For instance, skills might pertain to ability to conduct quantitative or qualitative research analysis; the knowledge to establish meaningful research questions; and the values to support the academic mission of the department, college, or university. The traditional tenure process assumes a human capital approach to success in the academic profession (Ramos and Wijesingha 2017; Wijesingha and Ramos 2017). An individual pursuing a tenure track position must effectively exhibit and confirm human capital (skills, knowledge, and values) in teaching and learning; research, scholarly and creative activities, and institutional and professional service.

For teaching and learning, performance in the classroom, course delivery, student support and academic outcomes generally are key indicators for this category. Student course evaluation reports and new courses development can help to demonstrate teaching requirements. The rapport established between the instructor and students is therefore important. However, the social and cultural context prevalent in society at large may become an unmeasured factor that influences student evaluations of Black Canadian academics. The Black professor may also face expectations of students (Henry, Dua, Kobayashi et al. 2017) and, by extension, communities to advocate on their behalf for the culturally appropriate and institutional values purported by the university as part of its mission. For instance, Black physics professors may not be experts in contemporary political or social issues, yet students or the institutions may expect them to be sensitive to or even engage in discussions pertaining to Black Canadian issues. Therefore, institutions need to acknowledge and facilitate the development of mechanisms to take into account these broader contributions to the university or college.

For research, scholarly, and creative activities, there is no singularly defined measure to determine what constitutes the meeting of expectations in this category. The publication of a single paper that revolutionizes a profession and brings new insight to a research area may be sufficient. For the majority of researchers and academics, it is the accumulation of their body of work over several years that leads to the attainment of the necessary standard in research, scholarly and creative activities, such as journal articles, peer review conference presentations, and books for arts and science or performances, manuscripts, and shows.

Collaborative research is becoming increasingly important. The ability of Black Canadian academics to become members of collaborative research groups is therefore a determinant of their ability to achieve the research expectation associated with tenure requirements. For individuals, the opportunity to work with their research/thesis supervisor or members of their supervisory team is often the first mechanism for becoming a member of a collaborative team, building on the research conducted in their thesis (e.g., it is helpful for individuals to aim to attain one or two publications based on their thesis). In institutions, collaborative research teams and departments' sponsored seminars can be a significant determinant of the research output of new faculty members. An individual's participation in academic conference activities (e.g., by presenting a paper, volunteering to review journal submissions or conducting book reviews) can assist in building bonds with collaborative research teams.

Academic departments may further define effective research as scholarly or creative activities in relation to "impactfulness" measured by journal publications in a high-impact journal, and books published by well-known publication presses; or performance at a well-known centre.[3] The Black community may define effective research in terms of impact on the well-being of community members or inclusive social progress for all Canadians (e.g., submitting a report or letter to a task force on community health or policing). Some Black Canadian academics may consider that there are competing goals or definitions between institutional and community "impactfulness." However, this does not always have to be so. It is worthwhile considering that outstanding research on sickle cell anaemia can contribute to the literature as well as foster the betterment of individuals and families within the community. Excellent research in any field can inspire the next generation of academics and leaders from the community and beyond. The pursuit of excellence in any profession can serve the dual expectation of community and societal institutions while enabling the achievement of one's own sense and definition of professional success.

For institutional service activities, it is important to recognize that many, although by no means all, universities operate on a bicameral system involving a senate and board of directors/governors. The senate represents the highest body for the determination of the academic standards and matters of the university or college, while the board provide oversight on the operational, administrative, and resource/financial matters, strategies, and policies of the institutions. As a result, an individual's participation in academic governance by serving on a senate or board committee represents contributions to the institution's service activities.

Academic institutions engage with the communities they serve. Participation in these activities constitutes additional institutional service obligations. For instance, a group of individuals may get together to offer a tutoring program to high school students within the community every weekend. However, there may be no formal organization to write a letter of commendation for individuals attempting to develop their dossier to be submitted as part of the tenure process. Volunteering for a well-known established organization may allow for such a letter to be written and to be weighted greater in balance; however, this volunteer work may not support the sharing or transfer of social capital back to an intended community. Communities with well-established organizations may have differing experiences. The individual and the institution must therefore be sensitive about how these factors may influence the choices and the documentation of activities in support of institutional service.

Honig (1998) and Walters (2004), referring to credentialing theory, suggest that the degree, publications, academic awards, and research grants signal or predict future productivity or effectiveness within the profession and do not necessarily indicate ability. Perna (2005) also investigated differences in faculty tenure and promotion between men and women using the U.S. National Study of Postsecondary Faculty database and found that productivity (i.e., human capital) variables were more important in predicting tenure and promotion outcomes between men and women than social capital/network or family ties. Productivity variables included quantity and quality of education (e.g., highest degree), amount of on-the-job training (e.g., years in current position), number of recent referred publications, and number of recent presentations.

Lutter and Schröder (2014), like Perna (2005), suggest that tenure is primarily dependent on scholarly output, including publication record. However, Lutter and Schröder (2014) indicated that symbolic capital (e.g., reputation) and social capital (e.g., social network – who one knows) can affect labour market outcomes. Perna (2005) further highlights the importance of mentorship and access to institutional networks in providing information to the individual on the expectations, conduct, and activities of the academic institution as important in supporting the success of women faculty members. Additionally, the intersections of race and gender may further influence outcomes and experiences in different ways for Black males and for Black females in the academy (Henry, Dua, James et al. 2017).

Wijesingha and Ramos (2017) examined tenure and promotion of racialized female and male faculty in eight Canadian universities in what is believed to be the first such study of its kind in Canada. The study "confirms that controlling for human capital and cultural or identity taxation washes away the differences between being tenured and promoted for female faculty. Differences for racialized faculty remain, offering evidence of racial discrimination in the academic system" (15–16). Fearon and Wald (2011) provided additional evidence at a broader level for the Canadian economy. Henry and Tator (2009, 8) explained that in sectors such as education and post-secondary in particular, a number of factors combine to create an environment "characterized by deep ruptures and abiding forms of individual, institutional, and systemic inequity." In a highly competitive academic job setting, the strength of reference letters or period taken to complete the PhD may influence the chances of acquiring a tenure track position. As a result, the human capital framework must be augmented by other socio-cultural factors embodied in concepts such as "frayed careers" and "social capital."

On Frayed Careers: Do We All Have to Follow the Same Pathway?

Sabelis and Schilling (2013) note that the normalized image of the career trajectory is accumulative and linear, but life is non-linear, and women's lives – shaped by the social expectations of gender – cannot necessarily follow careers uninterrupted as a result of the "rhythmicity in working life" (129). The standard academic career trajectory assumes linearity, competition, and consistency – uninterrupted (e.g., a career path directly from undergraduate to master's to PhD to tenure track position to the attainment of tenure). For many Black academics, uninterrupted academic career paths may not be guaranteed. Acknowledging the "interrupted" experience, Sabelis (2010) proposed the term "frayed careers," Sabelis and Schilling (2013) recognizing it tends to be experienced by those considered to be marginalized, in particular those at the intersections of race, gender, and citizenship status. Sang et al. (2013, 160) note, for instance that "careers of women and migrant academics can be characterized as frayed careers as these academics tend to hold precarious posts with long routes to tenure, and difficulties of access to prestigious posts." In other words, academia may be experienced as a site of struggle over who does and does not belong to it (Wacquant 1989, 4). Sang et al. (2013) posit that experiences differ, depending on "where they stand at the crossroads of differing marginalized identities" (160). In this case, Sang et al. (2013) discuss first-generation migrant women professors whom they recognized as subject to "double discrimination"

and having the status of "double outsiders," regardless of being categorized as an elite migrant.[4] However, when conducting research among
migrant women faculty, the authors found that they did not view their
career in such terms and, indeed, utilized greater levels of agency, connectedness, and entrepreneurial flair to mobilize their resources in order to achieve career success (160).

An important resource utilized by Black academics to aid professional
development is social capital. Bourdieu (1986, 1988), who developed
the concept of capitals and their role in social practice, also explored
the value of social capital in fostering relationships within the academy.
For instance, Sabelis and Schilling (2013) illustrated how a participant
was able to carve out a niche, making her double expected disadvantage
from gender and race/ethnicity become an advantage by community
relationships, assisting in accessing knowledge and data for community-based research publications. This is similar to Dr. Williams's own experience, where she was able to draw on her own experiences as a recent
immigrant and her connections to her community in the Greater Toronto Area to develop a distinct and accepted research question for her
dissertation (Williams 2014).

Connectedness is therefore not only about obligation but can also
be an invaluable asset outside and within the academy. Academics are
agents active and acting in the field of post-secondary education "by the
fact that they possess the necessary process to be effective, to produce
effects, in this field" (Wacquant 1989, 6–7). Therefore they are bear-
ers of capitals carrying differing potentials and positions. Bourdieu and
Wacquant, (1992) suggest that one's own position and the parameters by
which they are judged within the profession may shape the perception
of one's chances of success in the profession. Being away from the site/
field, such as accepting employment in other sectors or as part-time or
on contract, may deprive one of the ability to be included in meetings,
collaborative research teams, and activities that enhance the ability to
display additional skills that are required, if given a chance to compete
for a permanent position in the department. These are additional considerations that may lead to a delayed, interrupted, or "frayed career"
trajectory.

It is therefore no surprise then that mentorship is a valuable resource
for academics. It is directly tied to networks or network centrality, and
speaks to the depth and breadth of social capital (Lin and Huang 2005).
However, Henry, Dua, Kobayashi et al. (2017) showed that among racialized minority academics most had experiences of being a mentor but
not in being mentored. It must be emphasized here, however, that this
is not to suggest that aspiring Black academics set their sights away from

the needs of their community members to focus only on the strategies that will create opportunities for professional success (e.g., tenure). As emphasized in Sang et al. (2013), choices made are also embedded in personal and social values. In fact, moments of mentorship and guidance may be nurturing and provide the motivation and resilience for continued effort and realization of excellence.

With regard to community engagement, it does require interest and desire to provide guidance to those who need it. Dr. Williams notes that, as a contract faculty member, there had been opportunities to support students in the everyday by motivating them, showing interest, providing a sense of belonging, and making herself available to answer questions they may have had about their career plans. For Dr. Williams, as other Black women academics, experience in this setting is valuable for personal development and sense of pride in being able to give back in a meaningful way. Spending time and committing to the expression of these values may not be visible and therefore not acknowledged by institutions. However, mentorship and contributions to the community must be pursued by racialized faculty members to facilitate social progress and building of community cultural wealth that benefit all.

Social Capital

Social capital, according to Bourdieu (1986, 4), is "made up of social obligations ('connections')"; this capital is "convertible, in certain conditions, into economic capital." While Lutter and Schröder's (2014) analysis was consistent with that of Perna (2005), meaning tenure was primarily dependent on scholarly output (e.g., publication record – human capital), Lutter and Schröder suggested that symbolic capital (e.g., reputation of institution where PhD is earned) and social capital (e.g., social network – whom one knows) also influenced labour market outcomes. Specifically, Lutter and Schröder (2014) found social capital had a small positive effect on the probability of being tenured, with publication record being the greatest factor. Generation of publications is developmental and often benefits from the availability of social and research networks such as academic association and online networks (e.g., Research Gate).

Goddard (2003) uses Coleman (1990) to suggest that social capital involves three components: relational network, social trust, and social norms. Meanwhile, Scrivens and Smith (2013) identify four components of social capital: personal relationships, social network support, civic engagement, and trust and cooperative norms. On the other hand, Yosso (2005, 77) takes a different approach, based on Oliver and Shapiro

(1995) by instead emphasizing community cultural wealth, which includes familial capital, social capital, navigational capital, resistant capital, linguistic capital, and aspirational capital. There are commonalities in each of the definitions presented for social capital. What is particularly common is that communities can act as a resource that is shared across members, depending on their own positionality and social status within the community (Grischow and McKnight 2008). Social capital reflects a community network aggregation, while human capital is dominated by individual characteristics and qualities (Putman 2000; Scrivens and Smith 2013). Indeed, the OECD (2010) Centre for Educational Research and Innovation suggest that realized outcomes are determined through the interaction of human capital and social capital.

The quality of social capital is becoming a topic of consideration when community social capital is investigated. Anthias (2007) introduces an important consideration of social capital: if it cannot be converted to economic capital or be useable in some other way to create advantage, then it cannot be considered a form of social capital. In other words, social capital is valued for its use-value (i.e., quality) in affecting outcomes and decisions in socio-economic engagement (DeFilippis 2001). With this form of social capital, aspiring and established Black academics would have to consider and assist in developing useable forms of social capital that are valued by the evaluators of their credentials and contributions to the organization or society. As noted by Li (2003) in Sang et al. (2013, 164), "There is a consistent argument that migrants who adopt and conform to the mainstream culture are welcomed and more likely to be settled and included, than those whose cultural specificities lie outside that mainstream." On the other hand, the migrant women participants in the United Kingdom discussed in Sang et al. (2013) utilized a combination of qualifications, abilities to conduct research, publish papers, supervise research projects and students, and take on administrative and managerial responsibilities as different forms of resources towards success. Importantly, for some participants their research was directly related to their community, and the strength of their association with their community enabled them to identify a distinct research area to aid in their career.

The involvement of community members in activities and governance of post-secondary institutions (e.g., university board of directors and other bodies) facilitate the establishment of linkages and understanding of the history and social context of the Black community within the fabric of the university, including its policies, curriculum, and course offerings. Without courses in Canadian Black history and African and Caribbean studies, Black Canadian academics with PhD research training in these areas may find it difficult to garner teaching positions in their area of specialization. The connectedness between the community and academia therefore affects the potential of Black Canadian academics to gain tenure track and eventually tenure level positions within colleges and universities. Therefore, the community must look outward and inward to address considerations such as the diversity and representation of faculty members at post-secondary institutions that reflect the diversity of the Canadian mosaic. Correspondingly, academic institutions need to establish community outreach initiatives to facilitate university-community engagement for communities that may not have a history of involvement within academic institutions. This means looking at the composition of its board, senate, and university committees and taking deliberate action to build inclusion. Equity, diversity, and inclusion must therefore not only be defined simply by the demographics of the student population or even faculty and staff members. Without a deep level of social inclusion, deficits in useable community social capital will impede the success of members of the Canadian Black community in academic institutions, even as these individuals possess all the necessary human capital requirements.

The social capital available to the Black Canadian academics is therefore related to the capacity of the community's cultural wealth as well as the relational network, social trust and norms, and civic engagement. A high level of social capital within the community provides individuals with a stronger platform for launching their academic career. For instance, the sophistication of community organizations provides the institutional foundation for academics to conduct service activities, as well as to receive official letters of acknowledgment for Black Canadian academics to use in demonstrating a portion of their institutional service contributions. The participation of community organizations in establishing scholarships, bursaries, research foundations, and funding research grants as well as partnering in community-based research can facilitate Black Canadian academics and the next generation in achieving their academic professional aspirations.

Honig (1998) and DeFilippis (2001) point to the need for a critical view of social capital. The evolution of the community depends on the proportion or propensity of effort to activities that support the building of specific kinds of social capital. The social capital developed by a community implies a reaction to the challenges and opportunities that prominent community members and social influencers identify as priorities and the mechanisms to be pursued in support of community and/ or personal progress (Grange et al. 2013). Black Canadian academics must be recognized as members of multi-social networks that may lead to hybridity and are situated in the context of an evolving definition of Canadian society and identity (Reynolds 2013).

A community with a contemporary history influenced by slavery, and forged by the civil rights movement and anti-discrimination action due to historical and contemporary experience may, for instance, legitimately develop a high level of resistant capital relative to the level of navigational capital within the community. When confronted with conflicts within the workplace in a university or college, members of the community may advocate and even initiate actions based on the use of the community's high resistant capital capacity. On the other hand, the collegial governance framework within colleges and universities tend to value and reward the use of navigational capital to negotiate and seek compromise and resolve conflict, as opposed to confrontation or positional bargaining. It is unlikely that the history and social context of a people can be erased or should be diminished, since it is a part of what defines them and represents their contributions to the diversity and social resilience of society. In fact, fostering greater navigational capital, while maintaining resistance capital capacities, can assist the Black Canadian academic to harness social capital characteristics to advance professional success and community progress.

Community social capital cannot be confined or abstracted from the interaction of the Black community with broader societal institutions and other communities. This sets the stage for bonding and bridging social capital (Putnam 2000). Bonding social capital relates to the utilization of community social capital/wealth to bond members to the engagement, involvement, and a sense of belonging to the community. For instance, a community organization may have social norms that direct the individual to attend meetings/sessions several times each week that may increase the bonds amongst individual community members but crowd out the development of relations (bridging) across other communities. The community reasonably exhibits both bonding and bridging social capital characteristics simultaneously.

Communities facing social capital deficits may tend to exhibit more bonding social capital as a way to reduce the loss of its capacity as well as to generate social cohesion in support of social resiliency to overcome the adversity of discrimination or marginalization. The more welcomed a community feels, the less it will tend to foster primarily bonding social capital. Bonding social capital implies an individual's obligation to comply with the norms and social engagement within the community. In societies that are not as inclusive, the social contract established between the individual and the community – for access and support based on and utilizing the community's social capital – involves the community expecting the individual to return value and to contribute to the betterment of the community (Brown III 2001). When this social contract is broken more exclusively, the community may implement social suasion or punishment to reinforce the contract, as well as to ensure that the community social capital is not depleted by those who would access it without making any reciprocating or replenishing contributions. Consider, for instance, individuals getting an academic scholarship through the efforts and fundraising of a community organization, yet they view themselves as having no obligations or responsibilities to mentor youth or conduct research in relation to uplifting the community.

The bridging social capital of the community can be equally important. Highly inclusive societies tend to exhibit greater alignment between community and broader societal values and interests. For instance, it can facilitate community members serving on the board or committees of a college or university, which may directly affect the policies and practices aimed at supporting diversity hiring practices and inclusive education initiatives that will influence the hiring and success of Black Canadian academics. Further, a Black Canadian academic may be asked by a community member how to draft a cover letter for a tenure track position. Consequently, bridging social capital is valuable, yet it is not separate from bonding social capital, since it is the bonds between the individual and the community that support the individual who is building bridges between groups. As Yosso (2005) suggests, social capital represents a community resource to be utilized for supporting professional success, but it must be replenished if it is to continue to be available as an asset and network for promoting individual, community, and societal success.

Conclusion

This chapter explored two expectations facing Black Canadian academics. It illuminates challenges and opportunities for the community and institutions looking towards these individuals to make a contribution to the betterment of the communities and institutions. It suggests that successes in academic professions and in the community can be attained through a combination of bonding and bridging social capital. The combination of social capital components (navigational and resistance social capital characteristics) and types (bonding and bridging social capital) defines the quality of social capital. The formation of academic peer group associations (e.g., the *Black Canadian Studies Journal*) is material in supporting research and publication by members of the Black community and others. The association could expand its role by establishing professional development support in teaching and learning; research, scholarship, and creative activities, and institutional service; as well as the documentation needed for a tenure track dossier. Sessions are also needed on the development of research agendas, engaging in practice interviews and presentations, grant submissions, and the formation of a research network. Many universities and fields consider the "impact-fulness" of journal publications as important in the tenure and promotion process. As a result, Black Canadian academics must appreciate that they will need to build bridging tools through publications and research that span a range of journals and measures of impactfulness. Academic institutions must examine their tenure and promotion processes to adequately recognize community service as service to the university's mission.

The personal experiences of the two authors suggest that the building of human capital and drawing on the different components of community social capital (e.g., resilience and navigational capital) can assist in overcoming challenges precipitated by a "frayed careers" trajectory and social economic disparities where race is a significant determinant. The support provided by individuals and institutions within the Black communities cannot be underestimated. This chapter embodies a sense of optimism and represents a mechanism for building and sharing social capital within the community.

NOTES

1 According to Desjardins (2012, 7),

> The overall proportion of tenured or tenure-track positions for doctorate holders working full-time in Canadian universities decreased by 10 percentage points between 1981 and 2007, decreasing from 79.8% in the 1980/1981 academic year to 70.3% in the 2006/2007 academic year. The decline was even more pronounced for professors under the age of 35. In 1980/1981, one-third of professors under age 35 (35%) held a full-time tenured or tenure-track position; 25 years later, this was true for only 12% of professors in that age category, a decrease of 23 percentage points.

2 Additionally, society through the media may influence community expectations by suggesting that members of the Black Canadian community should be doing something about the challenges in their community.

3 It is important for academics to know the list of top journals, publishers, artistic and/or performance outlets in their field along with the requirements for publication/performance within their area. This principle is as relevant for the mathematician as it is for the musician – every profession has its

markers and rules for success and, whether one agrees with them or not, it is often necessary to demonstrate aptitude in the field based on the established peer group and markers prior to choosing to break new, innovative ground. The authors deliberately use the term "often necessary," since there are no absolute rules, and some individuals may leap beyond the usual bounds and frameworks and take the rest of us along with them.

4 The authors note that the women in this study came from privileged backgrounds. The majority came from "advanced" economies and all identified as heterosexual.

REFERENCES

Anthias, F. 2007. "Ethnic Ties: Social Capital and the Question of Mobilisability." *The Sociological Review* 55 (4): 788–805. https://doi.org/10.1111/j.1467-954X.2007.00752.x.

Bourdieu, P. 1986. "The Forms of Capital." In *Handbook of Theory and Research in the Sociology of Education*, edited by J. Richardson, 9–21. New York: Greenwood Press.

Bourdieu, P. 1988. *Homo Academicus*. Stanford, CA: Stanford University Press.

Bourdieu, P., and Wacquant, L. 1992. *An Invitation to Reflexive Sociology*. Chicago: University of Chicago Press.

Brown, M., III. 2001. "The Historically Black College as Social Contract, Social Capital, and Social Equalizer." *Peabody Journal of Education* 76 (1): 31–49. https://doi.org/10.1207/S15327930PJE7601_03.

CAUT. 2018. *Underrepresented and Underpaid: Diversity & Equity among Canada's Post-Secondary Education Teachers*. https://www.caut.ca/sites/default/files/caut_equity_report_2018-04final.pdf.

Cheong, P., Edwards, R., Goulbourne, H., and Solomos, J. 2007. "Immigration, Social Cohesion and Social Capital: A Critical Review." *Critical Social Policy* 27 (1): 24–49. https://doi.org/10.1177/026101830707220.6.

Coleman, James. 1990. *Foundations of Social Theory*. Cambridge, MA: Harvard University Press.

DeFilippis, J. 2001. "The Myth of Social Capital in Community Development." *Housing Policy Debate* 12 (4): 781–806. https://doi.org/10.1080/10511482.2001.9521429.

Desjardins, L. 2012. *Profile and Labour Market Outcomes of Doctoral Graduates from Ontario Universities*. http://www.heqco.ca/SiteCollectionDocuments/LabourMarketOutcomesDoctoral_ENG.pdf.

Fearon, G., and Wald, S. 2011. "The Earnings Gap between Black and White Workers in Canada: Evidence from the 2006 Census." *Industrial Relation* 66 (3): 324–348. https://doi.org/10.7202/1006342ar.

Goddard, R. 2003. "Relational Networks, Social Trust, and Norms: A Social Capital Perspective on Students' Chances of Academic Success." *Educational Evaluation and Policy Analysis* 25 (1): 59–74. https://doi.org/10.3102 /01623737025001059.

Grange, H., Fearon, G., Sloly, P., Hunter, M., Dowdy, D., Beckles, M., Campbell, A., and Shelton, S. 2013. *Towards a Vision for the Black Community.* http://www .jcaontario.org/wp-content/uploads/2010/05/TOWARDS-A-VISION-FOR -THE-BLACK-COMMUNITY-October-2013.pdf.

Grischow, J., and McKnight, G. 2008. "The Power of Social Capital: Historical Studies from Colonial Uganda and the Gold Coast." *Canadian Journal of African Studies* 42 (1): 98–128. https://doi.org/10.1080/00083968.2008 .10751374.

Henry, F., Dua, E., James, C.E., Li, P., Ramos, H., and Smith, M. 2017. *The Equity Myth: Racialization and Indigeneity at Canadian Universities.* Vancouver: University of British Columbia Press.

Henry, F., Dua, E., Kobayashi, A., James, C., Li, P., Ramos, H., and Smith, M. 2017. "Race, Racialization and Indigeneity in Canadian Universities." *Race Ethnicity and Education* 20 (3): 300–314. https://doi.org/10.1080/13613324.2016.1260226.

Henry, F., and Tator, C. 2009. *Racism in the Canadian University: Demanding Social Justice, Inclusion and Equity.* Toronto: University of Toronto Press.

Honig, B. 1998. "What Determines Success? Examining the Human, Financial, and Social Capital of Jamaican Microentrepreneurs." *Journal of Business Venturing* 13: 371–394. https://doi.org/10.1016/S0883-9026(97)00036-0.

Lewis, A. 1955. *The Theory of Economic Growth.* Homewood, IL: Richard D. Irwin.

Li, P. 2003. "Deconstructing Canada's Discourse of Immigrant Integration." *Journal of International Migration and Integration* 4 (3): 315–333. https://doi .org/10.1007/s12134-003-1024-0.

Lin, S., and Huang, Y. 2005. "The Role of Social Capital in the Relationship between Human Capital and Career Mobility: Moderator or Mediator?" *Journal of Intellectual Capital* 6 (2): 191–205. https://doi.org/10.1108 /14691930510592799.

Lutter, M., and Schröder, M. 2014. *Who Becomes a Tenured Professor, and Why?* Max Planck Institute for the Study of Societies. https://www.mpifg.de/pu /mpifg_dp/dp14-19.pdf.

Munro, D. 2015. *Where Are Canada's PhDs Employed?* http://economicdevelopment .org/2015/01/where-are-canadas-phds-employed/.

Oliver, M., and Shapiro, T. 1995. *Black Wealth/White Wealth: A New Perspective on Racial Inequality.* London: Routledge.

Organization for Economic Co-operation and Development (OECD). 2010. *Social Capital, Human Capital and Health: What Is the Evidence?* OECD Publication: Centre for Education Research and Innovation (CERI).

Perna, L. 2005. "Sex Differences in Faculty Tenure and Promotion: The Contribution of Family Ties." *Research in Higher Education* 46 (3): 277–307. https://doi.org/10.1007/s11162-004-1641-2.

Putnam, R. 2000. *Bowling Alone.* New York: Simon and Schuster.

Ramos, H., and Wijesingha, R. 2017. "Academic Production, Reward, and Perceptions of Racialized Faculty Members." In *The Equity Myth: Racialization and Indigeneity at Canadian Universities,* edited by F. Henry, E. Dua, C.E. James, P. Li, H. Ramos, and M. Smith, 46–59. Toronto: University of Toronto Press.

Reynolds, T. 2013. "'Them and Us': 'Black Neighbourhoods' as a Social Capital Resource among Black Youths Living in Inner-City London." *Urban Studies* 50 (3): 484–498. https://doi.org/10.1177/0042098012468892.

Sabelis, I. 2010. "Career Cultures: Rhythms of Work from a Gender Perspective." In *Geschlecht und Innovation. Gender Mainstreaming im Techno-Wissenschaftsbetrieb* (Internationale Frauen-und Genderforschung in Niedersachsen, Teilband 4), edited by W. Ernst, 201–218. Berlin: LIT Verlag.

Sabelis, I., and Schilling, E. 2013. "Editorial: Frayed Careers: Exploring Rhythms of Working Lives." *Gender, Work and Organization* 20 (2): 127–132. https://doi.org/10.1111/gwao.12020.

Sang, K., Al-Dajani, H., and Ozbilgin, M. 2013. "Frayed Careers of Migrant Female Professors in British Academia: An Intersectional Perspective." *Gender, Work and Organization* 20 (2): 158–171. https://doi.org/10.1111/gwao.12014.

Scrivens, K., and Smith, C. 2013. "Four Interpretations of Social Capital: An Agenda for Measurement." OECD Statistics Working Papers. OECD Publication.

Spafford, M., Nygaard, V., Gregor, F., and Boyd, M. 2006. "'Navigating the Different Spaces': Experiences of Inclusion and Isolation among Racially Minoritized Faculty in Canada." *Canadian Journal of Higher Education* 36 (1): 1–27. https://doi.org/10.47678/cjhe.v36i1.183523.

Universities Canada. 2019. *Equity, Diversity and Inclusion at Canadian Universities. Report on the 2019 National Survey.* https://www.univcan.ca/wp-content/uploads/2019/11/Equity-diversity-and-inclusion-at-Canadian-universities-report-on-the-2019-national-survey-Nov-2019-1.pdf.

Wacquant, L. 1989. "For a Socio-Analysis of Intellectuals: On *Homo Academicus.*" *Berkeley Journal of Sociology* 34: 1–29. http://www.jstor.org/stable/41035401.

Walters, D. 2004. "The Relationship between Postsecondary Education and Skill: Comparing Credentialism with Human Capital Theory." *The Canadian Journal of Higher Education* 34 (2): 97–124. https://doi.org/10.47678/cjhe.v34i2.183458.

Wijesingha, R., and Ramos, H. 2017. "Human Capital or Cultural Taxation: What Accounts for Differences in Tenure and Promotion of Racialized and

Female Faculty." *Canadian Journal of Higher Education* 47 (3): 54–75. https://doi.org/10.47678/cjhe.v47i3.187902.

Williams, K. 2014. *Jamaican Middle-Class Immigrants in Toronto: Habitus, Capitals and Inclusion.* Unpublished PhD dissertation, Queen's University.

Williams, P.J. 1992. *The Alchemy of Race and Rights.* Cambridge, MA: Harvard University Press.

Yosso, T. 2005. "Whose Culture Has Capital? A Critical Race Theory Discussion of Community Cultural Wealth." *Race Ethnicity and Education* 8 (1): 69–91. https://doi.org/10.1080/1361332052000341006.

PART THREE

Blackness: A Complicated Canadian Conversation

Commentary on Part Three: "Killing Us Softly" – with Questions

ANNETTE HENRY

These five chapters, grouped under the heading "A Complicated Canadian Conversation," are peppered with questions – questions asked of the authors and at times questions the authors ask themselves, all in a context of white normativity. After considering who was asking the majority of questions, what was being asked, and from whose point of view, one can conclude that the few verbal exchanges in these chapters did not involve conversations at all, but rather blunt, curt, clipped exchanges, slips of the tongue, imposing and impolite inferences, presuppositions, and interrogations that corrode the heart and challenge the presence and integrity of the Black Canadian body and intellect in public and intellectual spaces. Each author underscores the ontological (un) (be) longing that accompanies the Black state of being when subjected to constant importuning. By no means, then, are these questions part of any conversation. They represent, for the most part, white attempts at Black subjection. This questioning will be my main focus.

What's your background? Where are you from? I mean where are you really from? Where were you born? Where are your parents from? Where is that accent from? Are you from Jamaica? How long have you lived here? Where did you grow up? How can you live there, in an expensive neighbourhood, when I cannot? Under the white gaze, our presence and the authenticity of our words are questioned.

Underlying these tiresome questions is the white historical belief that one's Black presence is anomalous, if not dangerous (Henry 2015). Such questions are pervasive and invasive, whether by strangers or colleagues. African American historian Chana Kai Lee's (2008) response to the questioning of her colleague in women's studies reflects the frustration brought about by the frequent request for authentication of a Black person's words and experience. After suffering a stroke while teaching, barely capable of speech and still in the hospital, her white colleagues in women's studies badgered her with questions doubting the state of her illness, questioning her request for sick pay as well as how her classes would get taught. Lee recounted, "I was insulted. I could not take it." She blasted a colleague during a phone call: "I do not need you or anyone else questioning my integrity after all that I have been through. Fuck this job!" (212).

Indeed, Lee's response at a fragile time of illness evokes the commodification and dehumanization that Black people experience. If not vigilant, the grating questions that accompany the white gaze may cause us to question our own decisions, identities, authority, or our very Blackness. Henry Daniel asked himself, "Who am I fooling, and why am I really here?" and "Do I look much better without my dreadlocks? Why did I shed them?" (chapter 11). White normativity attempts to set limiting parameters on who we are / should be / can be with complete disregard for our own self-definition for what Juliane Otok-Bitek, a Black woman, an African, an Acholi, a Ugandan, a scholar, a poet, and a mother among other identities, names the "poly-selves." She ponders, "How do we name the poly-selves of us? Poly-selved compared to who? The mono-selved folk in our company?" (chapter 13). She underscores "the here and there of place and diaspora," the cultural and geographic memories embedded in the self. Daniel emphasizes the "fragmented subjectivities" that are a product of a system that causes us to live in more than one psychic, spiritual, and epistemic location at once.

More Than Skin Deep

Similar to Otok-Bitek, Jan-Therese Mendes points out the multidimensionality and heterogeneity of Blackness as well as the quotidian ways in which we dwell in these intersections and tensions (chapter 15). Both authors also remind us that even Black people may subscribe to homogenizing views of what and who a Black person can be, or whose Blackness is legitimate, authentic, or acceptable, or what ontologically makes one Black, dismissing the range of intersections and variegations of Blackness. Indeed, insider-outsider tensions can be religious, racial, cultural, physical, social, political, and historical, and often quite palpable. As Twine (2000) argues, the idea of "racial insiderness may simply create a different set of pluses and minuses, rather than eliminate them" (13).

Otok-Bitek's research travels and Mendes's research participants illustrate how contexts and events may change ideas of the Black self or even the realization of the self as Black. Consider Paulita, Mendes's Panamanian research participant. She identified as "Hispanic" before her conversion to Islam and before wearing a hijab. "I realized I look

African so I identify now as a Muslim-Afro-Hispanic." She also stated, "I started to say 'I am Black' when I became Muslim because they [the white Canadian public] can't see my hair." Paulita mentioned her hair, a primary racial signifier, and in her opinion, a mark of her Latina-ness, and perhaps a demarcation away from Blackness. Her former and current identifications might be informed by how race and racism are configured in Panama's racial schema (Craft 2017; Telles and Paschel 2014) as well as Canada's racialization where, as Paulita discovered, one does not escape one's African heritage easily. "Displacement is a place of identity," as Stuart Hall (1996) has written, and migration can be a place of re-identification. Mendes's discussion of hijabi women underscores the many possible angles of Black (un)belonging that include religion, clothing, skin colour, and hair in a larger normative context inimical to Blackness. Although Subreenduth and Rhee (2010) discuss skin colour, one can extend the list to include the aforementioned characteristics to argue that they also "can be a source of discrimination and oppression in one's own community" (338), especially under the legacy of coloniality and white normativity.

"All Things Bright and Beautiful" White People Made Them All

The school that I attended as a child held a morning assembly in which we sang a hymn with the lyrics, "All things bright and beautiful … The Lord God made them all," imparting the white epistemic view of how the world works. Similarly, through taking part in Western colonial education, Black people are subjected to the Eurocentric epistemic project, learning that all things progressive, scientific, intellectual, and innovative come from white people. At the same time, we witness the violence of white appropriative practice. Appropriation has been an unwelcome reality for diasporic Blacks since the Atlantic slave trade, and in less institutionalized ways before that time (Klein and Vinson III 2007). Our bodies, our reproductive systems, our labour, our artistic, cultural, and intellectual production have been commodified and appropriated. We are expendable and disposable objects of property. Black cultural and intellectual production are co-opted, even in university settings. Little wonder, then, as Delice Mugabo recounts in chapter 14, that white Québécois feminists feel no shame in claiming a proto-theory of the well-known Black feminist concept of intersectionality, forerunner the Black feminist theory, despite its historical Black feminist intellectual tradition that predates Crenshaw's formulation in the 1990s (Collins 2000). A stunning display of white supremacist appropriation! The Québécois feminist claim outperforms the boldness of most white feminists who tend to erase race, giving a mere lip service to the Black feminist tradition, and misconstrue the concept for their self-interest.

Conversations That Make Sense

This brief examination of questions allows us to glimpse daily experiences of systemic racism in a world of white discomfort with Black people. Even though our lives are questioned in our intellectual environments, even though our presence and work are scrutinized, we find ways to carry out our work and thrive, although we were never meant to survive (Lorde 1997). Daily we push through many forms of oppression and dehumanization, focusing on our commitments to our work, those for whom we are doing our work from our own epistemological and theoretical perspectives.

In these inimical contexts, it helps to draw from the power of community as Emmanuel Tabi encourages (chapter 12), especially when we feel feeble or falter. And we all do, whether junior or senior scholar. These communities of Black support can multiply and be found in places far from where we are located. It is in such spaces of comfort that "complicated conversations" can truly take place in the true etymological meanings: *com-plicare* – to weave, to fold together; *conversare* – to turn about; to ponder. I share a personal example here. Although separated by department at the three universities where I have worked, I have valued nothing more than having another Black female faculty member on the campus. (And usually there were only a few on the entire campus.) Together we can "turn over," "turn around" to ponder and weave together the fact of an event, a happening, or an injustice. In these spaces, without invasive questioning, we can have conversations that make sense to our lived experiences. Here we do not need to justify our research, our presence, or our humanity.

REFERENCES

Collins, P.H. 2000. *Black Feminist Thought: Knowledge, Consciousness and the Politics of Empowerment.* 2nd ed. New York: Routledge.
Craft, R.A. 2017. "The Politics of Race in Panama: Afro-Hispanic and West Indian Literary Discourses of Contention." *New West Indian Guide/Nieuwe West-Indische Gids* 91 (3–4): 364–366. https://doi.org/10.1163/22134360-09103060.
Hall, S. 1996. "Minimal Selves." In *Black British Cultural Studies: A Reader,* edited by H. Baker Jr., M. Diawara, and R.H. Lindeborg, 44–46. Chicago: University of Chicago Press.

Henry, A. 2015. "'We Especially Welcome Applications from Visible Minorities': Reflections on Race, Gender and Life at Three Universities." *Race, Ethnicity and Education* 18 (5): 591–610. https://doi.org/10.1080/13613324.2015.1023787.

Klein, H.S., and Vinson, B., III. 2007. *African Slavery in Latin America and the Caribbean.* Oxford: Oxford University Press.

Lee, C.K. 2008. "Journey toward a Different Self: The Defining Power of Illness, Race, and Health." In *Telling Histories: Black Women Historians in the Ivory Tower,* edited by D. White, 45–54. Chapel Hill: University of North Carolina Press.

Lorde, A. 1997. *The Collected Poems of Audre Lorde.* New York: Norton.

Subreenduth, S., and Rhee, J.E. 2010. "A Porous, Morphing, and Circulatory Mode of Self-Other: Decolonizing Identity Politics by Engaging Transnational Reflexivity." *International Journal of Qualitative Studies in Education* 23 (3): 331–346. https://doi.org/10.1080/09518390903156215.

Telles, E., and Paschel, T. 2014. "Who Is Black, White, or Mixed Race? How Skin Color, Status, and Nation Shape Racial Classification in Latin America." *American Journal of Sociology* 120 (3): 864–907.

Twine, F.W. 2000. "Racial Ideologies and Racial Methodologies." In *Racing Research, Researching Race: Methodological Dilemmas in Critical Race Studies,* edited by F. Twine and J. Warren, 1–34. New York: NYU Press.

11 Fitting [Out-Fitting] In

HENRY DANIEL

A Prologue: Who Is He Fooling and What Is He Really Doing There?

They encountered each other in the parking lot, the one that was reserved for upper administration.

The dean looked at the professor, who was on his way to another parking lot much farther away, and started voicing what he probably thought was a compliment. Stopping abruptly, he tried to swallow the final words of the sentence.

"You look so much bet—."

The professor smiled politely. Both knew exactly what the rest of the sentence was going to be and both silently agreed not to pursue the issue. The professor had cut his dreadlocks. After all, he thought, the dean seemed like a *mensch* and surely didn't intend any bias.

In fact, he was the one who encouraged the professor when the latter's million-dollar grant application to set up a performance research centre was not allowed to leave the university on grounds that it was not likely to succeed at the federal level. The inside story was that an assistant professor without tenure in an arts facility wouldn't have much chance of success at that level.

This dean was also the same one who commented at the professor's hiring interview that the job was contingent on completing his PhD, even though the requirement for the position specified an MFA or equivalent experience. The professor was ABD at the time, with an MA and an extensive and enviable international career at the highest professional level in his field.

Back then he still had his dreadlocks. Now, in the parking lot more than seven years later, and with his title changed to associate professor, he had shed them. The dean had also retired but was recalled to head a new faculty.

Who Am I and Why Am I Really Here?

I remember precisely when and why I first started growing dreadlocks. It was a long time ago in the Caribbean, before I became a professional dancer and choreographer.

My last attempt came out of pure frustration. I had gotten tired of driving the three hours from Münster to Amsterdam every time I needed a haircut.

Why not grow some dreadlocks again?

Now, a few years on from the comment in the parking lot, with more than a little "salt-and-pepper" on my head and the title of full professor next to my name, I wonder about the numerous "slips" of the tongue I had experienced from colleagues and strangers en route.

Who am I fooling, and why am I really here?

Do I really "look much better" without my dreadlocks?

Why did I shed them? Why are they still lying in the top drawer of my cupboard amidst the socks and underwear? And how many other discarded masks still lie in the cupboards of my house?

The term "fragmented subjectivities" comes to mind.

Four different deans and a number of institutional reorganizations at the faculty and departmental levels later and I'm still trying to fit into a system that continues to see me as "other."

Tracy McMullen riffs on Curtis Mayfield's gospel-inspired "People Get Ready, There's a Train a'Comin'" (1965). She claims that there is no need to get ready for a future that is already here. McMullen also suggests that the African American tradition of improvisation offers perspectives on notions of the self, hope, and the future that reveals a great deal about being in a world that "does not erect fictitious boundaries around a self that cannot, in fact, be located" (McMullen in Heble, and Wallace 2013, 266).

My essay "Performing the Now: Mingus' Pithecanthropus Erectus" (2017) looks at the life and work of musician/composer Charles Mingus.[1] Following McMullen, it argues that the postcolonial, post-slavery, post-institutional "self" does not quite exist and thus has little to prop itself up against or gather around. It can, however, begin to recreate itself as an individuality through a constant search by way of a strategic set of improvisational ideas that eventually open up possibilities for *becoming* (Daniel 2017).

I think about what I have become, or rather about what I have given up to become.

Who am I fooling, and what am I really doing here? Do I look much better without my dreadlocks? Under whose gaze?

Fitting [Out-Fitting] In

This chapter concerns itself with the performativity of identity from the perspective of a Black male artist and scholar working in a school for the contemporary arts within the Canadian university system. Having spent the greater part of my life in countries outside my own native land[2] and in the professional arena as dancer, performer, choreographer, media artist, and scholar, one can say that I have acquired a fair degree of experience about the nature of discourses on performance and the performativity of identity. Since I regularly lecture on and challenge many of these ideas in my intellectual and artistic work – at the same time encouraging my students to do the same – the thematic of this book gives me an opportunity to comment on some of my experiences within a wider context.

Three issues compound the challenges someone like me faces in an average day. The first is that my job as a dance and performance studies scholar sits squarely in the realm of what is known as research/creation in Canada and, as such, is considered already on the margins of valid academic research. Second, in promoting an approach to art scholarship that intersects with a wide spectrum of disciplines, I am often confronted with the borders that many of these disciplines erect to protect their domain. Third, my own immigrant Caribbean/Black African slave ancestry background makes me extremely sensitive to what I see as a certain "colonization of minds" that the dominant forms of discourse foster within academia, and the difficulty people like me encounter in trying to offer alternative approaches.

The point here is that I am no stranger to the prejudices constituted against race, language, academic discipline, and all the other subtle – and not so subtle – discriminatory practices the "guilty" face inside and outside academia. Given that many of these biases are grounded in historically established configurations of inequality and affect what takes place in the classroom, the boardroom, in adjudication panels where research funding priorities are determined, and in hiring, promotion, and tenure committees where one's performance is being assessed, this chapter is a study in "fitting in" as I am tasked to help "outfit" a generation of students who, all too often, are more concerned with what they are entitled to than what unique potentials exist in such settings.

So "What's Your Background?"

Most of us working in the arts are fairly acquainted with some form of this question. I call it the "establishing an artistic genealogy" question. We always want to know what others' artistic lineage is, how they got to where they are now, and who their mentors or artistic influences were along the way. In many ways, the question is similar to another ambiguously worded one that people who have one or another language accent, racial origin, or deviation from some tacitly agreed norm encounters. This is the "Where are you from?" or, "Where are you really from?" question. When positioned within the context of academia, where disciplinary categories, theoretical and conceptual frames within particular knowledge fields, and the "impact value" of one's own research within a socio-political economic sphere plays a large role in situating someone's work, these questions converge in a dynamic space that generates a great deal of tension, not to mention misunderstandings and downright fallacies. To put it another way, a wide range of personal and institutional prejudices comes into play, and when the neoliberal politics of university administrators are added to the mix,[3] important things get sacrificed.

To be fair, the above-mentioned questions are often asked out of sheer curiosity, and sometimes in an unguarded or naive manner to elicit information, start a conversation, or simply to check out the competition. However, these situations also present a rich field of investigation for people like me: artists/scholars whose research involves detailed examinations of human beings "performing" their way through the structures of privilege, entitlement, and institutional power. These mises en scène are composed of so many different layers that it is not difficult to lose one's sense of self while playing a number of scripted roles. Acknowledging that others genuinely want to know more about one's background, to better locate one in the intellectual machinery, so to speak, the issue soon becomes one of how far can such performances last before one or more of the many layers or masks we perform begin to reveal themselves. The fascinating thing about these encounters is that, no matter what one suspects about the nature of one's own exclusion from particular orbits of institutional power, there is almost never any overt admission of such exclusivity until the proverbial slip of the tongue. When such slips occur, and they infrequently do, the supporting cast can be left with debilitating feelings of being mere placeholders fulfilling some kind of institutionally mandated role that helps promote a vaguely articulated notion of inclusivity. To put it even more colourfully, one can find oneself playing the role of the "spice" that adds taste to a dish but that must not be confused with being the meal itself, or even having a real influence on the decisions made at table. Such realizations are always painful for the ego. Unfortunately, or perhaps fortunately, the stories I have to tell here are minor narratives in a larger discussion on notions of "diversity" and "inclusivity," or what I call here "fitting [out-fitting] in."

First of all, how does one "fit into" a paradigm, research or otherwise, that essentially ignores the validity of one's dance, choreographic, and performance practices as critical modes of knowing? Second, how can such "embodied" practices inscribe themselves within institutions of power when the actors themselves and the very methods they use to investigate that knowledge are already perceived as unworthy, or barely tolerable at the margins of serious research? Third, who constructs the ontological and epistemological bases that can support this type of knowing, and/or the perceptive lenses and inscriptive practices through which such knowledges can be recognized and promoted? These are all extremely difficult questions to even begin to consider here, but unless they are faced head-on, I believe the particular "colonization" of minds that currently substitute for real critique in certain quarters of the academy will continue. More importantly, unless there is a critical mass of these "bodies of difference" in the practice room and lecture halls of the academy to engage in such dialogue, we are being profoundly delusional in our use of the terms "diversity" and "inclusivity."

A colleague of mine spoke quite frankly at a recent scholarly gathering[4] about the fact that there are quite distinct approaches to and notions of diversity and inclusivity in the part of Canada from which I write. Acknowledgment comes first for the First Nations community; after all, the term itself undeniably calls for such recognition. After this comes the Chinese-speaking community and the substantial contributions they make to help keep the economy vibrant, an economy that relies to a great extent on a booming real estate business and a growing tech industry (Holmes 2016). Third in line comes the South Asian or "Indian" community who form a powerful and important cultural presence, and only then, if there is any goodwill left, could one perhaps begin to talk of a Black community. Having experienced this prioritization as an unwritten rule in my years of living amongst this "diverse" community, I understood what my colleague meant. These statements, to my mind, were certainly not derogatory or prejudicial by any stretch of the imagination. However, this individual was called to task by a member of the audience, another colleague, who warned against articulating a tendency toward discrimination against Asians that was already tacitly promoted in the community. Theoretically, I saw her argument. However, I felt the point became lost amidst a particular kind of sensitivity – or institutional practised conservatism – that always seems to mollify glaring problems that require address, at the same time drawing attention away from policies that are themselves inherently discriminatory.

Caught in such a set of maddeningly contradictory circumstances, one is forced to take a step back and evaluate one's own position within what could easily turn into "competitive oppression exceptionalism."[5] Such attitudes serve no helpful purpose whatsoever and indeed create even more unwanted tensions within and across racial groups. One could be forgiven for asking whether we can ever move away from such dichotomized modes of thinking. What, then, are we really trying to achieve here, and what could be the role of the artist as intellectual within a system that not only ignores the potential of such a presence, but actively forces it into a set of frames that deny its very potential? Indeed, one can ask whether it is really possible for new theoretical and conceptual frames to emerge from an institutionalized framework that forces people like me to "fit in" to something that fundamentally was not designed to accommodate difference.

Admittedly, these same questions have dogged my extended residence in countries on both sides of the Atlantic throughout a professional career as dancer and choreographer. Then, however, the issue had more to do with how I saw myself being presented within the framework of other people's choreographic ideas, and my own struggle to articulate an individual creative voice that could "speak" about such a predicament. These international performance stages were precisely the locations where bodies like mine desperately strove to "train" a different type of gaze, one that could offset the negative effects of a colonial past. Now, as a scholar, I encounter some of the same institutional barriers, and I am again forced to ask, When will we be ready for such conversations and in what kinds of forms will these conversations come? Damned if I can, damned if I can't! If I'm cast in the role of trying to perform new identities for my own survival, then perform I must. However, and in the meantime, the feeling persists that one's greatest performances come from daily trying to negotiate a space to exist within institutions that do not truly recognize the modes of knowing and the structures for framing the knowledge that people of difference bring. We always seem to be trying to fit into an uncomfortably limited and limiting space. And for bodies and minds accustomed to wide open physical and mental vistas, this is quite disconcerting.

"Where Are You From? I Mean Where Are You Really From?"

These two questions, especially when they follow one another, always provoke a deep sense of frustration and a consequent re-examination of the notion of self that any person of colour, immigrant, or "outsider" feels within a system. Identity, and the structures of identification one finds oneself inhabiting, is so complex that one always wonders which "you" is really under examination. Responses can be dangerous. Which part of me is out of place? And why does it appear to others that I do not belong? These are more than rhetorical questions; they are foundational aspects of what one "is" and/or intends to "become," and hence profoundly philosophical.

As the only tenured Black faculty member in a department of more than thirty full-time faculty at the time of writing, and perhaps a further quarter of that number of part-timers, I am already a minority. But is race really the only criterion that determines the issue of belonging, or fitting in? And are there other less obvious criteria that are being applied that I am unaware of? When my mostly white and mostly female students in a studio class comment on what they see as a "cultural" approach to the physical practices that I offer, what exactly do they mean? And what about the more "diverse" student population in my lectures and seminars, and the theoretical approaches and perspectives that I offer there? Since the sum total of this material is not necessarily "Black" by any stretch of the imagination, does the comment about "a cultural thing" mean that it's not "original" or that the material is in some way flawed?

In Rotterdam, where I was a guest artist, I once had the director at a well-known contemporary dance academy call my studio practice "Afro-Caribbean Limón." This person was referring to my approach to a dance technique I was trained in at the Juilliard School and performed through repertory works in the José Limón Dance Company of New York for many years. It amused me that this colleague chose to ignore the fact that all of these so-called modern and/or contemporary dance techniques have had substantial input from Black bodies throughout their development[6] – input that is unacknowledged in many of the written histories that continue to be disseminated. Ironically, he also recognized that there was something I added to the technique simply by performing it. This point is lost on many of these writers, who should actually know better. Another relevant point is that during each day I do not encounter more than three or four Black students on my way through the halls of the department I teach in. Very rarely do I have three at the same time in any of my lecture courses, and never have I had more than three at any one time in the studio courses that I teach. This is quite shocking for someone whose work attempts to address precisely such absences. However, the more important issues at stake here, and the questions that need to be asked should be, Where are these people, and why are they not here? Do my teaching practices or those of colleagues like myself across the university not accommodate what they are looking for?

Of course, it could simply be that there are not many of "us" people of colour in the city in the first place. Or that those who are around do not think the programs offered are worthy of their time and effort. Whatever the case, the onus seems to be on me to go find and invite them in, which in turn poses the question: Is that part of the reason I was hired in the first place? Am I expected to go find and bring these diverse student populations into the institution? And if this is indeed the case, why aren't my substantial and ongoing efforts to do so not being supported by said institution? Growing up in a place where we were taught that Columbus "discovered" the Americas more than half a century ago, and that he was followed by others who brought our ancestors here through an ignominious trade, the issue of how to go about dismantling deeply embedded modes of thinking has always been of concern to me.

But how does one go about de-colonizing a mind, starting with one's own? This is a question the Kenyan writer Ngũgĩ wa Thiong'o himself wrestled with. Part of his solution was to go back to writing in his own indigenous tongue, where I believe he felt more embodied in the rhythm, syntax, metre, colour, and tone of the language. Perhaps the way for us who have been deprived of our indigenous languages to resist the dominant forms of discourse that continue to foster the types of biases I mentioned earlier must take place in the spaces between the verbal and the non-verbal. And if so, the arts must play a key role in these initiatives. How, then, do we get the relevant bodies to help de-colonize the physical spaces of the institutions we are hired to teach in, and how can we permeate the strategic "barriers" that have been erected to protect disciplinary domains? Lastly, what options do people like me have – those of us with a background embedded in a history of slavery and colonization? How can we react to the rhetoric of a dominant discourse that still continues to shape the minds and bodies of those we are charged to educate? These questions will certainly not be addressed without the establishment of a certain "critical mass." But where will that critical mass come from?

Oh! You're a Professor? What Do You Teach?

My first response to these questions is almost always to say that I teach dance, or that I teach theatre and performance studies. This of course elicits the inevitable follow-ups: "What kind of dance?" and "What is performance studies?" "You mean you can actually get a PhD in dance?" By this time, I am already preparing for the upcoming explanation of what studies in dance, theatre, and performance studies actually entail. More importantly perhaps, I try to explain how all of these interests combine to form a comprehensive approach to teaching, scholarship, and research. Amidst the genuine surprise and obvious confusion, I'm usually enjoying the entertainment for what it's worth, trying to discover more about the nature of the personality standing in front of me. The scene is a truly fascinating one, and the reader would be correct in thinking that any anthropological and/or auto-ethnographically minded person would already be constructing a case study: "Kafka's Ape revisited," if you wish.[7] And if, as "Red Peter," one is consigned to a continual reportage of gratefulness to the academy for enabling one's *Entwicklung* or "evolutionary development," then one can be forgiven for seeing the entire charade for what it is worth: an extended and ongoing performance of identity that's taken more than half a century to unfold. Walcott and others are indeed correct in their observations. His claim that "the colonial history that gave rise to contemporary life in the West [still] haunts our present" (Walcott 2014, 96) is evident in all aspects of these same everyday lives.

Perhaps already sensing what lay ahead, soon after my own appointment as an assistant professor in a Canadian university I created a new dance and performance work titled *Relatively Well-Centred* (2000). This would be the first in Canada of a choreographic model I had begun developing much earlier in the United Kingdom and other parts of mainland Europe – mostly Germany – in academic, professional, and community dance institutions. This model included using students I was assigned to teach in a number of different disciplinary areas, faculty members from across the university, and professional artists working in the "real world" outside academia. To my mind at the time, the response to this first work was quite strange; I thought either no one understood the work or my colleagues were too polite to comment about what they saw. I received absolutely no critical feedback outside the cast and creative team, something that baffled me, since I assumed that in such an environment critical dialogue was expected, encouraged, and even demanded. Even gentle probing failed to squeeze much out of my colleagues.

Relatively Well-Centred utilized text from Franz Kafka's *Ein Bericht für eine Akademie* (A report to an academy) (1917), Mari Evans's *I Am a Black Woman* (2007), and Virginia Woolf's *Orlando* (1928). Its aim was to explore some of the issues that were inherent in these writings, and the critique of culture, gender, race, and the academic enterprise that they posed. The work was also part of a larger strategy to position dance and other performance practices as valid modes of investigation and of strategies for knowing, able to hold their own with any intellectual pursuit. *Relatively Well-Centred*, as the title suggests, looked at how bodies within a system enter a state of dynamic equilibrium, in this case how they become relatively fixed in elliptical paths or orbits around one another. This habit of drawing inter- and trans-disciplinary references is strategic to both my studio practices and my intellectual/theoretical work. Indeed, it is a crucial aspect of a research methodology that attempts to look at the simultaneity of human "being" in its complex dimensions. Such an approach underlines the idea that we human beings enjoy an existence in bodies that have complex histories, are embedded in multiple domains, have "selves" and memories that exist simultaneously in different spatio-temporal orbits, and can be investigated by methodologies that do not obey prescriptive disciplinary categories.

Relatively Well-Centred utilized the basic concept embedded in an ellipse, which describes a trajectory that is quite different from that of the circle. The structure of the circle is described by an object that sits at the centre of a path in relation to another object that rotates around it with equal radii everywhere. The ellipse, on the other hand, suggests that there are two centres around which an object travels: one visible and the other invisible. The "visible" centre "pulls" the rotating object towards it, while the "invisible" source of energy drags it away such that the viewer sees an elongated path. The idea behind this mise en scène was that for every performer "onstage," an invisible "force" existed that shaped the movements of the "orbiting subject." One could read into this the idea that every phenomenon or movement action is influenced by two main sources, one visible and the other invisible, which together stabilize a moving subject into an elliptical path. In short, there are always at least three forces at work that determine an individual's actions, and these forces are never equal.

In *Relatively Well-Centred* all of the white performers onstage were "shadowed" by pre-recorded images of Black bodies on a screen behind, creating a doubly centred "elliptical path" with the audience as observing subjects. Additionally, the entire music in the work consisted of African-influenced drumming patterns, voice, and percussion executed by the only Black colleague I had in the department – a highly skilled musician lecturer who had spent decades accompanying dance classes in the department and running a biennial field school to Ghana until his retirement in 2015. However, none of this music was obviously recognizable as such, since it was electronically manipulated into something quite "other" than. My musician colleague never appeared live on stage, nor did I, but we were both forces instrumental in determining the trajectory of the audience's perspectives. This, in short, was my critical response to the fact that the program had so few persons of colour visibly at work in the current structures and systems of institutional power. This, to be sure, was just one layer of the work. The other layers spoke for themselves, and audibly so through the texts of Kafka's *Report*, Woolf's *Orlando*, and Evans's *Black Woman*.

This initial effort to introduce what I hoped would stimulate critical dialogue was met by polite silence. Even as I sought feedback, no one said a word about what I saw as the most important aspect of the work, namely, how to introduce a lively debate about diversity and inclusivity through an individual artistic practice and to offer a critique of the institution that seemed not to encourage what it was actually advertising as part of its social and educational mandate. A decade later, and after much effort in developing new works with varying degrees of criticality, I re-choreographed and restaged a section of *Relatively Well-Centred* as *The Report* (2011), this time using just Kafka's text in the original German, with the translation of my former playwright colleague Marc Diamond.[8] *The Report* presented white bodies performing classical ballet steps *en pointe*, steps transformed by a contemporary vocabulary that challenged the ballet's own form of institutionalization of dance. The "ape" role was reprised by the original Canadian/Filipino actor-performer. There were no references to Black bodies or their virtual representation onstage in this version. However, my attempts to create inter-, cross-, and transdisciplinary dialogues, to position studio-based or process-based research with dance on a more secure footing with other forms of academic research continued, and if I may say so, with much success internally (via university-based grants) and externally (via multi-year federal funding).

What's Ahead?

Those of us with a past embedded in the experience of the Atlantic slave trade have inherited a peculiar relationship to the descendants of those who enslaved our forefathers and the institutions they created to keep them in check. We have become trapped in each other's orbits, rooted in each other's gazes, if you wish. Escape demands becoming something "other than" – radically shifting a focus that forever recreates and/or perpetrates an illusion that presumes its own truth. But what could this radical shift be, and from whence can it come? I firmly believe that a new and more diverse set of bodies must infiltrate and thus radically change the current institution and the discourses it attempts to proliferate. These bodies must challenge what has become normative, actively promote shifts in perception, and expose the many possibilities that lie hidden between the yes/no, subject/object dichotomies of an inherited rationalist mode of thinking and being. As McMullen (2013) argues, we are dealing with a future that is already here, and something other than must describe that future.

> I don't subscribe to your version of diversity
> I don't believe in its inclusivity practices
> I don't wish to represent anything
> I want to make work that contributes to a radical perceptual shift
> – Henry Daniel, 2021

NOTES

1 Charles Mingus was born in Nogales, Arizona, on 22 April 1922 of mixed heritage: African American, German American, British, Chinese, and Native American (Horton 2007). He died in Mexico on 5 January 1979 at the age

of fifty-six, soon after working on music for an album with the Canadian singer/songwriter Joni Mitchell.

2 I was born in Trinidad and educated at Naparima College, an all-boys secondary school founded by Canadian Presbyterian missionaries for the sons of Indian indentured servants who were brought in to replace the "emancipated" African slaves in the mid-nineteenth century.

3 See Hall, Massey, and Rustin's (2015, 16) critique of neoliberalism's project as "a reassertion of capital's historic imperative to profit – through financialisation, globalisation and yet further commodification," and Bill Readings's (1996) critique of the university and its administrative manipulation of teaching and research objectives.

4 This exchange took place at the "Continuing Conversations," 15 October 2015 roundtable discussion at the Djavad Mowafaghian Cinema, Goldcorp Centre for the Arts, Simon Fraser University, Vancouver. The discussion was part of a three-day seminar dedicated to remembering and continuing the work of British public intellectual Stuart Hall. http://www.henrydaniel.ca /news/.

5 This term is used by interdisciplinary scholar and critic Rinaldo Walcott (2014, 96).

6 Contemporary dance techniques such as Graham, Limón, and Horton have all had major influences in their developmental process from Black dancing bodies since the early part of the twentieth century. Dance historian Brenda Dixon-Gottschild (1996, 2003) has written extensively on the Black influence on modern and contemporary dance, including George Balanchine's neo-classic ballet, by a Black movement and music aesthetic.

7 I'm referring to Franz Kafka's story (1917) about an ape who is captured somewhere in Africa and trained in Europe to become human. After a rigorous education, "Red Peter" is asked to make a report to an academic committee about his transformation.

8 Teacher, theatre director, playwright, novelist, opera librettist Marc Diamond died suddenly at his home in Vancouver on 17 November 2005, aged sixty-one. http://www.sfu.ca/~gotfrit/Marc_Diamond.htm.

REFERENCES

Daniel, H. 2011. *The Report*. http://www.henrydaniel.ca/the-report.

Daniel, H. 2017. "Performing the Now: Mingus' Pithecanthropus Erectus." In *Jazz Cosmopolitanism from East to West*, edited by Y. Hui and T. Whyton, 42–57. Zhejiang: Zhejiang University Press.

Dixon-Gottschild, B. 1996. *Digging the African Presence in American Performance: Dance and Other Contexts*. Westport, CT: Greenwood Press.

Dixon-Gottschild, B. 2003. *The Black Dancing Body: A Geography from Coon to Cool*. New York: Palgrave Macmillan.

Evans, M. 2007. *I Am a Black Woman*. New York: Morrow.

Hall, S., Massey, D., and Rustin, M. 2015. "After Neoliberalism: Analysing the Present." In After *Neo-Liberalism?: The Kilburn Manifesto*, 4–15. Baltimore, MD: Project Muse.

Heble, A., and Wallace, R., eds. 2013. *People Get Ready: The Future of Jazz Is Now!* Durham, NC: Duke University Press.

Holmes, R. 2016, 3 February. "Without Affordable Housing, Vancouver Risks Becoming an Economic Ghost Town." *The Financial Post*. https://financialpost.com/entrepreneur/fp-startups/without-affordable-housing-vancouver-risks-becoming-an-economic-ghost-town.

Horton, A. 2007. *Charles Mingus and the Paradoxical Aspects of Race as Reflected in His Life and Music*. Unpublished PhD thesis, University of Pittsburgh.

Hui, Y., and Whyton, T., eds. 2017. *Jazz Cosmopolitanism from East to West*. Hangzhou: Zhejiang University Press.

Kafka, F. 1917. "Ein Bericht für eine Akademie." https://www.projekt-gutenberg.org/kafka/erzaehlg/chap002.html.

McMullen, T. 2013. "People, Don't Get Ready: Improvisation, Democracy, and Hope." In *People Get Ready*, edited by A. Heble and R. Wallace, 265–280. New York: Duke University Press.

Readings, B. 1996. *The University in Ruins*. Cambridge, MA: Harvard University Press.

Walcott, R. 2014. "The Problem of the Human: Black Ontologies and 'the Coloniality of Our Being.'" In *Postcoloniality – Declononiality – Black Critique: Joints and Fissures*, edited by S. Broeck and C. Junker, 93–105. Frankfurt: Campus Verlag.

Woolf, V. 1928. *Orlando: A Biography*. London: Hogarth Press.

12 The Caged Bird Still Sings in Harmony: The Academy, Spoken Word Poetry, and the Making of Community

EMMANUEL TABI

Writing with Community as a Quest for Freedom

I am often asked why it is important for me to localize my writing within the context of race, class, and gender. The simple yet consistent answer I provide is, "I need to." I need to write about the things in the world that both trouble and excite me. I have the privilege to express my anger, joy, distrust, and sadness to two powerful yet separate communities.

The first community is more familiar to me; it is an audience that has few restraints and judgments, an audience from which both my courage and imagination have grown within. This audience is Toronto's exuberant and massively talented spoken word poetry community. I have been sharing my poetry and music within the spoken word community and, to a larger extent, Toronto's arts scene for approximately fifteen years. Within this community I have the freedom to speak about my entire human condition. Though I have the liberty to write poetry and music on any issue my soul desires, the themes within my artistic expression often return to matters that relate to gender relations, race, and class oppression.

The second community I traverse is the academic community. I have been mentored and encouraged by a collective of academics who have provided a space for me. I have learned that as a graduate student it is not necessary for everyone to be on your side, but it is imperative that you do have a "tribe" that you can return to, a tribe that knows your strengths, weakness, and goals, a tribe that can grow with you and encourage your evolution.

I often write about issues surrounding gender, race, and class oppression, for it is a means for me to exercise the pain that has been built up within me over the years of existing as a Black male within a Eurocentric society. This pain became increasingly clear to me throughout the process of writing this chapter. The first few drafts began more as rants, talking about how misunderstood I felt as a Black person within Canada, and how distrusting I had become of "the system." The result was a draft, though passionate, still lacking structure, leading the reader through a wild adventure of confused words and pain-filled metaphors. In these moments I was reminded of how deep the trauma due to social oppression can be, and how difficult it is to be clear and concise when communicating the moments that wound. Pain does not wait for the right time to be expressed. Pain explodes, pain moves with unpredictable trajectories and is often unintelligible. This I realized was the plight of many Black academics within Canada who write about race. It is through writing this chapter – as a novice scholar who is in the middle of writing his PhD thesis, a situation I will address next – that my already reverent respect for those Black Canadian academics who have gone before me deepened.

The main point of this chapter remains that in order for me to be successful, I needed both the academic and spoken word communities to support me through this work. I do not place the importance of one community over the other, but as I will show in this chapter, both communities have worked in concert with one another to support me through very difficult moments.

This chapter rises from my personal narrative through my PhD journey. This chapter is also an example of the intersections of the communities inside and outside of the academy, and how these intersections inform, nurture, support, and guide this journey. I will speak to my heritage and my constant negotiation with my Canadian identity, and how these negotiations then led to the pursuit of my doctorate at the Ontario Institute for Studies in Education/University of Toronto (OISE/UT). Then I will discuss the moments during a road trip across Canada that was problematic and concerning, and the support I received in order to work through these moments. I will conclude by highlighting the "brotherhood" that formed with four very special young men as my mother fell ill last summer. These stories speak to and reflect the importance of having a community surround you that can be nurturing, while simultaneously providing the opportunity to nurture others, and to pass on the wisdom that has been provided. These experiences show that we are constantly changing within the academy, and the importance of having support as we change, grow, and heal. Life continues while we are in graduate school, and we bring to the academy the reality of our sometimes complicated lives. For racialized graduate students, the pain and difficulty of oppression is our reality, and amidst our deadlines, aspirations, and projects, we still have to maintain a difficult discussion within ourselves about what it means to be, in my case Black and an academic, knowing the systemic and expressive forms of racism that "being Black" affords in Canada.

An African proverb states, "It takes a village to raise a child." I invoke this same wisdom to describe the support required for graduate students, for as children, we graduate students are experiencing a new reality, which is daunting, terrifying, and exciting, and much like a child, we need consistent guidance and direction. My experiential narratives in this chapter show how important it is that graduate students, particularly Black graduate students, be part of a community that encourages and uplifts them through the work they pursue, for we bring to this work the pain and reality of being racialized folx in Canada, navigating intersectional identities (Crenshaw 1991), as well as the need to know how to live through these realities while traversing academia.

Writing as a Method of Becoming

Born in Guelph, Ontario, to a mother of Grenadian descent and a father of Ghanaian heritage, my Black identity was shaped and nurtured within both diasporic and traditional African ideologies, customs, and ways of being. My mother being a Pentecostal preacher and my father being a bank executive instilled within our family a foundation of justice, morality, hard work, and discipline. These experiences and observations provided me with a schema of what was possible, as well as strategies to navigate race and gender biases.

Despite being immigrants, my parents reinforced the fact that I was Canadian, even though when I went to school, I was told otherwise. This became really confusing, especially when classmates of mine who were not born in Canada, yet were white, were never questioned about which country they came from. Within these moments I learned that being "Canadian" was traditionally correlated with whiteness. Nevertheless, I continued to identify with being Canadian.

Being Canadian did not imply that I must conform to whiteness, nor that I would be divorced from the boldness, intelligence, and resolve of my parents' cultures. Instead, my African and Caribbean roots informed my Canadian identity. Canadian heroes such as Oscar Peterson provided for me examples of people who were Canadian, Black, and excellent. Furthermore, my parents often talked about Black heroes such as Muhammad Ali, Maurice Bishop, Nelson Mandela, Maya Angelou, and Kwame Nkrumah. We would spend many hours during my childhood watching documentaries of Black freedom fighters. I learned at an early age that though racism is real, painful, and at times overwhelming, it is not a reason for me to give up, but instead a reason for me to rise up. With fortitude and provision, I can become whatever I put my mind to. As a graduate student, I do my best to honour the direction of the memory of the freedom fighters who have gone before me. I remain fascinated and inspired by those who continue to combat and resist all forms and expressions of oppression.

My time at OISE/UT has instructed, nurtured, and protected my anti-oppressive lens. It has provided me with further opportunities to name and confront systemic issues that plague our society. During my time at OISE/UT, I was invited on a voyage of a lifetime, an undertaking and adventure that would trouble what it means to be Black in Canada.

The Negotiation of Blackness in Canada

In the summer of 2013, two of my close friends and colleagues had the ambitious idea of driving from Toronto to Victoria Island, British Columbia, as we were to present at the annual Canadian Society for the Study of Education (CSSE) conference. I was excited! Being Canadian, I had an innate desire to drive across the country. The three of us represented and lived in three very different racial paradigms. One of my colleagues is white and a very proud Canadian. My other colleague grew up in South America and has lived in both the United States and Canada. I knew that the opportunity to drive across the country with phenomenal people was rare, so I took advantage of the offer and began a journey that would be both beautiful and challenging.

As we drove through Canada, it became clear that my colleagues and I experienced Canada in very different ways, particularly its legislative buildings. My white Canadian colleague was excited to see the legislatures in major Canadian cities we drove through and often looked at them with awe and pride. I recall appreciating the architecture of the buildings, while experiencing angst at the sight of statues of white men who benefited from the occupation of Turtle Island and the oppression of First Nations people. Standing before these buildings, I was reminded of the Eurocentric hegemonic and patriarchal discourse perpetuated through Canada's historic imagination. The legislative buildings function as a pedagogy of ignoring, a symbol that those who can identify with these statues or see themselves within the statues have access to and benefit from the laws that are passed within them. The statues are more than statues to me; they functioned as "Keep Out" signs – signs that illustrate who belongs and who does not, a discursive hegemonic space that immediately alienates me from the land in which I was born. What is emphasized through these buildings and monuments is the "greatness and strength" of a white man, it assumes that he shaped this country by his own hand, that he constructed Canada through fairness and justice, thus re-establishing whiteness within a heroic saviour trope.

I am a proud Canadian, but whether that label is perceived as credible is tied to the spaces my Black body occupies. When I travel to Africa, Europe, and the Caribbean, I tell people I am Canadian and they take it as such. Yet it is here in Canada where I am asked where I am really from, or where my parents are from. So not only do these buildings not represent me. I am also reminded through legislation, comments, and statues of "Canadian heroes" that this land does not represent me, nor does it belong to me. These moments establish what Awad Ibrahim (1999, 353) explains as the *social imaginary*, "a discursive space or representation in which they [Blacks] are already constructed, imagined and positioned and are thus treated by the hegemonic discourses and dominant groups, respectively, as Blacks." Nothing at the legislature allowed me to imagine myself in connection with the long-standing existence of Blackness in Canada that resulted from the American Revolution, the War of 1812, and the Underground Railroad. The silence surrounding stories of resilience, strength, courage, and knowledge of early Black settlers establishing themselves in Canada tells to me that it is also unimportant within the colonial project we identify today as being Canada. In sum, it seems, my life and my being Black in Canada is of little or no significance.

My understanding of what it meant to be a Black Canadian was further reinforced through the deferential treatment of police officers towards my white friend and colleague as we continued our journey to Victoria Island.

Observations of Privilege

I still recall the police siren interrupting the morning sunrise as we drove through Wisconsin. We had driven through the night in order to keep to our schedule. My white colleague had been driving almost 150 kilometres an hour and had not noticed the police officer. I have had encounters with police officers. Some were positive and others were negative because I was simply "driving while Black." The horror stories of police encounters in America began to trickle into my mind as I began to wonder how this scenario would play out. I exchanged glances with my Latinx colleague, who had just awakened from a nap, as she had driven for much of the night. The police officer approached the driver's side of the car. My white colleague greeted him with a smile and a hurried explanation for why she had exceeded the speed limit. My Latinx colleague and I both knew that as people of colour, the less you said to a police officer the better. The police officer had a polite conversation with the driver. "This is how white people live, huh?" I thought to myself. My white college showed little mistrust, for what did she have to fear? Her reality did not include innocent people that look like her being murdered by police officers. Instead she was interacting with someone she had little doubt was there to protect and serve her. At the end of the exchange, my white colleague received a sheet of paper that astounded me: a written warning informed her that if she were to be caught speeding again, she would receive a speeding ticket. I was shocked and confused. Not only had she been driving above the speed limit, she had been driving at a speed that usually ends with a significant fine. I was immediately brought back to the moment when I was given a speeding ticket while driving in traffic, or the speeding ticket I received while approaching a red light. The privileges afforded to my colleague were astounding, and she had expected no different.

We arrived at the conference after four days on the road. My colleagues and I bonded and grew from our experiences on our trip. I also had the pleasure of spending time with Professor Ibrahim of the University of Ottawa (one of the co-editors of this volume), a man who has been a guiding light, a mentor, and a father figure for me during my academic journey. I was quick to tell him about my experiences with the legislative buildings and the police officer. I did not know how much I needed to speak to a Black person/man about these issues, as it sounded like a story that was/is too familiar to Black people. Besides being a mentor, Professor Ibrahim has written about his own racist interactions with the police in Toronto during his time in graduate school. Our lived experience as Black people is our site of research, Professor Ibrahim reminded me, and it is our site of theory making. Our lived experience, he continued, appoints us to speak, so we must write it. Prof. Ibrahim more than understood my experiences; our conversation provided me with great comfort and relief. He encouraged me to write about these experiences because, he argued, no one can bear witness for the witness and no one can write our stories exactly the way we can.

That evening, Professor Ibrahim invited me to dinner with four other prominent Canadian Black scholars: Boulou de B'beri, Handel Kashope Wright, and Tamari Kitossa. We shared many stories and strategies of how to traverse academia as people of the African diaspora. They were attentive and encouraging as I told my stories. Seeing these scholars, hearing their stories of struggle, triumph, perseverance, and courage instilled in me the confidence that I too could find my place within academia. Though the challenges would be many, with this support, coupled with a strong work ethic and courage, I would have a successful career. This energy moved with me to my conference presentation, where I spoke with boldness and confidence. My presentation was really well received, and I felt that I was making a home for myself. I left the conference with renewed and invigorated confidence.

My colleagues were waiting for me after my presentation and greeted me with smiles and hugs. They too had had a strong conference and felt invigorated! While driving to catch the ferry to Vancouver, we spoke about all the writing we would do during the rest of our summer. It was exciting having our ideas acknowledged and appreciated by other scholars who were participating in fascinating and meaningful work. We were filled with dreams of endless funding and tenure; it felt as if we could accomplish anything! It was in the midst of our discussion that yet again my white colleague was pulled over for speeding. I had a strong feeling that this ticket would be a hefty one and cringed at the thought of having to face yet another police officer. The officer came to the window and was greeted by a flurry of apologies from my colleague. He jokingly asked us where we were going in such a hurry. My white colleague professed that we were trying to reach the ferry in time and we were driving back to Toronto. Without hesitation, the policeman engaged my colleague in conversation about his time on the force and how nice the summer was, as if they were old friends. I had had enough. I was angry. I immediately began to reminisce about the experiences that I and many Black folx have had with police officers. I was reminded that being a person of colour in Canada often means negative interactions with state representatives such as the police. I felt as if I were a second-class citizen within my own country, but most importantly, I no longer felt the joy, confidence, and sense of promise with which I had left the conference only twenty minutes earlier.

While on the ferry, I called Professor Ibrahim while choking back tears of frustration. I so wanted to return to that safe space amongst a group of people that believed in me. I didn't want to feel fear. I did not want to feel alone. Professor Ibrahim spoke to me with grace and wisdom, returning me to my centre: "You have to write this out, my son," he said. "You can't let this rest within you. You have to write it down. Only in putting it on paper, in naming it while it is fresh will you be able to witness and see the trauma you just went through." This was strong advice. I did not have to remain within this negative energy. In fact I refused to.

For the remainder of the trip, I wrote. I wrote about my previous experiences with police officers, I wrote about the racial and social climate of Canada and the United States, I wrote my poetry. And it was in doing this I gained strength, perspective, and power. Though I have the privilege to express myself through academic writing, it is through poetry that I make sense of the worlds around me. It is as if poetry provides the language I need to make sense of the passion and the pain. It is a place absent of judgment, a place where I can hide, heal, and feel what is personal as it evolves into what is political. Audre Lorde states, "Our poems formulate the implications of ourselves, what we feel within and dare make real (or bring action into accordance with), our fears, our hopes, our most cherished terrors … and there are no new pains. We have felt them all already. We have hidden that fact in the same place where we have hidden our power. They surface in our dreams, and it is our dreams that point the way to freedom. Those dreams are made realizable through our poems that give us the strength and courage to see, to feel, to speak, and to dare" (1984, 39).

The assertion of Lorde (1984) that "there are no new pains" communicates that there are others who have experienced similar difficulties. I needed the mentorship of an individual who has gone through this pain to help walk me through it, in essence to not only show me that I will be OK, but to show me *how* to be OK. My time at CSSE 2013 taught me the importance of having a community that maintains academic excellence while overcoming injustice that depresses and traumatizes many people of colour. With the right support, I am realizing now, I can overcome the residue of racism. In writing this chapter and through my academic writing, my hope is to find strategies and opportunities to heal from racial oppression. Since then, as I began to write more, my sense of responsibility grew, and the foundations of my dissertation began to evolve into a program that would bring me into community with like minds and souls.

Gaining Courage through Community

As a researcher, I wanted to use my privilege as an academic to provide a platform from which members of Toronto's spoken word poetry community could speak. Education and social justice is a motivation for many spoken word poets I have met, and their wisdom and experience needed to be shared alongside other curriculum theorists. Moreover, this was an opportunity to present, particularly, images of Black male youth in Toronto who were doing their best to uplift and encourage other youth who were having a hard time within the K–12 education system. Furthermore, I wanted to provide a counter-narrative that did not speak only to Black male youth being failed within our education system. I knew I would learn a great deal about the many ways that these young men would provide support for Toronto's most vulnerable communities.However I was not aware of the role they would play in supporting me. It was through their support that I realized how invaluable they are to Toronto.

My research explores how four young community leaders within the Greater Toronto Area use spoken word poetry and rapping as a means of community education and activism, particularly during the height of the Black Lives Matter Toronto movement. I came to this research topic through my previous work, which examines the educational trajectories of Black male youth in Toronto. It has been well documented (Dei 1997; James 2012) that Black males have some of the lowest average measured academic performances when compared to other ethnic groups, specifically between grades 7 and 8 and 9 to 12 (Toronto District School Board 2007). Though I whole-heartedly agree with this line of research, I have also found that the conversation surrounding Black male youth and education often fosters a narrative that produces only part of the story. Though statistics on the academic achievement of Black male youth is troubling, terms such as "academic troubles" and "failure" have become synonymous with Black males in school, and academic success is often aligned with Eurocentric customs and ideologies (Gosine 2008). Though the narrative surrounding Black masculinity and schooling often ends with many young Black men dropping out of school, this is not where their journey of education ends. The Black young men who participated in my study continue to educate themselves and many other young people outside of schools. Their strategies have allowed them to traverse Ontario's education system despite racial and class oppression. In turn, they have developed curriculum that teaches young people how to gain and maintain a strong sense of self-worth in the face of oppression, thus insulating their message of courage, strength, and knowledge of self within the cultural production of spoken word poetry and rapping. Moreover, these four young men, aged twenty-one to twenty-nine, and whose pseudonyms are Efe, Ebele, Kofi, and Tashi Delek (TD), are a small representation of young Black people who are often forgotten within narratives surrounding Toronto's most vulnerable and marginalized communities. Interestingly, all four used rapping or spoken word to help communicate their message of unity, self-awareness, courage, and education. During my time with these young men, individually and as a group, I was reminded of the importance of being part of a community of like-minded individuals who not only understood my lived experience as a Black male in Canada, but who have also survived and overcome similar experiences. In our focus group meetings, which was part of my PhD research methodology, we were able to bare our souls and speak to the many times we Black men have had to combat racism, as adults and as children. We discussed strategies and coping mechanisms that were beneficial to us, and coping mechanisms that were detrimental to us. We also spoke about where we were the problem, and instances where our performances of hegemonic masculinity perpetuated patriarchal standards, thus reinforcing our male privilege. These were challenging, informative, and healing moments as we traversed the instances within our lived experiences in which we inhabited the role of both the oppressed and the oppressor.

Though I was not surprised that this project galvanized a brotherhood among these four young men and me, I could not have fathomed the depth and fullness of our connection, as well as the support and comfort they provided me during the most difficult moments I have yet to face in my life, in which my mother lost her battle with cancer.

The Foundations of Brotherhood

It was a Thursday, and the five of us were meeting in a boardroom on the tenth floor of OISE where we could observe the sun setting over the Toronto skyline. Despite the fullness and depth of the summer sunset that filled the room, my heart was downcast, as I had found the day before that my mother's cancer had returned. If it had been any other meeting, I would have cancelled, but meeting with "the brotherhood" was more than a meeting; it was a safe and comforting space, a cypher of souls, a space where I could be myself and grow in strength with some of the greatest minds I have had the benefit of meeting. Individually and collectively these young men held me together. During my time in the research field, I was in contact with all four men almost daily, so few things occurred in my life or theirs that escaped us. It was Kofi who hugged me after a spoken word gathering, and it was in this moment that I cried, only for the second time since my mother's diagnosis. I was able to finally release my fears surrounding my mom's battle. I fondly recall sitting on a cement block with Efe at 12:30 a.m. outside Toronto General Hospital. I was spending the night with my mom. Efe knew this, so he came by to keep my company and lighten my spirit. The day my mom passed away, I called TD to give him the news. He immediately took the time off work and came with me to the hospital. "As hard as this is, man, your mother's death does not change your purpose," TD encouraged me. Ebele reached out to me daily, encouraging me and standing with me, even at my mother's funeral. It was these moments that led me to believe that everything was going to be all right. My mother would often say, "Where there is great pain, grace abounds even more." The grace these young men leant to me was of great encouragement, and through my conversations with them and the time I spent with them in the community, I learned that they plant these same characteristics within the soil of the community. They spend time caring for the seed and doing their best to ensure the health of not only the seed, but also the soil and the community – a community they saw that I was part of.

As a budding academic, I know that I will spend countless hours alone preparing for classes, marking, and writing. Nevertheless, I will not be able to contribute most fruitfully if I do not have the support of my community. During my PhD journey, I have received support from two separate communities, both the academic and the spoken word community. As an educator, I have accepted the role of a conduit, as mentor and mentee. Regardless of my position within the many relationships I will find myself part of, I will need a community surrounding me in order to survive – a community, a tribe of *critical friends*, people who will have the courage to be honest, and the kindness to encourage within me hope and love, making me a better person, a better citizen, and most importantly a better educator.

REFERENCES

Crenshaw, K. 1991. "Mapping the Margins: Intersectionality, Identity Politics, and Violence against Women of Color." *Stanford Law Review* 43 (6): 1241–1299. https://doi.org/10.2307/1229039.

Dei, G.J.S. 1997. "Race and the Production of Identity in the Schooling Experiences of African-Canadian Youth." *Discourse: Studies in the Cultural Politics of Education* 18 (2): 241–257. https://doi.org/10.1080/0159630970180206.

Gosine, K. 2008. "Living between Stigma and Status: A Qualitative Study of the Social Identities of Highly Educated Black Canadian Adults." *Identity* 8 (4): 307–333. https://doi.org/10.1080/15283480802365304.

Ibrahim, A. 1999. "Becoming Black: Rap and Hip-hop, Race, Gender, Identity, and the Politics of ESL Learning." *TESOL Quarterly* 33, 349–369. https://doi.org/10.2307/3587669.

James, C.E. 2012. "Students 'at Risk': Stereotypes and the Schooling of Black Boys." *Urban Education* 47: 464–494. https://doi.org/10.1177/0042085911429084.

Lorde, A. 1984. *Sister Outside*. Berkeley, CA: Crossing Press.

Toronto District School Board. 2007. "2006 Student Census, Grades 7–12: System Overview." Toronto: TDSB.

13 States of Being:[1] The Poet & Scholar[2] as a Black, African, & Diasporic Woman

JULIANE OKOT BITEK

Poet[3]

> & so I'm on my hands & knees
> picking up words off the floor between finger & thumb
> you said you'd remember me
> you said you'd know me anywhere
> you said many many many things

Scholar

In the spaces between fallen words we find ourselves homeless, situated in a space for which where you come from doesn't exist except perhaps in that amorphousness that is Africa. Diaspora, semantic for the dispersal, determines the spaces between where we are & where & how we think about home. What words can we find among the ones on the floor that will describe our various selves, we who are of here & there, of there & sometimes nowhere else? How do we name the poly-selves of us? Poly-selved compared to whom? The mono-selved folk in our company? To those who never left home? Then how is it we find spaces of solidarity with those who never left home & were displaced from their social & also intimate selves? We are contained in a minority that reminds us of numbers, not depth, not history, not substance. Elsewhere we are the dominant ones. We are the major; we are no minors, we are no minority except here, in this place we now call home.

We see that there was never empire, that the colonial endeavour was a scam & that there are words beyond the scattered ones on the floor with which to create another world around us. For now, these will suffice. Let us begin.

Poet & Scholar Both[4]

Black Poet[5]

Because if you're black then your blackness is part of your identity as
a poet. If you're white, you'll hardly ever be called a white poet. The
politicization of blackness in identity is often played against politeness,
the note: you're black, you're a poet. In Canada, in this most non-racist
(a term from Marlon James (2016) on a video for *The Guardian*)[6] country, where we're known for our politeness & the manner with which we
thank the bus driver, each of us loudly, each of us, each of us, each of
us clearly earnest about the importance of thanking the bus driver as if
 we owe, we owe & some of us are going to work & forgot our bus pass
  at home & some of us are going to school & we forgot the bus pass
  at home
 & some of us have no change
 & some of us are just so entitled that we tell the driver clearly: I got
  no change
 & sometimes the driver says nonchalantly, go ahead
 & sometimes the driver says I got no ride for you, or something to
  that effect[7]
so what is it going to be for me today, bus driver? What?

Canadian Poet[8]

This means I live among the most non-racist[9] people that can fit in this
country. This means that a paper on the nuances of blackness in the academy is necessary work. This means that if we don't do the work, it will hardly
be taken up by our non-racist friends, relatives, & colleagues. Arguably,
the need to insist on the nation as one of politeness, of a peace-making
history, is also to insist on the yin-yang image of United States & Canada.
The image of a Canada as the kinder, gentler cousin of the United States
functions as denial of the common spaces[10] of history & the present.

Black Canadian Poet & Scholar[11]

& so now I get to write on these unceded lands. I think about the extent to which my Canadian identity betrays[12] the black self & in turn the
extent to which my Canadian identity (& how a Canadian identity) functions as part of the oppressive settler community pitted against the First
Nations people on whose land I think, live, work, & love. My Canadian
self knows about travel & knows about not belonging. My black self knows

about dislocation & knows about the history of dislocation, ours & that of Indigenous people. I hold a Canadian passport & travel as a Canadian citizen, not as a black Canadian citizen. I live in Canada as a black Canadian woman. I am also African. I am also Acholi from Uganda. I am also a poet. I am also a scholar, poet & scholar, both. But the gaze & my reaction to the gaze functions in the most unoriginal way: by presenting race & gender, simplifying & complicating the singular[13] self.

African Canadian Poet[14]

> Diaspora, the African diaspora
> diaspora is to describe a people by their journey
> to a place from somewhere else
> Most of those elsewheres don't even know each other
> Continent wide dispersals at different times
> To imagine us as dandelion seeds at the mercy of a breeze
> Today across the Sahara
> Today across the Mediterranean
> Today across the continental floor over the border at Zimbabwe
> from Africa (don't you know?)
> & into South Africa
>
> Overland   over clouds
>
> Contained in metal   planes
>
> Contained in chemical sprays
> to keep African bugs in Africa[15]
> even the ones that tried to come with us
> Africa-diasporan woman
> Seed. Dispersal. Memory

Ugandan Poet

> & now back on home ground
> as part of a panel where the "Role of the Diaspora" is a thing.

At the 2015 Writers International Festival in Kampala someone makes a point about whether the African diaspora should be included within the borders of our national or continental writers. We on the panel are asked to comment on what it means to be an African writer living in the diaspora. There is a brief debate about the proximity & accessibility to publishing opportunity that diasporic writers have, well, those who live in the West. There's commentary on location-specific writers: how do they know anything about how we live, here, in Africa? My response is a poem I'd written in response to being aware of the deadly news around the 2012 Walk to Work protests & what it was like to be away, suspended in a not-here-not-there moment.[16]

Siyanda Mohutsiwa (2016) set off a firestorm of debate on what it means to her to read work by Africans living in the diaspora. "I'm over it: immigrant literature," she wrote. Frustrated by the alienation she felt from reading books by African writers living in the diaspora who write about life in the West, Mohutsiwa longed for literature beyond the white gaze, unfiltered by African immigrant experience & unencumbered by the need to translate & explain the text to a non-African reader. The problem is that there are many ways of being African, that in these myriad ways of being are best understood by one who has to be severally. Lost. Away from home. Stranger.

There's something to be said for the ability to express ways of unbelonging & belonging. I sit in my living room in Canada with the TV on & my laptop on my lap. I am watching the wedding of Prince William & Kate, the Duchess of Cambridge, while following the Walk to Work protests in Uganda in April 2011. During these protests that begin in Kampala & spread throughout the country, there is a fierce clampdown by the government – tear gas, live bullets, beatings. People are hurt. People are killed. "Stuff to Do When Your Hometown Is Burning" comes from the experience of being away from home, in the "safety" of the West, & attempting to carry on with "normal" activities in the knowledge that your hometown is under fire.

Woman Scholar[17]
Black Woman Scholar[18]
African Woman Scholar[19]
Vancouver Poet[20]
Canadian Researcher[21]

In Tarime, Tanzania, I'm directed to the city hall offices to get some information. At the records office, I introduce myself. I make it clear that I'm not here to do interviews but would like to visit some sites of interest to my research project. What university are you affiliated with? I'm asked. The University of British Columbia. Colombia? No. The university's name is University of British Columbia. There's a British Columbia? Yes, that's the name of the province in Canada where my university is. What is the research project about? The Kagera War. So why are the Canadians interested in the Kagera War? It's not the Canadians, I try to say. It's me. I'm the one interested in it. But you work there. Yes, I do. & you carry a Canadian passport? Yes, I do. So why are you Canadians interested in the Kagera War? I fumble with the words on floor. The limitations of my Swahili language skills are severely tested as I try to explain that the Kagera War provides the context with which to think about memory, alienation, & how we think about history. He doesn't bite. I have nothing to tell you, he says. Leave. Leave now.

Western-Trained Academic of African Descent Doing Research in Africa

"Good to see you!" My friend welcomes me when I get to London. "Are you visiting for a while?" "I'm here to do research." We laugh. Between us we get it immediately. For too long the stream of researchers has been one way: Westerners to the African continent. Of course, this is the beginning of my research travel. Soon enough I will be one of those researchers adding to the stream of Western researchers headed to Africa. Some of my research participants live in London, & while it is a brief moment of mirth, the point is well taken – that it should be a funny thing that an African goes to Europe to conduct research.

African Academic Doing Research in Europe

At the British Library, one must register to use the library. In the form to be filled out one must enter a number of questions, including ethnicity. Black, black British, black (African?) American, West Indian … there's no section for African Canadian. So I can only be African.

Foreign[22]
So where are you from?
Where were you born?
Where are your parents from?
Where is that accent from?
Are you from Jamaica?
You must be from Ghana.
Where are you from?
Where are you from?
How long have you lived here?
Where did you grow up?
I like your skin
I like your hair/may I touch your hair?
Your skin is so soft
Where are you from?
I'm just curious – where did you grow up?
Where are you from?
Where are you from?

One of the best things about living in Canada is the diversity
  I love it – where are you from?
  Is it hot where you come from?
  Do you ever get sun-burned?
  You lucky you don't have to wear sunscreen – where are you from?
  I am Black & foreign
  Black, foreign & female[23]
  Don't ever let me forget that
  & don't ever let me forget
  That my Blackness & my femaleness
  Must inform the way I be here
  I am also daughter[24]
  Also daughter,[25] sister,[26] mother

Historical Self[27]

Claudia Rankine presents a moment when there's a recognition that in a historical past this moment could not have happened. A historical self recognizes the slave & the master ancestors whose descendants you are. In the moment, there may be a performance of power (Rankine 2014, 7), a reminder: you used to be our slaves. Moments like when the man barges in front of you in a line then apologizes for not seeing you (77). Invisibility (17) & reclamation (156). But also exhaustion (62).

I'm in London in the fall of 2014, when the Tower of London is draped in red flowers to commemorate the centenary of the British dead from the First World War. The image is reproduced over all local & international media. As I am engulfed in images of the red poppy, a metaphor for spilled blood, beauty, & patriotism, I think about the historical silence around the fact of a world war in which everyone was involved, beyond the British borders, beyond European borders. I think about the silence around the contributions of the colonized during both world wars over the years & the weight of this silence now, a hundred years during which it has come to surface, these contributions, these lives cut short, these needless deaths for an ungrateful[28] colonial master. I think about the fact that the British sprayed nerve gas into the caves where the Acholi people of Lamogi retreated to as they resisted the British. How silent this is in the context of our unrecognized war dead[29] from that & other wars. How silent this is in the context of discussions of how deadly the nerve gas was during the trench wars & the gas chambers that characterized the Holocaust of the Jews by Nazi Germany during the Second World War. How silent the context of culpability & responsibility from the ones who colonized & settled on this unceded[30] land on which I live. I'm so tired.

Social Self[31]

Invisible (or Visible Self)[32]

At the airport in Edmonton after a recent visit there, I hand my board-ing pass to an airport employee who must scan it in order for the gate to open into the security section where my luggage & self will be scru-tinized along with others. He asks me where I'm going. Vancouver, I answer. Is that your final stop? Yes, I answer. Do you live there? Yes, I do. Where in Vancouver do you live? By City Hall, right behind Vancouver General Hospital. That's an expensive neighbourhood. Yes, it is. I live in subsidized housing. Is there subsidized housing over there? Yes, there is. I used to live in Surrey, he says. I moved out here because the price of housing over there is too much. What I also hear: how do you live in Vancouver? Why do you live there? How can you live there, in an expen-sive neighbourhood when I cannot?

Who are those people whose presences are not questioned? & why? The man interrogating me is a brown man. His gaze is specific to me, illustrating the machinations of power. The female black body as the least vulnerable, one that can be swallowed up, unacknowledged. Among the murdered & missing women, there we are, there we are: un-named, invisible, visible & not.

Place-Specific Self

In Canada & especially in this unceded territory, I live as a politicized body: black, female, middle-aged. I watch the lists get checked off. Professor, I never had a black professor before, a student tells me, as does another & another & another ever since I started to teach. Once, a student felt comfortable to express her fear of black men.

Why do you think black men are scary? I asked, mirroring her words.

It's what I see on TV & movies, she said.[33]

I think about my familial relations. Are the black men in my life scary? Are they scary to me? Are they scary because they might resemble what-ever scary black men images are up for consumption on TV & in the media? Are they scary because they are black? The brothers, son, father, cousins, friends of mine, these men that I love, are they scary?

On the bus on these unceded lands a couple of kids are chatting as a seat becomes available next to me. One says to the other: you wanna sit? The other mumbles. His friend responds quickly, loudly enough: what, are you racist? Then he turns to look at me. His friend mumbles some-thing to him. The bus rambles on. No one else makes a comment. We sit in silence. The seat beside me remains empty. The bus rambles on, on this home & native land.

Acholi Self

On the bus to Madi Opei from Kitgum, Uganda, a woman is having a conversation with the person next to her. An overheard conversation already in medias res. It was so cold, the woman says. It was so cold it looked like it was raining milk. No way, her friend responds. I'm telling you. It was really, really cold. & when the milk landed it seemed to disappear on the ground like water. People around her laugh. It's funny, this story of a wet snow. It's so completely out of context during this dry season at the same time of the year, in January. Milk falling from the sky is so out of context where the dust clouds are already forming in the early morning. Not enough dew to hold on to the dust. It hasn't rained for a couple of months. The landscape is a red brown. I laugh, too. Having grown up on books illustrated with apple trees that look like oak trees dotted in red, I know that this woman's experience in that cold place need not permeate the reality of this hot, dry place. It is funny that it should be so cold that milk falls from the sky & disappears into clear rivulets. It is a very, very funny story.

Relational Self

At home & unencumbered. At home in Gulu & unencumbered because even those that might try to locate me, to carve me out of the everyday with their "Where are you based?" don't diminish me. It means that they know, they must know, that I am of this land. In any case, "where are you based" is a Kampala question. The answer depends on when/where & if I feel like it. Sometimes, Canada. Sometimes Vancouver. Sometimes nowhere, here, I'm just at home. After all these years of exclusion, I decide that it's probably no one's business where I'm from, located, born, live unless I want it to be. Relational because in Gulu there are many folks with familial connections with whom I can relate. I might not look like, walk like, dress like, sound like, be like I'm from there but what are you going to do? Where are you going to go?

Sometimes I get asked: Gang wu tye kwene? I can always say my home is in Mican, where my paternal homestead is. Or as I sometimes do, Holy Rosary where my mother's people are. Or my ancestral home of the Pacwa people where I claim my ancestry. It's all my home, this place, this physical place, this place that will always, always receive me. & then I return home to Canada where I cannot even say hello or be greeted in the language of the people on whose unceded land we live.

Invisible Self

One of the most important social events in northern Uganda in 2015 was the commemoration of the martyrdom of Archbishop Janani Luwum on 16 February at Wii Gweng, near Kitgum. I was there, along with thousands of other well-wishers. My ex-partner's father was one of the speakers at the event. He had been one of the last people to see the archbishop alive. Afterwards, I went to greet him. In the traditional Acholi fashion, I was on my knees to greet him & we exchanged pleasantries. Nothing special about a woman on her knees to greet someone else, especially an older person, especially this man who is so admired. After I greeted him I sat on a chair beside him & had a little visit between us. Our hands were still linked. We laughed a bit.

On reflection, I recognize that if I had stuck out my hand to greet him while standing & him sitting, I would have called attention to myself. I would have been making a public statement in my gesture that this man was not worthy of my respect, that I imagined myself in a superior stance to him. & knowing what I know about the colonial gesture of establishing superiority, this is not a position I will adopt. Here, on my knees, I express my respect for an older person that I love & admire while retaining the opportunity for private visit in a public space. Not every encounter needs to be political.[34] Not every encounter needs to privilege my Western-ness, my now-ness, my "been away so long[35] I forgot how to behave in public" self-ness. I'm glad for the invisibility that my cultured self (& the extent to which I'm steeped inside an Acholi identity) allows me. In that moment, my kneeling body is a powerfully aware one, one that is at home, one that feels at home & yet does not feel disempowered by someone else that might have (or even might still) deem it so.

Webbed (Related Self)

My doctoral fieldwork[36] took me to several cities. I had the opportunity to spend some time in Arusha, Mwanza, Bukoba, Musoma, Kampala, Lira, Kitgum, Gulu, Butiama, Tarime, London, & Lokung. I introduced myself at every interview, & every time there was the recognition of my father's name, sometimes a vignette – who my dad was, what *Song of Lawino* (Bitek 1984) meant to them, why my dad remains an important voice today. It was quite clear that three decades after his demise my father was still holding the door open for me. The people I interviewed welcomed me as a niece, daughter of a friend or someone they admired. In those encounters, my identity as a Canadian scholar, a black person, a poet was of no consequence. In London, for example, the door opened at the

264 Juliane Okot Bitek

home of one of the people I'd gone to interview. Hello, I said & started to introduce myself. Come right in, the old man said, taking me by the arm. I first knew you as a two-year old sitting on my lap as I visited your parents' home in Nairobi. I walk into his London home & I walk into a story in which I would learn that there was indeed a connection between the event that I was researching & the generosity of my parents who took care of the Ugandan exiles in the home I grew up in. The history of the country is the history of the family, mine, several, all. Echoes of historical events can be traced through stories as rememory (Morrison 1988), softly spoken, quietly remembered & yet powerfully resistant to the dominant narrative through which contemporary Uganda is understood.

I think & write about rememory as decolonizing practice in these unceded territories, from this non-racist country, from a place where anti-racist work is the stuff of headlines & radical resistance. I recognize the need to "signify[37] the archive" & to hold on to my blackness & African-ness as part of the work of being a scholar & poet. I remain aware that such privilege is not available to everyone.

NOTES

1 I write along with Claudia Rankine's *Citizen: An American Lyric*, in which she argues that location, history, & a culture of racism & sexism are at odds with the black woman self that she is & that her perspective permeates the experience of other black folks but is also uniquely hers as "an aspect of life for all black bodies" (Rankine 2014, 25). I'm not American. I am an Acholi diasporic woman. I am African. I am Canadian. I have lived in Canada for twenty-seven years. In all this time, there has been & still is an everyday practice of distancing from my surroundings from which I am reminded that I am not of here.

2 This form illustrates the intersections that I occupy in my various identities. Am I ever just one self? Can I be only a scholar, only a poet? When one of my annotated poems was published in a scholarly journal I recognized that I needn't always have to pick between poetry & the conventional essay. Here I present an argument in a form that considers creative use of space & pushes the conventions for the location of knowledge, citations, & creativity on the page. I use travel vignettes & stories from Vancouver to make the point about disorientation, dislocation, belonging, & rejection. I extend the endnote as a space for dialogue with the main body of the text as well as the reader. The endnote has spent way too much time as the space for credit, as the space for limited talk, like the commercial kitchen where any & all talk is related to food production. The endnote here is like the

kitchen we grew up in, the heart of the house, the place where all nutrition comes from, both food & story. "Kitchen poets," Edwidge Danticat writes in the epilogue for her short story collection *Krik? Krak!*, are the "thousand women urging you to speak through the blunt tip of your pencil" (Danticat 1996, 219). Kitchen poets may be located in the kitchen, & it is also in the kitchen that generations of women incorporate their stories within the daily activities. Cooking & braiding, as Danticat explains, are methods & metaphors for surivival for women who pass on knowledge through story-telling. Anishnaabeg scholar Leanne Simpson identifies storytelling as "the lens through which the Nishnaabeg people can envision [them]selves out of the imperial cognitive" (Simpson 2011, 33). I employ stories to engage the reader & create a space through which we can come together to see what is. This form allows me to be both poet & scholar, to perform the intersections & celebrate narrative as dialogue. I remain inspired by Junot Diaz's *The Brief Wondrous Life of Oscar Wao* (2008), a novel that carries several narratives in the footnoted sections, a novel approach to the novel. A formal essay would have betrayed my poet voice.

3 Okot Bitek (2016): a poetic response to the twentieth anniversary of the 1994 Rwanda Genocide.

4 Okot Bitek (2012).

5 Okot Bitek (2013a, 43).

6 In a video for *The Guardian Online,* Jamaican novelist Marlon James (2016) makes the distinction between non-racist & anti-racist. The non-racist is the one who doesn't practise racism, may detest racism, but will stand by & witness while the anti-racist will do the work to end racism. Non-racist, especially in these days of Indigenous resurgence, the Can-lit scandals, and post-Charlottesville might also describe the reluctance of the beneficiaries of white privilege to challenge white supremacy.

7 Having taken the bus consistently for the last twenty-five years, I have witnessed all these responses. Should've thought to mark when drivers reject a non-paying patron & when they don't. By far, from observation, a young person is more likely not to get a free ride on the bus.

8 *Okot Bitek* (2014). This poem was commissioned by Simon Fraser University Centre for Dialogue. It was among five poems commissioned to celebrate Chief Bobby Roberts.

9 This is not a benevolent term. I understand this term as Marlon James (2016) defines it. See also Nikesh Shukla's article (2016) in which he discusses Marlon James's position on the relationship between diversity and action.

10 Phanuel Antwi (2013) presents the insidiousness of denial (of anti-black racism) & the lively presence of the KKK in Canada. "A public lack of memory averts our analytical gaze from recognizing the work of practices, that of

anti-Black feeling behind … it leaves a public memory of lack" (141). Antwi notes that lacking in the archive is the black fear, anger & resistance (141) & subsequently an archive that is lacking (142). The contemporary form of this lacking is in the figure of the polite Canadian. Sorry, sorry & thank you to the bus driver.

11 Afuwa and Okot Bitek (2015).

12 "I am reminded each time I return to Haiti: the exile's joy & the resident's anguish – it can also be the other way around – the exile's joy & the resident's anguish" (Danticat 2011, 46). As opposed to Salman Rushdie's (1992, 431) image of the exile as "fall[ing] between two stools," Danticat imagines moments of joy & anguish, both & sometimes singularly.

13 Fanon's "Look! A Negro!" (1991, 93–4). In the gaze of a little white child a grown man is reduced to an object, a collection of insults, a nightmare & reduction into ash. Rankine takes on the power of the gaze as debilitating in its banality: "You're not sick, not crazy / not angry, not sad – it's just this, you're tired" (*2014*, 145).

14 A few weeks leading up to Black History Month in 2013, I was invited to read a poem from the *Great Black North* anthology. There was some resistance to my poem "Diaspora" because it was not a "celebratory" poem, and as such it was deemed to not fit with the joyful theme of Black History Month at city hall in Vancouver. One of the editors, Kevan "Scruffmouth" Cameron, wrote an email in defence of keeping the poem as part of the line-up:

> Much of the work of Juliane Okot Bitek is concerned with identity, and the movement of the diasporic African into a new space. In the struggle with self to transform this new space into a familiar place, we find the poetic expression from a perspective that questions the rituals and traditions of the society in the effort to overcome the loneliness and solitude of leaving home. In Vancouver, it would be a contradiction to impose censorship on a poet who is speaking to the freedom to express herself through her artwork. As an editor of *The Great Black North*, we selected this poem because it offered an authentic sentiment from a diasporic African; just as the creative and cultural contributions of [Jeni] Legon and [Joe] Fortes enhanced this place that they chose to live even though they originally came from the Americas and the Caribbean. (Personal email)

I was finally able to read the poem as part of the City Hall Black History Celebrations. The initial resistance to including "Diaspora" is an illustration of the parsing between black and African.

15 According to the British Airways website, it is a WHO requirement to spray the cabin with insecticide to and from specific destinations. While some airlines spray the cabin before the passengers embark, BA practice is to spray the cabin before take-off, warning passengers to cover their mouths and noses if they want to.

16 Okot Bitek (2015b).

17 In Butiama, the caretaker for the Julius Nyerere Museum recognizes my last name after I'm done with the guest book. Are you related to Okot p'Bitek the writer? Yes, I say. He's my dad. That is so cool! He gushes. The only other books I ever sell in this museum, aside from books by Mwalimu Nyerere, are your dad's books. But I just ran out, see? I see that there are only three copies of books by Mwalimu Nyerere. This is so cool, the man repeats himself. & then: Do any of your brothers write?

18 *In Lose Your Mother*, Saidiya Hartmann (2008) writes about returning to Ghana as a researcher and as a black woman.

19 Yolande Bouka (2015) provides great insight on how the "skinfolk connection" that allows her to connect with her fieldwork informants isn't sufficient for the identities she claims, none local for her in Rwanda.

20 Under the auspices of Vancouver's Poet Laureate Rachel Rose, I am one of the Vancouver poetry ambassadors. In my capacity as a poet ambassador, I have given a talk on poetry at a First Nations college, performed poetry at the farmer's market, & attended meetings. I am a Vancouver poet.

21 I conducted fieldwork as part of my doctoral research, which took me to Uganda, Tanzania, & Britain between the fall of 2014 & winter of 2016. I left Canada & returned between country visits, & every time I struggled with what it meant to be African & return to a home in Canada. I struggled in the field with what it meant to be affiliated with a Canadian university, even as I appreciated the association, as I was a sponsored researcher & have benefitted largely from SSHRC as well as other grants from the university. It was in Tarime, Tanzania, that my Canadian identity and affiliation was most dramatically challenged.

22 A man sidles up to the stool beside me in a Vancouver bar. You mind if I sit here? No, I answer. So where were you born? What does that have to do with anything? I'm defensive. I want to ask him what business is it of his where my mother's labour pangs ended. I was born in ———— Scotland, he says. Good for you, I answer. You Scottish? No, he says. My mother is from ———— and my father is from ————. So he's British. I won't answer that question in the various ways it comes. Sometimes it shows itself in the most direct way. A man calls my attention as I walk down the steps at the local library. Sister! Hi! Where are you from? Uganda, I say. Habari gani? Mzuri, I answer. You have a coffee waiting for you whenever you finish whatever you'll be doing there. Asante sana. I'm still going to be doing a reading over here. Ala! the man exclaims. You're part of the event? Yes, we sisters are everywhere. After the reading my new African brother is nowhere to be seen. Whether the question is to distance myself from this land or to establish a solidarity that is limited to old expectations of a woman's role in society – the effect is all the same. Either I don't belong or I don't perform as expected.

23 On how many first days can I call the students to attention and get "We're waiting for the instructor"? How many times during the term does a student, two, more, express in astonishment how they've never had a black instructor before, sometimes how they never expected to take a class in English from an African woman?

24 I'm at the same event as an African professor in Vancouver. Every time I'm in your company, he says, I feel uncomfortable. I'm taken aback but I do have a glass of wine in my hand. Why?," I ask. Because I loved your dad's work so much. I first read your dad in high school and have referred to him throughout. I don't know what to expect from you.

25 Some time ago (20 April 2016) I made a comment on social media in response to an excerpt by Winston Churchill. Arinaitwe Rugyendo, a Ugandan journalist, responded, "Now you sound just like your legendary father." Seriously, though? Seriously?

26 So the public library lists one of my publications under my sister's name. Yes, they will edit it to reflect that the poem is indeed my creation, so they assure me.

27 A man is set off at an event in Vancouver. First, at the woman next to him: Get on with it, bitch! Then profanities at the presenter, a black academic & poet (who is visiting!) but still takes it upon himself to chastise the man. You can't talk to her like that. Motherfucker! The man yells at the poet professor. N*****! Go back to where you came from! He goes on & on. On & on. We're in an art gallery in Vancouver downtown. Most of the audience is white. We (four) black people are the true targets the objectification of the man's ep-ithets. No one else fits. No one else relates. No one reaches out. Non-racist. No one checks in. Non-racist. The gallery is intact. Non-racist. We are not. Non-racist. The walls are white. Non-racist. We are not. The people seem fine. We are not. The man disappears into the night after spitting on the glass doors behind him so that we remain enclosed in the man's disgust. We are nothing but the blackness of ourselves in a non-racist city in a non-racist country. Where else/when else but at night in an art gallery that there is such an illustration of the exclusionary lives & disconnectedness with black people through a historical & contemporary experience of discrimination, racism, & sexism; nowhere else but in an art gallery that the audience can remain de-tached, that the collection of eyes at the scene is illuminating for some & real for others. A poem inspired by this event, "Under What Conditions Do Black Poets Write?" is published by *The Capilano Review* (Okot Bitek 2017).

28 As if they could be anything but ungrateful.

29 In "Remembrance Day Reflections" (Okot Bitek 2013b) I write about what it means for those of us who remember our dead from wars beyond the Canadian war experience. How, indeed & when else can you engage in a public memorial of the war dead when we don't carry our own in our hearts?

Remembrance Day as the day to be grateful for the sacrifices of the dead in the struggle for our freedom remains a naive way & perhaps misguided attempt to justify war while ignoring the suffering of citizens at home. At the time I was thinking about the suffering of the Mi'kmak First Nations in Elsipogtog. Fighting for freedom? Whose freedom? Which freedom?

30 So where are my screams? I can't hear my own screams. I can't hear my own screams.

31 Same Scottish man above asks if he can sit next to me. Go ahead. Thank you, he says. You're welcome. I turn to talk to my son, who's taken me for a beer on Mother's Day. May I sit here? the man asks my son. Sure you can, he answers. I turn back to the man. I already said you could. What the hell, man. I have to ask *him*. He's the man, the Scottish man says. He's the man, the Scottish man says in the presence of me, the mother.

32 Of course, there's a way to be seen. The gaze that determines who you are makes you invisible in your black visibility.

33 "Why do you feel comfortable saying this to me?" (Rankine 2014, 10).

34 In an interview with Kim Turcot DiFruscia, Veena Das defines the political as your reaction to the way the world makes claim to you. My experience as a black African woman scholar poet Ugandan Canadian Acholi woman is that there are several claims. My political stance therefore lies in the spaces in which I choose how to respond & not, for instance, what the liberal feminist position has laid out for me as a contemporary woman.

35 While attending a funeral in Arua, I help to attend to guests. Pouring warm water for guests to wash their hands from a cup into a plastic bucket is done before meals. I'm on my knees, as is the social norm, to offer & allow guests to wash their hands before a meal. I could've done it while standing – it's rough on the lower back. Afterwards, I return to sit next to my cousin who says, I didn't think you'd remember how to do that. I thought you'd be too Western for that. I tell him that I am not disempowered by this service. I tell him that I haven't forgotten, but also that it's much easier on the body to control the pour of water while on my knees. I have lived in Canada for more than a quarter century now. Not long enough to forget that there is some good from where I come from. Long enough to recognize that there is enough bad behaviour towards the people on whose unceded territories we live. The colonial legacy in Canada & its shadow are a constant source of shame for me.

36 My dissertation research is on the memory of a naval ship that sank in Lake Victoria during the Kagera War between the governments of Uganda & Tanzania & the Ugandan exiles who fought alongside them. "History, Memory & Alienation" (Okot Bitek 2015a) attempts to connect the quiet story of that event with contemporary narratives of Ugandans as victims, villains, or victors.

37 Antwi (2013, 143).

REFERENCES

Afuwa, and Okot Bitek, J. 2015. "Rooted: A Diaspora Playlist." *Our Schools/Our Selves* 24 (3): 35–52.

Antwi, P. 2013. "A Lack of Public Memory: A Public Memory of Lack." In *Trans/ Acting Culture, Writing, and Memory: Essays in Honour of Barbara Godard*, edited by C. Karpinski, J. Henderson, I. Sowton, and R. Ellenwood, 12–23. Waterloo, ON: Wilfrid Laurier University Press.

Bitek, O. 1984. *Song of Lawino and Song of Ocol*. Nairobi: Heinemann Publishers.

Bouka, Y. 2015. "Researching Violence in Africa as a Black Woman: Notes from Rwanda." http://conflictfieldresearch.colgate.edu/wp-content/uploads /2015/05/Bouka_WorkingPaper-May2015.pdf.

Compton, W., and Sarojini, R., eds. 2015. *The Revolving City: 51 Poems and the Stories behind Them*. Vancouver: Anvil Press.

Danticat, E. 1996. *Krik? Krak!* New York: Vintage.

Danticat, E. 2011. *Create Dangerously: The Immigrant Artist at Work*. New York: Vintage.

Díaz, J. 2008. *The Brief Wondrous Life of Oscar Wao*. New York: Riverhead Books.

Fanon, F. 1991. *Black Skin, White Masks*. New York: Grove Press.

Hartman, S. 2008. *Lose Your Mother: A Journey along the Atlantic Slave Route*. New York: Farrar, Straus and Giroux.

James, M. 2016, 13 January. "Are You Racist? 'No' Isn't a Good Enough Answer – Video." *The Guardian*. https://www.theguardian.com/commentisfree/video /2016/jan/13/marlon-james-are-you-racist-video.

Mohutsiwa, S. 2016. "I'm Done with African Immigrant Literature." okayafrica, 9 February. http://www.okayafrica.com/news/im-done-with-african -immigrant-literature/.

Morrison, T. 1988. *Beloved*. New York: Plume.

Okot Bitek, J. 2012. "A Chronology of Compassion or Towards an Imperfect Future." *International Journal of Transition Justice* 6 (October): 394–403.

Okot Bitek, J. 2013a. "Diaspora." In *The Great Black North: Contemporary African Canadian Poetry*, edited by V. Mason-John and K. Cameron, 43–44. Calgary: Frontenac House.

Okot Bitek, J. 2013b. "Remembrance Day Reflections." Zócalo Poets, 11 November. https://zocalopoets.com/2013/11/11/remembrance-day-reflections -juliane-okot-bitek/.

Okot Bitek, J. 2014. "A Love Letter or Considering Reconciliation in Canada." *subterrain* 67 (16 September): 14.

Okot Bitek, J. 2015a. *History, Memory & Alienation*. Unpublished PhD diss., University of British Columbia.

Okot Bitek, J. 2015b. "Stuff to Do When Your Hometown Is Burning." In *Revolving City: 51 Poems and the Stories Behind Them*, edited by W. Compton and S. Saklikar, 40–43. Vancouver: Anvil Press.

Okot Bitek, J. 2015c. "What to Do When Your Hometown Is Burning." In *The Revolving City: 51 Poems and the Stories Behind Them,* edited by W. Compton and S. Saklikar, 40–43. Vancouver: Anvil Press.

Okot Bitek, J. 2016. *100 Days.* Edmonton: University of Alberta Press.

Okot Bitek, J. 2017. "Under What Conditions Do Black Poets Write?" *The Capilano Review* 3 (31): 77–84.

Rankine, C. 2014. *Citizen: An American Lyric.* Minneapolis, MN: Graywolf Press.

Rushdie, S. 1992. "Imaginary Homelands." In *Imaginary Homelands: Essays and Criticism 1981–1991,* 12. London: Vintage.

Simpson, L. 2011. *Dancing on Our Turtle's Back: Stories of Nishnaabeg Re-Creation Resurgence and New Emergence.* Winnipeg: Arbeiter Ring Publishing.

Shukla, Nikesh. 2016, 21 October. "Marlon James Calls for Action on Diversity Instead of Just Talk." *The Guardian.* http://www.theguardian.com/books/2016/oct/21/marlon-james-calls-for-action-on-diversity-instead-of-just-talk.

14 Intersectionality in Blackface: When Post-racial Nationalism Meets Black Feminism

DÉLICE MUGABO[1]

Nou led, Nou la.
The women who came before me were women who spoke half of one language and half another. They spoke the French and Spanish of their captors mixed in with their own African language. These women seemed to be speaking in tongues when they prayed to their old gods, the ancient African spirits. Even though they were afraid that their old deities would no longer understand them, they invented a new language, our Creole patois with which to describe their new surroundings, a language from which colorful phrases blossomed to fit the desperate circumstances. When these women greeted each other, they found themselves speaking in codes.
– How are we today, Sister?
– I am ugly, but I am here.

– E. Danticat (1996)

Edwidge Danticat's famous essay "We Are Ugly, but We Are Here" speaks poignantly of the history of Haitian women fighting and surviving from sea to distant sea and through slavery to dictatorships, all while creating a language to preserve the names of their foremothers and their spirits – words that testify to their trials and carry their visions. Forging a grammar of our suffering as well as of our resistance and our creativity remains, for me, one of the most fundamental tasks of Black feminist activism in Quebec today. Black feminist thinkers in the province find imaginative and resourceful ways to resist and reject the ideological formations that seek to discipline our thinking and the reach of our analyses and intellectual contributions. The nuances of Blackness that I explore in this chapter are not about the difference that it sometimes makes to be francophone while Black in Canada, nor am I trying to figure out if there is more or less anti-Black racism in universities in Quebec, compared to other provinces. The question that I explore here is about the kind of strategies that we, as Black feminists, use to write about Blackness and anti-Blackness in a context where Black feminist thought is reformulated in Quebec universities to serve white nation-building.

The deficit of Black studies programming is a stark reality across Canada. There has been an interdisciplinary minor in Black and African diaspora studies at Dalhousie University since 2016, and more robust Black studies programs are under way at York University and Queen's University. It is important that such initiatives not be limited to the Canadian metropolitan areas. Indeed, there needs to be Black studies programming across the country to avoid reproducing the geographical assumptions about Blackness belonging only in a few urban centres. There are also endowed chairs in fields related to Black diaspora studies at Dalhousie University, Queen's University, and York University (Walcott 2014). Much more recently, a number of Canada Research chairs have been appointed on Black culture and politics at Dalhousie University, McGill University, McMaster University, Ryerson University, University of Alberta, and University of British Columbia. The overall lack of Black studies programming is in many ways compounded in French-language universities in Quebec, where something akin to French republican ideologies – whose goals of assimilation and universalism seek to destroy difference at the expense of equality and inclusion (Keaton 2010) – about race and difference actively disqualify public recognition of anti-Blackness. This same process is a precondition for the production (and policing) of a Quebec national discourse that celebrates equality, justice, and fairness as national virtues.

Throughout the 1990s, the Black Students Network at McGill University critiqued the colonial nature and direction of the African Studies program and organized for an Africana Studies program that would address Black life in North America that came up against institutional opposition. In 2016, Black students at Concordia University and supportive professors began a campaign to have a Black Studies program at the institution (Dragonroot Media 2016). There are no African Studies, much less Africana or Black Studies programs, at any of the fourteen French-language universities in Quebec. Efforts at Université de Montréal were quickly shut down in 2015. At the University of Ottawa – an English- and French-language institution – Quebec and Canadian nationalist ideologies have shaped the responses of the faculty and white student body to francophone Black students' organizing on campus. For example, BlackCollectiv's efforts in 2014 for a Black Studies program at the University of Ottawa met a brick wall from professors and the administration. Not only was the referendum that year for the creation of a centre for racialized students defeated, but a website with a picture of a half-naked Black female student and member of BlackCollectiv was circulated campus-wide to mobilize against the referendum.

University campuses, student federations, and academic networks – having historically been ground zero for Quebec nationalist movements, political parties, and unions – are key spaces where foundational myths are formed, reconceptualized, and strengthened. I agree with Walcott (2014) that "the nation-state is the most significant site of violence launched at Black personhood," and "therefore Black Studies in most instances always offers at least a critique of the state, if not nation-state continually" (4). What French-language universities reject is not only Black studies, but the scrutiny and the questions that Black life in the province unveil about Quebec as a settler colonial nation and a central actor in French imperial rule. Elements of francophone academia in Quebec have halted or impeded Black student organizing and scholarly research that is focused on a Blackness that is rooted or routed in Quebec.

Quebec nationalism – understood here in its broadest terms, therefore not simply in relation to political independence – is based on the idea that the French language is what demarcates the territory of Quebec and its people from the rest of the continent, as well as what unifies its population *regardless* of race and ethnicity. Key to the distinct nationhood thesis is the myth of double colonization that has at its basis that although they descend from the initial French settlers, the French-Québécois were colonized by the British Crown (and later on by U.S. capital). The French-Québécois use a narrative of victimhood that not only hides the white supremacy that they have always wielded, but also amalgamates their political project to that of subjugated peoples worldwide.

There is a long history of Quebec writers, thinkers, and academics using Blackness and Black thought to reinforce white nation-building. Pierre Vallières's (1971) autobiography, titled *White Niggers of America*, is most emblematic of this anti-Black politics of innocence-making. Throughout the 1960s and 1970s, Quebec intellectuals read Fanon and Césaire, studied the Black Panthers, formed relationships with exiled Haitians in Montreal, and "building upon perceived historical injustices – as a people abandoned by France and colonized by the British – [they constructed] a politically useful collective identity" (Cornellier 2017, 32). What is also important to observe is how this self-fashioning as "white niggers" and as a colonized people has been based on highlighting "certain [French-Québécois] peoples, relations, and histories while treating others as given, namely those associated with indigenous dispossession, settler colonial occupation, and the Black experience in Montreal" (33).

Most recently, as a result of the synergy between the white feminist and nationalist movements in Quebec, intersectionality theory has become the latest example of how white, French-Québécois academics use Black thought to enshrine nationalist politics. Jonathan Durand-Folco's (2013) long essay advocating for what he calls an "intersectional nationalism" in Quebec is the predictable outcome of the appropriation of Black women's intellectual labour in academic and activist movements. Durand-Folco is a well-known public intellectual in Québec recognized for his work with Québec Solidaire (QS), a leftist provincial political party describing itself as feminist, environmentalist, and sovereigntist (QS 2006). In his article, Durand-Folco spells out how, in the context of Quebec, an intersectional analysis cannot be limited to race, gender, and class, but must also take into account the "historic national oppression of francophone Quebecers" (4, my translation). Durand-Folco predicts that adapting intersectionality to the Québécois context will make for an "egalitarian and emancipatory nationalism" (4, my translation), even though he admits to not having a profound knowledge of the intersectional approach.

For Durand-Folco, an example of "pluralist nationalism" is found in QS, because it understands the Quebec nation as "defined by the francophone community's own history, but transformed little by little by successively integrating elements from other communities. The Quebec nation is therefore open to outside contributions since it's not based on ethnic origin but voluntary membership in the Quebec polity" (Durand-Folco 2013, 12; my translation). We find here one of the founding myths that is integral to any discussion of Quebec: the nation was not founded through slave-holding white settler colonialism but by forward-thinking francophone people with windows open on the world. Further, race is later evacuated from Durand-Folco's version of intersectionality, since the Quebec nation is the outcome of a "'decolonial nationalism' that is born out of the desire of working-class francophones to emancipate themselves from the oppressive anglophone bourgeoisie and the Canadian federal government" (23, my translation). Durand-Folco goes even further and writes that the Quebec Left embodies and concretizes all that intersectionality is about: "In general, the Left can be defined as the political application of the intersectional critique, or as the articulated struggle against all forms of domination. If we recognize national oppression in the context of Quebec as a fact, then a consistent Left must clearly support the struggle for national emancipation" (24, my translation). We see here a catch-all intersectionality whose only loyalty is to the national struggle. The reconfiguration of intersectionality within the Quebec feminist movement and Quebec Left facilitates and propels national social projects that still cannot imagine Black life and Black freedom.

The next section of the chapter proceeds with a brief overview of the genealogy of intersectionality in Black women's intellectual labour, as a way to foreground my analysis. I then use my own experience in the French-language university system, namely at Université du Québec à Montréal (UQAM), to argue that anti-Blackness is foundational to the nation-building project at the core of Quebec's post-secondary education system. As Williams (1988) so poignantly captured it, we do not write lived stories simply by mere indulgence, but as "a recapturing of that which had escaped historical scrutiny, which had been overlooked and underseen" (5). Furthermore, Williams explains, it would be too dangerous to leave these stories in the white hands of those who would not only rewrite the past but also the future. Lastly, I offer examples from the high-profile debate about the place of intersectionality among white feminist scholars in Quebec to tease out further the specificity of anti-Blackness in francophone Quebec. Throughout, I demonstrate how the continued history of Black women's resistance in the province, dating back to slavery under the French regime in New France, is elided in Left academic spaces in favour of a politics of nation-building that is based on a narrative of white francophone innocence and/or martyrdom.

On Intersectionality and Black Women's Intellectual Labour

The ideas behind intersectionality have a long history among Black women intellectuals, from nineteenth-century thinker Anna Julia Cooper through to the civil rights–era writing of Angela Davis, from Audre Lorde's tracing the poetics of resistance to Patricia Hill Collins conceptualizing the matrix. Yet contemporary understandings of inter-sectionality usually begin with Kimberlé Crenshaw's 1989 essay, which specifically exposed how anti-discrimination law's treatment of gender and race as separate, unconnected categories erased the experiences of Black women and ensured that the specific discriminatory experiences of Black women had little weight under the law. Crenshaw's (1991) innovation was to articulate a manner to marry the rich tradition of Black feminism with anti-discrimination law, thereby accounting for the specific ways that Black women were "invisible in plain sight," to borrow Crenshaw's more recent expression (as cited in Adewunmi 2014).

Fast forward nearly three decades, and in mainstream feminist theory and practice, intersectionality is often depoliticized and shed of its Black feminist raison d'être. Without irony, Black women's contribution to contemporary theorizations of the concept, as well as its original Black, race-critical *political* trajectory have fallen to the wayside. For example, Jennifer C. Nash (2014) argues that intersectionality "is treated as a kind

of remedy [that] can effectively cure women's studies of violent histories of exclusion" (53). She then explains how ideas about feminism's
future that are made possible by intersectionality often go hand-in-hand
with ideas about practising intersectionality without Black women. For
Nash, these movements away from Black feminist thinkers "shift intersectionality from a preoccupation with multiple marginalization toward
an interest in structures of domination more generally" (54), including about how privilege circulates. Sirma Bilge (2010) writes that one
strategy that is used to dissociate intersectionality from race is taking
whiteness into account "only as an identity dissociated from white racial
power structures" (24). Bilge's argument about the "whitening" of intersectionality dovetails with Nash's (2014) argument that "doing" intersectionality in a manner in which we are subject of neither a *feminism-past*
nor a *feminism-future* constructs Black women as always out of time (61).
In other words, Black women's intellectual labour must be erased for
intersectionality to reach its latent potential *for* white feminism. This
move to transcend Black women's bodies and construct intersectionality
as belonging to all is particularly salient in the Quebec academy, where
white Québécois thinkers and writers have a long history of using Black
thought to claim authority and power over space, land, and politics.

King's (2015) writings on the commodification of intersectionality
also provides a stark reminder of what is at stake in academic spaces.
She explains that "the extent to which a theory or intellectual project
has been rendered a commodity within the institution also corresponds
to the ways that it is allowed to circulate and change in form, content,
and value in the institution. Commodities tend to hide the labor that
produces them" (123). While I trace the ways in which Black women's
labour is hidden or erased in my analysis, I do so not only as a critique,
but also as a way to "write ourselves into existence" again and again.
To be clear, just as Nash (2014) does, I too "presume a fundamental
relationship between black women's bodies and intersectionality" (46),
if for no other reason than Crenshaw's path-breaking investigation of
the particular harm and inherent injustice that Black women experience
through the law. Subsequently, I am particularly perplexed by the ways
in which Black women disappear from intersectionality once it is in the
hands of white feminist scholars in Quebec. Nikol Alexander-Floyd's
(2012) observations help us understand how this apparent interest in
intersectionality in particular and Black feminist thought in general
has not translated into an engagement with Black feminist scholarship
coming out of Quebec and the rest of Canada: "The emphasis on race,
class, and gender in academe or the showcasing of black female authors
… coexists with appropriations of black women's work. The visibility

does not translate into authority to retain voice or serve as a shield from appropriation" (13).

In Quebec, Black women also have an intellectual and activist history through which important critiques emerged about the pervasive injustices that continue to shape our lives. Myriam Chancy (1993), a Black feminist scholar who was born in Port-au-Prince and raised in Quebec City, has written about how the denial and erasure of Black women's history in Canada specifically amounts to being forced to survive without our mother or our roots. For her, Black women writers in Canada have been crucial to "uncover[ing] the connections between us as Black women at the same time as re-discovering that which has been kept from us: our cultural heritage, the language of our grandmothers, ourselves" (12). What Chancy signifies is how Black women's histories of resistance across Canada as well as the history of their ideas and dreams are important in the ways that they help us to survive.

I present in the next two sections the main positions on intersectionality in Quebec, interspersed with some of my own experiences doing activism alongside nationalist white feminists. While the first position considers intersectionality as a divisive concept that fractures the universal woman at the centre of (white) feminism, the second one sees it as a useful conceptual tool that allows white women to sharpen their feminist analysis. What both have embedded in them is the absented presence of Black women.

Black Feminist Genealogies in Quebec

We have no way through but to create ourselves. This life insists we make a cabal out of these words, gather them into a riot of gestures, a plot against their own inscription. I, like the maroons of La Goyave, remember that words can be no bigger than the woman for it is all contained in her mouth.

– Felicia Denaud (2020)

What sustained me during my time as a student at UQAM and as an activist in the largely white feminist movement were the ears and shoulders my sistafriends lent me at the many dinners we had together, creating methods and moments to (re)build our spirits. I had never considered sharing some of these stories publicly until Malinda Smith generously approached me about contributing to this volume. I immediately thought of Yasmin Abdullahi Ali and Sumaya Ugas, the Muslim Black feminist writer-creator-poet-researcher duo behind *Somali Semantics* (2015), whose work in Montreal, Ottawa, and Toronto has been instrumental in getting

Black women and girls to "write ourselves into existence." I accepted the invitation to write this chapter because it is important for me that Black political reflections from or about Quebec be housed in Black archives. I also took the very deliberate decision to write in English as an act of defiance to the ways in which discourses around the preservation of the French language in Quebec have been used as strategies to control Black speech and its reach. Indeed, the geographical unruliness of Blackness causes great anxiety in Quebec, for Black movement connotes a certain kind of disloyalty to or betrayal of the Quebec national project. In other words, the fact that Black people in the province consider their liberation not tied to Quebec's but to each other, everywhere, unveils how anti-Blackness remains foundational to the project of Quebec as a post-racial francophone society.

In *States of Race*, Smith (2010) reminds us that, "with any storytelling, there is a need to differentiate between narratives that sustain the status quo and counternarratives that ... interrogate stories in which the socially powerful construct a form of shared reality in which its own superior position is seen as natural and is reinforced in everyday institutional practices" (41). In addition, Tiffany Lethabo King's (2015) work on today's neoliberal university reminds us that testimonies are important "to track the way in which institutional power works off the record in ways that structure racism, sexism, ageism, and other forms of violence in the academy" (116). Indeed, inspired by both Smith and King, I construct a counter-narrative that includes testimonies of my own everyday experiences precisely because they "capture everyday speech acts that might otherwise remain unremarked on or undocumented because of their off-the-record nature" (116). By foregrounding my own storytelling, I aim to build the type of counter-narrative that challenges the erasure of Black women's lives in Quebec.

Quebec is a former slave-holding society and French colony conquered by the British in 1763. As the focus in New France shifted from resource extraction to settlement in the seventeenth century, successive colonial administrators lobbied the French Crown to allow them to import slaves (Gay 2004). Although the vast majority of slaves were indigenous to the borderlands around present-day Wisconsin, Illinois, and Ohio, over a quarter of them during the French regime were Black. While enslaved Black people were usually bought in the Caribbean, others were brought to New France as bounties of wars waged in the United States, and records even allude to ships arriving in New France directly from Africa with enslaved Black people (82).

The two most famous enslaved Black people in Quebec are both women. First, Marie-Joseph-Angélique, born in Portugal and later brought to New England, was an enslaved Black woman in Montreal who was found guilty of burning down the city and punished by public hanging and immolation in 1734 (Cooper 2006). Prior to that, she had attempted to flee, providing glimpses of the impossibility of Black life in New France. Second, Marie-Thérèse-Zémire was bought in Saint-Domingue (now Haiti) and is known widely today for being portrayed in the famous *Portrait of a Haitian Woman*, by François Malépart de Beaucourt (Nelson 2004). Zémire's eventual life in New France coincided with the period following the Haitian Revolution, thus her opportunity to lead a life free of slavery disappeared with her bondage in Montreal. The lives of Marie-Joseph Angélique and Marie-Thérèse-Zémire teach us a great deal about geographies of Black struggle, genealogies of Black women's resistance, and white women's role in the bondage of Black people (both were eventually owned by French settler women), all of which bear the mark of a history that fundamentally contradicts Quebec's foundational myth of white innocence.

In actuality, what we learn from Black women's enslavement and forced migration to New France is how their sense of freedom had to, by definition, exceed the confines of the territory and the nation that held them captive. Likewise, Deonne Minto (2008) talks about how Black Montreal writer Mairuth Sarsfield "offers visions of ways in which Black subjects, who choose not to seek national recognition, may move in and out of the here and there of national spaces while claiming elsewheres, that is to say, other spaces not necessarily mapped by the nation" (142). Also taking a cue from Rinaldo Walcott (2000), I ask whether women's/gender studies in French-language universities in Quebec can tolerate the repetitive and disruptive returns of Blackness. And what can Quebec academia not bear to hear in regard to Blackness and the nation? Indeed, the Black feminist intellectual tradition that emerges from/in this place is dissonant. One key ground of contestation in recent feminist scholarship in Quebec is the relative usefulness of the concept of "intersectionality" to (white) women's equality and/or nationalism. Given the concept's origins in Black feminist intellectual traditions, its rejection, misappropriation, and/or misuse is noteworthy (Bilge 2013). To help us better situate the nature and the context of my critique, we should first be clear about what we mean when we talk about intersectionality.

Nowhere to Hide: Anti-Black Feminism in and out of the Classroom

In what language does one seek connections to the past when, divided through enslavement and colonization, so many of us have been forced to acquire languages which would serve only to wedge us further apart? Perhaps the answer

to systemic oppression and marginalization lies not so much in the language we choose to write and speak as in what we choose to say in speech and writing.
– Myriam J. Chancy (1993)

Anti-intersectionality

I became involved with the Fédération des femmes du Québec, the largest feminist organization in Quebec (and in Canada) in 2009. In 2011, it launched the historic Estates General of Feminist Action and Analysis (États généraux, or ÉG) – a two-year process that engaged women from all over Quebec in a review of feminist action and analysis. I was elected to be a member of the steering committee and eventually as one of the ÉG's three spokespersons. One of the main reasons for leaving my studies and UQAM completely in the winter of 2012 was the intimate experiences I had while working with white feminist academics who thwarted Black feminist approaches to activism in Quebec. It was through my work during the ÉG that I learned how white feminist activism and intellectual production together form a force that is particularly anathema to Black feminisms. In my later reading, the white feminist movement aligned a praxis and an analysis that resulted in the subjugation of Black feminisms in their Quebec nation-building project. This realization, combined with the everyday forms of racial violence that I experienced, led me to leave the mainstream feminist movement permanently.

At the first meeting of the ÉG's steering committee, as we were discussing the different ways to guide each stage of the process, the women of colour (WOC) who were members of the committee felt strongly that we should adopt an intersectional approach to discuss the many issues that would be debated during the two-year process. One white woman in particular (I will call her R.S.) appointed herself as the committee's expert on *all* feminist thought by virtue of the role she occupies at UQAM and in a network of feminist scholars in francophone academia, undermining Black and other WOC committee members who had particular knowledge of our own intellectual traditions. In a statement that quickly shut down further discussion on the topic that day, R.S. said to the committee members, "Well, intersectionality is very fashionable, but we should keep in mind that the federal government encourages groups to adopt that model *as part of its federalist agenda.*" Her observation that intersectionality is misused by the state is certainly not particular to Quebec and Canada (see Walcott 2017). As Tiffany Lethabo King (2015) reminds us, "Intersectionality is often co-opted by the state and incorporated into the statist and corporate diversity-management apparatus" (119). That said,

R.S.'s critique was not along the same lines as King's. As I have explained elsewhere (Mugabo & Jahangeer 2014), "The best way to discredit something or someone in Québec is by branding them [a] 'federalist'" (33), so R.S.'s critique of the federal government's co-optation of intersectionality was instructive on several levels.[2]

In a second illustrative example, at the wrap-up meeting of the steering committee of the ÉG over two years later, a well-known white feminist from the second-largest union in Quebec (I will call her C.N.) proclaimed to everyone around the table that while her assessment of the project as a whole was not *only* negative, she nonetheless felt that it had been hijacked by "intersectionality extremists." The two Black women and two Arab women around the table immediately recognized that she was referring to our tireless refusal to back down on the importance of centring racialized women's experiences in our analyses. The fact that she used the highly loaded term "extremists" to characterize, and indeed, racialize our work only compounded the sense of isolation we felt in that space. I would like to think through R.S.'s and C.N.'s comments along with some recent feminist scholarship illustrative of their statements in francophone Quebec. Their arguments point to how behind a certain opposition to intersectionality is in fact a warning to white society to beware of a Black feminist organizing and academic production that exceeds its (U.S.) boundaries and perverts what makes the Quebec feminist movement distinct.

Isabelle Marchand and Sandrine Ricci's (2010) text on the challenges that "ethnic diversity" poses to the feminist movement in Quebec presents the history of intersectionality as one in which white feminists granted Black women's requests for inclusion (67). As Nash demonstrates, intersectionality is easily instrumentalized to propel white feminism forward. Marchand and Ricci go on to argue that critiques by WOC in the United States made their way to Quebec first with Black women in the 1970s and then further with WOC in the early eighties. This common historiography of "borrowed blackness" (Alexis 1995) erases at least a century of Black feminist struggle in the province against the state, and in opposition to white women organizing in defence of white supremacy in Quebec. As in several other texts that look at the history of feminist movements in Quebec (e.g., Descarries 1998; Dumont 2008), Black women and other WOC appear only in the seventies or eighties, seemingly out of nowhere and often only to appeal to white feminist benevolence. This erasure of the long history of Black feminist organizing and writing, and the sudden appearance in the 1970s, is related to how the French-Québécois had throughout the 1960s referred to themselves as "white niggers," thus conflating their economic exploitation with the history and legacy of slavery. Once the French-Québécois took full control of their economy and created institutions to match their power, this self-racializing paradigm became much less relevant. Nonetheless, Black women in Quebec therefore appear as a surprise, for white feminists now have to figure out what to do, i.e., how to neutralize the Black bodies that were behind the Black ideas they had no more use for.

It was particularly telling how during the ÉG, white feminist activists and scholars alike dealt with the "issue" of intersectionality. At times, they agreed that an intersectional approach was useful to understand and transform their organizing and analysis around issues of class, ableism, settler-colonialism, and transnational politics, for example. What became clear, though, is how their own anti-Blackness was a hindrance to the full acceptance of intersectionality as a worthy tool of analysis and practice when it came specifically to Black women, who, as we have seen, are largely responsible for its intellectual origins. Indeed, I participated in a training session aimed at different women's groups and shelters on "doing" intersectionality in their clinical and/or community work, and a white practitioner who was also in attendance emphatically stated her refusal to include an introduction to the Black feminist roots of intersectionality to her co-workers because (white) women would never listen, much less apply it in their feminist work.[3] She eventually made a concession with the trainer that she would move the introduction to the end of her own workplace presentation, so that her colleagues would "buy into" intersectionality *before* finding out it comes from Black women's intellectual labour.

Further, it is no coincidence that much of the feminist movement's discourse in Quebec echoes the larger nationalist cause. Both require non-white people in Quebec to align anti-racist or anti-colonial change with their nation-building project. The feminist movement's calls to protect the integrity of a universal feminist project and subject must be read as an artefact of a specific racial *and* national project.

"Just like Black Feminists": White Feminists Usurping Black Feminist Thought

Every day, white Québécois women ask us, in French, where we come from, and with dumbfounded eyes, with a gaze thirsting for exoticism, for the misery of others, for the violence of others, seeking the "beautiful" and the "ugliness of others."
– Octavia Pierre (2015; my translation)

A second approach to intersectionality among white feminists in Quebec consists of rewriting the genealogy of the term to argue that white

French-speaking women in the province during the 1960s had actually conceptualized their political positions in parallel ways. Geneviève Pagé (2016), a white feminist political scientist at UQAM, argues that the feminist movement must embrace an intersectional approach in order to understand the struggles of Québécois women more effectively. Pagé then explains that Quebec is unique because "it is a society between France and the United States with its windows open on the world ... and with its 'white niggers' still hoping to be masters in their own home, always immersed in the Other's language but desiring French-language propriety" (202; my translation). In her introduction, we learn that Quebec is a cosmopolitan society ("windows open on the world"); the federal government continues to control it ("hoping to be masters in their own home"); the French language remains paramount; and last but not least, the Québécois continue to be the "white niggers" of the Americas. In all, Pagé's argument is about convincing the Quebec feminist movement that it can embrace intersectionality without negating its foundational myths.

Pagé further builds her argument by explaining that during the Quiet Revolution in sixties and seventies Quebec, "radical (white) feminists adopted an analytical framework grounded in global decolonial struggles inspired by Fanon, Memmi, and Césaire" (Pagé 2014, 206; my translation). She then explains that as a result, the term "white niggers of America," popularized by Vallières (see above), served to articulate the class, linguistic, and religious hierarchies that marked the "colonized" position that (white) Québécois people occupied on the continent. "Influenced by decolonial theories and struggles of the Third World," Pagé reminds us that "language became a marker that established belonging to a class and a race. Revolutionary feminists then saw the Quebec liberation struggle as a decolonial struggle and conceived of themselves as racialized subjects" (206; my translation). Pagé does acknowledge that such a position presented some difficulties; namely, it elided Indigenous peoples as colonized subjects and made it appear as if Quebec's experience was symmetrical to that of "other colonized countries." Regardless, Pagé maintains that through their intellectual labour white feminists in Quebec offered a proto-theory of intersectionality: "[Québec feminists] established relevant bases for what could have become a theory of the intersectionality of oppressions. Indeed, despite downplaying some of the privileges of white feminists compared to racialized women 'from here or abroad' (to use their own terms), the feminism-nationalism nexus was materialized through providing a basic understanding of how different oppressions interact" (206, my translation)

In a later article, Pagé (2015) goes on to argue that not only did white feminists of that era recognize multiple oppressions active in their lives, but *"just like Black feminists at the time"* (208; emphasis mine, my translation), they also saw how these systems interacted. In the end, radical Quebec feminists articulated the beginnings of what *could have* become "a three-way intersectional analysis" (208; my translation), but unfortunately, laments Pagé, eventually "realizing their privilege on a global scale, contemporary feminists in Quebec rarely use the racial colonial framework to describe present-day linguistic oppression" (208; my translation). Pagé presents us with two interrelated arguments supporting the use of intersectionality within the Quebec feminist movement.

On the one hand, Pagé demonstrates the type of affinity with Black women's intellectual labour that is common in white feminist spaces, performing what Alexander-Floyd (2012) identified as post-racial forces that emphasize "gender and racial representation while short-circuiting more far-reaching social and political change" (2). In the same way as her predecessors sought to appropriate Black pain and suffering through the "white niggers" moniker, Pagé insists on making a specious connection with Black women without any engagement with the work of a single Black feminist in Canada. Alexander-Floyd (2012) has argued that we need to be wary of how scholars set out to re-vision and redesign intersectionality, wanting to give it greater appeal in ways that undermine Black women and their potentially transformative power: "In order to avoid further (neo)colonization of this term, intersectionality research must be properly understood as the purview of researchers investigating women of color. Scholars who do not focus on women of color as political actors should develop new terms, concepts, and approaches in order to illuminate other experiences and investigate the questions at the center of their research" (19).

Indeed, we must unsettle research in Quebec that centres white feminists, the history of white feminism, or even the contributions that white feminism makes to Quebec nation-building by subjugating concepts that were developed by and for Black women organizing their own resistance.

On the other hand, Pagé downgrades Black women's specific contribution to feminist theory and action through a remarkable re-reading of her predecessors' work. If we are to believe Pagé, white feminists in Quebec articulated a "proto-genesis" of the concept by linking gender, class, ethnicity qua race, and language. Bilge (2010) has deftly pointed out that one of the techniques used to "whiten" intersectionality is to deny its innovative character by pointing to previous theorizations by white women, although most all but excised race. According to Bilge, such efforts inevitably "erase intersectionality's insurgent roots and embodied political positionalities" (22). Ultimately, Black women appear in

Pagé's account as a trope through which to assert a form of nationalism on the path to a presumed universal (white) women's liberation.

On Flight and Resistance

Excluded is too benign a word for the denial of history and must now be used carefully as must all words which begin as oppositional tools and become co-opted by state institutions, and the white cultural establishment. Perhaps we should talk again about the repression of our cultures by this concept of "whiteness." We haven't been excluded, we've been repressed, and we don't need access, we need freedom from the tyranny of "whiteness" expressing itself all through our lives.

– Dionne Brand (1998)

I have pointed to the ways in which the Quebec feminist movement and nationalist movement engage in anti-Blackness in their intellectual and activist work. In particular, I focused on the widespread misuse and misappropriation of intersectionality in each movement. My first argument focused on examples of the *rejection* of the concept by white feminists as a way to caution against Black feminist organizing and academic production and the perversion of the Quebec feminist movement. It also pointed to how any discussion of Black women's intellectual labour must be scuttled to create the political conditions for its support. My second argument focused on the *appropriation* of intersectionality by white feminist and nationalist thinkers as a way to reinvent 1960s-era feminists as radical anti-racist thinkers or to expunge race from the concept's genealogy. In either case, both the *rejection* and *appropriation* of intersectionality are unmistakably connected: both require concerted effort to ignore the Black feminist labour that continues to propel the concept forward intellectually and politically.

Whether we understand these efforts in Quebec in King's terms of the commodification of intersectionality, in Bilge's (2014) terms of its whitening, or in a combination of both, the resounding popularity of intersectionality in feminist circles has done little to support Black women's calls for freedom. In fact, as my analysis suggests, they may compound the centuries-long erasure of Black women from the history of Quebec, in ways that further trivialize our resistance and survival.

Disillusioned with the narrow educational options available to me as a Black feminist at Quebec's most "progressive" post-secondary institution, I came into my Black feminist self through the education that I received from a community of radical Black thinkers that I found in Montreal, Toronto, Vancouver, Paris, and Rotterdam, as well as the vast and energizing community of Black activist-scholars on social media whose intellectual generosity knows no bounds. While I am not advocating for Black students to leave French-language universities en masse, I do want to propose a different way of understanding how and why francophone Black students move for their education. I would argue that if movement has always been at the centre of Black struggles and strategies of resistance, we must consider that part of moving is also about collectivizing and planting our ideas and looking for space(s) to think and to imagine otherwise. Even if a white Quebec nationalist analysis would qualify my piece as defamatory or treasonous, what matters to me is how my analysis of being Black in Quebec is read by my people, francophone Black women, men, and children in Quebec.

NOTES

1 I am particularly grateful to Octavia Pierre, Darryl Leroux, Michèle Spieler, and Leila Bdeir for the comments, suggestions, and guidance they provided in writing this chapter.

2 As I have explained, "there were referenda in 1980 and 1995 on whether or not Québec should leave Canada and become a sovereign state. Québec politics has largely been based on the sovereigntist versus federalist axis. Although different political options have emerged in the last ten years in Québec, the Left has historically been identified as predominantly sovereigntist, hence why so many Leftist groups and organizations in Québec are associated with the sovereigntist project" (Mugabo 2016, 3).

3 Sara Ahmed (2017) addresses this particular kind of citational erasure.

REFERENCES

Abdullahi, Y., and Ugas, S. 2015. *Somali Semantics*. https://issuu.com /somalisemanticszine/docs.

Adewunmi, B. 2014, 2 April. "Kimberlé Crenshaw on Intersectionality: 'I Wanted to Come up with an Everyday Metaphor That Anyone Could Use.'" *New Statesman*. http://www.newstatesman.com/lifestyle/2014/04/kimberl -crenshaw-intersectionality-i-wanted-come-everyday-metaphor-anyone-could.

Ahmed, S. 2017. *Living a Feminist Life*. Durham, NC: Duke University Press.

Alexander-Floyd, N.G. 2012. "Disappearing Acts: Reclaiming Intersectionality in the Social Sciences in a Post-Black Feminist Era." *Feminist Formations* 24 (1): 1–25. https://doi.org/10.1353/ff.2012.0003.

Alexis, A. 1995, 8 May. "Borrowed Blackness." *This Magazine* 28: 14–20.

Bilge, S. 2010. "Beyond Subordination vs. Resistance: An Intersectional Approach to the Agency of Veiled Muslim Women." *Journal of Intercultural Studies* 31 (2): 9–28.

Bilge, S. 2013. "Intersectionality Undone: Saving Intersectionality from Feminist Intersectionality Studies." *Du Bois Review* 10 (2): 405–424. https://doi.org/10.1017/S1742058X13000283.

Bilge, S. 2014. "Whitening Intersectionality: Evanescence of Race in Intersectionality Scholarship." In *Racism and Sociology*, edited by W.D. Hund and A. Lentin, 175–205. Berlin: Lit Verlag Münster.

Brand, D. 1998. *Bread out of Stone: Recollections, Sex, Recognitions, Race, Dreaming, Politics.* Toronto: Vintage.

Chancy, M.J.A. 1993. "Black Women Writing, or How to Tell It Like It Is." *Canadian Woman Studies/Les Cahiers de la Femme* 14 (1): 12–15.

Cooper, A. 2006. *The Hanging of Angélique: The Untold Story of Canadian Slavery and the Burning of Old Montreal.* Athens: University of Georgia Press.

Cornellier, B. 2017. "The Struggles of Others: Pierre Vallières, Quebecois Settler Nationalism, and the N-Word Today." *Discourses* 39 (1): 31–66. https://doi.org/10.13110/discourse.39.1.0031.

Crenshaw, K. 1989. "Demarginalizing the Intersection of Race and Sex: A Black Feminist Critique of Antidiscrimination Doctrine, Feminist Theory and Antiracist Politics." *University of Chicago Legal Forum* 1: 139–167.

Crenshaw, K. 1991. "Mapping the Margins: Intersectionality, Identity Politics, and Violence against Women of Color." In *The Public Nature of Private Violence*, edited by M.A. Fineman and R. Mykituk, 93–118. New York: Routledge.

Danticat, E. 1996. "We Are Ugly, but We Are Here." *The Caribbean Writer* 10: 137–141.

Denaud, F. 2020. "Renegade Gestation: Writing against the Procedures of Intellectual History." *Black Intellectual History: A JHI Blog Forum*, 23 October. https://jhiblog.org/2020/10/23/renegade-gestation/.

Descarries, F. 1998. "Le projet féministe à l'aube du XXIe siècle: un projet de libération et de solidarité qui fait toujours sens." *Cahiers de recherche sociologique* (30): 179–210.

Dragonroot Media. 2016, 8 November. "Bring Black Studies to Concordia: An Interview with Anthony and Shannon." https://soundcloud.com/dragonrootmedia/black-studies-at-concordia-interview-with-anthony-and-shannon?in=dragonrootmedia/sets/dragonroot-radio-archives.

Dumont, M. 2008. *Le féminisme québécois raconté à Camille.* Montreal: Les Éditions du Remue-ménage.

Durand-Folco, J. 2013. "Oppression nationale et intersectionalité: entre nation et intersection." *Ekopolitica: Journal d'écologie politique et de démocratie radicale.* Accessed 23 December 2015. Link no longer active.

Gay, D. 2004. *Les Noirs du Québec, 1629–1900.* Quebec: Septentrion.

Keaton, T.D. 2010. "The Politics of Race-Blindness: (Anti)Blackness and Category-Blindness in Contemporary France." *Du Bois Review* 7 (1): 103–131. https://doi.org/10.1017/S1742058X10000202.

King, T.L. 2015. "Post-Identitarian and Post-Intersectional Anxiety in the Neoliberal Corporate University." *Feminist Formations* 27 (3): 114–138. https://doi.org/10.1353/ff.2016.0002.

Marchand, I., and Ricci, S. 2010. "Sexisme et racisme: la diversité ethnoculturelle, défi au mouvement féministe." In *L'intervention féministe d'hier à aujourd'hui: portrait d'une pratique sociale diversifiée*, edited by C. Corbeil and I. Marchand, 65–92. Montreal: Les Éditions du remue-ménage.

Minto, D.N. 2008. "Here, There, and Elsewhere: Migratory Spaces of (Un)Belonging in Mairruth Sarsfield's *No Crystal Stair* and Tessa McWatt's *This Body*." In *Comparing Migration: The Literatures of Canada and Québec*, edited by C. Khordoc and M. Carrière, 141–152. Bern: Peter Lang.

Mugabo, D. 2016. *Geographies and Futurities of Being: Radical Black Activism in a Context of Anti-Black Islamophobia in 1990s Montreal.* Unpublished master's thesis, Concordia University.

Mugabo, D., and R. Jahangeer. 2014. "The Charter of Québec Values, Intersectionality & Being a Black Feminist in Montreal: An Interview with Délice Igicari Mugabo." *Upping the Anti: A Journal of Theory and Action* (16): 28–41.

Nash, J. 2014. "Institutionalizing the Margins." *Social Text* 32 (1): 45–65. https://doi.org/10.1215/01642472-2391333.

Nelson, C. 2004. "Slavery, Portraiture and the Colonial Limits of Canadian Art History." *Canadian Woman Studies/Les cahiers de la femme* 23 (2): 22–29. https://cws.journals.yorku.ca/index.php/cws/article/view/6300/5488.

Pagé, G. 2015. "'Est-ce qu'on peut être racisées, nous aussi?': les féministes blanches et le désir de racisation." In *Le sujet du féminisme est-il blanc? Femmes racisées et recherches féministes*, edited by N. Hamrouni and C. Maillé, 133–154. Montreal: Éditions du Remue-ménage.

Pagé, G. 2016. "Sur l'indivisibilités de la justice sociale ou Pourquoi le mouvement féministe québécois ne peut faire l'économie d'une analyse intersectionelle." *Nouvelles pratiques sociales* (3): 200–217. https://doi.org/10.7202/1029271ar.

Pierre, O. 2015. "La 'vérité' sort de la bouche des blancs." L'égalité est un concept radical. http://unconceptradical.tumblr.com/post/113069811483/la-vérité-sort-de-la-bouche-des-blancs.

Québec Solidaire. 2006, February. "Nos Principes." https://quebecsolidaire.net/propositions/nos-principes.

Smith, M.S. 2010. "Gender, Whiteness, and 'Other Others' in the Academy." In *States of Race: Critical Race Feminism for the 21st Century*, edited by Razack, M. Smith, and S. Thobani, 37–58. Toronto: Between the Lines.

Vallières, P. 1971. *White Niggers of America.* Toronto: McClelland and Stewart.

Walcott, R. 2000. "'Who Is She and What Is She to You?': Mary Anne Shadd Cary and the Impossibility of Black/Canadian Studies." *Atlantis: A Women's Studies Journal* 24 (2): 137–146. https://journals.msvu.ca/index.php /atlantis/article/view/1598.

Walcott, R. 2014. "Shame: A Polemic." *The CLR James Journal* 20 (1): 1–5. https:// doi.org/10.5840/clrjames20142018.

Walcott, R. 2017. "Why the City's Intersectionality Awareness Week Proposal Is All Crossed Up." *NOW*, 19 July. https://nowtoronto.com/news/city -intersectionality-awareness-week.

Williams, P.J. 1988. "On Being the Object of Property." *Signs* 14 (1): 5–24. https:// doi.org/10.4324/9780429500480-10.

15 Re-spatializing the Boundaries of Belonging: The Subversive Blackness of Muslim Women

JAN-THERESE MENDES

How does the *"where* of race" (McKittrick 2006, xiv) at once speak to the spatial and psychic geographies of Black Muslim women's dominations as well as to the ways the re-imagining of a historical past can be employed to subversively re-narrate the self into/as being in meaningful place? In what ways do these women respond to the dominant directives that authoritatively inscribe their bodies (Narayan 2009) into a particular kind of "necessary" difference by decisively re-configuring the boundaries of racial belongings in order to sanction the political sites for their affirmed dwellings? Engaging with the generous narratives of five women I interviewed between 2010 and 2011 in Toronto, Canada, this chapter examines the specific methods by which those who identify as Black and Muslim recognize and respond to their racist-sexist-Islamophobic oppressions. As part of my graduate ethnographic research,[1] I conducted thirteen in-depth, semi-structured interviews of women between the ages of eighteen and seventy whose sites of national-cultural descent can be, incompletely, located throughout the Americas, the Caribbean, as well as western and northeastern Africa. These women's words illustrate an inventive re-articulation of the self specifically from and through the strategically inhabited site of an interpellated Blackness that works to historically and socially place them beyond the confines of the Canadian white nation, even as they continue to live within its hostile socio-geographic borders.

In his foundational essay "Introduction: Who Needs Identity?" (1996) Stuart Hall explains that "identities are constructed through, not outside, difference" and always in "relation to the Other" (4). Elaborating on identity formation, Hall further continues, "Identities can function as points of identification and attachment only *because* of their capacity to exclude, to leave out, to render 'outside,' abjected. Every identity has at its 'margin' an excess, something more ... So the 'unities' which identities proclaim are, in fact, constructed within the play of power and exclusion, and are the result, not of a natural and inevitable or primordial totality but of the naturalized, overdetermined process of 'closure'" (5). Employing Hall's theoretical renderings of identity across a selection of his works alongside Katherine McKittrick's (2006) and Sara Ahmed's (2000a, 2000b) analyses of the ideological cultivation of certain bodies as persistent Others, I first explore how Black Muslim women might be positioned as an "excess" whose abject yet imperatively proximal selves are made to function as a dark difference that affirms dominant attachments to a definitively white Canadian identity. As part of this contingent process of identification the women of my study are forcibly located amongst those who make up this outside through their initial interpellation into a Black identity. Yet, what might appear as an "effective suturing" into the subject-position (Hall 1996, 6) of Blackness reveals the possibilities that arise as women step into the expected position but come to occupy it as a historical-political "resource" (4) by articulating and re-signifying their oppressions through enunciations of an Africanness.

Following Yasmeen Narayan's (2009) work on the "(re)-production and re-circulation" (607) of dominant norms, the subject is understood to not *simply be passively inscribed* but also to *respond* to violating, dictating reflections by engraving and sculpting the contours of their own body (613). To enter into the Black subjectivity that already directively marks the surface of the skin and dictates the recognizable form of the body might indeed make the claiming of an African ancestral past – however fantasmic (see Hall 1996, 4) – an illustration of the subject's responsive engraving. Hence, for some of these Muslim women the self is effectively and affectively re-engraved as African as they describe, navigate through, and at times reach beyond the violences that operate in their present. Black Muslim women's conceptualizations of their inhabited Africanness does not, however, equate to "a unified social imaginary" (Scott 2013, 4), considering that the affirming redrawing of the borders of belonging also includes regulative movements towards as well as away from each other. Rather than imagining these recirculating boundaries of inclusion and exclusion as misplaced or as unfortunate fracturings within a collective these fluctuating terms of racial authenticity can instead be read as illuminating the complexities – if not sheer messiness – of the project to find place for the subjugated self. Black Muslim women's experiences therefore verify Hall's (1996) assertion that identity is indeed intertwined with "the process of becoming rather than being" (4).

Securing the White Nation: The Safety of the Recognizable, Always Knowable Other

Describing the entanglements of "the production of space" with the violently subjugating yet efficiently tuned "geographic frameworks" that order the world, McKittrick explains that dominations "naturalize both identity and place" (2006, xv). In this way, racist-sexist oppressions take repetitive shape as "spatial acts" (xvii) as they delegate the places where "subaltern bodies" commonsensically and unalterably belong (xv). Within the context of settler-colonial Canada (of and in which McKittrick writes) it is the space of the nation that is effectively produced as normatively white terrain. For Canada to be naturalized as white and peopled by bodies that reflect this dominant truth, persons who do not belong (or, properly belong in the spaces that are designated to be "out of place" [xv]) must be readily available as the measurable difference – the relation of Otherness – against and through which Canadian identity can take shape and enact the desired closure (see Hall 1996, 4–5). Himani Bannerji (2000) thus fittingly declares, "Concomitant with this mania for the naming of 'others' is one for the naming of that which is 'Canadian.' This 'Canadian' core community is defined through the same process that others us" (65). To this I would add that the insistence on clearly defining those who are Other is not a frenzied fixation on categorization as the word "mania" might suggest, but rather reflects a meticulously crafted and carefully wielded system meant to secure what may otherwise be a less verifiable belonging for the white settler-colonial nation. In this regard, those who are numbered amongst the authentic "we" of the nation come to recognize the boundaries of a national identity that envelopes bodies like their own through the availability of the bodies of those who are knowable through their outsiderness.

Thinking through the construction and recognizability of strangers/ strangeness, Ahmed (2000a) enquires into the degree to which encounters with those who are recognized as strange entails determining "the contours or boundaries of the body-at-home" (38) through the gestures that first allow the "unmarked body" of those who are "*in-place*" (46; italics in original) to remove from and thus move past the proximal stranger (20, 22, 38). Ahmed (2000b, 49) explains that the stranger is not solely the unknown figure located in a site that is out of sight but also comprises those who are nearby and thus hold a "co-presence" in social space (Ahmed 2000a, 38). Strangers are accordingly "*already recognised as not belonging, as being out of place*" as soon as they have crossed into the spatial "home" of bodies at home (Ahmed 2000b, 49, italics in original). If strangers are already distinguishable as strange in the moment of encounter and in the imaginings that precede their physical arrival, then any threat posed to the *core community* of authentic Canadians would not emerge from a site of unknowability. As such, I instead ask, What kind of interruption or disturbance might unfold if strangers occupy the "wrong" or unexpected type of Otherness that deviates from the strangeness through which bodies such as theirs are normatively understood? Further, how does the re-inscribing of Others from a mixed-matched strangeness into the familiarly strange stranger (Ahmed 2000b, 50; Kassam 2011, 560) confirm "a discourse of survival" by the white nation/subject whereby survival means always being able to comprehend and stabilize the foreignness of those who live where they can never belong? The narratives of Black Muslim women offer insights into these very queries.

Reading Muslim Bodies into Blackness, Responding to the Interpellation

> I started to say "I am Black" when I became Muslim because they [the white Canadian public] can't see my hair [under the hijab]. All they can see is my skin colour and I am a Black Muslim ... It's only when I came to Canada that I had to think, "What am I?" It's not enough to say I'm from Panama, I'm Hispanic, and I speak Spanish.

Paulita's recounting notes the demand to realign her conceptions of self with the dominantly comprehensible and familiar racial-historical "truths" that already appear to inscribe the surface of her skin with the visible, cogent, and meant-to-be-static signifiers for the Black subject. The recognition of the "not enough" therefore conveys the work of a disciplining reading of Paulita's body that *compels her citation* of the racial norm (see Butler 1993, 232) in Canada so that her named and claimed identifications become *enough alike* with the knowledges of difference that already know her darkness as Black. Hall (1996) explains that identities are "points of temporary attachment to the subject positions which discursive practices construct for us" (6) as such, what can be understood as an "effective suturing" entails the subject's investment in the subject-position that has hailed them – which in turn requires that the suturing is conceived as an "*articulation*" (6; italics in original). Paulita is thus hailed by the subject-position of Blackness which she "step[s] into" (Hall 1995, 8) and effectively invests in by articulating a link between the way she physically appears and the racial and spatial identifications this appearance is meant to invoke (see also Fanon 1994), which is not a Latinaness. Yet the complexities of this interpellation must be further unpacked because Paulita's words point us towards the layers behind and before this attachment's successful embodiment.

Shortly after immigrating to Canada from Panama, Paulita converted to Islam and donned the hijab. Because it is the visibility of her hair, meaning its particular texture, that Paulita understands to partially signify her Latinaness, its invisibility within the diaspora following her conversion and decision to wear the hijab becomes a kind of out-of-sightness that she conceives to obscure this earlier identification. As a result, a space evidently emerges for the *effective suture* into a hailing Black subjecthood to be made possible, in accordance with "interior-ized" normative directives (Narayan 2009, 612) that collapse darkness into Blackness. Reflecting on Hall (2002), Narayan contemplates the ways subjects respond to "authorizations and injunctions," as reflected in "the practices of multiple others towards the self *and* others both in-side and outside the familial home(s)" (611). She goes on to argue that there is a *simultaneous* and *continuous* engraving, carving, and sculpting of the body – of the self into being – as the subject distinguishes between the self and others and alters external prohibitions into imperatives that are seemingly their "own" (611). Although in our interview Paulita describes her Panamanian life as devoid of conceptions of race amidst what she experienced as ethnic homogeneity, following Narayan's reasoning, notions of what a Latina is or is not (and thus what a Latina looks like and what she does not) would nonetheless arise from injunctions reflected in the practices of others within Panama; that is, injunctions that norma-tively correlate certain bodies with specific "biological" and "cultural" *traits* (611). The texture of one's hair would therefore be inscribed onto the surface of the body by others as being indicative of Latinaness and simultaneously taken up as well as re-engraved into the subject's sense of the traits that compute with this/their identity. Moreover, because Paulita's identification as Latina first requires an Other in order to come into formation, in the way of all identities (Hall 1996, 4), Black bod-ies may in fact be the contrasting Others against which constructions of Latinaness take shape. Specifically, Black people can be imagined to be those who have dark skin but do not or cannot have what is recognized as "Latina hair" – a difference of Blackness Paulita later inhabits as a hijabi Muslim woman in Canada once her hair is out of sight.

I further suggest that normative directives within a Canadian context would also compel Paulita's re-sculpting away from a Latina identity and into the Black subject-position as part of the process of ensuring the forever recognizability of the familiarly strange stranger, here be-ing the Muslim woman. That is, while the Otherness of Muslims can be knowable through Blackness, Latinaness does not accord with what makes the foreignness of Muslims readily comprehensible and unceasingly available. To be at once Latina, Muslim, in hijab, *and* with dark skin is an unexpected kind of strangeness. In Canada, as within other Western countries, the veil is dominantly made to function as what is synonymous with Islam, while its presence on the bodies of women is used to unquestionably locate them as Muslim (Kassam 2011, 557; Zine 2006, 242). The bodies of Muslim women who wear and are recognized through the hijab are therefore employed, according to Jasmine Zine (2006), as symbolic referents for "social difference" (242). The hijab confirms that these women are foreign to and thus do not authentically belong within (or amongst) the "we" of the Canadian nation (246). Muslim women are therefore one of the always knowable Others whose presence within Canada, again, assures the white nation/subject of what they are not (Kassam 2011, 559–60). Veiled women must remain recognizable through the difference they inhabit to secure a national identity's constant verification and renewal. For Paulita this means that in donning the hijab her surface is inscribed as/into the locatable and verifiable outsiderness of the Muslim who dwells in the home that is not their own, as she is simultaneously instructed out of a primary identification with Latinaness and into the Blackness that is read on her skin and can be digested along with her hijab. In line with the feats of what Edward Said (2000) describes as "successful nationalisms," a "falsehood" is then ascribed to an identity through which this woman orients herself (176) in order to reorient her difference into commensurable place.

Writing on ideologies of *nation-purity* that maintain the impossibility of Black people's national belongings, McKittrick (2006) imitates the sentiments of a dominant voice as she attests, "Black people *in* Canada are geographically un-Canadian – their bodies (and therefore their histories) tell us so" (99). As part of the violent legacy of nation building, Black people's subjugations have continued to include their methodical un-writings from the legitimized and legitimizing sites from where belongings can take spatial and cultural shape within the constructed borders of an intently, if not zealously, guarded Canadianness. Black bodies are at once imagined to be forever approaching, vying for entry, from the elsewhere they must come (95, 99; see also Tettey and Puplampu 2005b, 40–1) and are despised as the perpetually proximal Others who have already arrived and insolently move within regulatively white space. Comprising one manifestation of the stable near-to-us difference that allows for the constitution of the white nation/subject, Black people are the familiarly strange strangers who can be identified by dark contrast (see Massaquoi 2007). Moreover, Black women in particular are *managed* as racial-sexual bodies through dislocating and subjugating readings that "assum[e] that black femininity is altogether knowable" (McKittrick 2006, xv). The "effective suture" verified through the now matter-of-fact articulation of her Blackness, of her Black Muslimness, might then mean for Paulita to occupy the correct kind of categorical strangeness. But of course, even with the appropriate suture, this woman never ceases to be numbered amongst the many Others whose surfaces are used to reinforce the national *drive* to *permanently* "kee[p] the foreign [discernibly] foreign," to borrow from David Theo Goldberg (2009, 182). Without any clear indication of being accepted by the white nation/subject following the proper stepping into a Black subject-position, one must question why Paulita nonetheless accommodates, invests in, and thus articulates the prescription. Refusing the disingenuous and re-subjugating supposition of a subordinate obedience, I suggest that what is unfolding would inaccurately be defined as a passive inscription (see Narayan 2009).

Re-imagined Roots, Performing Diasporic Belongings

In taking up the Black subject-position into which she is directively situated, I surmise that Paulita gainfully acquires or enters into a specific site of social-historical "resource" (Hall 1996, 4). In particular, I argue that an inscribed racial positioning is not simply embodied in the precise ways dominant dictates demand but can also be disruptively re-articulated as an imaginative platform from which the self can access a diasporic sense of locatedness that is otherwise hard to find. Explaining the paradoxical and highly contingent play between language and meaning, Hall (1991) states, "You have to be positioned somewhere in order to speak. Even if you are positioned in order to unposition yourself, even if you want to take it back, you have to come into language to get out of it" (51). To refuse to claim the Black subjectivity that has already claimed her – even before the moment of articulation[2] – would mean to risk a sort of unspeaking placelessness (that is, if we can first assume that a refusal is actually within the range of choice for the subject). Specifically, because Paulita's appearance does not accord with what being Latina is dominantly imagined to look like and thus is not a subject-position that continues to hail her within a Canadian context, the self that attempts to speak from this incomprehensible place of Latinaness may have an indecipherable voice as she infringes on the rules of intelligibility. Although to be Black renders one as out-of-place, this marginal positionality is not constructed entirely as a non-place. Black subjecthood is also invested in as a marginal site of language from which one can possibly begin to reconfigure situatedness within a white nation that is at once hostile to and dependent on their certain Otherness. Paulita tellingly asserts, "I realized I look African so I identify now as a Muslim-Afro-Hispanic ... I'm African because of my skin colour ... I am a shade of them." Paulita not only invests in Black subjectivity but specifically names it through an Africanness. By asserting that she *looks* and therefore *is* African, this Muslim woman re-inventively locates herself amidst the African diaspora in Canada in a way that possibly positions her both within and beyond the confines of Canada for a broader sense of place, as a re-narrated historical past situates her within a self-affirming kind of "elsewhere" that enables her to speak into and against her silencings. In this way, Paulita does not merely obey and/or replicate external prescriptions (Narayan 2009, 613) seeing that, in comprehending her Blackness as reflective of an African identity, she performs a self-engraving that at once registers and responds to controlling injunctions by approaching this Africanness as a meaningful site of inhabitance. Africa is, of course, the ultimate elsewhere from which foreign Black bodies are dominantly imagined to come. For Paulita to think of Blackness alongside or as synonymous with Africanness is then not an unexpected connection and can very well be considered as part of the interpellation. What remains central in this woman's confident declaration, however, is that in attaching to an African sense of self she begins to alter her spatial knowings of the world (McKittrick 2006, xxvi). Hereby, feeling one's Africanness may be the affective means for entry into certain historical and social forms of space-making.

Claiming a Violent Past to Name an Oppressive Present

The narrative of Zahra, a woman who has grown up as a Muslim in Canada, offers an alternative illustration of the social and political effectivity of historical re-imaginings when sculpted through an invested Blackness. Zahra states, "I didn't grow up thinking I was Black. The idea of Blackness is very new to me ... Someone came up to me ... and he was like, 'Zahra, are you Black first, Hispanic first, or Muslim first?' I was like, 'Black first? I'm not Black!' But then I was like, 'Oh, I have to be. I didn't get this colour by the sun. There has to be *slavery* in my history somewhere that has made *me, me.* "

By assuming the Black identity authoritatively inscribed from without, Zahra accordingly "steps into the place of recognitio[n]" that another has prescribed (Hall 1995, 8). However, not only is the dictated Black subject-position responsively imbued with the signifiers for an

Africanness, as reflected in Paulita's experience, but Zahra's re-imaginings decisively draw a connection between her subjectivity and the transatlantic slave trade. The psychic-social act of self-engraving, for Zahra, therefore includes the re-narration of parts of herself into and through slavery's "historical violence and rupture" (6) as she lays bodily and ancestral claim to the memory of what is a painful past. Even as Zahra invokes and seemingly re-writes the self through a discourse of discovered or recovered origins that roots her within an African past and potentially brings her into communion with an African diasporic present, it is not necessarily an affirmed, essential, or verifiable Africanness or an African "homeland" that this woman seeks (Anthias and Yuval-Davis 1992, 4–5; Foster 1996, 18; Hall 1991, 58; Tettey and Puplampu 2005a, 4–5, 7). Instead, I propose that in attaching to the enslavement of both newly imagined and declared ancestors, Zahra acquires what Hall calls "the symbolic language for describing what suffering [is] like" (1995, 13).

Also from Panama, having immigrated to Canada with her family as a small child, Zahra's hijab and dark skin visibly represent cues for the foreignness into which her racial-sexual body is so knowingly and functionally written. Notably, she speculates that her hijab is the primary sign of difference to which a white Toronto public responds, as part of growing Islamophobic fervour. At the same time Zahra concedes that her dark body is also figured as Black (and plausibly has always been so), even as her Muslimness is experienced as the target of the most overt oppressions. It is then only with the enunciated hailing that Zahra describes the acquisition of a language to classify encounters with discrimination (experienced both before and after the perceived interpellation) as specifically anti-Black racist. Zahra begins to be able to name the racist oppression that has been unnameable following her own enunciation of what already is, her publicly recognizable and thus appropriate Blackness (Mendes 2011, 115–16). Slavery as a historical possession here operates within a liberatory politic whereby racist violences are linked to and can be comprehended through a longer story of subjugation. The nightmare of slavery gives voice to and aids in comprehending the traumas of her present. Zahra's anti-Black racist, sexist, and Islamophobic dominations would, of course, not cease to inflict their degradations, as if incapacitated by the moment of recognition and the subject's self-engraving (McKittrick 2006, xvii). What I suggest emerges is a psychic-discursive site for the re-signification of such dominations wherein an inscribed and invested Otherness is configured as a space for the subject's own knowings. The subject's very body can be what becomes the site of their "counter-politics" (Hall 1991, 53).

Specifically, the visible signs of difference that are made to render them as the familiarly strange stranger unexpectedly proffer a discourse from which Others can identify (and identify with) the legacy of their outsiderness, begin to critically articulate the feeling of subjugation, and thus partially "recast the meanings" of their oppressions (McKittrick 2006, xvii) by approaching them as a kind of rooted knowledge. Knowledge therefore points towards one's roots but also performs a radical historicizing that interrupts the dominant imaginings of their outsiderness as something that naturally "just is" (xv).

Returning to the encounter Zahra defines as pivotal to her resignified racial identity, a notable detail is that, unlike Paulita's experience, it is not the authoritative readings of a dominant white public that direct Zahra into the appropriate subject-position. Rather she is absorbed into a Black man's sense of what makes Blackness recognizable. The subject who has presumably already been hailed and has *stepped into the recognition* thus affirms their investment in the racial interpellation as they re-carve the bodies of other Others by the same terms that controlling marks the surface of his own skin. Even so, repeating the knowability of the Black subject may nevertheless be more than the simple obedience to and replication of the directive, since, in naming Zahra as Black, the process of a responsive engraving is potentially being enacted by identifying the members of a could-be collectivity and a maybe-belongingness. What remains problematic, however, are the particular ways this carving reinstitutes Black and Muslim women's racial-sexual bodies as forever locatable, always available, and of course already knowable, before and/or despite the knowledges through which women comprehend or spatialize themselves (McKittrick 2006, xv). Zahra is definitively located within three forms of Otherness, suggesting that Black, Muslim, and Latina subjectivities can conceivably be occupied simultaneously – if unequally – according to the imaginings of those who are also Othered. What becomes Zahra's task within what is presumptively the limits of her power for this Black man is to give a cogent hierarchical order to these multiple identities. With reference to Hall, Narayan explains that the subject does not unrestrictedly select identifications from an array that lie before them for the choosing but instead secures a "will" only as they respond to reflections of the self mirrored in others (2009, 612). Accordingly, Zahra's will arguably never rested in the picking or ordering of her precise identities but emerges through her capacity to re-stylize the meaning of these selves from within and thus introduce a "variation" on the directives that repeatedly inscribe her surface (see Butler 1993, 33, 145). Even as Zahra's investment in an enslaved ancestry confirms her successful

attachment to a prescribed Blackness, her re-styling of this subject position importantly introduces anti-Black racism as a discourse for her
political re-imaginings, mobilized through her re-narrated lineage. It is
also important to note that such a mobilization of identity at no point
discounts the realness of the re-narrated past (see Forte 2010, 195; Hall
1996, 4; McKittrick 2006, 32–3).

Black like Me? Structuring the Boundaries of Acceptable Blackness

Notably, the experiences of some of the women of this study reveal that
once a Black identity is attached, it may be used to judge, contest, or
deny the validity of other women's places within this subject-position.
In particular, the national borders that organize continental Africa are
appropriated as the racial-culture boundaries that decide the authenticity of claims to Blackness in Canada. Women's stories therefore include
varying conceptions of racial belongings that refract or converge from
each other through assertions such as: Somalis are not Black; Somalis *are*
Black; Somalis and Ethiopians are "not *that* Black"; all people of African
descent are Black; or continental Africans' cultural dissimilarities from
Black Canadians' discounts them from personal narratives of Blackness.
Although each of these Muslim women contends with a white landscape
that relentlessly dislocates her from a legitimate and situated dwelling,
such trials do not result in a boundless affinity. Only an Africanness that
is spatialized in particular ways are admitted into the Blackness they
are inscribed into and now effectively occupy within an imaginatively
claimed diaspora. Hall's (1996) suppositions on the contingency of
identifications are thus confirmed here. Identification does not eliminate difference *once secured*; on the contrary, one woman can be counted
within the "constitutive outside" that partially reinforces another's sense
of being in place (2–3). One is then left to ask, Why is there a re-draw-
ing of the perimeters that decide inclusions and exclusions into or away
from legitimate inhabitances of Blackness? Moreover, why are these limits engendered through the bodies of others who are comparably Othered? McKittrick (2006) maintains that Black women both contribute
to geographies and hold investments in "spatial politics" as a result of
the very ways they are fictitiously consigned to the outsides of spatial
productions (54). As such, Black Muslim women's decisive orderings
of what appears to be the African geographies of Blackness may in fact
exemplify one aspect of this spatial politic and creative capacity. Perhaps
instead of asking why, as if in lament, it is therefore more apt to enquire
into what such racial boundaries do and/or potentially interrupt. To
regulate the qualities that make up a verifiable Black identity (as one

who is already dominantly figured into this foreignness) conveys an investment in the production or configuration of racial space that is neither anticipated nor wholly controlled by the forces of the white nation/subject. Even as these women are rendered uninterruptedly knowable, there might be something psychically or socially liberating in not being unquestionably recognizable to each other. In these unanticipated ways, geographies of belonging can be produced, approached, or possibly entered into with a complexity that takes into account individual complexities that would not be considered by controlling inscriptions of the familiarly strange stranger. At the same time, it seems like more than mere coincidence that the enduringly stigmatized and infantilized African nations of Somalia and Ethiopia are specifically named as part of the re-spatalized outside. If the marginalized subject indeed relies upon and employs the bodies of others "as receptacles to contain what the self cannot recognize themselves 'to be'" (Narayan 2009, 613), the invested process of ordering the acceptable African geographies of Blackness might include a defensive divorcing from the undesirable or "wrong" kind of Africanness. Hence, there becomes a sort of Africanness that is "too much" outside what one can risk recognizing oneself within, amidst the ongoing attempt to re-situate into a locatedness that is so often or otherwise beyond reach. Past this erected racial-spatial frontier may only rest, to quote Edward Said (2000), "the perilous territory of not-belonging" (177).

Eby, a woman from Somalia raised in a Muslim family, details what it can feel like to be in this space of "too much" and outside:

> Once you're classified as an *outsider* it's really hard to self-identify ... I was not accepted by one group and rejected by the other. The number of fights I would get into in high school because of this question ... it would be the same thing being told [by Black peers] over and over again, "You're not Black because you're Somalian." And that goes back to Somalian girls *saying they're not Black* themselves. It was a vicious cycle ... [I]t was like a way for each group to self-guard their own *identity*, their own *insecurities*. What really pissed me off was "you're not Black." I was like ... "What?! I'm from *the Motherland*, do you understand? I'm from *the hold* of Africa. How am I *not* Black? I'm *more* Black than you!

To be able to proclaim her Blackness in Canada would first follow from a directive hailing into which Eby has both stepped and evidently resculpted from within by establishing a recent and verifiable tie to continental Africa – to the "Motherland" – as what evidences an indisputable Black identity. And, of course, to assert that she is "more Black" than those whose ties to Africa may be more historically distant – if not ambiguously or fantasmically crafted in the space of diaspora (Forte 2010, 195) – participates in the very regulation of Blackness Eby contests (Narayan 2009, 613). Even so, it is not an effort to unhinge or distance the unverifiable African from a Black identity that this woman's words convey, but rather a deep yearning to be recognized as Black by those selves she also and already reads within this subject-position. It is clearly not enough to be directively written into a Black subjectivity by the white nation/subject for an affirming self-engraving to follow, for Eby, since, as she painfully expresses, self-recognition remains difficult without acknowledgment by other Others (Hall 1995, 8). To silence this woman's Africanness out of a legitimate Blackness, however, might be what acts as the effective vehicle by which other women can speak themselves into the possibility of a secure kind of place (5).[3]

(Not) Knowing Each Other: The Hijab as What Incites or Unlatches the Closure

The exclusion from the site of racial authenticity that Eby experiences as a wound that confounds further indicates that the signifiers that determine comprehensible and acceptable qualities of a Black identity cut past the flesh and across religious-racial lines, since it is non-Muslim Black peers who explicitly reject this Somali Muslim woman's proclamations of Blackness. Notably, the narratives of women who wear the hijab convey that it can be a visible Muslimness that particularly renders their Blackness incomprehensible to Black women who do not identify as Muslim. Confusion, hesitation, aversion, and/or explicit Islamophobia are perceived to fill the affective space of the public encounter between themselves and non-Muslim Black women. This is a space of feeling that they imagine would otherwise be imbued with the immediate sense of elation or respite that can sometimes arise in the moment of meeting another Black woman in the inhospitable terrain of white supremacist society. Aiya, a convert to Islam born in Canada and of mixed Caribbean heritage, explains, "I think when Black women who are not Muslim see me, they see me as *Muslim* and *different* and step back a little bit – because of the scarf. I'm sure if I had no scarf on they'd be like, 'Hey! It's a sister!'" Paulita and Zahra of course understand their dark skin to fixate them as incontestably Black within the controlling gaze of the white nation/subject and a re-inscribing non-Muslim Black patriarchy, despite or even because of their hijabs. Even so, non-Muslim Black women do not necessarily invoke or rely upon the same cues of racial demarcation within their own productions of and political investments in space (McKittrick 2006, 54). While Black Muslim hijabi women's perpetual, multiplied Otherness assures a white Canada of its authenticated whiteness, for Black women who are not Muslim (yet are still always Othered) this difference might visibly and viscerally represent the form of outsiderness that cannot ensure a maybe-belongingness and thus is not what they should understand themselves to be alike to.[4] It is then not into these carefully guarded racial-social spaces that Black Muslim women can expect to gain access.

In counter-response to their rigidly maintained Otherness, Black Muslim women nonetheless reveal a concentrated willingness to temporarily relinquish the social-cultural and national boundaries set between each other that they otherwise employ to autonomously spatialize an acceptable complicated Blackness. As a means of garnering some sense of psychic relief from anti-Black racism and/or Islamophobia within the public spaces where these aggressions are felt to be most acute, the strategically produced racial-geographic closure briefly opens up or falls away – thus, allowing for a momentary re-spatialization of oppression through instances of what I call "spontaneous solidarity." Within the South Asian or Arab majority mosque (where anti-Black racism often shapes how women experience the religious institution), or on the streets of an anti-Black racist and Islamophobic Toronto, to be acknowledged by another Black Muslim woman through an act as fleeting as the locking of gazes performs as an affirming, humanizing interruption. Tahisia, a convert to Islam of Zimbabwean heritage, offers a poignant account of the closure's unlatching within the mosque on the rare but valued occasion that another Black woman happens to be present. She states, "You're *aware*. You know where they're sitting, you know where they're praying. There's this contact – eye contact. An extra 'Yeah, we understand, we're in this together' ... [I]t feels nice." In these moments women identify each other through the visible cues that also make them unalterably knowable within dominant directives: dark bodies in hijab. Yet the gazes through which women register and hold each other in these impromptu moments are different. Something more is happening here that is radically and defiantly nourishing. Black Muslim women's self-engravings allow for an inventive and potentially disruptive embodiment of their relegated Otherness, even though the racial inscription is not intended to be to their benefit. They begin to imagine an affirming situatedness, inciting a fluidity that introduces social and political possibility into hostile places. It is not that women imagine that the differences between them dissolve at the very instant of the humanizing recognition, but rather the violent hold of the oppressive dictate temporarily or perhaps incrementally widens into more liveable space as women acknowledge one another's existence. Thus the pleasure, the brief respite that is spontaneously shared affirms not a dominant subjectivity but each other.

Conclusion

As selves who are meant to be unalterably situated and ceaselessly recognizable within a naturalized outsiderness, Black Muslim women's lived experiences powerfully convey their imaginative capacity to re-conceptualize hailing inscriptions into meaningful sites for a re-stylized, affirming embodiment of space. While dominant directives mark the surface of these women's necessarily proximal bodies with the instructively appropriate symbols for the familiarly strange stranger against which an authentic Canadian identity can be verifiably constructed and reassuringly maintained as white, covert potentialities follow the effective suture. Hence, Muslim women are not simply inscribed into the knowable Otherness of Black subjectivity but respond to/against the controlling dictates by inventively occupying the interpellated identity as a platform for an alternative self-articulation and self-recognition whereby Africanness is unexpectedly inhabited as a historical-political resource. Such subversive enunciations, however, do not unquestionably become the stuff of collectivity, since Black Muslim women are not necessarily recognizable to each other from within the suture. Instead, an imaginatively claimed African identity in Canada appears as that which regulates the boundaries of what women consider to be a legitimate Black identity. Hereby their investments in the production and politics of space are illustrated through the distinction between acceptable and undesirable African geographies of Blackness. In the silencing of some other Others out of or away from a social and spatially verified Black subjectivity, a sense of maybe/could-be belonging is defensively secured. Appearing across religious lines, the Blackness of Muslim women who wear the hijab is also defensively denied as a "wrong" kind of outsiderness by Black women who are not Muslim. The same barriers that Black Muslim women erect between each other through a qualified Blackness are thus temporarily relinquished as an interlude to their acute oppressions from which their subjugation in public spaces can be momentarily re-spatialized and unsettled through women's spontaneous solidarities. Of course, Black Muslim women's capacities for affirmative, resistive, and re-spatializing invention is more complexly interwoven with ambiguous practices of articulation and shaped by pain, celebration, and narrative-makings than can be effectively captured in this chapter. What I hope nonetheless remains evident is the possibility for the psychic-social unhinging of racist-sexist-Islamophobic controls – even when temporary, messy, and conflicting – as these women effectively and affectively speak.

NOTES

1 Interviews were conducted between September 2010 and January 2011 in the Greater Toronto Area and its surrounding suburbs, for my master's thesis in religious studies. While all narrative quotes are taken directly from my thesis, newer analysis has partly emerged from a paper I presented at the 2014 John Douglas Taylor Conference: Contemporary Orientations in African Cultural Studies (McMaster University, Hamilton, Ontario, Canada).

2 That is, Paulita's dark skin may have already been dominantly read as a cue for Blackness prior to the donning of her hijab and thus before her own enunciation of a Black identity.

3 It would be worthwhile to consider whether these Somali women desire to remove from what they might perceive to be the more perilous outsiderness of Blackness, within Canada. Such an unwillingness to invest in the Black subject-position perhaps illustrates the unsuccessful suture.

4 Alternately some of the women of this study also describe a counter-experience wherein their hijabs signify a Muslimness that also un-writes their Blackness for a dominant white Toronto public. Women explain that the hijab sometimes "forfeits" or "cancels out" their Blackness as a dominant imagination reads them as South Asian or Arab – and thus as the familiar Muslim woman. Yet, for some, this same disappeared Blackness resurfaces in any instance that the hijab is removed and the texture of their hair reveals the physical cue for a now indisputable Black subjectivity – experiences that appear in contrast to Paulita's.

REFERENCES

Ahmed, S. 2000a. *Strange Encounters: Embodied Others in Post-Coloniality*. New York: Routledge.

Ahmed, S. 2000b. "Who Knows? Knowing Strangers and Strangerness." *Australian Feminist Studies* 15 (31): 49–68. https://doi.org/10.1080/713611918.

Anthias, F., and Yuval-Davis, N. 1992. *Racialized Boundaries: Race, Nation, Gender, Colour, and Class and the Anti-Racist Struggle*. London: Routledge.

Bannerji, H. 2000. *The Dark Side of the Nation: Essays on Multiculturalism, Nationalism and Gender*. Toronto: Canadian Scholars' Press.

Butler, J. 1993. *Bodies That Matter: On the Discursive Limits of "Sex."* New York: Routledge.

Fanon, F. 1994. *Black Skin, White Masks,* translated by R. Philcox. New York: Grove Press.

Forte, J. 2010. "Diaspora Homecoming, Vodun Ancestry, and the Ambiguities of Transnational Belongings in the Republic of Benin." In *Global Circuits of Blackness: Interrogating the African Diaspora,* edited by J. Rahier, P. Hintzen, and F. Smith, 174–201. Urbana: University of Illinois Press.

Foster, C. 1996. *A Place Called Heaven: The Meaning of Being Black in Canada.* Toronto: HarperCollins.

Goldberg, D. 2009. *The Threat of Race: Reflections on Racial Neoliberalism.* Malden, MA: Wiley-Blackwell.

Hall, S. 1991. "Old and New Identities, Old and New Ethnicities." In *Culture, Globalization and the World System: Contemporary Conditions for the Representation of Identity,* edited by A. King, 41–68. Minneapolis: University of Minnesota Press.

Hall, S. 1995. "Negotiating Caribbean Identities." *New Left Review* 1 (209): 3–14.

Hall, S. 1996. "Introduction: Who Needs Identity?" In *Questions of Cultural Identity,* edited by S. Hall, and P. du Gay, 3–17. London: SAGE Press.

Hall, S. 2002. "On the Way Home." Lecture at the Institute of Psychoanalysis. London.

Kassam, S. 2011. "Marketing an Imagined Muslim Woman: *Muslim Girl* Magazine and the Politics of Race, Gender and Representation." *Social Identities* 17 (4): 543–564. https://doi.org/10.1080/13504630.2011.587308.

Massaquoi, N. 2007. "An Unsettled Feminist Discourse." In *Theorizing Empowerment: Canadian Perspectives on Black Feminist Thought,* edited by N. Massaquoi and N. Nathani Wane, 75–94. Toronto: Inanna Publications and Education.

McKittrick, K. 2006. *Demonic Grounds: Black Women and the Cartographies of Struggle.* Minneapolis: University of Minnesota Press.

Mendes, J. 2011. *Exploring Blackness from Muslim, Female, Canadian Realities: Founding Selfhood, (Re)claiming Identity and Negotiating Belongingness within/against a Hostile Nation.* Unpublished master's thesis, McMaster University.

Narayan, Y. 2009. "On Post-Colonial Authority, *Caribbeanness,* Reiteration and Political Community." *Cultural Studies* 23 (4): 605–623. https://doi.org/10.1080/09502380902950997.

Said, E. 2000. *Reflections on Exile and Other Essays.* Cambridge, MA: Harvard University Press.

Scott, D. 2013. "On the Very Idea of a Black Radical Tradition." *Small Axe* 17 (1): 1–6. https://doi.org/10.1215/07990537-1665398.

Tettey, W., and Puplampu, K. 2005a. "Continental Africans in Canada: Exploring a Neglected Dimension of the African-Canadian Experience."

In *The African Diaspora in Canada: Negotiating Identity and Belonging*, edited by W. Tettey and K. Puplampu, 3–23. Calgary, AB: Calgary University Press.

Tettey, W., and Puplampu, K. 2005b. "Ethnicity & the Identity of African-Canadians: A Theoretical & Political Analysis." In *The African Diaspora in Canada: Negotiating Identity and Belonging*, edited by Tettey and Puplampu, 25–48. Calgary, AB: Calgary University Press.

Zine, J. 2006. "Unveiled Sentiments: Gendered Islamophobia and Experiences of Veiling among Muslim Girls in a Canadian Islamic School." *Equity and Excellence in Education* 39 (3): 239–252. https://doi.org/10.1080/10665680600788503.

PART FOUR

Black Pasts, Black Futurity

Commentary on Part Four: Surviving Anti-Blackness: Vulnerability, Speaking Back, and Building Black Futurity

SHIRLEY ANNE TATE

Introduction

The seven chapters in part 4, "Black Pasts, Black Futurity," by the Black Graduate Students' Collective, Delores V. Mullings, OmiSoore H. Dryden, Jennifer Kelly, Adelle Blackett, Barrington Walker, and Malinda S. Smith, locate Canadian universities as zones of Black (un)belonging. Black Canadian (un)belonging, being without whilst precariously located within academia and the nation state, resonates with Western Hemispheric Black experience (see Christian 2012; Gabriel and Tate 2017; Jansen 2019; Emejulu and Sobande 2019; Bernardino-Costa et al. 2018). These chapters on Black life in the face of anti-Blackness speak back to white supremacy in the academy and social life through thoughts of engaged scholars in the Black community on past and present strengths, vulnerability, and activism as the starting points for survival, agentic possibility, and building Black futurity.

Anti-Blackness: Vulnerabilities and Activism

The Black Graduate Students' Collective (Jan-Therese Mendes, Charmaine Lurch, Mosa McNeilly, Evelyn Amponsah, and Ola Mohammed) remind us of the continuing necessity to establish Black studies within the academy through using the example of the decades-long struggle at York University. Here Black students continue to engage in scholarship on Black life and the production of Blackness as the locus of epistemology and pedagogy, staking a claim to be and belong to the university space in a context of Black unliveability and invisibility. In staking this claim they become Black on their own terms rather than within the institutional framing of "the Black student/academic/ administrator." Unliveability and invisibility point to institutional anti-Blackness.

For Mullings, misogynoir (Bailey and Trudy 2018) – that is, anti-Black woman misogyny – thrives in Canadian academia within the hypervisibility of Black women's bodies, even whilst their expertise is undermined and questioned. The violence of anti-Blackness continues to circulate and cause harm, such as at the levels of affect (Mendes; Blackett), psyche (Mullings; Kelly), knowledge production and epistemological affirmation (Lurch and McNeilly; Amponsah; Mullings; Dryden; Walker), and career possibilities and progression (Kelly; Smith). Anti-Blackness is institutionalized, as Dryden's chapter uses witnessing to show. Dryden begins with an analysis of the majority report at York University to illustrate that the harm of anti-Blackness continues, because "university established policies and practices are incapable of disrupting anti-Black racism," even with "the institutionalization of inclusion and diversity, welcoming environments and harassment and discrimination free zones."

Such institutionalized anti-Blackness, we *know*, we *feel* viscerally, whether through vicarious experiences or our own. Delores Mullings uses critical race auto-ethnography to engage with "the scars etched deeply" in her psyche because of the racism, sexism, and white power and privilege she experiences within the social work classroom focused on community service learning. Here an anti-oppressive perspective is paramount, but Black women professors are at increased risk of negative stereotyping and character assassination amid student claims of victimhood. This is the "fire" through which she has to walk as "social work students echo the normal mantra calling for the eradication of the Black woman faculty member's body." Using Black feminist auto-ethnography, Jennifer Kelly interrogates "the mutual embrace of racism and neoliberalism in higher education." Meditating on her own struggles within "the ivory tower" as a Black woman department chair at the University of Alberta, she reflects on the lack of support for Black academics in leadership roles who she sees as occupying a "border positioning." In the university, as in other institutions, "leadership is about performing sameness both physically and ideologically," whilst "institutional whiteness" disempowers and disables social change, curtailing Black faculty careers and dismissing Black complaints of racism. Malinda S. Smith shows the complexity of "Black Canadians" and "their experiences in universities" as a visible minority defined in the Employment Equity Act (1985) as non-white and non-Indigenous. Smith uses her "diversity gap research," where she developed an "intersectional equity approach to disaggregated data collection and analysis" to support her claim that "Black Canadian students, professors, and administrators often face an opportunities gap and barriers to advancement, realities reflected in the underrepresentation in the professoriate and in university leadership." She illustrates that equity in

Canadian university spaces has been about gender – read white women – with "identifiable infrastructure and resources that aim to achieve these ends." In marked contrast, racial equality and racial justice "have never been prioritized." Further, Smith's focus on the leaky Black student/ faculty/administrator/academic pipeline and individuals' experiences whilst in universities of racism, negation, being constituted as bodies out of place and lack of safety or support, completes a dire picture of Canadian anti-Blackness in educational institutions.

   Pervasive anti-Blackness is to be expected, if, like Barrington Walker, we take a perspective of the "historical present and its attendant anti-Black violence." Walker points out that the struggle for substantive rights has framed the Black experience in Canada throughout the history of Black presence, from enslavement, to indenture, to contemporary forms of un-freedom within "stupefying innocence" of Indigenous dispossession, white settler colonialism, enslavement, indenture, and BIPOC death as foundational in the creation of the Canadian racial state. This ensures that Black Canadians live over-policing, hyper-incarceration, higher unemployment, precarious employment, lower life expectancy, higher school dropout rates, and lower-than-average incomes.

Academic Activist Community and Agentic Survival

Even within what Smith describes as a period of "Black Canadian studies resurgence after a 1980s effort waned," Black faculty and students continue to have to survive anti-Blackness in classrooms and graduate programs, from colleagues and university administration, but also from each other. As Blackett shows in her pan-African "love story," harm from each other is worrying because of what seems to be a continuing political necessity to narrowly define who counts as "Black" and "African." For Blackett, we should invoke a Du Boisian expansive Black radical tradition, "insisting on the significance of our truth that flows through lived multiple but linked community experience." We could also, of course, include Marcus Garvey's (2004) pan-Africanist expansive view of Blackness here. For Blackett, there is a necessity "for now" to "be as one" politically. Indeed, we can also see this urgent need for unity in difference in the shared experiences of anti-Blackness and misogynoir within university spaces across all of the chapters. Blackett echoes Walker when she reminds us that white privilege as a form of property emerges through "the subordination of Blacks as the objects of property through slavery and the dispossession of Indigenous people of their land," which goes largely unchallenged within institutional claims that "equity matters." Her call for engaged critical scholarship and pedagogy that "sustains resistance to (re)colonizing spaces that promise freedom" speaks to the need for a Black feminist anti-racist decolonial politics and community.

The space of continuing pain, which universities often are for Black faculty and students, is also a "generative" one for politics, epistemology, and methodology as the Black intellectual speaks "her truth," inhabits university spaces, re-presents universities to herself, and engages in other visions of community. This means that, as in the Black radical tradition, "the university cannot and is not permitted to be our whole world, to define us" (Blackett in this volume). The chapters in this section make clear the urgency of decolonization and anti-racism if Black futurity is to become possible in universities that have failed to be cognizant of the particularities of Black experiences, expectations, and positionings. They also reinforce why the much-feted Canadian politeness and "niceness" (Smith 2003; Razack, Smith, and Thobani 2010), which insists on the governance of multiculturalism by consensus, has not yet engaged the struggle against anti-Blackness, decolonization, and anti-racism in universities.

Anti-racism, Decolonization, and Building Black Futurity

The chapters (see especially Dryden, Kelly, and Smith) question what more must be said and done within contexts with institutionalized equity policies, procedures, and bureaucracies to enable the long-awaited work of decolonization and anti-racism to finally begin. The issues presented here are well known, not just by Black scholars but by university administrations themselves. Yet we continue to see a strange inertia amidst a flurry of diversity activity where, as Sara Ahmed (2006) reminds us, equity, particularly racial equity, remains a non-performative, it is never achieved. The burden for leading change falls on those who experience anti-Blackness through an institutional whiteliness (Yancy 2015a, 2015b; Tate and Page 2018) produced by a white intersubjective matrix as a social, psychological, and phenomenological reality that whites see as benign (Yancy 2015a, 2015b). The chapters show that institutional whiteliness remains because white faculty, administrators, and students continue to benefit from the racial contract and its epistemologies of ignorance (Mills 1997, 2007), that Walker calls the "Canadian racial contract," in which Black people, and Black women in particular, continue to be located at the bottom of the racial hierarchy (Pateman and Mills 2007).

As shown by the Kelly and Dryden chapters, when faced with this Black truth, the usual reaction is white fragility (DiAngelo 2011, 2018) – which is a drawing inwards, a movement away from the discomfort caused to white Canadian niceness by experiences of anti-Black racism at white hands. The usual individual responses are either the speech of no response, denial (read: "I didn't know"), or projection and blaming Black faculty/students/administrators for being a "problem" (read: "You are taking this too personally"). And all of this while the institution's response continues to be "The problem is unconscious bias" (Tate and Page 2018). We continue to hear these all-too-familiar and problematic white Western Hemispheric responses to systemic inequities and note that they change nothing. So inured are we to these responses that if they do *not* occur, we are left to wonder, "What happened?" That happening is never a happy one, of course, but merely a prelude to more institutional pain and Black suffering under systems characterized by white supremacy.

These chapters show recurring suffering as anti-Black racism and misogynoir continue in universities, but they also show us how we can get past suffering and pain to action, individual thriving within toxic institutions, and Black futurity. Black scholars' strategies include "divesting in hegemonic, institutionalized whiteness ... investing in Black futures by redirecting professional energies to preparing the next generation of Black and racialized students to succeed in a sometimes hostile learning environment" (see Smith). This politics and commitment to action emanates from what Blackett describes as the vocation of the Black scholar whose focus is on pan-African love, where Black community is "home ... told through our truth, through the temporal recognition of the responsibility ... to be as one." Further, Black women faculty's "specific lived experiences" must not be devalued, nor should there be collusion with racist stereotypes "of the incompetent and illegitimate Black woman professor," as these "serve as a method ... to avoid reflexivity about the hegemonic nature of whiteness and white privilege" (see Mullings). As such, Black scholars, administrators, and leaders must "be adept at ... intersectional analysis ... to recognize the ways in which racialized power operates through institutional whiteness" (see Kelly). Black scholars, students, and administrators must be alive to the fact that the institutional whiteliness that undergirds equality and diversity in "Canadian academic institutions that claim to be 'welcoming' and 'inclusive'" means that claims to commitment to addressing racism can never be fulfilled. Awareness must then lead to political action, as in #BlackOnCampus, and addressing "the fallacy of race neutrality and the ineffectiveness of simply uttering 'this is a welcoming place'" (see Dryden).

In his critique of BLM in Canada, Walker reminds us that activists should look to history to engage aspects of the Black radical traditions: "Black Marxism, pan-Africanism, Garveyism, [and] Rastafarianism."

Without this engagement, "emancipatory possibilities are foreclosed, because the archive of Black freedom is not adequately mined." Remaining within the radical tradition of Black feminism, like bell hooks (1989), the Black Graduate Students' Collective embrace the margin as a position of radical possibility. From marginality they name oppression but also move "the apex of our discourse from overcoming to becoming. We move our discourse of countering, troubling, and interrupting violences and erasures by inhabiting and transforming spaces with the nuances of our multilayered presence, co-creating futures of belonging." It is in this Black futurity of presence becoming that decolonization will do its work to unsettle and transform institutional racism, anti-Blackness, and misogynoir as the un-ending sites of Black suffering intent on reproducing Black faculty, administrators, and students as white stereotypes. As Glissant (1997) reminds us, the work of decolonization will have been done when we go beyond white stereotypes and make ourselves anew, refuting the necessity of relationality with whiteliness to come into being. This entails a profound Black unsuturing from whiteness (Yancy 2015a, 2015b; Hall 1996).

Audre Lorde (1934–92) reminds us that in analysing Black suffering, Black feminist anti-racist action and caring for the self are necessary for Black futurity (Lorde 1980, 1988, 2007). Reading the chapters and thinking about the possible futures they lay out where Canadian universities and society are called to account for anti-Black dehumanization, I draw four lessons that intersect with Audre Lorde's work and insights – speaking against silencing, agency, empowerment, and building community. These lessons emerge powerfully from this section's chapters as methods for ensuring Black futurity. Lorde (1980) locates herself as a warrior in her response to the pain and silencing of cancer when compounded by the intersections of racism, sexism, and homophobia. She speaks out even as pain's despair alienates her from her body, making her see herself from a distance. In "The Transformation of Silence into Language and Action," Lorde writes about the activism initiated through words as a source of power to combat the lack of agency. She also insists on Black plurality in which we cannot be known only as and through skin.

Lorde analyses the erotic as a power located in our unrecognized feelings. We must recognize our deepest feelings to end the suffering caused by anti-Blackness, and as we come to see ourselves as subjects. This is the selfhood project of empowerment through affective transformation engaged by these chapters. As I read, I *feel* these chapters being utterly against Black suffering and self-negation, even whilst they speak agency with and through them. Following Lorde's erotic politics, within these chapters, subjectivities are reinforced at the same time as a political community is formed within and through the affective space produced by writing Black pain. This enables affective attachment and the construction of communities of Black scholars, intellectuals, and activists to develop ways of being beyond the anger caused by, and the pain of, anti-Blackness. After Lorde had been diagnosed with cancer for a second time, she located self-care as a radical political act (1988). It is not self-indulgence (see Smith). It is about self-preservation which is a practice of political warfare in a hostile world in which we "return the gaze" (Bannerji 1998; Razack 1998), stare down our pain in the face of hate, disdain, contempt, and hostility which often feels like, and is, too much to bear. This political warfare based on well-being is essential for Black futurity. The self-care produced from the writing in these chapters, where Black scholar activists as readers can see themselves, their thoughts, knowledge systems, experiences, and methodologies reflected, helps us to go beyond mere survival. It helps us to thrive as we see and bring into being the Black feminist decolonial anti-racist futurity, which must be aimed for.

In this section contributors ask that we not give in to the negation of the pain of institutional and societal anti-Blackness in our everyday and university lives. They instead encourage us to recognize our pain and to use it as a starting point for agency. Speaking opens us up to vulnerability, but also illuminates the way forward through breaking institutional silencing, building communities of love, trust, and support, and continuing the necessary work on a politics of Black feminist decolonial anti-racist liberation.

REFERENCES

Ahmed, S. 2006. "The Nonperformativity of Antiracism." *Meridians* 7 (1): 104–126. https://doi.org/10.2979/MER.2006.7.1.104.
Bailey, M., and Trudy. 2018. "On Misogynoir: Citation, Erasure, and Plagiarism." *Feminist Media Studies* 18 (4): 762–768 https://doi.org/10.1080/14680777 .2018.1447395.
Bannerji, H. 1998. *Returning the Gaze*. Toronto: Sister Vision Press.
Bernardino-Costa, J., Maldonado-Torres, N., and Grosfoguel, R. 2018. *Decoloniadade e Pensamento Afrodiaspórico*. Brasilia: Autêntica.
Christian, M., ed. 2012. *Integrated but Unequal: Black Faculty in Predominantly White Space*. New Jersey: Africa World Press.
DiAngelo, R. 2011. "White Fragility." *International Journal of Critical Pedagogy* 3 (3): 54–70.
DiAngelo, R. 2018. *White Fragility: Why It's So Hard for White People to Talk about Racism*. Boston: Beacon Press.

Emejulu, A., and Sobande, F., eds. 2019. *To Exist Is to Resist: Black Feminism in Europe*. London: Pluto Press

Gabriel, D., and Tate, S.A., eds. 2017. *Inside the Ivory Tower: Narratives of Women of Colour Surviving and Thriving in British Academia*. London: IOE/Trentham Books.

Garvey, M. 2004. *Selected Writings and Speeches of Marcus Garvey*. Mineola, NY: Dover Publications.

Glissant, E. 1997. *Poetics of Relation*. Ann Arbor: University of Michigan Press.

Hall, S. 1996. "Introduction: Who Needs Identity?" In *Questions of Cultural Identity*, edited by S. Hall and P. du Gay, 3–17. Thousand Oaks, CA: SAGE Press.

hooks, b. 1989. "Choosing the Margin as a Space of Radical Openness." *Framework: The Journal of Cinema and Media* 36: 15–23.

Jansen, J.D., ed. 2019. *Decolonisation in Universities: The Politics of Knowledge*. Johannesburg: Wits University Press.

Lorde, A. 1980. *The Cancer Journals*. San Francisco: Aunt Lute Books.

Lorde, A. 1988. *A Burst of Light: Essays*. Ann Arbor, MI: Firebrand Books.

Lorde, A. 2007. *Sister Outsider: Essays and Speeches*. Berkeley, CA: Crossing Press.

Mills, C. 1997. *The Racial Contract*. Ithaca, NY: Cornell University Press.

Mills, C. 2007. "White Ignorance." In *Race and Epistemologies of Ignorance*, edited by S. Sullivan and N. Tuana, 11–38. New York: State University of New York Press.

Pateman, C., and Mills, C. 2007. *The Contract and Domination*. London: Polity.

Razack, S. 1998. *Looking White People in the Eye: Gender, Race and Culture in the Courtrooms and Classrooms*. Toronto: University of Toronto Press.

Razack, S., Smith, M.S., and S. Thobani, eds. 2010. *States of Race: Critical Race Feminism for the 21st Century*. Toronto: Between the Lines Press.

Smith, M.S. 2003. "'Race Matters' and 'Race Manners.'" In *Reinventing Canada: Politics of the 21st Century*, edited by J. Brodie and L. Trimble, 108–130. Hoboken, NJ: Prentice Hall.

Tate, S.A., and Page, D. 2018. "Whiteliness and Institutional Racism: Hiding behind (Un)Conscious Bias." *Ethics and Education* 13 (1): 141–155. https://doi.org/10.1080/17449642.2018.1428718

Yancy, G. 2015a. "Dear White America." *The New York Times*, 24 December.

Yancy, G. 2015b. "Introduction." In *White Criticality beyond Anti-Racism: How Does It Feel to Be a White Problem?*, edited by Yancy, xi–xxvii. Washington, DC: Lexington Books.

16 (Re)situating Black Studies at York University: Unsilencing the Past, Locating the Present, Routing Futures

THE YORK UNIVERSITY BLACK GRADUATE STUDENTS' COLLECTIVE[1]
JAN-THERESE MENDES, CHARMAINE LURCH, MOSA MCNEILLY,
EVELYN AMPONSAH, AND OLA MOHAMMED

Althea Prince (2001) recalls efforts by students and faculty in the early 1970s to establish a Black presence at York University (55). Her narrative laments the efforts of subsequent scholars at the university strategizing to establish a Black intellectual community without reflecting on the broader historical context of this work. Hence, Prince offers a corrective that interrupts the ways forgetting and subsequent erasures of the past can culminate in its disjointed repetition (55–7). Taking Prince's call to acknowledge the past seriously, this chapter describes our current efforts as five Black graduate students in various academic disciplines to recognize, build upon, and insert ourselves into this historical narrative as part of the ongoing task to situate Black studies as a critical component of York University. The theoretical aspects of our research enquire into and are shaped by what it means to be Black students engaged in scholarship on Black life without institutional or structural support. By locating our work and ourselves within the university, this chapter aims to describe some of the ways Black scholarship and life are institutionally rendered unliveable and perpetually relegated to the regions of the academy that are intended to be kept out of sight and out of mind. Our writings intentionally resound with the ways this peripheral, meant-to-be discarded Blackness can alternatively be politically inhabited as a resistive, inspiring, and enduringly valuable space of knowing as well as being. With contributions from selected members of the Black Graduate Student Collective (BGSC), this chapter provides details about how we seek to do this work by offering one another emotional support; asserting the legitimacy of cultural production as artists within a larger Black community; encouraging and mentoring the prospective scholarship of Black undergraduates as part of noting and upsetting the systemic and cyclical oversight in allocating resources and space to meet these students' needs; as well as by representing, archiving, and promoting Black graduate work in the conscious effort to seek out and speak with/to the historical narrative(s) of Black scholarship. Our main objective is to convey how, in collaboratively working to forge a centralized, social-intellectual community through the BGSC, we enact a formal/ized speaking back. We locate and establish Black student activism, past and present, as a collective force that can begin to make demands on/of the institution as we mobilize community, consciously locate our scholarship, and re-imagine the work that lies ahead at York University.

Emotional Support: Affirming the Affective Knowledges of Black Bodies in Place

Jan-Therese Mendes

By conveying the perpetual reluctance of Canadian academic institutions to recognize the existence of and/or the necessity to respond to racial concerns, except when compelled by "racial crisis," Francis Henry et al. (2006) recount, "During the mid-1980s ... York University established a committee on race and ethnic relations only because a graduate student in a residence was consistently subjected to racial harassment. The student was first told by the manager of the residence that she was *'too sensitive.'* When she complained to her department, little was done ... Concluding that the university was not prepared to deal with the issue, she mobilized her fellow students of colour" (245; emphasis added). What does it mean to be "too sensitive" in the midst of racial aggressions within the Canadian academy? How does the charge of being too sensitive also mean to be too emotional or to have the wrong kind of emotions in the particular space of the university? From which bodies does the affective or emotional reaction to quotidian institutionalized racism appear to be in excess, inappropriate, or uncomfortably out of place? Alternatively, how can the collective acknowledgment of the realness of the "psychic pain" (Ahmed 2014, 31) of racist encounters within the university operate as a type of critical support between Black graduate students whereby the emotional is witnessed and affirmed as a legitimate site of knowing and of being (Boler 1999; Henry 1998)? In this formulation the recognition of pain acts not as a cultivated or fetishized woundedness but as an affective politic (see Ahmed 2012). Although Henry et al. (2006) detail a series of events that are now decades past, the minimizing or disappearing of lived encounters of racist violence by/within the university remains as a familiar visceral experience or "bad feeling" for students of colour in general and Black graduate students in particular. As such, the critical narratives of Black

Canadian scholars – writing of their own or others' confrontation with institutionalized racial hostilities – communicates the disparagement of one's needs (Bullen 2007, 155); the continual negation of one's being (Carty 1991, 13); as well as the perpetual senses of alienation, isolation, and discontent (Bullen 2007, 155; Mogadime 2002, 142, 145) that continues amid the vested reproduction of Eurocentric power and privilege (Douglas 2012, 50; Carty 1991, 16, 34).

Megan Boler (1999) emphasizes that education as a social institution not only structures our values and possible becomings but also operates as a primary mechanism for "maintain[ing] the status quo … and of enforcing social control of the nation's citizens" (xiv).Boler thus puts forth the premise that within the realm of education emotions are conjointly made to function in the interest of social control (xiv), working in part to discipline and to subjugate (xxi). To "feel *power*" thus entails comprehending and performing "our appropriate roles of subordination and domination … through learned emotional expressions and silences" (xvii), which enunciate the dictates of "dominant discourses of emotion" that regulate and shape students in the affective realm of the classroom or the institution at large (xiv, 5). Extending this reasoning to think through some of the realities of Black scholars,[2] we propose that notions of rational and thus rightly felt feelings neither encapsulate the embodied expressions that oppose or call attention to racial injustice. That is, such upsets as these are not to be counted amongst the right feelings by or against the proper people; rather they are always "too much" as emotions in-excess and out of place. Silences discipline. Without the dominant institutional-cultural space for the hurt of anti-Black racism to be either spoken or heard the void of this emotional silence silences, while it simultaneously disciplines Black selves into subordination. Dolana Mogadime's (2002) writings on Black women in graduate school in Canada relay the questions of doubtful belonging that students pose to themselves as they are met with the seeming comfort and content of white graduate colleagues while their own unhappiness pervades (145). As Sara Ahmed (2012) suggests, it is the whiteness around which the institution is oriented that must be made comfortable or maintained in its comfort. Accordingly, non-white-appearing bodies are expected to "minimiz[e] the signs of difference" in order to not disturb this quality of ease (41). The contentment Black graduate students read in surrounding white bodies is therefore a comfort that belongs to whiteness. Specifically, the emotionality of being comfortable (which is perhaps the "happiness" Black students register as being outside their own state of feeling) is made to appear as a "bodily trait" of whiteness that *secures a social hierarchy* "between emotions" (Ahmed 2014, 3, 4). The affective expressions of Black pain, hurt, lonesomeness, anger, or discontent can be conceived as "lower," "unruly emotions" (3) (again, the "too much" or "too sensitive") whose threat to an "elevated" (3) white comfort and happiness must be disciplined back into invisible place.

Returning to our early queries we thus ask, What would it mean to re-orient and re-inhabit the site of emotions as a legitimate space as/for Black graduate students whereby the existence of our psychic pain can be acknowledged through/despite its institutional silencings and also accorded the status of alternative, productive knowledges? Borrowing from and inspired by Black Canadian feminist scholars' assertions of the resistive possibilities that can emerge as Black women intellectuals validate and incorporate ways of knowing that come from the "outside" (see Carty 1991, 23; Henry 1998, 126–7; Wane 2002, 176), we of the BGSC aim to claim the affective as an *appropriate*, acceptable mode of knowing. Specifically, we register the pain of racism as a persistent truth of what it means and how it feels to reside within the university as Black selves since the anti-Black racism that orients our social worldstakes familiar affective shape within the institution of higher learning. In this way, uncomfortable feelings that are meant to be relegated to the academic outside are recognized and thus repositioned as part of the emotional knowledges of bodies *inside* (i.e., both how our bodies feel on the psychic plane of our "insides" as well as how we feel as bodies inside the academy, however marginal). A critical component of verifying these knowledges is the necessary practice of bearing witness to one another's pain through our shared narratives. The experiences of racist aggressions that are often endured during our graduate seminars, (in)formal encounters with university faculty and staff, and at times during the tutorials we lead become occurrences that – through the interchange of their retelling and a conscious listening – are able to occupy a legitimized platform of emotional knowing. In this way, dinners, car rides to and from conferences, spontaneous telephone conversations and text messages, periods of pause during or after meetings, impromptu connections at artistic events, hushed exchanges in the library book stacks, pointed divulgences following a tense seminar, as well as intermittent or organized exchanges throughout an assembly of the BGSC are all moments that become critically imbued with our recountings. Painful chronicles are therefore affectively documented as well as collectively authenticated through a supportive listening and its likely lament. Here the sometimes violent yet often, subdued ache of the racist encounter is recognized as "a happening in the world" (Ahmed 2014, 30) through each other so that our response to the ache is not a poorly disciplined emotion but a valid visceral articulation to what indeed hurts.

Considering the potential trappings of politicized identities that are structured through *ressentiment*,[3] Wendy Brown (1995) describes, and perhaps cautions against, what can become an investment in one's subjection (70) and an attachment to one's own exclusion (74). In particular, Brown explains that politicized identities whose existence stems from and requires the continuance of their exclusion come to rely upon this marginalization as a "site of blame" to locate suffering so that pain is ultimately entrenched as the foundation of the political (74). It is important to emphasize that even as we affirm the realness of our wounds, it is not the hurt of institutional anti-Black racism in itself that we attach to or seek to maintain; our pain is neither held onto as a form of "good" feeling in the pursuit of collective organizing nor in the desire for a recognition or displacement of suffering. In acknowledging the emotional as a knowledge and presence, pain does not operate as *the* centre of our politics but is instead critically understood to be an element that can be a part of the political. In this way, emotional support within the BGSC does not rely upon or evoke an ideology of absolute sameness, which assumes stable, mirrored, and thus wholly shareable experiences of racist subjugation since our social locations and identities (i.e., mixedness, queerness, being a parent) refuse this form of collapse. We instead offer each other the opportunity to be heard and seen (even if not fully understood) as feeling selves whose emotional responses, needs, and modes of knowing can be affirmed as being in place.

Reimagining Black Presence in the Academe: Through Research Methodologies Grounded in Art and Performance

Charmaine Lurch and Mosa McNeilly

Dash, and other cultural producers, present new epistemologies, in fact create sight and knowledge where there was not any before ... [She] invents a new optic ... that enables one to see what the limits of modernity's privileged epistemology of sight hides.

– Tiffany Lethabo King (2013)

As Black women artists and researchers, we engage with ideas through embodied methodologies. These methodologies centre visuality and performance as critical languages of discourse and counter the primacy of the written word in academia. Positioning the Black female subject as a multiply-inscribed site of research, we challenge the systemic anti-Black racism that affects the erasure of Black scholarship. By claiming physical

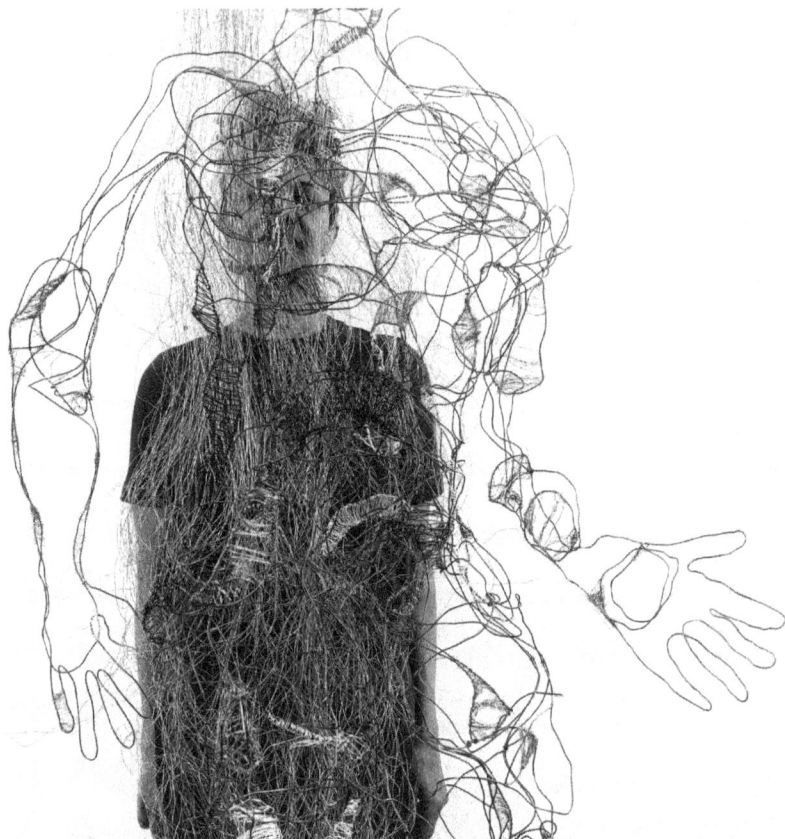

Figure 16.1. *Sycorax Scene II*, by Charmaine Lurch, 2020. Photo print on archival paper, 24" x 24" (courtesy of the artist). Photo by Hannah Zbitnew.

and epistemological space in which our work can exist, we contribute to fostering a robust and resilient Black student presence in the academe.

Charmaine Lurch

Envisioning Black studies at York University, particularly work that is grounded in arts-based research centred on the Black female subject, requires me to consider space as integral to marking past and making current Black presence visible. I'm thinking about space in two ways – physical and psychological space – to organize and share ideas, and further, to manage the way our work is disseminated and consumed.

Creating and claiming space can aid Black students in manoeuvring the often inhospitable terrains of the university industrial complex.

Grace Kyungwon Hong (2008) examines this terrain through a Black feminist lens. Hong draws on Barbara Christian's (1994) descriptions of mechanisms of exclusion – the very structure and design of the systems of learning and the representations of knowledge, and how they work to keep Black feminists out. Christian suggests that the "fetishization of Black feminism as intellectual inquiry" can lead to violence against Black women scholars and serve to exclude them from involvement in "Black feminist inquiry" (96). This kind of violence sets in place the ("absent presence/ present absence" McNeilly 2015) of Black feminists from "encoding and decoding" (Hall 1993) the shared and psychological spaces we work in.

Tina Garnett, in her graduate studies at York University, described a common experience that many Black students must navigate. She says, of her ongoing efforts to get paid for her work as a graduate assistant, "The institutional barriers are exhausting, in conjunction with the academic research being personal and taxing on our very existence" (T. Garnett, personal communication, 9 January 2016). These sentiments, echoed across faculties, reveal the many micro-aggressions we confront in institutional spaces. How do we begin to address these aggressions? And how can we interrupt the systems of structural erasure, leave signs, and make maps so that others can follow? Creating archives, reciting names, and managing Black collective knowledge in the university remains critical in addressing these issues. This imperative to create archives has mobilized members of the Black Graduate Students Collective to inscribe our poetics, past and present, and imagined futures on the walls in the halls of the academe.

In response to my painting *Affair 1969* at the Body | Institution | Memory Symposium, Trinidad 2014, Marsha Pearce points out how art is used to challenge the erasure of Black presence within the university industrial complex.[4] The painting references the Sir George Williams Affair, 1969, an example of institutional racism that has been described as the largest student riot in Canadian history. Charges of racism were brought against a white professor who was failing all the Black students in his class. This resulted in a peaceful protest that turned into a riot when met with police aggression (Austin 2013). "Lurch attends to the question: How does the body signify in the context of memory and institution? She provides answers, first in relation to memory, by pointing us to the way in which the body can act as a signifier of a particular position in an event or experience: the students who participated in the sit-in of 1969; the onlookers and so on; as well as Lurch as artist many years later" (Pearce 2013, 2).

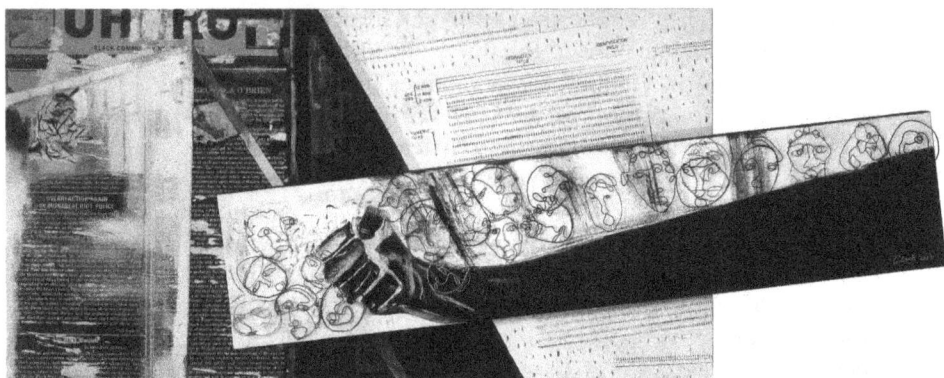

Figure 16.2. *Affair 1969*, by Charmaine Lurch, 2015. Acrylic and wire on wood, 24" x 62" (courtesy of the artist). Photo by Charmaine Lurch.

Sharing this painting and my research on this historical event has shown me how very few Black students, and people in general, know of this significant Canadian event. The Sir George Williams Affair has made clear the extent to which Black activism in academia has been erased from Canadian consciousness; however, though invisible, their collective action set mechanisms in place for reporting injustices and initiating procedures and policies, which laid the foundations that are available to *all* students today. It changed the way universities respond to students. Arts-based theoretical research can help to remind us of the work that has been done and what still is left to do. This is not just a story about collective Black activism. It's also about how these forms of art can be used to tell this story so it's not lost; and to share this history with a new student body so they can build on what has been done before.

As Black graduate students, sharing our personal encounters with racism is never easy. Anthony Stewart eloquently illustrates that discrimination, inherent to the systemic structures within academia, pressures Black people "admitted to the club" to stick to specific formulaic behaviours. Stewart describes his decision to discuss a personal experience of a racist incident instead of his planned talk on Chinua Achebe's *Things Fall Apart* (1958), and how it taught him a valuable lesson: "It would have been right for me to talk about Achebe in the expected way – academically, dispassionately, according to the frame of reference we'd agreed upon in advance – but to incorporate into the seminar room the personal experience of the only person in the room who had actually encountered the effects of racial devaluation in the post-colonial world was to breach the rules of the club and, as I felt at the time and on numerous occasions since, to risk my membership in the club altogether" (Stewart 2004, 36).

Stewart illustrates the importance of breaching the rules in order to claim psychological space for our voices to be heard. We also need physical space in the institution to form connections across the academy, where we can provide intellectual support, build archives, and create and maintain community (Prince 2001). In this way we build an empowered and resilient graduate collective.

In the Faculty of Environmental Studies at York University there are few cultural production courses that offer opportunities to study the intersections of race, gender, and class through arts-based research. These courses rely on two small community arts spaces – Crossroads and Wild Garden Media Centre – where much of the coursework is developed and shared. Crossroads attracts projects, performances, installations, and workshops with themes on social and environmental justice. Though this is not a designated space for Black students, it is one of the few spaces in the Faculty of Environmental Studies where Black students gather informally. The enormous efforts of a few professors and graduate assistants provide, protect, and forge this workshop space. Though this institutional space comes with many limitations, the seminal works produced at Crossroads by students of colour are able to have an audience of peers, faculty, and community members. The inaugural event, the Contemporary Urgencies of Audre Lorde's Legacy (2013), brought together over five hundred activists, scholars, artists, and organizations from around Toronto, including Women and Gender Studies Institute at the University of Toronto; and Community Arts Practice Program and the Faculty of Liberal Arts and Professional Studies at York University. Crossroads was the venue in which we workshopped our collaborative production, *Refusing the Imaginary of Fungibility: The Black Female Body in Flux*, and provided the space we needed to move our work forward.

Mosa McNeilly

In a sombre palette of black, brown, and white, the stylized torso of a Black woman fills the frame. A large bird flies out from behind her head across a dark sky. Her face, reminiscent of an African ceremonial mask, is tilted at a dramatic angle. With one breast exposed, she holds one hand to her solar plexus and extends the other palm forward. The diamond-shaped spiral pattern on her dress echoes the zig-zag pattern of her locks. The dichotomy of her gentleness and strength is conveyed by two contrasting styles in the rendering of her body – fluid, brown, hand-drawn lines and thick, black, angular shapes.

Figure 16.3. *Mystic Warrior*, by Mosa McNeilly, 1989. Mixed media monoprint on mulberry paper, 24" x 37" (courtesy of the artist). Photo by John Scully.

I begin with a work of art depicting a Black woman to convey the polyvalence of Black feminist cultural production as a critical form of discourse. Employing an image serves to privilege visuality; the description of the work suggests an engagement with radical imagination as a frame of reference to decipher the embedded layers of meaning; and an artwork of and by a Black woman signals the centring of Black female subjectivity. In order to access the knowledges layered within such a hybrid, a critical engagement with a pastiche of methodologies is required. Engaging visuality, Black feminist thought, Black radical imagination, and embodied knowledge production are critical modes of research and distinct vocabularies of discourse. These modes and vocabularies counter the coloniality of academic research that disregards and discredits Black diasporic knowledges – how they move, how they are understood, and how they are allowed to exist in academia. I embark here on theorizing a performative work entitled *Refusing the Imaginary of Fungibility: The Black Female Body in Flux,*[5] to illustrate the engagement with the modes of research I am proposing, as King states, "My interdisciplinary method is committed to a simultaneity of vision. This simultaneous and syncretizing way of seeing and knowing is an epistemic tradition of Black and Women of Colour cultural workers, spiritualists and intellectuals" (King 2013, 17).

Incorporating visual art, installation, and movement, Charmaine Lurch and I co-created and mounted a collaborative performance that speaks to the construct of the Black female body as fungible. In this work we respond to Tiffany Lethabo King's (2013) dissertation, *In the Clearing*, and pay homage to Julie Dash's lush cinematic masterpiece, *Daughters of the Dust* (1991). We offer our audience a glimpse of the decolonized Black female body through the eyes of two Black women artists gazing upon one another.

Contrapuntal, embodied, and improvisational, this performance integrates drawing, movement, and installation. Banners hung from the ceiling represent the optic of simultaneous vision, in which we explore visual representations of disappearance and emergence, presence and absence. We represent the disappeared Indigenous presence with two ceremonial shakers resting upon a piece of deer hide, reminiscent of an altar, and echoing the Indigenous cosmologies of ceremony and communion with the land. A sterling silver tea set, filled to overflowing with soil, represents the settler's consumption of the land that he exploits, and the imposing presence of the settlement, even in the absence of the settler himself. A long piece of white paper with drawing materials suggests this as a site of imminent cultural production.

The action begins with repetitive movement motifs symbolic of the toil of Black female labour on the plantation – scooping, lifting, digging, planting, washing clothes, sweeping, and stirring the cauldron. We take turns replacing each other and imitating each other's movements. As each one is replaced, she disappears and re-emerges from behind the banners in a cyclical flow representing flux.

As the piece progresses, we set out to transform fungibility into solidarity by overwriting the dehumanization of the Black female body with sensuality and transformed vision. Unravelling the motifs of repetitive movement, we begin to occupy and define space in individual irreplicable ways. By shifting into moving in simultaneity rather than sequentially, and then by allowing our movements to interact with each other, we trouble fungibility and reimagine it as solidarity. By taking turns draping each other in cloth and drawing one another, and by virtue of the

Figure 16.4. Digital still of Charmaine Lurch from *Refusing the Imaginary of Fungibility: The Black Female Body in Flux,* by Charmaine Lurch and Mosa McNeilly, 2014 (courtesy of the artists). Performed at Crossroads Gallery, York University, 2014. Film footage courtesy of Allos Abis.

stillness that this engenders, we draw the audience into contemplating the transformation of the Black female body into an embodied subject. We reimagine the Black female body as a site of humanity worthy and capable of tenderness and love.

Each time we performed *Refusing the Imaginary of Fungibility,* Lurch and I were affected by the responses from Black women in the audience – tears, resonance, and heartfelt gratitude. We reflected on how the agency of Black women's embodied practices of art and performance within the context of academia can counter the violences of erasure and catalyze the spiritual work of healing. Black women's responses reveal that this work speaks to those who possess a "hunger for transcendence" (Somé 1997, 18); those who recognize the oppressions and thirst for freedom. By modelling the centring of Black female subjectivity, by

Figure 16.5. Digital still of Mosa McNeilly from *Refusing the Imaginary of Fungibility: The Black Female Body in Flux*, by Charmaine Lurch and Mosa McNeilly, 2014 (courtesy of the artists). Performed at Crossroads Gallery, York University, 2014. Film footage courtesy of Allos Abis.

reorienting the representation of our knowledges and our bodies, we move from the margins of "modernity's secularized episteme" (Alexander 2005, 7) to the centre of the discourse and praxes that our work engages. Working through embodied research methodologies to reframe a humanizing imaginary of Black female subjectivity suggests a palimpsestic repertoire of praxes geared towards freedom.

As Black women artists and researchers, it has been our experience that presenting art and performance as theoretical work remains on the periphery of what is considered academic discourse. Discussing Barbara Christian's analysis of Black feminist presence in the academy, Hong states that "she makes an important point in which the conditions for knowledge production are determined by assumptions about what counts as knowledge" (Hong 2008, 103). As part of the Black Graduate Students

Figure 16.6. Digital still of Mosa McNeilly and Charmaine Lurch from *Refusing the Imaginary of Fungibility: The Black Female Body in Flux*, by Charmaine Lurch and Mosa McNeilly, 2014 (courtesy of the artists). Performed at Crossroads Gallery, York University, 2014. Film footage courtesy of Allos Abis.

Collective, we were able to respond to these assumptions by presenting our artistic work in the unexpected context of academic panels at conferences. Art and performance are often cloistered and framed as enhancements to the substance of the conference – the literary discourse. Being part of a panel enabled us to interrupt the normative constructs of "what counts as knowledge" (Hong 2008) by occupying and using space in unconventional ways. Transforming space in the intimate setting of seminar rooms affects and implicates the audience in visceral ways, demanding more than participating as passive spectators. Working through research methodologies grounded in art and performance, our work can encourage other Black students to reimagine Black presence in the academe and centre creative ways of knowing and producing within and as part of the collective.

A Pedagogy of Support for Black Undergraduate Students

Evelyn Amponsah

As part of our praxis, the BGSC works to encourage the prospective scholarship of Black undergraduates at York University. We situate this work as part of a larger historical tradition within the African-Canadian community that has seen parents and community members step in and up to fill gaps in the education system (Calliste 1996). As graduate students who are also teaching assistants, we recognize our unique and advantageous position within the academy to connect with and support Black undergraduate students. Further, as graduate students, who have gone through the process of applying for and successfully getting into graduate school, we have knowledges that would support Black undergraduates interested in taking up similar endeavours. Working to support Black undergraduate students is important to the BGSC as our investment in anti-racism, specifically anti-Black racism, requires that we not only think about how we are affected by anti-Blackness but how Black undergraduates are as well. We further recognize that the lack of support and resources from the university dedicated to Black undergraduates at York University is part of a cycle that makes the academy "anything but comfortable for faculty and students of colour" (Caliste 2000). While we fully understand the ways in which anti-Black racism is imbedded in the systemic nature of the academy, we endeavour to do what we can, in the ways that we can to create space for future Black graduate work at York. Canadian political philosopher C.B. Macpherson (2014) includes in his definition of possessive individualism,[6] a lack of intergenerational mentoring. The BGSC refuses to participate in the possessive individualism we see in the academy and instead recognize that "anti-racism entails a recognition of the individual and collective responsibility to use multiple positions and differential locations of power, privilege and social disadvantage to work for change" (Dei 2000).

In the fall of 2014, I was assigned as the teaching assistant for Intro to African Studies, a second-year course at York University. On the first day of tutorial I was surprised to see that the entire class of twenty-five students were all African descended. Over the course of the semester, a unique bond developed. I attribute this to a classroom of Black students being engaged by a teaching assistant who had an investment in anti-racism and anti-Black racism. Dei and Calliste (2000) define anti-racism as "an action-oriented, education and political strategy for institutional and systemic change that addresses the issues of racism and the interlocking systems of social oppression" (13). I walked away from this experience realizing how significantly positive it could be for Black students to be in an academic setting with other Black students and a Black instructor in a moment of high racial tension as the killing of Michael Brown and the protests in Ferguson were the backdrop to the semester. While students were attempting to digest the tragedies relating to Black bodies and police brutality in the media, each class was an opportunity to be action-oriented around anti-Black racism, creating space to not only unpack the tragedies but also to ground students in the historical conditions that such violence arises from.

Being in a classroom with all Black students reminded me of the significant population of Black undergraduate students at York University and prompted me to think about and share a concern expressed by Dei and Kempf (2013, 123): "We must face some difficult challenges to assess whether some teachers possess the requisite qualifications, knowledge, and skill sets to teach the young learners of culturally and racially diverse populations." What opportunity would have been missed and what opportunities are missed when instructors who have a "skills deficit" (Dei and Kempf 2014) in anti-racism are the authorities in teaching spaces? As Black graduate students, many of us have access to and are invested in scholarship that aims to promote anti-racism. As members of the BGSC, we have made a commitment to Black studies at York University and therefore have both an opportunity and a responsibility to fill the skills deficit that many teachers in the university in general lack. As we are aware that there may not always be the opportunity to be TAs in classrooms, or that the reach in these cases is limited to our students, the BGSC provided anti-Black racism talks on campus open to all students and teaching assistants. The goal of these conversations was to provide strategies for students and teaching assistants to address racism in classrooms. The first workshop we held saw an attendance of over thirty people – a racially diverse group of students from various disciplines, graduate students and teaching assistants. The numbers tell us that many students are not only concerned with but also invested in anti-racism.

York University, along with many other universities, has made a commitment to increase representation among groups that are historically under-privileged and under-represented. In the past these commitments were recognized through access programs (James and Manette 2000). "Access programs [were] often understood to be post-secondary institutional responses to the ideological disruption to the university ethos" (76). While these access programs translated into larger representation for marginalized groups, there still needed to be more work done in how these groups were engaged in the academy. For James and Mannette (2000, 86), "Access, then, is more than just gaining access into the university; for, once in university, students must be provided an academic environment in which the curricula, pedagogy and social relationships are conducive to their learning, welcoming of their participation in all areas of university life and responsive to their needs, interests and expectations."

The experiences of many Black students at York indicate that students are not being provided with the previously mentioned supports. The BGSC aligns its mission with a historical tradition that has seen Black students at Canadian universities fill this gap. Frederick Ivor Case (1996, 206) notes, "The tradition of resistance to the cultural determination of our children and to the psychological limits placed on their growth continued until the 1960s when African Canadian university students of York University and University of Toronto together with other educators founded the Black Education Project and the Transitional year program."

This, Case states, was the initiating of the first major school-community-university partnerships. Case further notes other examples of school-community-university partnerships including visits from high school students to university campuses with a focus on or on visits to programs where certain groups are underrepresented, such as female high-school students visiting programs that are dominated by males. York University Black Students Association (YUBSA) at York University continues this type of partnership through their mentoring program that targets Black high school students interested in post-secondary education. While there is support for mentoring Black high-school students, there is indeed a gap for mentoring Black undergraduate students to encourage and promote graduate scholarship. The BGSC recognized this and directed energy to filling this gap. To begin, we facilitated a "Applying While Black" workshop, which focused on providing Black undergraduate students with support on options for graduate school, how to apply, writing statements, and choosing schools.

Our interest in promoting Black undergraduate access to graduate school is rooted in our concern for shaping the academy in a way that produces significant change. We attribute the lack of Black faculty to racist hiring practices, but we also see it as a result of systemic barriers that prevent Black people from accessing and completing PhD programs. By supporting a group of interested individuals to apply for graduate school, we hope to increase the number of Black undergraduates securing graduate school spots, therefore increasing the number of graduates in both master's and PhD programs, leading to an increase in the number of Black faculty at universities. We further position ourselves on admissions committees in our various departments, where we are part of reviewing graduate application forms. This task is particularly important because we know that admission committees seldom recognize work on Blackness as important or scholarly. Notable here is the experience of one BGSC member who sat on an MA admission committee where she was the only woman and only Black person. The other members were three older white men who were faculty members and one other white male who was a graduate student. While reviewing the files, the chair repeatedly skipped over her when it was time for input on files. Though a specific incident, the BGSC recognizes that representation on admission committee is necessary for increasing representation of Black graduate students.

We do this work in the interest of students but also in the interest of the limited number of Black faculty who supervise Black graduate students. Essentially becoming our "school parents," these faculty support us not only because our research interests align, but also and often more so because they understand the lack of support and the disadvantages Black graduate students face in the academy. These faculty members are just as overworked and under-resourced as students, while also facing anti-Black sentiments in the academy. Might it be possible that through inspiring and promoting more Black undergraduates to take up graduate work, we might reduce the pressure on faculty and isolation of Black graduate students in general? We look to these faculty members as our mentors within the academy. They over-extend themselves so that we may do important work. We therefore model our relationships with Black undergraduates after the relationship we have with these faculty. We must reciprocate their kindness, support, and love in order to support Black undergraduates, even if this adds an additional layer of work on us.

Henry A. Giroux (2002) identifies neoliberalism as the defining economic paradigm of our time. He looks specifically at the ways in which the university is increasingly run like a corporation, more concerned with spending less and making more, rather than an investment in critical scholarship. While this section is both a narrative and an account of what the BGSC is doing to support Black undergraduate students, it is also a critique of the university and its participation in neoliberalism, which sees the university downloading its responsibilities onto students. If students do not do this work, then it will not be done at all, and the BGSC recognizes that this work must be done. It would irresponsible of us to suggest that all Black graduate students can invest time and energy in this work and to not acknowledge that the gaps identified are a shortcoming of the university. Students, much like Black faculty, are overworked, under-paid, and are expected to produce, produce, produce. We have taken up this work and are committed to ensuring our success; however, this work should not fall solely on students who are already under-privileged, over-worked, and under-resourced. Giroux (2002, 457) tells us, "The current regime of neoliberalism and the incursion of corporate power into higher education present difficult problems and demand a profoundly committed sense of collective resistance." The BGSC participates and attempts to organize as part of this collective resistance; we also show our resistance through our support and commitment at the grassroots level.

Grammarians of the York Black Studies Archive

Ola Mohammed

In a statement published on 28 March 1991 in *Excalibur,* The Ad-hoc Committee for the Rights and Dignity of the Black Academic Community recalled the efforts of a group, along with students and allies, to combat anti-Black racism that had been published in the same school newspaper the previous February. Beyond the committee's recounting of the earlier event, they wrote,

> In the same spirit that we recognize that the dismissal of the editor was only a small step towards addressing the issue of institutional racism ... we are conscious that Excalibur does not exist in a vacuum and are convinced that this is part of the larger problem of institutional racism which goes unchecked at this university. Institutional racism has manifested itself in a number of ways. We feel that it is noteworthy that Toronto is the home of the largest Black population in Canada. We at York constitute the largest Black academic community in Canada. The issues that Black students faced in the 1970s are the same issues which Black students face in the 1990s. (1991, 8)

This clear identification of structural anti-Black racism that the ad hoc committee recognized as part of York's historical mistreatment of Black intellectuals is not a part of narratives that publicly celebrate York as a progressive institution. Rather, they exist in what we connect to Anthony Bogues's definition of *a different set of archives.* Traditionally archives are understood as "both documents of exclusion and monuments to particular configurations of power" (Bogues 2012, 31). When thinking of Black intellectual life, and its presence in traditional academic archives – particularly in Canadian academic institutions – the anti-Blackness is as Rinaldo Walcott identifies, so deep that "no dean, vice-president, or president of a Canadian university is known to have ever uttered any public commitment such as increasing Black faculty – or, for that matter, increasing Black graduate students" (2014, 275–6). And so, when the disproportionately few Black graduate students at York[7] come in response to public narratives that advertise York as a supportive space to do and house our work, attend, and experience our presence as "only one of requiring representative bodies and not one of intellectual and political contributions" (Walcott 2014, 276), it encourages us to further investigate the institution.

We recognize as a collective of Black graduate students, along with our historical and undergraduate counterparts, the institutional mechanisms that attempt to exclude and regulate Blackness at York, and choose – much like Black students and faculty in the past – to come together and insert ourselves into the historical narrative by taking on the "role of grammarians of our order" (Wynter 1992, 55). The role of grammarian, as Wynter references Eritrean anthropologist Asmarom Legesse, suggests that "all mainstream scholars ... are well-versed in the techniques of ordering a select body of facts within a framework that is completely consistent with the system of values ... of the society to which they belong. It is only by the 'trained skills' which we bring to the orders of such facts, that intellectuals as a category are able to ensure the existence of each order's conceptual framework" (55). By integrating the logic of the Black intellectual grammarian along with contributing and promoting the alternative archive, we as the BGSC take our mandate of "forging a centralized space for graduate scholarship by black students within the academy" (BGSC Executive 2015, 1) as crucial to our survival within academe.

What grounds our praxis of being grammarians of this alternative archive created by and for Black students within the academy is what many leading Black Canadian scholars identify as the theoretical basis on Black Canadian thought: the logics of diaspora (Hudson and Kamugisha 2014; McKittrick 2014; Walcott 2003, 2014). This idea of drawing from multiple sources to explain/inform our own experiences was demonstrated through our first formal coming together as a group, with the encouragement and support of Dr. Kamala Kempadoo, as a panel that demonstrated the rigorous intellectual work being produced by Black graduate students at York at the Second Biennial Black Canadian Studies Association Conference in 2015 at Dalhousie University, in Halifax, Nova Scotia. The overwhelming positive response we received from the audience during and after the panel from fellow graduate students, Black community activists, and Black scholars reifies the value in pursuing collective work. As a notable Black Canadian scholar said to us in response to our panel,

> Apart from being theoretically rigorous and aesthetically engaging, the panel for me was a performance of intellectual, interventionist praxis. Others have made strong appeals for Black studies in Canada but your "panel" illustrated how strong and engaging the work is that is already

being undertaken by grad students, even without organized Black Studies and therefore makes an eloquent tangential case for the establishment of a proper, interdisciplinary program of studies. The fact that you are already mentoring undergrads only further indicates how exciting the work you are already doing on making Black studies into what Roger Simon used to call "a project of possibility." (H. Wright, personal communication, 26 May 2015)

This description of the BGSC as "a project of possibility" feels like the perfect descriptor of what this journey has been thus far for us and what we hope continues beyond our time at the institution. Despite the fact that there is no Black Canadian studies program in Canada, we intend to utilize the BGSC as a tool/space for archiving the work of graduate students, scholars, artists, professors, and the Black community at York and beyond in order to continue to push for formal recognition of this field at the institution and avoid the erasure of Blackness.

Conclusion: Reflecting on the Future

In the always-changing, always-moving flow of the institution, we, the Black Graduate Student Collective at York University stop. We stop to reflect on the past histories of Black studies at York, asserting that though Black studies was not and is not permanently acknowledged through the institution, it was and continues to be here. We engage with the past, bring it to the present to claim, stake place and space, and say we are here. We stop to contend that even if the university continues to erase us, we will not be erased, and rather than wait for the institution to legitimize our bodies, our work, our scholarship, we legitimize ourselves.

We, the BGSC, emerge as a disruption/interruption of what many of us have come to know as the public narrative of York University – a narrative that hails the institution as a place for those who wish to work against the status quo, the radicals, the free thinkers, the outsiders. What we find instead is that we are still outside. While it is critical to name the oppressions, we move the apex of our discourse from overcoming to becoming. We move our discourses of countering, troubling, and interrupting violences and erasures by inhabiting and transforming spaces with the nuances of our presence, co-creating futures of belonging. In 2014, York's "This Is My Time" campaign asked students to envision the university as a place of endless possibilities, yet possibility is continually denied to the Black populace. By stopping, we make the time and the space for our own possibilities. By envisioning different futures we push forward as the collective of Black graduate students at York University.

NOTES

1 Established in 2015, the York University Black Graduate Students' Collective ("BGSC" or "Collective") is a group of Black graduate students in various disciplines at York University who are interested in forging a centralized space for graduate scholarship conducted by Black students within the academy. BGSC's intention is to form a social-intellectual community of Black graduate students at York University. By doing this, the BGSC locates and reclaims past and present Black scholarship as a distinct part of York University. The collective inserts itself into and as part of this historical narrative in order to contextualize and promote Black studies within one of Canada's most diverse institutions. This chapter is a result of a panel organized for the Second Biennial Black Canadian Studies Association Conference held at Dalhousie University in 2015, featuring members of the collective and as a result is written by five of the six panellists who were present.

2 Which of course, would include those of us who are Black women for whom these sexist regulations always appear alongside our racial subjugation.

3 Brown refers specifically to Nietzsche's conception of ressentiment, described as "the moralizing revenge of the powerless, 'the triumph of the weak as weak'" as incited by liberalism's presumption of the "self-reliant and self-made capacities" of the liberal subject yet simultaneous denial of their situatedness, which propels this same subject into a failure whose hurt or pain they desire to displace through a vengeful infliction of harm (1995, 67–8).

4 Marsha Pearce was the discussant for Charmaine Lurch's presentation, "Embodied Memory: The Sir George Williams Affair," as part of a panel, "Visual Arts and the Body" at the "Body | Institution | Memory: A Symposium," 25 October 2013, University of the West Indies, St. Augustine Campus, Trinidad. Ms. Pearce personally shared her response papers with the author.

5 The first performance was a culminating course project for Jin Haritaworn's "Feminist Perspectives in Environmental Studies" course at Crossroads, York University, December 2014. As part of a panel with doctoral students Evelyn Amponsah, Jan-Therese Mendes, Ola Mohammed, and Sam Tecle, with support from Kamala Kempadoo (York University), we presented at the Second Biennial Black Canadian Studies Association Conference 2015: Community, Empowerment & Leadership in Black Canada, May 2015, at Dalhousie University in Halifax, Nova Scotia; chaired by Afua Cooper, James R. Johnston Chair in Black Canadian Studies. Our panel was entitled "Being Black: Re-Imagining Subversion in/through Black Graduate Scholarship at York." The panel was invited by Handel Kashope Wright (University of British Columbia) to present at Congress 2015 at the University of Ottawa, in June 2015, at an event entitled Black Café. With support

from Joy Manette (York University), we presented an altered version of our panel under a new title, "Unknowable, Unintelligible, Unreadable Blackness: Approaches to Black Studies in Canada." This event was hosted by Handel Kashope Wright, Awad Ibrahim (University of Ottawa), and Tamari Kitossa (Brock University).

6 Canadian political philosopher C.B. Macpherson famously termed "possessive individualism" whose manifestation is in the lack of intergenerational mentoring, a refusal of collective work, especially if it occurs without the promise of individual reward, a reluctance to engage in institution building, an unwillingness to cite other Black scholars, especially if they work outside of the discipline (or, even worse, if they work outside of the academy), and the sour trumpeting of individual achievement through the dubious celebration of the "Black first" based on an entrepreneurialism that uncritically mines the deep ethos of the academic marketplace while inscribing oneself within a white supremacist discourse of individual Black exceptionality (Hudson and Kamugisha 2014, 3).

7 According to the York University website, the school prides itself on being the second-largest university in Ontario, third-largest in Canada, home to 5,900 graduate students, runs a $1 billion operating budget, and is home to Canada's largest liberal arts program.

REFERENCES

Achebe, C. 1958. *Things Fall Apart*. London: Heinemann.

Ahmed, S. 2012. *On Being Included: Racism and Diversity in Institutional Life*. Durham, NC: Duke University Press.

Ahmed, S. 2014. *The Cultural Politics of Emotion*. Edinburgh: Edinburgh University Press.

Alexander, M.J. 2005. *Pedagogies of Crossing: Meditations on Feminism, Sexual Politics, Memory, and the Sacred*. Durham, NC: Duke University Press.

Austin, D. 2013. *Fear of a Black Nation: Race, Sex, and Security in Sixties Montreal*. Toronto: Between the Lines.

BGSC Executive. 2015. BGSC Club Constitution and By-laws.

Bogues, A. 2012. "And What about the Human?: Freedom, Human Emancipation, and the Radical Imagination." *boundary 2* 39 (3): 29–46. https://doi.org/10.1215/01903659-1730608.

Boler, M. 1999. *Feeling Power: Emotions and Education*. New York: Routledge.

Brown, W. 1995. *States of Injury: Power and Freedom in Late Modernity*. Princeton, NJ: Princeton University Press.

Bullen, P.E. 2007. *Facing Intolerance: Toronto Black University Students Speak on Race, Racism and In(e)(i)quity*. Unpublished PhD thesis, University of Toronto.

Calliste, A. 1996. "African Canadians Organizing for Educational Change." In *Educating African Canadians*, edited by K.S. Braithwaite and C.E. James, 87–106. Toronto: James Lorimer & Company.

Calliste, A. 2000. "Anti-Racist Organizing and Resistance in Academia." In *Power, Knowledge and Anti-Racism Education: A Critical Reader*, edited by A. Calliste and G.J. Dei, 141–160. Halifax, NS: Fernwood Publishing.

Calliste, A., and Dei, G.J. 2000. "Mapping the Terrain: Power, Knowledge and Anti-Racism Education." In *Power, Knowledge and Anti-Racism Education: A Critical Reader*, edited by Calliste and Dei, 11–22. Halifax, NS: Fernwood Publishing.

Carty, L. 1991. "Black Women in Academia: A Statement from the Periphery." In *Unsettling Relations: The University as a Site of Feminist Struggles*, edited by H. Bannerji and L. Carty, 13–45. Toronto: Women's Press.

Christian, B. 1994. "Diminishing Returns: Can Black Feminism(s) Survive the Academy?" in *Multiculturalism: A Critical Reader*, edited by David Theo Goldberg. Boston: Blackwell Publishers.

Christian, B. 2005. "But What Do We Think We're Doing Anyway: The State of Black Feminist Criticism(s), or My Version of a Little Bit of History." In *New Black Feminist Criticism, 1985–2000*, edited by G. Bowles, M. Giulia Fabi, and A. Keizer, 5–19. Urbana: University of Illinois Press.

Christian, B., Bowles, G., Fabi, M., and Keizer, A., eds. 2007. *New Black Feminist Criticism, 1985–2000*. Urbana: University of Illinois Press.

Community Arts Program (CAP). 2015. *The Contemporary Urgencies of Audre Lorde's Legacy*. http://cap.info.yorku.ca/the-fires/student-projects/litanies -for-our-survival-visual-and-performative-conversations-with-audre-lorde/.

Dash, J. 1991. *Daughters of the Dust*. [Motion picture]. USA: Kino International.

Dei, G.J., and Kempf, A. 2013. *New Perspectives on African-Centred Education in Canada*. Toronto: Canadian Scholars' Press.

Douglas, D. 2012. "Black/out: The White Face of Multiculturalism and the Violence of the Canadian Imperial Academic Project." In *Presumed Incompetent: The Intersections of Race and Class for Women in Academia*, edited by G. Gutiérrez, Y. Muhs, C. Nieman, Z. González, and A. Harris, 50–65. Boulder: University Press of Colorado.

Forsythe, D. 1971. *Let the Niggers Burn: The Sir George Williams University Affair and Its Caribbean Aftermath*. New York: Our Generation Press.

Giroux, H. 2002. "Neoliberalism, Corporate Culture, and the Promise of Higher Education: The University as a Democratic Public Sphere." *Harvard Educational Review* 72 (4): 425–462. https://doi.org/10.17763/haer.72.4 .0515nr62324n71p1.

Hall, S. 1993. "Encoding, Decoding." *The Cultural Studies Reader* 4: 90–103.

Henry, A. 1998. *Taking Back Control: Black Women Teachers' Activism and the Education of African Canadian Children*. New York: State University of New York Press.

Henry, F., Tator, C. Mattis, W., and Rees, T. 2006. *The Colour of Democracy: Racism in Canadian Society*. Toronto: Thomson Nelson.

Hong, G.K. 2008. "'The Future of Our Worlds': Black Feminism and the Politics of Knowledge in the University under Globalization." *Meridians: Feminism, Race, Transnationalism* 8 (2): 95–115. https://doi.org/10.2979/MER.2008 .8.2.95.

Hudson, P.J. 2014. "The Geographies of Blackness and Anti-Blackness: An Interview with Katherine McKittrick." *The CLR James Journal* 20 (1/2): 233–240. https://doi.org/10.5840/clrjames201492215.

Hudson, P.J., and Kamugisha, J. 2014. "On Black Canadian Thought." *The CLR James Journal* 20 (1/2): 3–20. https://doi.org/10.5840/clrjames201492216.

Ivor, F.C. 1996. "School-University Partnerships: The Challenge of Commitment." In *Educating African Canadians*, edited by K.D. Braithwaite and C.E. James, 205–215. Toronto: James Lorimer & Company.

James, C.E., and Manette, J. 2000. "Re-Thinking Access: The Challenge of Living with Difficult Knowledge." In *Power, Knowledge and Anti-Racism Education: A Critical Reader*, edited by A. Calliste and G.J. Dei, 73–90. Halifax, NS: Fernwood Publishing.

King, T. 2013. *In the Clearing: Black Female Bodies, Space and Settler Colonial Landscapes*. Unpublished PhD thesis, University of Maryland.

Lorde, A. 2007. *Sister Outsider: Essays and Speeches*. Berkeley, CA: The Crossing Press.

McKittrick, K. 2014. "Wait Canada Anticipate Black." *The CLR James Journal* 20 (1/2): 243–249. https:doi.org/10.5840/clrjames2014984.

McNeilly, M. 2015. Sipping Freedom: Engaging Black Radical Imagination, Confronting Middle Passage Memory, Embodying the Sacred. MES thesis published in the Faculty of Environmental Studies Outstanding Graduate Student Paper Series, York University.

Mogadime, D. 2002. "Black Women in Graduate Studies: Transforming the Socialization Experience." In *Back to the Drawing Board: African-Canadian Feminisms*, edited by N. Wane, K. Deliovsky, and E. Lawson, 129–157. Toronto: Sumach Press.

Pearce, M. 2013. From transcript of panel discussion, "Body, Institution, Memory." UWI St. Augustine Campus.

Prince, A. 2001. *Being Black: Essays by Althea Prince*. Toronto: Insomniac Press.

Rumi, J., and Green, M. 1997. *The Illuminated Rumi*. New York: Harmony Books.

Somé, M.P. 1997. *Ritual: Power, Healing and Community*. New York: Penguin.

Stewart, A. 2004. "Penn and Teller Magic: Self, Racial Devaluation and the Canadian Academy." In *Racism, Eh?: A Critical Inter-Disciplinary Anthology of Race and Racism in Canada*, edited by C. Nelson and C. Nelson, 33–40. Concord, ON: Captus Press.

Walcott, R. 2003. *Black Like Who? Writing Black Canada*. Toronto: Insomniac Press.

Walcott, R. 2014. "Shame: A Polemic." *The CLR James Journal* 20 (1/2): 275–279. https://doi.org/10.5840/clrjames201492318.

Wane, N.N. 2002. "Carving Out Critical Space: African-Canadian Women and the Academy." In *Back to the Drawing Board: African-Canadian Feminisms*, edited by N. Wane, K. Deliovsky, and E. Lawson, 175–196. Toronto: Sumach Press.

Wynter, S. 1992. "'No Humans Involved': An Open Letter to My Colleagues. *Forum N.H.I.* 1 (1): 42–73. http://carmenkynard.org/wp-content/uploads /2013/07/No-Humans-Involved-An-Open-Letter-to-My-Colleagues-by -SYLVIA-WYNTER.pdf.

17 Community Service Learning and Anti-Blackness: The Cost of Playing with Fire on the Black Female Body

DELORES V. MULLINGS

I feel enraged that much of my daily labor is anchored in convincing others of my humanity.

– Griffin (2012)

Introduction

Employing autoethnography, this chapter discusses the deep scars on one Black woman faculty member's body; it explores the experiences associated with facilitating community service learning (CSL) in social work undergraduate courses to mostly white-presenting students, in a small urban centre in eastern Canada. Given its fashionable concern with anti-oppression, why should a discussion about the psychic scars of sexism and anti-Black racism centre on a school of social work? Social workers see themselves as social justice champions with a praxis founded on an anti-oppressive perspective; however, racism, sexism, and whiteness are inherent in social work education and practice (Brown 2019; de Montigny 2013; Gosine and Pon 2011). One may expect faculty in other disciplines to experience discrimination, but on the basis of the social work agenda, as a Black woman I should not experience anti-Black racism and sexism from students, faculty, and staff in a school of social work. Regardless of discipline, Black women faculty thrive and achieve scholarly success in post-secondary institutions – all in spite of oppressive practices and policies. However, understanding and mastering the Eurocentric system of meritocracy and what is considered "legitimate" scholarship has taken on a new dimension: that of CSL.

Through this recent pedagogical strategy, post-secondary administrators have imposed additional expectations on the teaching and learning environment with little consideration of its negative impact on women professors of colour. Black women's experiences of anti-Black racism and sexism are amply demonstrated in the literature (Berry 2009; Douglas 2012; Evans 2007; Gregory 2001; Griffin 2012) where they discuss the challenges that they experience under traditional teaching conditions in the professoriate. Pedagogically, CSL is non-traditional, and this means increased workload for students and professors, as well as the need for students' openness and flexibility in working with community members. Therefore, encouraging professors to use the CSL pedagogy increases the risk for negative stereotyping and character assassination of Black women professors. Administrators also do not take into account white power and privilege and that the power differential between Black women faculty members and white students exacerbates the potential for discriminatory student behaviour in the CSL context.

Similar to other areas in academe, social word administrators have embraced CSL; however, CSL adds complexity to the teaching and learning environment, which is in turn linked in my experience to increased student anxiety. A vicious cycle is set in motion wherein the potential racist conduct of students is given free play by projecting their anxieties onto me, the instructor. When (especially white) students are anxious, scared of failing, or pressured with life circumstances, they are more likely to resist teaching opportunities seen as different from the norm. Black women professors are inherently different by their very nature of being Black and female. I assert that with the introduction of CSL, the professor's Blackness, femininity, and idiosyncratic pedagogy are seen as anomalies. Therefore, while students already racially harass Black women professors when they teach in traditional ways, these faculty members are additionally harassed when they introduce CSL into the classroom.

In Canada, the scholarly literature on social work pedagogy has not substantively addressed the dynamic interaction between CSL and the subject of anti-Black womanism in the social work classroom. This chapter will add to the literature on Black women professors' experiences in academe and makes transparent the anti-Black racial and sexual harassment they encounter when they introduce CSL to predominately white students. Despite the limits I identify here, CSL pedagogy can be liberating both for students and professors, so I want to encourage other Black women professors in social work to use this teaching and learning tool, but with careful consideration of the pitfalls hidden from public view and overshadowed by administrative excitement and approval of this purportedly bias-free pedagogy.

The Black Woman Professor and Critical Race Theory

For a Black woman faculty member, critical race feminism (CRF) is an appropriate framework to analyse my teaching and learning experience in facilitating CSL courses to predominantly white undergraduate social work students. CRF is used to challenge racist and sexist norms in academic institutions, including unearthing biases in educational structures, curricula, student perceptions of racialized faculty, and low expectations of racialized students (Harley 2008; Ladson-Billings 2005; Verjee 2012; Villalpando and Delgado Bernal 2002). It is therefore relevant to this autoethnographic discussion of gender and racial harassment and discrimination in higher education in the context of CSL. The arguments I present in this chapter focus on my experience and student feedback. Autoethnography helps to legitimize me as a researcher, makes visible my experiences of sexism and racism, and connects these experiences to a larger institutional social context beyond my control. I provide a literature review of Black women faculty, CRT, and CSL, which prefigures the introduction and analysis of my students' course and instructor feedback. My story is based on a nuanced cultural understanding as a Black female faculty member of anti-Blackness, whiteness, and sexism. I offer recommendations to address a lack of administrative commitment to CSL pedagogy. The literature review that follows draws from and echoes the voices of other faculty of colour who have been affected by racism and sexism in the academy.

Literature Review

Black women faculty face multiple barriers and discrimination, including sexism, racism, ableism, and heterosexism in the academy. They are considered intellectually inept and face what Evans-Winters (2007) calls extraordinary scrutiny. Other than from Black women professors themselves (Nelson 2012; Henry 2019), there is little or no attempt to critically examine their history of enslavement's afterlife and its impact in intergenerational trauma. Although they are academically qualified, the idea of meritocracy evades them in their encounter with employment discrimination as precarious workers in part-time and sessional positions (see Douglas 2012, 51–2; Henry et al. 2017). Black women faculty members frequently enter the professoriate later in life, so they frequently balance home, career, and community responsibilities (Evans 2007; Harley 2008). They routinely assume the Mammy role (discussed below) as leaders in addressing ethnic and diversity problems and concerns, and servitude roles, including committee work such as supervising Black,

Indigenous, and racialized graduate students, community liaison, and social justice advocacy (Evans 2007; Turner 2002).

The heavy service workload and other systemic barriers for Black women professors – such as unfair course evaluations; unavailability of mentors; exclusion, isolation, lack of recognition of community-engaged pedagogy; and the emphasis on traditional research paradigms and peer-reviewed publications in the tenure and promotion process – are further disadvantages (Bradley and Holcomb-McCoy 2004; Gregory 2001; Harley 2008; Wallace et al. 2012). Harley (2008) suggests that Black women professors are "referred to as maids of academe" and as such experience "race fatigue" resulting from being overworked and undervalued (20–1). Engaged in low-level administration work, they rarely advance to upper-level administration. Indeed, Smith (2018) reviewed academic leadership in Canada's fifteen research-intensive universities (U15) and found no Black women among the 278 senior administrators. Rather, they tend to experience heightened surveillance and are held suspect as radicals who want to challenge the status quo (Harley 2008), especially as they integrate critical perspectives in their teaching and research scholarship. Bailey and Zita (2007) argue that their discipline (philosophy) has presented "White ways of knowing, seeing, anthologizing, evaluating, being, nation building, and judging" as the norm (viii). I assert that social work is similarly suffused with a culture of whiteness: this is evident in the failure of Jennissen and Lundy (2011) to address the inherent racism in the social work profession. I suggest that as a practice and extension of white framing inherent in social work, CSL is a pedagogical method that mirrors and perpetuates racism in the academy.

Community Service Learning

CSL combines community-engaged participation with reflection (Furuto 2007; Lemieux 2007; Humphrey 2014) and provides the space for students to collaborate and develop relationships with community partners (DePaola 2014; Phillips 2007). An important aspect of CSL is reciprocity, in which students and community partners jointly decide on the co-creation and completion of service projects, and learn from and teach each other throughout the process (Cooper, Cripps, and Resiman 2013; Gardinier 2016; Phillips 2007). CSL can help students learn about civic engagement (Gardinier 2016; Gerstenblatt and Gilbert 2014; Vergee 2012); share power with faculty and community members (Mullings 2016; Lemieux 2007); and gain a better understanding of racism and oppression (Espino and Lee 2011; Green 2003), poverty (Baggerly 2006; Sanders, McFarland, and Bartolli 2003), social justice (Cipolle 2010;

DePaola 2014), health (Mitschke and Petrovich 2011), and social responsibility (Maistry 2014; Verjee 2012). Mullings (2013) suggests that, when successfully applied, CSL helps students to interrogate their identities, social relations and structures, and knowledge, as well as confront their racism and other biases. However, the current understanding of CSL demonstrates a heightened market commodification emphasis on students being community-engaged in order to learn directly in the community-based setting, where they will ultimately be employed.

CSL, with the centrality of neoliberalism, has become a novelty such that many institutions lay claim to a corporatized version of community engaged learning and teaching. Students are seen as pawns (Tight 2013) or consumers in a market-driven economy (Brown, Hesketh, and Williams 2003; Olson and Peters 2005; Tomlinson 2016). In the neoliberalist climate of political sexiness CSL is something of a dog and pony show where racialized people are minoritized and disadvantaged communities are exploited, all under the guise of working in partnership and collaboration. With respect to CSL, Verjee (2012) conducted a qualitative study of racialized students, faculty, and staff at the University of British Columbia. "The women in this study spoke of daily micro-aggressions and trauma of being unseen, unheard, devalued, silenced, delegitimized, disempowered, scrutinized, disciplined, and perceived as inferior" (60). Green (2003) discusses white students' whiteness, classism, and racism in her own reflection of facilitating CSL. One can therefore understand why the predominately white student body, with its sense of entitlement, frequently resists CSL and harasses Black women faculty who introduce these unique educational opportunities in the classroom. On cue, students regularly display their white entitlement steeped in racial superiority, even as they are positioned to work with the most vulnerable people in society. The next section frames this discussion of CSL within critical race feminism.

Theoretical Orientation: Critical Race Feminism

Critical race feminism (CRF), a splinter group of the CRT movement, takes up feminism by centralizing race and gender, and acknowledging other forms of intersecting social hierarchies such as class, disability, and sexual orientation. The major tenets of CRT include the endemic nature of racism; the notion of meritocracy, objectivity, and neutrality; colour blindness – specifically, colour invisibility; counter-storytelling; whiteness as property; and interest convergence (Aylward 1999; Bell 1992, 1995; Crenshaw 1995; DeCuir and Dixson 2004; Delgado 1989, 1995; Delgado and Stefancic 2012; Haney-López 2007; Ladson-Billings 2009; Ladson-Billings and Tate 1995). CRF employs CRT tenets and extends them to specifically include a gendered lens. "Fundamental to Critical Race Feminism is the idea that women of colour are not simply white women plus some ineffable and secondary characteristic, such as skin tone, added on" (Wing 1997, 3).

CRF recognizes the inherent power embedded in social, legal, and political relationships and further suggests that racialized women's experiences are different from those of white women (Wing 2000). Ladson-Billings (2009) demarcates three different types of stereotypical Black women and, by extension, Black women faculty: Mammy, Sapphire, and Jezebel. With her soft body, Mammy's life purpose is to happily care for white people and their families while neglecting her own. Sapphire "is stubborn, bitchy, bossy, and hateful"; she is a harpy or shrew who is extremely difficult to deal with, having no redeeming feminine qualities. The "Jezebel image is that of a woman who is physically attractive and seductive; she is a conniving temptress who cannot be trusted" (91). Black women professors are frequently categorized into at least one of these roles and stereotyped as what I refer to as temporarily allowed trespassers. As temporary entities in a site of the reproduction of power, it is easy for white bodies to brand them as illegitimate. Black female faculty members are allowed passage but only under certain conditions, and they are kept on the margins and easily expelled or exterminated through the application of white power and privilege.

My understanding of CRF is aligned with Solórzano's (1998) arguments that "a critical race theory in education challenges the dominant discourse on race and racism as they relate to education by examining how educational theory, policy, and practice are used to subordinate certain racial and ethnic groups" (122). Proponents of CRF argue that racialized women must be the architects of their stories and that such stories must be created by and for women with lived experiences. Given that I identify as a Black woman faculty member and CRF centralizes race and gender, among other identity markers, this framework is suited to analyse the research data, capture the covert racism embedded in my teaching environment, and highlight my experiential knowledge in higher education. CRT "foregrounds the role of race and racism in contexts where pervasive and overt forms of structural and interpersonal racism [exist]" (Truong, Graves, and Keene 2014, 5). Berry (2009) argues that teacher education programs contain gatekeepers for women of colour who make it difficult for them to find allies to support their aspirations of becoming educators. Berry (2010) proposes "a classroom praxis of engaged pedagogy from a critical race feminist perspective" (20). Few (2007) articulates a research model that combines Black feminism with CRF as a tool to honour Black women's lives.

Pratt-Clarke (2010) outlines a transdisciplinary model of social justice education that examines the relationship between Black women and Black men in Detroit's Black communities and critically analyses the Detroit male academy's social and political power. Evans-Winters and Esposito (2010) contextualize and discuss Black girls' education and experience in the United States, including how they are stereotyped and the strategies of resilience that they employ. Regina Austin (1989) ponders how racialized feminist scholars should approach the Sapphire caricature and questions if we should "renounce her, rehabilitate her or embrace her and proclaim her our own" (540). She suggests that racialized women faculty should critically adopt the Sapphire role and use their position to unapologetically challenge discriminatory social structures as well as defend and advocate for racialized women's lived realities and aspirations. Similar to Verjee (2012), this chapter discusses racism and sexism in the context of CSL pedagogy.

Autoethnography and Student Data

I employ autoethnography (AE) research methodology to personalize this chapter in order to make transparent the implications of my Black womanhood experiences as an educator teaching predominately white students. I employ this method to also demonstrate that the racism of students constitutes epistemic violence, which results in psychological trauma for Black women professors. Chang et al. argue that "[autoethnography] is a qualitative research method that focuses on self as a study subject but transcends a mere narration of personal history" (Chang et al. 2013, 18). AE enables researchers to self-disclose according to their comfort level with publicly displayed emotions and perspectives. To this end, "autoethnographers use personal stories as windows to the world, through which they interpret how their selves are connected to their sociocultural contexts and how the contexts give meaning to their experiences and perspectives" (Chang et al. 2013, 19). In my discussion, I include Anderson's (2006) analytic AE methodology, which combines external data from the students and my emotive expression.

As mentioned above, this study is framed in the form of an analytic autoethnography (Anderson 2006) where I present my narrative as a Black female faculty member. I interpret and discuss the behaviour of predominately white students as a group that is external to me (Atkinson 2006). My personal experiences are framed in the context of the bigger story of racism and sexism. The narrative of this autoethnography presents data drawn from students' course questionnaires as well as my personal experiences as primary data. Points of consideration include the idea of culture as identity, both for the individual and the group. Racialized people's identities take many forms, each reflecting different forms of culture: private/public, informal/formal, racialized/non-racialized, and female/male/trans. Chang describes group culture as "individuals who can actively interpret their social surroundings" (2008, 44). Where racism and sexism are concerned, autoethnography makes transparent that individuals are forced to interpret their social surroundings, in my case being a Black female faculty member in a predominantly white Canadian institution. Arising from this autoethnography I offer a discussion aimed at raising the consciousness of faculty, students, and administration toward a more substantive engagement with anti-Blackness and anti-oppression consideration. Data were gathered for this chapter from undergraduate students' course feedback.

In the winter term of 2017, I taught three sections of a social work course to undergraduate students at an eastern Canadian university in the School of Social Work. I use data (results $n = 60$) gathered from the 2017 winter semester course equivalency questionnaires, the university's formal course evaluation. There are three qualitative questions: Q14 and Q15 are standard on the questionnaires, and Q26 is an instructor-supplied question, which I inserted. Questions 14 and 15 ask students to comment on the best aspects of the course and to suggest improvements. Question 26 asks students to comment on their own performance in the course. Twenty students were enrolled in each of three different sections for a total of sixty students: fifty self-identified as cisgender females and six as cisgender males. Given the small sample (total of 4) of self-identifying gender non-conforming, gay, lesbian, and trans people, they are grouped together to preserve students' privacy and anonymity. With respect to racial distribution, fifty-eight students self-identified as local or white (all were white presenting), and one each identified as Aboriginal and South Asian. The response rate for each of the three sections of the courses are as follows: 89 per cent (S2), 50 per cent (S3), and 65 per cent (S4). In the section below, I present a context and my motivations for pursuing CSL.

Arriving at and Navigating Fire Hazards in Social Work Spaces

I became inspired to influence SW education because of my experience in undergraduate and graduate classes where professors spoke to students, expected us to listen, and then regurgitate what they told us. I was equally dismayed at the lack of relevance my undergraduate social work education had for Black people. I objected to what I believed was, and still is, an uncritical, Eurocentric, paternalistic, imperialistic, impractical, and one-dimensional education geared towards primarily young white women students' understanding of the world around them. I decided then that I wanted to contribute to the transformation of social work education and ultimately social work practice. When I got the opportunity to assume a full-time tenure track position, I took the position hoping to influence the social work profession. Following the dream was not a challenge, but moving to a different province and cultural milieu away from everything that was familiar and almost everyone that I loved was.

I am a Black Canadian woman of African Caribbean descent, the biological mother of two living adult children, and a member of a large extended family. I emigrated from Jamaica at the age of fifteen and have since called Southern Ontario "home." Because of my tenure track position, I left that "home" when I moved to a small urban centre in eastern Canada. I moved away from my family with my then-fourteen-year-old daughter and my belongings. I cried from grief at my departure at the airport, and when I landed in the new province I cried again, both for my loss and for the potential opportunities in my new community. The province in which I relocated is a settler society (Ahluwalia 2001) like much of Canada and populated with majority people of European descent. I felt that my lived experiences as a Black heterosexual, spiritual (not religious), single mother of African Caribbean descent rendered me unique in this province. Having dark complexion, long locks, and a muscular physique further made me more visible. While the white culture in this province is considered unique and friendly, that friendliness is only surface deep. After ten years, I am still lonely in my new "home." I miss my family, friends, cultural foods, familiar sounds, and feeling a sense of belonging, but I believe I have something to offer the university community, and specifically my own faculty, so I stay.

I approach my scholarship, teaching, and learning from the perspective that students are invested in their education and want to contribute to their own learning. I concur that the "banking model" of education (Freire 1982) is designed to cultivate uncritical system-focused students who follow the principles of the status quo without challenge or questions. Frowning on traditional educational paradigms, I charted a course to transform social work education when I embraced transformative pedagogies including CSL through which I, ironically and deliberately, centre students' needs in the classroom. I create the space for students to challenge and be challenged, to expand and excel while receiving support and encouragement. As much as the condition and context allow, I share power with students by co-creating a shared environment in such areas as assignment due dates, course literature, class structure, guest speakers, and community partnership. My experience with CSL pedagogy has been rewarding but also littered with trauma and violence that I suffered at the hands of students and administrators. Still, I am committed to CSL as a tool to fulfil my vision of transformation in social work education and practice. Below, I present an outline of how I organize a CSL class.

Organizing a Community Service Learning Class

In the first class, I introduced CSL concepts, approaches, and examples from past courses. Similar to Mullings (2016), I provided the outline, guidelines, and explanation for the first assignment, which required each learner to propose a potential term project, including which community group(s) each might partner with. These proposals were submitted in the second week of class, graded, and returned the third week. During the third week of class, learners showcased their individual suggestions for a CSL project, and each of the classes voted for one project they would work on with community partners for the entire semester. They formed partnerships as follows: section two (S2) with the Autism Society to bring awareness to a specific discriminatory policy; section three (S3) with several community groups to advocate for a supervised injection site in the province; and section four (S4) with the province's largest public library and a not-for-profit community literacy organization.

In keeping with CSL concepts, each class project could move forward only with community collaboration and partnership. In order to keep abreast of CSL projects, help was required to communicate through Desire to Learn (D2L), the university's teaching and learning interface, to provide or seek project updates, clarification, and support for tasks to be completed. I established this mode of participation to support and guide learners as they progressed through the course. By week four, students were becoming acquainted with the concepts and principles of CSL. Each week, learners were also required to provide updates on their projects during class, get suggestions and support from me, ask for assistance from classmates, and to discuss challenges, successes, and learning. Many students were communicating through private Facebook groups (of which I was not a member) rather than using D2L to communicate. There were tensions about the CSL projects, but some students seemed to embrace the CSL concept and we conversed easily about it in class. I further made myself available outside of class time to review D2L posts, answer questions relevant to the project(s) and assignments, and support students with course work by meeting them individually and holding tutorials. The following section presents a thematic analysis of students' questionnaire comments.

Searching for the "Mammy": Finding Jezebel and Sapphire

For the purposes of this discussion, I use only Q15, which asks students, "What aspects of this course could be improved and how could they be improved?" Using Glesne and Peshkin (1992), I conducted a thematic analysis of the data and grouped sub-themes into two major categories: students as victims, and racist stereotypes and characterization. Twelve recurring sub-themes (confusion, fear, intimidation, anxiety, crying, sleeplessness, bowel dysfunction, lack of clarity, unclear instructions, lack of guidelines, clearer deadlines, and lack of support) related to students' victimhood. In addition, thirteen recurring themes emerged about my character, which are grouped into the category of racist stereotypes (bully, inconsiderate, unreasonable, intimidating, misuse power, abusive, disorganized, lack of support, conflict with students, disrespectful, insensitive, difficult marker, negative attitude).

Student Victimhood

This section discusses students' comments that highlight the themes of the larger category reflecting student victimhood. Students commented that they did not feel comfortable or confident they would pass the course and this created anxiety for them. As noted by one student, "This course was also very anxiety prone. I never felt confident that I was going to succeed during this whole course. I spent the entire semester in fear that I was not going to pass" (S3).

In spite fear and anxiety, some students identified that I cared for students. However, some students also felt that I had unrealistic expectations and was disrespectful. One student wrote,

> Dr. Mullings is a brilliant woman and I believe she has a big heart and cares about her students, however, she has unrealistic expectations, is not considerate and I feel that she expects student to be able to read her mind. The assignments in this course were unclear, we would be told one thing by her in class and then she would expect another. I am aware and understand that this is a difficult course but the amount of tears, stress and anxiety students experience as a result of this course and its instruction is not worth the negative impacts on students mental health. I genuinely worried for the mental health and stability of some of my classmates during the semester because of this course. It made us all feel like no matter what we did it would never be good enough and honestly made me question even wanting to be in involved with this school of social work. I was outraged several times throughout the semester because of this course and upset that the school

of social work allowed such chaotic environment that was not conductive to the learning to exist. Several times throughout the semester students were treated with disrespect, there were many times that we had to individually wait outside of Dr. Mullings office for hours and I'm not exaggerating when I say hours because Dr. Mullings wanted to meet with us individually. (S2)

Similar to the quote above, some students had strong reactions to being asked to meet with me individually to discuss their assignments and felt inconvenienced because they had to wait. Repeatedly, they suggested that assignment instructions were unclear without realizing that it was they themselves who were unclear in how they approached their projects.

Students seemed ambivalent about how to describe aspects of my scholarship and often conflated characteristics with roles and responsibilities. CSL pedagogy is often a messy process; however, students consistently remarked that I was unorganized and did not provide sufficient feedback and guidance to them. Simultaneously, they absolved themselves of the responsibility for their own learning: "I think although if this course was based on CSL, we were not provided enough feedback to be successful as we would have been if there was more guidance. I understand that we were responsible for our own learning, but the way the course was conducted was very unorganized, and a lot of pressure on us as students" (S4).

Pedagogically, faculty and students spend more time interacting when engaged in CSL activities than in traditional educational environments. This is because CSL pedagogy by its very nature is more time consuming (Hains and Smith 2012). All three sections of the course were engaged in CSL but students seemed confounded by CSL's non-linear concepts and seemed to expect me to assume leadership for their CSL projects and to engage in traditional teaching practices. Thus in relation to CSL, one student wrote that a "better understanding of what 'reflecting' is rather than 'telling' would have been useful for writing papers" (S4). Students also expressed racial stereotyping in their feedback.

Racist Stereotypes

Some students liked the concepts of CSL and the actual assignments but felt that I was unapproachable and were, therefore, uncomfortable in asking questions, particularly since they believed that I used my personal power to intimidate them. While they suggested being intimidated in person, the tone in the feedback seemed less so: "You could have been more approachable. I loved the layout of this course but the biggest thing I struggled with is not feeling comfortable asking you questions. It really sucked that your awesome assignment and activities were not as appreciated because of how you used your power as a professor to intimidate students" (S2).

Some students talked about their panic about rigorous assignment grading. They did not feel that the process helped them to learn or feel confident. Rather it stifled their freedom and caused them to feel stagnant: "The degree of difficulty to which the assignment were marked just made the students panic ... [W]e were filled with anxiety and stress around the last assignment because nearly all of us were counting on it to pass the course. I don't feel that this made us work more productively, I think for some people it stressed them out to the point where they just doubted everything and what they were writing and clammed up" (S2).

At least four students echoed that I should not be "allowed" to teach the course and they questioned why the SSW and the university would allow me to organize the class in such a manner. Students suggested that I bullied them, was frequently cruel, flaunted and abused my power, was late for appointments, and accused students of racism when they tried to challenge me. I was also seen as incompetent and for several students, the worst professor they have ever had:

> Dr. Mullings should not teach this course. I am not sure why she gets away with the things she does. She flat out bullies her students, both face to face and over D2L, she grades arbitrarily without any suggestions for edits or anything to her rhyme or reason to what she does, she is frequently cruel, all the while she claims to be a "learner" too and that CSL makes us all equal, yet she does things to flaunt and abuse her power, such as making a post telling students they must meet with her the next day at 8:30 a.m., without thought to how they may have other classes, jobs or kids, and then she herself does not bother to show up for half an hour! And if anyone disagrees with her or tells her that her behaviour makes them uncomfortable she accuses them of being racist. In five years at the university I have never had a worse professor. I would rather drop out than ever take a course with her again, and I will suggest to anyone considering social work that they should think twice if they value their mental health and this course is still taught by this professor. It is an absolute shame on the faculty that she is allowed to behave this way. (S3)

Within the two major themes – student victimhood and racist stereotypes – students positioned themselves as innocent, mentally fragile, race-neutral victims while racially stereotyping me as a bully, disorganized, and incompetent.

My Interactions with the Students

I supported students with unwavering commitment: I had weekly sched-uled office hours; I met with students for two of the four assignments to provide individualized coaching and feedback before and after sub-mission. In addition, I supported students during class time, on D2L, and elsewhere outside of normal business hours. I was active on social media (Twitter and Instagram); reviewed documentation, (e.g., ethics forms, invitations, flyers, etc.); offered guidance about community re-sources; attended activities (e.g., public presentations, bake sales, and book drives); coached students (once after 10:00 p.m.) in preparation for a radio interview; edited final reports; and hosted a tutorial to help students prepare for the final paper. Despite this high level of instruc-tional engagement, students rendered my work invisible and described me as a caricature of the bad, unapproachable, and intimidating Black woman professor and, more aptly, the bitchy and bossy shrew. Regardless of my work ethic, which consistently exceeded my responsibilities, stu-dents regularly complained about my perceived deficiencies.

Students suggested that I could have supported them more by provid-ing supplemental information and clarity around grading. Their claim about arbitrary grading lacks foundation as, along with me, there were three teaching assistants who graded the assignments and provided a grading rubric and feedback to students for each assignment. The stu-dents were more upset and offended, one may argue, by my perceived power and the inferred fact that I used that power to structure a CSL non-traditional environment. I created supplemental information and posted them on D2L in the second week of class. Interestingly, students did not assume responsibility for their learning, but instead expected me, like the Mammy, to mother them. Similar to Henry (2015), some students perceived that, as a Black woman professor, I am incompetent since I failed to provide information to help them feel safe, nurtured, and cared for. Furthermore, they suggested that I created anxiety and fear in them and threatened their mental health. By this terror-inducing behaviour, for them, I embody the personas of Sapphire and Jezebel who are extremely difficult to please, so that no matter how well students performed it was assumed I was never satisfied with them. Students re-linquished their responsibility in the CSL projects and tried to hold me fully accountable for their anxieties and self-prophesying fear – which was ostensibly created by my Black female body.

Some students claimed the course was too focused on race; as a re-sult, they refused to accept the complexities of social justice issues that centred race. The perceived dangers of examining race enables and reifies social work students: their "insulated environment of racial privilege builds white expectations for racial comfort while at the same time lowering the ability to tolerate racial stress" (DiAngelo 2011, 59). Black women's bodies have paid the price for whites feeling safe, sheltered, and well cared for as they revel in their illusionary tales of what it means to be academics in Canadian universities. The mostly white students in social work CSL classes vociferously engage in sexism and racism and, even as they expectantly watch the potential demise of the Black female body, they claim ignorance and innocence.

In general, the mostly white student cohort positioned themselves as frail and vulnerable victims of a cruel Black woman professor who in this case is unreasonable, unapproachable, and merciless, causing them to feel anxiety, panic, and stress. As George Yancy notes, "A key feature of the social ontology of whiteness is that whites attempt to avoid discussing their own social, political, economic, and cultural investments in whiteness" (2004, 4). The students who relied on the device of projection avoided seeing how they benefit from CSL and the embodied experience of Blackness, which presented them with the opportunity of learning through critical engagement with community individuals. Their whiteness allowed them to envision CSL instruction from a safe place, but CSL challenged their sense of safety, and rather than acknowledging their areas for growth – emotionally and scholastically – they portrayed me as Jezebel. Overall, the students refused to see their complicity in maintaining whiteness and their investment in insulating themselves through white fragility and victimhood. Similarly, they failed to see how their sense of entitlement and superiority privileged them in dictating to the university the merits of my qualifications and authority to occupy space as a faculty member.

Playing with Fire

My approach to facilitation is CRT, in which I coach students to consider situations or ideas that are not part of their lived experiences. My pedagogical practice invites students to engage with their whole selves and to link cognitive and emotional intelligence. They are encouraged to "think with their hearts and bellies," "dig deeper," and "peel back the layers" of complexity in the deconstruction of power relations. I personally enjoy facilitating social work education, performing in the front stage and working in the backstage to promote student excellence. But in spite of my love for this profession, I hurt every day in some way, shape, or form. The hurt is akin to burns one sustains from being in a fire. I did not envision these deadly attacks, wounds, wars of words, and silences – violence that I experience in social work classrooms. In deed, mi ah play wid fiyah (I'm playing with fire). My experiences in social work spaces are similar to what other Black and racialized women have noted. I experienced what Lazos (2012) alludes to: "When women and minorities enter their classrooms, their students, too, have expectations about them. Their majority counterparts do not face this obstacle. As women and minority instructors labor to make their classrooms friendly and warm (so that they can get decent student evaluations), they must ponder how their conduct will be perceived by their students in the context of their gendered and raced role expectations. From the get-go, the task is daunting" (175).

It is normal for white bodies to think that I am intimidating and insensitive, even before they meet me. Racism influences all political and social structures, including those in academe, and the power differential between white elites and racialized people harms our lives (Aylward 1999; Crenshaw 1989; Austin 1989; Delgado and Stefancic 2012; Ladson-Billings and Tate 1995; Mullings 2015). In almost every semester, students lodge complaints against me, citing my incompetence, abusive behaviour, social injustice, and violence. Predictably, administrators summon me to their office to account for my behaviour based on what they suggest are students' concerns (read: complaints similar to the data above). Quantitatively, respecting my university's collective agreement and the standards of professional excellence, my scholarship meets and in some instances exceeds the "norm" (see Wallace et al. 2012). Yet, in spite of it all, I am still considered incompetent and inferior by students and administrators alike. In my faculty I am marginalized, my work rendered invisible, and my body imagined as subhuman (see Griffin 2012, 141).

Whiteness and white fragility shape my experience of the classroom. From administrators' offices up to and including the vice president and provost, I must always directly or indirectly respond to their summons and defend myself against white students' concerns. The stigmatization and discipline that I endure are analogous to being in a prison of a different kind, albeit without walls and bars. I am regularly shamed, scrutinized, and rarely given an opportunity, unlike my white colleagues, to learn and grow. I have brought my concerns to my faculty association, and they have suggested that none of my experiences are grieveable on the basis of the collective agreement; however, they have been keeping a record of my reported incidences of racism and sexism.

By the very nature of my being a Black woman, working with authority as a knowledge holder, I have dared to challenge the dominant narrative of white privilege grounded in the ideology of objectivity, meritocracy, equal opportunity, colour invisibility, and race neutrality (Ladson-Billings and Tate 1995; Mullings 2015; Williams 1991; Wing 1997). I am a Black woman faculty member whom mostly all white students regularly resist and shame. Such public flogging does not occur with white professors, especially white men, no matter how ineffective or inappropriate they are. The future social workers in my classroom suggest that I frequently play the race card, while implying that their own critiques and violence are race neutral and colour invisible. In my case, when students see the Mammy (Hill Collins 2002) but experience the opposite, I am accused of neglecting my servile duty to feed them information and care for them emotionally and physically by organizing the classroom to protect their fragility and entitlement to privilege. I am therefore the perfect Sapphire – combative, hard, unsympathetic, bossy, cruel, and bitchy (Hill Collins 2002; Ladson-Billings 2009). As Jezebel I am the angry Black woman: my words of hope, power sharing, and creativity are seductive to some, but for these students I cannot be trusted because my "foreign" words and actions provoke debilitating anxiety and distress among students before, during, and after they leave a class that I facilitate. For them, the state of whiteness must prevail, hence my status as a temporarily allowed trespasser must cease and I must be driven out of the faculty and university.

Discussion: Walking through Fire

Following the principles of autoethnography, my story is important, as it gives voice to my own perspective of the stereotypical characteristics of my personhood and in the enclosure of my Black body. I do not deny that others may have endured abuses in academe. However, my words make visible my personal experiences of anti-Black racist and sexist violence, inclusive of the "white gaze" (Yancy 2008). I foreground my expulsion in and from academe because I am Black and female. As argued by McKittrick (2011), "The intellectual work of honouring complex racial narratives that name struggles against death and a black sense of place can be, paradoxically, undermined by the analytical framing of racial violence" (949). My experience of racial and sexist violence supports claims by Wallace et al. (2012) and Douglas (2012) that the academy is built upon and maintained by the ideology of whiteness and thereby marginalizes, exploits, and victimizes racialized students and faculty.

   In my experience, students and faculty are hesitant to accept CSL pedagogy, but university administrators continue to advance its virtues because governments, corporations, and community organizations increasingly demand that the burden of training be placed on the academy.

The CSL context therefore places the Black female body significantly at risk, given CSL's inherent lack of formal structure, sharing of power with students, facilitative process, and involvement of community individuals. Moreover, the commodification of education where students are the consumers, the ones to be pleased and pampered, are taught but not placed in a position in which they may become emotional or upset is paramount. Gates, Heffernan, and Sudore (2015) posit that social work faculty are increasingly being forced to act as customer service representatives in social work programs. As consumers, students expect more and more from their institutions and their professors. As a Black woman, I am expected to be their "maid in academe" (Harley 2008) – wet nurse, nanny, surrogate mother, counsellor, faculty, and housekeeper.

Servitude work is insufficient guarantee of safety from white fright and fear. Fear of the Black body necessitates surveillance and profiling (Mullings 2015). White fright (Myers 2013) or white fear of the Black body demands extermination and dismemberment in the minds of white students, and administrators in my case. The frailty and fragility of white social work students are frequently reflected in the fear in their eyes and the convulsing of their bodies during interactions with me in class or privately in my office. Seemingly out of fear, social work students echo the normal mantra calling for the eradication of the Black woman faculty member's body. In their infinite wisdom, being certain of positions steeped in whiteness and white power, these students call for the eradication – in essence the extermination – of my Black female body from one of the major institutions of whiteness and a hub of white power. What does this say about the minds of these future social workers, who carry the angelic disposition of moral saviour and champion of human rights? It confirms Yancy's (2008) assertion that a white female student who yelled "Bullshit" in his lecture about his experiences of racism and whiteness "was lying to herself, concealing from view the reality of her own racism in relationship to those moments on elevators or in other social spaces where she engaged in perceptual practices that criminalized or demonized the Black body" (228). So too are these social work students lying to themselves and concealing their own transgressions aimed at the erasure of the Black female body.

These students, like those in DuRocher's (2011) Jim Crow South, were born, bred, and cultivated with anti-Blackness in their cultural life-blood (media, stories, national histories, etc.). DuRocher discusses how white children learn about power and whiteness at an early age by witnessing the racial domination of African Americans in the Jim Crow South. An example was provided to demonstrate the point: Ruben Stacy, a homeless African American farmer was jailed for frightening a white woman. He was taken from jail and lynched, and his remains were hanged on a tree by a noose around his neck with his hands tied in front of his body. white families from nearby visited the site to take pictures with the corpse, and "several white girls in their Sunday dresses stand around Stacey's body, their whiteness framing him" (1). While I would not equate being gazed upon as lynching, I do suggest that students' whiteness frames my body during my interactions with them. This gazing helps them to frame their whiteness in such a way as to suggest that my body is problematic in the learning and teaching space and should be disposed of. Indeed, their survival and existence depend on violating the Black body. Their gate-keeping role is to ensure the erasure of the Black woman faculty's body.

On the issue of the Black body's disposability, McKittrick (2011) explains how "geographies in the Americas are connected to practices of domination and deliberate attempts to destroy a black sense of place" (947). The geography of the Canadian post-secondary institution on the East Coast, a white settler society, is indeed hostile territory for the Black woman's body. This notion of non-belonging surfaces in every course that I facilitate and, while efforts are consistently made to push me out, I am locked up figuratively in a maze where I am punished and regulated for disobeying the rules and confines of whiteness. This is the type of institutional regulation that Dorothy E. Roberts (1999) hinted at in relation to Black women's bodies and reproduction, in my case knowledge production and reproduction. My Black body is always on the front lines and therefore in the line of fire of white aggression. For me, there is always the struggle to be heard and seen in an environment that forces me to simultaneously remain invisible.

Conclusion and Recommendations

Through autoethnography, this chapter extends the discussion of racial and sexual discrimination in higher education to include the impact on the Black female body specifically in the context of CSL. This is a discussion that has received scant attention in social work education. Increasingly Black women are occupying space in higher education; simultaneously, post-secondary administrators are changing the teaching pedagogical expectations by implementing CSL. There are common themes in my experience as a Black woman faculty member: the Black female body is disciplined, stigmatized, scrutinized, and regulated in ways that maintain whiteness in social work, a discipline that is supposedly predicated on a social justice platform and prides itself for working to help those who are disadvantaged, to ultimately reduce social injustice. In my perception of the cultural environment, anti-Black stereotyping comes from all sectors of the university community, but I argue that administrators collude and are complicit with anti-Black sexist stereotypes that help to perpetuate the violence I have experienced. As CRF argues, racism is endemic, and therefore it is considered normal and ordinary in everyday life (Austin 1989; Berry 2009, 2010; Crenshaw 1989; Few 2007; Wing 1997). CSL pedagogy can legitimize students' fear and create a breeding ground for increased racist attitudes and behaviour.

DePaola (2014) notes that traditional education assumes that students enter the classroom space with little or no knowledge or life experience and are therefore primed to only accept knowledge. CSL, on the other hand, positions students as knowers who have knowledge to contribute to their education and to others', inclusive of their instructors (Baugher and Frantz 2013; Haber-Curran and Tillapaugh 2015). CSL pedagogy is challenging and time consuming. Students are entrusted with aspects of their learning; this mode of engaging is not linear and eschews facilitators imposing a set structure. In my experience, this mode of instruction is a source of anxiety for students and motivates their longing for the safety of the traditional classroom structure. During CSL activities, students insist that I direct their activities and shape their experiences, and on many occasions, some resist taking responsibility for their own learning. For some students even at the end of the semester they are not comfortable in making their own decisions. The university promotes a consumer-driven environment with students thereby reifying, as Tomlinson (2016) notes, a "dominant conception of contemporary students is therefore as rational investors who have embarked on higher education as a means of maximising future economic outcomes" (151). Students' wanting to be told what is "right" supports their perspective of how to prepare to enter their field armed with a precise type of knowledge, and they see any deviation from this notion as an obstacle in their education and potential success in the marketplace.

If university administrators are committed to CSL pedagogy, they – and indeed faculty associations – must work with the union to adjust the university infrastructure to support Black women professors, especially when they experience racism, sexism, stereotyping, and harassment. CSL structure and expectations must include naming and making transparent sexism and racism, in addition to ensuring students assume responsibility for their learning. Administrators and colleagues must stop comparing Black women faculty to each other and other racialized groups of women and men. Black women are not saints and, because they can simultaneously be victims and victimizers, they are not above reproach and moral culpability. However, some of the statements and questions that are frequently directed to me include "Students are like that with me too and I'm white"; "How do you know its racism?"; "Maybe it's your pedagogy and has nothing to do with the colour of your skin"; and "X person is Black and s/he/they don't have these problems." These comparisons devalue Black women faculty's specific lived experiences and they create further collusion with the racist stereotype of the illegitimate and incompetent Black woman professor within the caricature of Sapphire. Further, such comparisons divide and serve as a method for students to avoid reflexivity about the hegemonic nature of whiteness and white privilege. Schools of social work have the power and obligation to provide leadership for CSL. Further, programs and policies must be implemented to address institutional sexism and anti-Black racism, including mentorship and retention programs, challenging students' stereotyping and harassment of Black women faculty, and validation of the professors' experience.

REFERENCES

Ahluwalia, P. 2001. "When Does a Settler Become a Native? Citizenship and Identity in a Settler Society." *Pretexts: Literary and Cultural Studies* 10 (1): 63–73. https://doi.org/10.1080/713692599.

Anderson, L. 2006. "Analytic Autoethnology." *Journal of Contemporary Ethnography* 35 (4): 373–395. https://doi.org/10.1177/0891241605280449.

Atkinson, P. 2006. "Rescuing Autoethnography." *Journal of Contemporary Ethnography* 35 (4): 400–404. https://doi.org/10.1177/0891241606286980.

Austin, R. 1989. "Sapphire Bound!" Faculty Scholarship at Penn Law. https://scholarship.law.upenn.edu/faculty_scholarship/1347.

Aylward, C. 1999. *Canadian Critical Race Theory: Racism and the Law.* Halifax, NS: Fernwood Publishing.

Baggerly, J. 2006. "Service Learning with Children Affected by Poverty: Facilitating Multicultural Competence in Counseling Education Students." *Journal of Multicultural Counseling and Development* 34 (4): 244–255. https://doi.org/10.1002/j.2161-1912.2006.tb00043.x.

Bailey, A., and Zita, J. 2007. "The Reproduction of Whiteness: Race and the Regulation of the Gendered Body." *Hypatia* 22 (2): vii–xv. https://doi.org/10.1111/j.1527-2001.2007.tb00978.x.

Baugher, S., and Frantz, G. 2013. "The Inlet Valley Project Reflections on an Early Model for Interdisciplinary and Cross-Cultural Service-Learning Courses in Landscape Architecture." *Landscape Journal* 32 (1): 113–130. https://doi.org/10.3368/lj.32.1.113.

Bell, D. 1992. *Faces at the Bottom of the Well: The Permanence of Racism.* New York: Basic Books.

Bell, D. 1995. "Who's Afraid of Critical Race Theory?" *University of Illinois Law Review* 4: 893–910. https://heinonline.org/HOL/LandingPage?handle=hein .journals/unilllr1995&div=40&id=&page=.

Berry, T. 2009. "Women of Color in a Bilingual/Dialectal Dilemma: Critical Race Feminism against a Curriculum of Oppression in Teacher Education." *International Journal of Qualitative Studies in Education* 22 (6): 745–762. https://doi.org/10.1080/09518390903333913.

Berry, T. 2010. "Engaged Pedagogy and Critical Race Feminism." *Educational Foundations* 24: 19–26. https://files.eric.ed.gov/fulltext/EJ902670.pdf.

Bradley, C., and Holcomb-McCoy, C. 2004. "African American Counselor Educators: Their Experiences, Challenges, and Recommendations." *Counselor Education and Supervision* 43 (4): 258–273. https://doi.org/10.1002/j.1556 -6978.2004.tb01851.x.

Brown, C. 2019. "Anti-Oppression through a Postmodern Lens: Dismantling the Master's Conceptual Tools in Discursive Social Work Practice." *Critical Social Work* 13 (1): 34–65. https://doi.org/10.22329/csw.v13i1.5848.

Brown, P., Hesketh, A., and Williams, S. 2003. "Employability in a Knowledge-Driven Economy." *Journal of Education and Work* 16 (2): 107–126. https://doi .org/10.1080/1363908032000070648.

Chang, H. 2008. "Autoethnography." In *Autoethnography as Method*, edited by Chang, 43–58. Walnut Creek, CA: Left Coast Press.

Chang, H., Ngunjiri, F., Hernandez, K., and ProQuest. 2013. *Collaborative Autoethnography*. Walnut Creek, CA: Left Coast Press.

Cipolle, S. 2010. *Service-Learning and Social Justice: Engaging Students in Social Change*. Toronto: Rowman & Littlefield.

Cooper, S., Cripps, J., and Reisman, J. 2013. "Service-Learning in Deaf Studies: Impact on the Development of Altruistic Behaviors and Social Justice Concern." *American Annals of the Deaf* 157 (5): 413–427. https://doi.org /10.1353/aad.2013.0003.

Crenshaw, K. 1989. "Demarginalizing the Intersection of Race and Sex: A Black Feminist Critique of Antidiscrimination Doctrine, Feminist Theory and Antiracist Politics." *University of Chicago Legal Forum* 1: 139–167. http:// chicagounbound.uchicago.edu/uclf/vol1989/iss1/8.

Crenshaw, K. 1995. *Critical Race Theory: The Key Writings That Formed the Movement*. New York: New Press.

DeCuir, J., and Dixson, A. 2004. "'So When It Comes Out, They Aren't That Surprised That It Is There': Using Critical Race Theory as a Tool of Analysis of Race and Racism in Education." *Educational Researcher* 33 (5): 26–31. https://doi.org/10.3102/0013189X033005026.

Delgado, R. 1989. "Storytelling for Oppositionists and Others: A Plea for Narrative." *Michigan Law Review* 87: 2411–2441. https://doi.org/10.2307 /1289308.

Delgado, R. 1995. *Critical Race Theory: The Cutting Edge.* Philadelphia: Temple University Press.

Delgado, R., and Stefancic, J. 2012. *Critical Race Theory: An Introduction.* New York: NYU Press.

de Montigny, G. 2013. "The Essentialism of Whiteness: Abandoning Empirical Engagement." *Journal of Social Work* 13 (6): 633–651. https://doi.org /10.1177/1468017312475279.

DePaola, T. 2014. "Collaborating for Social Justice through Service Learning." *New Directions for Community Colleges.* https://doi.org/10.1002/cc.20089.

DiAngelo, R. 2011. "White Fragility." *The International Journal of Critical Pedagogy* 3 (3): 54–70. http://libjournal.uncg.edu/ijcp/article/view/249/116.

Douglas, D. 2012. "Black/Out: The White Face of Multiculturalism and the Violence of the Canadian Academic Imperial Project." In *Presumed Incompetent: The Intersections of Race and Class for Women in Academia,* edited by G. Gutierrez y Muhs, Y. Niemann, C. Gonzalez, and A. Harris, 50–64. Boulder: University Press of Colorado.

DuRocher, K. 2011. *Raising Racists: The Socialization of White Children in the Jim Crow South.* Lexington: University Press of Kentucky.

Espino, M., and Lee, J. 2011. "Understanding Resistance: Reflections on Race and Privilege through Service-Learning." *Equity & Excellence in Education* 44 (2): 136–152. https://doi.org/10.1080/10665684.2011.558424.

Evans, S. 2007. "Women of Color in American Higher Education." *Thought & Action,* 131–138. https://eric.ed.gov/?id=EJ1070865.

Evans-Winters, V., and Esposito, J. 2010. "Other People's Daughters: Critical Race Feminism and Black Girls' Education." *Educational Foundations* 24: 11–24.

Few, A. 2007. "Integrating Black Consciousness and Critical Race Feminism into Family Studies Research." *Journal of Family Issues* 28 (4): 452–473. https://doi .org/10.1177/0192513X06297330.

Freire, P. 1982. *Pedagogy of the Oppressed.* New York: Herder.

Furuto, S. 2007. "Components of Service Learning as Pedagogy in Social Work Education." In *Social Work and Service Learning: Partnership for Social Justice,* edited by M. Nadal, and M. Sullivan-Cosetti, 21–39. Toronto: Rowman & Littlefield.

Gardinier, L. 2016. *Service-Learning through Community Engagement: What Community Partners and Members Gain, Lose, and Learn from Campus Collaborations.* New York: Springer.

Gates, T., Heffernan, K., and Sudore, R. 2015. "Social Work Students as Market Consumers: Faculty Perceptions of Customer Service Expectations." *Social Work Education* 34 (7): 881–894. https://doi.org/10.1080/02615479.2015.1065811.

Gerstenblatt, P., and Gilbert, D. 2014. "Framing Service Learning in Social Work: An Interdisciplinary Elective Course Embedded within a

University-Community Partnership." *Social Work Education* 33 (8): 1037–1053. https://doi.org/10.1080/02615479.2014.935731.

Glesne, C., and Peshkin, A. 1992. *Becoming Qualitative Researchers: An Introduction.* White Plains, NY: Longman.

Gosine, K., and Pon, G. 2011. "On the Front Lines: The Voices and Experiences of Racialized Child Welfare Workers in Toronto, Canada." *Journal of Progressive Human Services* 22 (2): 135–159. https://doi.org/10.1080/10428232.2011.599280.

Green, A. 2003. "Difficult Stories: Service-Learning, Race, Class, and Whiteness." *College Composition and Communication* 55 (2): 276–301. https://doi.org/10.2307/3594218.

Gregory, S. 2001. "Black Faculty Women in the Academy: History, Status, and Future." *Journal of Negro Education* 70 (3): 124–138. https://doi.org/10.2307/3211205.

Griffin, R. 2012. "I Am an Angry Black Woman." *Women's Studies in Communication* 35: 138–157. https://doi.org/10.1080/07491409.2012.724524.

Haber-Curran, P., and Tillapaugh, D.W. 2015. "Student-Centered Transformative Learning in Leadership Education: An Examination of the Teaching and Learning Process." *Journal of Transformative Education* 13 (1): 65–84. https://doi.org/10.1177/1541344614559947.

Hains, B., and Smith, B. 2012. "Student-Centered Course Design: Empowering Students to Become Self-Directed Learners." *Journal of Experiential Education* 35 (2): 357–374. https://doi.org/10.1177/105382591203500206.

Haney-López, I. 2007. "'A Nation of Minorities': Race, Ethnicity, and Reactionary Colorblindness." *Stanford Law Review* 59 (4): 985–1063. https://heinonline.org/HOL/LandingPage?handle=hein.journals/stflr59&div=31&id=&page=.

Harley, D. 2008. "Maids of Academe: African American Women Faculty at Predominately White Institutions." *Journal of African American Studies* 12 (1): 19–36. https://doi.org/10.1007/s12111-007-9030-5.

Henry, A. 2015. "'We Especially Welcome Applications from Members of Visible Minority Groups': Reflections on Race, Gender and Life at Three Universities." *Race Ethnicity and Education* 18 (5): 589–610. https://doi.org/10.1080/13613324.2015.1023787.

Henry, A. 2019. "Standing Firm on Uneven Ground: A Letter to Black Women on Academic Leadership." In *African Canadian Leadership: Continuity, Transition and Transformation,* edited by T. Kitossa, E. Lawson, and P. Howard, 82–95. Toronto: University of Toronto Press.

Henry, F., Dua, E., James, C.E., Li, P., Ramos, H., and Smith, M. 2017. *The Equity Myth: Racialization and Indigeneity at Canadian Universities.* Vancouver: University of British Columbia Press.

Hill Collins, P. 2002. *Black Feminist Thought: Knowledge, Consciousness, and the Politics of Empowerment.* New York: Routledge.

Humphrey, K. 2014. "Lessons Learned from Experiential Group Work Learning." *Social Work with Groups* 37 (1): 61–72. https://doi.org/10.1080/01609513.2013.816919.

Jennissen, T., and Lundy, C., eds. 2010. *One Hundred Years of Social Work: A History of the Profession in English Canada, 1900–2000.* Waterloo, ON: Wilfrid Laurier University Press.

Ladson-Billings, G. 2005. "The Evolving Role of Critical Race Theory in Educational Scholarship." *Race Ethnicity and Education* 8 (1): 115–119. https://doi.org/10.1080/1361332052000341024.

Ladson-Billings, G. 2009. "'Who You Callin' Nappy-Headed?' A Critical Race Theory Look at the Construction of Black Women." *Race Ethnicity and Education* 12 (1): 87–99. https://doi.org/10.1080/13613320802651012.

Ladson-Billings, G., and Tate, W. 1995. "Toward a Critical Race Theory of Education." *Teachers College Record* 97 (1): 47–68. https://www.unco.edu/education-behavioral-sciences/pdf/TowardaCRTEduca.pdf.

Lazos, S. 2012. "Are Student Teaching Evaluations Holding Back Women and Minorities? The Perils of 'Doing' Gender and Race in the Classroom." In *Presumed Incompetent: The Intersections of Race and Class for Women in Academia,* edited by G. Gutiérrez y Muhs, C. Niemann, Z. González, and A. Harris, 71–84. Boulder: University Press of Colorado.

Lemieux, C. 2007. "Service Learning in Social Work Education: The State of Knowledge, Pedagogical Practicalities, and Practice Conundrums." *Journal of Social Work Education* 43 (2): 309–325. https://doi.org/10.5175/JSWE.2007.200500548.

Maistry, M. 2014. "Community Engagement, Service Learning and Student Social Responsibility: Implications for Social Work Education at South African Universities: A Case Study of the University of Fort Hare." *Social Work/Maatskaplike Werk* 48 (2): 142–158. https://doi.org/10.15270/48-2-95.

Maynard, R. 2007. *Policing Black Lives: State Violence in Canada from Slavery to the Present.* Halifax, NS: Fernwood.

McKittrick, K. 2011. "On Plantations, Prisons, and a Black Sense of Place." *Social & Cultural Geography* 12 (8): 947–963. https://doi.org/10.1080/14649365.2011.624280.

Mitschke, D., and Petrovich, J. 2011. "Improving Social Work Students' Understanding of Health and Social Justice Knowledge through the Implementation of Service Learning at a Free Community Health Clinic." *Journal of Human Behavior in the Social Environment* 21 (1): 97–108. https://doi.org/10.1080/10911359.2011.535733.

Mullings, D. 2013. "Service Learning: A Teaching Tool to Help Students Acknowledge Their Own Racism." *Race Equality and Teaching* 32 (1): 15–21. https://access.portico.org/Portico/auView?auId=ark:%2F27927%2Fphx2c2c1km.

Mullings, D. 2015. "The Racial Institutionalization of Whiteness in Contemporary Canadian Public Policy." In *Unveiling Whiteness in the 21st Century: Global Manifestations*, edited by V. Watson, D. Howard-Wagner, and L. Spanierman, 12–25. New York: Lexington Books.

Mullings, D. 2016. "Caring for Older Black LGBTQ People: A New Challenge for the Social Work Profession." In *Queering Social Work Education*, edited by S. Hillock and N. Mulé, 23–34 Vancouver, BC: UBC Press.

Myers, K. 2013. "White Fright: Reproducing White Supremacy through Casual Discourse." In *White Out*, 131–146. London: Routledge.

Nelson, C. 2012. "Resisting Invisibility: Black Faculty in Art and Art History in Canada." *Equity Matters.* https://www.ideas-idees.ca/blog/resisting-invisibility-black-faculty-art-and-art-history-canada.

Olssen, M., and Peters, M. 2005. "Neoliberalism, Higher Education and the Knowledge Economy: From the Free Market to Knowledge Capitalism." *Journal of Education Policy* 20 (3): 313–345. https://doi.org/10.1080/02680930500108718.

Phillips, A. 2007. "Service Learning and Social Work Education: A Natural but Tenuous Connection." In *Social Work and Service Learning: Partnership for Social Justice*, edited by M. Nadal and M. Sullivan-Cosetti, 12–23. Toronto: Rowman & Littlefield.

Pratt-Clarke, M. 2010. *Critical Race, Feminism, and Education: A Social Justice Model.* New York: Springer.

Roberts, D. 1999. *Killing the Black Body: Race, Reproduction, and the Meaning of Liberty.* New York: Vintage Books.

Sanders, S., McFarland, P., and J. Bartolli, J. 2003. "The Impact of Cross-Cultural Service-Learning on Undergraduate Social Work Students' Perceptions of Culture, Race, and Economic Justice." *Journal of Baccalaureate Social Work* 9 (1): 19–40. https://doi.org/10.18084/1084-7219.9.1.19.

Smith, M. 2018. "Leadership Diversity Matters at Canada's U15 Research-Intensive Universities." News release. Academic Women's Association University of Alberta. https://uofaawa.wordpress.com/awa-diversity-gap-campaign/the-diversity-gap-in-university-leadership-2018/.

Solórzano, D. 1998. "Critical Race Theory, Race and Gender Microaggressions, and the Experience of Chicana and Chicano Scholars." *International Journal of Qualitative Studies in Education* 11 (1): 121–136. https://doi.org/10.1080/095183998236926.

Tight, M. 2013. "Students: Customers, Clients or Pawns?" *Higher Education Policy* 23 (3): 291–307. https://doi.org/10.1057/hep.2013.2.

Tomlinson, M. 2016. "The Impact of Market-Driven Higher Education on Student-University Relations: Investing, Consuming and Competing." *Higher Education Policy* 29 (2): 149–166. https://doi.org/10.1057/hep.2015.17.

Truong, K., Graves, D., and Keene, A. 2014. "Faculty of Color Teaching Critical Race Theory at a PWI: An Autoethnography." *Journal of Critical Thought and Praxis.* https://doi.org/10.31274/jctp-180810-42.

Turner, C. 2002. "Women of Color in Academe: Living with Multiple Marginality." *Journal of Higher Education* 73 (1): 74–93. https://doi.org /10.1080/00221546.2002.11777131.

Verjee, B. 2012. "Critical Race Feminism: A Transformative Vision for Service-Learning Engagement." *Journal of Community Engagement and Scholarship* 5 (1): 57–63. https://digitalcommons.northgeorgia.edu/jces/vol5/iss1/7.

Villalpando, O., and Delgado Bernal, D. 2002. "A Critical Race Theory Analysis of Barriers That Impede the Success of Faculty of Color." In *The Racial Crisis in American Higher Education: Continuing Challenges for the Twenty-First Century,* edited by W. Smith, P. Altach, and K. Lomotev, 56–68. New York: SUNY Press.

Wallace, S., Moore, S., Wilson, L., and Hart, B. 2012. "African American Women in the Academy: Quelling the Myth of Presumed Incompetence." In *Presumed Incompetent: The Intersections of Race and Class for Women in Academia,* edited by G. Gutiérrez, Y. Muhs, C. Nieman, Z. González, and A. Harris, 421–438. Boulder: University Press of Colorado.

Williams, P.J. 1991. *The Alchemy of Race and Rights.* Cambridge, MA: Harvard University Press.

Wing, A., ed. 1997. *Critical Race Feminism: A Reader.* New York: NYU Press.

Wing, A. 2000. "Introduction: Global Critical Race Feminism for the Twenty-First Century." In *Global Critical Race Feminism: An International Reader,* edited by Wing, 1–15. New York: NYU Press.

Yancy, G. 2004. *What White Looks Like.* New York: Routledge.

Yancy, G. 2008. *Black Bodies, White Gazes: The Continuing Significance of Race.* Lanham, MD: Rowman & Littlefield.

18 Blackness and the Limits of Institutional Goodwill

OMISOORE H. DRYDEN

In 1983, then university president Ian MacDonald convened the Presidential Special Review Committee to explore the "charges of racial and sexist harassment against five York University students on the York Campus" (Committee against Racial Discrimination at York University [CARDY] 1984, 1). According to the 1984 *Majority Report of the Presidential Special Review Committee on Charges of Racial and Sexist Harassment of York University Students and on Metro Toronto Police Conduct on the York University Campus*, the special review committee was established "in the wake of allegations of racial and sexist harassment made by a Black female [graduate] student, Janice Joseph" (1). The majority report documents the anti-Black racism experienced by Joseph and other Black York University students, as well as the ways in which institutional policies and practices failed to disrupt anti-Black racism. The majority report provided a number of recommendations, including the creation of a new office within the university that is responsible for the "receiving, reviewing and resolving complaints specifically related to racial harassment and other over expressions of racial intolerance" (56). In 1988, the Centre for Race & Ethnic Relations (CRER) was established.

In this chapter, I argue that university-established policies and practices are incapable of disrupting anti-Black racism. I am interested in the divide between the student activism in support of Black life and the institutionalization of "inclusion and diversity," "welcoming environments," and "harassment and discrimination-free zones." Through mapping the trajectory of Joseph's experience, 1992 Black student activism, and the creation and trajectory of CRER, I think through the ontological problem made of Blackness, Black subjectivity, and the attempts to disrupt (diverse forms of) anti-Black racism. I base my analysis on documents produced in and by the university alongside my own archives, reflections, and experiences, as a student and as an employee at York University.[1]

I engage in this analysis cognizant of the dialogue already occurring with, for example, Delia D. Douglas's "Black/Out: The White Face of Multiculturalism and the Violence of the Canadian Academic Imperial Project" (2012); Tamari Kitossa's *Implicit Racism: The Need for Deep Diversity at Brock University* (2016); and Annette Henry's "We Especially Welcome Applications from Members of Visible Minority Groups" (2015). In my recounting of anti-Blackness, Black subjectivity, and Blackness at York University, I make use of Rinaldo Walcott's description of Blackness. He states that Blackness is "to signal it as a sign, one that carries with it particular histories of resistance and domination. Blackness is also a sign which is never closed and always under contestation ... allow[ing] for a certain kind of malleability and open-endedness which means that questions of blackness far exceed the categories of the biological and the ethnic" (Walcott 2003, 27).

And as Frank Wilderson posits, "*Blackness* refers to an individual who is by definition always already void of relationality" (Wilderson 2010, 18).

Janice Joseph, a Black woman from St. Kitts, was a PhD student and a teaching assistant who lived in graduate residence at York University. Joseph was subject to sexist-racism from her neighbour, Grant Austin, a white man and a third-year undergraduate student. According to the majority report, Joseph and Austin lived in the same on-campus student apartment building. Their apartments were side-by-side and shared a common wall. On a number of occasions, Austin left flyers, including those from Kentucky Fried Chicken, posters, and other forms of litter outside of Joseph's door. In the notes he posted on, and the letters he slipped under, her door, Austin often referred to Joseph as "missie" or "little girl." One note stated, "They sure didn't make them smart when they made them *Black*" (CARDY 1984, 4; emphasis in original note). By 1983, the harassment Joseph was experiencing had escalated and increased in intensity. Austin began to bang on the adjoining walls throughout the day and night. According to the majority report, Joseph stated that she began to fear for her safety and had contacted York University's Safety and Security Office[2] requesting that they intervene. However, on the occasions that security officers *did* attend to speak to Austin, he refused to answer his door (7). Feeling frustrated with the lack of support and guidance offered by the university, Joseph posted an open letter (7) in *Excalibur*, the university student paper, appealing for help.

In response to this letter, and in an attempt to resolve this situation, three Black men – Ike Hendrickson, Barrington Morrison, and Vernie Green (each a student at York University) – decided to intervene by visiting Austin (CARDY 1984, 7). Hendrickson, Morrison, and Green approached Austin's apartment and knocked on the door, intending to have a conversation. However, not only did Austin refuse to answer the door (as he had done with Safety and Security officers), but he also called the police (an action he did *not* take with Safety and Security officers). According to the report, "While the students were attempting to engage [with Austin] in a dialogue, approximately eight policemen arrived in the corridor. All three [Black] students expressed, during their testimony, astonishment that so many policemen arrived so quickly in the short span of time between the first knock on the door and the subsequent attempted dialogue through the closed door (8).

Hendrickson, Morrison, and Green were accosted by the police officers, patted down, and threatened with arrest.

The majority report details the police harassment and brutality that these young men endured. It recounts how one of the officers addressed the students with comments such as "I hate you niggers" and "You are a bunch of thieves and troublemakers" (CARDY 8). The same officer, it is documented, asked for Hendrickson's identification and after looking at the document, tossed it onto the ground instead of returning it directly to the student (8). Hendrickson, Morrison, and Green asked the university's security officers in attendance to document the police's "racial abuse and harassment" (iii). According to the report, "The offending officer waived his hand toward the York Security officer and said, 'Keep out of this,' to which the York Security officer responded, 'I don't want anything to do with it'" (9).

In thinking through experiences of Joseph, and the intervention attempted by Hendrickson, Morrison, and Green, the engagement of Jared Sexton's work with Lewis Gordon is productive. Specifically, Gordon's discussion draws attention to "the twin axioms of white superiority and black inferiority" (Sexton 2010, 27), and the "negative categorical imperative – above all don't be black" (Gordon, as cited by Sexton 2010, 27). Outside Austin's door, Hendrickson, Morrison, and Green were treated as the recognizable dangerous stranger. They were considered to not-belong in that space by Toronto police, and when they turned to the agents of the university for assistance, their identity as student was once again denied. These actions by Safety and Security officers made them "junior partners" to Toronto police.

On 1 June 1983, William Farr, vice president (Finance & Employee Relations) "conducted a hearing into complaints made by Janice Joseph against Mr. Grant Austin" (CARDY 1984, 85). Farr determined that Austin did act in a "harassing and insulting manner" but concluded that Austin did not constitute a physical threat of Joseph. As a penalty, Austin was not "to be" allowed to live in residence. The majority report includes a copy of a letter, written by the Presidential Special Committee to

President Ian Macdonald on 21 June 1983 asking to appeal the decision made by Farr at the disciplinary hearing. The committee insisted that "in light of the seriousness of the charge, and that this is a precedent setting decision, we recommend that Mr. Austin be expelled from the University immediately" (93).

Although the special committee was mandated to provide effective solutions that would "ensure that people on the York Campus conduct themselves in a manner that reflects the behavioural standards and expectations of the York Community" (CARDY 1984, 2), it would seem that President Macdonald refused this request from the special committee. The majority report states that as of 13 October 1983, Austin was still enrolled as a student and taking courses and had continued his sexist and racist harassment of Joseph (v).

According to the majority report, "Mr. Macdonald emphasized that he did not want the Committee's work to be *merely* an exercise in public relations. He asked the Committee to demonstrate York's commitment to provide effective solutions that will equip the University to quickly come to terms with these difficult situations" (CARDY 1984, 2; emphasis added). As such, the mandate of the committee included providing recommendations on mechanisms that could "as far as it is possible, ensure that people on the York Campus conduct themselves in a manner that reflects the behavioural standards and expectations of the York community" (2).

At the conclusion of the Presidential Special Committee, the majority report[3] (written by a majority of the total committee members) made twenty-five recommendations. CRER opened in 1988; however, the creation of this office only *partially* responded to the concerns outlined in the majority report, or the committee's twenty-five recommendations.

How are Black students to respond when the recommendations of the majority report are not addressed? What options are made available to Black students to have the institution respond and intervene in the disruption of anti-Black racism?

On 12 March 1992 at York University, students protested anti-Black racism in the university. This protest was in response to a number of racist incidents, including: a Black woman student being physically assaulted by a bouncer at the Underground;[4] York Security officers harassing Black students studying in the library; York Security officers asking Black students in the student centre to produce identification, because they "look too young to be students"; a parking lot attendant telling a Black student, "This is not the jungle"; and a Black student who was told by a professor, "Your kind of people make me want to puke" (Dryden personal archives). During the protest we chanted, "No Justice

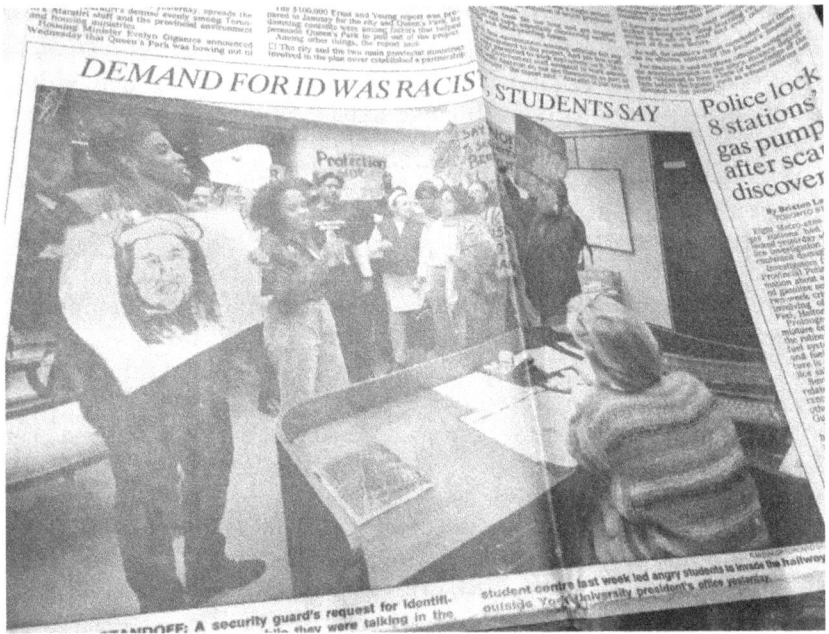

Figure 18.1. *Toronto Star*, 13 March 1992.

No Peace," "Respect Due," "No Apartheid at York," "Say No to Security Brutality," "By Any Means Necessary," and "Stop the Harassment, Fire the Racists" (Dryden personal archive). Black students (I was a student at the time) organized a response to this anti-Black racism and racial profiling.

We occupied the president's office, and before agreeing to leave we demanded to have a public meeting with President Harry Arthurs, then executive director of safety and security, Pam MacDonald, and the general manager of the Student Centre, Rob Castle. At the meeting, which occurred on 16 March 1992, we presented a list of demands,[5] which included an investigation into Safety and Security by an external body, and the hiring of another full-time staff person for CRER. President Harry Arthurs did not attend this meeting, but every member of the senior administration was in attendance, including then vice president finance, William Farr. Farr informed us that while President Arthurs was away,[6] Farr was the acting president and could make any necessary decisions.[7]

We were seeking justice and yet turned to the university to provide that justice through reviews and restructuring of existing systems. Many

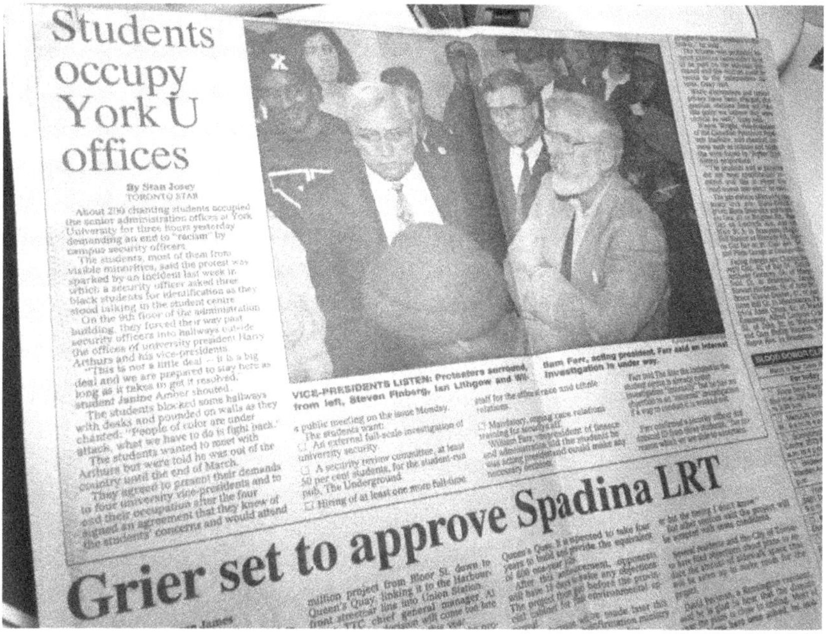

Students occupy York U offices

By Stan Josey
TORONTO STAR

About 200 chanting students occupied the senior administration offices at York University for three hours yesterday demanding an end to "racism" by campus security officers.

The students, most of them from visible minorities, said the protest was sparked by an incident last week in which a security officer asked three black students for identification as they stood talking in the student centre.

On the 9th floor of the administration building, they forced their way past security officers into hallways outside the offices of university president Harry Arthurs and his vice-presidents.

"This is not a little deal – it is a big deal and we are prepared to stay here as long as it takes to get it resolved," student Janine Amber shouted.

The students blocked some hallways with desks and pounded on walls as they chanted: "People of color are under attack, what we have to do is fight back."

The students wanted to meet with Arthurs but were told he was out of the country until the end of March.

They agreed to present their demands to four university vice-presidents and to end their occupation after the four signed an agreement that they knew of the students' concerns and would attend

VICE-PRESIDENTS LISTEN: Protesters surround, from left, Steven Finberg, Ian Lithgow and William Farr, acting president. Farr said an internal investigation is under way.

a public meeting on the issue Monday.

The students want:

An external full-scale investigation of university security.

A security review committee, at least 50 per cent students, for the student-run pub, The Underground.

Hiring of at least one more full-time staff for the office of race and ethnic relations.

Mandatory, ongoing race relations training for security staff.

Grier set to approve Spadina LRT

Figure 18.2. *Toronto Star*, 12 March 1992.

of us felt that the system could work effectively if it were tweaked and changed in a few significant places. The flyer for the protest was titled "Action Now" and above the list of grievances was the statement, "This is your university. It should be a safe and non-threating environment for all students" (Dryden personal archive). Our demands at the large public meeting on 16 March included timelines and deadlines for when each demand was to be met. And while some students continued to work with the university to ensure that the demands were met, other students returned to their studies, exams, final papers, jobs, family responsibilities, and other activist projects. And this is the climate of student activism. The institution can afford to wait out students – wait for students to drop out or return to studies and then graduate. There was a university institutional discourse that ultimately alienated students who were not fully versed on the mechanisms of the academic system. Yet, in this disciplinary structure, a new review committee was established to review the work of the Safety and Security Department, and a person was hired in CRER. I posit that these "wins" suggested that a commitment had been made to address the larger issues of anti-Blackness in the university, but those commitments were not specified or fully spelled out and therefore not executed.

York University opened CRER in 1988 and David Trotman[8] was appointed as director. At the end of Trotman's term in 1990, Chet Singh[9] became the first full-time advisor. Also in 1990, CRER and the Sexual Harassment Education & Complaint Centre (SHEACC)[10] began to share resources, included office space. In 1992, in response to the above detailed demands, a second full-time advisor, Teferi Adem,[11] was added to the staff. It was only a few years later that Singh left the university to pursue other endeavours and I was hired[12] to work in the centre.

Commitments to address anti-Black racism meant finding creative and strategic tools that would compel the university to move beyond minimum requirements (as outlined by provincial human rights legislation) and engage in maximum efforts to disrupt racism. I'm reminded of Mohanty, who argues, "Cultures of dissent must work to create pedagogies of dissent rather than pedagogies of accommodation" (Mohanty 2003, 216). The separation of racial harassment from sexual harassment, as signified in these two distinct and separated offices and policies,[13] meant that as Audre Lorde stated, Black women were "too alien to comprehend" (Lorde 1984, 117) and therefore outside the boundaries of normative delimited understandings of racism and sexism. As a Black woman working in the office, there was an underlying belief that my "racism work" was not complicated with the interlocking realities of sexism and/or homophobia.[14] And there were regularly occurring moments when Black women walked into the office, needing a determination to be made: was their concern "more" about sexism or "more" about racism? Kimberlé Crenshaw states, "The intersectional experience is greater than the sum of racism and sexism, any analysis that does not take intersectionality into account cannot sufficiently address the particular manner in which Black women are subordinated. Thus, for feminist theory and antiracist policy discourse to embrace the experiences and concerns of Black women, the entire framework that has been used as a basis for translating 'women's experience' or 'the Black experience' into concrete policy demands must be rethought and recast" (Crenshaw 1989, 140). In other words, how can the experiences of Black women be better represented in the complaint procedures in the university?

Returning to Janice Joseph, the majority report acknowledged the sexism that informed the type of racism to which she was subject: "Janice Joseph suffered both sexist and racist abuse" (CARDY 1984, 24). It then goes on to state, "The nature of Janice Joseph's complaint was sexist as well as racist and constituted an attack against her as a womon [sic] and as a Black person" (55). The special committee felt that the reluctance to acknowledge sexual violence on campus was "the same reluctance we [the special committee] have detected throughout our enquiry, to name racism when it occurs" (24). In this assessment of Joseph's experience, we witness both the difficulties to speak about the interlocking realities of sexism and racism, but also the attempts of the committee to fully capture the misogynoir[15] Joseph was experiencing.

There was an attempt to address harassment and discrimination, in the wording of the policy and procedures framework in the university, following the release of the 1999 decision in *Law v Canada (Minster of Employment and Immigration)*. In this decision Justice Iacobucci states that there must be an allowance to address and articulate the ill effects of a situation based on one or more grounds. The documentation of new directions by the Supreme Court and proposed (at the time, yet now realized) changes to provincial human rights practices effectively demonstrated the need for the university to think through and develop procedures that would allow for a more detailed accounting of the types of harassment and discrimination complainants were experiencing. It was the hope that the untouched underlying social structures and the occluded complexity of meaning would be disrupted if the system were able to address and recognize the complexity of everyday experiences, to move beyond just simply addressing discrete "symptoms." This meant combatting the belief that citing more than one ground of harassment and/or discrimination meant that the complainant was attempting to manipulate the system (unfairly) in the complainant's favour.

While on paper, university and college institutions may include words "on one or more grounds," the practice in institutions has become more committed to gatekeeping and risk management. As such, human rights offices were now used to ensure the university's reputation was protected (see Ahmed 2012; Schmidt 2015) – a practice that also occurred at York University.

In the early 2000s, SHEACC, along with CRER underwent another restructuring. With the addition of a new special assistant to the president on human rights, both centres became part of the larger office, newly titled the Centre for Human Rights and Equity. The President's Office made this change with little input from the larger university community. I left the university in 2004, and it was at this time that another much larger change occurred. An external review of the Centre for Human Rights and Equity occurred, again initiated by the President's Office, and the recommendations of this review included creating a Centre for Human Rights, which effectively closed SHEACC and CRER and also removed race and ethnic relations/sexual harassment/sexual and gender diversity advisors. Staff in the office were required to be "generalists," not "specialists."

The challenges in the university are not isolated from the larger Canadian landscape. Canadian multiculturalism, through both federal legislation and national narratives, becomes the obstacle that makes Blackness and anti-Blackness difficult to image in the nation.[16] If considered as a form of public relations, multiculturalism suggests that the nation is established within and maintains *good will* (Ahmed 2012, 143). Thus when issues of anti-Black racism are raised, it is cast as "disgruntled voices," unappreciative of the nation and its commitment to tolerance through neoliberal narratives of multiculturalism, and not a serious, isolated incident. Canada's enduring espousal of multiculturalism makes it difficult to have anti-Blackness understood as endemic to, and within the fabric of, Canadian nation-making; thus "the Black" remains unable to fully traverse the boundary between inclusion and exclusion.

I thought I left this particular form of work (institutional, fighting from within) behind, yet when I was a pre-tenure professor, at a small, predominately white institution in northern Ontario, I found myself returned to the institutional labour of "inclusion and diversity," "welcoming environments," "harassment and discrimination-free zones" as part of my university service. As Sara Ahmed (2012) has argued, there was much resistance to this work, both from the institution (committed to a colour-blind[17] politics of inclusion) and me (I did not want to take on this role as the only full-time Black/person of colour faculty member). Participating in this work meant that I addressed the fallacy of race neutrality and the ineffectiveness of simply uttering "This is a welcoming place." But my presence on campus also meant that my Blackness in public view would animate the already anti-Black discord. This was realized on 28 February 2016 when posters on my office door where torn off and covered with graffiti. The misogynoir of this incident was poorly understood and existed outside the parameters of the university's official harassment and discrimination policy. And I must state again that the anti-Black (sexist) racism I experienced on the job is neither unique nor an isolated experience.

The trajectory from Janice Joseph's experiences in 1983 continued in 2015. For example, #BlackOnCampus videos were popping up and spreading across Canadian university and college campuses (Francis 2015). On 27 November 2015, students and faculty protested at the University of British Columbia demanding that the "many manifestations of racism at the university" be addressed (Tseghay 2016). And on 16 January 2017, the CBC's *The Current* spoke with PhD students Huda Hassan (University of Toronto) and Sam Tecle (York University), and

Dr. Malinda Smith (University of Alberta) about anti-Black racism in Canadian academia. Canadian academic institutions that claim to be "welcoming" and "inclusive" are not committed to disrupting and addressing racism generally, and anti-Black racism specifically. This chapter is just a tiny look into some of the history of anti-Black racism in Canadian universities.

NOTES

1 My paid position with the university was that of advisor on race and ethnic relations and sexual and gender diversity. This was an administrative position that reported to the senior executive of the university. The position was responsible for providing services to all levels of the university community.
2 In 2017, at the writing of this chapter, the name of security services at York University is York Security Services. However, at the time of these racist events, the department had a slightly different name.
3 The members of the Presidential Special Committee wrote two reports. I was unable to locate a copy of the minority report. Although detailed recommendations were made on the conduct of Toronto Police Services on campus and York University's Safety and Security officers, no substantive actions were taken. The majority report also included three additional subsections: "Disciplinary Procedures," "The Standing Committee for Race Relations," and "The Centre for the Protection of Human, Civil, and Legal Rights and Charter of Rights for Students."
4 The Underground is a restaurant/pub located in the basement of the York University Student Centre.
5 1. We demand a full-scale investigation into security conducted by an external body, in consultation with the director of race and ethnic relations;
   2. We demand the formation of a security review committee for the Underground comprising at least 50% students;
   3. We demand the hiring of at least one more full-time staff person for the Office of Race and Ethnic Relations to deal with racial discrimination on campus;
   4. We demand an annual review of security, by an external body in cooperation with the Office of Race and Ethnic Relations, to check for discriminatory behaviour;
   5. We demand any officer found guilty of discriminatory behaviour be fired immediately;
   6. We demand a commitment to mandatory and ongoing race relations training of security staff (Dryden personal archives).

6   Later we found that President Arthurs was not out of the country, as stated in the meeting and cited in the *Toronto Star*, but was in fact on campus that day.

7   William Farr, as stated by the *Toronto Star*, "confirmed a security office did demand ID from three students, 'for no reason which we are able to ascertain'" (1992, A6).

8   Dr. Trotman became the first Black person to hold the position of master of a college at York University (Founders College). Before his appointment in the CRER, Trotman was the coordinator of the Latin American & Caribbean Studies Program at York University.

9   Chet Singh is the founding member of the Dub Poets collective and former board member of the Ontario Arts Council. He is recognized as a pioneer of dub poetry and spoken word in Canada. Singh is a human rights activist. He is also a college professor.

10 I have little documentation on how the Sexual Harassment Education & Complaint Centre (SHEACC) was instituted in the university. Nor do I have access to the history of advisors. What I am familiar with is that during this time (1988–92) SHEACC was in operation. In the 1990s there were two full-time advisors (both white women): Dale Hall (who now works as the human rights advisor to the president at George Brown College), and Siobhan McEwan (who now lives in Australia and works as a clinical psychologist). The demands to hire a second full-time advisor in CRER were, in part, to mirror the staffing complement of SHEACC.

11 In 2012, Teferi Adem was the recipient of the William P. Hubbard Award for Race Relations awarded by the City of Toronto. He has worked at the Ethiopian Association and as the Diversity Program coordinator at the Alzheimer Society of Toronto. Teferi Adem, a social worker and a human rights consultant, has a long, vibrant, and rich history of anti-racism work in the city of Toronto.

12 I began my employment as an advisor-in-training and I reported to the vice president of campus relations and student affairs, Elizabeth Hopkins. At that time, my role was to provide supportive "anti-racist counselling and information to individuals or small groups; do initial intake of 'complaints'; maintain complete, detailed and confidential notes and files; offer anti-racist education workshops to student groups; assist with dispute resolution; work with the Centre for Race & Ethnic Relations Advisory Board; assist in the collection and maintenance of resource materials for the centre; represent the centre on committees and tasks forces; maintain contact with external and internal anti-racist groups, agencies, centres, associations and clubs; attend weekly working meetings with other advisors and the vice president; attend staff meetings between CRER/SHEACC regularly, and assist when necessary in general office operations" (Dryden personal archive).

13 The Policy Concerning Racism was vastly different from the Sexual Harassment Policy (which included provisions for gender harassment). For example, the Policy Concerning Racism consisted of these four statements:
1. York University affirms that the racial and ethnocultural diversity of its
   community is a source of excellence, enrichment and strength.
2. York University affirms its commitment to human rights, and, in particular, to the principle that every member of the York community has a
   right to equitable treatment without harassment or discrimination on the
   grounds prohibited by the Ontario Human Rights Code, including race
   and ethnicity.
3. York University acknowledges its on-going responsibility to foster fairness
   and respect, to create and maintain a positive working and learning environment and to promote anti-racism.
4. Anyone in the York community who infringes a right protected by the
   Ontario Human Rights Code shall be subject to complaint procedures,
   remedies and sanctions in the University's policies, codes, regulations
   and collective agreements as they exist from time to time, and to such
   discipline (including rustication or discharge) as may be appropriate in
   the circumstances.

14 There are still occasions where I am confronted with/vexed by the question, "What is more important to you, your race or your gender (sex,
orientation)?"

15 Moya Bailey, a Black queer feminist scholar, first used the term "misogynoir" in 2010 (Bailey 2010, np), and she conceived of the term in order
to better capture the specific type of harassment and discrimination
(anti-Black sexism/sexist racism) Black women encounter and confront.

16 Canada's anti-Black, racist, historical, and contemporary realities are often
nationally and publicly obscured by narratives that frame Canada as innocent and free of the "ugly" realities present elsewhere.

17 The politics of colour-blindness is an indication of racial anxiety, not race
neutrality, as is argued. The claim that one does not see colour does nothing to disrupt the ways in which decisions are made based on the systems of
white supremacy.

REFERENCES

Ahmed, S. 2012. *On Being Included: Racism and Diversity in Institutional Life.*
Durham, NC: Duke University Press.
Bailey, M. 2010, 14 March. "They Aren't Talking about Me …" Crunk Feminist
Collective: Where Crunk Meets Conscious and Feminism Meets Cool. http://
www.crunkfeministcollective.com/2010/03/14/they-arent-talking-about-me/.

CBC. 2017. "Black PhD Students Call Out Inequity in Canadian Academia." *The Current*, 16 January. https://www.cbc.ca/radio/thecurrent/the-current-for -january-16-2017-1.3934687/black-phd-students-call-out-inequity-in -canadian-academia-1.3934776.

Committee against Racial Discrimination at York University (CARDY). 1984. *Majority Report: Special Review Committee on Charges of Racial and Sexual Harassment and on Metro Toronto Police Conduct on the York University Campus.* York University.

Crenshaw, K. 1989. "Demarginalizing the Intersection of Race and Sex: A Black Feminist Critique of Antidiscrimination Doctrine, Feminist Theory and Antiracist Politics." *University of Chicago Legal Forum*. https:// chicagounbound.uchicago.edu/uclf/vol1989/iss1/8.

Crenshaw, K. 1991. "Mapping the Margins: Intersectionality, Identity Politics, and Violence against Women of Color." *Stanford Law Review* 43 (6): 1241–1299. https://doi.org/10.2307/1229039.

Douglas, D. 2012. "Black/Out. The White Face of Multiculturalism and the Violence of the Canadian Imperial Academic Project." In *Presumed Incompetent: The Intersections of Race and Class for Women in Academia*, edited by G. Gutiérrez y Muhs, Y. Nieman, C. González, and A. Harris, 50–65. Boulder: University Press of Colorado.

Francis, A. 2016. "Canada Students In Canada Get Behind the #BlackOnCampus Movement." *The Huffington Post*, 20 November. https:// www.huffingtonpost.ca/2015/11/20/black-on-campus-canada_n_8612482 .html.

Henry, A. 2015. "'We Especially Welcome Applications from Members of Visible Minority Groups': Reflections on Race, Gender and Life at Three Universities." *Race Ethnicity and Education* 18 (5): 589–610. https://doi.org /10.1080/13613324.2015.1023787.

Kitossa, T. 2016. *Implicit Racism: The Need for Deep Diversity at Brock University.* http:www.brockpress.com/2016/03/implicit-racism-the-need-for-deep -diversity-at-brock-unversity/.

Law v Canada (Minister of Employment and Immigration), [1991] 1 SCR 497.

Lorde, A. 1984. *Sister Outsider: Essays & Speeches*. Berkeley. CA: Crossing Press.

Mohanty, C. 2003. *Feminism without Borders: Decolonizing Theory, Practicing Solidarity*. Durham, NC: Duke University Press.

Schmidt, P. 2015. "Colleges Respond to Racist Incidents as If Their Chief Worry Is Bad PR, Studies Find." *The Chronicle of Higher Education*, 21 April. https:// www.chronicle.com/article/Colleges-Respond-to-Racist/229517.

Sexton, J. 2010. "People-of-Color-Blindness: Notes on the Afterlife of Slavery." *Social Text* 103 (28): 31–56. https://doi.org/10.1215/01642472-2009-066.

Toronto Star. 1992, 13 March. "Demand for ID Was Racist Students Say."

Toronto Star. 1992, 13 March. "Students Occupy York U Offices."

Toronto Star. 1992, 17 March. "York U Agrees to Demands."

Tseghay, D. 2016. "Challenging Anti-Black Racism on Canadian Campuses." RandkAndFile.ca. https://www.rankandfile.ca/challenging-anti-black-racism-on-canadian-campuses/.

Walcott, R. 2003. *Black Like Who: Writing Black Canada.* Toronto: Insomniac Press.

Wilderson, F., III. 2010. *Red, White & Black: Cinema and the Structure of U.S. Antagonisms.* Durham, NC: Duke University Press.

19 Leadership in Neoliberal Times: A Road to Nowhere

JENNIFER R. KELLY

Re-production, especially in its Marxist-feminist sense, refers not only to the explicit use of power within institutions, but to the conditions of consciousness that enable the maintenance of existing institutional patterns, habits and structures. It thus refers to the patterns of thought that condition patterns of action, and set the limits of possibility to the working conditions of the academy.

– Franklin (2015)

This chapter highlights critical scholarship on race and racialization to examine leadership and administration within academic institutions constituted as "white." Specifically, I describe and analyse my own experiences as a Black woman administrator in a university. Women racialized as other than white still face racism – they are still subject to racialized power as enacted through institutional whiteness. Drawing on critical social theory literature, I tease out how these racialized and gendered social intersections and interactions play out in our advanced neoliberal times. The chapter allows for recognition of what James and Valluvan (2014) describe as the "mutual embrace of racism and neoliberalism in higher education" (1). My main task here is to raise a political and ideological question: Who can Black academics rely on to support their leadership?

Introduction

While leadership within the Black community has historically been an important discussion point in North America (from Sojourner Truth, Harriet Tubman, Angela Davis, bell hooks, Frederick Douglass, Marcus Garvey, W.E.B. Du Bois, Frantz Fanon, and Martin Luther King Jr., through to the present day), it is paramount that consideration of leadership extends beyond our own communities, that the discussion is not just contained or related to aspirations within the Black communities but recognizes possibilities that border the community. While the experiences of an administrator in a university setting might be perceived by some as external to the real issues facing the Black community,[1] in actuality the university and Black communities can be considered as border communities: spaces where people cross back and forth, even if the traffic is limited. This border positioning can be viewed in relation to my role as chair, administrator, or academic leader, someone who is approached by folks from different Black communities about navigating the off-putting bureaucracy of universities. For example, someone approached me about how to publish a book; someone else wanted advice on returning to study; and a few request support with getting a job. In a similar vein of reciprocity I take the university into the lives of Black community members to carry out research on people's lived experiences. The shift in the 1990s towards discussion of equity in employment led to small gains in representation of previously excluded equity groups in universities, but as noted by several Black Canadian scholars, although some inroads have been made into the "ivory tower" (Henry and Tator 2009; Smith 2014), there is still a struggle for bodies racialized as non-white. The equity group that has gained the most over the past thirty years from changes in policies have been women, and more significantly women racialized as white (Smith 2014). Women racialized as non-white (e.g., African descent, Aboriginal) are still not part of the mainstream and are still outside the corridors and bathrooms of power.

Historically, Black women and men have been able to find solace primarily through leadership within Black-led organizations. My recent archival work on the African Methodist Episcopal church in Alberta provides ample examples of such leadership in the early 1920s, especially among women.[2] Further, from the early twentieth century through to the mid-1970s, the Black-led Chicago-based International Union of the Brotherhood of Sleeping Car Porters demonstrates how those workers fought for their labour rights and broadened civil rights for all Canadians (Cui and Kelly 2010; Mathieu 2001).[3]

Despite strong leadership demonstrated through many of the Black-led organizations, recent shifts that allowed a few of us to lead within historically white organizations have manifested racialized dynamics. The literature indicates that while becoming a leader in a white institution might be presumed by some as success for Black academic leaders, this change in position can create "disempowering experiences ... [for] leaders in predominantly white organizations" (Stanley, cited in Davis and Moldalano 2015, 6). In examining these disempowering experiences and the culture that operates within traditional institutions such as universities, we find inequities reinforced through a structural apparatus that is gendered, raced, and neoliberal. This neoliberalism constitutes higher education as a market, a space of differentiation where traditional understandings of leadership re-inscribe forms of masculinity associated with whiteness that reproduces the status quo rather than changing the institution. So we see that leadership is about performing sameness both physically and ideologically. The disempowering experiences can be identified as a form of "institutional whiteness" (Ahmed 2013), and I would argue that this institutional whiteness is at the heart of the inability of universities to take up social change in any serious way. As Sara Ahmed (2013) has indicated, having a diversity policy is not enough to be able to claim that an organization is inclusive. In addition to institutional whiteness, a university culture of neoliberalism is also under scrutiny in this chapter – an ideological structure and context within which the categories of race, gender, and criticality are nested. Regarded as an episteme, or "a *historical a priori*" (Foucault 2002, 127; emphasis in the original) that structures and organizes certain types of knowledge and speech as acceptable during our present era, neoliberalism is also a conundrum; it is always doing more than one thing. Although free-market supporters advocate for a classic economic laissez-faire market, we find instead that the supposed free market is often massaged and unlocked by the state, or in this instance by administrators within universities. This opening up of universities to the market is more about creating a space within which the cult of individualism can deepen and flourish. So as a Black female administrator I am not only contoured by race, gender, and criticality (ideology) but also by free market initiatives: fluidity of faculty labour, larger class sizes, growth of online learning fostered through technological innovations, and push for international students who bolster university funds through higher tuition fees.

In the methodology for this chapter I draw on feminist scholarship and auto-ethnography by placing myself within a social context that allows for self-reflexivity. Thus I examine and analyse my own experiences as a Black administrator in a university setting dominated by a neoliberal economic framework wherein experiences are mediated through race, gender, and specific masculinized understandings. By examining discourse, I tease out how these racialized and gendered social intersections and interactions played out in my life as a chair, within an advanced neoliberal time of fast capitalism (Agger 1989). Although my reflections are based on personal anecdote, I think that we can learn a broader lesson about how racialized and gendered ideology operates within institutions historically constituted as white. Although I am cautious that the emphasis on the individual might overwhelm broader institutional structures, "I also know that my personal story could be almost anyone's: the thing about reproductive mechanisms is that they are by definition generic. My experience is very recognisable" (Franklin 2015, 22). I am particularly interested in the "how" of institutionalized whiteness and with issues of complicity in reproduction of inequities and contradictions in thinking whereby those of us who are interested in change and social justice end up being part of the broader processes of reproduction of inequities. I find Sara Ahmed's comment on sexism insightful for understanding how complicity in race and inequities occurs: she indicates clearly the necessity to show how sexism (and in my case, racism) is a set of attitudes that are institutionalized, a pattern that is established through use, such that it can be "reproduced *almost* independently of individual will" (Ahmed 2014, 10). This idea of reproduction of inequities, despite the will to do otherwise, is interesting, especially for those of us who know that just placing racialized bodies into positions of leadership is not enough to bring about social change. I take up Sara Franklin's suggestion that "the question of how we understand the means by which the academy is reproduced helps us to ask sharper questions about our own reproductive practices, as well as to intervene in the means of reproduction we want to challenge" (Franklin 2015, 14). I see this chapter as prodding me to ask sharper questions.

By generating data to guide analysis of the main issues of racialization, gender, and criticality I will share three encounters with faculty members (three men and one woman racialized as white). To ascertain what can be learned about leadership in a university setting I have sorted my data into three themes: the unexpected chair; creating a crisis; hear no evil, see no evil, speak no evil. The four faculty members are folks whose areas of scholarship can be identified with a traditional masculinized form of educational administration and leadership and who are able to use racialized power to enact institutional whiteness to ensure that only specific forms of change take place and change does not fundamentally challenge their own power within their areas of scholarship or the organization. For me, these encounters relay the production/reproduction of racialized power as enacted through institutional whiteness.

The Unexpected Chair

Entitlement

I make a phone call to a woman I have known since my graduate student days and who became a faculty member the same year as I did. We both ran for the

position of department chair. She has been friendly before the interviews for the
position. Once I am announced as chair, things change. On the night of the an-
nouncement I ring to suggest how we could work together for the department. On
the other end of the phone she is cool, if not cold. "Jenny you know I am fond of
you, but I don't want to talk to you. I am going to appeal the decision." I said to
her "OK" and put the phone down.

So What to Make of the Encounter?

Well, certain types of bodies in certain institutional spaces have become
so normalized that Other bodies raced and gendered seem to be an
abomination. I know that because when I was interviewed and selected
as chair of my department in 2010, those in opposition to my selection were not just surprised but startled. I was able to recognize those
who were not my supporters because they did not congratulate me or
offer to support me in any way. I think this sense of some folks being
entitled to becoming leaders and others assumed incapable of leading but rather of only following directions was clearly illustrated and
made obvious to me. It is a stereotype that has haunted Black folks since
manumission and before – our supposed inability to take the initiative,
to come up with ideas (Kelly and Wossen-Taffesse 2012). While some
might say being selected as chair was just a surprise because I had not
been mentored into a chair role nor identified for succession planning,
I would pose the counter-argument as to why harassers did not let it go
at being surprised. Why take the time to consistently meet, plan, and
escalate minor issues, to make sure they always reinterpret negatively
what I have said? It would seem that it was more than just a surprise; it
challenged their sense of being.[4]

I thought long and hard about the non-conversation with my colleague on the phone and concluded that what she expressed was her
surprise that I was chosen over her. I came to see this incident as indicative of her sense of entitlement,[5] a sense that it was unbelievable
that I had been chosen. That sense of naturalness and entitlement
haunted my time as an administrator. Through discursive practices,
I have been constituted as an unexpected chair – one who was neither
expected nor the "natural" successor to the outgoing white male or
his self-appointed successor. I was regarded as not entitled to become
part of the decision-making hierarchy. I was not the chosen one.
I began to become aware that a few of my department colleagues
regarded white folks, especially men, as more natural at undertaking
the role of chair – a role that only a certified administrator could assume. While some were vocally hostile, others expressed ambivalence

about the fact that I was the first woman to be chair of the department and also a woman racialized as Black. My being chair was something to be resisted.

Regardless of traditional university expectations of collegial governance whereby administration is open to all academics to participate, the colleague who became chair had to be white, preferably male, and committed to following the rules. When these expectations of white entitlement are linked to broader governance structures in the neoliberal university, we begin to see a desire for administrators who support individualism, specific types of knowledge production, administration through the expert qualified through certification, and concern with the broader international framework for education rather than more home-based equity issues. For those who are pedagogically against the shift in educational institutions to advanced neoliberalism and fast capitalism (with its strong tendencies towards revenue generation on the backs of international students and communities not traditionally served by universities), speaking out becomes problematic, especially when linked to non-white bodies. This became evident to me when as a chair I spoke against the growing advanced neoliberalism, and larger class sizes, a culture driven by technology rather than pedagogy, and the inherent inequities that such changes would produce in our undergraduate program. My reluctance to support neoliberal policies was perceived by fellow academics as akin to an uppity Black, as going beyond my station, and thus any authority traditionally associated with the role of chair was no longer valid. This was not just my perception. After one particularly tense meeting about my department's role in our faculty's undergraduate program, a sympathetic faculty member noted that what had occurred in the meeting was one of the most blatant examples of racism they had perceived in the faculty.

For many academics present at the meeting, the disrespect shown towards me went unnoticed and the power and privilege of the undergraduate chair to mete out such treatment was ignored, maybe because "privilege is not visible to its holder; it is merely there, a part of the world, a way of life, simply the way things are" (Wildman and Davis 1995, 893). It is this "simply the way things are" that prevents those within academia from recognizing how power works with and through bodies to maintain privilege. The naturalness of how the males, and surrogate women racialized as white, are assumed to be leaders was akin to Sara Ahmed's suggestion that "maybe an institution is like an old garment: it acquires the shape of those who tend to wear it, such that it becomes easier if you have that shape. Privilege can be thought of in these terms: that which is wearing" (Ahmed 2014, 146).

Creating a Crisis of Leadership – Sense of Disorder

Only White Folks Know How to Make Decisions – Policies Are Neutral and Fair

Policies were often quoted. For example, the supposed inability to be flexible when rewarding faculty yet the ability to circumvent procedures when rewarding favoured individuals. One colleague in particular consistently attempted to demonstrate my supposed incompetency and lack of rule-following and knowledge of policies, which he usually communicated by telling me how he wanted things done. Having taken this stance he would immediately ignore department policy, without following processes, in order to establish what he wanted for himself.

As institutions of higher education, universities supposedly live by a sense of meritocratic and bureaucratic fairness that operates through neutral policy and its application. Yet for me policy is a two-headed Hydra that is both visible and invisible. As part of institutional whiteness, policy was regarded as inflexible without reference to context, as though it existed in a vacuum. It was considered that progressive social change should always be subservient to policy unless it serves institutional whiteness. In this instance I was expected to act as if the world is a simple place where all one has to do is administer. We just need to follow the rules and ignore any need for social change or social justice. Policy was decoupled from domination without regard for history or context within which policy operates. In particular I was keen to promote opportunities for Indigenous students within our MEd program. This was viewed as abusing my position by those who wanted the resources to be directed in their favour.

I can appreciate Sara Ahmed's comment that "for some bodies mere persistence, 'to continue steadfastly,' requires great effort, an effort that might appear to others as stubbornness or obstinacy, as an insistence on going against the flow. You have to be insistent to go against the flow and you are judged to be going against the flow because you are insistent" (Ahmed 2014, 144).

As a woman racialized as Black and trying to do the business of administration differently, I was perceived as lacking the ability to know and follow rules and policies. But I noted that always following the rules and ignoring the ways in which inequities get reproduced through these rules is one of the greatest predictors of reproduction of the status quo. This idea of a Black female administrator being inherently incompetent is a discourse that is evident within many societies constituted as white.[6] It never seems to occur to my harassers that my challenge to rules and how they play out might be deliberate rather than accidental.

As part of creating a crisis of leadership, the group of faculty that strongly support institutional whiteness also present themselves as victim, under the reign of an authoritarian, mad, Black woman who doesn't know the rules.

Another Event

Our international and Aboriginal graduate students bring forward some concerns to the department council concerning marginalization of their knowledge and experiences in some of the courses that are taught by the group of males and their feminized surrogate. The group, absent from the council, take offence once they hear about the student concerns and demand to know who the students are so that they can bring disciplinary action against them.

The Emails Follow

Email as the main form of communication among academics has become a tool/weapon through which dominance is enabled and reinforced. It is a tool of power, depending on who sends the email to whom, who is blind copied, who is not included, etc. Foucault has schooled us into ways in which power operates at the capillary level. It is not just top-down. So presenting themselves as the victims of an authoritarian chair is an effective tool to wield if one regards power as only ever top-down. It is a clever ruse to turn the tables on those we are oppressing, to make those we are oppressing take the burden of responsibility for our negative actions. Thus when a member of that specialization group used his phone to photograph a private document distributed in a closed meeting and to then send copies to colleagues via email, it heightened a sense of panic among his colleagues and presented an opportunity to challenge my authority in how I dealt with the issue:

Hi Jenny, I am writing to indicate my grave concern with the letter of February 12, 2014, presented at department council and again today at the selection advisory committee meeting. I am including my colleagues in this correspondence, because they have been implicated in this letter and I feel they ought to be aware of my concerns.

Or

As I attempt to analyse and de-escalate the male posturing surrounding the students' concerns, the same male colleague takes my response and my use of the term "Eurocentric" as an insult rather than a fact:

I am also perplexed by the accusation that [here he quotes me] *"students are concerned with the issue of Eurocentrism within the curriculum. It is a systemic problem that they are identifying not an individual one." This is a critique that I have heard numerous times from faculty members and students who have no knowledge of our field of study. It is offensive and irritating. I have made the case with my colleagues many times about the diversity in our field of study. I am not sure why this is necessary.*

The multiple cc'd email is used to great effect, since my harassers are now able to make me respond to a lot of folks who are not really involved in the topic under discussion. The point, of course, is not just the topic under discussion but is also the use of their power to indicate that the department is under threat. Only these good old white guys and a couple of good old white gals can really solve the problem – whatever it is. The cc'd email to those in authority above me is also a useful tactic. In this instance the dean is cc'd to ensure that she is receiving the message that there is disorder and mayhem, that the department is not being run effectively, that disorder is the norm. It is another tactic to create a climate of disorder. Policies are not being followed and some folks are not happy.

Since much of this bullying is often carried out in public, one would expect that fellow academics would call their bluff and see what power plays and games are going on. But in neoliberal times the identity of an academic is not the same as during the 1960s and 1970s, when disorder and rebellion was an acceptable (even if not uniform) identity for an academic. Today there is no expectation of academic dissent. Many academics have reconstituted their identities around individualism in the era of neoliberalism so that their worth is now demonstrated through the number of articles they write, and administrators' assessments of their excellence (Davies 2003). How important and vital their research/production is to the brand of the university ranks above all other concerns. In addition, the threat of reprisal from these male supporters of institutional whiteness or the surrogate women who align themselves with masculinized power is evoked as a tool of subordination for fellow academics – especially women. While many of these women, who themselves are oppressed elsewhere, would seemingly agree with my position and analysis on departmental issues, they would not step forward to offer support to me as a woman. For some, their reluctance to support me publicly can be attributed to their recognition that the male detractors and surrogate women had authority within the broader institution and might well end up on their tenure and promotion committees or other groups that operate behind closed doors. For other women it was too much to risk and not their fight. Analysis of this lack of gendered support compels one to ask, On what basis does present-day feminism operate? Was feminism more about making it into the institution and traditional male space than changing those masculinized spaces?

Hear No Evil, See No Evil, Speak No Evil

Silence and Consensus

In a society with a deep mythic attachment to consensus and conformity constituted through colonialism, white supremacy, and nativism, Canadians have come to view themselves as nice people. Silence rather than speaking up is equated with being "nice." Yet much of that silence is a vital part to reproducing relations based on dominance of one group over another. Such silencing constitutes conflict as problematic, speaking out, and speaking truth to power is certainly not valued. Most of my colleagues who observed the harassing emails publicly turned a blind eye to the constant harassment. The nearest I got to support from those racialized as white was one colleague who, when I pointed out to her how colleagues copied on the harassing emails ignored the bullying, thought about my comment and then emailed offering to support me if I wanted to bring a case of harassment. But overall there was a strong culture of silence. The exceptions were some students and some Indigenous/Aboriginal women in my department. Students were perceptive in private and brought to my attention how they saw racialized/gendered power being enabled during our department council. Indigenous women drew on their own racialized and gendered experiences and encounters with this group of men and women to understand what was going on for me. But again, without support from higher administration, they were also vulnerable to the male-dominated group responsible for the harassment and supportive of institutional whiteness.

The importance of secrecy and silence in undermining my leadership was demonstrated time and time again, especially when I underwent reselection for the position of chair. I had decided not to run, since I believe in collegial governance, that folks should take turns, and that I had given a great deal of my personal and academic life to the position. However, I was persuaded by supporters within the department who feared that changes I had initiated in the department might be overturned when I left. I submitted my name, and amid a flurry of other departmental and faculty fall term activities had to undertake an application, presentation, and interview for the chair position. I also asked the dean that the chair selection be delayed until the next term. But she decided she could not make that decision alone and would have to use a doodle poll to find others' perspectives on whether the selection should wait until after the fall term. After seeing the dean's decision to go ahead, based on the loss of the poll by one vote, I should have taken a run for the position more seriously and recognized the need to rally supporters and challenge the selection process. One can never assume that things will run smoothly. The result was that the selection committee (which included one man who had consistently threatened me) allowed anonymous letters to be submitted and shared as evidence of my leadership without my ever knowing what crime I was accused of. Requests for basic points or contents of the letters to be shared, while the letter writers remained anonymous were refused under the university's interpretation of the Alberta Freedom of Information Protection. The one letter that was not redacted contained untruths that, had I been asked, could easily have been refuted. There was no way to challenge what took place and it demonstrated to me how easily secrecy can work in selection and hiring to maintain the status quo.

Discussion

In a final reflection, I have three points to make about leadership in neoliberal times.

Institutional whiteness is produced/reproduced when people know they won't be challenged on their action; they know they can get away with it. This getting away with producing and reproducing institutional whiteness can be regarded as a form of ideology, "a system of cultural values and normative discourses that instruct individual subjects in how to behave, how to know their place, how to serve and how to obey. And we should not forget that although the operations of power can be complicated and hidden, they can also be obvious and blunt" (Franklin 2015, 31). In my experience with senior leadership in my university, they use the obvious and blunt when the common sense of neoliberalism is critiqued and when the threat comes in the racialized body of a woman. The lack of senior institutional support enabled those women and men racialized as white to undermine my leadership, ensure I was not reappointed, and enabled a direct cut in my salary and pension. In my interaction with senior university administration on race and racism, it seemed that most of them had been "taught to see racism only in individual acts of meanness" (Mackintosh 1989, 1). The idea of a culture of institutional whiteness (institutional racism) that is enabled through the actions of individuals such as themselves was not regarded as a possibility. Having to consistently explain the racialized, gendered, neoliberal push was futile and tiring, especially when I was faced with day-to-day harassment. For example, in response to my complaint that the process for chair selection was flawed, a senior administrator responded, "I am unable to offer any comment about the particular process as I was not ... at the time and have had no communication with the former Dean about the selection" (personal communication with senior administrator, 2016). Such a comment seems to brush off my request for a review of the chair selection process while absolving the institution of responsibility to act when inequities are reported. I wonder who takes responsibility or is accountable for actions that are blatantly unfair and help to reproduce institutional whiteness. Administrators need to be aware that institutional whiteness is not about people wearing white hoods, it is in patterns of behaviour and "can also be institutionalized informally – in associational patterns, longstanding customs or sedimented social practices of civil society" (Fraser 2000, 114).

Those to whom I appealed for support were unwilling and unable to view the issues of complaint as complex, about more than one thing. They were unable to recognize the way in which my experiences were raced, gendered, and laced together with neoliberal ideology. In response to this willful ignorance of those in authority, I suggest that anyone taking up a senior position in higher education should thoroughly understand institutional whiteness and be able to wield an intersectional analysis to deconstruct institutional whiteness. Intersectionality theory – which came out of Black feminist theorizing to challenge the ways women racialized as non-white were structurally and politically marginalized by white feminists – would be an appropriate tool and should be required of senior administrators. This would enable a more relational approach to address inequities and to recognize that we have multiple identities.

In this age of entrepreneurialism, it is not evident to senior administrators in higher education that knowledge and the experiences of people racialized as non-white should be a supported or valued. It seems that for senor administrators "the study of race and racism is anachronistic and inward looking, ill-equipped to compete in the market place that demands novelty, interdisciplinarity and conformity" (James and Valluvan 2014 3). Priorities in today's economic climate are linked to revenue generation. Those who can bring money-earners to the university are recognized for their individual "get-up-and-go," for their entrepreneurial spirit, and their ability to go where no one else has been. Issues of race and equity are concerned with group identities and pluralism, whereas advanced neoliberalism is concerned with the individual entrepreneurial self and technologies of the self. In other words, academics are regarded as entrepreneurs who can generate income for the institution and for that we may be awarded extra monies at the faculty evaluation committee or we may be deemed "excellent" by those higher in the administrative structure for increasing the university's brand value. Thus equity within universities becomes associated with individual entrepreneurial spirit, ensuring the brand rather than an ethical collective responsibility.

Traditionally, within theories of oppression it has been assumed that those who are conscious of their own oppression will be able to more easily recognize and identify with the oppression of others and thus be able to act as an ally in broader struggles against oppression and domination. Critical theory has worked on the assumption that development of a collective consciousness around one's own oppression will mean an opening up of empathy towards others. But there is no automatic recognition of oppression of others through one's own experiences. For example, do those fighting for gender or LGBTQ issues necessarily seek an alliance with those seeking to remedy inequities on the basis of race and class? Nancy Fraser (2000) has long argued for the need to work not just on issues of recognition but also redistribution. I would argue, as second-wave Black feminist Hazel Carby (1982) has done, that we need to complicate our understanding of the ways in which oppression works, for there is no automatic full alignment of Black women with white women who are racialized as white. I also implicate myself in some decisions made under pressure while the idea of trying to be consensual was taken up. In some ways a sharper sense of purpose and determination to challenge may have worked out better for bringing about change. I now argue that to be an effective administrator/leader within an institution, one needs to be adept at analysis – specifically, intersectional analysis. To be able to recognize how racialized power operates through institutional whiteness is absolutely essential. It is not enough to be good at following rules or just shuffling the papers that cross our desks. In this historical period of late and fast capitalism, leadership requires a creative, critical, and intellectual approach. Collegial governance becomes even more important, as effective leadership increasingly entails the analytic skills one brings to the job. Those who are able to draw on critical intellect rather than mere rule following are sorely needed in leadership roles and administrative structures today. The question is raised: Can administrators ever be other than purveyors of the status quo (or in our present era, neoliberal policies) within institutions racialized as white? To repeat Sara Ahmed, "You have to become insistent to go against the flow" (2014, 144).

NOTES

1 For example, Black Lives Matter is a life-and-death campaign taking place in North America.
2 See my article with Thashika Pillay, which discusses women and leadership in 1920s Alberta (Kelly and Pillay 2016).

3 In 1978 the BSCP merged with the Brotherhood of Railway Clerks, now known as the Transportation Communications International Union.

4 After years of struggle and monies I have finally managed to access a number of redacted emails that indicate clearly the path of collusion and messages that these so-called colleagues and senior administrator folks used to plot against me.

5 This sense of entitlement created around leadership roles reminded me of my days canvassing for the Labour Party in the United Kingdom when working-class folks were willing to support the Tory government of Margaret Thatcher because the Tories were in some way our betters and thus had a natural propensity and right to be rulers.

6 This discourse has been identified and highlighted by Gonzalez and Harris (2013) in "Presumed Incompetent: Continuing the Conversation Part I,"a special issue of the *Berkley Journal of Gender, Law & Justice* 29 (2). This anthology explores the experiences of women of colour in higher education from a variety of perspectives.

REFERENCES

Agger, B. 1989. *Fast Capitalism: A Critical Theory of Significance.* Urbana: University of Illinois Press.

Ahmed, S. 2012. *On Being Included: Racism and Diversity in Institutional Life.* Durham, NC: Duke University Press.

Ahmed, S. 2014. *Willful Subjects.* Durham, NC: Duke University Press.

Carby, H. 1982. "White Woman Listen! Black Feminism and the Boundaries of Sisterhood." In *The Empire Strikes Back: Race and Racism in Seventies Britain,* 212–235. New York: Routledge.

Cui, D., and Kelly, J. 2010. "'Our Negro Citizens': An Example of Everyday Citizenship Practices." In *The West and Beyond: New Perspectives on an Imagined Region,* edited by A. Finkel, S. Carter, and P. Fortna, 253–277. Edmonton, AB: Athabasca University Press.

Davies, B. 2003. "Dissemination, or Critique and Transformation?" In *Disseminating Qualitative Research,* edited by C. Hughes, 110–122. London: Open University Press.

Davis, D., and Maldonado, C. 2015. "Shattering the Glass Ceiling: The Leadership Development of African American Women in Higher Education." *Advancing Women in Leadership* 35: 48–64.

Foucault, M. 2002. *The Archaeology of Knowledge.* London: Routledge Classics.

Franklin, S. 2015. "Sexism as a Means of Reproduction: Some Reflections on the Politics of Academic Practice." *New Formations* 86 (Winter): 14–33. https://doi.org/10.3898/NewF.86.01.2015.

Fraser, N. 2000. "Rethinking Recognition." *New Left Review* 3: 107–120. https://newleftreview.org/issues/ii3/articles/nancy-fraser-rethinking-recognition.

Freire, P. 1973. *Education for Critical Consciousness.* London: Seabury Press.

Gonzalez, C., and Harris, A. 2013. "Introduction: Presumed Incompetent: Continuing the Conversation (Part II)." *Seattle Journal for Social Justice* 12 (2): 284–299. https://digitalcommons.law.seattleu.edu/sjsj/vol12/iss2/1/.

Henry, F., and Tator C. 2009. "Manifestation of Racism in the Academy." In *Racism in the Canadian University: Demanding Social Justice, Inclusion and Equity,* edited by Henry and Tator, 22–59. Toronto: University of Toronto Press.

James, M., and Valluvan, S. 2014. "Higher Education: A Market for Racism?" *Dark Matter Journal,* 25 April. http://www.darkmatter101.org/site/2014/04/25/higher-education-a-market-for-racism/.

Kelly, J., and Pillay, T. 2016. "African-Canadian Women, Leadership and Adult Education." In *"Reclaiming a Past." Women, Adult Education, and Leadership in Canada,* edited by D. Clover, S. Butterwick, and L. Collins, 163–174. Toronto: Thompson Publication.

Kelly, J., and Wossen-Taffesse, M. 2012. "The Black Canadian: An Exposition of Race, Gender, and Citizenship." *Journal of Canadian Studies* 46 (1): 167–192. https://doi.org/10.3138/jcs.46.1.167.

Mackintosh, P. 1989. "White Privilege: Unpacking the Invisible Knapsack." *Bimonthly Journal of Women's International League for Peace and Freedom.* July/August, 1–6.

Mathieu, S. 2001. "North of the Colour Line: Sleeping Car Porters and the Battle against Jim Crow on Canadian Rails, 1880–1920." *Labour/Le Travail* 47: 9–41. https://doi.org/10.2307/25149112.

Smith, M. 2014. *Report on "Perpetual Crisis? Diversity with Equity in the Academy."* https://www.academia.edu/6475562/Malinda_S._Smith_Report_on_Perpetual_Crisis_Diversity_with_Equity_in_the_Academy.

Wildman, S., and Davis, A. 1995. "Language and Silence: Making Systems of Privilege Visible." *Clara Law Review* 35: 881–906. https://digitalcommons.law.scu.edu/lawreview/vol35/iss3/4/.

20 Vocation of the Black Scholar in the Neoliberal Academy: A Love Story

ADELLE BLACKETT[1]

We chose only hope and freedom and justice, and the spirits chose us to be black.

– Harding (1974)

Black study and resistance must begin with love.

– Kelley (2016)

On Blackness

"She's not Black – I mean, not African," said my guest – an academic from a postcolonial West African state, about me, to another West African colleague.

"She says she's Black," was the response, which preceded a conciliatory comment on the high quality of the Baoulé mask that hangs in my living room in Montreal, a mask that was made to be worn. And maybe it was the urgent, slightly embarrassed but not particularly convincing tone in which she reiterated my prior affirmation of Blackness, knowing that I would hear, that has stayed with me the most.

Like that mask, my forgiving smile worked overtime to convey some historical irony, but dull most of the pain. Yet in that moment it all came rushing back to me: the remnants of lived experiences from a Black Atlantic of no return where I had travelled extensively but that I thought we – Black academics – had moved through and past some time ago. Was it not in 1946 that the founder of modern sociology, W.E.B. DuBois, wrote *The World and Africa: An Inquiry into the Part Which Africa Has Played in World History*, embodying the inextricable links between Africa and its diaspora, insisting on the need to reclaim African history as world history, and positing that the world needs Africa?

DuBois himself reminds of his attempt to bring a pan-Africanist vision – through the framing of self-determination – to the Paris Peace Conference in Versailles in 1919. DuBois the careful empiricist incarnates the scholar who challenged the easy assumptions of universalism, knowing its ready coexistence with racial subordination (Morris 2015). Throughout his long life, he saw myriad examples of this apparent paradox – for example, he opined that the same Jan Smuts, prime minister of the Union of South Africa in 1945, could at once argue for the white supremacist suppression of Blacks while advocating for human rights in the UN Charter. DuBois situated the paradox plainly in the history of the slave trade: "The trade in human beings between Africa and America, which flourished between the Renaissance and the American Civil War, is the prime and effective cause of the contradictions in European civilization and the illogic in modern thought and the collapse of human culture" (DuBois 1947, 43). For DuBois, slavery and the colour-caste system, perpetuated through colonialism, were foundational, and global (DuBois 1935, 32).

Let me be clear: my academic guests were not acknowledging the perils of reductionist or overdetermined nativistic notions of "Africanness" that enact and perpetuate colonialism's work of othering and subordinating (Ngwena 2018), nor were they insisting on the historically specific ways in which understandings of race continue to move to re-enact DuBois's colour line in familiar yet vastly transformed ways across divided terrain (Hall 2017). My guest's "innocent" words were an ocean away from an expansive, Black radical tradition that DuBois embodied on both sides of the Atlantic – a tradition of insisting on the significance of our truth that flows through lived, multiple but linked community experiences, a tradition of recognizing the temporal urgency of "an ending" to Cedric Robinson magisterial work: "But for now we must be as one" (Robinson 2000, 318).

But for *now*. *As* one. We must be.

On Learning in Community

I was born and raised in Montreal, the daughter of Caribbean immigrants. I attended the local grade schools where most kids' parents were from elsewhere and mostly everyone in our working-class neighbourhood knew not to ask what our parents did for a living. We were proud of our families and communities, and through our complicity to centre other conversations, pushed back on societal presumptions of being able to define us through the hard work that our parents had to accept for pay – facile short-hand about "social class" and "the masses." In those rare spaces where consumerism could somewhat be held at bay – Black community-building camps, a summer in Barbados enjoying the stars, and in a loving home where friends could always come for food and fellowship – community self-love took hold. Survival strategies were multiple in a school that took students that other schools rejected, island-wide, and streamed more students into hairdressing and auto-mechanics than the fledgling enriched math and science program. Years later, as I sat as the only Black student in an undergraduate Canadian social history course at Queen's University, listening to a young white classmate explain at great length and with surprise that white supremacists held family picnics, it hit me hard: some of the smartest kids I have known were not in university classrooms. Some of the smartest kids I have known were too aware, too conscious, not sheltered enough from the weight of societal subordination to survive.

By the time I got to university, I already knew enough to understand that the formal educational system was not home. I had been fortunate enough to be schooled in pan-Africanism from a young age, and through community – a synthesis of those community members who spoke in the language of the "word" and the "river" – who understood synthesis between the acts of preaching and teaching in the spaces we inhabited (Harding 1981). I had learned a great deal from Dr. Daniel Kabasele, who migrated to Quebec from the Democratic Republic of Congo after earning a doctorate in France, and who missed no opportunity to infuse the study of classics like Albert Camus's *L'Étranger* with a solid dose of anti-colonial critique. My time in Quebec's pre-university cégep program with Dr. Leo W. Bertley was particularly formative. "Dr. Bertz" hailed from Trinidad and Tobago, earned his doctorate in history from Concordia University, and founded the Quebec Board of Black Educators. He insisted that I read Cheikh Anta Diop alongside his teachings on Greek mythology, invited literary giants like George Lamming to Montreal, edited the African Canadian newspaper, wrote books on African Canadian history, and protested apartheid in South Africa. These overqualified teachers (it is crucial not to walk past that point) fulfilled their vocation with conviction *and* insisted on claiming their status as "Dr." so that their students could at once see racism in employment and see how community members chose to survive so others could thrive.

Their teachings helped me to withstand the mix of cynicism and condescension with which I was confronted in university: Africa is at once omitted from world history, yet resurrected to lay blame not only for a panoply of contemporary failures of governance, but in particular, for complicity in the transatlantic slave trade. This can be expressed as two very similar questions: "Why, were you *not* told of this role? *Why* were you not told of this role?"

I have asked myself those questions repeatedly, but for different reasons. I am reminded of the questions every time I find myself wondering how deeply enslavement is claimed as a shared experience by those who look on Blacks of the African diaspora as distant cousins, robbed of any meaningful terms of belonging to Africa beyond a past that cannot be remembered and cannot be reclaimed. I am reminded of the questions every time acts of collegial sharing and solidarity are met in the neoliberal academy, not with mutual recognition and the collective kindness necessary for the preservation of our communities, but rather with academic extractive behaviour that rewards predatory, first-past-the-post claims of individual ownership by scholars who might well have *forgotten* that there might be another way. The question speaks to our collective ability to keep the vocation of the Black scholar alive in these troubled times.

On the Neoliberal Academy

Our moment is characterized by a neoliberalism increasingly understood not to conflate the free market with democracy or to eschew regulation in favour of laissez-faire, but rather as a historicized process to "encase" markets and "inoculate capitalism against the threat of democracy" and "contain often-irrational human behavior," "reorder[ing] the world after empire" (Slobodian 2018, 2–3). While all but the 1 per cent have been deeply affected, Black communities are "especially devastated by the economic crisis that for them has not only continued but deepened" (Dawson 2016, 156). Some even add that sometimes Black becomes a metaphor for demonized others (Temin 2017; Wright 1995). For the working class that resurrects its understanding of its name in the deeply racialized divides sown throughout slavery and colonialism, it is hatred that is emancipated (Butler 2016).

The academy, so far from a refuge, reflects, enacts, and repurposes itself in this neoliberal moment. "Equity matters" are not immune (Henry et al. 2017). Indeed, the neoliberal academy repackages racial justice claims as claims about the business case for diversity, about acquiring cultural competency, about acknowledging unconscious bias. Diversity is an objective to be managed and measured within all too predictable frames. Norms such as merit remain pristine and abstracted from equity, as the perpetuation of structural disadvantage is left untouched. The privilege that makes whiteness a form of property (Harris 1993) through the subordination of Blacks as the objects of property through slavery and the dispossession of Indigenous people of their land goes unchallenged.

And in this moment entrenched in the rise in white supremacy in society as a whole, should we really be surprised that this should embolden

entitled students to challenge their racialized and Indigenous professors' competency, as soon as they walk through the university doors?
The tales some colleagues have told are chilling (Guttiérrez y Muhs
et al. 2012). Similarly, the authors of *The Equity Myth* provide the data
to establish the persistence of inequality, and what is more, to illustrate
the performativity of equity policies (Henry et al. 2017; Ahmed 2017).
Equity policies have not brought us representation. The authors offer us
recommendations. But their very brevity, I suggest, is an avowal of the
authors' deeper critique.

The university, taken from its pedestal, *is* society, and worse, is in
Polanyian terms (2001), part of – indeed a sustaining or socially reproductive part of – post-industrial market society. Even as it designs more
equity policies, and makes overtures, and trumpets the desire to bring
more people in, it perpetuates exclusions.

And it seemed increasingly urgent and clear to me that we needed
to be able to start the inquiry elsewhere: can universities – and critical
scholars within them – be part of sensing and holding open an emergent, critical pedagogical posture that sustains resistance to (re-)coloniz-
ing spaces that promise freedom? Are universities in Canada positioned
to be at the vanguard of the kind of society we want to create?

Historian Robin Kelley has staked the claim that U.S. universities quite
simply are not up to the task. Like Stefano Harney and Fred Moten in
their work on the *Undercommons* (2013), Kelley questions the wisdom of
"acknowledging the university's magisterium in all things academic" while
"granting the university ... [considerable] authority" (Kelley 2016, n.p.).
Harney and Moten ultimately challenge the university's very ability to
be a place of enlightenment; they do not consider it a place of refuge.
In this vision, the task is not to decolonize the university. They centre
alternative images – the maroon, the fugitive, those who refuse to allow
themselves to be encircled by the narrow universe of a neoliberal academy, claiming instead the spaces "in the hold" that remain constantly
in motion, places that refuse to be settled, places that retain possibility.

On Vocation

There is much that is compelling in this work, and its clear-eyed vision
offers its own solace and call to movement. And it is precisely the element
of refusal – to draw on Audra Simpson's work (2014) – to continue to do
things in the same way, to continue to accept the same premises, refusal
to be other that is required of decolonization. And that refusal opens
up possibilities. Throughout Harney and Moten's trenchant critique, another call resonates – one that has been pivotal to my own thinking and

rooting in what it means to be a Black scholar, too often the only one, in my discipline and in university settings. The call has kept me going back to get what's ours. It is called *Sankofa*.

When I think of the fugitive slave, I too think of a body and soul in motion, who carries an archive of knowledge – through music, through quilts, through knowledge of the land and stars. "When the First Quail Calls, Follow the Drinking Gourd" is a spiritual about the North Star; another spiritual, "Wade in the Water," evokes the river. That archive of knowledge survives, in the struggle to construct a promised land despite ongoing dispossession, by grounding in a deepened knowledge of self, of ancestors, of history, and insistent on the need to reclaim and recreate, and to be, as one.

There is a persisting pain involved in continuing to carry forward an archive of knowledge that came from elsewhere, that enslaved Africans insisted on bringing with them, of holding on to, even when "haunted by night by a nagging sense of nobodyness," with "the ache and anguish of living in so many situations where hopes unborn have died" (King 2010, 127). It bears remembering that grappling with Blackness and nothingness have never been far from those who have inhabited the word and the river. Generative movement emerges from those spaces: the celebration by which "the slightest, most immeasurable reversal of emphasis – that Afro-pessimism and Black optimism are not both nothing other than one another" (Moten 2013, 742). What thinkers like King, Harding, and Robinson have taken from their own engagement with the enslaved, with their *ancestors*, with community, is an "ontological affirmation of Blackness that consistently beat back the prevailing logic of Black inferiority" (Kelley 2017, n.p.).

Like so many of the visionaries from Africa and the African diaspora, DuBois wrote his breathtaking tome *The World and Africa* as a matter of vocation. He modestly professed that his book was "the sort of thing at which every scholar shudders" (Dubois 1947, xi), given its breadth and what he referred to as his modest preparation and his recognition that it should be the "research of a lifetime" (DuBois 2015, xii). Recall, of course, DuBois the careful empiricist (Morris 2015) had been preparing for this treatise since he became the first African American to earn a PhD at Harvard University in 1895 and throughout his life of scholarly engagement that was always deeply rooted in community. He traced pathbreaking scholarship about Black life in America that understood the colour bar as antithetical to democracy (DuBois 1899, 2015). Moreover, DuBois expressed the sense of urgency and responsibility that he felt, incredibly, to establish the equal humanity of "Black Africans." He added, "I am faced with the dilemma, that either I do this now or leave it for others who have not had the tragedy of life which I have, forcing me to face a task for which they may have small stomach and little encouragement from the world round about" (DuBois 1947, xii).

Although "passport issues" prevented him from accepting an invitation to independence celebrations by Prime Minister Kwame Nkrumah, he wrote,

> Today when Ghana arises from the dead and faces a future in this modern world, it must no longer be merely a part of the British Commonwealth or a representative of the world of West Europe, Canada, and the United States. Ghana must on the contrary be the representative of Africa and not only that, but of Black Africa and the Sahara desert. As such her first duty should be to come into close acquaintance-ship and co-operation … All the former barriers of language, culture, religion, and political control should bow before the essential unity of race and descent, the common suffering of slavery and the slave trade, and the modern color bar. In all these places today, Black Folk writhe under color tyranny and oppression. (DuBois 1957, 2)

It is well known that DuBois was most assuredly present at Dr. Nkrumah's presidential inauguration in 1960, and subsequently moved to the Republic of Ghana, where he lived out his last days. He lived a life that embodied a process called for subsequently by the Rev. Dr. Martin Luther King in the meditation in his final book, *Where Do We Go From Here: Chaos or Community*: a "higher synthesis" (King 2010, 137).

On a Higher Synthesis

Dr. King's higher synthesis was built on a Hegelian frame and included his understanding of hybridity embodied in those who are the heirs of "a great and exploited continent" and the descendants of slaves, who are "neither totally African nor totally Western" and who should construct not a separate Black "nation within a nation" but rather an America "in which its multiracial people are partners to power" (King 2010, 55). And as he reflected on witnessing the Gold Coast's independence in 1957, Dr. King recalled that the Montgomery Bus Boycott had to be just a beginning, and that "freedom only comes through persistent revolt, through persistent agitation … through the pressure that comes about from the people who are oppressed" (King 1957, n.p.).

The Institute of the Black World (IBW) emerged out of the "morass of anger, disappointment and confusion" (White 2011, 2) that reigned after Dr. King's assassination in 1968, and the backlash and abandonment that Dr. King (2010) predicted. Vincent Harding took up Dr. King's

challenge to build a "higher synthesis" between currents on Black liberation that included the streets, by sustaining the IBW throughout the long
seventies (White 2011).

Education and Black Struggle: Notes from the Colonized World (Harding
1974) is a remarkable series that emerged from the IBW, and that included work by C.L.R. James, the man whom Cedric Robinson referred
to as "the teacher [Black students, the new Black intelligentsia] could
honor, a living, absorbing link between themselves and a past of which
most had only a vague notion" (2000, 285); and a range of other political and intellectual leaders, notably Walter Rodney and President Julius
Nyerere. The sense of the possible and the urgency of uprooting myths
and crafting alternatives flow through the pages. The significance of
resisting the loss of "hegemony over the interpretations" (White 2011,
192) about ourselves and our conditions permeated the IBW's work, as
did the need for constant critical inquiry about the relationship between
Black academics in the university and those who would never make it.

Harding introduces his own meditation entitled "The Vocation of
the Black Scholar and the Struggles of the Black Community" with a
reminder that nations no less than individuals are best known by calls on
us to join "ourselves and our work to the movement of the great black
river of the African diaspora" (Harding 1974, 23). Living pan-Africanism
becomes part of creating "a truth of relationships and linkages so often
denied and unseen by the world of white scholarship" (23). But while
naming those postcolonial Black scholars of the diaspora, Harding also
took a hard look at academia – both in white universities and in historically Black colleges. Without discounting the spaces that might be found
there, he argued presciently: "The vast majority of the black institutions
we need are yet to be born. To live the truth is to join in the process of
that birth, of that building" (26).

Truth appears repeatedly in Harding's work. The Black intellectual
needs to speak the truth to the people, their truth. Harding's claim is
the opposite of erasure practices that move us away from embodying
the kind of personal integrity that Dr. King understood was essential in
order to be "independent, assertive and respected" as "indispensable for
an authentic expression of power" (King 2010, 156). Harding (1974)
invokes "joining ourselves and our work to the movement of the great
black river of the African diaspora" as a way of creating "a truth of relationships and linkages so often denied and unseen by the world of white
scholarship" (23).

Must this all transpire through our universities? Certainly not, and
the fact that by the end of IBW's struggle to stay viable, it was working
to institutionalize Black studies programs within universities despite

ambivalence is no small indicator of the dilemma it had to face with eyes wide open. But what if we refused simply to hand over the universities as entities beyond ourselves? What if we stopped allowing universities to be the administration alone, including the administration that imagines itself as the vehicle through which equity happens? What if we challenged the disciplinary canon, creating that truth of relation that is "ongoing, never fixed, ever changing" (Roberts 2015, 147) and that has been so much a part of a historically rooted but emergent understanding of freedom that moves beyond the "innocent" scholarship in the postcolonial world that reifies, re-enacts, and retrenches divides? And in the neoliberal context, in the resolutely Quebec context out of which I have emerged – what if we allow ourselves to challenge in part because we still can – because in Quebec students can still pay less than $4000 for a university education without having to prove that they are the deserving poor? What if we insisted on claiming our ability to navigate the land via the stars, to make archives of quilts and songs, to wade in the waters? What if we do in fact claim our universities as our intersectional, collective, deliberately slowed down, and unrelentingly critical selves?

Legal scholar Charles Lawrence III expresses his sense of partial alienation from the role of "scholar" and the risk of assimilation that it entails. The dual subjectivity in DuBois's sense (1994), or multiple consciousnesses, to invoke legal scholar Matsuda (1989), is a positionality that enables Lawrence to remain alive to the "social realities that are unseen by those who live more fully in the world of privilege" (Lawrence 1992, 2239). But Lawrence looks back, and gets what's ours. Lawrence embraces "the Word," understood more fully as an interdisciplinary tradition of "teaching, preaching and healing ... wherein healers are concerned with the soul and preachers with the pedagogy of the oppressed" (2238).

The representation work goes well beyond the "diversity challenge," to challenge the culture of whiteness in academia (Henry et al. 2017). It is necessary to build critical mass; to change what it feels like to walk into a room and know that it is inhabited not just by the one but by the many multiple communities who comprise ourselves, our society; to re-present our universities to ourselves; to bring communities to catch a vision of ourselves that is other. Wherever we are situated along the spectrum of institutional insider-outsider, the Black radical tradition understands that the grounding is *other* – in this sense, the university cannot and is not permitted to be our whole world, to define us.

What if we really did take teaching seriously, in the Freirean sense, in which the teacher and the learner are each the other, in which a commitment to dialogue is part of what sustains counter-hegemonic challenge in a shared struggle against dehumanization, a challenge that takes place over land, is at once rooted but always in motion, never settled or self-satisfied or content, or to keep Vincent Harding's terms of movement, rooted in land and struggle, "the River"?

On Movement

Destabilizing the "universal" in the "university"; putting universities in their proper place; holding open spaces beyond it; and insisting on academics' genuine freedom to engage ... For Angela Davis, this means prioritizing social movements, "movements that are sufficiently open to allowing for the future emergence of issues, ideas, and movements that we cannot even begin to imagine today" (Davis 2017, 5).

Reflecting on Ghanaian independence in his contribution to *Education and Black Struggle*, C.L.R. James offers a prescient challenge to the virulent myth that Africans were "the takers," the ones to be taught by others, to the absence in dominant discourse of "the slightest hint that anything which took place there could instruct or inspire the peoples of the advanced countries in the management of their own affairs" (James 1974, 41). James was calling for a different kind of academic movement, which resonates with writing from Africa, through lived experience. The critical work of the neoliberal academy is replete with examples that identify spaces that may be alive with alternatives, including alternative trajectories of learning (Blackett 2017). Taking the Black radical tradition seriously operates a critical decentring of the West (Davis 2017); it requires the movement that James understood would be central to creating space for new ways of thinking, for alternative imaginaries. It is part of responding to Harding's most painful plea: "To identify the enemy is to point to our failure to believe in ourselves and our tremendous potentials" (Harding 1974, 16).

Like so much of this scholarship, the work is directional: it understands theories of freedom as necessarily tentative (Davis 2017). It theorizes the time and space of movement itself. As James famously proclaimed, "Time would pass, old empires would fall and new ones take their place, the relations of countries and the relations of classes had to change, before I discovered that it is not the quality of goods and utility which matter, but movement; not where you are or what you have, but where you have come from, where you are going and the rate at which you are getting there" (James 2013, 113).

It might seem counter-intuitive for me to add that in the neoliberal academy, this sense of time and movement must include sustaining the ability to respect life cycles and to slow academic performance down. I write this acknowledging the deep unease it elicits for me, as a Black academic who sees myself and so many of my community members raised to work twice as hard, as if it is our only salvation. Aldon Morris reminds the reader of an organic intellectual whose work ethic was unrelenting, and whose longsuffering wife Shirley Graham DuBois did most of the reproductive labour. And I cannot but pause. I write this reflection as a Black de facto single mother who has worked overtime to raise healthy children, despite the systemic racism that has kept their Beninese father with a doctorate in law and years of international experience from finding suitable employment in Quebec. I write this knowing the significance of the space this impossible reconciliation enables me to hold open. It leads me to reaffirm that part of what we need to be able to do is to speak truthfully, indeed to try to "find ways, stumbling ways, to live the truth" (Harding, 1974, 20) in academic spaces, to enable those who come after us to live them in healthy, embodied ways. And I am struck by Angela Davis's reminder – Davis whose first published article was written from prison, and who has used her place in academia to advocate prison abolition – that "we cannot fail to apprehend how central women have been to the forging of a Black Radical Tradition," the extent to which Robinson's work centres gender in that tradition,[2] and "the ways of theorizing history – or allowing it to theorize itself – that are crucial to our understanding of the present and our ability to collectively envisage a more habitable future" (Davis 2017, 241). For Davis, a Black Radical Tradition is necessarily a feminist tradition and links her own contributions to it (Davis 2017). A feminist tradition increasingly, non-essentially, and unapologetically, includes taking care of ourselves, to be our best selves for each other.

On Love

It would be conventional to walk past this final dimension, yet Robin Kelley insists that an integral part of a Black Radical Tradition of education is love – the kind of love that is inseparable from study, and indissociable from struggle, and inextricable from resistance. Kelley turns to James Baldwin's *The Fire Next Time* to theorize the politics of love. In retracing those footsteps, I recalled another of Baldwin's less well-known essays, "The Dangerous Road before Martin Luther King." It is a meditation on the kind of discerning leadership that Black communities have needed, and the love that Dr. King brought. Baldwin recounts his first meeting with Dr. King, the cleric's "genuine smile" and how he seemed to have come through so much "really unscarred." Baldwin's text is poignant, perceptive, and painfully premonitory: "I remember feeling ... as though he were a younger, much-loved and menaced brother, that he seemed very slight and vulnerable to be taking on such tremendous odds" (1998, 641). And Baldwin captures the essence of Dr. King's love: "The fact that King really loves the people he represents and has – *therefore* – no hidden, interior need to hate ... will ... continue to have the most far-reaching and unpredictable repercussions" (Baldwin 1998, 638–9).

Dr. King insisted on the importance of understanding love in relation to power, including institutional power, rather than dichotomizing it. In his higher synthesis, this power to justice would be cultivated. Dr. King argued instead,

> Power properly understood is nothing but the ability to achieve purpose. It is the strength required to bring about social, political or economic changes. In this sense power is not only desirable but necessary in order to implement the demands of love and justice. One of the greatest problems of history is that the concepts of love and power are usually contrasted as polar opposites. Love is identified with a resignation of power and power with a denial of love.... What is needed is a realization that power without love is reckless and abusive, and that love without power is sentimental and anemic. Power at its best is love implementing the demands of justice. Justice at its best is love correcting everything that stands against love. (King 2010, 37–8)

Love offers the only basis upon which to challenge the enemy that was at the heart of the IBW's call for a higher synthesis: the failure to believe in ourselves and our tremendous potential (Harding 1974). Harding's scholarly gifts and engagement in the world convey an "unfaltering belief" in the transformative power of love (Shenk 2014, n.p.). A higher synthesis in our understanding of the power of community self-love – in all the spaces we inhabit, and in particular in the spaces where we teach and learn – from our home places, to our community and spirit building spaces, to our schools and streets, and yes, to our universities – is absolutely vital.

Teaching in the post-secondary context *for decolonization* must entail quelling the perpetual unearthing of narrow Black nationalisms that "leave intact the circumstances and structures that perpetuate exclusion and marginalization" (Davis 2017, 246). This decolonial teaching may be best understood as an act of love, indeed fragmentary and fraught "islands" of decolonial love (Simpson 2013). I have argued that this teaching should root itself in the project of building beloved community. One small place to start is resisting the call to frame recognition claims in ways that perpetuate neoliberal understandings of the direction that the academy must take – divorcing them from the broader emancipatory claims that are inseparable from political recognition and redistribution. And our refusals of assimilation and embrace of a justice-filled love may create the space to imagine the startlingly unbounded directions in which our vocation as Black academics might take us, once we refuse the falsity of the question we are asked to address.

Why were you not told? Are you Black? Far from limiting freedom, these questions – even within the neoliberal academy, even in our homes – are openings to movement through liminal spaces, reminders of the catalytic power for reordering that emerges from the "most liminalized group" – the enslaved – who insist on resistance (Roberts 2015, 160). Building on Edouard Glissant's stages of freedom understood through the experience of slavery, Niall Roberts's indispensable and evocative *Freedom as Marronage* recalls that "responsibility is the last attribute of freedom" (Roberts 2015, 164). Maybe home is the first exile, not simply a place but a way of thinking and being, one that for Esi Edugyan (2014) "we leave in order to come back, changed, made new" (51).

The vocation of the Black scholar in an era of neoliberalism is a love story about home, one told through our truth, through the temporal recognition of the responsibility, for now, to be as one. It is part of that impossibly urgent, radically hope-filled movement to sustain and transform our frames for rebirthing and engendering knowledge wherever we are, including our universities. It is only from this specificity that we can begin to cultivate the kind of communities we want to live in.

NOTES

1 I am immensely grateful to the editors of this book for their close, careful reading of this chapter, and for their myriad expressions of community self-love in action. I also wish to acknowledge Dr. Dotse Tsikata's attentive comments, which have improved this text. Early versions of this text were presented at the Canadian Association of University Teachers' Equity Conference, 2018, and "Protest and Pedagogy: Black Protest, Black Lives and the University: Transnational Conversations," Concordia University, 2019, where the ideas received thoughtful engagement. Finally, I thank my McGill University research assistants, Zakia Jahan, BCL & LLB 2020, and Fanta Ly, BCL & LLB candidate, for valuable support as I finalized this chapter. Any errors are my own.

2 While it is true that Black Marxism centres W.E.B. DuBois, C.L.R. James, as well as novelist Richard Wright in framing the Black Radical Tradition, Davis reminds the reader that to engage with Robinson's work as a whole, "we cannot fail to apprehend how central women have been to the forging of a

Black Radical Tradition" (Davis 2017, 241). She quotes Robinson himself, who insists that "all resistance, in effect, manifests in gender, manifests as gender. Gender is indeed both a language of oppression [and] a language of resistance" (Quan 2005, 47).

REFERENCES

Ahmed, S. 2017. *Living a Feminist Life*. Durham, NC: Duke University Press.

Baldwin, J. 1998. *Collected Essays*. New York: The Library of America.

Blackett, A. 2017. "Follow the Drinking Gourd: Our Road to Teaching Critical Race Theory and Slavery and the Law, Contemplatively, at McGill." *McGill Law Journal* 62 (4): 1251–1277. https://doi.org/10.7202/1043165ar.

Blackett, A. 2018. "Slavery Is Not a Metaphor." *The American Journal of Comparative Law* 66 (4): 927–935. https://doi.org/10.1093/ajcl/avy041.

Butler, J. 2016. "Trump Is Emancipating Unbridled Hatred." Zeit Online, 28 October. https://www.zeit.de/kultur/2016-10/judith-butler-donald-trump-populism-interview.

Davis, A. 2017. "An Interview on the Futures of Black Radicalism." In *Futures of Black Radicalism*, edited by G. Johnson and A. Lubin, 241–248. London: Verso.

Dawson, M.C. 2016. "Hidden in Plain Sight: A Note on Legitimation Crises and the Racial Order" *Critical Historical Studies* 3 (1). https://doi.org/10.1086/685540.

DuBois, W.E.B. 1899. *The Philadelphia Negro: A Social Study*. Philadelphia: University of Pennsylvania Press.

DuBois, W.E.B. 1935. *Black Reconstruction: An Essay toward a History of the Part Which Black Folk Played in the Attempt to Reconstruct Democracy in America, 1860–1880*. New York: Russell & Russell.

DuBois, W.E.B. 1947. *The World and Africa: An Inquiry into the Part Which Africa Has Played in World History*. New York: Viking Press.

DuBois, W.E.B. 1957. "Letter to His Excellency, Dr. Kwame Nkrumah, Prime Minister of the Gold Coast," 7 February. http://credo.library.umass.edu/cgi-bin/pdf.cgi?id=scua:mums312-b146-i353.

DuBois, W.E.B. 1994. *The Souls of Black Folk*. Mineola, NY: Dover Publications.

DuBois, W.E.B. 2015. *The World and Africa: An Inquiry into the Part Which Africa Has Played in World History*. Mansfield Center, CT: Martino Publishing.

Edugyan, E. 2014. *Dreaming of Elsewhere: Observations on Home*. Edmonton: University of Alberta Press.

Gutierrez y Muhs, G., Niemann, Y., Gonzalez, C., and Harris, A., eds. 2012. *Presumed Incompetent: The Intersections of Race and Class for Women in Academia*. Boulder: University Press of Colorado.

Hall, S. 2017. *The Fateful Triangle: Race, Ethnicity, Nationalism*. Cambridge, MA: Harvard University Press.

Harding, V. 1974. *"Vocation of the Black Scholar and the Struggles of the Black Community." In Education and Black Struggle: Notes from the Colonized World,* 3–29. Cambridge, MA: Harvard University Press.

Harding, V. 1981. *There Is a River: The Black Struggle for Freedom in America.* New York: Harcourt, Brace and Company.

Harney, S., and Moten, F. 2013. *The Undercommons: Fugitive Planning and Black Study.* Wivenhoe: Minor Compositions.

Harris, C.l. 1993. "Whiteness as Property." *Harvard Law Review* 106 (8): 1707–1791. https://doi.org/10.2307/1341787.

Henry, F., Dua, E., James, C.E., Li, P., Ramos, H., and Smith, M. 2017. *The Equity Myth: Racialization and Indigeneity at Canadian Universities.* Vancouver: University of British Columbia Press.

James, C.L.R. 1974. "African Independence and the Myth of African Inferiority." In *Education and Black Struggle: Notes from the Colonized World,* edited by Institute of the Black World, 33–41. Cambridge, MA: Cambridge Harvard Educational Review.

James, C.L.R. 2013. *Beyond a Boundary: 50th Anniversary Edition.* Durham, NC: Duke University Press.

Kelley, R. 2016. "Black Study, Black Struggle." Boston Review, 7 March. http://bostonreview.net/forum/robin-d-g-kelley-black-study-black-struggle.

Kelley, R. 2017. "Winston Whiteside and the Politics of the Possible." In *Futures of Black Radicalism,* edited by G. Johnson and A. Lubin, 241–248. London: Verso.

King, M., Jr. 1957. "The Birth of a New Nation," 7 April. https://kinginstitute.stanford.edu/king-papers/documents/birth-new-nation-sermon-delivered-dexter-avenue-baptist-church.

King, M., Jr. 1967. "Where Do We Go From Here?" The Martin Luther King, Jr. Research and Education Institute. https://kinginstitute.stanford.edu/encyclopedia/where-do-we-go-here-chaos-or-community.

King, M., Jr. 2010. *Where Do We Go from Here: Chaos or Community?* Boston, MA: Beacon Press.

Lawrence, C.R. 1992. "The Word and the River: Pedagogy as Scholarship as Struggle." *Southern California Law Review* 65 (5): 2231–2298.

Matsuda, M.J. 1989. "When the First Quail Calls: Multiple Consciousnesses as Jurisprudential Method." *Women Rights Law Reporter* 11 (1): 7–10.

Morris, A. 2015. *The Scholar Denied: W.E.B. DuBois and the Birth of Modern Sociology.* Berkeley: University of California Press.

Moten, F. 2013. "Blackness and Nothingness (Mysticism in the Flesh)." *South Atlantic Quarterly* 112 (4): 737–780. https://doi.org/10.1215/00382876-2345261.

Ngwena, C. 2018. *What Is Africanness? Contesting Nativism in Race, Culture and Sexualities.* Pretoria: Pretoria University Law Press.

Polanyi, K. 2001. *The Great Transformation: The Political and Economic Origins of Our Time.* Boston, MA: Beacon Press.

Quan, H.L.T. 2005. "Geniuses of Resistance: Feminist Consciousness and the Black Radical Tradition." *Race and Class* 47 (2): 39–53. https://doi.org/10.1177/0306396805058081.

Roberts, N. 2015. *Freedom as Marronage.* Urbana: University of Chicago Press.

Robinson, C. 2000. *Black Marxism: The Making of the Black Radical Tradition.* Chapel Hill: The University of North Carolina Press.

Shenk, J. 2014. "Vincent Harding: 'Don't Get Weary though the Way Be Long.'" *The Mennonite.* https://themennonite.org/feature/vincent-harding-dont-get-weary-though-way-long/.

Simpson, A. 2014. *Mohawk Interruptus: Political Life across the Borders of Settler States.* Durham, NC: Duke University Press.

Simpson, L.B. 2013. *Islands of Decolonial Love.* London: ARP.

Slobodian, Q. 2018. *Globalists: The End of Empire and the Birth of Neoliberalism.* Cambridge, MA: Harvard University Press.

Temin, P. 2017. *The Vanishing Middle Class: Prejudice and Power in a Dual Economy.* Cambridge, MA: MIT Press.

White, D.E. 2011. *The Challenge of Blackness: The Institute of the Black World and Political Activism in the 1970s.* Gainesville: University of Florida Press.

Wright, R. 1995. *White Man, Listen! Lectures in Europe, 1950–1956.* New York: Harper Collins.

21 The Changing Same: Black Lives Matter, the Work of History, and the Historian's Craft

BARRINGTON WALKER

Introduction

In their manifesto, the founders of Black Lives Matter state that they are making "an ideological and political intervention in a world where Black lives are systemically and intentionally targeted for demise. It is an affirmation of Black folks' contributions to this society, our humanity and our resilience in the face of deadly oppression" (Black Lives Matter 2016). These words could have been written at any point during the past 400 years of Blackness in Canada, and it would have been relevant and resonant in every era of slavery and (un)freedom (the latter being the forms of servitude and bonded labour that come to replace formal chattel slavery after emancipation or abolition). If slavery and its immediate aftermath was a condition that was framed by violence and its ever-present threat, its legacy haunts us still in the structural violence that frames the Black condition in modern-day Canada. And this structural violence produces and is a product of the metronomic violence that permeates the lived experiences of Black people that is suffered on the body and in the psyche.

This chapter is a short meditative piece on the historian's craft, what I call "the work of history" and the complicated historical present of Black Lives Matter, with a reflection on its possibilities and limits in its partial understanding of Black freedom struggle. Black Lives Matter is a product of long histories of freedom struggle, but its engagement with history has been limited and, as a consequence, it has had mixed results. Black Lives Matter was founded in the United States by three Black queer women – Alicia Garza, Patrice Cullors, and Opal Tomati – in response to George Zimmerman's murder of Trayvon Martin, an unarmed seventeen-year-old Black boy in the Florida community of Sanford (Garza 2014). What distinguishes this movement from its

nineteenth- and twentieth-century predecessors is its birth and prolifer-
ation on social media and its eschewing of the leadership and brokering
models of earlier movements. BLM spread throughout the United States
in the wake of similar incidents of anti-Black violence finding its way
across the border into Canada, where chapters have been established in
Toronto, Ottawa, Montreal, Vancouver, and Edmonton (Migdal 2016).
In this chapter, I continue and engage a conversation from previous,
recent, and forthcoming work that examines the challenges and possibilities of thinking about movements such as BLM against and through a
history of Black Canadians' struggle and journey from fungible property
to rights-bearing citizens and subjects (B. Walker 2010, 2012, 2021).

I argue further that when one considers BLM in light of the history of
slavery and the early post-slavery eras in Canada, one is struck by the continuities that emerged around the fragility of Black freedom and Black
peoples' ongoing struggle to achieve full citizenship in different historical periods. In the eighteenth and early nineteenth centuries, Black
freedom was circumscribed by the sceptre of slavery and unfreedom.
The same is true of the carceral logics that inform the racial landscapes
of the twenty-first century for Black citizens who have founded BLM –
effectively the panoptic techniques of surveillance that migrated from
the plantation to prison/city of the nineteenth and twentieth century.
This chapter begins with a discussion of Black modernity's "changing
same," then moves to discussion of the troubled histories of slavery, freedom, and the circumscribed nature of legal freedom or "unfreedom" in
Canada, eschewing straightforward and linear notions of Black peoples'
march from slavery to freedom. Last, it takes up brief discussion of the
work of history, the role that it has played in subjugating Black people,
and the part that insurgent historical practice has had in pushing against
their subjugation and conventional understandings of time and space.

The Changing Same

Katherine McKittrick has argued that much of the history that marked
the experience of modernity in the Atlantic world – a modernity that
is very much the product of Blackness – is the idea of "the changing
same" (McKittrick 2002, 33). This is shown through the work of Leroi
Jones in his classic text *Blues People*, a treatise on the Black experience
in white America that was written in 1963. Here Jones famously wrote,
"And Rhythm and Blues is 'new' as well. It is contemporary and has
changed, as jazz has remained the changing same" (Harris 2004, 312).
Leroi Jones, who later renamed himself Amiri Baraka, was referring to
the ways in which free jazz embodied continuity and change, the past and

the present. Baraka argued that unlike the avant-garde music of the time that was played by white musicians, which was consciously arbitrary and cacophonous, free jazz, which was rooted in the African American tradition, was a little different in that it incorporated noise. It was, as one critic put it, "rooted in the shouts of the black church and the hollers of the field, sounds saturated with the history of slavery. Furthermore, from its inception to the present, ethnomusical sounds, such as shouts, screams, and grunts, have been associated with the black musical tradition. In essence, the music is a contemporary way into African American history and tradition, into ethnic identity and through sound and for, into what Baraka has called the 'changing same,' that cultural community that persists in changing forms 'the present moment of the past'" (313).

I want to take up this idea of the changing same for thinking about the deep historical ties between the history of early post-slavery Canada and the forms of unfreedom that marked it, Black Lives Matter in Canada, and the social conditions and historical forces that gave birth to it as precisely this, a "present moment of the past." Like the seemingly cacophonous jazz sounds that that were a quintessential expression of the Black modern and all of the tensions and complexities that lay therein, I suggest that Black Lives Matter is simultaneously part of a deep historical archive of Black freedom struggle in North America. Moreover, it is a social movement that pivots on and moves through today's landscape of anti-Blackness. In its current incarnation, however, I suggest that BLM has only partially mined the historical archive of which it is a part.

Slavery, Freedom, and Unfreedom

Whilst most works on the history of Black people in the Atlantic world chart their journey from slavery to freedom, in the Loyalist era Black people found that this journey could easily lapse into bondage, from freedom to unfreedom. In 1775 Lord Dunmore, the governor of Virginia, declared martial law in his colony and found himself in the desperate position of having to search for reinforcements as he was in the midst of a terrible war of attrition with the rebels-cum-Patriots who were fighting for an independent country and succession from the British Empire. Dunmore declared "all indentured servants, Negroes or others (appertaining to Rebels) free, that are able and willing to bear arms, [join] his Majesty's troops as soon as may be, for more speedily reducing this Colony to a proper sense of duty, to his Majesty's crown and dignity" (J.W. St.G. Walker 1992, 1).

Within a week of Dunmore's proclamation, 300 Black men decided to bear arms against their former masters in a military outfit that would be named the "Ethiopian Regiment." The success of this tactic as a recruiting device was immediately evident to both sides in the struggle, and a precedent had been set that aligned the Loyalist cause with the "personal aspirations of the Black 20 percent of the colonial population" (J.W. St.G. Walker 1992). Dunmore, for his part, was seen as one of continental America's most loathsome and formidable enemies. American slave owners viewed the governor's strategy of exploiting their slaves' desire for freedom as yet another brazen affront from their old colonial masters. This insult was made plainly visible on the uniforms of the Ethiopian regiment, which had the words "LIBERTY TO SLAVES" emblazoned across the front. And yet, James W. St.G. Walker reminds us, the crucial point is that although Dunmore's proclamation gave many slaves the opportunity to free themselves, their emancipation was not his primary goal. The rebels, Walker points out, also freed the slaves they found on Loyalist plantations. Thus the proclamation was a tactic of war rather than a moral pronouncement on the evils of the institution of slavery. The amoral aspects of this policy are also the reason the British never adequately prepared for Blacks who chose to respond to the opportunity the British presented them.

In 1779, British commander Henry Clinton's Phillipsburg Proclamation turned the trickle of freedom offered by the Dunsmore Proclamation into a veritable flood: "To every Negro who shall desert the Rebel Standard, full security to follow within these lines any Occupation which he shall think proper" (Walker 1992, 2). Until then, only those Blacks who were capable of military service were accepted as refugees. The Phillipsburg Proclamation changed the course of history. After it was issued, it opened the floodgates to include many more Blacks in what would become a mass movement among the slaves in search of their freedom.

However, a razor-thin line demarcated Black freedom from unfreedom. Many slaves who were set free by the British before they arrived or by their masters upon their arrival found that when they touched the soil of the "promised land" of Nova Scotia, new arrangements – such as indenture – bound their labour and re-established the hierarchies that predominated during the days of slavery. As historian Harvey Amani Whitfield has noted, Nova Scotians struggled to assert their agency and build communities in the face of severe economic hardship – a "contracting economy" – and racially segmented labour markets pushed them to the bottom of the socio-economic hierarchy (Whitfield 2006). The indentures of John Harris and Heton Horton illustrate the tenuousness of Black freedom in early nineteenth-century Loyalist and "refugee" Nova Scotia and the liminality of the position occupied by those in semi-slavery, the not-quite-human non-citizen. And of course, whilst these stories provide a window on the highly contested nature of Black freedom, they are silent on the original dispossession of First Nation peoples and its relationship to the Black experience, which has provided fruitful debate amongst scholars who study the relationship between Blacks and Indigenous peoples in North America (Madden 2009 Sexton 2014; Walker 2021).

An example of this liminality can be found in 1786, when John Harris, "a Black Man," entered into an agreement with a white planter. Harris, the agreement read, "doth bind himself as a servant to be put to any plantation or farm work to William Stone from the date hired to the fourteenth of July next to come providing the said William Stone to find him in provisions during said time" (Black Loyalists 2016). Similarly, in 1817, fourteen-year-old Horton indentured himself to George Deinstadt, a farmer, at the behest of his mother, a widow. The terms of his indenture stipulated that the boy was to serve "his [Deinstadt's] lawful commands [and] everywhere readily obey." In return, the young Horton was to be apprenticed as a cordwainer (shoemaker), receiving "sufficient meat, drink, clothing, lodging, and washing, fitting for an apprentice, during said term of six years, four months & twenty two days and shall permit & allow him to attend night school one quarter of a year in every year during said term and provide for him paper and pens and other necessities and pay the schoolmaster's fees" (Black Loyalists, 2016).

The grim reality that Black people in the Loyalist era had to turn to such arrangements speaks to the threadbare promise of freedom under the British flag. When Black people freed themselves by absconding to British military lines during the American Revolution and the War of 1812, it was an important exercise of their agency that has been well established in the literature. Blacks in Nova Scotia and New Brunswick scratched out a living on the margins of the economy, working their small farms and engaging in small-scale entrepreneurial activity. So Black people's exercise of their freedom was no mere academic undertaking; it could and did have substantive dimensions. Nonetheless, the reality of white supremacy and racialized class relations meant that the "mighty experiment" of Black freedom in the Loyalist era had mixed results, at best.

Black freemen did not have uniform experiences before coming to British North America. Some had been free, others occupied the relatively lofty positions of house slaves or skilled artisans, and still others were part of the army of field hands that fuelled the U.S. plantation economy. This latter group had had no opportunity to amass personal wealth, nor, of course, did they have the chance to learn a skill that might enable them to carve out a place in an economically challenged region once they arrived. They invariably had only their wits or their labour-power to fall back upon. The former was useful, but it produced limited returns. The latter, in a market saturated with cheap labour where jobs at the bottom of the occupational hierarchy were jealously guarded by white labourers, facilitated indentureship as a solution to the problem of how the dominant culture was to maintain social control over a presumably unruly Black population. This population was unruly precisely because this was a society that, whilst it had one of the largest free Black populations in the Atlantic World, was also a society with slaves. The post-1783 free Black populations of Nova and New Brunswick offered the perfect opportunity for marronage for those who were still enslaved. This, coupled with the fact that though the law recognized slavery as a property right of whiteness, ensured the courts placed the onus upon slave owners to provide evidence of their property right (and this was exactly the opposite in Britain's former colonies in the United States). Thus indenture served multiple ends. Indentured labour was an old/new labour agreement, as old as slavery, but reconfigured in the Loyalist era to secure Black labour and keep it at the lowest rung of the labour hierarchy. In so doing, it reinforced the relationship between racialized capitalism and social control, thus reinforcing the commonalities between Black slavery and Black freedom. The relationship between the two is key to understanding profiling, carding, and mass incarceration of Blacks in North America – themes against which BLM has mobilized and to which this chapter will refer in the final section. Most importantly, I suggest, BLM has mobilized against the forces of history by engaging in insurgent intellectual praxis. In this way they have a lot in common with activists and insurgent intellectuals of the Black historical condition.

History's Work and the Work of the Black Historian

The Black Lives Matter movement is impressive, but it is by no means perfect. As many authors in this volume point out, it has its limitations when it is placed alongside other Black social movements that have come before it. There are serious questions about whether true social transformation can occur via social media, a medium that has been funded by white capital and supresses Black aspirations for freedom through its relentless algorithmic expressions of white supremacy. Nonetheless, as I noted in my introductory comments, this chapter is a meditation on the imperative of intellectuals who focus on the historicity of Black modernity to come to grips with the importance of the history of this movement, which is a product of history and an articulation of it. The Black Lives Matter movement is product of the long history of slavery/

capitalism/colonialism, of anti-Black violence, and the commodification and systematic dehumanization of Black people. This long history of dehumanization and commodification along with the history of Black people's resistance, BLM signifies the refusal to accede to the "naturalness" or inevitability of subordination and the desire to assert and reassert Black dignity and humanity across space and time as the quintessence of the Black modern.

Capital *H* History – what Public Enemy's Flava-Flav famously called "his story" – has, from the beginnings of the era of European colonization, worked to create race, racisms, and Blackness, while it has also attempted to reduce the life changes of those deemed Black (Public Enemy, track 2, 1990). The work of history in the lives of African-descended people in the diaspora, and most profoundly in the West, has been the unfolding of this reality in the face of many histories, spaces, and places: the holds of slave ships, auction blocs, plantations, plantation houses, ghettos, neighbourhoods, churches, slums, and prisons.

While the history of Blackness in the West is also largely – though not easily or simply reduced to – histories of violence, the creation and development of formal academic disciplines have also played a role in perpetuating this violence. What I allude to is not novel or original. Whilst violence is at the very heart of Black modernity in the West, the origins of this violence are not only physical but also epistemic. The physical forms of violence and erasure that have characterised so much of the Black modern are ultimately expressions of and made possible only in the first instance by epistemic violence. Anti-Blackness is embedded in the epistemic foundations of the natural sciences, social sciences, and humanities, including history. For Hegel, world historical individuals were those – European-descended men – who realized their place in history and moved it by actualizing the conditions in and through which they seized their freedom. The philosophy of history of Hegel and other foundational European thinkers created the intellectual soil out of which the formal discipline of history grew.

Starting in the early twentieth century, Black scholars of the Black historical condition pushed back, placing Black people at the centre of their own history as individuals and groups who claimed the mantle of their own freedom. In W.E.B. DuBois's seminal *Souls of Black Folk*, he argued that, despite the protestations of many that the U.S. Civil War had "naught to do with slaves," "and yet no sooner had the armies, East and West, penetrated Virginia and Tennessee that fugitive slaves appeared within their lines. They came at night, when flickering camp-fires shone like vast unsteady stars along the black horizon: old men and thin, with gray and tuffed hair; women, with frightened eyes, dragging whimpering hungry children; men and girls stalwart and gaunt, a horde of starving vagabonds, homeless, helpless, and pitiable in their dark distress" (1965, 222)

In spite of his patrician Victorian upper-class distain that illustrated his social class and its attendant attitudes and outlook towards lower-class Black people, DuBois placed Black people at the centre of the events that embroiled the United States in a war with itself. While he argued that the war was tangentially about slaves), his more substantive observation was that the ex-slaves turned the war from one of secession into a war over slavery and the meaning of citizenship and liberty. This was, as we shall see below, also evidenced in an earlier era where the issue of Black freedom was front and centre in North America.

C.L.R. James's *Black Jacobins* was a salvo against a notion of history that placed Europeans and Europe qua Europe at its centre, while writing Black people out of history. James argued that San Domingo, France's West Indian colony, was the pillar of the French empire's economic wealth and stability. The revolt of these slaves and the emergence of Haiti as an independent nation was the subject of his book. But more than this, he wrote Black people into the narrative of modern history as its movers rather than the passive, commodified objects of historical sources that emanate from Eurocentric scholarship: "The revolt is the only successful slave revolt in history, and the odds it had to overcome is evidence of the magnitude of the interests that were involved. The transformation of slaves, trembling in hundreds before a single white man, into a people able to organize themselves and defeat the most powerful European nations of their day, is one of the great epics of revolutionary struggle and achievement" (1989, ix).

James's work not only recasts the French Revolution with slaves at its centre, but something more. James, an ardent student of Marxist/ materialist Hegelian method, sought to situate Black people as world historic individuals and movers of their history.

But as Fred Moten argues in *Black and Blur*, Cedric Robinson's *Black Marxism: The Making of the Black Radical Tradition* pointed to the limitations of C.L.R. James's work (Robinson 1983). Robinson felt that it did not come to grips with the nature of the Black radical tradition, even whilst it illustrated "a lyric disruption of a certain Europeanized notion of public/national history and historical trajectory as well as exterior/ African disruption of the interiority of European lyric" (Moten 2017, 9). Moten further observes, "While the European radical tradition had been formed by and in relation to the bourgeoisie a black radical tradition had been formed independently, by another tradition of radical resistance, another and separate revolutionary culture, another origination of resistance outside of the historical trajectories of either Marx or Hegel, not in between them at the same time as in excess of their oppositional limitations, the one racial, the other classed. That is to say, in Robinson's terms, that 'black radicalism … cannot be understood within the particular context of its genesis'" (Moten 2017, 9).

Anthony Bougues has elaborated upon Robinson's observations about the genesis of Black radical thought, situating the work of C.L.R. James and other exemplars of the Black radical tradition in a space of intellectual praxis that transcends borders and cuts across space and time in its (non-essentialist) iterations. The Black radical tradition, Bougues suggests, consists of "ideas, practices, cultural and literary forms" that are marked by African and African Diasporic elaborations (Bougues 2011, 484). These ideas, practices, and literary forms are expounded by university-trained intellectuals and activists. Activist groups such as Black Lives Matter, in response to the historical genealogies that frame Black life in the present moment, is an iteration of the historical dynamic of Black resistance.

The Colour of Freedom

Black Lives Matter is an organic response to the conditions that shape Black life under the conditions of late modernity. It is important for the historian for two reasons. First, the movement is the most recent iteration of Black social movements in a long history of such movements that began with Black people's resistance to slavery. Second, the movement exists inside and outside of conceptions of linear time, just as Black people do. The social media apparatus in and through which Black Lives Matter has grown is a product of the twenty-first century and the new sorts of identities, mobilizations, and configurations it opens up in relation to Blackness and Black life. Nonetheless, the central jeremiad at its centre – the insistence on the sanctity of Black life in the context of white supremacist logics that are driven towards Black erasure and death – is the lament of the slave, the freedman, the sharecropper, and the denizen of the segregated semi-rural community, the ghetto, the slum. Black Lives Matter was born in response to police killings of Black people. But these killings are symptomatic of the broader structures of societal and historical inequality. They are embedded in the historical present and its attendant anti-Black violence.

In the introduction to his foundational *Colour of Justice: Policing Race in Canada* David Tanovich stated, "The colour of justice in Canada is white. The unequal impact of our criminal justice system begins with police surveillance" (Tanovich 2006, 1). If the colour of justice in Canada has been white, then so too has been the colour of freedom. whiteness in Canada in the eighteenth and early nineteenth century meant freedom from the semi-serfdom and quasi-slavery of indenture: it also meant the freedom to own Black people and to colonize Indigenous Canadians). Similarly, in the early twenty-first-century whiteness is the badge that greatly militates against the likelihood of arbitrary police stops, arrest, or violent confrontations with law enforcement.

The second point of Black Lives Matter's relevance for the historian is that its direct action against the criminal legal system awakens us to the sameness of Black people's exploitation. Policing and the racialized surveillance that has come to characterize it in urban areas is a continuity from slavery to the contemporary criminal legal system that robs Blacks of their liberty, lives, and livelihood in Canada. They are less likely to receive bail in the early stages of adjudication. They also suffer disproportionately harsh sentencing in Canada's courts. And once imprisoned, the conditions of the imprisonment for Blacks (and First Nations peoples) tend to be harsher than that of whites (Luck 2016).

But of course racialized policing and its attendant techniques of surveillance and the disproportionately high representations of Blacks in Canada's prisons is built on a foundation of a long historical archive of judicial and extra-judicial anti-Blackness. Since the mid-nineteenth century, Canada has been mythologized as a haven for people of African descent. While it was a legal haven from slavery since the British abolition of slavery in 1833, custom and law supported white supremacy and Canadian Jim Crowism (B. Walker 2010). Theatres, restaurants, movie theatres, and nightclubs often had informal colour bars; hospitals, schools, and even graveyards were segregated racial landscape in Nova Scotia, Ontario, Quebec, and the prairies. Racially selective federal immigration laws (as well as bureaucratic practices of selecting immigrants) tended to screen out Blacks at our borders (Backhouse 1999; B. Walker 2010).

Legally supported cultural and societal Canadian Jim Crowism shaped Blacks' experiences in the criminal justice system as well (B. Walker 2010). The unequal sentencing patterns that characterize today's justice system have their roots in the nineteenth and early twentieth century. Alongside the disproportionately harsh sentencing of Black defendants was the permutation of racially charged discourse throughout trials that constructed them as the worst threats to dominant social (and sexual) order. Black people were also seen as members of a childlike race, who, because they lacked the cognitive ability necessary for premeditation, were fitting, if pitiful, objects toward whom white clemency and the celerity of British justice could be extended (B. Walker 2010).

Conclusion: Racial Chronotopes and the Changing Same

Today's landscape of anti-Blackness is built on the edifice of the past, but it has taken on newer forms of expression and newer modes of deployment and circulation. The larger story I have tried to tell in this piece is that of the dance between what we historians like to call "continuity and change." In particular, historians of Black Canada continue to grapple with how "Black time" folds in on itself, with the past impinging upon the present, and the present shaping the lens through which we view our past. We are alerted to the importance of history as a foundation for understanding today's moment while pointing to the of history for grasping the possibilities of our future as Black peoples in a place where we are rooted but do not belong.

But what complicates the Canadian story is that half of the tension – the past – has been obscured and even obliterated from the national memory. Canadians – even some Black ones – are simply not cognizant of the sheer weight of anti-Black racism in this country. We might ask ourselves about the possibilities to articulate historically based grievances for recognition of Black humanity when the country's founding narrative is of benign discovery and settlement punctuated by what Constance Backhouse – citing poet and scholar Dionne Brand – has called a "stupefying innocence" (Backhouse 1999, 14) around Canada's deep investment in territorial dispossession of First Peoples, colonization, slavery, and creation of a racial state.

If we skip ahead to the present – the moment I call the historical present – we find that Black life is out of the clutches of slavery but not free from its shadow, its burdensome legacy. Black Lives Matter in Canada – and Toronto in particular – is part of a global movement against the brutal policing of Black people in North America and throughout the world. While the shooting of Andrew Loku in Toronto and the obfuscation of the role of the police and Ontario's Special Investigations Unit was the catalyst for much of the protest we witnessed in Toronto, this again is more of the changing same. Toronto has a long and deep archive of anti-Black police violence dating back to the shootings of Lester Donaldson and Michael Wade Lawson, which spurred the development of the Black Action Defence Committee (B. Walker 2015). It is as if we were watching these events unfold yet again. The actors have changed, as have some of the details, but the narrative remains the same. And yet, amongst the BLM leadership, there is often an lack of attention to the lessons to be drawn from these histories. Scant attention is paid to the struggles of forbears who fought against anti-Blackness in Canada and beyond. BLM also pays little attention to how we might imagine Black freedom beyond their insistence that we not be killed by law enforcement. The relative lack of engagement with Black radical traditions – Black Marxism, pan-Africanism, Garveyism, Rastafarianism – means that emancipatory possibilities are foreclosed, because the archive of Black freedom is not adequately mined by BLM. Radical politics are limited to the body and intersectional identities. The lack of a substantive challenge to capitalism (racial and colonial) and the flattening of radical politics to primarily the politics of identity means that BLM is a fundamentally conservative movement. Tamari Kitossa (2019) has also pointed to the neoliberalism that pervades BLM.

To be a Black Canadian or American is to exist in a post–civil rights era of hard-won victories from modern states who have been compelled to recognize Black humanity in the forms of now quite old anti-discrimination acts, officially colour-blind immigration policies, refugee policies, official multiculturalism, and affirmative action policies. And yet these official measures cannot ensure Black equality beyond formal equality, nor overcome what Charles Mills calls the "racial contract" amongst whites that excludes non-whites from the benefits and privileges of civil society (Mills 1997, 11). Neoliberalism has not meant the retreat of the state, as some suggest, but rather its strategic retreat in areas that characterize the gains of the post–civil rights era and its ferocious ascendance in the security and carceral state.

Black Canadians suffer pernicious forms of hyper-policing, particularly carding (as was noted in an open letter to the city of Toronto posted on Rabble.ca in November 2016), hyper-incarceration, higher unemployment, lower life expectancy and the incongruity of higher school "drop out" rates amongst our young people, lower than average incomes and labour precarity amongst far too many who hold postgraduate degrees. The struggle for substantive rights has framed the Black experience in Canada throughout our history. It is through understanding this difficult and still incomplete journey from a white property right to demanding the rights of citizenship that we can make sense of the emergence of Black Lives Matter and its limitations as well as our continued resilience and resistance to those who continue to deny our humanity

REFERENCES

Backhouse, C. 1999. *Colour-Coded: A Legal History of Racism in Canada, 1900–1950.* Toronto: The Osgoode Society for Canadian Legal History.

Black Lives Matter. 2016. "Herstory." http://blacklivesmatter.com/herstory/.

Black Loyalists. 2016. "Our History, Our People." http://blackloyalist.com/cdc/index.htm.

Bougues, A. 2011. "Pan Africanism and the Black Radical Tradition." *Critical Arts* 25 (4): 484–499.

DuBois, W.E.B. 1965. "The Souls of Black Folk." In *Three Negro Classics*, edited by J.H. Franklin, 207–390. New York: Avon Books.

Garza, A. 2014. "A Herstory of the #BlacklivesMatter Movement by Alica Garza." The Feminist Wire. http://www.thefeministwire.com/2014/10/blacklivesmatter-2/.

Harris W.J. 2004. "'How You Sound??': Amiri Baraka Writes Free Jazz." In *Uptown Conversation: The New Jazz Studies*, edited by B.H. Edwards, J. Griffin, and R.G. O'Meally, 312–325. New York: Columbia University Press.

James, C.L.R. 1989. *The Black Jacobins: Toussaint L'Overture and the San Domingo Revolution.* New York: Vintage Books.

Jones, L. 1963. *Blues People: Negro Music in White America.* Westport, CT: Greenwood Press.

Kitossa, T. 2019. "African Canadian Leadership and the Metaphoricality of 'Crisis': Towards Theorizing, Research, and Practice." In *African Canadian Leadership: Continuity, Transition, and Transformation*, edited by T. Kitossa, E. Lawson, and P. Howard, 91–98. Toronto. University of Toronto Press.

Luck, S. 2016, 20 May. "Black, Indigenous Prisoners Over-Represented in Nova Scotia Jails." CBC News. http://www.cbc.ca/news/canada/nova-scotia/black-indigenous-prisoners-nova-scotia-jails-1.3591535.

Madden, P. 2009. *African Nova Scotian–Mi'kmaw Relations.* Halifax: Fernwood Publishing.

McKittrick, K. 2002. "'Their Blood Is There, and They Can't Throw It Out': Honouring Black Canadian Geographies." *Topia: Canadian Journal of Cultural Studies* 7: 27–37. https://doi.org/10.3138/topia.7.27.

Migdal, A. 2016, 24 August. "Black Lives Matter Protests Death of Abdirahaman Abdi across Canada." The Globe and Mail. http://www.theglobeandmail.com/news/national/black-lives-matter-protests-death-of-abdirahman-abdi-in-cities-across-canada/article31531189.

Mills, C. 1997. *The Racial Contract.* Ithaca, NY: Cornell University Press.

Moten, F. 2017. *Black and Blur: Consent Not to Be a Single Being.* Durham, NC: Duke University Press.

Ridenhour, E., Sadlier, E., and Shocklee, K. 1990. "Brothers Gonna Work It Out." Recorded by Public Enemy, Chuck D, and Flava Flav. On *Fear of a Black Planet* Compact disk. New York: Def Jam Records and Columbia Records.

Robinson, F. 1983. *Black Marxism: The Making of the Black Radical Tradition.* Chapel Hill: University of North Carolina Press.

Sexton, J. 2014, 19 December. "The *Vel* of Slavery: Tracking the Figure of the Unsovereign." *Critical Sociology.* https://doi.org/10.1177/0896920514552535.

Tanovich, D.M. 2006. *The Colour of Justice: Policing Race in Canada.* Toronto: Irwin Law.

Tator, C., and Henry, F. 2006. *Racial Profiling in Canada: Challenging the Myth of a "Few Bad Apples."* Toronto: University of Toronto Press.

Walker, B. 2010. *Race on Trial: Black Defendants in Ontario's Criminal Courts, 1858–1958.* Toronto. University of Toronto Press and the Osgoode Society for Canadian Legal History.

Walker, B. 2012. *The African Canadian Legal Odyssey: Historical Essays.* Toronto: University of Toronto Press and the Osgoode Society for Canadian Legal History.

Walker, B. 2015. "Playing the Race Card: Policing Toronto the Good." *Torontoist,* 15 May. http://torontoist.com/2015/05/playing-the-race-card-policing-toronto-the-good/.

Walker, B. 2021. "Critical Histories of Blackness in Canada." In *Unsettling the Great White North: Black Canadian History,* edited by M.A. Johnson and F. Aladejebi, 31–49. Toronto: University of Toronto Press.

Walker, J.W. St.G. 1992. *The Black Loyalists: The Search for a Promised Land in Nova Scotia and Sierra Leone 1783–1870.* Toronto: University of Toronto Press.

Whitfield, H.A. 2006. *Blacks on the Border, Black Refugees in British North America, 1815–1860.* Burlington VT: University of Vermont Press.

22 Charting Black Presence and Futures in the Canadian Academy

MALINDA S. SMITH

Introduction

This chapter maps the Black presence and representations of Black scholars and scholarship in the Canadian academy, with an eye to charting Black futures. "Black Canadians," one of ten visible minority or "non-white" groups in Canada, are diverse and complex (Statistics Canada 2019). The Government of Canada defines "visible minority" in *The Employment Equity* Act (1986) as "persons, other than Aboriginal peoples, who are non-Caucasian in race or non-white in colour" (Statistics Canada 2017). The ten visible minority or non-white groups are Black, Arab, Chinese, Filipino, Japanese, Korean, Latin American, South Asian, Southeast Asian, and West Asian. Visible minority is a state-legislated construct, what Marx (1996) refers to as race-making. It is a relational concept that differentiates non-whites from hegemonic whiteness and Indigeneity. At times racial borders – shaped by colour, culture, and nationality – obscure diversity within the categories and their intersections. The concept is contested, and the United Nations, among others, have advocated to discontinue its use (CBC News 2007; Edwards 2011; Grant and Balkis Balkissoon 2019; Woolley 2013). The concept can obscure the specificities of each social group that falls under its broad rubric; still, the concept non-white has the potential to mobilize a counter-hegemonic response to hegemonic whiteness reflected in all major Canadian institutions and social relations.

All of the conceptual limits – and possibilities – of visible minorities as non-whites need not be rehearsed here. Despite some notable changes, such as the replacement of the pseudo race-scientific concept of "Caucasian" with "white," and the shift from "Aboriginal" to "Indigenous," the concept "visible minority" is useful for benchmarking university data to broader societal data over time and space. For my more specific purpose, it is necessary to disaggregate the ten visible minority groups in order to make visible the specificities of the Black experience, and to chart the Black academic pipeline and pathways into and through the academy. It is also worth noting that other commonly used concepts to replace visible minorities, such as "people of colour" and "racialized groups," also pose similar conceptual challenges: although they can ignite counter-hegemonic solidarity to unsettle whiteness, they can also obscure specific Black experiences.

In Canada, Black scholars are less likely than non-Black peers to be hired as a professor, more likely to be unemployed and underpaid, and are absent in leadership positions at all levels (CAUT 2018a, 2018b; Ramos and Li 2017; Smith 2018a, 2018b; Universities Canada 2019). Black Canadian students, professors, and administrators often face an opportunities gap and barriers to advancement – realities reflected in the underrepresentation in the professoriate and in university leadership. These barriers are compounded at the intersections of Blackness, gender, sexual orientation, abilities, class, and generation. In this chapter, I build on my diversity gap research (Smith 2016, 2019b), where I developed an intersectional equity approach to disaggregated data collection and analysis to unsettle diversity silos and transform the dominant institutional equity architecture and infrastructure that reproduce racialized and gendered social hierarchies. Most university equity programs were designed to advance gender equity, and there are identifiable infrastructure and resources that aim to achieve these ends. Racial equity, let alone racial justice, has never been prioritized and has received inadequate institutional resources. There is no infrastructure designed to address, for example, racism, including anti-Black racism, racialized harassment, or persistent underrepresentation of Black faculty or the Black student experience (MacDonald and Ward 2017a, 2017b). Without disaggregated visible minority data, institutions cannot identify and address the barriers each group faces, the systems and structures that produce and sustain inequities, and what is necessary to transform the social injustice of sameness (Essed and Goldberg 2002). While the available data herein do not enable us to tease out Black diversity and scholarship (Statistics Canada 2019), we can analyse Black scholars in relation to racialized scholars generally, and the predominantly white professoriate and university leadership.

Charting Black Canadian Studies Resurgence

My efforts to explore the nuances of Blackness, chart Black academic pipelines, amplify engaged scholar activism, and map institutional innovations are occurring in a moment that might broadly be conceived as a Black

Canadian studies resurgence after a similar effort in the 1980s waned (Kitossa 2012). As Francis (2019) notes, the emergent "field of Black studies is slowly getting its due recognition at Canadian universities, thanks to the tireless work of Black scholars and student activists" and, moreover, this resurgence is the result of grassroots efforts: "For decades, Black scholars and students in Canada have found ways to bring Black studies into the academy. Now, thanks to the work of this network of scholars and students, the field is getting formal recognition, funding and space."

The past decade has witnessed growing numbers of new and mid-career scholars working in Black Canadian studies. At least five grassroots and institutional developments amplify and reinforce this resurgence. First, Black, African diaspora, and Caribbean studies programs are increasing in number. As well, university transition-year programs facilitate the entry of Black students. A second and related development of note is the endowment of scholarships and fellowships named after Black trailblazers, and Black postdoctoral fellowships aimed at cultivating future Black professors. A third, primarily student-led development is Black graduation ceremonies to celebrate Black student achievement. A fourth area of growth is in knowledge mobilization through Black studies speaker series profiling renowned Black intellectuals and activists, and Black studies research chairs. A fifth institutional development is Black student associations and Black and racialized faculty caucuses to advocate for collective interests and professional well-being.

The first development of note is the creation of courses, certificates, minors, and degree programs in Black Canadian studies. These initiatives build on earlier African studies programs at Carleton University, McGill University, the University of Calgary, University of Toronto, the University of British Columbia, and York University. They also include Caribbean studies programs, such as at the University of Toronto and the Caribbean Studies Certificate at Ryerson University. There are many undergraduate Latin American and Caribbean studies programs, including at Carleton University, McGill University, and a master's at Guelph University. While few Caribbean Studies Institutes continue to exist, the Harriet Tubman Institute for Research on the Global Migration of Africans at York University is distinctive for its focus on the worldwide Black experience. The Brock Institute for Canada-Caribbean studies, which was established in 2019, has formed a partnership with the University of the West Indies. Both the African and Caribbean studies programs are strengthened by scholarly associations that meet at the Congress of the Humanities and Social Sciences, and by professional journals. While some of these programs are complementary, the early established programs had few, if any Black scholars and tended to be among the first to face budget cuts. Moreover, the curriculum, research, and scholarship generated in these Latin American and Caribbean studies programs do not centre specifically on the Black experience.

A new generation of Black Canadian studies scholars have mobilized with Black students to create new minors and certificates, including the Black African Diaspora Minor and Certificate at Dalhousie University, the Black Canadian Studies Certificate and Minor at York University, the Africana Studies Minor at Brock University (and a minor under exploration at Concordia University). Black scholars insist that Black professors and university leaders matter to decolonizing research, teaching, mentoring, and training future students (see Francis 2019; The Link 2017; Yaboha 2016). There is also a related development with the creation of pathways to the academy for Black students with transition year programs (TYP). One of the earliest TYPs began at Dalhousie University in 1970 with the aim of increasing access and success of Black and Indigenous students. The University of Toronto's TYP inaugurated by Karen S. Braithwaite, among others, built on its early Black community roots, and since then has been expanded to include Indigenous peoples and diverse genders, orientations, and abilities.

Moreover, initiatives are emerging out of university working groups on racism, slavery, and colonialism. Queen's University, for example, is coming to terms with its history of institutional racism, which led to Black students being expelled and banned from the Faculty of Medicine in 1918 and lasting until 1965 (Dannetta 2019; Rideout 2019). The expulsion ended the medical careers of at least two of the fifteen students. After decades of denial, Queen's Principal Daniel Woolf and Dean of Medicine Richard Reznick acknowledged the expulsion and ban on Black medical students and offered an institutional apology on 16 April 2019 to right the wrong (Dannetta 2019; Rideout 2019). Queen's will include this history of anti-Black racism in a course to be taught in the School of Medicine, and has established a mentorship program during clerkship and residency and a $10,000 entrance scholarship for Black medical students (Rideout 2019). Another more limited example from McGill University was the Provost's Working Group on Principles of Commemoration and Renaming, which examined the role of the university's founder, James McGill, in slavery and colonialism. I say "more limited" in part because, despite having only eight Black professors and fewer Indigenous scholars, several of them are renowned slavery and anti-colonial scholars, yet two white scholars not known for research on slavery and colonialism were tapped to lead that working group. Perhaps in the most significant example, Afua Cooper at Dalhousie University, led the Scholarly Panel on Lord Dalhousie's legacy of race and slavery. The panel's mandate included responding to the question, "What did it mean to celebrate 200 years of existence in the context of racism, anti-Blackness, and knowledge about the founder's view and actions toward people of African descent?" (Cooper 2019). The final report included thirteen recommendations focused on regret and responsibility, recognition, and repair through concrete measures to transform the legacy. While few, such initiatives mark a new direction for Canadian universities.

Second, while there have been a number of scholarships honouring trailblazing Black scholars in the academy for some time, new ones continue to be created. Among those named after Black trailblazers include the Abraham Beverley Walker Scholarship at the University of New Brunswick, the Kenneth J. Melville Bursary at McGill University, the Maynier-Fuld Scholarship at the University of Toronto, and the Robert Sutherland Fellowship at Queen's University (see Smith in this volume). Likewise, new scholarships, such as the Viola Desmond Bursary at Saint Mary's University, have been established to support graduate students, awarding the first two in 2019. A few universities have also established postdoctoral fellowships with the potential to more proactively create future Black scholars. These include the 2021 Provost Postdoctoral Fellowship for Black and Indigenous researchers at the University of Calgary, the 2019 Provost Postdoctoral Fellowship for Black and Indigenous researchers at the University of Toronto, and the 2019 Provostial Research Scholars in Institutional Histories, Slavery, and Colonialism at McGill University, which aim "to address and confront its historical legacy of wrong towards historically subordinated groups" (Geitmann and Lecky, 2018). These McGill Provostial Research Scholar positions also centre Black and Indigenous scholars who remain significantly underrepresented at these universities.

A third initiative, which emerged in response to the Black student experiences of discrimination and marginality, celebrates Black student achievement. At the University of Toronto and McGill University, students have initiated Black graduation ceremonies, in which each "honours excellence and aims to empower students who still face challenges" (McQuigge 2017). Influenced by similar programs at Harvard and Yale, Jessica Kirke first proposed the idea at the University in Toronto in 2017. Kirke highlighted, "I've experienced, and have seen, that black students are more likely to be talked over and interrupted in the classroom" (as cited in McQuigge 2017). Given the fact that micro-aggression "takes a toll" on Black students, the ceremony was envisioned to celebrate Black student survival and success. Subsequently, in May 2019, Christelle Tessono, a political science student and president of McGill Black Students Network, co-organized that university's first Black graduation ceremony. For Tessono, "The point is to assert our history here on campus, as well as our successes" (as cited in Shalom 2019). After conducting research for a history class, Tessono more fully understood that "Black students have always been in leadership positions at McGill. In the 1940s, they were presidents of their residences, their halls, they were on varsity teams ... They were presidents of debate teams and they were extremely involved on campus" (Shalom 2019). The under-representation of Black students and professors alike is reflected in the curriculum and amplified in the anti-Black stereotypes in some university classrooms. "Sometimes you really can't believe the things people say about the developing world, mostly about African nations," Raphael Ajima noted. "But you learn not to get shocked. You let it go" (as cited in Shalom 2019).

Fourth, Black Canadian studies research and the Black experience in the academy are expanding (Francis 2019; Henry 2016). One institutional development that is fundamental to Black knowledge production and mobilization is creating research chairs and speaker series that foreground Black intellectuals and activists in Canada and the African diaspora. They also serve as a reminder that academic events featuring all-white or all-male panels (manels) are rooted in and reproduce hegemonic whiteness in the academy. The reproduction of whiteness in the professoriate and university leadership is a stark contrast to what exists in the student body and the broader society (Smith 2018, 2019b). Three examples of speaker series serve to highlight interdisciplinarity, the diversity of Black intellectuals, and the breadth of scholarly interventions: the Robert Sutherland Visitorship at Queen's University has included speakers such as Ken Wiwa, Faith Nolan, and Lawrence Hill; the 2015 Race Literacies: A Black Canadian Scholars' Series by professor Annette Henry included Dionne Brand and David Chariandy, among others (Henry 2016; Werb 2015); and the 2020 Thinking While Black-Lind Initiative Speaker Series at the University of British Columbia profiled renowned African Diaspora intellectuals.

These Black speaker series complement the work of Black studies research chairs. The oldest research chair, the James R. Johnson Chair in Black Canadian Studies at Dalhousie University, is named after the university's first Black graduate. Launched in 1996 through the activities of Bev Samuels, among others, it has supported scholars in law (Esmeralda Thornhill, 1996–2003), social work (David Divine, 2004–11), history (Afua Cooper, 2011–19), and public health (OmiSoore H. Dryden as of 2019). Another major research chair is the Jean Augustine Chair in Education in the New Environment at York University. Named after the first Black woman elected to the Parliament of Canada, the inaugural chair, education professor S. Nombuso Dlamini (2010–16), focused on

Black urban education in teaching, research, community engagement, and university-community alliance (Armstrong 2016). The priorities of the subsequent Jean Augustine Chair in Education, Community, and Diaspora held by education professor Carl James (since 2016), aimed to expand access, equity, and inclusivity in education through collaboration and university-community engagement. In 2021 a record number of federal government-funded Canada Research Chairs (CRCs) fuelled research in Black studies, including Charmaine Nelson as a Tier 1 CRC in TransAtlantic Black Diasporic Art and Community Development at NSCAD; Christiana Sharpe as a Tier 1 CRC in Black Studies in the Humanities at York University; Andrea Fatona as a Tier 2 CRC in Canadian Black Diasporic Cultural Production at OCAD University; and Grace Adeniyi as a Tier 2 CRC in African Urban Futures at Queen's University. In February 2021, the University of Alberta advertised a Tier 1 CRC in Black Studies, with the successful candidate to be based in the English and Film Studies.

A fifth development is the growth of Black students associations (BSAs) and Black faculty caucuses. Many of the earliest BSAs were created in professional fields, primarily in law and medicine, as shown in table 22.1, with other undergraduate and postgraduate associations emerging in the early 1990s. The number of BSA-related organizations expanded between 2016 and 2019, including at Memorial University in Atlantic Canada, the University of Windsor and the University of Toronto in Central Canada, and the University of Alberta and Kwantlen University in Western Canada.

A consistent thread in all of these associations is the need for solidarity in the face of isolation and marginality, to strengthen cultural connections, provide support, combat discrimination, and give back to the broader community. The theme of self-help is also a consistent thread. "We thought, if nobody's going to help us, we'll help ourselves," says Ladan Mowild, the then president of the Black Students' Association at Memorial University (CBC News 2017). Mowild described the isolation, a common obstacle to a sense of belonging for Black students: "I was oftentimes the only person in my classroom, so I felt like that in itself was already hard to adjust to" (CBC News 2017). Similarly, when Black students at the University of Alberta created a BSA, they stressed the need to provide mutual support, to combat discrimination, as well as "giving back to the wider community" (McMaster 2019; Yousif 2018).

Although not as prevalent, several Black and racialized faculty and staff caucuses and networks have emerged on Canadian campuses for reasons similar to those for the students' associations. Among these are Dalhousie's Black Faculty & Staff Caucus, Queen's Black Faculty

Table 22.1. The Growth of Black Students Associations and Networks at Canadian Universities

Black Students Associations (BSAs)	Kwantlen University, Laurier University, McGill University, McMaster University, Memorial University of Newfoundland and Labrador, University of Alberta, University of Guelph, University of Toronto, Western University
Other Black associations	Black Association of Student Expression at University of Waterloo; Students of Caribbean and African Ancestry at Simon Fraser University; United Black Students at Ryerson University
Black Graduate Students Associations	National Black Graduate Network, University of Alberta, University of Toronto.
Black Law Students Associations	Dalhousie University, McGill University, Osgoode Hall, Queen's University, Thompson Rivers University, Université de Montréal, Université de Quebec à Montréal, University of Alberta, University of British Columbia, University of Calgary, University of Manitoba, University of Ottawa, University of New Brunswick, University of Toronto, University of Victoria, University of Windsor, Western
Black Medical Students Associations	University of Calgary, University of Ottawa, University of Toronto

Association, Ryerson's Black Faculty & Staff Community Network, the Black Faculty Working Group at the University of Toronto, and the York University Race Equity Caucus. These community-minded groups combat anti-Black racism and enable mobilization to address systemic inequities and improve representation and curriculum innovations.

The institutionalization and professionalization of Black Canadian studies is also buttressed by an insurgent Black Canadian Studies Association (BCSA). It was founded in 2009 on the final day of the "Knowledge Production and the Black Experience in Canada" symposium organized by Afua Cooper. During its early years, Cooper and a group of radical Black scholar-activists – notably Jennifer Kelly, Tamari Kitossa, and Charmaine Nelson, among others – led the BCSA through its early formation, including symposiums at the University of Alberta (2010), Brock University (2013), and Brandon University (2015). In 2017, the BCSA became a member of the Federation for the Humanities and Social Sciences and one year later began holding its conferences annually in concert with the Congress of the Humanities and Social Sciences (Kitossa 2012).

These institutional developments, among others, have also helped to focus attention on the Black student experience, the underrepresentation of Black professors, and curriculum gaps. As Henry (2016) notes,

"The practices in Canadian universities often ignore a varied and rich black intellectual tradition." Moreover, racism remains a taboo subject in the Canadian academy despite the distortions it creates: "Institutional racism promotes distorted contours of various disciplines, limits students' capacity for knowledge production and, in some subject areas, gives an erroneous view of the range of human possibilities, including what it means to be Canadian." Efforts to close the Black studies knowledge gap and its curricular and student experience impact further highlight why Black scholars matter, and why there is an urgent need to cultivate, hire, and retain them. The knowledge gap also limits the opportunities Black undergraduate and graduate students have to engage Black Canadian studies scholarship, and to experience Black professors as producers of knowledge rather than Blackness primarily as objects of study and undue scrutiny (Crichlow 2019; Nelson 2012; Mogadime 2015).

Charting Black Academic Pipeline

My next aim is to chart, for the first time, one iteration of a Black academic pipeline. The original data herein show that the underrepresentation of Black scholars does not stem from prevailing assumptions regarding workforce availability. The tendency to frame the underrepresentation of Black scholars as a function of qualification relies on an enduring stereotype that constructs Black-as-lack. Black scholars are more likely to be unemployed or underemployed, as well as underpaid, compared to their white counterparts and scholars from other racialized groups (CAUT 2018a, 2018b; Ramos and Li 2017; Smith 2018). Underrepresentation is tied to underemployment – blocked access to the academy. Once in the academy, the devalued status is reinforced by Black scholars being under-recognized and underpaid. These dynamics are a function of the intersections of anti-Black racism and discrimination on the one hand, and hiring and advancement policies rooted in cultural cloning and a preference for sameness on the other hand. Essed and Goldberg (2002) explain the reproduction of whiteness as follows: "By cloning we understand the reproduction of sameness which is deeply ingrained in the organization and reproduction of culture" (Essed and Goldberg 2002). This cloning reimagines the colonial racial order, reinforces the culture of whiteness in the academy (Henry 2004), and reproduces the racialized and gendered social hierarchies that systematically disadvantage Black students and professors.

The metaphor of the academic pipeline, particularly the concept of the "leaky pipeline," is widely used to account for the ways in which representation declines for social groups the further along the academic trajectory they move, and to call into question where and why some scholars tend to "leak out." In the Canadian academy, the pipeline metaphor has been used primarily in research on the status of women, whereas in the United States it is also used to account for gaps in Indigenous and racialized minority representation (Abiola 2014; Cross 1991; Jackson 2007). The pipeline metaphor has faced widespread criticism for limits in how it conceptualizes "the messy reality of inequality, discrimination, and corporate culture" (Gregg 2015; Garbee 2017), as well as what it assumes about the linearity of academic trajectories in and out of the academy: "Careers do not all flow along a single pipeline, or at the same pace ... And far from a single pipeline, there are clearly many different paths through academia" (Fyfe 2018). Despite the limits, the metaphor is a useful heuristic for thinking through and charting a Black academic pipeline in Canadian universities. For Black scholars the leaky pipeline might be too passive, given the systemic dynamics: with Black scholars we might be dealing with more of a ruptured or sabotaged pipeline. Either way, the metaphors can be useful in efforts to conceptualize and chart Black scholars' academic trajectories from K-12 to the professoriate to senior university leadership. Such an examination could lead to an effort to refocus attention on creating early pathways into the academy, such as from high school to TYPs; to identifying the structures, obstacles, barriers, stereotypes, attitudes, and biases that block access to colleges and universities; and to retention efforts to prevent "leaks" from the PhD to assistant professor, and from full professor to university leadership.

Black Student Experience: What Happens before University?

The Black academic pipeline or pathway begins pre-university. There is a significant body of research that maps the Black student experience from kindergarten to high school. This mapping is often framed in terms of the "race attainment gap" and the urgent need to close the "racialized achievement gap" (James and Turner 2017; Shah 2019), as well as a desire to prevent and transform the "school-to-prison pipeline" (Maynard 2017; Morgan 2016; Neigh 2018). The "Black and racialized achievement gaps are a red alert," according to Shah (2019). In the case of the attainment gap, the research reveals how systemic racial inequality and an opportunities gap affect disparities in educational performance, such as, for example, on test scores, school pushout (not "dropout") rates, and the streaming of Black students into technical programs and courses below their ability (Draaisma 2017; Gordon 2017; Rushowy 2015), as well as overall university attendance and degree completion rates.

In the case of the school-to-prison pipeline, the research suggests Black and Indigenous youth and adults alike experience discriminatory treatment in schools and the broader society. Black and Indigenous children disproportionately experience "interrupted childhoods" in the child welfare system (OHRC 2018), and Black and Indigenous youth and adults are disproportionately targeted by police for surveillance, harassment, arrest, and violence (Ontario Human Rights Commission 2017, 2019). The early policing of Black children and youth also results in disproportionately harsh punishment, suspensions, and expulsions from the school system (James 2002; James and Turner 2017; Salole and Abdulle 2015). One report to the Toronto District School Board (TDSB) found that of the 307 students who were expelled from Toronto public schools between 2011–12 and 2015–16, an astonishing 48% were Black, compared to 10% who were white (Naccarato 2017).

A study by Carl James (2017) using TDSB data and consultations with some 324 parents, school administrators in Toronto, Peel, York, and Durham regions, as well as students and teachers, highlighted a persistent pattern: the hope and promise of Black students are being dashed with disproportionately harsh suspensions, through streaming into applied rather than academic programs, despite their interests and often below their abilities, and by relatively lower applications from high school to postsecondary (James 2017; Draaisma 2017; Gordon 2017; Rushowy 2015):

- Suspensions: 42% Black; 18% white; and 15% other racialized groups
- Academic stream: 53% Black; 81% white; and 80% other racialized groups
- Graduation rates: 69% Black; 84% white; 87% other racialized groups
- Did not apply to postsecondary: 58% Black; 41% other groups

These disaggregated data highlight a number of key dynamics relevant to the pre-university academic pipeline: first, students with higher suspensions (Black) have lower graduations, and students with lower suspensions (white, other racialized) have higher graduation levels. Further, the data suggest at what point, and the reasons why, Black students are pushed out of schooling. As well, students in the academic stream have higher graduation rates and are more likely to attend postsecondary. The streaming and postsecondary application data show 58% of Black students do not – or are not encouraged to – apply to postsecondary institutions, compared to 41% of other groups, and where diversions from, and blockages to, accessing the higher education pipeline might occur. For Black scholars in the academy, the data show where a significant percentage gain access to the academy (e.g., technical programs, certificates below the bachelor's) as well as where many of these Black scholars might leak out (e.g., at the bachelor's level) of the academic pipeline.

The dominant focus on an attainment gap and the school-to-prison pipeline are to disrupt the pathways that lead away from higher education. They may also obscure Black achievements, despite the obstacles, biases, and everyday micro-aggressions that students in higher education experience. The growth of BSAs follow a radical Black tradition of self-help, solidarity, and mutual upliftment, and the need to mobilize against the tyranny of low expectations that prevent Black advancement.

The empirical data on representation and the metaphorical pipeline tell us one kind of story and constitute one way of thinking about the status of Black scholars in the academy. Numbers can never tell the whole story of the lived experience of being Black in the academy. Stories of everyday lived experiences matter, as they also reveal that despite over three decades of expressed commitments to equity, diversity, and inclusion in Canadian universities, Black and racialized students and faculty continue to be perceived as not belonging, as not "fitting in."

Black Student Experience: What Happens in Universities?

On Canadian campuses, student diversity stands in stark contrast to the diversity of the professoriate and university leadership. A closer examination of the everyday Black student experiences provides insight into why many Black students leak out of the academy. How does Blackness affect access to, and pathways through, the academy? How does being Black shape the student experience in Canadian higher education?

Charting the Black student academic pipeline in the Canadian academy is constrained by the availability of reliable race data (Henry 2016, 2017; James, Robson, and Gallagher 2017; MacDonald and Ward 2017b; Smith 2016). Over the past decade, there have been increased calls for race-based data collection (Government of Ontario 2019; Grant and Balkissoon 2019; Reynolds 2016). After an extensive investigation, MacDonald and Ward (2017a, 2017b) found that most of Canada's postsecondary institutions do not collect racial diversity data and, therefore, have a picture of their student body that is incomplete, at best. They also found that of the 83% of universities and colleges contacted, seventy-six could not provide any data on the racial diversity of their students. However, Canadian universities have some data on Indigenous students (Saucier 2018), on international students, and better data on women (Statistics Canada 2018). Efforts to address race-based inequities in higher education require rich student body data in order to understand Black student experiences and engagement, and to assess wide-ranging needs, such as academic, mentoring, and financial.

In what follows, I sketch the Black academic pipeline from high school to undergraduate and graduate students in Canadian universities. Figure 22.1 shows the representation of Black scholars relative to

Figure 22.1. Educational Attainment of Black Scholars by Gender, 2016

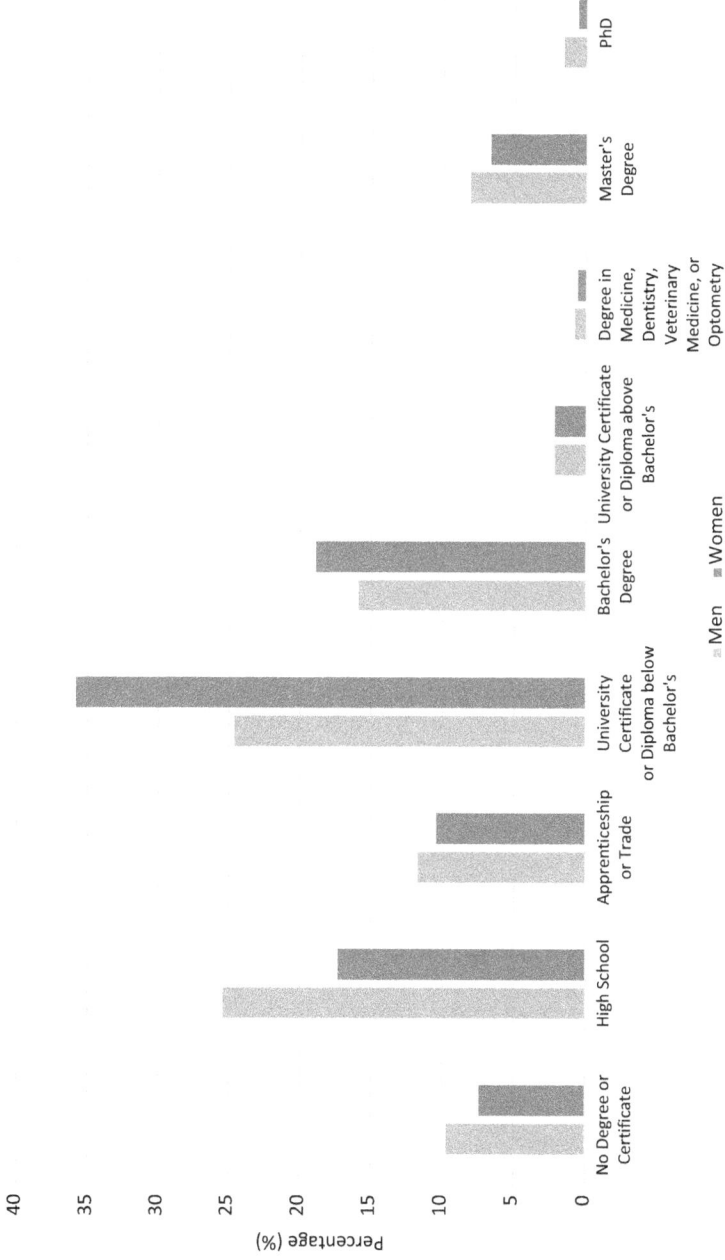

Source: Adapted from Statistics Canada, Census 2016.

Figure 22.2. Representation of Black Students in Canadian Universities

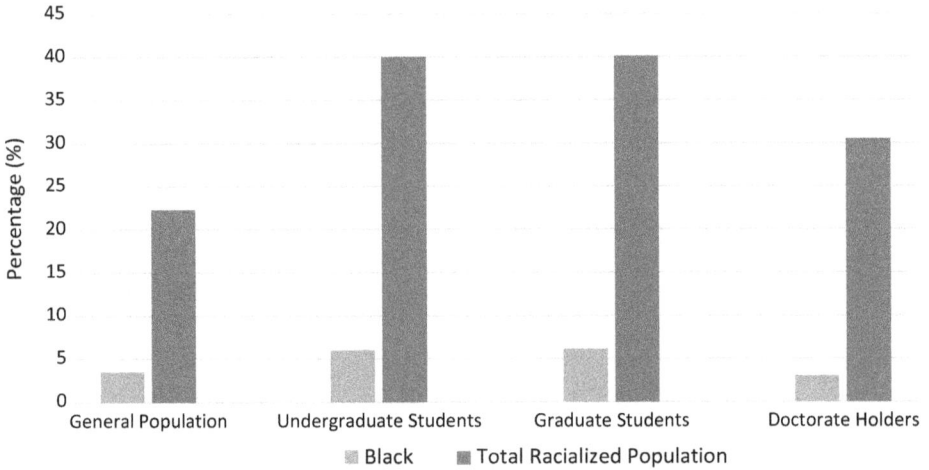

Source: Adapted from M.S. Smith (2018); Universities Canada (2019, 12).

the overall racialized minority population in higher education. At the undergraduate level, Black women have higher levels of educational attainment than Black men but leak out faster at the graduate level, leaving higher numbers of Black men with advanced degrees. Figure 22.1 also shows significant numbers of Black men who are streamed into apprenticeships and Black women who obtain certificates below the bachelor's degree. At the graduate level, particularly at the master's level, more Black men obtain advanced degrees than Black woman. A significant percentage of Black scholars leak out of higher education before or during doctoral studies.

Figure 22.2 shows the overall representation of Black scholars in the Canadian academy in relation to the total racialized student population. Overall, racialized students constitute 40% of undergraduate students, 40.1% of graduate students, and 30.5% of all doctoral degree holders. The proportion of both Black undergraduate and graduate students enrolled in postsecondary programs in Canada is nearly double their proportion in the broader society. Black students constitute 6% of the undergraduate student population and 6.1% of the graduate student population in Canadian universities. At 3%, the percentage of Black doctoral holders is roughly proportionate to the percentage of the Black Canadian population at 3.5%.

Despite the obstacles, the proportion of Black students pursuing undergraduate and graduate programs is nearly double their proportion of the Canadian population. This is a story that is often obscured by the dominant focus on the attainment gap rather than an opportunity (restricted or de-nied) gap, as evident in Hadiya Roderique's story. "My parents moved to Canada to offer me the promise of the North American dream," Roderique wrote in a widely circulated *Globe and Mail* article. "But on my way to be-coming a lawyer, I learned that success isn't necessarily about merit. It's also about fitting in. As a person of colour, that's a roadblock that comes up again and again" (Roderique 2017). Black students often excel because of self-help and with the mentoring and emotional labour invested by already overloaded Black and racialized faculty (Zoledziowski 2018). Black students often succeed not because of the higher education system, but despite the barriers, biases, and everyday experiences of systemic anti-Blackness, with its under-studied impact on student – and faculty and staff – health and well-being (Arday 2019; Chanicka 2018a, 2018b; Green 2016).

Stories of the lived experience tend to fall into three themes: first, the stories of isolation and alienation; second, the pervasiveness of disrespect; and third, the experiences of racial profiling and carding. Together, these experiences make Black students feel as if they are out of place, as if they do not belong. "A lot of times Black students come to the school and feel like they're doing it alone," says Anyika Mark, president of the Black Students' Association at the University of Toronto (Vendeville 2018). According to Mark, "You go to your class of 1,500 stu-dents at Convocation Hall, and you're like, 'Why are there no people who look like me?'" (as cited in Vendeville 2018). Jamar Adams-Thompson had a similar experience of being Black in theatre school: "I got here and I realized, 'Wow, there is almost no one … [like] me.' That was a bit of a hit … I kind of had to take the goggles off and realize it's not just up to the older generation to fix this, it's up to me" (Haggert 2019). The experience of being the only Black student in a class or program shapes the Black student experience of isolation, but it also affects career aspi-rations. For Tiffany Gordon, a doctoral student in philosophy, it was not only that the professoriate – like much of the humanities in Canada – was predominantly white and male. The curriculum was also centred almost exclusively on white male European thinkers, furthering the alienation of Black students and making it difficult to connect with mentors who were aware of these barriers. It mattered when Gordon experienced bet-ter faculty representation in her field of interest: "Being surrounded by philosophers and academics of colour, who were successful professors, made me think there might be room in philosophy for me" (as cited in Zoledziowski 2017). Julia-Simone Rutgers, a journalism student, had the opposite experience. "I was really noticing that I didn't have any kind of adult figures to go to and talk to about this stuff because most of the adult figures in my school are white people" (as cited in Zoledziowski 2017).

A second kind of lived story is of Black students mobilizing for self-help and survival to counteract a lack of institutional support, and the invaluable role of accidental and informal mentors. In January 2017, Black doctoral student Huda Hassan posted the following message to Twitter: "If you're a black woman applying to grad school & would like a writer+phd student to revise your statement, email me" (Hassan, @hudahassan, 4 January 2017). Hassan received over 2,300 responses, including 120 applications from Black women wanting to pursue graduate studies. Hassan was driven to extend the offer on the basis of her own experiences as a Black woman in doctoral studies. The tweet led to an informal network of self-help through virtual mentoring: "I did luckily receive support from strangers who were black women, who were all already in academia, and who already understood how important it was for me to not only get support from them and get into this program but that it was a very lonely process" (CBC Radio 2017). This kind of virtual self-help is needed, noted Sam Tecle, a member of the Collective of Black Graduate Students at York University, who also saw the decline of Black students at the graduate level. "We don't populate these spaces as we're supposed to," Tecle stated. "We don't form critical masses in our departments so very often we have to seek support or communities of care by our own making ... just to make sure we kind of survive and finish" (CBC Radio 2017).

The lonely experience was also true for Chika Stacey Oriuwa, as the only Black medical student, and isolation took a health toll. Professors unfamiliar with the Black student experience can also provide unhelpful advice. According to Oriuwa, she was told not to speak about race or on what it is like being a Black woman in science, technology, engineering, and mathematics. However, she soon found helpful Black mentors: "At the start of med school, I found it challenging to take ownership of my identity as a Black woman in medicine. I doubted myself and my competencies, and felt that I needed to be perfect to prove my worthiness amongst my peers. These unrealistic, self-imposed expectations caused me to struggle, which led me to become physically and mentally unwell. Thankfully, I had the support of incredible Black physician mentors" (Oriuwa 2019).

The third prevalent theme in the Black student experience was of being made to feel out of place and unwelcome on university campuses, intensified by encounters with anti-Black racism and especially the sometimes unthinking use of the n-word. "I felt devalued. I felt deeply humiliated and angered that he said something like this," was how health student Chizoba Oriuwa described her English professor at Western University who casually used the n-word in class. Despite the course being a requirement, this compelled her to seek a better learning environment in an alternative class (Rodriguez 2019). Some Black students face degrading and humiliating campus experiences, particularly young Black men. When Shelby McPhee attended the

BCSA conference at the June 2019 Congress, two white women followed, photographed, and called campus security after falsely accusing him of stealing a laptop. McPhee said he "felt embarrassed ... and I felt there was no safe place for me at UBC or for my colleagues that had come from the Black Canadian Studies Association" (as cited in Larsen 2019; see also Smith et al. 2021). Jamal Boyce, a Black student and student association vice-president at the University of Ottawa, was skateboarding on a campus street in June 2019 when he was stopped and carded by campus security. Deciding to walk away, he was followed by the security guard, arrested, and handcuffed on a busy street and held for two hours (Ranlakhan 2019). Boyce shared his experience on social media, tweeting, "This was [a] humiliating and messed up experience. @uOttawa security used their authority to harass and demean me. Is this how students will continue to be treated on campus @uOttawa?" (Ranlakhan 2019). This experience led the University of Ottawa to review and develop a new policy on carding; however, anti-Black racist incidents continued to occur. In all cases, Black students expressed frustration at the inadequate institutional mechanisms to address the prevalence of anti-Black racism on campus and in classrooms, as these created conditions of disadvantage and harmed the student experience.

Black Professors in the Canadian Academy

The preceding analysis suggests much work needs to be done to make Canadian universities more welcoming and inclusive spaces for Black students. This is also true for the Black professoriate. The CAUT (2010) found that "university teachers who self-identify as Black constitute 1.6% of all university teachers, while comprising 2.2% of the overall labour force" (4). It also highlighted the fact that overall, racialized "minority university teachers earn well below the average of all professors and are more likely to experience unemployment" (1). Changes to these inequities have been glacially slow. A major finding of CAUT's April 2018 report was that, "whereas there has been a slight improvement in the representation of Black university teachers over the past decade (from 1.8% in 2006 to 2.0%) in 2016, the growth in the proportion of Black workers in the labour force has been greater (from 2.2% to 3.1%)" (CAUT 2018b, 14).

Representation of Black University Professors

Table 22.2 shows the representation of Black university professors and college instructors in relation to disaggregated visible minority professors and the majority white professors in the Canadian academy. Representation is racialized and gendered. Black professors and college instructors, particularly women, are significantly underrepresented in

Table 22.2. Representation of Black and Racialized* Professors and College Instructors at Canadian Universities and Colleges, 2016

	University professor		College professor		Total labour force	
	Number	%	Number	%	Number	%
White	59,365	77.55	80,895	82.59	12,742,720	75.07
Male	32,390	42.31	38,190	38.99	6,668,455	39.29
Female	26,980	35.24	42,695	43.59	6,074,265	35.79
Total visible minority	16,150	21.10	14,135	14.43	3,590,560	21.15
Male	10,140	13.25	6,030	6.16	1,838,680	10.83
Female	6,010	7.85	8,110	8.28	1,751,885	10.32
Black	1,555	2.03	2,350	2.40	518,600	3.06
Male	1,020	1.33	1,250	1.28	257,855	1.52
Female	535	0.70	1,105	1.13	260,750	1.54
South Asian	3,895	5.09	3,330	3.40	899,820	5.30
Male	2,550	3.33	1,435	1.47	504,435	2.97
Female	1,345	1.76	1,895	1.93	395,380	2.33
Chinese	4,325	5.65	2,710	2.77	732,355	4.31
Male	2,575	3.36	950	0.97	364,680	2.15
Female	1,760	2.30	1,765	1.80	367,680	2.17
Filipino	195	0.25	755	0.77	436,220	2.57
Male	110	0.14	280	0.29	179,260	1.06
Female	90	0.12	480	0.49	256,960	1.51
Latin American	1,080	1.41	1,045	1.07	244,970	1.44
Male	595	0.78	410	0.42	125,450	0.74
Female	490	0.64	635	0.65	119,515	0.70
Arab	1,820	2.38	1,410	1.44	202,580	1.19
Male	1,260	1.65	705	0.72	125,935	0.74
Female	560	0.73	705	0.72	76,650	0.45
Southeast Asian	320	0.42	335	0.34	151,810	0.89
Male	160	0.21	120	0.12	73,710	0.43
Female	165	0.22	210	0.21	78,100	0.46
West Asian	1,500	1.96	840	0.86	124,435	0.73
Male	1,035	1.35	395	0.40	70,845	0.42
Female	475	0.62	445	0.45	53,595	0.32
Korean	530	0.69	320	0.33	87,115	0.51
Male	330	0.43	105	0.11	43,375	0.26
Female	200	0.26	215	0.22	43,740	0.26
Japanese	460	0.60	445	0.45	43,600	0.26
Male	220	0.29	115	0.12	18,760	0.11
Female	235	0.31	325	0.33	24,840	0.15
Other	455	0.59	600	0.61	149,055	0.88
Male	290	0.38	270	0.28	74,380	0.44
Female	165	0.22	330	0.34	74,680	0.44

Sources: Created from Statistics Canada, Census 2016; CAUT Almanac, unpublished data; CAUT (2018b).
* Racialized minorities data are drawn from visible minority categories in the 2016 Census.

the Canadian academy. There are approximately 3,905 Black professors and college instructors teaching in Canadian universities and colleges. Of these, 60% – 2,350 – are employed at colleges, while 40% – 1,555 – are employed as university professors.

Average Income of Black University Professors and College Instructors, Age 25+

Table 22.3 draws on 2016 Statistics Canada Census data to show the average income of racialized and Black university professors and college instructors at Canadian universities and colleges relative to the overall average for male and female workers. The findings of a racialized and gender wage gap are consistent with those outlined in Ramos and Li (2017) using 2006 census data. The 2016 census data show Black scholars experience a wage disparity compared to their white counterparts, and some racialized minority professors – particularly Chinese, South Asian, and Southeast Asian – although by no means all racialized scholars. Some racialized scholars, such as Filipinos, Japanese, and West Asians, also experience racialized and gender wage gaps. While many Canadian universities pursue pay equity reviews for women, few, if any, examine the racialized wage gap or engage in an intersectional analysis of race, Indigeneity, and gender data.

A Black Academic Pipeline in Canadian Universities

Figure 22.3 presents a novel representation of the Black academic pipeline in the Canadian academy, from undergraduate and graduate studies, to the professoriate, to university leadership. This is, I believe, the first time a Black academic pipeline has been charted in the Canadian academy. As discussed earlier, the educational achievement of Black undergraduate and graduate students exceeds their proportion in the general population. However, Black professors as full-time academic staff are underrepresented relative to their proportion in the population. Black scholars are also underrepresented in senior university leadership, which remains overwhelmingly white and predominantly male (Smith 2019a, 2019b; Universities Canada 2019), followed by white women and to a lesser extent non-Black racialized minorities.

With a few notable exceptions, Black scholars are absent from senior leadership positions. Figure 22.3 shows that 91.7% of university senior leadership positions are white, 8.3% are racialized minorities, and of these only 0.8% are Black. There is little representational diversity among university provosts, 98.7% of whom are white. The greatest racial diversity is found among vice presidents, but these positions are also 85.4% white and a mere 1.3% Black.

Table 22.3. Average Income of Black and Racialized Professors and College Instructors at Canadian Universities and Colleges, 2016

	University professors		College professors	
	Earnings ($)	+/– average earnings (%)	Earnings ($)	+/– average earnings (%)
All workers	102,298	0.00	62,529	0.00
Male	110,713	0.00	69,490	0.00
Female	91,366	0.00	56,552	0.00
White	105,297	2.90	64,363	2.90
Male	114,832	3.70	71,007	2.20
Female	93,898	2.80	58,533	3.50
Total visible minority	90,011	−12.00	50,972	−18.50
Male	96,557	−12.80	59,045	−15.00
Female	77,908	−14.70	44,932	−20.50
South Asian	94,246	−7.90	54,582	−12.70
Male	101,419	−8.40	62,442	−10.10
Female	79,642	−12.80	48,728	−13.80
Chinese	97,001	−5.20	50,783	−18.80
Male	104,379	−5.70	71,648	3.10
Female	84,929	−7.00	39,451	−30.20
Black	90,363	−11.70	52,164	−16.60
Male	94,951	−14.20	49,269	−29.10
Female	81,803	−10.50	55,552	−1.80
Filipino	80,279	−21.50	51,800	−17.20
Male	76,031	−31.30	54,691	−21.30
Female	85,981	−5.90	50,074	−11.50
Latin American	72,871	−28.80	46,169	−26.20
Male	82,394	−25.60	54,809	−21.10
Female	59,901	−34.40	40,466	−28.40
Arab	88,245	−13.70	47,865	−23.50
Male	95,766	−13.50	58,625	−15.60
Female	68,274	−25.30	36,247	−35.90
Southeast Asian	98,919	−3.30	50,678	−19.00
Male	106,524	−3.80	53,026	−23.70
Female	91,212	−0.20	49,599	−12.30
West Asian	75,672	−26.00	47,616	−23.80
Male	80,282	−27.50	55,310	−20.40
Female	62,540	−31.60	40,495	−28.40
Korean	90,820	−11.20	34,448	−44.90
Male	94,326	−14.80	34,182	−50.80
Female	83,795	−8.30	34,583	−38.80
Japanese	78,851	−22.90	46,819	−25.10
Male	85,776	−22.50	78,054	12.30
Female	73,363	−19.70	35,226	−37.70

Note: Created from Statistics Canada, Census 2016 data.

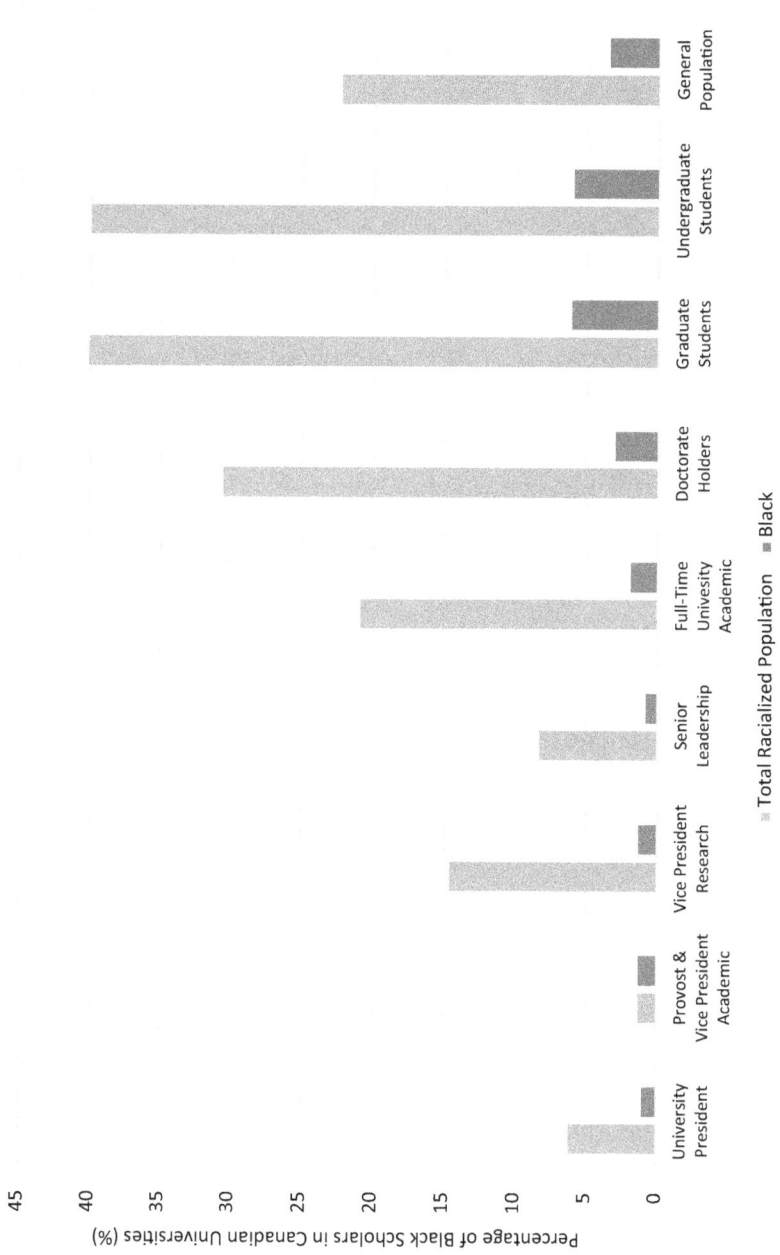

Figure 22.3. The Black Academic Pipeline in Canadian Universities, 2019

Source: Adapted from M.S. Smith (2018, 2019a, 2019b, 12).

In trying to break into the professoriate, Black scholars, particularly Black women, have to engage in a twofold competition: "As a woman, or as a candidate of colour, you do not just compete with other applicants; you must also prove yourself in light of a dominant negative group image" (Essed 2004, 119). Black scholars often have to contend with the negative group image that frame Black-as-lack, and Black professors – rather than the structural conditions of their work life – are often perceived as less social and more rebellious, again reproducing colonial logics for subjection. These negative group images and stereotypes inform beliefs and decision-making around hiring, research, teaching, and service, as well as views about who should be tapped for university leadership positions. "Whereas racial segregation was designed to keep blacks as a group or class outside centers of power" (Collins 1998, 38), the new technologies of racial profiling, carding, and "surveillance now aim to control black individuals inside centers of power when they enter the white spaces of the public and private spheres" (20). The barriers that function to keep Black students and professors out of the academy also function to keep Black scholars down once they are in the academy (Palmer 2014). Black students and professors "find themselves condescended to and otherwise made to feel that they do not belong" and encounter conditions that include "a wide range of aggressive and unconscionable behaviors" (Misra and Lundquist 2015) that function as social mechanisms of control and containment. Few if any universities have tackled these barriers and mechanisms that function to maintain hegemonic whiteness and Black underrepresentation.

Rather than to a meritocracy, these racialized and gendered dynamics speak to double and shifting standards that too often stereotype Black scholars as less competent, despite all the evidence to the contrary, and Black and racialized women too often are "presumed incompetent" (Gutiérrez y Muhs et al. 2012, 3–8). In the selection and propagation of the professoriate through the hiring process, "privileging masculinities, whiteness, or European-ness, is not 'just' a matter of preference. Presumed homogeneity among human beings is always a matter of biased perception, not a natural given," according to Essed (2004). Institutional policies to address racial biases, harassment, bullying, and micro-aggressions rarely exist. Or, in the experience of too many Black scholars, policies that are "on the books" are non-performative (Ahmed 2012); they do not do what they purport. Instead, many of these policies tend to focus more on risk-management and protecting institutional reputation. For many Black scholars, these inadequately address how conditions of social injustice contribute to leaky academic pipelines.

Conclusion

In the Canadian academy, Black scholars face nearly insurmountable challenges that lead to a leaky Black academic pipeline from undergraduate to graduate school, and from the PhD to the professoriate and university leadership. As the cases of racial profiling discussed in this chapter illustrate, there are significant emotional and psychological costs to being a Black body perceived as "out of place" in Canadian universities. Despite the obstacles, Black students and professors have mobilized in associations and have developed self-help and survival strategies to confront a lack of institutional support and behaviours and practices designed to push them out or keep them down. Strategies used by Black scholars include divesting in institutional whiteness, while consciously and proactively investing in Black futures by redirecting professional energies to preparing the next generation of Black and racialized students to succeed in a sometimes hostile learning environment.

As Black scholars in the Canadian academy continue to chart alternative futures, often in spaces characterized by racialized and gender-based violence, it is necessary to recall the wisdom of Lorde (1988, 133): "Caring for myself is not self-indulgence, it is self-preservation, and that is an act of political warfare." This lesson learned from radical Black struggles was reinforced by Angela Davis (2014) when she, too, noted, "Self-care has to be incorporated in all of our efforts. And this is something new." With tender care, and loving self-care, Black scholars are charting Black Canadian studies futures through community self-help, collaborations, and ongoing political struggle. They are also deeply attuned to the political wisdom of Daurene Lewis, Canada's first Black woman mayor who advised, "If I could teach one thing to the next generation, it would be that no one should accept the status quo" (Lewis in Powell 2018).

REFERENCES

Abiola, U. 2014. "Three Layers of Underrepresentation: Academic Pipeline Issues for African Americans." In *Opportunities and Challenges at Historically Black Colleges and Universities*, edited by M. Gasman and F. Commodore, 57–74. New York: Palgrave Macmillan.

Ahmed, S. 2012. *On Being Included: Racism and Diversity in Institutional Life.* Durham, NC: Duke University Press.

Arday, J. 2019. "Racism in Academia Has Major Impact on BAME Staff Mental Health." *Times Higher Education.* https://www.timeshighereducation.com /blog/racism-academia-has-major-impact-bame-staff-mental-health.

Armstrong, N. 2016. "Dr. Carl James Is New Jean Augustine Chair and Has
Major Plans for It." *Pride: Canada's Daily African Canadian and Caribbean News
Magazine*, 25 May. http://pridenews.ca/2016/05/25/dr-carl-james-new
-jean-augustine-chair/.

Canadian Association of University Teachers (CAUT). 2010. "The Changing
Academy? A Portrait of Canada's University Teachers." *Education Review*
12 (1). https://www.caut.ca/docs/education-review/the-changing-academy
-a-portrait-of-canada-rsquo-s-university-teachers-(jan-2010).pdf?sfvrsn=14.

CAUT. 2018a. "Employment and Wage Equity Remain Elusive for Academics in
Canada's Universities and Colleges." https://www.caut.ca/latest/2018/04
/employment-and-wage-equity-remain-elusive-academics-canadas-universities
-and-colleges.

CAUT. 2018b. *Underrepresented and Underpaid: Diversity & Equity among Canada's
Post-secondary Education Teachers.* https://www.caut.ca/sites/default/files/caut
_equity_report_2018-04final.pdf.

CBC News. 2007, 8 March. "Term 'Visible Minorities' May Be Discriminatory,
UN Body Warns Canada." https://www.cbc.ca/news/canada/term-visible
-minorities-may-be-discriminatory-un-body-warns-canada-1.690247.

CBC News. 2017, 2 February. "'Not Much Diversity': MUN Black Students'
Association Aims to Provide Sense of Unity." https://www.cbc.ca/news/canada
/newfoundland-labrador/memorial-university-black-students-association-1
.3963181.

CBC Radio. 2017, 16 January. "Black PhD Students Call Out Inequity in
Canadian Academia." https://www.cbc.ca/radio/thecurrent/the-current-for
-january-16-2017-1.3934687/black-phd-students-call-out-inequity-in-canadian
-academia-1.3934776.

Chanicka, J. 2019a. "Marginalized People Face a Unique Mental Health
Struggle." *Huffington Post Canada*, 29 January. https://www.huffingtonpost.ca
/entry/marginalized-people-face-a-unique-mental-health-struggle_ca
_5cd5305ae4b07bc729759dd8.

Chanicka, J. 2019b. "Racist Micro-Aggressions Are Like Death by a Thousand
Cuts." *Huffington Post Canada*, 19 March. https://www.huffingtonpost.ca
/entry/microaggression-privilege-racism-discrimination_ca
_5cd53edce4b07bc7297632b6.

Collins, P.H. 1998. *Fighting Words: Black Women and the Search for Justice.*
Minneapolis, MN: University of Minnesota Press.

Cooper, A. 2019. *Report on Lord Dalhousie's History on Slavery and Race* https://
www.dal.ca/dept/ldp/findings.html.

Crichlow, W. 2019. "#BlackProfessorsMatter: Intellectual Survival and Public
Love." Federation for the Humanities and Social Sciences, 2 April. https://
www.ideas-idees.ca/blog/blackprofessorsmatter-intellectual-survival-and
-public-love.

Cross, W.T. 1991. "Pathway to the Professoriate: The American Indian Faculty Pipeline." *Journal of American Indian Education* 30 (2): 13–24. https://www.jstor.org/stable/24398108.

Dannetta, L. 2019. "Queen's Formally Apologizes for Black Medical Student Ban." *The Queen's University Journal*, 25 April. https://www.queensjournal.ca/story/2019-04-25/university/queens-formally-apologizes-for-black-medical-student-ban/.

Davis, A. 2014. "Public Lecture, Pacifica College Oregon." Vimeo. https://vimeo.com/94879430.

Draaisma, M. 2017. "Black Students in Toronto Streamed into Courses below Their Ability." CBC News, 24 April. https://www.cbc.ca/news/canada/toronto/study-black-students-toronto-york-university-1.4082463.

Edwards, S. 2011. "Canada Ready to Spar with UN over 'Visible Minorities.'" *National Post*, 5 July. https://nationalpost.com/news/canada/canada-ready-to-spar-with-un-over-visible-minorities.

Essed, P. 2004. "Cloning amongst Professors: Normativities and Imagined Homogeneities." *NORA: Nordic Journal of Feminist and Gender Research* 12 (2): 113–122. https://doi.org/10.1080/08038740410004588.

Essed, P., and Goldberg, D.T. 2002. "Cloning Cultures: The Social Injustices of Sameness." *Ethnic and Racial Studies* 25 (6): 1066–1082. https://doi.org/10.1080/0141987022000009430.

Francis. A. 2019. "The Growing Field of Black Canadian Studies." *University Affairs*, 7 August. https://www.universityaffairs.ca/news/news-article/the-growing-field-of-black-canadian-studies/.

Fyfe, A. 2018. "Women's Careers Are Not Like Pipelines: The 'Leaky Pipeline' Metaphor for the Lack of Women at Senior Levels of Academic Can Demotivate Those Whose Professional Paths Meander." *Times Higher Education*, 12 February. https://www.timeshighereducation.com/blog/womens-careers-are-not-pipelines.

Garbee, E. 2017. "The Problem with the 'Pipeline': A Pervasive Metaphor in STEM Education Has Some Serious Flaws." *Slate*, 20 October. https://slate.com/technology/2017/10/the-problem-with-the-pipeline-metaphor-in-stem-education.html.

Geitmann, A., and Leckey, R. 2018. "Working Group on Principles of Commemoration and Renaming." Office of the Provost and Vice Principal (Academic). Montreal: McGill University. https://www.mcgill.ca/provost/working-group-principles-commemoration-and-renaming.

Gordon, A. 2017. "Black Students Hindered by Academic Streaming, Suspensions: Report." *Toronto Star*, 24 April. https://www.thestar.com/yourtoronto/education/2017/04/24/black-students-hindered-by-academic-streaming-suspensions-report.html.

Government of Ontario. 2019. *Data Standards for Identification and Monitoring of Systemic Racism*. Toronto: Anti-Racism Directorate, Ministry of the Solicitor General.

Grant, T., and Balkis soon, D. 2019. "'Visible Minority': Is It Time for Canada to Scrap the Term?" *Globe and Mail*, 6 February. https://www.theglobeandmail .com/canada/article-visible-minority-term-statscan/.

Green, A. 2016. "The Cost of Balancing Academia and Racism." *The Atlantic*, 21 January. https://www.theatlantic.com/education/archive/2016/01 /balancing-academia-racism/424887/.

Gregg, M. 2015. "The Deficiencies of Tech's 'Pipeline' Metaphor." *The Atlantic*, 3 December. https://www.theatlantic.com/business/archive/2015/12 /pipeline-stem/418647/.

Gutiérrez y Muhs, G., Niemann, Y., González, C., and Harris, A., eds. 2012. *Presumed Incompetent: The Intersections of Race and Class for Women in Academia.* Boulder: University Press of Colorado.

Haggert, A. 2019. "'I Had No Idea How Difficult It Would Possibly Be': Being Black in Theatre." CBC News, 26 August. https://www.cbc.ca/news/canada /windsor/black-in-theatre-windsor-othello-1.5257651.

Henry, A. 2016. "Canadian Campuses Suffer from a Lack of Racial Inclusion: Universities Often Ignore a Varied and Rich Black Intellectual Tradition." University Affairs, 9 February. https://www.universityaffairs.ca/opinion /in-my-opinion/canadian-campuses-suffer-from-a-lack-of-racial-inclusion/.

Henry, F. 2004. *Systemic Racism towards Faculty of Colour and Aboriginal Faculty at Queen's University: Report on the 2003 Study, Understanding the Experiences of Visible Minority and Aboriginal Faculty Members at Queen's University.* https:// www.queensu.ca/provost/sites/webpublish.queensu.ca.provwww/files/files /SystemicRacism.pdf.

Henry, F., Dua, E., James, C.E., Li, P., Ramos, H., and Smith, M. 2016. "Race, Racialization and Indigeneity in Canadian Universities." *Race, Ethnicity and Education* 20 (3): 300–314.

Henry, F., Dua, E., James, C.E., Li, P., Ramos, H., and Smith, M. 2017. *The Equity Myth: Racialization and Indigeneity at Canadian Universities.* Vancouver: University of British Columbia Press.

Jackson, J.F.L., ed. 2007. *Strengthening the African American Educational Pipeline: Informing Research, Policy, and Practice.* New York: State University of New York Press.

James, C. 2017. "Towards Race Equity in Education: The Schooling of Black Students in the Greater Toronto Area." Toronto: The Jean Augustine Chair in Education, Community & Diaspora, York University. https://edu.yorku.ca /files/2017/04/Towards-Race-Equity-in-Education-April-2017.pdf.

James, C. 2002. "You Can't Understand Me: Negotiating Teacher–Student Relationships in Urban School." *Contact* 28 (2): 8–20.

James, C., Robson, K., and Gallagher, K. 2017. "Universities Have a Serious Data Gap on Race." University Affairs, 19 May. https://www.universityaffairs.ca /opinion/in-my-opinion/universities-serious-data-gap-race/.

James, C., and Turner, T. 2017. *Towards Race Equity in Education: The Schooling of Black Students in the Greater Toronto Area.* http://edu.yorku.ca/files/2017/04/Towards-Race-Equity-in-Education-April-2017.pdf.

Kitossa, T. 2012. "Black Canadian Studies and the Resurgence of the Insurgent African Canadian Intelligentsia." *Southern Journal of Canadian Studies* 5 (1): 255–284. https://doi.org/10.22215/sjcs.v5i1.298.

Larsen, K. 2019. "Nova Scotia Student Says He Was Racially Profiled at UBC-Held Congress." CBC News, 5 June. https://www.cbc.ca/news/canada/british-columbia/nova-scotia-student-says-he-was-racially-profiled-at-ubc-held-congress-1.4668201#:~:text=%22I%20felt%20embarrassed%20...,m%20paraded%20as%20a%20criminal.%22.

The Link. 2017. *Editorial: It's Time for a Black Studies Program at Concordia.* https://thelinknewspaper.ca/article/editorial-its-time-for-a-black-studies-program-at-concordia.

Lorde, A. 1988. *A Burst of Light: Essays.* Ithaca, NY: Firebrand Books.

MacDonald, J., and Ward, L. 2017a. "'The Rose-Coloured Glasses Are Off': Why Experts, Students Suspect Racism Under-Reported on Campuses." CBC News, 22 March. https://www.cbc.ca/news/canada/race-complaints-canadian-universities-1.3786176.

MacDonald, J., and Ward, L. 2017b. "Why So Many Canadian Universities Know So Little about Their Own Racial Diversity." CBC News, 21 March. https://www.cbc.ca/news/canada/race-canadian-universities-1.4030537.

Marx, A.W. 1996. "Race-Making and the Nation-state." *World Politics* 48 (2): 180–208. https://doi.org/10.1353/wp.1996.0003.

Maynard, R. 2017. *Policing Black Lives: State Violence in Canada from Slavery to the Present.* Winnipeg: Fernwood Publishing.

McMaster, G. 2019. "Black Sudents at U of A Launch New Group." Folio, 23 January. https://www.folio.ca/black-students-at-u-of-a-launch-new-group/.

McQuigge, M. 2017. "Black Graduate Celebrated at Special U of T Ceremony." CBC News, 22 June. https://www.cbc.ca/news/canada/toronto/university-of-toronto-black-graduation-1.4172742.

Misra, J., and Lundquist, J. 2015. "Diversity and the Ivory Ceiling." Inside Higher Education, 26 June. https://www.insidehighered.com/advice/2015/06/26/essay-diversity-issues-and-midcareer-faculty-members.

Mogadime, D. 2015. "The Nuances of Blackness and/in the Canadian Academy." Federation for the Humanities and Social Sciences, 20 January. https://www.ideas-idees.ca/blog/nuances-blackness-andin-canadian-academy-tool-engaging-equity-pedagogy-graduate-classroom.

Morgan, A. 2016. *The Blackening Margins of Multiculturalism: The African Canadian Experience of Exclusion from the Economic, Social and Cultural Promise and Prosperity of Canada.* African Canadian Legal Clinic. https://tbinternet.ohchr.org/Treaties/CESCR/Shared%20Documents/CAN/INT_CESCR_CSS_CAN_22907_E.pdf.

Naccarato, L. 2017. "Almost Half of TDSB Students Expelled over Last 5 Years Are Black, Report Says." CBC, 11 April. https://www.cbc.ca/news/canada /toronto/almost-half-of-tdsb-students-expelled-over-last-5-years-are-black -report-says-1.4065088.

Neigh, S. 2018. "Fighting the School-to-Prison Pipeline in Toronto." rabble.ca, 6 March. http://rabble.ca/podcasts/shows/talking-radical-radio/2018/03 /fighting-school-prison-pipeline-toronto.

Nelson, C. 2012. "Resisting Invisibility: Black Faculty in Art and Art History in Canada." Federation for the Humanities and Social Sciences, 2 March. https://www.ideas-idees.ca/blog/resisting-invisibility-black-faculty-art-and-art -history-canada.

Ontario Human Rights Commission. 2017. *Under Suspicion: Research and Consultation Report on Racial Profiling in Ontario.* http://www.ohrc.on.ca/en /under-suspicion-research-and-consultation-report-racial-profiling-ontario.

Ontario Human Rights Commission. 2018. *Interrupted Childhoods: Over-representation of Indigenous and Black Children in Ontario Child Welfare.* http:// www.ohrc.on.ca/en/interrupted-childhoods.

Ontario Human Rights Commission. 2019. *Policy on Eliminating Racial Profiling in Law Enforcement.* http://www.ohrc.on.ca/en/policy-eliminating-racial -profiling-law-enforcement.

Oriuwa, C.S. 2019. "In My White Coat I'm More Black Than Ever." *Flare*, 30 September. https://www.flare.com/identity/black-physicians-in-canada/.

Palmer, R.T. 2014. "Factors Affecting the Success of Black Males in PreK-12 and Higher Education." In *Black Men in Higher Education: A Guide to Ensuring Student Success*, edited by J.L. Wood and R.T. Palmer, 17–31. New York: Routledge.

Powell, L. 2018. "A Renaissance Woman – Celebrating Daurene Lewis, First Female, Black Mayor with Sculpture, Dedication, Words of Tribute." *Saltwire*, 11 September. https://www.thevanguard.ca/lifestyles/a-renaissance-woman -celebrating-daurene-lewis-first-female-black-mayor-with-sculpture-dedication -words-of-tribute-240445/.

Ramos, H., and Li, P. 2017. "Differences in Representation and Employment Income of Racialized University Professors." In *The Equity Myth: Racialization and Indigeneity at Canadian Universities*, edited by F. Henry, E. Dua, C.E. James, P. Li, H. Ramos, and M.S. Smith, 46–64. Vancouver: University of British Columbia Press.

Ranlakhan, K. 2019. "Black Student Carded, Cuffed at University of Ottawa, Prompting Review." CBC, 14 June. https://www.cbc.ca/news/canada /ottawa/university-human-rights-office-student-twitter-carding-1.5175864.

Reynolds, C. 2016. "U of T to Track Race-Based Data of Its Students." *Toronto Star*, 22 February. https://www.thestar.com/news/gta/2016/02/22/u-of-t-to -track-race-based-data-of-its-students.html.

Rideout, D. 2019. "Queen's University Moves to Right Historic Wrongs." *Queen's Gazette*, 16 April. https://www.queensu.ca/gazette/stories/queen-s-university -moves-right-historic-wrong.

Roderique, H. 2017. "Black on Bay Street." *The Globe and Mail*, 4 November. https://www.theglobeandmail.com/news/toronto/hadiya-roderique-black -on-bay-street/article36823806/.

Rodriguez, S. 2019. "'He Stripped Us of Our Dignity,' Western University Student Says of Prof Who Used N-Word in Class." CBC News, 29 October. https://www.cbc.ca/news/canada/london/western-prof-uses-n-word -1.5338315.

Rushowy, K. 2015. "End Streaming in Schools, Report to Toronto Trustees Recommends." *Toronto Star*, 7 October. https://www.thestar.com /yourtoronto/education/2015/10/07/end-streaming-in-schools-report-to -toronto-trustees-recommends.html.

Salole, A. and Abdulle, Z. 2015. "Quick to Punish: An Examination of the School to Prison Pipeline for Marginalized Youth." *Canadian Review of Social Policy* 72 (73): 124–168. https://www.proquest.com/openview/430a428018cb 6b67d84f1b2dd803f9ea/1?pq-origsite=gscholar&cbl=28163.

Saucier, D. 2018. "Reconciliation on University Campuses: 'Two Realities, Side by Side'?" *Maclean's*, 11 October. https://www.macleans.ca/education /reconciliation-on-university-campuses-two-realities-side-by-side/.

Shah, V. 2019. "Black and Racialized Student Achievement Gaps Are a Red-Alert." *The Conversation*. https://theconversation.com/racialized-student -achievement-gaps-are-a-red-alert-108822.

Shalom, F. 2019. "Inaugural Black Grad Celebrates Black Students at McGill." *McGill Reporter*, 6 June. https://reporter.mcgill.ca/inaugural-black-grad -celebrates-black-students-at-mcgill/.

Smith, M.S. 2016. "The Diversity Gap in Canadian University Leadership." Academic Women's Association, 18 August. https://uofaawa.wordpress.com /awa-diversity-gap-campaign/the-diversity-gap-in-university-leadership/

Smith, M.S. 2018. "Equity at Canadian Universities: National, Disaggregated and Intersectional Data." Academic Women's Association, 22 June. https:// uofaawa.wordpress.com/awa-diversity-gap-campaign/equity-at-canadian -universities-national-disaggregated-and-intersectional-data/.

Smith, M.S. 2019a. *Canadian U96 Universities: Leadership Pipeline by Position*. Edmonton, AB: The Diversity Gap.

Smith, M.S. 2019b. "U15 Leadership Remains Largely White and Male Despite 33 Years of Equity Initiatives." Academic Women's Association. https:// uofaawa.wordpress.com/2019/06/20/u15-leadership-remains-largely-white -and-male-despite-33-years-of-equity-initiatives/.

Smith, M.S., Golfman, N., Battiste, M., Crichlow, W., Dolmage, J., Glanfield, F., Malacrida, C., and Villeneuve, A.-J. 2021, 8 March. *Igniting Change: Final*

Report and Recommendations. Ottawa: Federation for the Humanities and Social Sciences. http://www.ideas-idees.ca/sites/default/files/sites/default/uploads /congress/igniting-change-final-report-and-recommendations-en.pdf.

Statistics Canada. 2017. "Visible Minority and Population Group Reference Guide, Census of Population, 2016." https://www12.statcan.gc.ca/census -recensement/2016/ref/guides/006/98-500-x2016006-eng.cfm.

Statistics Canada. 2018. "UCASS Revisited." https://www.statcan.gc.ca/eng /blog/cs/ucass-revisited.

Statistics Canada. 2019. "Diversity of the Black Population in Canada: An Overview." https://www150.statcan.gc.ca/n1/pub/89-657-x/89-657-x2019002 -eng.htm.

Universities Canada. 2019. *Equity, Diversity and Inclusion at Canadian Universities: Report on the 2019 National Survey.* https://www.univcan.ca/wp-content /uploads/2019/11/Equity-diversity-and-inclusion-at-Canadian-universities -report-on-the-2019-national-survey-Nov-2019-1.pdf.

Vendeville, G. 2018. "U of T Students to Host Second Black Graduation Ceremony." *UofT News.* https://www.utoronto.ca/news/u-t-students-host-second -black-graduation-ceremony.

Werb, J. 2015. "Canadian Black Scholars Deserve More Attention." UBC News, 10 November. https://news.ubc.ca/2015/11/10/canadian-black-scholars -deserve-more-attention/.

Woolley, F. 2013. "'Visible Minority': A Misleading Concept That Ought to Be Retired." *The Globe and Mail*, 10 June. https://www.theglobeandmail.com /opinion/visible-minority-a-misleading-concept-that-ought-to-be-retired /article12445364/.

Yaboha, S.G. 2016. "Black Consciousness at Concordia: Why This University Needs an Interdisciplinary Black Studies Minor." *The Link.* https:// thelinknewspaper.ca/article/black-consciousness-at-concordia.

Yousif, N. 2018. "Black Students at U of A Form New Group to Provide Support and Tackle Discrimination." *Toronto Star*, 16 December. https://www.thestar .com/edmonton/2018/12/13/black-students-at-u-of-a-form-new-group-to -provide-support-and-tackle-discrimination.html.

Zoledziowski, A. 2017. "Lack of Faculty Diversity Can Affect Studies and Career Aspirations." *The Globe and Mail*, 18 October. https://beta.theglobeandmail .com/news/national/education/canadian-university-report/lack-of -faculty-diversity-can-affect-studies-and-career-aspirations/article36637410/.

Zoledziowski, A. 2018. "The Extra Load That Professors of Colour Have to Bear." *The Globe and Mail*, 3 June. https://www.theglobeandmail.com /canada/british-columbia/article-the-extra-load-that-professors-of-colour -have-to-bear/.

Contributors

Ali A. Abdi is a full professor in the Department of Educational Studies in the Faculty of Education at the University of British Columbia, Vancouver, British Columbia.

Evelyn Amponsah is the director of the Centre for the Advancement of the Interests of Black People, Toronto Community Housing Corporation, and a PhD candidate in social and political thought, and chair of the Black Graduate Students' Collective at York University in Toronto, Ontario.

Juliane Okot Bitek is an author, writer and poet, and assistant professor of Black creative writing in Black studies, gender studies, and English at Queen's University in Kingston, Ontario.

Adelle Blackett is a full professor, Canada Research Chair in Transnational Labour Law and Development, and director of the Labour Law and Development Research Laboratory in the Faculty of Law at McGill University in Montreal, Quebec.

Wesley Crichlow is a full professor and critical race intersectional theorist of criminology and justice in the Faculty of Social Science and Humanities at the Ontario Tech University in Oshawa, Ontario.

Henry Daniel is a full professor of dance and performance studies at Simon Fraser University, and the choreographer/artistic director of Full Performing Bodies in Vancouver, British Columbia.

George J. Sefa Dei (Nana Adusei Sefa Tweneboah) is the director for the Centre for Integrative Studies, and a full professor in the Department of Social Justice Education at the Ontario Institute for the Study of Education at the University of Toronto in Toronto, Ontario.

Delia D. Douglas is the anti-racism practice lead in the Office of Equity, Diversity and Inclusion at the Rady Faculty of Health Sciences and Ongomiizwin Indigenous Institute of Health and Healing, University of Manitoba, in Winnipeg, Manitoba. She holds a PhD in sociology from the University of California, Santa Cruz.

OmiSoore H. Dryden is the James R. Johnston Chair in Black Canadian Studies, and an associate professor in the Department of Community Health & Epidemiology, Faculty of Medicine, at Dalhousie University in Halifax, Nova Scotia.

Gervan Fearon is the president of George Brown College in Toronto. He previously served as president and vice-chancellor of Brock University in St. Catharines, Ontario (2017–21), and of Brandon University in Brandon, Manitoba (2014–17). He holds a PhD in economics and a chartered professional accountant and corporate directors designation.

Annette Henry is the David Lam Chair in Multicultural Education, and full professor in the Department of Language and Literacy Education, Faculty of Education at the University of British Columbia in Vancouver, British Columbia.

Awad Ibrahim is a full professor and curriculum theorist in the Faculty of Education at the University of Ottawa in Ottawa, Ontario.

Carl E. James is a full professor in the Faculty of Education, Jean Augustine Chair in Education, Community & Diaspora, and the director of the York Centre for Education and Community at York University in North York, Ontario.

Jennifer R. Kelly is a professor emerita and former department chair in the Department of Educational Policy Studies, Faculty of Education at the University of Alberta in Edmonton, Alberta.

Tamari Kitossa is an associate professor in the Department of Sociology at Brock University in St. Catharines, Ontario.

Charmaine Lurch is an interdisciplinary visual artist, a graduate of York University's Faculty of Environmental Studies, and a former member of York's Black Graduate Students Collective in Toronto, Ontario.

Mosa McNeilly is a visual artist and performer, graduate student in the Faculty of Environmental Studies, and member of the Black Graduate Students Collective at York University in Toronto, Ontario.

Jan-Therese Mendes completed her PhD in gender, feminist, and women's studies at York University in North York, Ontario, and is a postdoctoral fellow at University of Stavanger in Stavanger, Norway.

Ola Mohammed is a PhD student in social and political thought, and a member of the Black Graduate Students Collective at York University in Toronto, Ontario, Canada.

Délice Mugabo is an assistant professor in feminist and gender studies in the Institute of Feminist and Gender Studies at the University of Ottawa, in Ottawa, Ontario.

Delores V. Mullings is the inaugural vice-provost, equity, diversity, and inclusion, and a full professor in the School of Social Work at Memorial University of Newfoundland and Labrador in St. John's, Newfoundland.

Malinda S. Smith is the inaugural vice-provost and associate vice-president, research equity, diversity, and inclusion, a 2018 Pierre Elliott Trudeau Foundation fellow, and a full professor in the Department of Political Science at the University of Calgary in Calgary, Alberta.

Emmanuel Tabi is an assistant professor in the Department of Integrated Studies in Education at McGill University in Montreal, Quebec. He holds a PhD from the Ontario Institute for Studies in education at the University of Toronto.

Shirley Anne Tate is a full professor and Tier 1 Canada Research Chair in Intersectionality and Feminism in the Department of Sociology at the University of Alberta in Edmonton, Alberta, and honorary professor, chair for critical studies in higher education transformation at Nelson Mandela University in Port Elizabeth, South Africa.

Wisdom J. Tettey is a vice-president of the University of Toronto and principal of the University of Toronto Scarborough, Ontario, and former dean of the Irving K. Barber School of Arts and Sciences at the University of British Columbia-Okanagan. He holds a PhD in political science from Queen's University in Kingston.

Gina Thésée is a full professor in the Department of Didactics, Faculty of Education Science, at the University of Quebec at Montreal, Quebec.

Barrington Walker is the inaugural associate vice-president, equity, diversity, and inclusion, and a full professor of history at Wilfrid Laurier University in Waterloo, Ontario.

Kay-Ann Williams is an independent scholar and holds a PhD in geography from Queen's University in Kingston, Ontario.

Handel Kashope Wright is the inaugural senior advisor to the president on anti-racism and inclusive excellence; the director of the Centre for Culture, Identity and Education; and a full professor of educational studies at the University of British Columbia, and a senior research associate in the Department of Communications, University of Johannesburg, South Africa.

York University Black Graduate Students' Collective – individual biographies as above: Evelyn Amponsah, Charmaine Lurch, Mosa McNeilly, Jan-Therese Mendes, and Ola Mohammed.

www.ingramcontent.com/pod-product-compliance
Lightning Source LLC
Chambersburg PA
CBHW030233030426
42336CB00009B/80